This series is a translation of
DIETRICH BONHOEFFER WERKE
Edited by
Eberhard Bethge†, Ernst Feil†,
Christian Gremmels, Wolfgang Huber,
Hans Pfeifer†, Albrecht Schönherr†,
Heinz Eduard Tödt†, Ilse Tödt

Publication of this volume was assisted by a special grant from the Bowen H. and Janice Arthur McCoy Charitable Foundation, which generously supported the entire series.

DIETRICH BONHOEFFER WORKS

General Editors
Victoria J. Barnett
Wayne Whitson Floyd Jr.
Barbara Wojhoski

I0884163

DIETRICH BONHOEFFER WORKS, VOLUME 17

Indexes and Supplementary Materials

DIETRICH BONHOEFFER WORKS, VOLUME 17

DIETRICH BONHOEFFER

Indexes and Supplementary Materials

Edited by
VICTORIA J. BARNETT AND BARBARA WOJHOSKI

With the Assistance of
MARK S. BROCKER

With a Retrospective on the English Edition by
CLIFFORD J. GREEN

FORTRESS PRESS MINNEAPOLIS

DIETRICH BONHOEFFER WORKS, Volume 17

Some material in this volume was originally published in German in *Dietrich Bonhoeffer Werke*, edited by Eberhard Bethge et al., by Chr. Kaiser Verlag/Gütersloher Verlagshaus, Gütersloh, in 1999; Band 17, *Register und Ergänzungen*, edited by Herbert Anzinger and Hans Pfeifer. First English-language edition of Dietrich Bonhoeffer Works, Volume 17, published by Fortress Press in 2014.

New documents were originally published in the *Dietrich Bonhoeffer Jahrbuch/Yearbook*, Chr. Kaiser Verlag/Gütersloher Verlagshaus, Gütersloh, 2003—.

Jacket design: Cheryl Watson
Cover photo: Dietrich Bonhoeffer's desk at the family home on Marienburger Allee in Berlin.
Photo courtesy of Peter Frick.
Book design: HK Scriptorium, Inc.
Typesetting: Ann Delgehausen, Trio Bookworks

The paper used in this publication meets the minimum requirements for American National Standard for Information Sciences—Permanence of Paper for Printed Library Materials, ANSI Z329.48–1984.

Manufactured in the U.S.A.
18 17 16 15 14 1 2 3 4 5 6 7 8 9 10

Contents

General Editor's Foreword to the *Dietrich Bonhoeffer Works, English Edition* — vii
Victoria J. Barnett

The Translation of the *Dietrich Bonhoeffer Works, English Edition*: An Overview — 1
Victoria J. Barnett

The *Dietrich Bonhoeffer Works, English Edition*: A Retrospective — 9
Clifford J. Green

The *Dietrich Bonhoeffer Werke*: Afterword to the German Edition — 17
Wolfgang Huber

Additional Letters and Documents

DBWE 9, 1/80a. To Ernst Fritz Schmid — 29
DBWE 9, 1/85a. From Ernst Fritz Schmid — 31
DBWE 9, 1/94b. To Ernst Fritz Schmid — 32
DBWE 9, 1/96c. To Ernst Fritz Schmid — 33
DBWE 9, 1/99b. To Ernst Fritz Schmid — 35
DBWE 9, 2/2a. On Euripides's Philosophy — 37
DBWE 12, 1/106a. From Wilhelm Lütgert to Adolf Schlatter — 48
DBWE 13, 1/34a. Book Inscription for Herbert Jehle — 54
DBWE 13, 1/208a. To Ernst Cromwell — 54
DBWE 13, 1/209a. To Ernst Cromwell — 57
DBWE 13, 1/209b. To Ernst Cromwell — 58
DBWE 13, 1/210a. From Philipp Cromwell — 59

Comprehensive Chronology and Master List of Documents

Master Indexes

General Editor's Foreword to the *Dietrich Bonhoeffer Works*

The German theologian and pastor Dietrich Bonhoeffer has become one of the most influential Christian thinkers of all time. Barely twenty-seven years of age when the Nazi regime came to power in Germany, Bonhoeffer emerged immediately as a radical Protestant voice against the ideological co-optation of his church. He was one of the earliest critics of the Nazi regime and an outspoken opponent of the pro-Nazi "German Christians." From 1933 to 1935, he served as pastor of two German-speaking congregations in England, leading them to join the Confessing Church—the faction within the German Protestant Church that opposed the nazification of the Christian faith. He returned to Germany to become director of a small Confessing Church seminary and, after the Gestapo closed it, continued to work illegally to educate Confessing clergy. Throughout the 1930s, he attended ecumenical meetings, effectively becoming the voice of the Confessing Church throughout the European and American ecumenical world. In 1939 his ecumenical friends urged him to accept a position in New York. Rejecting the security of a life in exile, Bonhoeffer chose instead to join the ranks of the German conspiracy to overthrow the regime, like his brother Klaus and his brothers-in-law Hans von Dohnanyi and Rüdiger Schleicher. He was arrested and imprisoned in April 1943 and executed in the Flossenbürg concentration camp in April 1945.

In a eulogy published shortly after Bonhoeffer's death, his former professor and friend Reinhold Niebuhr wrote that Bonhoeffer's story "is worth recording. It belongs to the modern acts of the apostles. . . . Not only his martyr's death, but also his actions and precepts contain within them the hope of a revitalised Protestant faith in Germany. It will be a faith,

religiously more profound than that of many of its critics; but it will have learned to overcome the one fateful error of German Protestantism, the complete dichotomy between faith and political life."[1]

In the ensuing decades, Niebuhr's prescient insight that Bonhoeffer's life and work offered lasting insights for modern Christian experience and witness has been more than fulfilled. Bonhoeffer wrote hundreds of letters, sermons, and biblical reflections in addition to his published theological works. After 1945 Bonhoeffer's former student and close friend Eberhard Bethge worked with publishers to reissue and translate the books Bonhoeffer had published in his lifetime. In translation, these works—*Discipleship, Ethics,* and *Letters and Papers from Prison*—became classics, finding a wide readership among Christians throughout the world.

Yet there was a growing sense that these works should not stand alone—a realization of the significance of the biographical and historical context of his thought. Bonhoeffer's papers also included lecture notes that had been made by his students, documents from the German Church Struggle and ecumenical meetings, circular letters that were sent to his seminarians, sermons, extensive correspondence with theologians and religious leaders in Europe and the United States, and prison writings. Bethge published several early compilations of some of these documents (*Gesammelte Schriften* and *Mündige Welt*) and incorporated additional material into his magisterial biography of Bonhoeffer, which first appeared in English in 1970 and then, in a revised and unabridged edition, in 2000.

Bethge and leading Bonhoeffer scholars in Germany decided to publish new annotated editions of Bonhoeffer's complete theological works, together with most of the documents from the literary estate, including historical documents and correspondence to Bonhoeffer. The *Dietrich Bonhoeffer Werke* series was published by Chr. Kaiser Verlag, now part of Gütersloher Verlagshaus. The first German volume, a new edition of Bonhoeffer's dissertation, *Sanctorum Communio,* appeared in 1986; the final volume, Bonhoeffer's complete prison writings, appeared in April 1998. A seventeenth volume, an index for the entire series, appeared in 1999; this volume also included documents discovered after their respective volumes had been published. Whenever possible these documents have been included in the appropriate volumes of the English edition; documents that continue to be discovered are published in the *Dietrich Bonhoeffer Jahrbuch,* a series published by Gütersloher Verlagshaus.

[1.] Reinhold Niebuhr, "The Death of a Martyr," *Christianity and Crisis* 5, no. 11 (1945): 6–7.

Discussion about an English translation of the entire series began as soon as the first German volumes appeared. In 1990 the International Bonhoeffer Society, English Language Section, in agreement with the German Bonhoeffer Society and Fortress Press, undertook the English translation of the German *Dietrich Bonhoeffer Werke.* The project began with an initial grant from the National Endowment for the Humanities with Robin Lovin serving as project director, assisted by Mark Brocker. An editorial board was formed for the *Dietrich Bonhoeffer Works, English Edition,* staffed by Wayne Whitson Floyd Jr. as general editor, and Clifford J. Green of Hartford Seminary as executive director. Wayne Whitson Floyd Jr., at that time director of the Dietrich Bonhoeffer Center at the Lutheran Theological Seminary in Philadelphia, served as general editor from 1993 to 2004, overseeing publication of the first seven volumes as well as volume 9. Victoria J. Barnett, director of church relations at the U.S. Holocaust Memorial Museum, joined the project as associate general editor in 2002 and became general editor in 2004, joined by Barbara Wojhoski, a professional editor who prepared the manuscripts of the final volumes for publication.

The *Dietrich Bonhoeffer Works, English Edition* (*DBWE*) is the definitive English translation of Bonhoeffer's theological and other writings. It includes a great deal of material that appears for the first time in English, as well as documents discovered only after the publication of the original German volumes. The *DBWE* is a significant contribution to twentieth-century theological literature, church history, and the history of the Nazi era. Particularly in their portrayal of the daily implications of the Protestant Church Struggle in Nazi Germany and the response of Christians outside Germany, these volumes offer a detailed and unique glimpse of Bonhoeffer's historical context and its great challenges for the churches and for all people of conscience.

Each volume includes an introduction written by the *DBWE* volume editor(s), footnotes provided by Bonhoeffer, editorial notes added by the German and English editors, and the original afterword written by the editor(s) of the German edition. Additions to or revisions of the German editors' notes are enclosed within square brackets and initialed by the editor of the respective volume. When any previously translated material is quoted within an editorial note in altered form—indicated by the notation [trans. altered]—such changes should be assumed to be the responsibility of the translator(s). Where available, existing English translations of books and articles in German and other languages are cited in the notes.

Bonhoeffer's own footnotes—which are indicated in the body of the text by plain, superscripted numbers—are reproduced in precisely the same numerical sequence as they appear in the German critical edition, complete with his idiosyncrasies of documentation. In these, as in the accompanying

editorial notes, the edition of a work that was consulted by Bonhoeffer himself can be determined by consulting the bibliography at the end of each volume.

Each volume also contains a list of abbreviations frequently used in the editorial notes, as well as a bibliography of archival sources, sources used by Bonhoeffer, literature consulted by the editors, and other works relevant to that respective volume. Each volume also includes a chronology of important dates relevant to that volume, an index of scriptural references, an index of persons with relevant biographical information, and an index of subjects. Bibliographies at the end of each volume provide the complete information for each written source that Bonhoeffer or the various editors have mentioned in the current volume.

Bonhoeffer's literary estate—the notes, sermons, and other writings, as well as correspondence, and the personal library of materials that belonged to him and survived the war—was cataloged by Dietrich Meyer and Eberhard Bethge; this catalog has been published as the *Nachlaß Dietrich Bonhoeffer.* Most of the documents cited in the *Nachlaß* are collected in the Berlin Staatsbibliothek, although some documents remain in other archives. All documents listed in the *Nachlaß*, however, have been copied on microfiches that are now at the Staatsbibliothek in Berlin and in the Bonhoeffer collection at Burke Library, Union Theological Seminary, New York. References to any of these documents are indicated within the *DBWE* by the abbreviation *NL*, followed by the corresponding catalog number. Books in the bibliography from Bonhoeffer's own library are indicated by the abbreviation *NL-Bibl.*

Volumes 1–7 of the English edition, which contain only Bonhoeffer's own writings, retain his original organization of the material, either as chapters or as sections or unnumbered manuscripts. Volumes 8–16 contain collected writings from a particular period of Bonhoeffer's life, including correspondence from others and historical documents. With the exception of volume 8, these final volumes are divided into three sections, with the documents in each section arranged chronologically: (1) Letters, Journals, Documents; (2) Essays, Seminar Papers, Papers, Lectures, Compositions; (3) Sermons, Meditations, Catechetical Writings, Exegetical Writings. Documents are numbered consecutively within the respective sections. In editorial notes these items are labeled by the *DBWE* volume number, followed by the section number, document number, and finally the page number; for example, *DBWE* 9 (1/109), p. 179, ed. note 1, would refer to the English edition, volume 9, section 1, document 109, page 179, editorial note 1.

The *DBWE* also reproduces Bonhoeffer's original paragraphing (exceptions are noted by a ¶ symbol to indicate any paragraph break added by the

editors of the English edition or by conventions explained in the introductions written by the editor[s] of specific volumes). The pagination of the *DBW* German critical edition is indicated in the outer margins of the pages of the translated text. Where it is important to give readers a word or phrase in its original language, a translated passage is followed by the original, set within square brackets. All biblical citations come from the New Revised Standard Version (NRSV) unless otherwise noted. Where versification of the Bible used by Bonhoeffer differs from the NRSV, the verse number in the latter is noted in the text in square brackets.

The publication of the *Dietrich Bonhoeffer Works, English Edition* would not have been possible without the generous support of numerous individuals and institutions. The verso of the half-title page of each volume provides a list of supporters of that particular volume. The series as a whole is indebted to many individual members and friends of the International Bonhoeffer Society, and to family foundations, congregations, synods, seminaries, and universities. Special thanks are due the following foundations and donors for major grants: the National Endowment for the Humanities; the Lilly Endowment, Inc.; the Thrivent Financial for Lutherans Foundation; the Aid Association for Lutherans; the Stiftung Bonhoeffer Lehrstuhl; the Bowen H. and Janice Arthur McCoy Charitable Foundation; and Dr. John Young and Mrs. Cleo Young. The Lutheran Theological Seminary at Philadelphia and its former Auxiliary have provided space and ongoing support. We have been extraordinarily fortunate to work with Fortress Press. With thanks to the entire Fortress team, particular gratitude goes to Will Bergkamp, publisher and managing director, and his predecessors, editorial directors Michael West and Marshall Johnson. We owe a very special acknowledgment to Ann Delgehausen of Trio Bookworks, who managed the production of most of these volumes, for her skill and above all her patience.

The existence of this series in English and other languages is testimony to the international community of those who have found Dietrich Bonhoeffer to be a profoundly important companion in their own journey. That community would not exist without the wisdom, generosity, and dedication of Eberhard Bethge (1909–2000) and his wife, Renate. Bethge was himself a pastor in the Confessing Church. After 1945 he was convinced that the future of a living church in Germany depended on its addressing its failures under Nazism and on a new understanding of Bonhoeffer's lasting question, Who is Christ for us today?

The editors of this English edition are particularly grateful to the original editorial board of the German edition—composed of Eberhard Bethge†, Ernst Feil†, Christian Gremmels, Wolfgang Huber, Hans Pfeifer†, Albrecht Schönherr†, Heinz Eduard Tödt†, and Ilse Tödt. As liaison

between the German and English editorial boards, Hans Pfeifer gave steadfast and congenial support to his colleagues on both sides of the Atlantic. As work on the *DBWE* proceeded, a new generation of Bonhoeffer scholars in Germany has assisted us as well: Christine Kasch, Andreas Pangritz, Holger Roggelin, Christiane Tietz, and Ralf Wüstenberg. We also wish to acknowledge our debt to the editors of the individual German volumes, who have also been generous with their time and expertise: Eberhard Amelung†, Herbert Anzinger, Eberhard Bethge†, Renate Bethge, Otto Dudzus†, Ernst Feil†, Jørgen Glenthøj†, Hans Goedeking, Christian Gremmels, Hans Christoph von Hase†, Martin Heimbucher, Jürgen Henkys, Ulrich Kabitz, Carl-Jürgen Kaltenborn, Wolf Krötke, Martin Kuske†, Gerhard L. Müller, Carsten Nicolaisen, Hans-Richard Reuter, Martin Rüter†, Ernst-Albert Scharffenorth, Hans-Walter Schleicher†, Albrecht Schönherr†, Dirk Schulz, Joachim von Soosten, Reinhart Staats, Christoph Strohm, Heinz Eduard Tödt†, and Ilse Tödt.

We remain grateful to those whose original translations of Bonhoeffer's words introduced most of us to his work. It is only fitting, however, that this English edition be dedicated, finally, to the remarkable group of scholars who over the years have devoted their time, their insights, and their generous spirit to the translation, editing, and publication of these volumes. That dedication should begin with a special acknowledgment of the capable editorial leadership of Wayne Whitson Floyd Jr., who brought eight volumes to publication, and to Clifford J. Green, whose steady hand has guided the project throughout its existence and ensured the financial foundation for its completion.

The translators who have brought Bonhoeffer's words to new life in these volumes are Victoria Barnett, Douglas Bax, Claudia Bergmann, Isabel Best†, Daniel W. Bloesch, James H. Burtness†, Lisa Dahill, Peter Frick, Barbara Green, David Higgins, Nick Humphrey, Reinhard Krauss, Peter Krey, Nancy Lukens, Scott Moore, Mary Nebelsick, Marion Pauck, Barbara Rumscheidt†, Martin Rumscheidt, Anne Schmidt-Lange, Douglas W. Stott, and Charles West.

The following individuals serve on the editorial board of the *Dietrich Bonhoeffer Works, English Edition*: H. Gaylon Barker, Victoria Barnett, Mark Brocker, Keith Clements, Peter Frick, Clifford J. Green, John W. de Gruchy, Barry Harvey, Reinhard Krauss, Michael Lukens, Larry Rasmussen, and Barbara Wojhoski. In addition, James H. Burtness†, Wayne Whitson Floyd Jr., Barbara Green, James Patrick Kelley, Geffrey B. Kelly, Robin W. Lovin, Nancy Lukens, Paul Matheny, Mary Nebelsick, F. Burton Nelson†, and H. Martin Rumscheidt all previously served on the board, and many of them have continued to serve the project through its advisory committee.

In September 1943, Dietrich Bonhoeffer wrote his parents from prison: "In normal life one is often not at all aware that we always receive infinitely more than we give, and that gratitude is what enriches life. One easily overestimates the importance of one's own acts and deeds, compared with what we become only through other people."[2] Everyone who has worked on this project will, I believe, find meaning in those words and feel gratitude for Bonhoeffer's life and witness. It is a privilege to have been part of this long, deep, and rich conversation with Bonhoeffer's thought, and to extend that conversation to the readers of these volumes.

Victoria J. Barnett

[2.] Letter of September 13, 1943, *DBWE* 8, 2/57, p. 154.

Victoria J. Barnett

The Translation of the *Dietrich Bonhoeffer Works, English Edition*

An Overview

Introduction to the Index Volume

This volume includes translations of documents that were discovered after the publication of the *DBWE* volumes and indexes of the scriptural references and the primary subject references for the series. It also includes an alphabetized list of all the documents included in the sixteen *DBWE* volumes; a comprehensive chronology of significant dates in Bonhoeffer's life, career development, and thought, as well as key historical events; and a biographical index of all people referenced in volumes 1–16 and in the new documents included in this volume. It is intended primarily as a guide to help readers find their way through the sixteen volumes, particularly with regard to certain periods and events in Bonhoeffer's life and the evolution of his thought. With the exception of the master index of scriptural references, the indexes do not include page references but simply provide the respective volume reference; readers should refer to the indexes of the respective volumes for more-detailed references and cross-references. The editors especially thank Mark S. Brocker for his work in compiling the master biographical index.

The retrospective on the *Dietrich Bonhoeffer Works, English Edition,* by Clifford J. Green, executive director of the *DBWE,* and the afterword to the German edition, by Wolfgang Huber, chair of the German *DBW* editorial board, explore the history and significance of this series for future scholarship and research. In the following section, I summarize the particular challenges we faced in translating the *DBW* volumes and how the *DBWE* team of editors and translators addressed them.

Approach to Translation in the *Dietrich Bonhoeffer Works, English Edition*

The translation of the sixteen-volume German *Dietrich Bonhoeffer Werke* began in the 1990s. The first two volumes to be completed, *Act and Being* and *Life Together/Prayerbook of the Bible,* were published in 1996; the final volume published was *Theological Education at Finkenwalde: 1935–1937,* in 2013. Over the course of the project, twenty-two translators worked on the *Bonhoeffer Works,* and several volumes (8, 9, 11, and 15) were the work of more than one translator. Translation work on each volume was done in consultation with the respective volume editor and the general editor. By agreement with the German editorial board, the translation of each volume was also reviewed either by the respective German volume editors or by someone assigned to review the translation in their stead. The editorial and translation work on volumes 1, 2, 3, 4, 5, 6, 7, 9, and 16 was overseen by the first general editor, Wayne Whitson Floyd Jr., while Victoria Barnett and Barbara Wojhoski oversaw the work on volumes 8, 10, 11, 12, 13, 14, 15, and concluded the editorial work on 16. Some adjustments to the original editorial and translation policies were made for the second group of volumes, in part because of the change in the general editorial team and in part because the first group of volumes consisted of theological texts, while the second group consisted largely of correspondence and documents that were historical in nature.

The midseries transition in the general editorial team, the length of time during which the work proceeded, and the involvement of multiple translators mean that there is no single "voice" in this series and there is less consistency in translation than would be true of a single volume translated by one person. Throughout the life of the series, there has been regular consultation and discussion not just among members of the U.S. series team but also between the *DBW* and *DBWE* editors and editorial boards. This process made the translation of these volumes an ongoing "work in progress" during which some translation decisions made for earlier volumes were revised for the later volumes. In this regard, the *DBWE* editors are

particularly grateful to the invaluable assistance of two members of the German *DBW* project, Hans Pfeifer and Ilse Tödt.

Translators of these volumes were confronted by some additional challenges. One is the nature of translation itself, which at its best is both a science and an art form, an attempt to render meanings precisely and with an ear for nuance and eloquence. Depending on the context, the identical word can have very different nuances and meanings. Even in the original German texts, there were inconsistencies in how Bonhoeffer and his correspondents referred to certain ideas, events, and organizations such as ecumenical bodies. The editors of these volumes have tried to annotate and explain all such instances, and the master index of subjects and the master list of documents in this volume have been constructed to help readers recognize where such instances have arisen. It should be added that in both the German and the English editions the editors of the respective volumes had particular theological or historical expertise in the content of their volume and helped shape the translation accordingly. On the one hand, this has led to inconsistency in some of the translated terms. On the other, it means that each editor had a keen eye for the historical and theological accuracy of his or her respective volume, and readers who are particularly interested in the rationale for the translation of certain German texts should refer to the volume editor's introduction to the corresponding volume.

Several other factors unique to this series have shaped our approach to the translation of this material. These factors also help explain why these *DBWE* translations differ significantly from some of the earlier translations of Bonhoeffer's writings.

Nature of the Content in the *DBW/DBWE* Volumes

One such factor is the variety of the content of these volumes, as well as the fragmentary nature of some of the original texts. Volumes 1, 2, 3, 4, 5, 6, and 7 consist of Bonhoeffer's own writings, published (with the exception of volumes 6 and 7) in German during his lifetime. With the exception of volume 7 (which contains literary attempts), these are theological works for which previous English translations also exist: *Sanctorum Communio* (published as *The Communion of Saints* in America), *Act and Being, Creation and Fall, Discipleship* (previously published in English as *The Cost of Discipleship*), *Life Together* and *Psalms: The Prayerbook of the Bible* (published as one volume in *DBW/DBWE*), *Ethics,* and *Letters and Papers from Prison.* Many of these earlier translations were done for a more general readership and are markedly freer translations of the original German than the translations in *DBWE.*

The material in *DBWE* volumes 8, 9, 10, 11, 12, 13, 14, 15, and 16 is primarily biographical and historical, although each of these volumes also includes shorter theological and academic texts, such as sermons, Bible studies, and lectures. Most of the content of these latter volumes consists of correspondence between Bonhoeffer and his family, friends, and colleagues, as well as material written by other individuals, ranging from lecture notes taken by his students to bureaucratic church records to documents written by Nazi officials. Translation of these texts demanded careful attention to the nature of the document (bureaucratic versus personal communications, for example) and the tone of the author in the original German. Even in Bonhoeffer's own correspondence, his voice changes over time, from his student days until his years in prison, and he naturally expressed himself differently when writing to different kinds of correspondents.

Differences between the *DBWE* Documents and Existing English Translations

The documents published in the *DBW/DBWE* volumes are from Bonhoeffer's literary estate, which has been cataloged by Dietrich Meyer and Eberhard Bethge in their edited volume, *Nachlaß Dietrich Bonhoeffer: Ein Verzeichnis; Archiv, Sammlung, Bibliothek* (Munich: Chr. Kaiser Verlag, 1987). The documents that were cataloged in that volume were preserved on microfiche (housed at the Berliner Staatsbibliothek and Burke Library at Union Theological Seminary in New York). They include not only Bonhoeffer's papers but also copies of relevant material (such as correspondence and reports) from other archives that were microfilmed as well.

Some of these manuscripts exist as incomplete fragments, particularly the student notes made of Bonhoeffer's academic lectures and his seminars at Finkenwalde and texts by Bonhoeffer himself that exist only in draft form. While earlier translations of such material sometimes filled in the blanks, completing sentences and passages, the translation policy for *DBWE* was to follow the German closely, leaving incomplete phrases as they were and even including ellipses where the original German text was unreadable. All such instances have been carefully annotated in the *DBW/DBWE* volumes, and where necessary, additional information is included in the editorial notes. It should also be noted that even some of the "original" documents themselves were in fact transcriptions made by Eberhard Bethge, either of original handwritten documents (Bonhoeffer's handwriting was notoriously difficult to read) or, in the case of material that was disintegrating, as a preservation measure. Thus some of the documents preserved in the microfiche are in fact Bethge's transcriptions, complete with Bethge's (not

Bonhoeffer's) annotations and corrections, many of these made during the process of the publication of earlier anthologies such as *Gesammelte Schriften.*

In a very few instances, Eberhard Bethge organized material that in 1945 existed only in fragmentary form. The most striking case of this is the book *Ethik/Ethics* (*DBW/DBWE* 6). After 1945 Bethge compiled the incomplete manuscripts that Bonhoeffer had written during the early wartime years and published them in 1949 as the first German edition of *Ethik.* Debate about the order of manuscripts led to a second, rearranged edition that was published in 1963 (English edition, 1965). By the time of the *DBW/DBWE* publication, work done on these handwritten manuscripts and on Bonhoeffer's writing notes, especially Ilse Tödt's painstaking analysis of the different papers that had been used, enabled the editors of the German edition to reconstruct the order in which Bonhoeffer had probably written them. Following a basic *DBW* editorial guideline, the book was reorganized to reflect this writing sequence. Also, one manuscript previously in the appendix was incorporated into *Ethics,* while the other four were grouped with contemporary occasional pieces in *DBW/DBWE* 16,[1] which includes the documentation from the resistance period, covering the same period during which the *Ethics* manuscripts were written. As a result, there are significant differences between the original German *Ethik* and the early English translations of that book, and the *Ethik/Ethics* published as volume 6 of the *DBW/DBWE.*[2]

As the case of *Ethics* illustrates, the background and organization of some key Bonhoeffer texts were not established definitively by scholars until work began on the *Bonhoeffer Werke.* Some of the writings translated and published in early anthologies such as *No Rusty Swords* (1965), therefore, were based not on the German texts in the *Bonhoeffer Werke* (which reproduced the documentation exactly as found in the Bonhoeffer *Nachlaß* microfiches and include extensive annotation tracing the development of certain texts) but on the early German publication of Bonhoeffer's writings in the six-volume *Gesammelte Schriften* (1958–74).

[1.] These are the essays "State and Church" (2/10); "'Personal' and 'Objective' Ethics" (2/13); "A Theological Position Paper on the Primus Usus Legis" (2/18); and "What Does It Mean to Tell the Truth?" (2/19), which is in an appendix in the German editions but is called "Part Two" in the earlier translations of *Ethics.* The piece now published in *Ethics* is "On the Possibility of the Church's Message to the World."

[2.] For a more detailed explanation of the reordering of the *Ethics* manuscripts, see the introduction by Clifford Green to *DBWE* 6:1–44 and the comparison of the different editions on p. 477 of that volume.

Translation and Style Guidelines for the *DBWE*

At the beginning of the *DBWE* project, translators, editors, and representatives of the German *Bonhoeffer Werke* met several times to establish general translation guidelines for the English language edition, and consultations have continued throughout the life of the project. These consultations led to a list of translations for specific terms, particularly of the theological concepts that were central to Bonhoeffer's thought. At the same time, there was general acknowledgment of the complexity of conveying the meaning of such terms and the necessity of translating even key terms in different ways depending on the context. A primary example is the translation throughout *DBWE* of the German word *Gemeinde* as "church-community" when it refers to the larger theological sense of the church as the community of Christ in the world—a notion central to Bonhoeffer's understanding of the church. Yet in many places Bonhoeffer used *Gemeinde* to refer to a local congregation, and it can also be translated simply as "congregation."

Thus throughout *DBWE* there are variations in the translations even of key terms, and a great deal was left up to the discretion of the respective translators and editors, all of whom brought distinctive strengths and expertise to this project. Specific translation decisions made in the different volumes are discussed both in the editor's introduction to each volume and in editorial notes throughout. For reasons noted earlier, the translations of some terms were altered over the course of the series. With respect to the translation of historical terms and names of institutional bodies and church offices, an attempt was made at consistency, but even here there may be discrepancies across volumes. The subject index in this volume notes differing translations of some terms with cross-references to assist the reader. For example, the German word *Buße* can be translated variously as "repentance," "penance," or "penitence," depending on the context. This variation is indicated in the master index of subjects in this volume by including the German term in parentheses with all three entries and noting the appropriate cross-reference.

Gendered Language

One of the early decisions made by the initial *DBWE* team of translators, volume editors, and the first general editor was to follow a policy of nonsexist language where appropriate and possible in translating Bonhoeffer's theological writings.

This policy raised a number of issues that became more problematic with respect to the historical material in the second group of volumes.

In negotiating the complexities of this policy, for example, a common approach by translators was to translate passages that in the German were in the singular masculine as the more inclusive plural in English. Obviously, however, this meant a significant shift in tone and even meaning: with the shift from singular to plural, texts that in the German read almost autobiographically, with a heavy emphasis on the third-person masculine, were altered in the English translation to read much more generally and impersonally. It was also difficult to justify the change to nongendered inclusive language in Bonhoeffer's writings, including his correspondence, while retaining the gendered language of his correspondents, students, and others whose writings are included here. Thus with the change in general editorial leadership, and after much discussion among the editorial board members, this policy was abandoned for the second group of volumes, both for the historical and the theological material. Obviously this decision does not imply editorial support for sexist language and attitudes; it simply acknowledges that Bonhoeffer's language and attitudes reflected those of his times, and that the meaning of his texts as well as the context of his times and his church can best be conveyed by a close rendering of the German.

My general editor's foreword to the series, included in this volume, gives additional information about the conception of the series and concludes, as I do here, with great appreciation for all my colleagues who have worked on the German and the English volumes, and with special thanks to Fortress Press for its commitment to publishing these volumes, under the leadership of Marshall Johnson, Michael West, and Will Bergkamp.

CLIFFORD J. GREEN

THE *Dietrich Bonhoeffer Works, English Edition*

A RETROSPECTIVE

During his lifetime, Dietrich Bonhoeffer was known only to a small but influential group of people in the English-speaking world. We think of people like John Baillie and Reinhold Niebuhr, with whom he studied at Union Theological Seminary; fellow students like Paul Lehmann; Adam Clayton Powell, pastor of Abyssinian Baptist Church in Harlem; George Bell, the Anglican bishop of Chichester; Joseph Oldham, the English ecumenist; Gandhi's friend C. F. Andrews; Father Herbert Kelly at the Society of the Sacred Mission, Kelham; and the people he debated in the World Alliance for Promoting International Friendship through the Churches.

It was through his theological writings that Bonhoeffer first began to be widely known in the English-speaking world after the war. His study of the Sermon on the Mount and the Pauline letters was published in English by the Student Christian Movement Press in London in an abridged edition as *The Cost of Discipleship* in 1948. Bishop Bell wrote the foreword, and Bonhoeffer's brother-in-law, the jurist Gerhard Leibholz, wrote the first memoir[1] of his life. Seven years later, the translation of the first edition of his

[1.] See Bonhoeffer, *The Cost of Discipleship* (London: SCM, 1948), 9–28. The first American edition, published by Macmillan in 1949, also had a preface by Reinhold Niebuhr.

Ethics, edited by Eberhard Bethge, was published by SCM Press in 1955. But it was the first edition of his prison writings, published in London in 1953 as *Letters and Papers from Prison,* and in New York in 1954 as *Prisoner for God: Letters and Papers from Prison,* that made Bonhoeffer famous, not only in Britain and America but throughout the English-speaking world.

Meanwhile, Bonhoeffer's literary executor, Eberhard Bethge, began publishing volumes of Bonhoeffer's letters, addresses, sermons, and theology; the first four volumes of the *Gesammelte Schriften* appeared between 1958 and 1965.[2] These were organized thematically: ecumenism, Church Struggle, theology, and sermons. Two supplementary volumes of *Gesammelte Schriften* were published in 1972 and 1974, prompted in part by the extraordinary impact of Bishop John A. T. Robinson's 1963 book, *Honest to God,*[3] which stimulated even greater international interest in Bonhoeffer's life and work. Bethge's biography had been published in Germany in 1967 (English translations in 1970, 2000),[4] and these two additional volumes of the collected writings were organized not thematically but historically to parallel the biography; volume 5 focused on academic papers and sermons, volume 6 on more personal biographical sources such as letters and diaries. An important supplement to Bethge's collection of Bonhoeffer's writings was published by the Danish researcher Jørgen Glenthøj, who had scoured European and British archives to assemble over three hundred pages of letters, reports, and other documents, which he published in 1969 as *Dokumente zur Bonhoeffer-Forschung 1928–1945.*[5]

Only a selection of these seven volumes was available in English for many years. In 1965 Edwin H. Robertson produced the first volume of "letters, lectures and notes . . . from the collected works of Dietrich Bonhoeffer," under the title *No Rusty Swords.*[6] Two more volumes followed in 1966 and 1973, titled respectively *The Way to Freedom* and *True Patriotism.*[7] Occasionally other pieces appeared here and there, and perhaps in the most system-

[2.] Published by Chr. Kaiser Verlag, Munich.

[3.] John A. T. Robinson, *Honest to God* (London: SCM Press, 1963).

[4.] *Dietrich Bonhoeffer: Theologe, Christ, Zeitgenosse* (Munich: Chr. Kaiser, 1967). Abridged English-language edition edited by Edwin Robertson, translated by Eric Mosbacher et al. as *Dietrich Bonhoeffer: Man of Vision, Man of Courage* (London: Collins; New York: Harper, 1970); revised and unabridged ed. translated by Victoria J. Barnett, based on the 7th German ed., as *Dietrich Bonhoeffer: A Biography* (Minneapolis: Fortress Press, 2000).

[5.] Published as volume 5 of the series *Die Mündige Welt* (Munich: Chr. Kaiser, 1969).

[6.] London: William Collins; New York: Harper & Row.

[7.] London: William Collins; New York: Harper & Row.

atic form in the anthology edited by Geffrey B. Kelly and F. Burton Nelson, *A Testament to Freedom: The Essential Writings of Dietrich Bonhoeffer.*[8]

In addition to translations mentioned here—*The Cost of Discipleship* and the two edited posthumous volumes *Letters and Papers from Prison* and *Ethics*—several other volumes of Bonhoeffer's theology were published, mainly during the fifties and sixties: *Life Together* (1954);[9] *Temptation* (1955);[10] *Creation and Fall* (1959);[11] *Act and Being* (1961, 1962);[12] *Sanctorum Communio* (1963, 1964);[13] *Christology* (1966);[14] *The Prayer Book of the Bible* (1970);[15] *Fiction from Prison* (1981);[16] *Spiritual Care* (1985).[17] Of these, only the two dissertations and *Life Together* had been published by Bonhoeffer himself. The others, sometimes compiled from students' lecture notes as in the case of *Christology,* sometimes excerpted from the *Gesammelte Schriften,* reflected the personal interests of translators and editors, public desire to read more Bonhoeffer, and, frankly, the desire of publishers to have Bonhoeffer in their lists.

Thus by the 1980s, a large amount of Bonhoeffer's writing was available in English, but the composite as a whole was miscellaneous in several respects. The translation and editorial work was of varying quality. The rendering of Bonhoeffer's German was inconsistent. A translator of terms and ideas in one text may not have been aware of how the same idea had been handled in another part of the corpus. In short, Bonhoeffer in English not only lacked a large amount of the complete corpus; it also lacked a disciplined and consistent editorial policy and procedure for presenting the whole. Yet interest in Bonhoeffer continued to grow, not only among theologians and historians, but also among students, congregations, and the wider reading public. The need for a scholarly edition of all of Bonhoeffer's works was self-evident.

Providentially, German colleagues under the leadership of Heinz Eduard Tödt, and with the full cooperation of Eberhard Bethge, met in 1980

[8.] San Francisco: HarperSanFrancisco, 1990; rev. ed., 1995.

[9.] London: SCM Press; New York: Harper & Row.

[10.] London: SCM.

[11.] London: SCM; New York: Macmillan.

[12.] New York: Harper & Row, 1961; London: William Collins, 1962.

[13.] London: Collins, 1963; New York: Harper & Row, 1964, as *The Communion of Saints.*

[14.] London: Collins, 1966; New York: Harper & Row, 1966, as *Christ the Center.*

[15.] Minneapolis: Augsburg.

[16.] Philadelphia: Fortress Press.

[17.] Philadelphia: Fortress Press.

and decided to create a comprehensive, critical edition. As Wolfgang Huber writes, "While the new edition would not include every single text of Bonhoeffer that had been preserved, it was indeed to include everything essential," and it was to do so "in a consistent format and in accordance with uniform editorial principles."[18] To leaders in the English Language Section of the International Bonhoeffer Society, who were in regular contact with their German colleagues and with Eberhard Bethge, it was obvious that the new German critical edition would be translated into English in its entirety.

The *Dietrich Bonhoeffer Works, English Edition* is the result of a cordial and productive partnership between the Bonhoeffer Society (English Language Section) and Fortress Press, the developer and the publisher respectively. Preliminary discussions for the English edition began in the early 1980s as editorial work on the first German volumes commenced. Consultations and agreements with publishers who held the rights to the existing Bonhoeffer English translations were an essential prerequisite, as were inquiries to foundations and other funding sources. In March 1986, the board of directors of the Bonhoeffer Society appointed a translation committee chaired by Robin Lovin and with Michael Lukens as administrative secretary. This committee held its first organizing meeting with a group of potential translators and editors at Luther-Northwestern Theological Seminary, St. Paul, Minnesota, in September of the same year.

In 1989 the first grant to the project was awarded by the National Endowment for the Humanities, an auspicious start to the fund-raising. Robin Lovin was appointed project director for this grant, with Mark Brocker, then a doctoral student with Lovin at the University of Chicago, as research assistant.

Work on the first volumes—*Sanctorum Communio, Act and Being*, and *Life Together*—was already under way when the contract of January 6, 1992, between the Bonhoeffer Society and Fortress Press was signed. A separate contract covered the relationship between Fortress and the German publisher, Chr. Kaiser Verlag, Munich, the longtime publisher of Bonhoeffer, which was later incorporated into Gütersloher Verlagshaus.

In 1991 Robin Lovin was appointed dean of Drew University's School of Theology, and in 1992 Mark Brocker accepted a pastoral appointment in Oregon. The editorial board in 1992 therefore appointed Wayne Floyd Jr. as general editor. He served from 1993 to 2004 and was joined by Clifford Green in the position of executive director. Floyd saw into print most of the

[18.] See p. 20.

volumes of the A series, that is, the monographs that had been previously translated and now appeared in newly translated, fully annotated scholarly editions, and the first volume of the B series, volume 9, *The Young Bonhoeffer: 1918–1927.* In 2002 Victoria J. Barnett joined the project as associate general editor, and became general editor in 2004. She was joined by Barbara Wojhoski, a professional editor who prepared the manuscripts of the latter volumes for publication.

The work of the English-language editors and translators was very different from that of the German editors. The main tasks of the latter were to establish the text of the critical edition and to annotate it with appropriate notes, bibliography, commentary, and similar scholarly resources. Occasionally work of this sort had to be done by the editors of the English edition, especially when new documents were discovered, as happened with some regularity. The primary task of the German editors, not to oversimplify too much, was to take Bonhoeffer's words and put them on paper in a coherent edition.[19]

Translation is a very different task. The translators and editors had to communicate the *meaning* of Bonhoeffer's words in a different language. Hans Pfeifer, a leading member of the German *Herausgeberkreis*, and the liaison with the English-edition editorial board, once formulated the challenge this way: "You must turn our Aramaic into your Greek!" It was by no means a matter of substituting one set of words for another. The challenge was first to *understand* Bonhoeffer and then to *communicate* his meaning for people with a different history and culture. This work had to be done remembering that the *Dietrich Bonhoeffer Works, English Edition* would be read not only in the United States but also in Britain, Canada, South Africa, Australia and, indeed, throughout the world—including China, India, and countries in Africa. The translators and editors also had to be mindful that many readers of English would not have the detailed familiarity with German theological and political history that the German editors could assume—particularly the complex ecclesial and political history of Germany in the National Socialist period; notes had to be added to assist in that area and also with the subtleties of many German words. Attention also had to be given to changing social sensibilities that were altering English-language usage and vocabulary; readers will find the issues of translating gendered language and avoiding sexism discussed by the general editors in

[19.] To be sure, the German editors went to great pains in their notes to make Bonhoeffer's meaning as clear as possible, and these notes were indispensable resources for the translators.

their forewords in the volumes and also by several volume editors in their introductions.

Given such challenges, a very deliberate procedure was created by the editorial board and followed in every volume. Central to the project was collegial international cooperation, and critical review was intrinsic to every stage of translating and editing.

Special mention must be made of the role of Hans Pfeifer, the official liaison between the German and the English-language editorial boards. A leading Bonhoeffer researcher and scholar, Pfeifer was familiar with the Anglo-Saxon world through his early study at Princeton Theological Seminary. For years he attended the meetings of the editorial board, which were held during the annual meeting of the American Academy of Religion each fall. He was in constant touch with editors, translators, and the general editor via email, dealing with questions of language and meaning, theology and history. He frequently read and commented on large drafts of translation or even entire book manuscripts. His contribution to the series was indispensable, and his death in 2011 was grieved as a deep loss.

Ilse Tödt also played a special role in the English translation. As an editor or coeditor of several German volumes, for example, *Discipleship* and *Ethics*, with an encyclopedic knowledge of the German corpus and an excellent command of English, she read translation drafts with great care and provided detailed annotation, not to mention numerous cross-references and commentary. And on the rare occasion when a query led back to an original manuscript and Bonhoeffer's difficult handwriting, it was Ilse Tödt who addressed it.

The *Dietrich Bonhoeffer Works, English Edition* can be compared in scope to the translation of Karl Barth's *Church Dogmatics* and to the American edition of *Luther's Works*—though Bonhoeffer did not live as long or write quite as much as his fellow theologians. But a project that has taken over a quarter of a century from its initial preparations to its completion accumulates a great many debts. The editorial board, editors, and translators wish to express their gratitude to our German colleagues, upon whose excellent work our own edition rests. The edition itself is the result of the faithful, patient, and generous labors of a great company of devoted people who were committed to producing an English edition of Bonhoeffer worthy of the high standards set by his life and thought. Many universities, colleges, and seminaries in the United States, but also in the United Kingdom and South Africa, as well as church congregations and ecumenical organizations, gave time and practical support to editors and translators. Numerous funding sources, including foundations, synods, congregations, nonprofit organizations, and the numerous individual members and friends of the

International Bonhoeffer Society—all gratefully acknowledged in the front of each volume—provided the essential financial support for the project. And the many staff of Fortress Press who have worked on this edition during three decades have contributed both their professional talents and also genuine personal enthusiasm.

Attention should be drawn to the forewords of the general editors and the introductions of the volume editors that appear in each volume. There details about the development of the project, its policy discussions, and its personnel can be found. Editors' introductions to individual volumes also contain discussions of translation questions, sometimes in considerable detail, and discussions of key theological and historical aspects of the text. Attention should also be drawn to translations of the afterwords of the German volume editor or editors, which contain their insights and observations about the content of their volumes.

In November 2013, the editorial board completed its work and voted officially to disband. Records of the work of the project are being prepared for archiving as part of the Bonhoeffer collection in Burke Library at Union Theological Seminary, New York.

Now that the *Dietrich Bonhoeffer Works, English Edition* is complete, a different task lies ahead for theologians, historians, and biographers. This is not a new task, but it remains urgent. It is implied in Victoria Barnett's statement with which she opens her general editor's foreword to this volume: "The German theologian and pastor Dietrich Bonhoeffer has become one of the most influential Christian thinkers of all time."[20] This reflects the remarkable worldwide extent of interest in the writings and the life of Dietrich Bonhoeffer. The task ahead is to achieve a more complete and profound understanding of this theologian and historical actor. In the early years of Bonhoeffer interpretation, in both Europe and the English-speaking world, attention focused on his provocative ideas about humanity in modernity and his proposal for a "religionless, worldly Christianity." It was Bonhoeffer's *ideas* that fascinated readers. In recent years, public attention has focused more on Bonhoeffer the historical agent, on the *person* and his life, particularly his role in church and political resistance to the National Socialist regime.

Now that all of Bonhoeffer's writings are available in both German and English, we have both the need and the opportunity to *read Bonhoeffer whole.* No longer can one read a part of the corpus—such as the book *Discipleship* or the *Letters and Papers from Prison*—and take it in isolation as a key to the

[20.] See p. vii.

whole. Recently we have begun to see new research into characteristics of Bonhoeffer's thought as a whole and new analyses of the relation between texts such as *Discipleship* and *Ethics*. But much work remains to fully understand Bonhoeffer the thinker. Is it possible, for example, to create a synoptic interpretation of the different components of Bonhoeffer's unfinished *Ethics* manuscripts that displays these components in a coherent whole? An even more comprehensive task is to ask whether, in the diversity of Bonhoeffer's writings, exigent as they often are, a unifying project informs his thinking from beginning to end. A related question, as one *reads Bonhoeffer whole,* is the degree to which his theology and ethics are informed by Luther and the complex Lutheran tradition, and how we are to account for novel aspects of his thought, not only in his famous late writings but also in his earlier work, for example, his distinctive valuation of the Sermon on the Mount and his Christian peace ethic. Historians as well as theologians will seek to better understand topics such as Bonhoeffer's role in the resistance conspiracy, his attitude and actions with respect to Jews and Judaism in the Third Reich, and the continuing crucial interaction of religion and politics as exemplified in Bonhoeffer's Germany. If we understand reasonably well the meaning and import of the theologies of Bonhoeffer's older contemporaries—Karl Barth, Paul Tillich, and Reinhold Niebuhr—the edition now completed will enable us to reach a like understanding of Dietrich Bonhoeffer. To make available to theologians, historians, and a wide public readership the continuing challenge and inspiration of Dietrich Bonhoeffer is the aim of this now completed edition.

Wolfgang Huber

The *Dietrich Bonhoeffer Werke*

Afterword to the German Edition

I 937

Dietrich Bonhoeffer was born on February 4, 1906; he died on Hitler's gallows on April 9, 1945, at only thirty-nine years of age. His premonition that his life would remain a fragment was confirmed. In looking at the life of his parents, he sensed the uncompleted, fragmentary nature of his own life particularly strongly. Yet he added: "Precisely that which is fragmentary may point to a higher fulfillment. . . . Even when the violence of outward events breaks our lives in pieces, as the bombs do our houses, everything possible must be done to keep in view the way all this was planned and intended to be. At the very least, it will still be possible to recognize from what kind of material here we build or must build."[1] And to his friend Eberhard Bethge he expressed the hope that "one still sees, in this fragment of life that we have, what the whole was intended and designed to be, and of what material it is made." In this context he spoke of fragments that "must remain fragments" "because only God could perfect them."[2]

A biography bears such a fragmentary character, which in Bonhoeffer's case was molded by an unusual connection between the testimony of his life and theological existence. Precisely in its fragmentary character, the

[1.] Letter of February 20, 1944, to his parents (*DBWE* 8, 2/114, p. 301).

[2.] Letter of February 23, 1944, to Bethge (*DBWE* 8, 2/115, p. 306).

impact of his life unfolded in effect far beyond the German-speaking world, the realm of the Protestant church, and the field of academic theology. Our responsibility is to see to it that this fragment remains recognizable and discernible. Its impact is not in our hands. And its ultimate completion can only be a divine matter.

938 On May 12, 1997, Eberhard and Renate Bethge gave Dietrich Bonhoeffer's papers to the Library of the Prussian Cultural Foundation [Staatsbibliothek der Stiftung Preußischer Kulturbesitz]. On April 5, 1998—also in the Berlin Staatsbibliothek—the completion of the sixteen-volume collected works of Dietrich Bonhoeffer was celebrated. Now, with the seventeenth volume, additional material and the general index can be published. With this, the responsibility for safeguarding the "fragments" has concluded, and in a striking way it is now evident "what the whole was intended and designed to be."

This edition is intended to do justice to the continuing significance that is due Dietrich Bonhoeffer's life and work for church and theology, for German history and the ecumenical world. It intends to make his legacy available for the long term. For that reason, it meets the standards of a critical historical edition, but at the same time the effort has been made to make Bonhoeffer's written legacy accessible to all readers, irrespective of their previous theological knowledge. It was still possible for friends and students of Dietrich Bonhoeffer, as contemporary witnesses, to work on this edition; in the fellowship of members of the younger generation, they have given this edition its form. Now this great theologian's work, in an edition prepared for lasting value, stands ready for the coming generations.

II.

It was anything but self-evident that the lasting significance of Dietrich Bonhoeffer's literary work would be recognized. During his lifetime he published, in addition to his dissertation and postdoctoral dissertation, four separate works of varying scope and a series of essays. He was denied an academic reputation; he was limited through bans on teaching and public speaking. In the final years of his life, that which he put on paper was written under the proviso that he had to disguise the circumstances under which he wrote it. After 1945 his participation in the conspiracy against
939 Hitler was for some a reason for additional reservations. Because of this, for some time after his violent death, none of the church, academic, or state institutions was particularly interested in the preparation of his works.

It was rather a personal risk that his friend Eberhard Bethge took in 1949 with the publication of the *Ethics* fragments, followed by the 1951

publication of his letters and papers from prison, under the German title *Widerstand und Ergebung.*[3] The risk was borne as well by Chr. Kaiser Verlag and its director, Fritz Bissinger, who during the 1930s had already overseen the publication of Bonhoeffer's writings by the publishing house. Now, however, a completely new phase began. The miracle that the *Ethics* manuscripts as well as the prison writings had been preserved was followed by the miracle of their impact. The breakthrough came with *Letters and Papers from Prison.* This book kept more people in the Christian faith than could have been anticipated, even in the Federal Republic of Germany. It encouraged a confessional resistance where necessary—as, for example, in South Africa. It helped people endure their situation in the minority—as in Japan. It stimulated a rethinking of the church—as in the German Democratic Republic.

Out of this, the question emerged about the context for these writings. After 1958 Eberhard Bethge began to publish various letters and essays, journal entries and sermons, notes from academic lectures, and other documents in the *Gesammelte Schriften* (Collected writings).[4] These volumes fitted together like the concentric growth rings of a tree and were read avidly by many as soon as they appeared. Ecumenical breadth, spiritual life, the courage of ideas and action united in a manner that opened up the Christian faith in a new way. Eberhard Bethge's great biography of his friend, which appeared in 1967, made the person and his works accessible in an unprecedented fashion. For the publisher, the significance of the legacy entrusted to it is evident in the fact that Ulrich Kabitz, who had been with the publisher since 1960, was freed for two years to assist almost exclusively with the work on the biography.

The organization of the *Gesammelte Schriften* and the supplementary
material published by Jørgen Glenthøj in 1969[5] was provisional. Just as 940
a volume appeared, new documents surfaced. Ernst Feil, one of the most prominent Bonhoeffer researchers even at the time, was the first to have the courage to draw the necessary consequences. "Almost seductively," he wrote Ulrich Kabitz on April 21, 1969, "almost seductively" the question had

[3.] [Literally, "Resistance and Submission"; the title of the first English edition was *Letters and Papers from Prison,* first published in 1953 by SCM Press (UK) and Macmillan (US). The early German and English editions were abridged; the complete prison letters and papers first appeared as *DBW* 8 (1998) and *DBWE* 8 (2010).—VB]

[4.] [A six-volume series, it has never been translated into English in its entirety.—VB]

[5.] [*Die Mündige Welt,* vol. 5: *Dokumente zur Bonhoeffer-Forschung 1928–1945,* published by Chr. Kaiser Verlag in 1969.—VB].

occurred to him "whether under all these circumstances one should still consider it too early to envisage a new edition of the *Gesammelte Schriften*."

The question was at the same time justified and farsighted. But it would not be until a meeting on June 6–7, 1980, that the decision was made, after many lengthy preliminary considerations. In 1981 the plan for the new edition was put into motion. It was to consist not only of the *Gesammelte Schriften*, however, but of Bonhoeffer's entire work. This plan was built on the foundation of Eberhard Bethge's edition, but with Bethge's agreement and his tireless support, it went further. While the new edition would not include every single text of Bonhoeffer that had been preserved, it was indeed to include everything essential, and it did so in a consistent format and in accordance with uniform editorial principles.

In the last half century, Eberhard Bethge's previous editions have had their own impact. Older readers may prefer to keep their old, trusted editions of *Ethics* or *Letters and Papers*. But at the same time, old and young alike will understand the value of the additional material they find in our edition. This is particularly true with respect to *Letters and Papers*, where the additional material sheds new light on Eberhard Bethge's contribution to the theological conversation with his friend.

The decision to have a new edition of the *Dietrich Bonhoeffer Werke* had many fathers and mothers. It would have been inconceivable without the admirable willingness of Eberhard and Renate Bethge to devote themselves to this great task, which meant that they also faced revising previous decisions. It would have been inconceivable without those who were prepared to take on the publishing responsibility, initially Manfred Weber and Ulrich Kabitz of Chr. Kaiser Verlag, and then Hans-Jürgen Meurer of Gütersloher Verlagshaus/Chr. Kaiser. It would have been inconceivable without the perseverance of the editors: Herbert Anzinger at the beginning and for a long time, and in the final phase of work, Hans Pfeifer. It would have been
941 inconceivable without the engagement of the editorial board members. In addition to Eberhard Bethge and Hans Pfeifer, they included in particular Bonhoeffer's contemporary Albrecht Schönherr; Ernst Feil, the definitive interpreter of Bonhoeffer's theology; and Christian Gremmels, the chair of the German section of the International Bonhoeffer Society, who took on one of the most difficult editorial burdens, *Letters and Papers*.

But above all, the step toward a new edition would have been inconceivable without the inspiring perseverance of Heinz Eduard Tödt, who until his death on May 25, 1991, was the chair of the editorial board. No one else shaped and pressed ahead with the work on this edition like he did; he brought and kept the circle of editors and staff together, both internally and externally. He himself set the standard through his work on the new

edition of *Ethics*. And through the research project on the "Bonhoeffer-Dohnanyi resistance circle"[6] that accompanied the edition, he contributed significantly to the research on the context in which Bonhoeffer's works arose. Only gradually and without any particular moment of discovery did Tödt, who was only twelve years younger than Bonhoeffer, become aware of his theological resonance with Bonhoeffer. He drew the consequences in the edition. Among the editorial board members, he is the only one who could not enjoy the completion of this edition, which owes him immeasurable gratitude.

Ilse Tödt worked on this edition together with him. Whoever closely looks at the sixteen volumes that precede this one will find that no name appears more frequently than hers among the volume editors. She is explicitly named in six of the sixteen volumes. But even where she is not named, she was involved—with her perfectly developed capacity to decipher Bonhoeffer's handwriting, with her knowledge of the different kinds of paper Bonhoeffer used, and as the person responsible for a number of indexes and countless sections of the text.

On October 6, 1990, when a renewed bout with cancer kept Heinz
Eduard Tödt from this work once more, he wrote me: "With this I am giving 942
you the task of assuming the duties of chairperson for the *DBW* editorial
board during the period of my illness." That was to remain so.

III.

In 1981 work on the new edition began. On February 4, 1986, Bonhoeffer's eightieth birthday, the first volume—*Sanctorum Communio*—reached the public. In a foreword on behalf of the editorial board, Heinz Eduard Tödt explained the project and its significance for the ongoing influence of Dietrich Bonhoeffer's theology. Sixteen volumes, with about 8,000 pages, were announced; a separate index volume was planned early. Although the number of announced volumes remained the same, the sixteen volumes now encompass 9,278 pages, plus the addenda.[7]

Heinz Eduard Tödt spoke of ten years of difficult work. This turned into eighteen years, if one calculates the time before the first volume appeared.

[6.] [This was a multiyear project (*Forschungsprojekt zum Widerstand des Bonhoeffer-Dohnanyi-Kreises gegen den Nationalsozialismus*) under Tödt's direction at the University of Heidelberg.—VB]

[7.] [The sixteen volumes in *DBWE*, the English edition, encompass 9,130 pages. —VB]

Thirteen years passed between the publication of the first volume and the appearance of the index volume. For almost two decades, more than thirty colleagues worked to present Bonhoeffer's texts reliably and in historical-critical form, worked on the necessary commentaries, and made the historical context accessible. The first eight volumes of this edition are being translated by Alberto Gallas into Italian. The entire sixteen-volume edition is also appearing in an English-language edition that will be overseen by an editorial board led by Wayne Floyd and Clifford Green.[8] The translations of individual works into other languages will also follow the new edition.

When the first volume of this edition was presented to the public, there were separate celebrations on Bonhoeffer's eightieth birthday in the
943 two parts of Berlin; the content of the celebrations was rather different as well. The plans for the edition, however, had been agreed upon by the two Bonhoeffer societies in still-divided Germany; this was expressed in the composition of the editorial board as well as the selection of those assigned to each volume. Now the division of Germany, at least externally, has been overcome for ten years. And it can be hoped that the era in which Bonhoeffer was instrumentalized politically by one side or the other is also behind us.

Bonhoeffer's legacy can unfold in that which he himself has to say. And that which distinguishes and must distinguish us from Bonhoeffer can be articulated. This too is part of the mature Christian existence that he encouraged as no one else did. In the treatment of Bonhoeffer and his legacy, maturity [Mündigkeit] is the only correct attitude, maturity that makes us capable of responsibility.

Bonhoeffer's works will continue to have an impact, not because the author is enveloped in the aura of a saint but rather because his work deserves this impact—and even more, because his witness of faith and his theological inspiration will prove itself even in the twenty-first century as a source of encouragement and as a challenge to our own thinking and action. For this reason the work on the preservation of his literary legacy has been worthwhile.

[8.] [Victoria J. Barnett became assistant general editor in 2002. In 2004 Barnett and Barbara Wojhoski became general editors for the remaining volumes of the *DBWE* series.—VB]

IV.

Several important distinctions from previous editions should be explicitly noted. The most important is the clear general organization of this edition. The distinction between the first series of monographs (volumes 1–8) and a second series of biographically organized volumes (volumes 9–16) proved to be the correct one. The material in the second series volumes has been consistently presented in three sections: letters and documents in the first section; essays, scholarly works, and academic lectures in the second; sermons and exegeses in the third. Within these sections, the documents have been organized chronologically. All the texts that had been published previously were compared again to the originals, and new commentary was added; in addition to these were a large number of newly discovered texts 944
or texts being published for the first time. Important phases of Bonhoeffer's life have been documented for the first time or extensively reworked. The academic lectures have now been documented in a methodologically clear fashion. The existing student notes taken at the time or later were not combined as in earlier editions; more often in the *DBW* volumes one set of notes has been selected, with additions from other notes indicated in the editorial notes. In every case, the manuscripts were consulted again. This has allowed for important improvements to the text—even for very well-known passages.

In 1986 Heinz Eduard Tödt noted with regret that Bonhoeffer's correspondence with his fiancée, Maria von Wedemeyer, at the time was not accessible. Fortunately this correspondence in the meantime has been largely published, even if unfortunately not in the scope of this edition.[9]

Some important material could not be incorporated into this edition but was published as a supplementary volume[10] or in a separate form.[11] Letters and documents from Bonhoeffer's immediate circle were edited as

[9.] These letters were published in English as *Love Letters from Cell 92: The Correspondence between Dietrich Bonhoeffer and Maria von Wedemeyer, 1943–1945*, trans. John Brownjohn with a postscript by Eberhard Bethge (Nashville: Abingdon Press, 1995). [It was possible in 2006 to include ten letters written by Bonhoeffer to Maria von Wedemeyer in the English *DBWE* 16 volume.—VB. Fourteen letters to and from Maria von Wedemeyer were also included in *Dietrich Bonhoeffer Auswahl*, ed. Christian Gremmels and Wolfgang Huber (Gütersloh: Gütersloher Verlagshaus, 2006), 5:185–226.—WH]

[10.] Bonhoeffer, *Zettelnotizen für eine "Ethik,"* ed. Ilse Tödt (Munich: Chr. Kaiser, 1993); this was a supplementary volume for *DBW* 6.

[11.] Ilse Tödt, ed., *Dietrich Bonhoeffers Hegel-Seminar 1933*, according to notes made by Ferenc Lehel, Internationales Bonhoeffer-Forum 8 (Munich: Chr. Kaiser, 1988).

a supplementary volume.[12] Another set of correspondence was linked in the publisher's catalog to the *DBW* edition.[13] In the future there may be additional individual supplementary volumes of this nature.[14]

945 The individual texts of Dietrich Bonhoeffer that were not included in the *DBW* volumes have been explicitly listed in the respective volumes[15] and can also be found in the catalog.[16] These can be viewed in the microfiche of Bonhoeffer's papers,[17] and the originals can also be viewed in the Manuscript Department [Handschriftenabteilung] of the Staatsbibliothek der Stiftung Preußischer Kulturbesitz in Berlin.

It was a particularly fortunate coincidence that with the completion of this edition the long-awaited international bibliography compiled by Ernst Feil was published.[18] This included an extensive list of sources as well as the secondary literature published between 1933 and 1996—in no fewer than sixteen different languages.[19]

Those who have worked on the individual volumes represent diverse personal, academic, confessional, and political backgrounds. They were

[12.] Dorothee Andersen, Eberhard Bethge, and Gerhard Vibrans, eds., *So ist es gewesen: Briefe im Kirchenkampf 1933–1942 von Gerhard Vibrans, aus seinem Familien- und Freundeskreis und von Dietrich Bonhoeffer* [This is how it was: Correspondence of Gerhard Vibrans, from his family, friends, and Dietrich Bonhoeffer, during the German Church Struggle], supplement to the *Dietrich Bonhoeffer Werke* (Gütersloh: Gütersloher Verlagshaus, 1995).

[13.] Hilde Enterlein and Albrecht Schönherr, *Lass es uns trotzdem miteinander versuchen: Brautbriefe aus der Zeit des Kirchenkampfes 1935–1936*, ed. Albrecht Schönherr, with an introduction by Otto Dudzus (Gütersloh: Chr. Kaiser Verlagshaus, 1997).

[14.] [The most important is the complete edition of the "Finkenwalde circular letters": *Finkenwalder Rundbriefe: Briefe und Texte von Dietrich Bonhoeffer und seinen Predigerseminaristen 1935–1946*, comp. Eberhard Bethge and Otto Berendts, ed. Ilse Tödt, supplement to the Dietrich Bonhoeffer Werke (Gütersloh; Gütersloher Verlagshaus, 2013).—WH]

[15.] [The texts omitted from each volume are listed at the conclusion of that volume in the appendix "Unpublished Material from Bonhoeffer's Literary Estate."—VB]

[16.] Dietrich Meyer and Eberhard Bethge, eds., *Nachlaß Dietrich Bonhoeffer: Ein Verzeichnis; Archiv—Sammlung—Bibliothek* [Dietrich Bonhoeffer's literary estate: A bibliographic catalog; Archive, collection, library] (Munich: Chr. Kaiser Verlag, 1987).

[17.] [Copies of the complete microfiche are in the Burke Library at Union Theological Seminary in New York and the Staatsbibliothek Berlin.—VB]

[18.] *International Bibliography on Dietrich Bonhoeffer*, ed. Ernst Feil, with Barbara E. Fink (Gütersloh: Chr. Kaiser/Gütersloher Verlagshaus, 1998).

[19.] [Since the conclusion of the German *DBW* edition, newly discovered documents have appeared in the *Dietrich Bonhoeffer Jahrbuch*, published by Chr. Kaiser/Gütersloher Verlagshaus. At this time of publication, five issues of the *Jahrbuch*, which also includes scholarly articles and new research on Bonhoeffer, have been published. Wherever possible these new documents were included in the appropriate volume of the *DBWE* edition; those that appeared too late for inclusion appear in the present volume.—VB]

brought together through their common responsibility for this edition. The individual accents they brought were not evened out but could be expressed particularly in the afterword of each volume. Despite all the differences between those involved, a homogenous edition has emerged that conforms to a single standard.

Two of those who worked on the German edition were unable to live to see its completion: Jørgen Glenthøj and Martin Kuske. We remember them too with great gratitude.[20]

V.

Whichever volume and whichever set of questions open the wealth of Dietrich Bonhoeffer's writings to the reader, one always encounters the connection between teaching and life, truth and existence, theology and church. The cantus firmus of Bonhoeffer's life's work can perhaps be described this 946
way: in Christ, God unconditionally opened himself to the reality of this world; for that reason this world cannot be fatalistically left to itself. Just as God's kingdom encompasses all reality, neither the individual Christian nor the church can simply withdraw from certain areas of this reality.

Bonhoeffer passionately connected theology with the reality of human experience. This shaped his understanding of God right up to speaking of the powerlessness of God on the cross; it shaped his picture of church right up to speaking of the "church for others"; it shaped his conception of Christian faith right up to the pointed expression that faith was not a special area of human existence but rather an "act of life." This openness to experience in his theology helps explain Bonhoeffer's particular capacity to interpret his own era, which is also extremely instructive with respect to other eras. The historical distance certainly helps us notice the ways in which these texts are connected to their times, but precisely this can bring to light—in a way that transcends our distance from that era—the meaning of Christian existence, church action, and theological reflection, for today and tomorrow, in a way that inspires and gives us an orientation.

The value of thought, speech, and writing was not minimized but rather put in its proper place when Bonhoeffer in a March 1938 sermon said: "The life of a Christian consists not of words but of experience. No one is a Christian without experience. We speak here not of life experience but of

[20.] [Since the completion of the German edition in 1998, a number of those involved have died, including Eberhard Bethge, who died in 2000. See also the general editor's foreword, p. xii.—VB]

the experience of God. But it is also not about various experiences of God but about the experience that lies in the probation of the faith and of the peace of God, the experience of the cross of Jesus Christ. Only the patient ones experience. The impatient ones do not experience anything."[21]

Wolfgang Huber
On behalf of the editorial board

Berlin, April 9, 1999
The fifty-fifth anniversary of Dietrich Bonhoeffer's death

[21.] Sermon of March 9, 1938, *DBWE* 15, 3/2, p. 475.

Additional Letters and Documents

DBWE 9, 1/80a. To Ernst Fritz Schmid[1]

Berlin, June 19, 1924

Dear Fritz:[2]

Only a few days ago, as I was visiting Held[3] and Dreier[4] on my trip back from Italy,[5] I learned that you very suddenly took the leap to get out.[6]

[1.] Handwritten in pencil. Bonhoeffer's address is handwritten at the end of the letter by Ernst Schmid: "Berlin-Grunewald, Wangenheimstr. 14." Letter in possession of Lotte Schmid (Augsburg). First publication in M. H. Schmid, "'Befreundest du dich etwas mehr mit der modernen Musik?': Ernst Fritz Schmid in musikalischem Briefwechsel mit Dietrich Bonhoeffer," in *Musik in Baden-Württemberg,* ed. G. Günther and W. Salmen (Munich, 2004), 11:49–61. In the German text, Bonhoeffer's shorthand for "and," "rather," and "against" have been deciphered. Ernst Fritz Schmid (1904–60) was a musicologist who taught at Tübingen from 1935 to 1937, when he resigned as a civil servant; he was president of the German Mozart Society from 1951 to 1958. For more about him, see *In memoriam Ernst Fritz Schmid (1904–1960): Ein Gedenkblatt für seine Angehörigen und Freunde* (Recklinghausen: Bauer-Druck, 1961), and the article by M. H. Schmid cited above. Previously published in *Dietrich Bonhoeffer Jahrbuch/Yearbook* 2 (2005/2006): 37–40. Transcription by Lotte Schmid and Ilse Tödt. Edited by Christian Gremmels. English translation by Victoria Barnett.

[2.] In connection with his joining the "Hedgehog" academic fraternity (see *DB-ER,* 48–51, and *DBWE* 9, 1/35), Bonhoeffer wrote his parents at the end of May 1923 about Ernst Fritz Schmid: "I chose my fraternity bodyguard on Thursday. I chose Schmid, the son of the resident philosopher, who is in his third semester and is studying zoology. He also plays violin a lot, so we play music together quite a bit." See also the message of July 7, 1923, to his parents: "I now spend a lot of time with Fritz Schmid. There at the house we play a lot of good music. There are not many concerts here, as you know, so it makes it very nice" (*DBWE* 9, 1/97, p. 61), and Bonhoeffer's curriculum vitae (*DBWE* 9, 1/96, p. 60), a handwritten entry in the Hedgehog fraternity "Foxes Book" in the 1923 summer semester.

[3.] Robert Held was a Tübingen student friend of Bonhoeffer's and a member of the Hedgehogs (see ed. note 8 below) since the 1923 summer semester; he later became an attorney in Stuttgart. On Held, see *DBWE* 9:570; and Renate Bethge and Christian Gremmels, eds., *Dietrich Bonhoeffer: A Life in Pictures,* trans. Brian McNeil, centenary ed. (Minneapolis: Fortress Press, 2006), 35.

[4.] Wilhelm Dreier was a Tübingen student friend and member of the Hedgehogs (see ed. note 8) after the 1923 summer semester. He later became a merchant in Bremen. On Dreier, see *DBWE* 9, 1/81 and 1/96b, and Bethge and Gremmels, *Life in Pictures,* centenary ed., 35.

[5.] Bonhoeffer's parents made it possible for Dietrich and his brother Klaus to study in Rome (April–June 1924); see Bonhoeffer's Italian diary, *DBWE* 9, 1/57. Regarding the return trip, see Bonhoeffer's letter in June 1924 to his twin sister (*DBWE* 9, 1/80, p. 129): "I also stayed in Zurich for a couple of hours and then traveled on to Horb, where two members of the Hedgehog fraternity were waiting to take me on a short excursion into the Black Forest." [This note combines notes 3 and 6 from the German version published in the *Bonhoeffer Yearbook.*—VB]

[6.] The "Hedgehog Association of Tübingen" (see ed. note 8) informed Schmid on June 2, 1924, that the organization "unanimously . . . approved" his resignation.

Since I am literally [. . .][7] still affected by the case, do write me about what specifically drove you to this; ultimately you are certainly not the only one who was not exactly made happy by the association,[8] and now you have simply left those of us who are not an insignificant part of the association, so we will have to work further on the same cause with one less man to support us, for naturally we too could get out for many reasons. That would then leave a pretty assortment of Hedgehogs. Now of course you did not have much in common with many of them at all, so the association also didn't give much to you. But do write me. Since we last saw each other, I have not heard anything more from you. I myself spent the large portion of the w[inter] s[emester] in bed with a slight concussion,[9] so I didn't hear anything about you from the others either. Did music lead you along this reclusive path? Someone just told me that you wanted to join the Youth Movement.[10] The entire matter is not very clear to me. I just set up a

[7.] Illegible.

[8.] Bonhoeffer's father had already been a member of the Tübingen Hedgehogs. See K. Bonhoeffer, "Lebenserinnerung," in *Karl Bonhoeffer: Zum Hundertsten Geburtstag am 31. März 1968*, ed. Jürg Zutt, Erwin Straus, and Heinrich Scheller (Berlin: Springer-Verlag, 1969), 32. At the beginning of May 1923, Bonhoeffer wrote his parents to ask: "Yesterday evening I was up at the Hedgehog fraternity house. . . . I liked the people fairly well and would like very much to join them for the one semester that I am here. Now, I don't know what you would think about my staying here for a second semester. . . . Please write as soon as you can and tell me what you think about my staying here for a second semester" (*DBWE* 9, 1/33, pp. 56–57). Together with his brother-in-law Wilhelm Dreß (see 1/94b, ed. note 7), Bonhoeffer broke from the group in 1933, "after some of its members exalted the Nazi *Gleichschaltung*, or 'synchronization' of society, as a fulfillment of ancient ideals. His resignation is recorded in the March 1936 senior members' bulletin" (*DB-ER*, 49; see also W. Dreß, "Dietrich Bonhoeffer in Tübingen," in *Theologia viatorum* 12 [1975]: 23–24).

[9.] The result of a fall while ice skating; see *DB-ER*, 56.

[10.] On the events leading up to this, see W. Gerstenberg, "Der Historiker Ernst Fritz Schmid," in *In memoriam Ernst Fritz Schmid (1904–1960): Ein Gedenkblatt für seine Angehörigen und Freunde* (Recklinghausen: Bauer-Druck, 1961), 16: "The young students' spirit, striving for freedom, was later driven out of inner necessity toward the Youth Movement. For many years Schmid was close to the Finkenstein Bund. The Finkenstein Bund, which was committed to the idea of lay music (with song weeks, apprenticeships, youth camps), had a great influence through its initiatives (founding of the magazine *Musik und Kirche* and the rediscovery of the work of Heinrich Schütz) on the renewal of Protestant church music (brass choirs, new organ works). On the Finkenstein Bund, see W. Blankenburg, "Singbewegung," in *Religion in Geschichte und Gegenwart*, 3rd ed., vol. 6, cols. 45–46; and "Die Finkensteiner Bewegung," in *Die deutsche Jugendmusikbewegung in Dokumenten ihrer Zeit: Von den Anfängen bis 1933; Auswahl und Zusammenstellung der Dokumente*, ed. Wilhelm Scholz and Waltraut Jonas-Corrieri (Wolfenbüttel: Möseler, 1980), 197–324. See also Hans Pfeifer, "Die Bedeutung der Jugendbewegung für Dietrich Bonhoeffer," in *Dietrich Bonhoeffer Jahrbuch/Yearbook* 1 (2003): 74–92.

quintet with Krauß[11] and Häring,[12] tomorrow the "Trout quintet,"[13] I don't get around to listening much nor to my own production. What are you doing in this regard? Are you becoming somewhat more favorably disposed toward modern music? If you see Weynand[14] sometime, tell him that I will write him very, very soon. Did he receive our card from the Black Forest, and did you get mine from Rome? Warm greetings to you from your

Dietrich Bonhoeffer

DBWE 9, 1/85a. From Ernst Fritz Schmid[1]

Morgenholz, August 28, 1924

Dear Bonhoeffer!

Today is the last day in our home up here in the mountains, and I *do want* still to send you a greeting. We will have been here almost 14 days and are hiking through the mountains in the area—unfortunately all too seldom, due to the terrible weather. The card shows approximately the view from our home. Sunday we head back to Tübingen. Best regards,

Your E. F. Schmid, student of music, Tübingen: Hirschauerstr. 3

[11.] Paul Krauß was a medical student and member of the Hedgehogs since the 1920 summer semester. He later became a professor of medicine in Göppingen; see *DBWE* 9, 1/49, pp. 73–74. [In *DBWE* 9 his name is spelled "Kraus."—VB]

[12.] According to an April 6, 2003, letter from Lotte Schmid, "this could be the son of the Tübingen theology professor Dr. Theodor Häring. Prof. Häring shows up several times in the Schmid family history."

[13.] In a June 1924 letter to his sister Sabine, Bonhoeffer wrote: "Tomorrow we will have an evening of music here. We'll play the *Forellen Quintet* [Trout quintet]. Two members of the Hedgehog fraternity will play the first violin and cello, Miss Rohloff the viola, Klaus the second cello, and I the piano. We intend to practice regularly during the week" (*DBWE* 9, 1/80, pp. 129–30).

[14.] Udo Weynand, a law student and Hedgehog member since the 1923 summer semester; see *DBWE* 9, 1/47, p. 71, and 1/55, p. 79.

[1.] *NL*, C17; handwritten postcard: E. F. Schmid. First published in M. H. Schmid, "'Befreundest du dich etwas mehr mit der modernen Musik?': Ernst Fritz Schmid in musikalischem Briefwechsel mit Dietrich Bonhoeffer," in *Musik in Baden-Württemberg*, vol. 11 (Stuttgart: Gesellschaft für Musikgeschichte in Baden-Württemberg, 2004), 56. Previously published in *Dietrich Bonhoeffer Jahrbuch/Yearbook* 2 (2005/2006): 41. Transcribed and edited by Christian Gremmels. Translation by Victoria Barnett.

DBWE 9, 1/94b. To Ernst Fritz Schmid[1]

Berlin-Grunewald, November 21, 1925

Dear Fritz,

I've let my reply wait a bit, even though I took care of the most important thing right in the two days after I received your letter. Since I do not personally know the director of the cathedral choir[2] I turned to the director of the high school choir,[3] whom I know very well, with the request that he and his wider circles (naturally he has connections to the cathedral choir) take an interest here. I hope to have some success with this. If I don't hear anything more from him in a few weeks, I will get back in touch with him. I was very happy to hear that you are now marching in seven-league boots toward your goal. I would indeed be very interested in seeing a work of yours sometime, because I simply can't imagine that you have bypassed Brahms and those writing the most recent music entirely unmoved and secretly, as in the time in Tübingen. By the way I apparently have kept up with you more than you have me, since I have heard some things from Dreier[4] and Breyhan,[5] whom I got to know in Bremen. I am now staying this final semester till my doctoral exams[6] here; there is a huge amount of work, so that I don't get around to playing music much. I am this dull studier, as students sometimes have to be, and because one really feels like

[1.] Handwritten in pencil. In possession of Lotte Schmid (Augsburg). First published in M. H. Schmid, "'Befreundest du dich etwas mehr mit der modernen Musik?': Ernst Fritz Schmid in musikalischem Briefwechsel mit Dietrich Bonhoeffer," in *Musik in Baden-Württemberg,* vol. 11 (Stuttgart: Gesellschaft für Musikgeschichte in Baden-Württemberg, 2004), 57. Previously published in *Dietrich Bonhoeffer Jahrbuch/Yearbook* 2 (2005/2006): 42–43. Transcribed by Lotte Schmid and Ilse Tödt. Edited by Christian Gremmels. Translation by Victoria Barnett.

[2.] Hugo Rüdel was conductor and director of the Berlin cathedral choir from 1909 to 1933; see *150 Jahre Staats- und Domchor Berlin: Unbekannte und unveröffentlichte Briefe und Dokumente, ausgewählt und eingeleitet von W. Dinglinger,* Deutsche Vergangenheit: Stätten der Geschichte Berlins 95 (Berlin: Edition Hentrich, 1993), 86–106.

[3.] Siegfried Ochs was director of the choir of the state academic high school for music in Berlin from 1920 to 1928; see D. Schenk, *Die Hochschule für Musik zu Berlin* (Stuttgart: F. Steiner, 2004).

[4.] Wilhelm Dreier; see *DBWE* 9, 1/80a, ed. note 4.

[5.] Christian Breyhan (1903–77); law student; member of the Hedgehogs since the 1921/1922 winter semester. He became a senior government finance president.

[6.] Bonhoeffer's dissertation, *Sanctorum Communio: A Theological Study of the Sociology of the Church* (*DBWE* 1), was completed in July 1927 and accepted by the theological faculty of the University of Berlin on August 1, 1927 (see *DBWE* 9, 1/105, pp. 174–77). Regarding the background of the dissertation, see the comment in a letter of March 13, 1926, from Richard Widmann: "What do you say about this proposition? For once, take the church as a sociological reality seriously and draw the consequences from it" (*DBWE* 9, 1/96, p. 156).

nothing other than a more or less elastic sponge, soon sated, I'd like to be able to work somewhat more independently, i.e., first take care of my postdoctoral exam as soon as possible; then I will see what's next. But I do think that it will still be the academic career path. At the moment I'm reading up together with Dreß[7] (who says hello to you). I met Dramblé[8] recently; I found him remarkably unchanged. Excuse the pencil; my pen was stolen. So I will keep up my interest in your songs, perhaps something or other will come of it.

With best regards, your
Dietrich Bonhoeffer

DBWE 9, 1/96c. To Ernst Fritz Schmid[1]

Berlin-Charlottenburg, March 25, 1936

Dear Fritz,

Many thanks for the notebook that you sent me a few days ago.[2] I was really happy to hear something again from you, even if it's only to receive something you sent,[3] but only today have I made myself take it on. I was

---

[7.] Walter Dreß, the husband of Bonhoeffer's youngest sister, Susanne. Regarding their preparation together for the exams, see the correspondence between Dreß and Bonhoeffer in *DBWE* 9: 1/89a, 89b, 93a, 93b, 94a, 96a.

[8.] Not identified.

[1.] Handwritten in ink; with an envelope (stamped: "Charlottenburg 2, 25.3.26, 6-7N") addressed to: "Mr. Ernst Fritz Schmid, Munich, Kurfürstenstr. 35." Forwarding address: "Tübingen, Württemberg, Hirschauerstr. 3" (the address of Schmid's parents). Letter in possession of Lotte Schmid (Augsburg). First published in M. H. Schmid, "'Befreundest du dich etwas mehr mit der modernen Musik?': Ernst Fritz Schmid in musikalischem Briefwechsel mit Dietrich Bonhoeffer," in *Musik in Baden-Württemberg,* vol. 11 (Stuttgart: Gesellschaft für Musikgeschichte in Baden-Württemberg, 2004), 58–59. Previously published in *Dietrich Bonhoeffer Jahrbuch/Yearbook* 2 (2005/2006): 44–45. Transcribed by Lotte Schmid and Ilse Tödt. Edited by Christian Gremmels. Translation by Victoria Barnett.

[2.] "In Partitur Gebrachtes bzw. Herausgegebenes" (M. H. Schmid, in *Musik in Baden-Württemberg,* 11:58). [This seems to have been either musical scores that Schmid had composed or music composed by others that he was publishing.—VB]

[3.] L. Lechner, *Neue Teutsch Lieder mit fünff und vier Stimmen,* published by E. F. Schmid, Augsburg, 1926 (according to Schmid, in *Musik in Baden-Württemberg,* 11:59). See also E. F. Schmid, "Bericht über geistliche und weltliche Abendmusik mit Werken alter Meister in württembergischen Städten im Juli 1926," in *Die deutsche Jugendmusikbewegung in Dokumenten ihrer Zeit von den Anfängen bis 1933,* ed. Wilhelm Scholz and Waltraut Jonas-Corrieri (Wolfenbüttel: Möseler, 1980), 296–300 (cf. *DBWE* 9, 1/80a, ed. note 10).

genuinely interested by the movements. Unfortunately I lack sufficient capacity to imagine how this will sound in a choir. At the next opportunity I will see if I can have it sung for four voices. Yet for me there is something very questionable in all this kind of music; as beautiful as it is in harmony, melody, and voicing, it just doesn't fit the innermost part of us human beings living today. There is absolutely no doubt that it strikes certain parts of us (particularly the desire for the naive), and it's just as certain that this is especially valuable. But I cannot help but see in all this a piece of lost romanticism, which one can love very much, but which, for a human being who has seen a factory and has serious problems on his mind, is simply not possible to listen to with the entire soul. And if you were to say to me that precisely that which is essentially music is only to be found here, then I would have to draw the consequence that the contemporary era is in its innermost depths unmusical. And then to lead such an era back to that which is "essentially music" (and in addition to do so through historicizing, not in one's own productivity!) does seem to me to approach inauthenticity. I would be interested to know whether you don't also think that this old music is basically unproblematic, naive, unbroken, and if that is the case, then, all things considered, I don't believe that it's so easy to find a synthesis for today's broken etc. era. I believe that which can be achieved with this kind of music *has* been achieved, and nothing would be more perverse than to diminish what in its own era were good tendencies, through the drive to collect them and the antiquarian odor.[4] Well enough of this. I know that you are of a different view, but it's precisely because of this that I'm writing so clearly. Basically this is not a very pleasant thank-you letter. But you do know how it is intended. I'm doing well. I have a lot to do—since the beginning of the holidays I'm playing more piano again, tomorrow Beethoven with a very good violinist. I'll be here again in summer.

With best regards and thanks from your
Dietrich Bonhoeffer

[4.] With respect to Bonhoeffer's catchwords in his critique of the musical conception in the "Singing Movement" ("desire for the naive," "lost romanticism," "historicizing"), cf. H. J. Kaiser, "Der Erziehungsbegriff in der Jugendmusikbewegung: Ortsbestimmungen," in *Die Jugendmusikbewegung: Impulse und Wirkungen*, ed. Karl-Heinz Reinfandt (Wolfenbüttel: Möseler, 1987), 134–59. On p. 142 Kaiser states: "It is revealing here that the creation of a new musical culture is expected from the new kind of experiencing a *past musical culture*"; a characteristic of this is a "'regression' to the existing music," "toward works of art in the emphatic sense of the *past* . . . on the one hand, and toward the folk music of *past* centuries on the other."

DBWE 9, 1/99b. To Ernst Fritz Schmid[1]

Berlin-Charlottenburg, October 5, 1926

Dear Fritz,

Thank you for your letter. I have learned from this that one should reply to letters quickly, for your great outpouring of temperament would certainly have been more understandable to me a half year ago than today. For a half year in my life always means a very great distance, and I believe that since then I have become rather different, let's say, I hope so in any case. Not that the special opinions have changed that greatly, but what does that matter?—Opinions are superficial. I believe we would recognize each other with difficulty if we could free ourselves entirely of the externals. To speak just briefly to the matter, I believe you can be certain that I am anything but an admirer of a group of people that you somewhat pharisaically dismiss. But: ultimately we belong together with the cynics etc.,—perhaps not gladly, but that doesn't matter. That in itself is a motive for me to regard their production more calmly. In such difficult moments they wish to reject the very ones who scream the most for community with Nietzsche-like violent gestures, and I don't care much for that. The consequence of this feeling of solidarity is naturally not at all resignation or a repulsive genius cult, which would be nothing but dishonesty. As unpleasant as I personally find most of these apparitions, I nonetheless make the effort to like them despite or in their unpleasantness, not the works but the human beings who stand behind them—because they do remain *that* in all their sloppiness. Otherwise I would see myself as a pharisee. I can omit the fact that it appears to me that much in your description simply doesn't fit, for that can't be contested. With all this only *one* thing appears dangerous to me, that one hopes, without contradiction from the other, to observe, support him, and now become the bringer of joy to the people [Volk]. The truth is *never* with *one* human being, who would then become God; that it [i.e., the truth] is there at all is illuminated only out of the contradiction of the other (Socrates). The consequence for every single one of us is the highest modesty and the observation of his own minutiae. One person thinks one thing, the other

[1.] Handwritten in ink. Envelope stamped: (illegible), 10.26, and addressed to "Mr. Ernst-Fritz Schmid, Munich, Herzogstr. 33 II 1." In possession of Lotte Schmid (Augsburg). Previously published in M. H. Schmid, "'Befreundest du dich etwas mehr mit der modernen Musik?': Ernst Fritz Schmid in musikalischem Briefwechsel mit Dietrich Bonhoeffer," in *Musik in Baden-Württemberg*, 11:59–61. Previously published in *Dietrich Bonhoeffer Jahrbuch/Yearbook* 2 (2005/2006): 46–48.Transcribed by Lotte Schmid and Ilse Tödt. Edited by Christian Gremmels. Translation by Victoria Barnett.

something else; it doesn't help at all that through this both mean the same thing! Each should do in his own place what he can take responsibility for,[2] and nothing more can be demanded than that he modestly acknowledge his *limits.*[3] But no limit*less* judgment of the other. Perhaps limitlessness will lead once again to a "great man," for which one hopes so longingly; I would decide every time for the limited existence in *genuine community* with *each one* (the neighbor), even if the great man is not forthcoming. There is much less danger in the manifestations of decline than in the limitlessness, and that means the pharisaical quality of the "ideal" plans for remedies. In my view the main thing is genuine life in community, not the heroic and the glittering manifestations of culture.

The entire Bach festival[4] is now behind me, and I am still strongly under its powerful effect. Nonetheless it drove me to write this letter; one should wish only to acknowledge the limits! Only in this way does one honor the infinite!

By the way, recently I have almost exclusively played old music, this just to orient you. My qualms consist of many things, but that isn't the issue here. The impression that I receive from Bach[5] etc. Schütz[6] is overwhelming every time.

Pardon the coarse "stationery," but I didn't have anything else. I am working on my dissertation about "the ideal of Christian sociology and the church";[7] I hope to be finished with it around Easter. I get around to music somewhat more during the holidays, admittedly much too little. [If] you

[2.] On this, see Bonhoeffer's demand to do what is necessary "in a given place" (*DBWE* 6:225 and 268).

[3.] This is early evidence of the theme of "limit/limits," the theological implications of which would preoccupy Bonhoeffer throughout his writings: in *Sanctorum Communio* (see the use of the term "barrier" [*Schranke*], *DBWE* 1:45ff); in his inaugural lecture, "The Anthropological Question in Contemporary Philosophy and Theology" (*DBWE* 10, 2/7); in *Creation and Fall* (in the discussion of limits and boundaries, *DBWE* 3:85–87 and elsewhere); and in the *Letters and Papers from Prison* (*DBWE* 8, 3/137, p. 366 and elsewhere).

[4.] This was the fourteenth German Bach festival, held by the new Bach Society from September 30 to October 3, 1926, in Berlin.

[5.] Johann Sebastian Bach (1685–1750). On Bonhoeffer's appreciation of Bach's music, see Andreas Pangritz, *Polyphonie des Lebens: Zu Dietrich Bonhoeffers "Theologie der Musik"* (Berlin: Alektor-Verlag, 1994), 40–53.

[6.] Heinrich Schütz (1585–1672). On the rediscovery of Schütz's works during the 1920s, see U. Eckart-Bäcker, "Die Schütz-Renaissance aus dem Geist der musikalischen Jugendbewegung," in *Die deutsche Jugendmusikbewegung*, ed. Wilhelm Scholz and Waltraut Jonas-Corrieri, 92–101. For Bonhoeffer's appreciation of Schütz, see Pangritz, *Polyphonie des Lebens*, 25–39.

[7.] *Sanctorum Communio* (*DBWE* 1).

want to know something from me otherwise, it's between the lines of this letter. If you happen to hear from Barth and Gogarten,[8] you can think of me. I have a great deal from them. The letter has become long, but since it will be another half year before the next one, you'll have to just accept that. I hope things go well for you, and with best regards from your

Dietrich

DBWE 9, 2/2a. On Euripides's Philosophy[1]

[Preliminary considerations]

Realism, or the aspiration to bring only genuine human beings onto the stage, is almost too great in Euripides, for with this he destroys the original

---

[8.] In the reference to Barth and Gogarten, Bonhoeffer is also referring to the emergence of his dissertation, for which the debate among Karl Barth, Friedrich Gogarten, and Eberhard Grisebach was decisive (cf. *DB-ER*, 83, and *DBWE* 1:298).

[1.] *NL*, A 5, 1–2, 1; handwritten. Previously published in *Dietrich Bonhoeffer Jahrbuch/ Yearbook* 3 (2007/2008): 29–41. Edited by Hans Pfeifer. Translation by Victoria Barnett. (An introduction to this text by Hans Pfeifer appears on pp. 21–28 of that *Yearbook* edition.) This appears to be a draft essay written for Bonhoeffer's matriculation (*Abitur*) examinations; cf. the letter of August 18, 1922, to his grandmother, *DBWE* 9, 1/30. The clean copy was in the official matriculation files and probably burned during the wartime bombing of the Grunewald School (today known as the Walter-Rathenau Gymnasium) along with the school archives. In addition to the draft, there are excerpts from book 3, chap. 2 ("The beginnings of modern culture. Euripides") of Eduard Meyer, *Geschichte des Altertums* (History of Antiquity), vol. 4:1 (2nd ed., Stuttgart: J. C. Cotta, 1911), as well as numerous excerpts from Hermann Diels's *Fragmenten der Vorsokratiker* (the English translation of Diels cited throughout the notes is Kathleen Freeman, *Ancilla to "The Pre-Socratic Philosophers"* [Oxford: Basil Blackwell, 1948]), above all from Heracleitus, which have not been included here but are occasionally cited in the editorial notes. Bonhoeffer used the German-Greek edition of Diels (either the 1903 1st ed. or 1906 2nd ed.; Berlin); the citations, however, are from the 1934–37 5th ed., vols. 1–3, edited by Walther Kranz. Kranz was Bonhoeffer's Latin instructor in 1922 (see *DBWE* 9, 2/2, pp. 198–214). Bonhoeffer wrote a lengthy interpretation of Meyer's work and Wilhelm Nestle's *Euripides: Der Dichter der griechischen Aufklärung* (Stuttgart: W. Kohlhammer, 1901). In addition it is fairly certain that he read Ulrich von Wilamowitz-Möllendorf's *Euripides' Heracles*, 2nd ed. (Berlin, 1895) (reprints in 1906 and 1910). He probably also read Erwin Rohde, *Psyche*, vols. 2, 5, and 6. It is unclear whether he read the presentation on Euripides in Nietzsche's *The Birth of Tragedy out of the Spirit of Music*. He read Nietzsche's comment that in Euripides tragedy "died by suicide" (see Nietzsche, *The Birth of Tragedy and Other Writings* [Cambridge: Cambridge University Press, 1999], 54), in the Nestle book on Euripides.

Herbert Anzinger was instrumental in assisting with deciphering the handwritten manuscript. There were numerous strikethroughs [in Bonhoeffer's original manuscript—VB], which have not been replicated or noted here. The citations from Euripides use the customary verse numbers; additional bibliographic sources are noted.

character. Out of the demigod[2] he makes a coarse person of the world. One thinks of Admetus in *Alcestis*, *Hippolytus*, etc.

The best example is the fate of Heracles. In the saga the human being becomes God through his will alone. In Euripides sin is inserted [into the story]. The overestimation of human capabilities is belied.[3] Once he has overcome everything, only his id remains, to which he succumbs.[4] He is spellbound by the earth; he cannot free himself from blood; he must continue to murder; the madness has been well prepared. Immeasurable vanity displays itself.

Heracles's guilt is driven out through the love of Theseus. The Furies soften.

Disposition

A. *Introduction: Goal of this work*

B. *Explanation: Some philosophical problems*

I. Euripides as philosopher

(1) The pre-Socratic philosopher, Sophist

Heracleitus, Epicharmus,[5]

His emergence

(2) The world of the gods

Fate, demons, gods, anthropomorphism

Ζεύς-νοῦς[6]

II. The ethicist, the psychologist

Δίκη (Heracleitus)

Freedom of will

Written works

Goal of life? Religion yearning for death. Question not dealt with in writing. Significance of death and life. σῶμα-σῆμα[7]

Agnosia[8] a desire. [*Antiope*] fr. 205

Summary of the essential aspects in Euripidean philosophy

[2.] [In Greek mythology demigods were the "heroes" who possessed both divine and human qualities.—VB]

[3.] [This sentence remains unclear in the original German.—VB]

[4.] Cf. Wilamowitz-Möllendorf, *Euripides' Herakles*, 128–29.

[5.] Cf. W. Nestle, *Euripides*, 14.

[6.] "Zeus–Reason," e.g., fr. 1018; see Nestle, *Euripides*, 50.

[7.] "Body–Tomb." See Rohde, *Psyche*, 253n2; and Nestle, *Euripides*, 143: "Fundamental concept of Orphic teaching on the soul."

[8.] [Ignorance or absence of knowledge.—VB]

[*A. Introduction: Goal of the work*][9]

Pirithous 593[10]	
Bellerophon 294	Gods do no ill[11]
Iphigenia T. 391	Gods do no ill[12]
Thyestes 395	nothing without the gods[13]
The Suppliants 533	πνεῦμα [μὲν] πρὸς αἰθέρα[14]
πνεῦμα 488[15]	

πῶς ἂν δροσερᾶς ἀπὸ κρηνῖδος
καθαρῶν ὑδάπων τῶμ' ἀρυσαίμαν
ὑπὸ τ' αἰγείροις ἐν τε κομήτῃ
λεμῶνι κλιθεῖσ' ἀναπαυσαίμαν[16]

If one looks for a quotation that should condense the thoughts and ruminations of this man into one sentence, it can only be this statement. It expresses the entire laboriousness of a tortured, brooding heart, the yearning for rest [Ruhe] from the sensation of the time, that desire to sink for once into nothingness. All thought leads indeed to nothing; the human being is weak and void. These same moods are reflected in the pictures that have been preserved of him.[17] We see a deeply brooding, melancholy man before us who cannot get his bearings in this world . . .[18]

If in this work I attempt to express some of the philosophical problems of Euripides, it is self-evident that from the large amount of material I can only

[9.] The subtitles of Bonhoeffer's text have been bracketed to clarify the organization.

[10.] *Pirithous*, 596: "Is not death then better than to live badly?" or 598: "Fate stands by the side of him who has the right attitude."

[11.] *Bellerophon*, 292: "When gods do something hateful they are not gods." Cf. W. Nestle, *Euripides*, 126, who contrasted this statement with a quotation by Sophocles stating that nothing in which the gods engage is evil. Bonhoeffer apparently read both quotations and confused them with each other.

[12.] *Iphigenia in Tauris*, 393: "The divine is not irrational"; cf. W. Nestle, *Euripides*, 91.

[13.] *Thyestes*, 391: "Human beings have no power without the gods." [*Thyestes* was a play by the Roman philosopher and dramatist Seneca.—VB]

[14.] "(In death) the spirit returns to the ether," from *The Suppliants*, 533. Similarly in the Euripides drama *Helen*, 1014ff.

[15.] The German editor was unable to trace this citation.

[16.] "If I could the clear, cooling drink / myself create out of the bubbling fountain. / In the shadow of the poplar by the flowering meadow / encamped there the silence delights me." From *Hippolytus*, 208–11.

[17.] Regarding the pictures of Euripides, see Nestle, *Euripides*, 20–21 and 389n49.

[18.] This view of Euripides is very much influenced by Meyer (*Geschichte des Altertums*, 799). However, like the quotation above, it also reveals something about the particular interest of the author.

single out some things that appear especially important to me and naturally cannot make any claim to exhaust the subject. The goal of the work can only be to give a brief, as apt as possible characterization of Euripides's way of taking a position on several philosophical, ethical, and psychological questions.

[B. *Explanation: Some philosophical problems*
I. Euripides as philosopher]
In order to comprehend a person, we may not view him completely by himself, but we must always conceive of him in juxtaposition with his dramatic and philosophical predecessors and with his environment. This is true here, too, in order to be able to evaluate Euripides's significance.

It is clear indeed that as dramatists Aeschylus and Sophocles must be considered, besides several others. One must only have read one drama of the three poets to be able immediately to recognize the difference: to summarize it in very few words, the essential point is that Sophocles and Aeschylus portray human beings, heroes in the struggle with the anthropomorphic gods, while Euripides portrays human beings in conflict with φύσις.[19] Now this φύσις can be embodied in a human being or in a god as an antagonist. Aphrodite in *Hippolytos* embodies the power of love, Artemis its chastity. Phaedra has to struggle with both. The gods now[20] become plain forces or symbols for these.[21] Indeed, Euripides is far removed from any kind of anthropomorphism, but more on that below. Aeschylus and Sophocles believe in the existence of the gods. We see, therefore, not much in common with these essentials.[22] One wished to discover a great deal here, [. . .][23] but particularly in Heracleitus and Anaxagoras.

And here, however, it seems to me that Heracleitus's influence proves itself to be much stronger.[24] His entire teaching about the gods, the Δίκη, originates with this master; he has adopted some things literally. We wish to offer a proof that he has put Anaxagoras's teaching on stage. In [*Chrysippus*] fr. 839, verses 12, 13 sound almost literally like Anaxagoras, R.P. 150.[25] It

---

[19.] "Nature"; cf. Nestle, *Euripides*, 174–75.

[20.] This text is difficult to decipher in the original manuscript.

[21.] Cf. Meyer, *Geschichte des Altentums*, 796; and Nestle, *Euripides*, 92.

[22.] In the original manuscript this sentence has been corrupted by strikethroughs and unreadable insertions; it can be reconstructed only provisionally.

[23.] The ellipses indicate an unreadable passage.

[24.] Nestle, *Euripides*, 57 and 70.

[25.] This can only mean the famous fragment 17 about "coming into being" and "passing away"; cf. Freeman, *Ancilla to "The Pre-Socratic Philosophers,"* 85.

appears, therefore, that Euripides adopted a large portion of the teaching about the origins of the world from Anaxagoras.

As the third teacher next to these two, we must place the entire Sophist movement, whose most significant son, and at the same time the one who overcomes it, is Euripides. Just as any kind of relativism, any kind of psychology, is a symptom of the decline [. . .] of a culture, this is also true of sophism. With sophism, relativism moves for the first time very strongly into the foreground of philosophy. We find nothing of this in Sophocles and Aeschylus. One doesn't even begin to consider whether there are really gods, but rather one believed it and placed no boundaries on his fantasy in locating a second idealized Greek world on the Olympus of the blessed gods. So the gods became [. . .]

Before we now move on very specifically to Euripides's ideas, we must still set down several general presuppositions. Euripides was the first to bring problems of this nature onto the stage and to wrestle seriously with them at all. Thus in him we will not yet find a system and a train of thought without contradiction.[26] Everything is just getting started. Thus we may give consideration not to what he did but rather to the fact that he dared to make sophistic thinking popular. There is naturally not yet any trace of the ominous[27] consequence. One contradiction piles onto the other, so that it is made very difficult to peel away even an approximately unified idea. And there is something else to consider: one often doesn't know in a given sentence on which side he[28] is standing and finally he himself says (*Antiope*, 189): Out of anything one can . . . ,[29] i.e., everything is only proof of the possibility of another perspective. This must be seen as much more than a cry of desperation, that there is nothing certain, no knowledge, that everything [remains] unclear, as a eulogy for the guild of the orators, which he deeply despises. Euripides is not satisfied to have torn down the old, and with that he believes that he towers above the sophists; he wants to build the new and is no longer able to do so on this foundation.[30] This is the deep tragedy of his life. Thus we must regard everything that follows as the first attempt at a philosophical foundation on which to build something new that can replace the old. This also explains the many contradictions.

[26.] Cf. Nestle, *Euripides*, 9.

[27.] This word is difficult to decipher in the original manuscript.

[28.] [Euripides.—VB]

[29.] *Antiope*, fr. 189: "One can make a controversial discussion out of every matter, if one is skilled in oratory." Cf. Nestle, *Euripides*, 47. He sees in this a consequence of sophism: "With it relativism moves for the first time very strongly into the foreground."

[30.] Cf. Nestle, *Euripides*, 190.

After these premises we can move on to the essential task. We want to begin with [the] main question of the entire worldview: the question of God. The poet has never been in complete agreement with this question; but then is there any human being who is this way all the time? Why then are we surprised by this in Euripides? Do not all human beings have moments in which they believe that everything has deserted them and then they begin to doubt God? We find typical examples among the most pious people. How could we expect something different from a nature like that of Euripides? But above the entire research activity[31] of Euripides stands the sentence: "There is nothing (*Helen*, 1618) more useful for mortals than respectable doubt."[32] Thus he vacillates; deeply within he believes in the existence of this highest being, but reason makes him waver (fr. 288). That which comes from the gods is dark and incomprehensible; indeed they confuse everything, so that we honor them (*Hecuba*, 958). He flees to the mysteries, yet these too repel him; everything is lies and deception (fr. 789). Thus the poet expresses himself in the hours of crisis and despair, but he had long ago created a new god in the image of Heracleitus. The old polytheism is completely refuted out of the existence of [. . .]. Only one higher being exists, and this is the heracleitistic Δίκη (cf. Heracleitus, fr. 20, 28, et al.).[33] But Euripides stretches this concept much further. This Δίκη is the divinity not only of justice but of worldly reason, to put it briefly the world principle itself; it is παῖς Διὸς (*Andromeda*, 151), "παῖς χρονοῦ" (*Antiope*, 222).[34] It is often directly identified with χρόνος (*Orestes*, 559). This concept shimmers in all shades. ἀνάγκη (*Helen*, 514), τύχη (*Iphigenia in Taurus*, 478), μοῖραι (*Alcestis*, 12), if it is conceived impersonally, τὸ δαμόνιον (*The Phoenician Women*, 18), ὁ νόμος, ὁ θεὸς, when it is conceived personally.[35] But here too he finds no peace; he is tortured again and again by the thought of injustice on earth. Thus he attempts a theodicy in *The Suppliants* (200). Yet this place is so insignificant and superficial that it hardly suffices for a solution.[36]

[31.] This passage is difficult to decipher in the original manuscript.

[32.] Cf. Nestle, *Euripides*, 42–43.

[33.] Freeman, *Ancilla to "The Pre-Socratic Philosophers,"* 26. Here Bonhoeffer is following particularly clearly the excerpt on "the divinity of Euripides" in Nestle, *Euripides*, 145ff.

[34.] "Child of Zeus" and "Child of the Time"; cf. Nestle, *Euripides*, 149.

[35.] Necessity, fate, adroitness, divinity, law. Bonhoeffer here is citing Nestle, *Euripides*, 54, where the characteristics of fate are discussed (cf. Meyer, *Geschichte des Altertums*, 797). He identifies fate and justice more explicitly than Euripides and the other authors being dealt with.

[36.] This is almost literally from Nestle, 64–65: "superficial in the highest degree."

But new thoughts continue to come about his new divinity, which he portrays most comprehensively in *The Trojan Women* (884ff.): "O pillar of the earth, you have your throne on earth. Whoever you are, inscrutably to know, Zeus, whether necessity of nature and spirit of the mortal, I beseech you, that you lead all mortals to justice along still paths."[37]

This place reminds us vividly of the well-known words from Faust.[38] God is conceived of as the immeasurable itself (this is [so] characteristic for the relation to Heracleitus) and immanent. It[39] lives on the earth, is at the same time law of nature and spirit of the human beings; briefly it is the very universe [das All], which it rules with reason. What a powerful advance[40] to a perspective like that of Sophocles and Aeschylus. If Euripides here apparently still summons the names of the gods, as at this point Zeus, these are only concessions to the spirit of the times [Zeitgeist]. He believes in the one rational spirit, which purposefully acts according to certain laws, immanent to the world and human beings.[41] God is acting in everything; the earth is mother of human beings (*Chrysippus*, 836).[42] Every passion is something divine. It is nature, therefore God, for precisely this, the emphasis on the power of φύσις, is a strong element in the conceptual world of Euripides (271 and elsewhere).[43] Peace is regarded as a goddess, i.e., as part of the universal god [Allgott]. It is often peculiar when the gods' names still appear in their old meaning, that is, still in the sense of ancient times. If at the very most even the name of the godhead, carried over as the principle of φύσις, is meant, then places such as fr. 436[44] are not at all understandable. The concept of ἀλάστωρ[45] deserves particular mention.

[37.] Cited in Nestle, *Euripides*, 146–47.

[38.] Goethe, *Faust* I, verses 3431ff. [These verses refer to Faust's *credo*, or confession of faith.—VB]

[39.] [The immeasurable.—VB]

[40.] [Bonhoeffer's handwriting is apparently difficult to decipher here; the German here reads *Fortschritt*, but an editorial note indicates the original German in the text may be *Unterschied* (difference).—VB]

[41.] Nestle, *Euripides*, 50; and Meyer, *Geschichte des Altertums*, 797ff.

[42.] This notion [i.e., of earth as mother—VB] continued in Bonhoeffer's thought and appears often in his writings. Cf. *DBWE* 3:38 and 134ff. and *DBWE* 10:378, 530, and 546.

[43.] Nestle, *Euripides*, 477n2: "Euripides says: Nature is everything." This corresponds not to the cited fragment but to fr. 265a and *Bellerophon*, 297.

[44.] Perhaps also 434.

[45.] The "spirit of revenge"; cf. Nestle, *Euripides*, 58ff.

This is naturally initially simply the spirit of revenge (*The Phoenician Women*, 1556), as already to be found in Aeschylus and Sophocles. That means it is a connecting link between human and God, but then it is conceived of in a personal sense. "The gods have thrown your ἀλάστωρ upon me,"[46] thus a personal spirit of revenge, meant to injure the other. This conception is, however, very unclear and confusing. The essential thing can be seen merely in the fact that Euripides portrays guilt, a crime, as something intended by God, even divine. He does not succeed in thinking this through to the end, to the solution of the problem of theodicy. But God acts only in the great things; coincidence is in the small matters, fr. 974: "God grasps the too much; coincidence the little things." Out of the one statement the inconsequent, unscholarly work is clearly characterized. But as noted before, all that is indeed irrelevant considering this one fact, namely, that he has made philosophy popular.[47]

[II. The ethicist. The psychologist]
We find the greatest contradictions in the relationship of the gods to human beings. On the one hand, the human being is entirely incapable of acting freely; on the other, he is in turn capable of rebelling against the power of the godhead (*The Phoenician Women*, 18; *Iphigenia in Taurus*, 1478–79; *Hecuba*, 864).[48] We already see the beginning of the dawn of the problem of free will; Euripides in terms of his entire understanding of life is a determinist, if one may already speak of this. The best proof of this is the entire figure of Phaedra in *Hippolytus*. Phaedra is the way she is only because this is how her ancestors were.[49] She cannot help this: fr. 32: Only bad fruit can come from a bad beginning. Fr. 6:[50] Noble sons come from noble women. Fr. 333: No good son comes from a bad father. Here we find the very first beginnings of our teaching about heredity. The human being is a tool in God's hand (*Hippolytus*, 1434).[51] He who acts in the φύσις of the human being does with that person what he will. Here the great contradiction consists in the fact that while human beings can rebel, it doesn't do them any

[46.] *Medea*, 1333.

[47.] Nestle, *Euripides*, ix.

[48.] See Nestle, *Euripides*, 183ff.

[49.] *Hippolytus*, 337ff.

[50.] This is an incorrect citation; the reference must be to *Alcmaeon in Psophis*, fr. 75: "Capable children come from capable men and those from bad ones are similar to the natures of their father."

[51.] "When a god imposes it, the human errs."

good, and on the other hand, God pursues and punishes those who are evil (fr. 559, fr. 255). Therefore, one has not yet penetrated all the way to the consequences, so one still regards this connection as something painful. Because Euripides cannot find any solution at all, he concludes this entire problem with the statement: "The human may sin when a god wishes it."[52] This is the one statement that we too can still write, albeit in a somewhat different sense within our views regarding this.[53] Euripides bore this question and agonized about it. Again and again he arrived at a contradiction that unsettled him and yet drove him to explore his sense of truth more.[54]

The relativity of all moral values [Sittlichkeitswerte] is naturally tied in an immediate sense to this solution to the problem of free will, although Euripides does not yet recognize it as such. Good and bad are relative terms and with that raised above any ethic, in the sense of an Aeschylus or Sophocles. ἄνθρωπος μέτρον πάντων χρημάτων. . . [The] individual bears his measure for virtue in his breast.[55] With the text in fr. 19: "What is bad? Only that which appears so to the one who does it," we stand on a moral "of what is beyond good and evil."[56] Euripides, however, must become shaky on this ground. Here he can go no further. In his eyes the human being has become a worthless thing, and yet all his interest lies in this human being. Heracles, the stormer of the heavens, attempts to become god but collapses. Only the love of a friend, apparently beyond any morality, can rescue him. How small and inferior the human being is, for "we know indeed what is good, but we do not do it"[57] says the man with experience of life in contrast to the idealistic Plato. Plato is only the man of construction, Euripides is of both, construction and reality, and this drives him to ruin.

How do things stand, however, with the purpose of life, if it is the case that the human being is a weak, unfree thing in the hands of the almighty Dike?[58] If there are no absolute moral concepts? Euripides did not find his

[52.] *Hippolytus*, 1434; cf. Nestle, *Euripides*, 184.

[53.] Here in the manuscript an insertion is noted but is not extant.

[54.] This sentence may be influenced by Nietzsche.

[55.] "Of all things the measure is Man" (Protagoras, fr. 1; translation from Freeman, *Ancilla to "The Pre-Socratic Philosophers,"* 125). See Nestle, *Euripides*, 46 and esp. n. 12: "Further I assert however: in v. 499ff in Euripides' 'Phoenician Women' and in Fr. 29 of 'Iolaus' we have nothing other than an application of the statement of the human as the measure of all things."

[56.] This is almost literally from Nestle, *Euripides*, 49. Cf. also Nietzsche, *Beyond Good and Evil*.

[57.] *Hippolytus*, 381–82; see Nestle, *Euripides*, 175.

[58.] [The goddess of justice.—VB]

way out of this problem; to be able to answer this he naturally had to return to the absolute concept of morality. For he praises ἀρετή[59] as the highest, and in summary he says once (fr. 526),[60] "The living must do good, for after death everyone is only shadow and dust." Nothing comes of nothing.

Therefore, do good for its own sake, for there is no reward after life. Our bodies become earth; our spirit returns to the universal spirit. (*Chrysippus*, fr. 836): "What comes from the earth returns to the earth, but what comes from the divine seed returns to heaven. Nothing dies of that which once was." Again an abundance of contradictions. The bad one is pursued by Dike, although good and evil are the same (cf. Heracleitus, fr. 58, 102).[61] Apparently a teaching of retribution!? From where does evil[62] come after death? We would have a certain solution if we had a doctrine in the sense of fr. 102 from Heracleitus. Then all life would be the expression and will of the highest godhead. But nowhere do we find this keystone or[63] argumentation, only [the] opposite perspective, as we observed.

But it would be petty and a sign of insufficient understanding of Euripides if we were to take umbrage at the many insufficient places in his system. These are indeed unessential matters. We have to see the essential in the fact that Euripides despite all acknowledgments cannot separate himself from the absolute morality. *With that, he unconsciously situates knowledge behind life.*[64] If these are the moral goals of life according to Euripides, then the other main goal, the essence of his own entire life, is the aspiration for knowledge. Euripides's sermon is to not[65] be satisfied with what is given and to have the courage to draw the most extreme consequences.[66] Only the one who strives for this has grasped the meaning of life, and it is he who longs to be out of this confusing existence [Dasein] filled with contradictions. For him all of life is a dying (Polydorus, fr. 638): "τίς [δ]

[59.] Virtue. Cf. Nestle, *Euripides,* 187 and 190.

[60.] "The decisive thing, even in [those of low descent—VB] low descent, is industriousness." The citation given in the text is not identified and hardly corresponds to what has been said previously.

[61.] Heracleitus, fr. 102: "To God, all things are beautiful, good and just; but men have assumed some things to be unjust, others just." Freeman, *Ancilla to "The Pre-Socratic Philosophers,"* 31.

[62.] Difficult to decipher in the manuscript.

[63.] This may be "of the."

[64.] In the left-hand margin here there are three exclamation marks.

[65.] *NL,* A 5, 2–2 begins here.

[66.] Here there are two exclamation marks in the margin.

οἶδεν, εἰ τὸ ζῆν . . ."[67] (cf. Heracleitus).[68] Nerve-wracking, tantalizing life drives Euripides to this perspective. Nothing is serendipity; everything must be achieved through travail. "Travail," one says, "is the father of high renown" (fr. 474). Frequently sensuality leads the human being into temptation. Thus he longs for rest [Ruhe], for nonbeing. In evil, ignorance is gain. Not to live is better than living badly (fr. 596); these thoughts appear almost Indian to us. Euripides never found this rest on earth; he digs through one problem after the other and all this with the sad result of the nothingness of everything that exists. We have never reached the solution of the problem, only always just up to the posing of the problem, he recognizes painfully.

What Euripides found was sad and horrifying. Thus he also never found tranquility in sophistry. Through strongly positive striving, he overcame this. He broke the power of the religion of the people, the mysteries; it was not enough for his love of truth. He tormented himself about the work, but oh, "the path to it is so narrow," as he himself said. Even as an old man, he found neither rest nor peace; he wandered to the court of Macedonia.[69] There he composed his final work, *The Bacchae*, as a memorial stone to his life, for in it he reflects his own colorful life, restless, tumultuous.[70] But it is precisely because it was so agonizingly long and nerve-wracking for his entire inner self, precisely because he never arrives at a certain solution of the problem, that posterity is grateful to him; he had a longer and deeper influence with the unresolved problem than did Sophocles with his seemingly resolved one.[71] Euripides wanted the best for his people and his city but was incapable of bringing this best alone to everyone. A new epoch of literature dawned with him. He often violated the ancient saga, in that out of the heroes he made human beings as they live and are. But this is indeed precisely what is characteristic of Euripides. If Aeschylus and Sophocles were poets of the old tradition, Euripides was a poet of struggling truth. He dared to bring human beings with all their passions onto the stage. Nothing was more important to him than truth, and his

[67.] μὲν ἔστι κατθανεῖν. "Who knows whether death is not life." Cf. Nestle, *Euripides*, 378n25; and Meyer, *Geschichte des Alterums*, 797.

[68.] Fr. 20: "When they are born, they are willing to live and accept their fate (death); and they leave behind children to become victims of fate." Freeman, *Ancilla to "The Pre-Socratic Philosophers,"* 26. See also Meyer, *Geschichte des Altertums*, 802.

[69.] Cf. Nestle, *Euripides*, 16.

[70.] On *The Bacchae* and its controversial significance, see Meyer, *Geschichte des Altertums*, 801; and Nestle, *Euripides*, 83.

[71.] Meyer, *Geschichte des Altertums*, 796–97.

most distinguished contribution for all times will have been that he showed this to his people.[72]

DBWE 12, 1/106a. From Wilhelm Lütgert to Adolf Schlatter[1]

Bergstr. 3, Neubabelsberg, October 1, 1933

Dear and honored friend,

I did remember your eighty-first birthday[2] together with Schaeder,[3] in Berchtesgaden, where we were in August with our wives. But I didn't get as far as writing, since there would have been so much to write that I didn't know where to start, much less where to stop. But now this request from Lietzmann, whose letter[4] I am simply enclosing, has pushed me to raise the issues to which I cannot

[72.] Nestle, *Euripides*, 6: "And Euripides found this platform, this pulpit for his sermon, in the theater of Dionysius, on the southern slope of the Acropolis of Athens. Here he condemned the Greek gods to death in name, at the festivals and in the sanctuary of a Greek god, with astonishing frankness, and proclaimed a new worldview, unwavering through misunderstanding, mockery and scorn, which followed him even to the grave."

[1.] Landeskirchliches Archiv Stuttgart (LKA), Best. 40/429; typewritten with handwritten corrections and signature. For more on Lütgert, see the article on him by Walter Sparn in *Theologische Realenzyclopädie* 21:497–500. Previously published in the *Dietrich Bonhoeffer Jahrbuch/Yearbook* 2 (2005/2006). It has been edited by Hartmut Ludwig, here with additional commentary in brackets by *DBWE* 13 editor Keith Clements. Translation by Isabel Best. [Bonhoeffer was assistant to Lütgert at the University of Berlin from 1929 to 1930. See *DB-ER*, 121, 129, 132, 136.—KC]

[2.] Schlatter's birthday had been on August 16. Cf. Werner Neuer, *Adolf Schlatter: Ein Leben für Theologie und Kirche* (Stuttgart: Calwer Verlag, 1996). [Schlatter was one of the most eminent German New Testament scholars of his generation. Bonhoeffer attended his classes in Tübingen in 1923. According to Bethge, Schlatter was the Tübingen theologian who interested Bonhoeffer the most and indeed the only one who had a lasting influence on him (*DB-ER*, 53). But Schlatter's positive attitude toward National Socialism in 1933 and his obstruction of the Bethel Confession aroused bitter indignation in Bonhoeffer (*DB-ER*, 54).—KC]

[3.] Erich Schaeder (1861–1936) was a professor of theology in Berlin. Martha Lütgert and Anna Schaeder were sisters.

[4.] Letter of September 29, 1933, from Lietzmann to Lütgert [not found, but reprinted in *Glanz und Niedergang der deutschen Universität: 50 Jahre deutscher Wissenschaftsgeschichte in Briefen an und von Hans Lietzmann (1892–1942)*, ed. Kurt Aland (Berlin: De Gruyter, 1979), 750–51], explaining "Neues Testament und Rassenfrage [The New Testament and the race question]" of September 23, 1933 [in *Die Bekenntnisse und grundsätzlichen Äußerungen zur Kirchenfrage des Jahres 1933*, ed. Kurt Dietrich Schmidt (Göttingen: Vandenhoeck & Ruprecht, 1934), 189–91]. Lietzmann wrote: "Couldn't you get Schlatter to follow your example? In my opinion, he would do the Protestant church a great service

give short shrift. You will decide for yourself, without my trying to persuade you, whether you can sign the statement.[5] It is only a small portion of the questions that have oppressed us here more than is realized, at least by my own brothers, friends, and acquaintances, who are far away from Berlin and aren't being so directly rattled, as we are, by the winds blowing around here.

I do find it regrettable that things have turned out, not without some responsibility on the part of those struggling in this arena, in such a way that the Aryan paragraph has become the focus—an unfortunate shifting of the fronts.[6] But even now, as I sit here writing to you,[7] a few of the most capable and serious theologians we have here, both academics and young pastors,[8] people close to

---

if he would throw the weight of his name into the balance of this theological statement, which, I agree with you, is quintessentially biblically based."

[5.] [The statement referred to was the Marburg expert opinion. The church leadership in Hessen-Kassel had requested "expert opinions" (*Gutachten*) from the theological faculties at the universities in Marburg and Erlangen regarding the theological validity of a church "Aryan paragraph." The Marburg theologians condemned the Aryan paragraph as unbiblical; the Erlangen theologians defended the exclusion of "non-Aryans" from the ministry.—VB] Schlatter replied on October 4, 1933: "With your judgment that the quarrel over the Jews has only symptomatic significance, I am wholly in agreement. [. . .] One can certainly subscribe to the New Testament–based assertions of the Marburg group. But the question of 'The Pastorate and the Jews' cannot be settled entirely by the quotations from St. Paul. This prevented me from signing the Marburg statement" [handwritten letter, reprinted in LKA Stuttgart, Best. D 40/421]. [The Marburg statement was signed by twenty-two New Testament scholars; however, Karl Heim, Alfred Juncker, and Julius Schniewind subsequently withdrew their signatures.—VB]

[6.] Here Lütgert does not mean the general opposition to the decision of the Old Prussian General Synod of September 5, 1933, which adopted the state "Aryan paragraph" for the church, but rather the interpretation that in doing so, the church had ceased to be the church of Jesus Christ. This was the position taken by Barth, Bultmann, and Dietrich Bonhoeffer, Lütgert's assistant, in his essay "The Aryan Paragraph in the Church" and other texts [*DBWE* 12, 1/96 and 2/16, et al.; see also *DB-ER*, 304–23]. [Upon Lietzmann's intervention, the corresponding position was struck from the draft declaration "The New Testament and the Race Question" in the words of the final sentence "*cannot* give up *without ceasing to be part of the church of Jesus Christ*" (cf. Lietzmann's letter of September 19 to Hans von Soden, in Aland, *Glanz und Niedergang*, 748–49). The Pastors' Emergency League statement of commitment of September 11, 1933, described the use of the "Aryan paragraph" as a violation of the church's confession.—KC]

[7.] On the Sunday when Lütgert was writing this letter, October 1, 1933, Bonhoeffer and Franz Hildebrandt went to the Old Lutheran church in Berlin-Wilmersdorf; they were considering moving their membership to this free church, since they felt obliged to leave the German Evangelical Church because of the "Aryan paragraph." But to their horror they found a swastika flag flying from this church, so that here clearly "there was no serious resistance to Nazism" (letter of July 30, 1973, from Franz Hildebrandt to Hartmut Ludwig). See *DB-ER*, 320.

[8.] Lütgert is referring to Bonhoeffer's circle of friends and students.

me, have been coming together to consider seriously whether they should leave the church or should abandon the German church and go to England.[9]

You can imagine that I earnestly warned them not to leave the German church on account of the Aryan paragraph.[10] But they claimed that this is only a symptom; and if even Lietzmann, who is close to the German Christians and with whom I remain in constant contact, if even he was so upset about the attitude of the synod that he spoke to me about it in the strongest terms,[11] then it is understandable that these young theologians who are close to Barth—those are the ones we are talking about here—are at the point of going into the catacombs,[12] which in my opinion no one yet has the right to do. However, I consider the attitude toward the Aryan question to be merely symptomatic of the situation, and one cannot just treat the symptoms and consider that curing them has healed the disease. But certainly these actions reflect the seriousness of the situation.

I don't know whether Fezer has returned to Tübingen[13] and whether he has given you his judgment about the state of affairs. When his coming here was being discussed, you wrote to me as if he were a friend of yours, so I don't like to pass judgment on him and his work.[14] But I would assume that you hear

---

[9.] See *DB-ER*, 298–300, 320, 321–22. Bonhoeffer's application to the Prussian Ministry of Culture for a leave of absence as lecturer at the Berlin faculty of theology, in order to become pastor to a German congregation in London as of October 1, 1933, had been approved by Lütgert on August 15, 1933 (*DBWE* 12, 1/83).

[10.] There is no documentation about this conversation.

[11.] Such a conversation between Lietzmann and Lütgert following the Old Prussian General Synod is not documented. At the Brandenburg provincial synod held previously, Lietzmann (as representative of the theological faculty) had voted against introducing the "Aryan paragraph," upon which the Nazi party leadership called for his dismissal as a university teacher [cf. Klaus Scholder, *The Churches and the Third Reich*, trans. John Bowden (Philadelphia: Fortress Press, 1988), 1:469.—KC]

[12.] Karl Barth had called for consistent rejection of the German Christians: "I maintain that the Evangelical Church ought rather to elect to be thinned down till it be a tiny group and go into the catacombs than make a compact, even covertly, with this doctrine" [*Theological Existence Today!*, trans. Birch Hoyle (London: Hodder & Stoughton, 1933), 50.—KC]

[13.] Karl Fezer, professor of practical theology in Tübingen, was more active in Berlin than in Tübingen from May to October, as spokesman for the faculty and theological adviser to Ludwig Müller, who later became Reich bishop. Cf. Jörg Thierfelder, "Karl Fezer—Stiftsephorous in der Zeit des Nationalsozialismus," in *Im Dienst an Volk und Kirche*, ed. Siegfried Hermle, Rainer Lächele, and Albrecht Nuding (Stuttgart: Quell Verlag, 1988), 132ff.

[14.] On hearing from Lütgert on June 5, 1933, that the Berlin faculty of theology had proposed Fezer for the chair in practical theology as successor to Friedrich Mahling,

from your son[15] about the reaction to these matters in Bethel. I was in Bethel myself recently and can only say that I have never seen Bodelschwingh so gravely concerned and indignant, so heavily laden with worries, as now.[16] It is not because the crisis in Bethel has been so long and drawn out, which may not be Fezer's fault but is at least due to his way of doing business.[17] Even all that is only symptomatic of the situation. The theological school is facing a real crisis, and it is only a part of the crisis confronting the Inner Mission and the church as well as Bethel.[18] You know about all that, but from the letters and visits I have been receiving since the beginning of this semester, I have seen that only here in Berlin is it possible to have an overview of the situation. That is because all those who are not German Christians are deprived of every possibility of expressing their views publicly. The church press is just as much under censorship as the political press. Things developed very quickly in such a way that it was no longer a question of Bodelschwingh or Müller—that actually was clear very soon.[19]

Schlatter wrote on June 9, 1933: "I have a great affection for Fezer. He has become a follower of Hitler out of his deepest convictions, doesn't wear the swastika just to exploit the turn of affairs [. . .] and honestly tries to cleave to the gospel, even in conjunction with the swastika" (LKA Stuttgart, Best. D 40/429 and 421).

[15.] Theodor Schlatter (1885–1971) taught at the theological school in Bethel from 1923 to 1933. On the "Vischer case," see ed. note 18.

[16.] On September 18, 1933, the board of the theological faculty, which Lütgert had chaired since 1911, discussed the political consequences for the faculty of being subject to the SA higher education office, the Führer principle, and so on, and the "Vischer case." The minutes of this meeting are in the Bethel Archives, 2/41-9.

[17.] Fezer had already been asked in June 1933 by the Prussian Ministry of Culture to investigate the "Vischer case" but had let it go until October 5, 1933.

[18.] The crisis threatening the entire church was the consequence of the political and ideological *Gleichschaltung* [i.e., synchronization with Nazi policies and ideology—VB] being promoted by the German Christians, as was evident in Bethel in the example of the Old Testament professor Wilhelm Vischer. Because he would not bow to the Nazi party's expectations, notably with regard to the "Jewish question," students who were party members had been boycotting his lectures and calling for his suspension since May 1933, until one year later Vischer himself was forced to resign. Regarding the "Vischer case," see Stefan Felber, *Wilhelm Vischer als Ausleger der Heiligen Schrift* (Göttingen: Vandenhoeck & Ruprecht, 1999), 59ff. [As the author of the section on "The Church and the Jews" in the Bethel Confession during the summer of 1933, Vischer attacked German Christian positions and even spoke of "religious anti-Semitism" (*DBWE* 12, 2/15, p. 379). Bonhoeffer refused to sign the final version of the Bethel confession after Vischer's wording was dropped. Cf. *DBWE* 12, 2/15, esp. ed. note 81 on p. 416.—VB]

[19.] Friedrich von Bodelschwingh was elected Reich bishop but resigned on June 24, 1933, under pressure from the Nazi party and the German Christians, making way for the election of Ludwig Müller on September 27 (see Scholder, *Churches and the Third Reich*, 1:340–54).

But that was the least of it. Even the constitution is as good and as bad as constitutions generally are. It depends whose hands have hold of the latch—that is what will be our undoing.[20]

When I look at these new people to whom not only we elders but also the young people will have to give way, I would rather not say what I think. And this is only the beginning. It is already an indication that neither Fezer nor Schumann made it into the Clerical Ministry.[21] No one acquainted with these matters and people expected any other outcome. But the semester that just ended has been the hardest politically that I have ever experienced. I was really only a spectator, since I have not given up my usual practice of staying out of church politics unless I had some duty to perform. But I had people coming daily to see me, people from the circle I couldn't avoid: my current or former lecture audiences. If I had turned away, it would have meant sacrificing whatever trust I had earned from them. The podium to which I keep being called is that of the Missions Conference, my old stomping ground.[22] Those evenings in the big auditorium developed into debates that went on into the night. I shall have to face another one tomorrow, where I am supposed to lecture on Judaism and Christianity, that same issue again. But I couldn't say no, and of course the tension is enormous.

But that is only my personal part of the debate. So far I have kept out of the synods and the political church campaigns. However, it is impossible to remove oneself from the general commotion over the seizure of power in the church by a political party with all the apparatus at its disposal. It amounts to a new culture war [Kulturkampf],[23] as in 1870–71, on a different front. The claim "we are the

---

[20.] Lütgert is referring to the German Evangelical Church constitution of July 11, 1933, which would not hinder the German Christians from pursuing their disastrous church policies (see Scholder, *Churches and the Third Reich*, 1:378).

[21.] Lütgert is referring to the German Christians' choice of personnel. The Clerical Ministry (Geistliche Ministerium), which with Reich Bishop Müller constituted the leadership of the German Evangelical Church, was (according to Art. 7.2 of the church constitution) to consist of three theologians and one attorney: Simon Schöffel (Lutheran), Joachim Hossenfelder (United), Otto Weber (Reformed), and the attorney Friedrich Werner. Fezer and Friedrich Karl Schumann had both represented the German Christians in the previous leadership of the church since July 1933 but were not named to the Clerical Ministry, in Fezer's case probably because he had advised against the choice of Müller as Reich bishop (see Scholder, *Churches and the Third Reich*, 1:462–63, 528–29).

[22.] The reference is to the Brandenburg Mission Conference, founded in 1892, which since April 1933 had been holding large forum discussions at the University of Berlin on "Christianity and Germanic Beliefs," in which Lütgert was a speaker. No documentation has yet been found on the one held October 2, 1933. See Archiv der Berliner Missionswerkes, Best. 1/7612, 7624, et al.

[23.] Lütgert is referring to the nineteenth-century Kulturkampf [of the German state against the Roman Catholic Church over church/state tensions about education,

church" is being asserted by every possible means. Of course you already know all this, but you are not experiencing the impact of it as directly as we are here. The way it is portrayed in the press prevents one from seeing where it is really coming from, if one is not right there experiencing it. There is no doubt that we have hard times ahead.

Until now, especially last semester, the great majority of the students here, apparently in contrast to those of other universities, were quite opposed to the German Christians.[24] Of course this may change under the severe pressure being put on them by the new church government. It would certainly change if Fezer came here. Last semester I had the largest numbers who have ever attended any of my private lectures. That too could change under this sort of pressure. But the open evenings were especially lively, and one had constantly to take care that no meat was there for the snoops whom one can now expect in every audience. But now I want to leave these disagreeable matters and just thank you again for your three gospel commentaries,[25] which were my daily nourishment last semester while lecturing on the history of Jesus. I was very happy to hear from your son that you are now working on the Letters to the Corinthians.[26] I am looking forward to seeing how my precious "Enthusiasts" will fare.[27]

As soon as I finish my systematics projects, of which I am now working on the first, I hope for enough health and energy to follow them with a book called *Freiheitspredigt und Schwarmgeister in Korinth*. But it will be awhile yet. In the

---

etc.], but of course the battles of the 1930s are generally called the "Church Struggle" (Kirchenkampf) and designated as such in the literature. Cf. Ernst Wolf's article "Kirchenkampf," in *Religion in Geschichte und Gegenwart*, 3:1443–53; and Olaf Blaschke's article "Kulturkampf," in *Religion in Geschichte und Gegenwart*, 4:1838–43.

[24.] During the 1933 summer semester in Berlin, 769 students matriculated in theology, of whom only "about 120 were German Christians. The great majority is pointedly against the German Christians" (from a letter of July 19, 1933, from Prof. Johannes Witte to the Prussian Minister of Culture, Geheimes Staatsarchiv Berlin, Best. PK, I. HA Rep. 76 Kultusministerium, Va sect. 2, tit. IV, no. 44, vol. 9, pp. 336–38.

[25.] Lütgert must be referring to Schlatter's earlier series of commentaries, "interpretations for readers of the Bible": 1. *The Gospel of Matthew*, 1895, 1916, 1947; 2. *The Gospels of Mark and Luke*, 1900, 1918, 1947. In his series New Testament Commentaries, 1. *Matthew the Evangelist* appeared in 1929; 2. *The Gospel of Luke* in 1931; 3. *Mark: The Evangelist to the Greeks*, not until 1935, so Lütgert cannot be speaking of it here.

[26.] See Adolf Schlatter, *Paulus, der Bote Jesu: Eine Deutung seiner Briefe an die Korinther* (Stuttgart: J. C. B. Mohr, 1934).

[27.] See Wilhelm Lütgert, *Freiheitspredigt und Schwärmgeister in Korinth* [The preaching of freedom and spiritual enthusiasts in Corinth] (Gütersloh: C. Bertelsmann, 1908). [On *Schwärmerei* (enthusiasm), see *DBWE* 13, 1/114b, p. 163, ed. note 13.—KC.]

meantime I am concentrating on the first article,[28] which the German Christians think they know better than the dialectical theologians. It is not the German Christians themselves, however, who make me want to do this. I am not writing for the moment, for today; on the contrary, what I find gripping is the centuries-long view that is opened up by such a theme.[29]

Now I will take no more of your time but send you my best regards.

Your faithful friend,
W. Lütgert

DBWE 13, 1/34a. Book Inscription for Herbert Jehle[1]

As a memento of a Christmas eve together and some church services at St. Paul's Church in London, in hope of some more nice hours.

Your Dietrich Bonhoeffer
Christmas 1933

DBWE 13, 1/208a. To Ernst Cromwell[1]

20 March 1935

Dear Ernst,

The many hours of compulsory silence that I have observed during the last few weeks have at least one good side. Now and then they provide enough

[28.] [I.e., of the creed.—KC]

[29.] See Wilhelm Lütgert, *Schöpfung und Offenbarung: Eine Theologie des ersten Artikels* (Gütersloh: C. Bertelsmann, 1934).

[1.] Handwritten in *Gebet für das Jahr der Kirche*, ed. K. B. Ritter (from the series Der deutsche Dom, published on behalf of the Berneuchen Circle by L. Heitmann, K. B. Ritter, and W. Stählin) (Kassel: Bärenreiter Verlag, 1933). First published in the *Dietrich Bonhoeffer Jahrbuch* 3 (2007/2008). Edited by Hans Pfeifer. Translated by Victoria Barnett.

[1.] The following four letters are part of the correspondence from Dietrich Bonhoeffer to Ernst Cromwell, who was one of Bonhoeffer's confirmands during his London pastorate. Cromwell was the son of a nonobservant Jewish father and a Protestant mother of Jewish descent from Nuremberg. The family had emigrated to England in March 1934. Born March 30, 1921, Ernst was baptized Protestant and before emigrating attended a Protestant school. In England, encouraged by his mother, Ernst was prepared for confirmation by Bonhoeffer and confirmed on February 24, 1935. Caught up in the British government's internment of "enemy aliens" in the spring of 1940, he was released to join the Pioneer Corps of the British army, studied after the war at Keble College, Oxford, and became a lawyer. He kept the letters because he was impressed by Bonhoeffer as a person; they were discovered in 2010.

quiet time to write a letter, and the pile of letters waiting to be answered gets visibly smaller. Today I will just send a brief greeting but not tell you a great deal; I'll do that in Scotland. I hope you are back at work now.

¶Did your father tell you that I received the news from Germany, at the last minute, that I have to be back there by April 15? This is now definite. In light of the most recent political decisions[2] over there, my heart sometimes stands still when I think of what awaits us, but the needs of the church are

---

There are twelve letters in all, ten written to Ernst, one to his father, Philipp, and one from his father to Bonhoeffer. Four were written during Bonhoeffer's time in London; because they were discovered too late to be published in *DBWE* 13, they are included here. The other eight letters have been published in *Theological Education at Finkenwalde: 1935–1937* (*DBWE* 14).

Bonhoeffer's letters to Ernst Cromwell were all written in German. Only the last of the twelve, the letter from Finkenwalde of March 27, 1936, was typewritten. The handwritten letters were initially transcribed by Jelena Beljin, assisted by Ralf Wüstenberg, and then thoroughly revised by Ilse Tödt. The German manuscript was edited by Clifford Green, who also provided the first draft of notes; additional contributions to the notes came from Victoria Barnett, Keith Clements, Ernst Cromwell, Stephen Plant, Toni Burrowes-Cromwell, and Ilse Tödt. No letters from Ernst Cromwell to Bonhoeffer have been found.

The German originals of the Cromwell letters will be published in the *Dietrich Bonhoeffer Jahrbuch/Yearbook* 6 (2014), with an introduction by Clifford Green. By agreement with Gütersloher Verlagshaus and Fortress Press, these letters have been published in English as *Letters to London: Bonhoeffer's Previously Unpublished Correspondence with Ernst Cromwell, 1935–36*, ed. Stephen Plant and Toni Burrowes-Cromwell (London: SPCK, 2013) and translated by Isabel Best. That edition also includes the transcript of an interview with Ernst Cromwell conducted by Stephen Plant, and an afterword by Toni Burrowes-Cromwell.

This letter (208a) is handwritten on both sides of two sheets; at the top of both sheets is the letterhead of the community: House of the Resurrection, Mirfield, Yorks. A handwritten addition under the date indicates that the letter was "answered." The Community of the Resurrection is an Anglican religious order in England that was founded in Oxford in 1892 by the Anglo-Catholic Charles Gore and settled in Mirfield, Yorkshire, in 1898. Keith Clements reports that at the time of Bonhoeffer's visit, the superior was Father Edward Talbot and the most venerable member of the community was the retired bishop and former superior, Walter Howard Frere. "At Mirfield it was the life of corporate prayer that touched Bonhoeffer most deeply; above all the way in which through the cycle of the daily offices in the course of each 24 hours the community prayed through the whole of Psalm 119" (Keith Clements, *Bonhoeffer and Britain* [London: Churches Together in Britain and Ireland, 2006], 85–86).

[2.] Germany had just regained the Saar after the plebiscite; many opponents of the regime had gone there for safety and were now arrested or went into exile; in early March the Reich made military service compulsory. On the church front, the Confessing Church established its provisional government in early 1935, and Gestapo pressures on the more radical elements of the Confessing Church were intensifying. The first mass arrest of Confessing Church pastors (seven hundred were arrested briefly) was in early March 1935 after they read a protest statement from the pulpit.

so urgent that there is no other way. The hours of silence here have come at just the right time for me. They are so full of all sorts of thoughts and feelings that they seem to pass by in a moment. The important thing, again and again, is not to become hardened and bitter or to worry unnecessarily, but to be able, time after time, to be immeasurably happy that there is such a great cause as Christianity, which can use the help of each of us in some way. And be happy that whatever comes, we are not alone; we are in fellowship.

¶In the next few days I must be sure and write to our circle of friends.[3] I've been going over in my head, day and night, what advice I should offer. It will be good, when I'm back over there, to be able soon to get our thoughts together on this. I've been thinking of you all a great deal in the past few days, and of you in particular. I wish the very best for all of you.

¶I'm leaving here on Saturday for two days in York, from there on to one more monastery, and then to Edinburgh. Say, do you think you could perhaps manage to leave by noon on Saturday, so as to be in Edinburgh by nine in the evening?[4] Three reasons: first, I shall have been in Edinburgh since Wednesday evening and am eager to be off on our walking tour. Second, I may have to be back in London a bit sooner than I planned (by the way, John and Inge[5] are *both* welcome to come; I've invited Inge too, but there still seem to be difficulties with timing). Third, I'd be happy to see a friend's face again, after these solitary days. But[6] do it only if it won't make *any* trouble for you at home, first of all; second, if you don't already have something planned for Saturday; and third, if you want to.

My best regards to all your family, and especially to you.
Dietrich

[3.] It is not clear to whom Bonhoeffer refers—whether these are the people in his London congregations who had refused in January 1935 to recognize the Reich church authorities, or his circle of closest friends like Niemöller in the German church situation.

[4.] In fact, apparently having celebrated the birthday at home with his family, Ernst arrived in Edinburgh on Sunday, according to his father's letter to Bonhoeffer dated Sunday, March 31; Ernst apparently brought this with him since it begins "Hiermit Ernst" [Ernst here brings]). This is also confirmed by Bonhoeffer's March 26 letter (1/209a below).

[5.] Note by Ernst Cromwell in the margin of his personal translation: "John and Inge are teenagers of the German parish in Forest Hill."

[6.] The following sentence and the closing were written in the left margin of the final page.

On *Monday,*[7] please write to me at: House of the Sacred Mission, Kelham, Newark, Notts.[8]

If I find no word from you there, I'll ring you on Wednesday or Thursday evening.

DBWE 13, 1/209a. To Ernst Cromwell[1]

Dear Ernst,

Thanks very much for your disrespectful letter; I'm looking forward greatly to your even less respectful presence on Sunday.[2] I'll expect you on the train that arrives at (+)[3] in Edinburgh. Then we can look around the city a bit more and continue that the next morning; the rest we'll leave for afterward, with the Cruesemanns.[4] I'd like to get up in the mountains as soon as possible, that is, by midday Monday.[5] By the way, I asked Mr. Ulbricht[6] to send a poncho for me to your address; please bring it with you. If *you* would like to have an anorak, just ring Mr. Ulbricht; there's another one at my place. I have one here for myself.

¶If you don't hear any more from me, we'll keep to the time as given above in any case! I don't know whether I should perhaps make a side trip to see

[7.] This sentence is written in the top margin of the final page.

[8.] Nottinghamshire.

[1.] Undated letter but probably March 26, 1935, handwritten on both sides and in the margins of both pages, on notepaper with the letterhead: Society of the Sacred Mission, Kelham Theological College. Kelham is near Nottingham, which means that after Mirfield Bonhoeffer first traveled northward to visit York for two days, then turned south, and arrived in Kelham on March 26. The letter is obviously dated before Ernst Cromwell's birthday on Saturday, March 30. The Society of the Sacred Mission was the third Anglo-Catholic monastery that Bonhoeffer visited. Founded by Father Herbert Kelly in 1893, the order originally intended to train missionaries for service in Korea. Housed in Kelham Hall since 1903, the order mainly trained priests for the Church of England until it closed in 1973. Bonhoeffer and Rieger were impressed by the lectures of Father Kelly and by the Old Testament scholar A. G. Herbert (Clements, *Bonhoeffer and Britain*, 85). For background on Ernst Cromwell and the publication of Bonhoeffer's letters to him, see ed. note 1, p. 54 of this volume.

[2.] In Edinburgh.

[3.] A circled cross, apparently referring to a time to be decided.

[4.] Gerhard Edward and Ingrid Elisabeth Cruesemann were confirmed by Bonhoeffer on Palm Sunday 1934.

[5.] This phrase inserted above the line.

[6.] Not identified.

Hahn[7] in Elgin[8] before Edinburgh. Then I wouldn't get to Edinburgh[9] until Saturday and couldn't pick up your letter at the post office. If there is any change, I shall ring you. However, I won't write to you again for your birthday,[10] I'll give a speech for you in person, a day late. I[11] wish you all a nice day, enjoy yourselves, and I will think of you especially on Saturday. My greetings to all the family, wish your grandmother a good trip home for me, and convey my thanks to your parents for their letter, which I was happy to receive. All the best to you!

Warm regards,
Dietrich

DBWE **13, 1/209b. To Ernst Cromwell**[1]

Dear Ernst,

Just a quick hello, to send in advance for your birthday (instead of dragging the money with me to Scotland) your summer[2] return ticket London–Edinburgh–London (3. 6/–).[3]

Get well soon!

Regards,
Dietrich

[7.] Kurt Hahn (1886–1974) was an influential German educator who emphasized experiential education; he founded the Salem School in Germany and Gordonstoun in Scotland, where he moved in 1933 following a brief imprisonment in Germany for his outspoken criticism of Nazi brutality; he later founded the Outward Bound organization. Brought up Jewish, he converted to Christianity in Scotland in the later 1930s. Hahn, like Gerhard Leibholz, was one of the German refugees in Britain to whom Bishop Bell turned for insight and advice. As of this publication it is not known whether Bonhoeffer actually visited Hahn, though he is mentioned as someone known to both of them. Hahn is also mentioned by Julie Bonhoeffer in her letter of October 24, 1935 (*DBWE* 14, 1/32, p. 107).

[8.] Elgin, where Hahn had established the Gordonstoun school in 1934, was about 170 miles north of Edinburgh.

[9.] From here to "hold" ("I'll give a speech for you") is written in the margin of the second page.

[10.] Ernst Cromwell's birthday in 1935 fell on Saturday, March 30.

[11.] From here to "convey my thanks" is written in the left margin of the first page and the remainder above the opening of the letter.

[1.] Handwritten letter, one sheet, undated but likely March 26 or 27, 1935, from Kelham, evidently before Ernst Cromwell's birthday on March 30. For background on Ernst Cromwell and the publication of Bonhoeffer's letters to him, see ed. note 1, p. 54 of this volume.

DBWE 13, 1/210a. From Philipp Cromwell[1]

Sunday, March 31, 1935

Dear Mr. Bonhoeffer,

Enclosed is a letter from Ernst, with all my good wishes and again many thanks. I hope the weather will clear up.

Baron Schröder's secretary hasn't rung me back this week either. He had promised to do so as soon as last week. It's possible that the baron is simply too ill, but they could tell me that.

If I don't hear any more from you, I shall post your letter early on Tuesday and then continue waiting, as before. One finds oneself losing the "backbone" to do anything more.

Following this unnecessary comment, I would ask you please to consider whether it seems useful to you to write to S. from there. If so, could it perhaps be added that the kind of work that Schröder does would, in my case, offer the rare possibility of a work permit, i.e., of productive help, and it seems worth trying also from the other perspective.

It strikes me as pathetic to write in this way. But the impending expiration of the work permit—on top of the rest—makes me uneasy. Please pardon me for taking up part of your holiday with this matter.

Yours very sincerely,
Philipp Cromwell

[2.] Inserted above the line.

[3.] Inserted above the line; Ernst Cromwell believes this was the cost of the rail ticket to and from Edinburgh, i.e., £3. 6. 0, three pounds, six shillings, no pence.

[1.] Handwritten, two pages; signature deciphered by Eberhard Bethge. This letter was not included in the publication of Ernst Cromwell's letters [*Letters to London: Bonhoeffer's Previously Unpublished Correspondence with Ernst Cromwell, 1935–36*, ed. Stephen Plant and Toni Burrowes-Cromwell (London: SPCK, 2013)] but is included here because of its connection to two other letters from Bonhoeffer: that of March 15, 1935, to Baron Schröder, and that of March 30, 1935, to Mr. Ryder in the baron's office; see *NL*, C 23, 1-1, (Dietrich Meyer and Eberhard Bethge, *Nachlass Dietrich Bonhoeffer: Ein Verzeichnis; Archiv—Sammlung—Bibliothek* [Munich: Chr. Kaiser Verlag, 1987], 136). Transcription by Ilse Tödt. For background on the Cromwell letters, see ed. note 1, p. 54 of this volume.

Comprehensive Chronology and Master List of Documents

Chronology 1906–1945

1906	
January 4	Dietrich and Sabine Bonhoeffer are born in Breslau.
1912	
Easter	Bonhoeffer family moves to Berlin due to Karl Bonhoeffer's appointment as director of the university psychiatric clinic.
1913	
Easter	Bonhoeffer begins school in the Friedrich Werder Gymnasium. His parents purchase a vacation home in Friedrichsbrunn.
1914	
July 28	Austria-Hungary declares war on Serbia, beginning World War I.
1916	
March	Bonhoeffer family moves to Berlin-Grunewald, Wangenheimstrasse 14.
1917	Bonhoeffer's brothers Karl-Friedrich and Walter are called for military service.
1918	
April 28	Walter Bonhoeffer dies in a field hospital in France of wounds suffered five days earlier.

November 9	Kaiser Wilhelm II of Germany abdicates. Social Democrat leader Philipp Scheidemann declares foundation of a new republic, the Weimar Republic.
November 11	War ends when Germany agrees to sign armistice. Over 9 million combatants, 6 million of them German soldiers, have died. U.S., Belgian, French, and British forces occupy the Rhineland.
December 25	German war veterans found the nationalist and anti-Semitic Stahlhelm.
1919	
Easter	Bonhoeffer enters Grunewald Gymnasium.
June 28	League of Nations formed; Treaty of Versailles signed. The Versailles treaty states that Germany is responsible for the war and orders it to pay reparations to the nations it has fought.
1920	
February 24	The first meeting of the National Socialist Workers Party (NSDAP, or Nazi party) is held in Munich. The party draws up its platform.
1921	
March	Confirmation of Dietrich and Sabine Bonhoeffer.
1922	
June 24	Walther Rathenau, the Jewish foreign minister of Germany, is assassinated by a right-wing group.
October	Benito Mussolini becomes prime minister and establishes a fascist government in Italy.
1923	During the "crisis of 1923," Germany's economy is devastated by inflation; unemployment grows. Unrest increases, generated by both Communists and Nazi activists. The first issue of *Der Stürmer,* the anti-Semitic Nazi newspaper, is published in Nuremberg; its slogan is "The Jews are our misfortune."
January	After Germany fails to meet its reparations payments, France and Belgium occupy the Ruhr.

March	Bonhoeffer takes his qualifying exams for the university. The Nazi party establishes a paramilitary organization, the SS (Schutzstaffel).
Summer semester	Bonhoeffer begins his theological studies in Tübingen, where he joins the "Hedgehog" fraternity.
November	Bonhoeffer briefly joins the Ulm Rifles troop, a part of the "Black Reichswehr," the paramilitary, nationalist, promonarchist group founded by Hans von Seeckt.
November 8–11	Hitler and Nazi party members attempt to gain control of Munich in the "Beer Hall Putsch," leading to his imprisonment for nine months. The Weimar government bans the pro-Nazi newspaper *Der Stürmer.*

1924

May 4	The Nazi party wins 6.6 percent of the vote in parliamentary elections, gaining representation in the Weimar parliament.
April–June	Dietrich and his brother Klaus travel to Rome, Sicily, and North Africa.
June–July	Bonhoeffer begins his third semester of studies, in Berlin.
Winter semester	Fourth semester, in Berlin.
December 20	Adolf Hitler is released from prison.

1925	General Erich Ludendorff founds the Tannenbergbund, an anti-Semitic nationalist group. The Nazi party begins to regroup with large rallies.
March 24	Publication of *Der Stürmer* resumes.
April 26	Election of General Paul von Hindenburg as president.
Summer semester	Fifth semester, in Berlin. Bonhoeffer concerns himself with Karl Barth's theology.
July 18	Publication of Hitler's book *Mein Kampf.*
August 19–30	Universal Christian Conference on Life and Work meets in Stockholm, establishing the Protestant ecumenical movement.
September	Bonhoeffer discusses his doctoral dissertation with Reinhold Seeberg.
Winter semester	Sixth semester, in Berlin.

October	Bonhoeffer preaches his first sermon, in Stahnsdorf.
1926	The Nazi party establishes a youth organization, the Hitler Youth.
February	Bonhoeffer begins assisting with children's worship services in the Grunewald church. Germany applies for membership in the League of Nations; Spain and Brazil veto its application in March.
Summer semester	Seventh semester, in Berlin.
Winter semester	Eighth semester, in Berlin.
1927	
April	Bonhoeffer begins the Thursday Circle for youth in the congregation.
Summer semester	Ninth semester, in Berlin.
July	Bonhoeffer submits his doctoral dissertation and registers for his examinations.
August 3–21	World Conference on Faith and Order held in Lausanne, establishing the other (besides Life and Work) branch of the international ecumenical movement.
October–November	Work on his sermon and catechetical lessons for November examination.
December	Doctoral examinations and defense of his doctoral thesis.
1928	
January	First theological exam; acceptance as a candidate for ordination by the consistory.
January 18	Bonhoeffer meets one last time with the children's worship assistants at Pastor Karl Meumann's; final meeting of the Thursday Circle.
January 22	Final children's service in Berlin.
February 8–15	Bonhoeffer travels to begin his assistant pastorate at the German church in Barcelona.
February 19	Installation service in Barcelona.
March 11	First sermon in Barcelona.
April 7–June 1	Bonhoeffer's brother Klaus visits.
April 23–ca. May 10	Tour of Spain with Klaus.

May 20	The Nazi party wins twelve seats in the German parliament.
June 27	Bonhoeffer substitutes for Pastor Friedrich Olbricht and begins work on his postdoctoral dissertation. Weekly children's services.
September 19–October 8	Bonhoeffer's parents visit him in Barcelona.
October 10	Postdoctoral dissertation plan takes shape after publication revisions for the dissertation *Sanctorum Communio* are almost complete.
November 13	Bonhoeffer begins his lecture series "Crisis and Hope in the Contemporary Religious Situation." First lecture: "The Tragedy of the Prophetic and Its Lasting Meaning."
November 27	Pastor Olbricht travels, leaving Bonhoeffer in charge of the congregation until just before Christmas. Dialogue circle with the secondary school seniors begins.
December 11	Second lecture: "Jesus Christ and the Essence of Christianity."

1929

January 10–13	Bonhoeffer travels to Majorca, where he conducts two services.
January 20	Heinrich Himmler becomes head of the SS.
February 3	Farewell sermon in Barcelona.
February 8	Third lecture: "Basic Questions of a Christian Ethic."
February 17	Departure for Geneva; Bonhoeffer spends a week there with his brother Klaus.
February 27	Arrival in Berlin.
Summer semester	Bonhoeffer becomes an academic assistant in systematic theology with Wilhelm Lütgert in Berlin.
June 28	German Evangelical Church day of mourning commemorating the tenth anniversary of the Versailles treaty.
August 3–4	Over one hundred thousand Germans attend a Nazi party rally in Nuremberg.
October 3	Reich chancellor and foreign minister Gustave Stresemann dies.
October 24	Collapse of the New York stock market ("Black Friday"), launching the Great Depression.

1930	Number of unemployed in Germany climbs from 3.2 million (January) to 4.38 million (December).
January 11	Bonhoeffer applies for a German Academic Exchange Service (DAAD) fellowship to study in the United States.
January 28	Bonhoeffer speaks with the German National People's Party parliamentary member Reinhard Mumm about financing the publication of *Sanctorum Communio.* German parliament accepts the Young Plan, against vehement nationalist opposition. Implementation of the plan is halted in 1931.
March 14	*Act and Being* is submitted for Bonhoeffer's postdoctoral degree.
March 28	Dissertation manuscript sent to Trowitzsch publishers.
April	Bonhoeffer visits the congregation in Barcelona, where he delivers a lecture.
April 19	Bonhoeffer returns to Berlin.
May 15	Bonhoeffer receives DAAD fellowship for study in the United States.
May 22	Bonhoeffer submits request to be excused from the preachers' seminary.
June 15	Bonhoeffer delivers address at the memorial service for Adolf von Harnack.
June 29	Bonhoeffer takes his catechetical examination in the Grunewald church children's service under Pastor Meumann.
July 5–8	Second theological examination.
July 12	Bonhoeffer delivers his trial lecture, "The Concept of Dialectic in the So-Called Dialectical Theology."
July 18	Bonhoeffer receives his postdoctoral degree for systematic theology.
July 20	Worship service with sermon exam in Teltow.
July 31	Public inaugural lecture: "The Anthropological Question in Contemporary Philosophy and Theology."
August 29	Denial of early ordination request, since Bonhoeffer has not reached the required age of twenty-five.
September 1	Meeting of the DAAD German exchange students going to the United States.
September 2	Delivery of the first copies of *Sanctorum Communio.*

September 5	Bonhoeffer departs for the United States on the *Columbus*.
September 14	In the parliamentary elections, the Nazi party wins 18 percent of the vote, becoming the second largest political party in Germany.
September 15	Bonhoeffer spends a week visiting the Boerickes in Philadelphia.
Late September	Bonhoeffer begins his year of study at Union Theological Seminary, where he becomes friends with two other European students, Erwin Sutz (from Switzerland) and Jean Lasserre (from France), and with U.S. students Paul Lehmann and Franklin Fisher.
October 25	Bonhoeffer visits the Negro Center in Harlem.
November 9	Bonhoeffer preaches a sermon on Armistice Day in the Memorial Methodist Church ("A message on war") on 1 John 4:16.
November 28–December 1	Visit with the Boerickes in Philadelphia.
December 1–4	Bonhoeffer attends Federal Council of Churches meeting in Washington, D.C., and visits Howard University with Franklin Fisher.
December 13–January 2, 1931	Bonhoeffer travels to Cuba with Erwin Sutz.
December 21	Bonhoeffer preaches in Havana on Deut. 32:48–52.

1931

January	Theologian Günther Dehn, a pacifist and religious socialist, is offered a professorship at Heidelberg but comes under attack by right-wing students; the job offer is withdrawn.
January 20	Bonhoeffer's mother writes Bonhoeffer of her fear that "a government of Nazis is coming."
January 31	Karl Barth delivers his lecture "The Crisis of the Protestant Church" before fourteen hundred listeners, sharply attacking Berlin church superintendent Otto Dibelius.
February 7	Dibelius responds with the lecture "The Responsibility of the Church: A Response to Karl Barth." On the same day, Dibelius writes Bonhoeffer about his possibly taking the position of student chaplain at the Technical College in Berlin.

May 5	After concluding their studies at Union, Bonhoeffer and Jean Lasserre leave by car for Mexico; Erwin Sutz and Paul Lehmann travel with them part of the way.
June 20	Bonhoeffer departs from New York by ship for Europe.
After June 26	Bonhoeffer returns to Berlin.
July 7	Conclusion of Paris negotiations about U.S. president Herbert Hoover's plan for an international debt moratorium.
July 10	Superintendent Max Diestel grants Bonhoeffer's request for leave from his church duties until October 1, 1931. Bonhoeffer spends three weeks in Bonn.
July 13	German banking crisis; there is a general run on banks, which stop payments.
July 15	Evening discussion at Barth's home with monks from Maria Laach. Bonhoeffer visits Maria Laach. First emergency decree regulating financial sector.
July 21–23	Seven Powers Conference in London to address the German banking crisis; short-term credits are extended to Germany.
July 23	Lunch with Karl Barth.
July 24	"Open Evening" at Karl Barth's home, organized by his students.
August 1	Bonhoeffer accepts a special position as assistant to Wilhelm Lütgert in the Department of Systematic Theology in Berlin.
August 4	Reich chancellor Heinrich Brüning's radio speech concerning the financial crisis.
August 14–27	Bonhoeffer participates in the British conference at Westcliff-on-Sea and St. Leonards-on-Sea.
August 27–29	Bonhoeffer may have participated in the Seaford Conference (Westhill).
August 29–31	Conference of the Youth Commission of the International Section of the World Alliance for Promoting International Friendship through the Churches in Cambridge.
September 1–5	Conference of the World Alliance for Promoting International Friendship through the Churches in Cambridge. Bonhoeffer is elected one of three youth secretaries and appointed to the Management Committee and the International Section of the

	World Alliance. The ecumenical meeting is attacked in the German press by nationalist theologians Paul Althaus and Emmanuel Hirsch.
September 3	Stock markets reopen.
September 21	German stock markets close.
October 1	Bonhoeffer begins service as student chaplain at the Technical College in Berlin-Charlottenburg.
October 10	Reich president Hindenburg receives the National Socialist party leader, Adolf Hitler.
October 11	Rally of the "national opposition" groups (National Socialist Party, German National People's Party, Stahlhelm) in Bad Harzburg; formation of the Harzburg Front.
October 20	Meeting of the Provisional Bureau for Ecumenical Youth Work.
October 28	Henry L. Henriod, secretary of the International Section of the World Alliance for Promoting International Friendship through the Churches, assigns Bonhoeffer to plan a French-German regional conference.
November 2	Semester begins. Bonhoeffer offers the lecture course "History of Twentieth-Century Systematic Theology" and the seminar "The Concept of Philosophy and Protestant Theology."
November 15	Bonhoeffer ordained by Ernst Vits. Appointment as city synodal vicar at the Zion Church (district III; present-day Berlin-Wedding and Prenzlauer Berg).
November 20	Great Britain implements stiff tariffs on imports.
November 21	Friedrich Wilhelm University informs Wilhelm Lütgert that Bonhoeffer can take the special position of assistant that has just come open.
November 25	Bonhoeffer becomes secretary of the Provisional Bureau for Ecumenical Youth Work.
Winter	German unemployment reaches its highest level (over 6 million).
December 4	France issues decree concerning imports from countries with foreign exchange controls.
December 8	The German government issues the fourth emergency decree for securing economic and financial institutions and for the protection of domestic peace.

December 14	Swiss announcement of the Swiss-German trade agreement.
December 24	U.S. president Hoover signs the moratorium for reparation payments and war debt.

1932

January 14	Bonhoeffer signs the contract for the special position as assistant at the Friedrich Wilhelm University in Berlin (the contract runs from August 8, 1931, to June 30, 1933).
January 28	Sino-Japanese War breaks out.
January 29	Decree by Reich Armed Forces minister Wilhelm Groener concerning the incorporation of the militias (*Wehrverbände*) into the armed forces.
February 2	Opening of the international conference on disarmament in Geneva.
February 4	Bonhoeffer delivers a talk at the Technical College, "The Right to Self-Assertion."
March 13	First primary for the Reich presidential election.
April 4	Bonhoeffer attends conference of the international youth secretaries in Epsom near London as well as the meeting of the planning group for the Gland ecumenical meeting.
April 5–8	Franco-British regional conference of the World Alliance for Promoting International Friendship through the Churches in Epsom.
April 10	Bonhoeffer in Berlin to participate in the main Reich presidential election (General Paul von Hindenburg is reelected).
April 11	Karl Barth delivers a talk in the main auditorium at Berlin University: "Theology and Mission in the Present."
April 13	SA and SS banned by an emergency decree at the recommendation of Reich Armed Forces minister Groener.
April 29–30	Theological conference of the Provisional Bureau for Ecumenical Youth Work at the Church Federation Office, organized by Wilhelm Stählin and Bonhoeffer.
May	Establishment of the *Deutsche Christen* (German Christians), a nationalist, anti-Semitic Protestant group that aligns itself with the Nazi party.

May 6	Semester begins. Bonhoeffer offers the lecture course "The Nature of the Church" and the seminar "Is There a Christian Ethic?"
May 12	Bonhoeffer preaches at the baptism of his nephew Thomas, son of Klaus and Emmi Bonhoeffer. Reich Armed Forces minister Groener resigns.
May 30	Brüning's cabinet falls.
June 1–2	Franz von Papen appointed chancellor by Hindenburg; organizes cabinet.
June 4	Dissolution of parliament.
June 16	Lifting of the ban on the SA and the ban on uniforms by emergency decree. Conference in Lausanne concerning the waiving of German reparation payments.
June 20	Prussian civil administration deposed; Reich chancellor Papen installed as Reich Commissar.
July 12–14	Franco-German regional conference in Westerburg, which Bonhoeffer organizes in his capacity as youth secretary of the International Section of the World Alliance.
July 18	General ban on demonstrations in Germany.
July 20	Papen assumes power in Prussia.
July 20–30	International Youth Peace Conference in Ciernohorské Kúpele (Czechoslovakia); Bonhoeffer arrives on July 25.
July 26	In Ciernohorské Kúpele Bonhoeffer delivers his talk "On the Theological Foundation of the Work of the World Alliance."
July 29	Bonhoeffer departs for Berlin earlier than anticipated.
July 31	Parliamentary elections in Germany. The Nazi party gets 37.3 percent of the vote.
August 1	After completing his year of church service, Bonhoeffer receives the position of assistant pastor.
August 12	Dissolution of parliament.
August 13	Negotiations collapse between the Reich government and Adolf Hitler regarding the participation of the Nazi party in the government.
August 16–17	Bonhoeffer spends two days at the vacation home of Jean Lasserre's family in Le Tremble, near Chamonix, France.

August 19–22	Conference of the Management Committee of the International Section of the World Alliance for Promoting International Friendship through the Churches in Geneva.
August 23	Meeting in Geneva of the group organizing the Gland conference.
August 25–31	Youth conference of the World Alliance for Promoting International Friendship through the Churches and of the Universal Christian Council for Life and Work in Gland, on Lake Geneva, Switzerland. Bonhoeffer chairs the German discussion group.
August 28	Bonhoeffer delivers an address at the Gland conference.
August 29	German note to France concerning the armaments question.
September 18	Official declaration of Great Britain concerning the Franco-German exchange on disarmament and equal rights.
September 25	Bonhoeffer attends the conference of student chaplains in Friedrichroda.
October	Bonhoeffer preaches at the baptism of his nephew Friedrich, son of Karl-Friedrich and Grete Bonhoeffer.
October 25	Supreme Court verdict on the dispute between Prussia and the German Reich.
November	Winter semester begins. Bonhoeffer delivers lecture "Creation and Sin" (published as "Creation and Fall") and "Review and Discussion of New Publications in Systematic Theology" and conducts a seminar on dogmatic exercises, "Theological Anthropology."
November 6	Reichstag elections: the Nazi party loses 2 million votes compared to the elections of July 31, 1932. General Kurt von Schleicher succeeds Franz von Papen as Reich chancellor.
November–December	Bonhoeffer delivers lecture "Christ and Peace."
December 3	Bonhoeffer's memorandum "The Social Gospel."
December 9–10	Bonhoeffer participates in the theological conference of the Provisional Bureau for Ecumenical Youth Work in Berlin.

1933

January 11	Dissemination of the Altona confession, written by a group of Hamburg pastors in the wake of a violent clash between Nazis and Communists in Hamburg-Altona, condemning extremist political violence.
January 30	Reich president Hindenburg appoints Hitler as Reich chancellor.
End of January–beginning of February	Meeting of the Executive Committee of the World Alliance and the Administrative Committee of Life and Work in Berlin.
February 1	Bonhoeffer's radio address "The Younger Generation's Altered View of the Concept of Führer."
February 23	Bonhoeffer gives a more expanded address on the Führer concept at the Technical College in Berlin.
February 27	Reichstag fire in Berlin.
February 28	Hindenburg's emergency measures "for the protection of people and state" suspend essential basic democratic rights; this is followed by excesses against Communists and Social Democrats. Bonhoeffer loses the vote on his application for a pastorate at St. Bartholomew's in east Berlin.
Beginning of March	Bonhoeffer repeats his expanded address on the Führer concept at the College of Political Science in Berlin.
March 5	Reichstag elections: the Nazi party and the German National Peoples' party (DNVP) win a combined 44.7 percent of the vote.
March 6–10	Bonhoeffer participates in the ecumenical conference in Dassel.
March 21	Opening ceremony of the Reichstag ("Day of Potsdam"). Malicious Practices Act (Heimtückegesetz) passed, barring all activity and speech critical of the state.
March 24	The Enabling Act grants dictatorial powers to Hitler.
End of March–beginning of April	Bonhoeffer develops theses concerning the question of the church membership of "non-Aryan" Christians.
April 1	Boycott of Jewish businesses throughout the Reich.
April 3–5	German Christians hold Reich conference in Berlin demanding a "synchronization of church and state."

April 7	Nazi regime passes Law for the Reconstitution of the Civil Service with the so-called Aryan paragraph, which orders the dismissal of Jewish and other "undesirable" civil servants from public service.
April 16	Bonhoeffer completes his essay "The Church and the Jewish Question."
April 25	Church president Hermann Kapler convenes the German Evangelical Church Committee (Kirchenausschuss) in Berlin to reform the constitution of the German Evangelical Church. Hitler appoints Chaplain Ludwig Müller, a German Christian, "confidential adviser and plenipotentiary in questions concerning the Protestant church."
May	Summer semester begins. Bonhoeffer lectures on Christology and conducts a seminar on Hegel's philosophy of religion.
May 4	Constitutional Committee of the Church Federation (Verfassungsausschuss des Kirchenbunds) begins discussions about a new church constitution; Ludwig Müller participates in the meetings.
May 6	The German Christians deliver to Evangelical Church Council president Hermann Kapler "Ten Principles" demanding among other things that the new Reich Church be a "church of the German Christians, that is, of Christians of Aryan race."
May 9	Young Reformation Movement founded in opposition to the German Christians.
May 16	New guidelines issued by the German Christians.
May 17	The German Christians nominate Ludwig Müller as their candidate for Reich bishop.
May 19	The Young Reformation Movement counters by nominating Friedrich von Bodelschwingh.
May 23	Lazarus church council in east Berlin turns down Bonhoeffer's application for a pastorate there.
May 27	Leaders of the regional churches elect Bodelschwingh Reich bishop; despite the German Christians' virulent campaigns against him, Bodelschwingh takes office.
June	Bonhoeffer's essay "The Church and the Jewish Question" is published.
June 7–8	Franco-German World Alliance meeting in Basel; Bonhoeffer does not participate.

June 19	Assembly of the German Student League (Deutsche Studentenschaft) on behalf of the German Christians. Most participants leave the auditorium when a resolution supporting Ludwig Müller is read. Bonhoeffer and Ernst Bronisch-Holtze report to the Reich chancellery concerning the assembly.
June 21	Pastor Friedrich Siegmund-Schultze expelled from Germany for assisting Jews.
June 22	About two thousand participants attend an assembly of the Working Committee of Protestant Students (Arbeitsausschuss evangelischer Studenten) to oppose the June 19 German Student League assembly. As one of the main speakers, Bonhoeffer demands that a Protestant council issue binding doctrinal statements clarifying the church's stand.
June 24	State commissioner August Jäger, appointed by the Prussian minister of culture, assumes leadership of all the regional churches in Prussia. Bodelschwingh resigns because of lack of support among church leaders.
July 6	In a statement sent to Hitler on July 12, 106 pastors from greater Berlin protest the installation of state commissioner Jäger.
July 11	Work on the new church constitution completed amid considerable political pressure.
Before July 14	Bonhoeffer's memorandum "The Jewish-Christian Question as Status Confessionis."
July 14	Publication of the new church constitution together with a Reich law confirming it and stipulating general church elections on July 23.
Mid-July	Church Foreign Office official Theodor Heckel inquires whether Bonhoeffer would accept a position in London as pastor to an overseas German congregation.
July 18	Bonhoeffer and Gerhard Jacobi protest to Gestapo chief Rudolf Diels in Berlin after election materials of the Young Reformation movement are confiscated; Diels threatens to send them to a concentration camp.
July 20	Signing of the concordat between the Reich government and the Holy See.

July 22	In a radio address regarding the church elections, Hitler unequivocally supports the German Christians.
July 23	In the church elections, the German Christians win approximately two-thirds of all seats in the regional church administrations throughout Germany.
July 24–25	The Young Reformation Movement withdraws from church politics and demands that a binding confession be formulated.
July 28	Bonhoeffer travels to London and on July 30–31 introduces himself to the congregations of the German Evangelical Church of Sydenham and St. Paul's German Reformed Church.
August 4	The Old Prussian church senate elects Ludwig Müller as bishop of the Evangelical Church of the Old Prussian Union.
August 5	Bonhoeffer in Bethel for preliminary talks concerning the Bethel confession.
August 15–25	Work on the Bethel confession results in the "August version."
August 24	Meeting of the (majority German Christian) Old Prussian provincial synods to elect representatives for the general synod. The Berlin-Brandenburg provincial synod adopts the state "Aryan legislation" for church officials.
August 29–September 4	International Youth Conference in Gland on Lake Geneva; because of church-political developments in Germany, Bonhoeffer does not participate.
End of August	Bonhoeffer's theses titled "The Aryan Paragraph in the Church."
September 5–6	The General Synod divides the Old Prussian church into dioceses, stipulates that sixteen of the nineteen representatives at the National Synod must be German Christians, and adopts the state Aryan paragraph.
September 9	Bonhoeffer writes to Karl Barth asking for his position on the August version of the Bethel confession.
September 11	Barth responds by letter.
September 12	Establishment of the Pastor's Emergency League to support pastors of "non-Aryan" descent.

September 15–20	Meeting of the World Alliance in Sofia, Bulgaria, which issues a statement condemning the Nazi racial laws. Bonhoeffer and Julius Richter visit the German embassy in Sofia afterward.
September 24	Petition to the National Synod drafted demanding that the introduction of the Aryan paragraph in regional churches be rescinded.
September 27	National Synod convenes in Wittenberg. Ludwig Müller elected Reich bishop, but the issue of the Aryan paragraph is not addressed.
Beginning of October	In Bethel Bonhoeffer and Hans Fischer work through the August version of the Bethel confession in light of the expert opinions that have arrived in the meantime. The official editorial conference, in which Bonhoeffer does not participate, does not take place until the final days of October.
October 4	In a conversation with the Reich bishop, Bonhoeffer refuses to represent the cause of the German Christians in his London pastorates.
October 6	Bonhoeffer meets with Church Foreign Office official Theodor Heckel.
October 14	Germany withdraws from the League of Nations.
October 17	Bonhoeffer begins his ministry in London.
October 24	Letter to Karl Barth explaining Bonhoeffer's decision to go to London.
November 13	Sports Palace rally of the German Christians in Berlin.
November 19	First suspensions of pastors in Germany.
November 21	Bonhoeffer's first visit to Bishop George Bell in Chichester.
November 27–30	Ministry conference in Bradford, Yorkshire.
December 20	Protestant Youth groups subsumed into the Hitler Youth.

1934

January 4	Ludwig Müller's "muzzling decree" prohibits any criticism by clergy and church officials of the Reich Church government.
January 25	Hitler meets with Protestant church leaders to discuss the church controversies.

January 31	Bonhoeffer attends ecumenical youth commission meeting in Paris.
February 8–9	Church Foreign Office delegation led by Theodor Heckel visits London.
February 13	Bonhoeffer attends Council of Brethren meeting in Hannover before going on to Berlin.
February 21	Theodor Heckel appointed bishop, overseeing the Church Foreign Office.
March 1	Reich Bishop Ludwig Müller places Martin Niemöller in involuntary retirement.
March 6	Complaint about Bonhoeffer sent to the Church Foreign Office; Bonhoeffer attends independent synod meeting in Berlin-Brandenburg.
April 12	August Jäger named "legal administrator" of the German Evangelical Church. Beginning of compulsory incorporations of regional churches into the Reich Church.
April 22	Confessional front issues the Ulm declaration in opposition to the Reich Church leaders.
May 10	Bishop Bell's Ascension Day message to the ecumenical world.
May 29–31	Confessional synod in Barmen, culminating in the Barmen Theological Declaration.
June 18	Bonhoeffer in Berlin; discusses participating in the Fanø ecumenical meeting with Karl Koch and Martin Niemöller.
June 30	Röhm putsch, in which under Hitler's orders the Nazi regime murders his party rivals as well as political opponents.
July 9	Interior minister Wilhelm Frick forbids public statements about the Protestant church dispute.
July 25	Austrian president Engelbert Dollfuss murdered.
August 2	Reich president Hindenburg dies; Hitler personally assumes both the presidency and the chancellorship.
August 18–30	Bonhoeffer arrives in Fanø.
August 20	Minister of education Bernhard Rust orders all civil servants to take a loyalty oath; Karl Barth refuses to swear the oath unless it is revised.
August 22	Ecumenical youth conference begins in Fanø.

August 24–25	"Lutheran Council" founded.
August 28	Bonhoeffer delivers peace speech at the ecumenical conference of the World Alliance for Life and Work in Fanø.
August 30	Resolution in support of the Confessing Church passed in Fanø under protest by Bishop Heckel.
September 3	Bonhoeffer attends Reich Council of Brethren meeting in Würzburg; reports on Fanø.
September 4–8	Bonhoeffer visits Jean Lasserre in Bruay-en-Artois and attends ecumenical French-German-British youth conference.
September 23	Installation of Reich Bishop Ludwig Müller.
October 6–12	Bishops Theophil Wurm and Hans Meiser placed under house arrest.
October 16	At the German embassy in London, the archbishop of Canterbury, Cosmo Lang, threatens to break ecumenical ties with the Reich Church.
October 19–20	Second Reich Confessional Synod in Dahlem; synod declares a state of emergency church law and establishes emergency governance of the Confessing Church.
October 26	Church commissioner August Jäger resigns.
October 30	Confessing bishops visit Hitler: Bishops August Marahrens, Meiser, and Wurm cleared.
November 1	Bonhoeffer receives invitation from Mahatma Gandhi.
November 5	German Protestant congregations in England break with the Reich Church government.
November 20	Church incorporation law rescinded; Reich Church project collapses.
November 22	First provisional church administration of the Confessing Church is established. Karl Barth and Martin Niemöller resign in protest from the Reich Council of Brethren.
November 25	Bonhoeffer sings in the chorus of the Brahms Requiem in London and then travels to Berlin, where he negotiates with Westphalian church president Karl Koch and the Ministry of Foreign Affairs.
December 22	Karl Barth loses teaching position in Bonn.

1935

January 4	Congregational councils of St. Paul's German Reformed Church and the German Evangelical Church of Sydenham refuse to recognize the Reich Church government or to accept the German Evangelical Church constitution.
January 13	Plebiscite held in the Saar territory (a majority of over 90 percent favor rejoining German Reich).
January 29	Bonhoeffer's memorandum to the ecumenical youth commission.
February 4	Bonhoeffer travels to Berlin for three days.
February 11	Bonhoeffer requests a leave of absence from St. Paul's from March 15 to September 15, 1935, to direct a Confessing Church preachers' seminary.
February 24	Confirmation service in Sydenham.
March 10	Final sermon in London before leave of absence.
March 16	Universal compulsory military duty instituted in Germany.
March 25	Bonhoeffer informs the Church Foreign Office of the six-month leave of absence he has been given from the London congregations.
March	Bonhoeffer visits the Anglican monasteries Society of John the Evangelist, Oxford; Community of the Resurrection, Mirfield; and Society of the Sacred Mission, Kelham; also the Woodbrooke Quaker center, Selly Oak, Birmingham.
April 15	Bonhoeffer meets with Bishop Bell in London, then returns to Germany.
April 26	Berlin-Brandenburg Preachers' Seminary of the Confessing Church of the Old Prussian Union established under director Dietrich Bonhoeffer; first session begins at Zingsthof.
May 1	New armed forces law goes into effect (renunciation of the armament restrictions of the Treaty of Versailles, introduction of universal compulsory military service in Germany on March 16).
May 11	Gestapo searches the office of the Reich Council of Brethren in Berlin for the first time.
May 13–14	Preparatory meeting with Joseph H. Oldham in Hannover for the World Church Conference in Oxford 1937.

May 15–17	Meeting of the administrative committee of the Universal Christian Council for Life and Work in Paris.
May 18	At the behest of Karl Koch, head of the Confessing Synod of the German Evangelical Church, Bonhoeffer flies to London to meet with Bishop Bell.
May 21	Hitler delivers his Reichstag speech outlining his thirteen-point "peace program."
May 22–23	Conference in Gohlfeld, Germany, of the "disrupted" church districts (in which governance was divided between German Christians and Confessing Church leaders).
June 4–6	Third synod of the Reich Confessing Church (after Barmen on May 29–31 and Dahlem on October 19–20, 1934) in Augsburg.
June 6	Police interrogation in Zingst concerning the June 2 worship service.
June 24	Preachers' seminary moves to Finkenwalde.
June 27	Meeting of the Ecumenical Council of the Provisional Church Administration in Berlin.
July 16	Decree merging the oversight responsibilities of the Reich and Prussia in church matters. Installation of the Reich Ministry for Church Affairs under Hanns Kerrl.
July 30	Retreat with Greifswald theology students in Finkenwalde till August 2. On July 31 Bonhoeffer delivers his lecture "Christ in the Psalms."
August 1–8	World Alliance youth conference in Chamby sur Montreux.
August 3–12	Bonhoeffer travels to London and to Chichester. Conducts farewell worship services on August 4 and 11 in St. Paul's German Reformed Church and the German Evangelical Church of Sydenham.
August 18–22	Meeting of the Universal Christian Council for Life and Work in Chamby sur Montreux.
August 20–25	Meeting of the Brotherhood of Assistant Pastors and Vicars of the Saxon Provincial Confessing Church in Hauteroda; on August 23 Bonhoeffer delivers his lecture "Contemporizing New Testament Texts." Bonhoeffer's essay "The Confessing Church and the Ecumenical Movement."

September 3	Lectures resume in the preachers' seminary after summer vacation.
September 8	Dedication of the provisional chapel in the Finkenwalde preachers' seminary.
September 12–28	George Bell, bishop of Chichester, in Germany for discussions about the German Evangelical Church.
September 15	At the National Socialist Reich rally in Nuremberg, Hitler announces the Nuremberg Laws, escalating the legal persecution of German Jews.
September 23–26	Confessing Synod of the Old Prussian Union in Berlin-Steglitz.
September 24	Law to Restore Order in the German Evangelical Church.
October 3	Reich Church Committee established under Wilhelm Zoellner.
October 8–11	Meeting of the Brotherhood of Pomeranian Vicars in Finkenwalde. Bonhoeffer's Bible study on "King David."
October 16	End of the first Finkenwalde session.
October 17	Regional Church Committee of the Old Prussian Union established under Johannes Eger.
November 4	Second Finkenwalde session begins.
November 12	Bonhoeffer's course on "Discipleship" begins at the University of Berlin.
December 2	Fifth implementation decree of the Law to Restore Order in the German Evangelical Church.
December 12	Bishop Marahrens declares his willingness in the name of the Provisional Church Administration to work together with the Reich Church Committee.
December 27	Establishment of provincial church committees in the Old Prussian Union.
1936	Bonhoeffer's resignation from the Hedgehog fraternity recorded in its alumni bulletin after some of its members openly support Nazi *Gleichschaltung* policies.
January 10	General assembly of the pastors of the Confessing Church of Pomerania in Stettin-Bredow. Bonhoeffer delivers statement "From Barmen to Oeynhausen" opposing the path to legalization for Confessing seminarians by the official church.

January 12	Old Prussian Union pulpit proclamation opposing the church committees. Confessing worship service in the provisional chapel of the Finkenwalde preachers' seminary and establishment of a local Confessing Church congregation.
January 15	Memorial service for Bonhoeffer's grandmother Julie Bonhoeffer in Berlin.
January 20	Hermann Ehlers, a lawyer with the Council of Brethren of the Old Prussian Union, comes to audit the Finkenwalde preachers' seminary budget.
February 14	Bonhoeffer's final lecture at the University of Berlin.
February 17–22	Fourth (and final) Reich Confessing synod in Bad Oeynhausen.
February 29	Departure of Finkenwalde seminarians for Denmark and Sweden.
March 7	German troops occupy the demilitarized Rhineland.
March 10	Finkenwalde seminarians return from Sweden and Denmark.
March 12	Election of the Provisional Administration of the German Evangelical Church (to replace the first Provisional Church Administration after the resignation of Bishop Marahrens) by the Reich Council of Brethren.
March 15	End of the second Finkenwalde session.
March 18	Council of the Evangelical Lutheran Church of Germany appointed as spiritual leadership of the "intact" regional churches of Hannover, Württemberg, and Bavaria.
March 29	Reichstag "election" (plebiscite for Hitler's policies; 99 percent vote yes).
April	Bonhoeffer and Eberhard Bethge vacation during Easter break in Friedrichsbrunn in the Harz Mountains. Bonhoeffer composes the guide to daily meditation.
April 15	Third Finkenwalde session begins.
April 20–24	Retreat with former session participants in Finkenwalde; April 21, Bonhoeffer's Bible study on "The Reconstruction of Jerusalem"; April 22, Bonhoeffer's lecture "On the Question of Church Communion."

April 27	Meeting of the heads of the educational offices and directors of the preachers' seminaries of the Old Prussian Union in Berlin.
May 20	Meeting of the Ecumenical Council of the Provisional Administration of the German Evangelical Church in Berlin.
June 4	Memorandum from the Provisional Administration of the German Evangelical Church, protesting many of the Nazi actions and laws, delivered to Hitler in the Reich Chancellery.
June 8–15	Evangelization trip undertaken by the Finkenwalde preachers' seminary.
June 17	Heinrich Himmler appointed *Reichsführer* SS and chief of the German police in the Reich Ministry of the Interior.
July 18	Germany and Italy intervene on behalf of General Francisco Franco in the Spanish Civil War.
July 23	Confessing Church memorandum to Hitler published in the *Basler Nachrichten*; arrest and imprisonment of those involved follows.
August 1–16	Olympic Games in Berlin.
August 5	As part of the series of Olympics events of the Confessing Church in Berlin, Bonhoeffer delivers an address on the history of the Protestant hymn. Withdrawal of Bonhoeffer's authority to teach at the university.
August 21–25	Meeting of the Universal Christian Council for Life and Work in Chamby sur Montreux.
August 23	Abbreviated version of the memorandum to Hitler read as a pulpit proclamation.
August 25	End of the third Finkenwalde session. Bonhoeffer and Eberhard Bethge travel in Italy till the beginning of September.
September 8–15	Meeting of the World Alliance Youth Commission in La Borcaderie/Neuchâtel.
October 17	Fourth Finkenwalde session begins.
October 19–23	Retreat with former seminarians in Finkenwalde. On October 20 Bonhoeffer conducts his Bible study on the epistles of Timothy and lectures on his "Confirmation Instruction Plan."

October 25	A German-Italian treaty establishes the Berlin-Rome Axis.
November 15	The Sermon on the Mount Bible week begins in the Finkenwalde Confessing congregation. Bonhoeffer delivers a sermon on the Beatitudes.
December 16–18	Confessing Synod of the Old Prussian Union in Breslau.
December 18–20	Disputation in the Finkenwalde preachers' seminary on how to preach the law.

1937

January 25–30	Evangelization trip undertaken by the Finkenwalde preachers' seminary.
February 12	Reich Church Committee resigns. Hans Böhm and Bonhoeffer travel to London for ecumenical discussions.
February 15	Hitler decrees that an election be held for a general synod of the German Evangelical Church.
February 16–24	Bonhoeffer in London (meeting of the Youth Commission of the World Alliance for Promoting International Friendship through the Churches; on February 19 and 24, Bonhoeffer visits George Bell).
March 15	End of the fourth Finkenwalde session.
April 12–17	Retreat with former seminarians in Finkenwalde.
April 18	Fifth Finkenwalde session begins.
May 11–13	Confessing Synod of the Old Prussian Union in Halle.
May 19–23	Working meetings of the Pomeranian and Provincial Saxon Confessing Church pastors in Finkenwalde. Bonhoeffer delivers his lecture "The Power of the Keys and Church Discipline in the New Testament."
May 31–June 4	Retreat with former seminarians in Finkenwalde.
June 9	Confessing Church prohibited from taking up collections. Professors at the Berlin Seminary prohibited from teaching.
June 14	Arrest of Wilhelm Niesel, educational adviser for the Old Prussian Union Confessing Church.
June 23	Meeting of the Reich Council of Brethren in Berlin canceled; eight members arrested.

July 1	Martin Niemöller arrested in Berlin-Dahlem; assets of the Pastors' Emergency League confiscated; office of the Provisional Administration of the German Evangelical Church closed.
July 4–10	Evangelization trip undertaken by the Finkenwalde preachers' seminary.
July 12–26	World Church Conference in Oxford, but without any German delegation.
August 24–27	Meeting of the Brotherhood of Provincial Saxon Assistant Pastors and Vicars in Stecklenberg in the Harz. On August 24 Bonhoeffer delivers lecture "The Power of the Keys and Congregational Discipline in the New Testament and among the Reformers."
August 29	Gestapo prohibits all Confessing Church educational and examination offices. Himmler issues an edict banning the Confessing Church's colleges and preachers' seminaries.
September 11	End of the fifth Finkenwalde session. Bonhoeffer and Eberhard Bethge spend two months with Bonhoeffer's parents in Berlin, then (in October) travel together on vacation to southern Germany.
September 25–29	Mussolini pays a state visit to Germany.
September 28	Gestapo closes the Finkenwalde preachers' seminary.
November 5	In a speech to military commanders and the foreign minister, Hitler announces his intent for the "conquest of new *Lebensraum* in the East" and its "Germanization" (in the Hossbach Protocol).
November 6	Italy joins the Anti-Comintern Pact, forming an "international political trio" (Berlin-Rome-Tokyo) to oppose Communism and the Soviet Union.
End of November	Twenty-seven former Finkenwalde seminarians arrested; publication of Bonhoeffer's *Discipleship* (*DBWE* 4).
December 5	Underground collective pastorates begin in Köslin and Groß-Schlönwitz; Bonhoeffer's official residence is now in Schlawe, as an "assistant pastor" under Superintendent Eduard Block.
Christmas	Bonhoeffer in the collective pastorate Groß-Schlönwitz.

1938

January 11	Bonhoeffer banned from Berlin and Brandenburg; shortly thereafter Karl Bonhoeffer manages to get permission for Bonhoeffer to visit his family.
January 24–25	Meeting of the "Brotherhood of Young Theologians in Pomerania" in Stettin.
February 4	Blomberg-Fritsch crisis; Hitler becomes the commander in chief of the armed forces; Joachim von Ribbentrop becomes foreign minister.
February 7	Martin Niemöller's trial begins; he is acquitted on March 2, 1938, but rearrested and taken to the concentration camp in Sachsenhausen.
February 26	Central order from Church Chancellery president Friedrich Werner concerning the "accepting into regional church ministry of those theologians trained by nonofficial institutions" ("legalization" of Confessing Church pastors).
March 12–13	German troops march into Austria; *Anschluß* (annexation) of Austria to the German Reich.
End of March	End of the 1937–38 winter session in the collective pastorates in Köslin and Groß-Schlönwitz.
April 10	Referendum on the *Anschluß* of Austria; 99 percent vote "yes."
April 20	Church Chancellery president Friedrich Werner in Berlin orders all pastors and church officials to take the loyalty oath to Adolf Hitler.
End of April (ca. April 25)	Beginning of 1938 summer session in the collective pastorates in Köslin and Groß-Schlönwitz.
June 11–13	Sixth Synod of the Confessing Church of the Old Prussian Union in Berlin-Nikolassee; discussions about the required pastors' loyalty oath.
June 20–25	Study conference for former Finkenwalde participants in Zingst; Bonhoeffer examines the biblical question of "temptation."
July 31	Second conference of the Sixth Synod of the Confessing Church of the Old Prussian Union in Berlin-Steglitz; church gives permission to take the loyalty oath.
August 6	Karl Barth's "open letter" to the Sixth Synod of the Confessing Church of the Old Prussian Union opposing its stand on the loyalty oath.

August 11	Bonhoeffer registers a protest with the Council of Brethren of the Old Prussian Union against granting clergy permission to take the loyalty oath.
August 17	Decree concerning middle names in passports, requiring "non-Aryans" to add either "Israel" or "Sarah."
August 18	Ludwig Beck resigns as chief of the general staff of the army, succeeded on August 27, 1938, by Franz Halder.
End of August	End of the summer sessions in the collective pastorates in Köslin and Groß-Schlönwitz.
September	Sudeten crisis between Germany and Czechoslovakia.
September 9–October 10	Bonhoeffer's sister and brother-in-law Sabine and Gerhard Leibholz and their children emigrate; Bonhoeffer and Bethge accompany them as far as Giessen; thereafter the two stay at the Leibholz home in Göttingen until October 10, 1938. Bonhoeffer writes *Life Together* (*DBWE* 5).
September 12	At the Reich party conference in Nuremberg, Hitler announces military assistance for the Sudeten Germans.
September 15	British prime minister Neville Chamberlain visits Hitler in Berchtesgaden.
September 19	Karl Barth's letter to Josef Hromádka in Prague, encouraging the Czechs to stand up against Nazi aggression "for the Church of Jesus Christ."
September 27	Peace prayer liturgy of the Provisional Administration of the Confessing Church for a worship service on September 30, 1938, amid anxieties that the Sudeten crisis will lead to war.
September 29–30	Munich agreement, ceding the Czech Sudetenland to Germany, signed by France, Britain, Italy, and Germany.
October 1	German troops enter the Sudetenland.
October 5	All Jewish passports recalled; any new passports had to be stamped with "J."
October 12	Bonhoeffer and Bethge depart Göttingen.
Mid-October	Bonhoeffer meets with Hans von Dohnanyi and several of his colleagues (including Reich minister of justice Franz Gürtner) in Berlin.
October 17–19	Beginning of the 1938–39 winter session in the collective pastorates in Köslin and Groß-Schlönwitz.

October 26	Meeting of the Pomeranian Council of Brethren; Bonhoeffer presents his report "Our Path according to the Testimony of Scripture."
October 31–November 2	Confessing Church Theological Society meets at the home of Ruth von Kleist-Retzow in Stettin.
November 3	Bonhoeffer must register at the military enlistment office in Schlawe.
November 9–10	The "Reich pogrom" (Kristallnacht; destruction of hundreds of synagogues and thousands of Jewish-owned shops in Germany; arrests of an estimated thirty-five thousand Jews).
November 10	Hitler delivers a secret address to members of the German press regarding a shift in propaganda toward preparing the German people psychologically for war.
November 20	Circular letter to the Finkenwalde brothers giving Bonhoeffer's reaction to the pogrom.
Christmas	Bonhoeffer in the collective pastorate in Groß-Schlönwitz; thereafter spends several days with his parents in Berlin.

1939

January 9–11	Confessing Church Theological Society meets at the home of Ruth von Kleist-Retzow in Stettin.
January 28–31	Seventh Synod of the Confessing Church of the Old Prussian Union in Berlin-Nikolassee ("Epiphany Synod"); rejection of legalization offers from the territorial consistories, declaration of solidarity with the "illegals."
January 30	Hitler's speech before the Reichstag; defends aggressive foreign policy, announces the "destruction of the Jewish race in Europe."
March 8	End of the winter session in the collective pastorates in Köslin and Groß-Schlönwitz.
March 10	Bonhoeffer and Bethge leave together for London; meetings there with Bishop George Bell and Willem A. Visser 't Hooft.
March 15–16	German troops enter Czechoslovakia.
March 23	German troops enter Lithuanian region of Memel.
March 29	Bonhoeffer meets with Leonard Hodgson (Faith and Order) in Oxford.

March 31	Britain and France guarantee Poland's independence.
April 3	Hitler instructs the armed forces to prepare for an attack on Poland. Bonhoeffer meets with Reinhold Niebuhr in Sussex, England, to discuss possible move to United States.
April 4	Church president Friedrich Werner and representatives of ten regional churches issue the Godesberg Declaration, demanding a German national church "free of Jews."
April 18	Bonhoeffer returns from London.
April 23	Bonhoeffer applies at the military enlistment office in Schlawe for a leave of absence for a trip to the United States from May 1, 1939, to May 1, 1940.
End of April	Collective pastorate at Groß-Schlönwitz relocated to Sigurdshof (Tychow near Schlawe).
April 28	Hitler addresses the Reichstag, renounces the Anglo-German Naval Treaty of 1935 and German-Polish Non-Aggression Pact of 1934.
May 6	Establishment of the Institute for the Study and Eradication of Jewish Influence on German Religious Life in Eisenach.
May 13	Bonhoeffer receives orders to report for duty in the armed forces on May 22, 1939.
May 20–22	Eighth Synod of the Confessing Church of the Old Prussian Union in Berlin-Steglitz ("Exaudi Synod").
May 22	Military alliance between Germany and Italy.
June 2	Bonhoeffer leaves for the United States via London, where he visits the Leibholzes.
June 6	Bonhoeffer meets with George Bell.
June 7	Bonhoeffer departs Southampton for New York on the *Bremen*, via Cherbourg.
June 12–July 7	Bonhoeffer arrives in New York, where he stays at Union Theological Seminary. In New York he is offered a position working with refugees.
June 20	Bonhoeffer speaks with Henry S. Leiper of the Federal Council of Churches and announces his decision to return to Germany.
July 6	Bonhoeffer meets with Paul Lehmann.
July 7–8	Bonhoeffer and Karl-Friedrich Bonhoeffer depart New York together

July 13	Bonhoeffer arrives in London, where he spends several days with the Leibholz family.
July 18	Confessing Church pastor Paul Schneider murdered in the concentration camp at Buchenwald.
July 25	Bonhoeffer departs London.
July 26–27	Visits to Confessing pastors Hans Iwand and Hermann Hesse in the Rhineland.
July 30	Bonhoeffer arrives in Berlin.
August 4–14	Bonhoeffer attends retreat with members of the Sigurdshof collective pastorate in Jershöft on the Baltic Sea; afterward spends several days there with members of the Köslin collective pastorate.
August 23	Nonaggression treaty signed between Germany and the Soviet Union with a secret protocol.
August 24–25	End of the summer session of the collective pastorates in Köslin and Sigurdshof.
August 26	Bonhoeffer and Bethge visit his parents in Berlin
August 29	Confidential Council of Clerical Advisors established by the German Evangelical church, includes August Marahrens, Johannes Hymmen, Walther Schultz.
September 1	Germany invades Poland.
September 2	Confidential Council of Clerical Advisors, with President Friedrich Werner of the German Evangelical Church, publicly state their support for the Führer and Reich.
September 3	Britain and France declare war on Germany.
September 9	Hoping to avoid military combat, Bonhoeffer applies for military chaplaincy.
September 27	Warsaw surrenders; formation of the Reich Central Security Office as the headquarters for all National Socialist police and security enforcement.
September 28	Soviet-German Friendship Treaty.
October	Beginning of the National Socialist "euthanasia" program ("T4 program").
October 6	Conquest of Poland concludes; Hitler addresses the Reichstag with his "offer of peace" to the Western powers if they will recognize the "new realities."
October 12–17	First deportation of Jews from Austria, Bohemia, and Moravia to Poland.
October 26	Establishment of the "General Government for the Occupied Polish Territories."

End of October	Beginning of the 1939–40 winter session in the collective pastorate in Sigurdshof; no longer possible to continue in Köslin.
November 8	Assassination attempt on Hitler by Johann Georg Elser in the Bürgerbräukeller in Munich.
December	First mass deportations of Jews and Poles from the Wartheland to the "General Government" region.
Christmas	Bonhoeffer at the collective pastorate in Sigurdshof, then travels to Berlin to be with his parents. While in Berlin, meets with ecumenical colleagues Nils Ehrenström and Hans Schönfeld and Confessing Church pastor Helmut Gollwitzer at the Gossner Mission house.

1940

Mid-January	Bonhoeffer returns to Sigurdshof from Berlin.
February 13–14	First deportations of Jews from the German Reich (Schneidemühl, Stettin, Stralsund) to Lublin.
February 27	Bonhoeffer's application for military chaplaincy rejected.
March 15	End of the 1939–40 winter session in Sigurdshof; return to Berlin.
March 18	Gestapo closes Sigurdshof.
March 19	Ludwig Beck, Hans Oster, Ulrich von Hassell, and Hans von Dohnanyi meet to discuss the "X report" (Dohnanyi's documentation of Nazi crimes).
March 24	Bonhoeffer meets with Hans Oster.
April–May	Bonhoeffer mostly in Berlin.
April 9	German invasion of Denmark and Norway.
Beginning of May	With Eberhard Bethge in Friedrichsbrunn.
May 7	Paul Braune and Friedrich von Bodelschwingh seek Karl Bonhoeffer's advice and assistance in opposing the "euthanasia" measures.
May 9	Braune meets with Dohnanyi. Oster communicates to Dutch military attaché Jacobus Sas in Berlin that the Germans will invade May 10.
May 10	Invasion of Holland, Belgium, Luxembourg, and France.
May 19	Bonhoeffer at the home of Herbert von Bismarck in Lasbeck.

June 4	Fall of Dunkirk.
June 5	Clergy meeting in Schlawe. Bonhoeffer takes physical for military service.
June 6	Beginning of the first visitation journey with Bethge to East Prussia.
June 8	Italy enters the war.
June 10–13	Meetings with clergy in East Prussia.
June 14	Paris taken without a fight.
June 17	Bonhoeffer in Memel. Surrender of the French armed forces.
June 22	Bonhoeffer in Danzig. Germany and France conclude cease-fire agreement.
June 25	Bonhoeffer returns to Berlin.
June 29–July 1	Lay and clergy meetings in Köslin.
July 2	Session of the Council of Brethren in Nowawes. Bonhoeffer comments on the political situation.
July 7	Second visitation journey to East Prussia. Königsberg. Theme: "The Order of Church Life."
July 8–9	Talks between the Council of Brethren and the southern German regional churches in Stuttgart.
July 8–10	Königsberg, pastors' retreat. Themes: "Protestant Confession," "Baptismal Grace and Baptismal Discipline," "Our Preaching Today," "The Prophetic Task of the Church," "Church and the Office of Ministry." Bible study on Matthew 7:13ff.
July 8–15	Hans Schönfeld and Nils Ehrenström in Berlin.
July 11	Bonhoeffer in Stettin for a session of the Council of Brethren; reports on present circumstances.
July 13–14	Weekend retreat in Blöstau dispersed by the Königsberg Gestapo.
July 15–17	Bonhoeffer continues visits to pastors in Pomerania.
July 19	Letter from Bishop Wurm to Reich minister Frick regarding the euthanasia measures.
July 20	Report from the Königsberg SD headquarters about the weekend conference in Blöstau arrives at the Reich Central Security Office.
July 23	Bonhoeffer in Danzig.
July 29	Return to Berlin. Bonhoeffer has discussion with Dohnanyi.
August 5	In Potsdam with Dohnanyi and Schönfeld.

August 6	Discussion with Dohnanyi about the draft of a law to be presented to Reich minister of justice Gürtner.
August 7	At the home of Ruth von Kleist-Retzow in Klein-Krössin.
August 13	Bonhoeffer returns to Berlin with Bethge, where at some point that month there is a meeting of Hans Oster, Hans Bernd Gisevius, Dohnanyi, Bonhoeffer, and Bethge at the Bonhoeffer home in Berlin.
August 18	Bonhoeffer attends Günther Dehn's worship service in Berlin-Friedenau.
August 22	Reich Central Security Office issues a ban on public speaking against Bonhoeffer and others on the grounds of subversive activity.
August 25	Third visitation journey to East Prussia, via Dirschau to Königsberg.
August 26	Contact made with the Königsberg branch office of Military Intelligence.
September 2	Bethge begins work at the Gossner Mission Society in Berlin.
September 4	Bonhoeffer required to register at his official place of residence in Schlawe and banned from all public speaking by the Reich Central Security Office for "activities that undermine the Volk."
September 15	Bonhoeffer in Berlin. Writes letter of protest to the Reich Central Security Office.
September 16	Bonhoeffer begins work on *Ethics* in seclusion at Klein-Krössin until about October 20.
September 24	Dohnanyi flies to Rome.
September 27	Tripartite Pact between Germany, Italy, and Japan.
October 9	Bonhoeffer in Klein-Krössin, continues work on *Ethics* manuscripts.
October 20	Back in Berlin. Sets up his library at home.
October 22	Beginning of the deportations of Jewish citizens from southwest Germany to Gurs in southern France.
October 28	Failed Italian invasion of Greece.
October 30	Bonhoeffer travels to Munich. Assignment to the Munich headquarters of the Military Intelligence Office.
October 31	Visit to the Ettal monastery.
November 4	Still in Munich, Bonhoeffer plans to return to Berlin.
November 15	Bonhoeffer in Jena.

November 16	Bonhoeffer travels from Jena to Munich. Wolfgang Staemmler arrested.
November 17	Bonhoeffer is guest at the Benedictine abbey in Ettal until February 1941; while there he writes and meets with other members of the resistance.
November 22	Arrival of Christine von Dohnanyi with her children in Ettal.
November 24	Adam von Trott in Geneva.
November 28–29	In Munich. Bonhoeffer visits the Chr. Kaiser publishing company.
December 7	Bonhoeffer visits Bishop Meiser.
December 8	Again in Ettal. Bonhoeffer mentions initial contact between Reich minister of justice Gürtner and Reich minister for church affairs Kerrl.
December 9	Bonhoeffer in Ettal.
December 16–19	Bonhoeffer in Munich. Bethge arrives.
December 21	Bonhoeffer in Ettal. Conversation with Gürtner. Announcement of the Ten Peace Points of British church leaders.
December 22	Dohnanyi expected in Ettal.
December 24	In Ettal Bonhoeffer attends Christmas Eve midnight service.

1941

January 7–10	Malvern Conference in England; confirmation of the Ten Peace Points.
January 14	Bonhoeffer's military exemption ("UK" classification) and assignment to the *Abwehr* approved.
January 18	Return to Munich. Bonhoeffer visits Prelate Neuhäusler.
January 20	Bonhoeffer writes to Bethge from Ettal: "In my work I am just coming to the question of euthanasia."
January 24	Dohnanyi on an official trip to Italy.
January 24–25	Bonhoeffer in Munich.
January 29	Minister of justice Gürtner dies suddenly.
January 30–31	Bonhoeffer in Munich at the Kalckreuth home.
January 31	Bonhoeffer's official residence transferred from Schlawe to Munich.
February 4	Catholic priest Johannes Neuhäusler, a resistance contact in Bavaria, arrested.

February 8	Bonhoeffer in Munich for Gürtner's funeral. Phone call from Christine von Kalckreuth in Ettal: Gestapo has asked her about Bonhoeffer. Swiss visa temporarily refused.
February 14	Consul Wilhelm Schmidhuber travels to Switzerland to resolve the visa problem for "non-Aryan" Christians and Jews being helped by Canaris's office.
February 16	Bethge in East Prussia until March 7.
February 17	Bonhoeffer in Ettal. Receives mail from Bishop Wurm.
February 24	Bonhoeffer leaves Munich on first trip to Switzerland.
February 25	In Zürich Bonhoeffer writes letters to the Leibholzes and Bishop Bell. Meets with Lore Schmid, Erwin Sutz, and others. Stays with the Pestalozzis.
February 26	Hans Schönfeld travels to Berlin and Belgrade until March 23.
End of February	Meeting of Oster, Dohnanyi, Hassell, and Baron Alexander von Falkenhausen in Berlin.
March 2	Bonhoeffer visits Erwin Sutz in Rapperswil.
March 4	Bonhoeffer visits Karl Barth.
March 5	Bonhoeffer visits Alphons Koechlin in Basel.
March 6–7	In Basel Bonhoeffer visits Barth in the morning on both days.
March 7	Bonhoeffer meets with Friedrich Siegmund-Schultze and Koechlin.
March 8–15	In Geneva Bonhoeffer meets with Visser 't Hooft, Nils Ehrenström, Adolf Freudenberg, Charles Guillon, Henry Louis Henriod, Henri d'Espine, Jacques Courvoisier, Frantz Leenhardt, Jacques de Senarclens.
March 18–19	Adam von Trott in Geneva, visits Visser 't Hooft.
March 19	Letter from Visser 't Hooft to Bishop Bell. Reich Chamber of Literature issues a ban on Bonhoeffer printing and publication.
March 20	Bonhoeffer visits the Pestalozzis in Zürich.
March 24	Bonhoeffer returns to Munich from Switzerland, communicates with Schmidhuber.
March 26	Bonhoeffer visits Ernst Wolf in Halle for advice regarding the publication ban. Bethge travels to Halle to meet Bonhoeffer.
March 27	Bonhoeffer in Berlin "after being away for five months."

April 1	Bonhoeffer in Ettal; receives letter from resistance figure Albert Lempp.
April 6	German attack on Greece and Yugoslavia.
Mid-April	Bonhoeffer in Klein-Krössin.
April 22	In Friedrichsbrunn Bonhoeffer writes letter of protest to the Reich Chamber of Literature.
April 25	Again in Berlin, Bonhoeffer invites Friedrich Perels and his wife for the afternoon.
April 28	Travels to Pomerania, Klein-Krössin.
May 6	Members of the Berlin Confessing Church theological examination commission arrested and imprisoned.
May 14	Bonhoeffer in Munich.
May 22	In Berlin Bonhoeffer visits lawyer Hans Koch with Dohnanyi.
May 25	In Berlin Bonhoeffer visits Hans Koch again with Dohnanyi in order to meet Arthur Nebe. Former Finkenwalde seminarian Horst Thurmann sent to Dachau.
May 30	Bonhoeffer writes Barth thanking him for sending *Church Dogmatics* 2/1.
June 1	Pentecost. Order issued by the Reich Chamber of Literature shuts down church presses.
June 1–4	Hans von Dohnanyi in Ettal.
June 7–19	Dohnanyi in Italy on official business.
June 11	Adam von Trott visits Visser 't Hooft in Geneva.
June 22	German troops invade the Soviet Union.
June 28	Order issued regarding civilian war duty for pastors.
July 6	Martin Bormann issues secret order regarding future church politics.
July 7–11	Hans and Christine von Dohnanyi on vacation with Schmidhuber in Venice.
July 12	Anglo-Soviet alliance treaty signed in Moscow.
July 15	Bonhoeffer travels to Munich.
August 1	News that Hans-Friedrich von Kleist-Retzow has been killed in action in Russia.
August 3	Memorial service for Hans-Friedrich von Kleist-Retzow in Kieckow.
August 5	Bonhoeffer with Bethge in Klein-Krössin.
August 7	Jürgen-Christoph von Kleist-Retzow killed in action in Russia.

August 19	Dohnanyi and Oster meet with Ulrich von Hassell.
August 20	In Berlin Bonhoeffer discusses salary with the Pastors' Emergency League.
August 25–28	In Munich and Ettal Bonhoeffer has conversations with Josef Müller and others. Friedrich Perels telephones from Salzburg.
August 29	Bonhoeffer's second journey to Switzerland.
August 30	Bonhoeffer visits Barth and Koechlin in Basel.
September 1	Jews are ordered to wear the yellow star and use Jewish first names (goes into effect September 19, 1941).
September 2	Bishop Wurm speaks before the regional church conference and openly criticizes National Socialist church politics.
September 3	Bonhoeffer visits Nils Ehrenström in Geneva.
September 4	In Geneva Bonhoeffer has conversations with Visser 't Hooft, Nils Ehrenström, Adolf Freudenberg, Jacques Courvoisier, Henry Henriod, Jean de Saussure, and others.
September 5–8	Bonhoeffer stays at Freudenberg's vacation home on Lake Champaix in Valais to work on a memorandum about William Paton's book *The Church and the New Order.*
September 10	Bonhoeffer visits Ehrenström in Geneva. Helmuth von Moltke meets Dohnanyi and Justus Delbrück in Berlin.
September 13	Reich regional governor Arthur Greiser bans "religious assemblies and religious associations in the Reich district of Wartheland."
September 15–24	In Zürich Bonhoeffer is guest of Otto Salomon.
September 19	Bonhoeffer visits Barth in Basel and, among other things, plans for a Christmas volume for the Confessing Church.
September 19–20	Nils Ehrenström in Berlin.
September 24	Fifteen governments of the Allied countries (including the Soviet Union) declare their support for the goals of the Atlantic Charter.
September 26	Bonhoeffer returns from Switzerland, probably to Berlin. In Berlin Moltke meets Ludwig von Guttenberg and Hans von Dohnanyi. Hans and Christine von Dohnanyi on an official trip to Italy until October 7.

September 29	Nils Ehrenström in Berlin until October 2.
End of September	Fabian von Schlabrendorff has his first conversation with Hans Oster.
October 10	Bonhoeffer in Munich.
October 15	Moltke meets Oster and Dohnanyi.
October 16	Mass deportations of Jewish citizens from Berlin, Cologne, Düsseldorf, Mönchen-Gladbach, Rheydt, Bonn, and Vienna.
October 18–20	Perels and Bonhoeffer prepare two reports about the deportation measures to pass on to military leaders and contacts abroad.
October 23	Order issued by the SS high commander and chief of the German police immediately prohibiting the emigration of Jews.
End of October	After discussions with Bonhoeffer, Willy Rott writes to Koechlin requesting help in rescuing Charlotte Friedenthal, Inge Jacobsen, and Emil Zweig (all of whom worked for the Confessing Church's Gruber office) from being deported.
November 8–9	Confessing Church synod in Hamburg; synodal commission chooses Bonhoeffer (in absentia) to prepare an elucidation of the fifth commandment (*primus usus legis*).
November 16	Moltke meets Oster and Dohnanyi to arrange a meeting with General Ludwig Beck on November 22 and another with the General Chief of Staff Halder.
November 17	Bonhoeffer in Berlin.
November 24	Hans Schönfeld in Berlin until December 8.
December 7	Japanese attack on Pearl Harbor.
December 8	Anthony Eden in Moscow. Josef Stalin demands the Curzon line as the postwar Soviet-Polish border as well as annexation of East Prussia to Poland.
December 9–10	Memoranda presented by Protestant church leaders (Wurm) and Catholic bishops' conference to the Reich Chancellery protesting National Socialist church politics.
December 11	Germany and Italy declare war on the United States.
December 12	Verdict in the trial of the Confessing Church examination commission announced; church superintendent Martin Albertz sentenced to eighteen months imprisonment.

December 14	Reich minister for church affairs Kerrl dies in Paris.
December 16	German offensive bogs down outside Moscow.
December 18	Adam von Trott visits Visser 't Hooft in Geneva.
December 19	Field Marshall Walter von Brauchitsch dismissed. Hitler becomes commander in chief of the army.
December 21	Bonhoeffer returns to Berlin.

1942

January 14	Arcadia Conference concludes between Franklin Roosevelt and Winston Churchill. Formation of a "Combined Chiefs of Staff Committee" (headquartered in Washington).
January 20	Wannsee Conference meets to coordinate measures for the "final solution of the Jewish question."
January 23	In Berlin, meeting between Helmuth von Moltke, Karl von Guttenberg, Justus Delbrück, Bonhoeffer, and his brother Klaus at the "Venetia."
February 1	Reich Commissar Josef Terboven installs a government in Norway headed by Prime Minister Vidkun Quisling.
February 14	Oster and Dohnanyi meet with Hassell; the conspirators note increased surveillance by the Gestapo.
March	Heavy Allied air raids on German cities begin. Hans and Christine von Dohnanyi in Italy.
March 24	Bonhoeffer writes Ernst Wolf regarding Rudolf Bultmann's demythologization thesis.
March 28	Oster and Dohnanyi meet with Hassell.
March 31	Bonhoeffer spends nine days with Bethge in Klein-Krössin, then travels on to Kieckow.
April 5	Bonhoeffer spends Easter in Kieckow. Norwegian Lutheran church issues "Kirkens Grunn," in protest against the Quisling government; many Norwegian bishops and pastors arrested.
April 8	Dohnanyi summoned back to Berlin.
April 9	Bonhoeffer gives first version of his will to Bethge.
April 10	Bonhoeffer embarks for Norway with Moltke. While in transit, he writes a letter to Swedish archbishop Erling Eidem.

April 13–15	Discussions in Oslo.
April 16	Bonhoeffer travels to Stockholm. Archbishop Eidem informed about Bishop Bell's upcoming trip to Sweden.
April 18	In Copenhagen Bonhoeffer takes flight back to Berlin.
ca. April 25	Adam von Trott visits Visser 't Hooft in Geneva; delivers to him a memorandum to the British government that he has composed together with Hans-Bernd von Haeften and Eugen Gerstenmaier.
April 27	Visser 't Hooft departs Geneva for London.
April 28	In Berlin Bonhoeffer receives Moltke's official report of their journey for review.
May 1	Reinhard Heydrich and Canaris conclude their "Prague Agreement" mutually limiting their functions. Telegram from Bishop Bell to Visser 't Hooft: "Visiting Sweden for three weeks commencing May 11."
May 5	Meeting between Visser 't Hooft and Bishop Bell in London. Delivery of the memorandum to Sir Stafford Cripps.
May 8	Bishop Bell received by G. W. Harrison in the British Foreign Office.
May 11	Beginnings of Bonhoeffer's third Swiss journey. He arrives in Zürich and stays with the Pestalozzis.
May 13	Bonhoeffer in Zürich; Bishop Bell departs by plane for Sweden.
May 15	Bonhoeffer's classification for his military exemption renewed. Bishop Bell meets with Archbishop Eidem in Sweden.
May 18	Hans Schönfeld departs Geneva for Berlin.
May 20	Bonhoeffer in Geneva. Investigations begin in Munich of Schmidhuber and Heinz Ickradt on suspicion of currency violations in connection with the "Operation 7" rescues.
May 21	Bonhoeffer in Zürich.
May 22–25	First meeting of the Kreisau resistance circle.
May 25	Bonhoeffer visits Barth in Basel; sends letter to Siegmund-Schultze from Zürich.

May 26	Bonhoeffer returns to Berlin. First meeting between Hans Schönfeld and Bishop Bell in Stockholm. Molotov signs the Anglo-Soviet alliance treaty in London.
May 27	Bonhoeffer prepares for trip to Sweden. Official passport issued dated May 27, 1942. Reich Central Security Office director Heydrich assassinated in Prague.
May 29	Second meeting between Hans Schönfeld and Bishop Bell in Stockholm.
May 30	Bonhoeffer flies to Stockholm. Schönfeld meets Bishop Bell in Uppsala.
May 31	Bonhoeffer travels to Sigtuna. Conversation between Bishop Bell, Schönfeld, and Bonhoeffer.
June 1	In Stockholm Bonhoeffer has second conversation with Bishop Bell. Schönfeld delivers his "Statement."
June 2	Bonhoeffer flies back to Berlin with Schönfeld.
Beginning of June	Bonhoeffer prepares a memorandum with Friedrich Perels concerning immediate steps to be taken in the church after the war.
June 8	In Klein-Krössin Bonhoeffer continues work on *Ethics*. Renews acquaintance there with Maria von Wedemeyer.
June 9	Bishop Bell's return flight to England.
June 12	Hans Schönfeld returns to Geneva; Visser 't Hooft returns there on June 14.
June 16	Bonhoeffer probably meets with the Freiburg circle to plan its memorandum (which outlined plans for German governmental organization after the coup).
June 19	Bishop Bell finishes his "Memorandum of Conversations" with Bonhoeffer and Schönfeld and delivers it the next day to the British Foreign Office.
June 20	Bonhoeffer in Munich.
June 21	Bonhoeffer in Berlin for three days of discussions with Dohnanyi.
June 24	Helmuth von Moltke meets with Bishop Wurm.
June 25	En route by train to Munich, Bonhoeffer writes Bethge: "But I sense how an opposition to all that is 'religious' is growing in me. . . . Because I believe that I am on the verge of some kind of breakthrough, I am

	letting things take their own course and do not resist"; mentions Maria von Wedemeyer.
June 26	Bonhoeffer flies to Venice with Dohnanyi.
June 30	Bishop Bell meets with British foreign minister Anthony Eden.
July 3–10	In Rome Bonhoeffer visits Father Robert Leiber and Rector Ivo Zeiger at the Vatican.
July 10	Bonhoeffer returns to Berlin.
July 13	Bishop Bell meets with British diplomat Stafford Cripps.
July 15–17	English "Peace Aims Group" meets in Oxford.
July 17	Eden gives negative answer to Bishop Bell about British support for the German resistance.
July 19	Moltke meets again with Bishop Wurm.
July 23	Bishop Bell sends telegram to Visser 't Hooft following Anthony Eden's reply: "Interest undoubted, but deeply regret no reply possible."
July 30	Bishop Bell reports to U.S. ambassador John Winant.
August 2	In Berlin Joachim Kanitz visits Bonhoeffer.
August 10	In Magdeburg Bonhoeffer has first meeting with the Confessing synodal commission on the topic of the "*primus usus legis*."
August 11	Bonhoeffer meets in Berlin with Carl Goerdeler and Bethge.
August 18–25	Bonhoeffer in Klein-Krössin.
August 22	Hans von Wedemeyer killed in action at Stalingrad.
August 26	Bonhoeffer returns to Berlin.
ca. August 28–30	Dohnanyi in Switzerland, conveys Bonhoeffer's letter of August 28 to Bishop Bell.
September 5	Charlotte Friedenthal (via "Operation 7") reaches Switzerland.
September 10	Munich Office of Military Intelligence applies for Bonhoeffer's travel visa to the Balkans, Italy, and Switzerland.
September 12–October 10	Hans and Christine von Dohnanyi travel to Italy on vacation.
September 16	Helmuth von Moltke flies to Oslo and Stockholm.
September 18–28	Adam von Trott in Sweden.
September 30	Remaining individuals rescued by "Operation 7" travel to Switzerland.

October 2	Bonhoeffer visits Ruth von Kleist-Retzow at the Berlin Franciscan hospital, where she has undergone an eye operation; meets once again with Maria von Wedemeyer.
October 3	Bonhoeffer travels by military train to Munich.
October 9	Bonhoeffer meets in Freiburg with Erik Wolf and Constantin von Dietze regarding the Freiburg memorandum.
October 10	Bonhoeffer returns to Munich.
October 14	Following urgent warnings, Bonhoeffer cancels journey and returns to Berlin.
October 15	Bonhoeffer meets again with Maria von Wedemeyer.
October 16–18	Second meeting of the Kreisau circle.
October 16–20	Dohnanyi breaks off his trip to Budapest because of warnings.
October 26	Bonhoeffer in Berlin. Faked documents are prepared. Maria von Wedemeyer's brother Maximilian killed in action on the eastern front.
October 28	Helmuth von Moltke meets with Catholic bishop Konrad Preysing.
October 31	Schmidhuber arrested in Meran.
November 1	During a worship service in Stuttgart, Bishop Wurm reads his "Thirteen Points" about the unification of the German Evangelical Church.
November 5	Bonhoeffer in Munich.
November 7	Bonhoeffer in Klein-Krössin.
November 8	Allied landing in northern Africa.
November 11	German troops occupy southern France.
November 14	Moltke tries in vain to get the Armed Forces High Command to stop the deportation of Jews.
November 17–18	Meeting of the Freiburg circle (without Bonhoeffer) regarding the memorandum. Dohnanyi speaks with senior military prosecutor Manfred Roeder regarding the Schmidhuber case.
November 19	Bonhoeffer in Berlin. Ruth von Wedemeyer forbids further letters to her daughter Maria.
November 24–25	German Sixth Army surrounded by Russian troops at Stalingrad.
November 27	Dohnanyi in transit to Rome and Switzerland.
November 29	First Sunday in Advent. Dohnanyi returns from Switzerland. Two meetings in November at the

	homes of Klaus Bonhoeffer and the Schleichers with conspirators Prince Louis Ferdinand, Carl Goerdeler, Jakob Kaiser, Wilhelm Leuschner, and Bonhoeffer.
December 3	Bishop Bell writes to Erwin Sutz and Harry Johansson.
December 11	The writer Jochen Klepper commits suicide with his Jewish wife and daughter.
December 12–13	Bonhoeffer visits Ernst Wolf in Halle with Oskar Hammelsbeck and Hans Böhm. Pastoral letter issued by the Catholic bishops regarding Nazi violations of human rights.
December 15	Bishop Bell meets with Anthony Eden.
December 20	Fourth Sunday in Advent. Eberhard Bethge and Renate Schleicher become engaged at the Marienburger Allee home. Ulrich von Hassell converses with the younger members of the Kreisau circle.
December 22	Members of the "Rote Kapelle" resistance group executed.
December 24	Bonhoeffer sends his letter "After Ten Years" to family and friends for Christmas.
December 31	Bonhoeffer spends New Year's Eve with the Dohnanyis in Sakrow.

1943

Beginning of January	German troops retreat from the Caucasus. Ernst Kaltenbrunner appointed head of the Reich Central Security Office.
January 3	Friedrich Perels composes his will.
January 13	Maria von Wedemeyer accepts in writing Bonhoeffer's marriage proposal, but the waiting period remains in effect.
January 14–15	Casablanca Conference, where Allied leaders demand Germany's unconditional surrender.
January 22	Ulrich von Hassell meets with Hans Oster and Carl von Guttenberg.
January 23	In Berlin Bonhoeffer writes to Maria von Wedemeyer: "We are holding our breath" in light of world events.
End of January	Freiburg memorandum completed.
February 2	Fighting ends in Stalingrad.
February 6–7	In Berlin Bonhoeffer meets with Walter Bauer about the Freiburg memorandum.

February 8	Bonhoeffer travels to Munich by train with Bethge and shares some of his recent work with him.
February 9	Bonhoeffer visits Josef Müller in Munich and prepares for the trip to Switzerland. Josef Müller travels to Rome.
February 10	People in Berlin strongly advise Bonhoeffer to cancel the journey to Switzerland.
February 11	In Munich Bonhoeffer meets with Hans Lokies.
February 12	Bonhoeffer returns to Berlin.
February 18	Goebbels proclaims "total war." Hans and Sophie Scholl arrested in Munich (executed on February 22).
March 10	Bishop Bell speaks in the House of Lords about the German resistance.
March 13	Bonhoeffer receives summons from Munich for military examination. Fabian von Schlabrendorff's assassination attempt on Hitler fails.
March 15	In Magdeburg Bonhoeffer makes presentation at the second session of the synodal commission (*primus usus legis*).
March 21	"Heroes' Memorial Day"; Colonel Rudolf von Gersdorff's assassination attempt at the Berlin armory fails.
March 23	Bonhoeffer visits Ruth von Kleist-Retzow at the Stettin hospital. Civil wedding ceremony of Renate Schleicher and Eberhard Bethge
March 26	Carl Goerdeler sends memorandum to the generals regarding the necessity for a coup.
March 31	Bonhoeffer family gathers in Berlin for Karl Bonhoeffer's seventy-fifth birthday.
Beginning of April	Maria von Wedemeyer begins training as a nurse at the Magdalena Home in Hannover.
April 5	Bonhoeffer arrested by military authorities with cooperation of Gestapo and taken to the Tegel Military Detention Center. Hans and Christine von Dohnanyi, Josef and Maria Müller, and Müller's secretary, Annie Haser, are arrested the same day. Hans Oster placed under house arrest.
April 12	First interrogation of Dohnanyi (and probably also of Bonhoeffer) and Oster, who denies knowledge of any special *Abwehr* commission for Bonhoeffer. German Africa Corps surrenders in North Africa.

April 14	Bonhoeffer writes first letter to his parents from prison.
April 17	Bonhoeffer is moved to a larger cell.
April 19	Beginning of the Warsaw ghetto uprising (crushed on May 16).
April 23	Good Friday. Dohnanyi sends a letter to Bonhoeffer in which he accepts total responsibility.
April 30	Christine von Dohnanyi is released from custody.
May	Bonhoeffer composes a wedding sermon for Renate and Eberhard Bethge.
May 13	Manfred Roeder confiscates defense documents in Dohnanyi's cell.
May 15	Eberhard Bethge marries Renate Schleicher.
May 23	Bonhoeffer's parents receive first permission to visit in Tegel prison. Maria von Wedemeyer and her mother visit Karl and Paula Bonhoeffer.
June 10	First draft of Bonhoeffer's letters to Manfred Roeder, between interrogations about "Operation 7."
June 12–14	Third meeting of the Kreisau circle.
June 15	Admiral Canaris is interrogated.
June 17	Renewed interrogation of Hans Oster, who revises his earlier statements, with negative implications for Bonhoeffer.
June 24	Maria von Wedemeyer receives visitation privileges.
July	Bonhoeffer works on his drama fragment (published as *DBWE* 7: *Fiction from Tegel Prison*).
July 8–10	Bethge travels to Switzerland on behalf of the military intelligence office, visits Barth and Visser 't Hooft.
July 10	Allied troops land in Sicily.
July 23	Field Marshal Wilhelm Keitel orders that charges of high treason be dropped in the case against Dohnanyi and Bonhoeffer.
July 25	Coup in Italy; Mussolini arrested.
July 30	Roeder informs Bonhoeffer that the interrogations are temporarily completed; indictment being prepared; writing privileges expanded. Bonhoeffer concludes drama fragment and begins novel fragment. He asks his parents to find an attorney.
August 1	Bonhoeffer's final letter to Roeder, defending himself against various charges.

August 3	Bonhoeffer writes his parents that he is expecting more information about his defense. Heavy air raids on Berlin.
August 8	Heavy bombardment of Hamburg and Berlin.
August 9	Hans von Dohnanyi is informed of the conclusion of the investigation and indictment. Maria von Wedemeyer returns home to Pätzig.
Mid-August	Bonhoeffer begins to write a novel.
August 17	Rüdiger von der Goltz is authorized as defense attorney for Bonhoeffer and Hans von Dohnanyi. Because of increasing air raids, essential sections of the Reich War Court are transferred to Torgau.
August 23	Roeder presents the report of his investigation. Intense air raids on Berlin during the night of August 23–24. Severe damage to the Bethges' apartment in Berlin-Dahlem.
September 3	Intense air raids on Berlin during the night of September 3–4. In Tegel prison Bonhoeffer transferred to cell 92, two floors lower. Allied troops land in southern Italy.
September 15	Eberhard Bethge is conscripted into the military, begins basic training in Spandau.
September 16	Indictments issued against Dohnanyi and Oster. Kurt Wergin is appointed as defense attorney for Bonhoeffer.
September 20	Bonhoeffer composes new will.
September 21	Indictment issued against Bonhoeffer.
October 1	In Copenhagen Moltke warns against the impending mass deportation of Danish Jews. Thanks to the initiative of the German navy attaché Georg Duckwitz, seven thousand Danish Jews are smuggled to Sweden.
October 3	Danish bishops read pastoral letter in the churches regarding the persecution of Jews.
October 16–19	Confessing Church synod in Breslau adopts two statements: "Exegesis of the Fifth Commandment" and the corresponding "Declaration to the Congregations." Bonhoeffer had participated in the preparation of both.
October 17	Karl Bonhoeffer writes to the president of the Reich War Court requesting Bonhoeffer's release from prison while awaiting trial.

October 27	Adam von Trott in Sweden (until November 13).
November 18	Bethge on leave in Berlin. First letters to him are smuggled out of Tegel. Reich War Court sets December 17 as Bonhoeffer's trial date.
November 18–23	Bonhoeffer's first letter to Eberhard Bethge.
November 23	Bonhoeffer makes yet another will after heavy air raids in Berlin. Composes "Prayers for Prisoners."
November 26	Air raids on the nearby Borsig factory. Dohnanyi, whose cell has been hit by an incendiary bomb, is taken to the Charité hospital with a brain embolism. Reich War Court severely damaged by air raid; trial documents destroyed by the fire. Bonhoeffer's parents, Bethge, and Maria von Wedemeyer visit him in Tegel together.
November 28	Bonhoeffer composes a report about his experiences during air raids. At the end of November, the Reich War Court orders Roeder to spend three days reconstructing the trial documents.
December 3	Dohnanyi's defense attorneys prepare a defense brief for him (first draft).
December 5	In a letter to Bethge, Bonhoeffer alludes to new theological themes; probably finishes his novel fragment.
December 13	Bonhoeffer writes Christmas letter to Maria von Wedemeyer.
December 15	Bonhoeffer works on the essay "What Does It Mean to Tell the Truth?" (*DBWE* 16, 2/19).
December 16	Attorney Kurt Wergin visits Bonhoeffer and announces postponement of the trial date.
December 23	Bethge on leave in Berlin; receives permission to visit Bonhoeffer in Tegel prison.
December 25	Bonhoeffer writes to Bethge (*DBWE* 8, 2/89): "Your visit stimulated a little work . . . and it encouraged and renewed in me the desire for my major work [*Ethics*]."

1944

January 1	Manfred Roeder transferred to Air District 4 as chief judge in Lemberg. Reich judicial councilor Helmuth Kutzner appointed to continue the proceedings against Oster, Dohnanyi, and Bonhoeffer.

January 4	Soviet army reaches the former eastern border of Poland.
January 5	Maria von Wedemeyer visits Bonhoeffer in Tegel.
January 8	Bethge travels through Berlin on the way to his unit in Italy.
January 15	Bethge writes Bonhoeffer from Rignano near Rome.
January 19	Solf resistance circle and Helmuth von Moltke arrested.
January 22	Dohnanyi removed from the Charité clinic and taken to the prison infirmary in Berlin-Buch.
January 23	Allies land near Nettuno.
January 27–28	Heavy air raids on Berlin. The prison guard Holzendorf, who has been secretly conveying Bonhoeffer's correspondence (Bonhoeffer refers to him as "Engel"), is killed in the city.
January 29	During the early morning hours, heavy air bombardment of Berlin, also striking the Borsig factory near Tegel prison.
January 30	During the night, heavy air bombardment of Berlin.
February 3	Birth of Dietrich Wilhelm Rüdiger Bethge.
February 4	Maria von Wedemeyer allowed to visit Bonhoeffer in Tegel prison on his birthday.
February 10	Max de Crinis, Karl Bonhoeffer's successor in the Charité clinic, declares Dohnanyi fit to stand trial.
February 11	Hitler orders Canaris's dismissal; the entire intelligence service is placed under the control of the SS Reichsführer Himmler.
February 12	With the imminent possibility of Dohnanyi's trial, Bonhoeffer hopes for a decision "in about a week." Reich War Court sentences Schmidhuber to four years, Ickradt to two years in prison.
February 16	Maria von Wedemeyer in Pätzig. Bethge's field unit is now in Velletri, near the Allied beachhead at Anzio-Nettuno.
February 19	Attorney Kurt Wergin in Tegel; Dohnanyi's illness prompts postponement of the trial again.
February 20	Maria von Wedemeyer receives permission to visit Bonhoeffer in Tegel. Admiral Canaris under house arrest in Burg Lauenstein.
February 21	Dohnanyi incapable of being interrogated. Bonhoeffer writes to Bethge (*DBWE* 8, 2/115):

	"As long as Hans is ill, nothing can be changed." (Bonhoeffer's own trial is postponed again.)
February–March	Bonhoeffer composes the story "Lance Corporal Berg" (*DBWE* 7:183–94).
March 4	Trial against Josef Müller ends with acquittal, but he remains in prison.
March 6	First daytime air raids on Berlin.
March 9	Bonhoeffer writes to Bethge that the trial has now been set for May.
March 10	Ruth von Wedemeyer receives permission to visit in Tegel prison.
March 14	Beginning of a new stage of interrogation (until May).
March 30	Maria von Wedemeyer receives permission to visit in Tegel prison.
Beginning of April	"Report on Prison Life after One Year in Tegel" (*DBWE* 8, 2/131) written for Berlin commander Paul von Hase.
April 4	Beginning of the Berneuchen Easter week in Bundorf.
April 11	Bonhoeffer writes to Bethge (*DBWE* 8, 3/132): "I have been told not to expect any change in my current situation for the time being."
April 15	Bonhoeffer interrogated in the Reich War Court.
April 22	Bonhoeffer writes to Bethge (*DBWE* 8, 3/135): "After being unproductive for so long, [I] feel more creative now that spring is coming."
April 26	Bonhoeffer writes to his parents that, after a year in prison, there is "a huge new dimension in one's life" (*DBWE* 8, 3/136).
April 30	Bonhoeffer writes first theological letter to Bethge (*DBWE* 8, 1/137), mentioning the question of "religionless Christianity."
May 3–4	Bonhoeffer is interrogated in the Reich War Court. (On May 5, writes Bethge [*DBWE* 8, 3/139]: "The result has been quite satisfactory. But since the question of the date is still unresolved, I am really losing interest in my case.")
May 5	Attorney Kurt Peschke submits the final version of Dohnanyi's defense brief. Bonhoeffer writes second theological letter to Bethge (*DBWE* 8, 3/139) on the "nonreligious interpretation of biblical concepts."

May 7	Intense daytime air attacks on Berlin.
May 9	Bonhoeffer writes to Bethge that "the next few weeks will bring such great and surprising events" (*DBWE* 8, 3/141).
May 11	Allied troops break out of the beachhead at Anzio-Nettuno, threatening German positions near Velletri and Rignano.
May 15	Bethge on leave from the front (special leave for the baptism of his son).
May 19	Renate and Eberhard Bethge receive permission to visit in Tegel prison (visitors' permit transferred to them by Paula and Karl Bonhoeffer). Heavy daytime air bombardment of Berlin.
May 21	Dietrich Bethge's baptism, at which Bonhoeffer's "Thoughts on the Day of the Baptism" are read. Maria von Wedemeyer attends and then visits Bonhoeffer in Tegel.
May 23–24	Allied offensive in Italy.
May 26	Discussion about securing a military chaplaincy for Bethge by approaching Military Bishop Dohrmann through Hans-Bernd von Haeften. Heavy fighting around Velletri.
May 29	A letter from Bonhoeffer to Maria von Wedemeyer is smuggled out of Tegel; it also contains a theological letter to Bethge (*DBWE* 8, 3/152) stating that God is no "stopgap."
June	General retreat of German troops in Italy. Dohnanyi falls ill with deliberately induced diphtheria and is transferred to the isolation ward in Potsdam. Investigation temporarily halted.
June 3	Bethge illegally visits Bonhoeffer in Tegel. Bonhoeffer's parents in Pätzig.
June 4–5	Resistance members Julius Leber and Adolf Reichwein arrested. Rome falls to the Allies.
June 5	Visiting privileges for Bethge. On the same day, Bonhoeffer sends his poem "The Past" to Bethge.
June 6	Allied invasion of Normandy.
June 7	Bethge returns to the Italian front.
June 8	Bonhoeffer's theological letter (*DBWE* 8, 3/161), on the topic of "Christ and the world come of age."

June 16	Bethge writes from Munich, again in transit to Italy.
June 17	Response to Maria von Wedemeyer's communication that for the time being she no longer intends to come to Berlin.
June 18	Bethge reaches his unit in Montevettolini.
June 21	Bonhoeffer writes to Bethge (*DBWE* 8, 3/166): "This morning we had the nastiest of all the air raids so far."
June 22	Soviet army offensive against the Center Army Group.
June 27	Maria von Wedemeyer receives permission to visit in Tegel prison.
June 30	Bonhoeffer's theological letter (3/170) mentioning "the claim [Inanspruchnahme] of Jesus Christ on the world that has come of age." General Paul von Hase visits Bonhoeffer in Tegel ("more than five hours!").
Beginning of July	Military investigator Helmuth Kutzner requests that Wilhelm Keitel halt the legal proceedings. Bethge with his unit near Florence; partisan skirmishes in the Apennines. Soviet army advances quickly to the west.
July 8	Bonhoeffer's theological letter (*DBWE* 8, 3/172) states: "One must not find fault with people in their worldliness but rather confront them with God where they are strongest." "By the way, it would be very nice if you didn't throw away my theological letters but . . . send them off to Renate from time to time. I might perhaps like to read them again later for my work." Bonhoeffer sends his poems "Who Am I?" (*DBWE* 8, 3/173) and "Christians and Heathens" (*DBWE* 8, 3/174) to Bethge. Composes poems "Happiness and Unhappiness" and "Night Voices in Tegel."
July 16	Bonhoeffer's theological letter (*DBWE* 8, 3/177) states: "Before God, and with God, we live without God."
July 18	Bonhoeffer continues the theological letter (3/177), referring to "participating in God's powerlessness in the world."
July 20	Claus von Stauffenberg attempts to assassinate Hitler and overthrow the regime. Coup fails. Stauffenberg, Ludwig Beck, Friedrich Olbricht, Werner von Haeften, and Albrecht Mertz von Quirnheim shot to death that evening.

July 21	Bonhoeffer writes to Bethge (*DBWE* 8, 4/178): "Later on I discovered, and am still discovering to this day, that one only learns to have faith by living in the full this-worldliness of life." In the Reich Central Security Office a "special commission" investigating the July 20 attempt begins its work (the arrests of Hans Oster, Paul von Hase, and Wilhelm Canaris follow).
July 23	Canaris is arrested.
July 25	Heinrich Himmler appointed commander of the Reserve Army.
July 27	Bonhoeffer writes to Bethge (*DBWE* 8, 4/180) that he is working on "the question of 'unconscious Christianity.'"
August 3	Bonhoeffer sends Bethge his "Outline for a Book" (*DBWE* 8, 4/187).
August 12	Carl Goerdeler arrested.
August 14	Bonhoeffer's first letter for Bethge's thirty-fifth birthday (*DBWE* 8, 4/190) states: "Indeed, the most important things in life are human relationships"; he also sends the poem "Stations on the Way to Freedom" (*DBWE* 8, 4/191).
August 18	Fabian von Schlabrendorff taken to Reich Central Security Office prison; Hans John and Friedrich Perels are arrested.
August 22	Hans von Dohnanyi transported from the isolation ward in Potsdam to the Sachsenhausen concentration camp.
August 23	Maria von Wedemeyer visits Bonhoeffer in Tegel, "so fresh and at the same time as steadfast and calm as seldom before" (*DBWE* 8, 4/193).
August 25	With Paris under Allied control, Charles de Gaulle returns.
August 27–28	Bonhoeffer composes his poem "The Friend" (*DBWE* 8, 4/196).
September 8	Arrests of Freiburg circle members Constantin von Dietze and Adolf Lampe.
After September 8	Interrogations of Canaris, Oster, and Alexander von Pfuhlstein at the Reich Central Security Office.
September 9	Beginning of German V-2 attacks on England.

September 22	Gestapo criminal investigator Franz Sonderegger discovers Dohnanyi's secret archive in the Armed Forces High Command outpost in Zossen.
September 25	Conscription of all men between the ages of sixteen and sixty for service in the German *Volkssturm* units.
September 27	Josef Müller taken to the Reich Central Security Office prison.
September 29	Bethge receives Bonhoeffer's poem "The Death of Moses" (*DBWE* 8, 4/197).
September 30	Margarete von Hase, widow of city commandant Paul von Hase (executed on August 8), finds refuge in the Schleicher home.
October	At Bonhoeffer's request, Maria von Wedemeyer moves in with Karl and Paula Bonhoeffer.
October 1	Klaus Bonhoeffer is arrested. Dietrich Bonhoeffer abandons his plan to escape.
October 4	Rüdiger Schleicher is arrested.
October 5	Friedrich Justus Perels is arrested. Letter to Maria von Wedemeyer with the poem "Jonah" (*DBWE* 8, 4/199).
October 8	Bonhoeffer is transferred to the prison at the Reich Central Security Office, first in cell 19, later cell 24.
October 15	Freiburg circle member Walter Bauer is arrested.
October 18	Bethge's unit near Mantua.
October 21	Aachen becomes first major German city to be occupied by the Allies.
October 28	Bethge learns of his imminent arrest in San Polo d'Enza and destroys the remaining letters he still has from Bonhoeffer (the "September correspondence").
October 30	Bethge is taken to the Lehrter Strasse prison in Berlin.
November 1	Freiburg circle member Gerhard Ritter is arrested. Bonhoeffer is interrogated again and describes it as "repugnant." That same week Himmler orders a halt to the gassings in Auschwitz.
December 16	Beginning of the Ardennes offensive.
December 19	Bonhoeffer writes letter to Maria von Wedemeyer with his poem "Powers of Good" (*DBWE* 8, 4/200) as "my Christmas greeting to you and my parents and siblings."

December 20	Indictments issued against Klaus Bonhoeffer, Rüdiger Schleicher, Friedrich Justus Perels, and others.
December 22	Maria von Wedemeyer writes Hedwig von Truchseß that Hedwig's husband, Dietrich von Truchseß, and Hans Jürgen von Kleist-Retzow have been arrested in Berlin.

1945

January 4	Reich Central Security Office director Ernst Kaltenbrunner reports to the Ministry of Foreign Affairs on Bonhoeffer's statements about Bishop Bell and English politics.
January 12	Beginning of major Soviet offensive on the German eastern front.
January 17	Bonhoeffer writes his last letter, to his parents regarding the people's sacrifice.
January 24	Helmuth von Moltke is executed.
January 29	Maria von Wedemeyer leads a group of youth fleeing the Soviet army on foot from Pätzig to the west.
January 31	Pätzig taken by the Soviet army; Ruth von Wedemeyer flees west to relatives in Oberbehme.
February 1	Dohnanyi is transferred to the underground prison at the Reich Central Security Office.
February 2	Goerdeler is executed. The Volksgericht (People's Court), presided over by Roland Freisler, sentences Klaus Bonhoeffer, Rüdiger Schleicher, Friedrich Perels, and Hans John to death.
February 3	Heaviest air attacks on Berlin to date. Freisler is killed in the bombing, which destroys the Volksgericht building.
February 4–12	Allied Big Three Conference in Yalta (Crimea): Stalin, Roosevelt, and Churchill agree to divide Germany into four occupation zones: the Soviet/Russian, American, British, and French.
February 7	Twenty prisoners are transported from the Reich Central Security Office underground prison; twelve (including Bonhoeffer and Josef Müller) are taken to the Buchenwald concentration camp, eight (including Canaris and Oster) to the Flossenbürg concentration camp.

February 13	Maria von Wedemeyer is in Berlin with Bonhoeffer's parents; adjutant's office of the Armed Forces High Command issues her a pass to travel toward Bundorf.
February 14–15	Dresden destroyed by air raids.
February 19	Maria von Wedemeyer writes to her mother from Flossenbürg (*DBWE* 8, 4/205): "Unfortunately my whole journey to Bundorf and Flossenbürg was completely in vain. Dietrich isn't here at all." Himmler meets secretly with Swedish Count Folke Bernadotte of the Red Cross about possible peace negotiations.
February 24	British prisoner officer Payne Best and General Friedrich von Rabenau arrive in Buchenwald; Rabenau shares a cell with Bonhoeffer.
March 8	Dohnanyi sends a secret message: "They have everything."
March 10	Allies take Cologne and Koblenz. In mid-March Hans von Dohnanyi is transferred to the state police hospital.
March 16	Schlabrendorff is acquitted in his trial but remains in custody.
April 3	Bonhoeffer is transported from Buchenwald concentration camp during Easter week.
April 4	The prisoner transport stops in Regensburg; meeting with some arrested members of the conspirators' families.
April 5	During the "midday meeting" at Hitler's headquarters, Hitler orders the executions of the conspirators after additional Zossen files discovered. The prisoner transport with Bonhoeffer continues on toward the Bavarian forest. Dohnanyi is taken back to Sachsenhausen.
April 6	At dawn the prisoner transport arrives at the schoolhouse in Schönberg. Following a summary court-martial in Sachsenhausen, Dohnanyi is sentenced to death.
April 8	Second Sunday after Easter. Bonhoeffer holds a devotional service for his fellow prisoners in the Schönberg schoolhouse and is then picked up. Best receives the farewell greeting for Bishop Bell before the continued transport to Flossenbürg, where a court-martial is held during the night of April 8–9.

April 9	Early morning executions of the Military Intelligence group: Bonhoeffer, Wilhelm Canaris, Ludwig Gehre, Hans Oster, Karl Sack, and Theodor Strünck; Dohnanyi executed in Sachsenhausen.
April 20	Indictment issued against Freiburg circle member Constantin von Dietze.
April 22–23	During the night of April 22–23, a group of prisoners from the Lehrter Strasse prison (where many political prisoners associated with July 20 were imprisoned) is executed by firing squad at the Lehrter train station; the group includes Klaus Bonhoeffer, Rüdiger Schleicher, Friedrich Justus Perels, and Hans John.
April 25	Other prisoners, including Bethge, are released from the Lehrter Strasse prison.
April 28	First Soviet soldiers arrive at the Marienburger Allee home. Mussolini, trying to flee to Switzerland, is captured and executed by Italian partisans.
April 30	Hitler commits suicide in the bunker of the Reich Chancellery in Berlin.
May 1	Josef Goebbels commits suicide in the bunker of the Reich Chancellery in Berlin.
May 2	German troops surrender in Berlin.
May 7	German armed forces surrender in Reims and on May 9 in Berlin.
May 30	From Geneva, Adolf Freudenberg telegraphs news of Bonhoeffer's death to London. Maria von Wedemeyer learns of it in June, Bonhoeffer's parents in Berlin only at the end of June through a visit by Hans-Bernd Gisevius and from the BBC broadcast of the London memorial service.

Master List of Documents for *DBWE* 8–17

Correspondence

Albers, Detlef, from—10
Albers, Detlef, to—10
Albertz, Martin, to—14
All Pastors Abroad, from the German Evangelical Pastors' Association—13
Althaus, Paul, to—10, 11, 12
Ammundsen, Ove Valdemar, from Ecumenical Youth Conference—13
Ammundsen, Ove Valdemar, to—12, 13, 14
Andrews, Charles Freer, from—13
Arnold, Eberhard, from Hardy Arnold—13
Arnold, Hardy, to Eberhard Arnold—13
Arnold, Hardy, from Edith Böker—13
Asmussen, Hans, to—13
Association of Congregations in London, from Theodor Heckel—13
Aulén, Gustav, to—14

Baillie, John, from—15
Baillie, John, to—15
Barth, Karl, from—12, 13, 14
Barth, Karl, to—12, 13, 14, 16
Barth, Karl, to Otto Salomon—16
Baumann, Eberhard, from—16
Baumann, Eberhard, to—16
Baumann, Eberhard, to Friedrich Onnasch—16
Beckmann, Joachim, to—16
Beckmann, Mr. and Mrs., to—14

Bell, George (*also* George K. A.), to—13, 14, 15, 16
Bell, George, from—13, 15
Bell, George, to Birger Forell—14
Bell, George, to Mahatma Gandhi—13
Bell, George, to Members of "Life and Work"—13
Bell, George, to Edward Keble Talbot—13
Bell, George, to the Editor of *The Round Table*—13
Bell, George K. A., from S. Payne Best—16
Bell, George K. A., from Anthony Eden—16
Bell, George K. A., from Hans Schönfeld—16
Bell, George K. A., from Willem Visser 't Hooft—16
Bell, George K. A., to Anthony Eden—16
Bell, George K. A., to Erling Eidem—16
Bell, George K. A., to Harry Johansson—16
Bell, George K. A., to Gerhard Leibholz—16
Bell, George K. A., to Hugh Martin—16
Bell, George K. A., to Erwin Sutz—16
Berlin Church Consistory, from Emil Karow—12
Berlin Office of the World Alliance for Promoting International Friendship through the Churches, to—12
Berlin Seminarians, to Friedrich von Bodelschwingh—12
Berlin Theology Students, to Friedrich von Bodelschwingh—12
Besig, Hans, from—13
Besig, Hans, to—13
Best, S. Payne, to George K. A. Bell—16
Bethge, Christoph, to—16
Bethge, Eberhard, from—8, 15, 16
Bethge, Eberhard, from Ruth von Kleist-Retzow—15, 16
Bethge, Eberhard, and Bonhoeffer, from Ruth von Kleist-Retzow—16
Bethge, Eberhard, to—8, 14, 15, 16
Bethge, Eberhard, to Paula and Karl Bonhoeffer—15
Bethge, Eberhard, to Renate Schleicher—16
Bethge, Eberhard, to Wolfgang Staemmler—14
Bethge, Eberhard and Renate, to—8
Bethge, Renate, from—8
Bethge, Renate, to—8
Beyer, Hermann Wolfgang, from—13
Beyer, Hermann Wolfgang, to—13
Bismarck, Herbert von, from—16
Bismarck, Spes von, to—15

Blanck, Ottonie, from—15
Blanck, Ottonie, to—15
Böckheler, Martin, from—14
Böckheler (*also* Boeckheler), Martin, to—14, 15
Bodelschwingh, Friedrich von, from—12
Bodelschwingh, Friedrich von, from Berlin Seminarians—12
Bodelschwingh, Friedrich von, from Berlin Theology Students—12
Boericke, Irma and Harold, to—12
Böker, Edith, to Hardy Arnold—13
Bonhoeffer, Julie, from—11, 14
Bonhoeffer, Julie, from Klaus Bonhoeffer—10
Bonhoeffer, Julie, to—9, 10, 13
Bonhoeffer, Karl, from—8, 9, 10, 13, 15, 16
Bonhoeffer, Karl, to—9, 10, 11, 15, 16
Bonhoeffer, Karl, to President of the Reich War Court—8
Bonhoeffer, Karl, to Reinhold Seeberg—9
Bonhoeffer, Karl, to Senior Reich Military Court Prosecutor—8
Bonhoeffer, Karl and Paula, from—8, 15
Bonhoeffer, Karl and Paula, from Eberhard Bethge—15
Bonhoeffer, Karl and Paula, from Gerhard Leibholz—16
Bonhoeffer, Karl and Paula, to—8, 9, 10, 11, 15, 16
Bonhoeffer, Karl and Paula, to Eberhard Bethge—8
Bonhoeffer, Karl-Friedrich, from—8, 10, 11
Bonhoeffer, Karl-Friedrich (*also* Karl Friedrich), to—10, 12, 13, 14, 15, 16
Bonhoeffer, Karl-Friedrich, to His Children—8
Bonhoeffer, Karl-Friedrich, and Margarethe, to—10
Bonhoeffer, Klaus, from—9
Bonhoeffer, Klaus, to—9, 10
Bonhoeffer, Klaus, to Julie Bonhoeffer—10
Bonhoeffer, Klaus, to Karl and Paula Bonhoeffer—10
Bonhoeffer, Paula, from—8, 9, 10, 13, 15
Bonhoeffer, Paula, to—8, 9, 10, 15, 16
Bonhoeffer, Paula, to Walter and Ilse Dreß—9
Bonhoeffer, Paula, Karl, and Dietrich, from Rüdiger Schleicher—16
Bonhoeffer, Sabine, to—9
Bonhoeffer, Susanne, from—9
Bonhoeffer, Susanne, to—9, 10
Bonhoeffer, Susanne, and Walter Dreß, to—10
Bonhoeffer, Ursula, to—9
Bonhoeffer Parents, Letters to—*see* Bonhoeffer, Karl and Paula

Brandenburg, Hans, to—11
Brandenburg, Willi, from—14
"Brotherhood of Young Theologians" in Pomerania,
from Werner de Boor and Gerhard Saß—15
Brothers (Finkenwalde), to—14
Brunner, Emil, to—16
Büchsel, Hans-Jakob, from—15
Büchsel, Karl, from—11
Büchsel, Karl, to—11
Bull, Paul, to—14
Burroughs, Arthur, from—12

Cavert, Samuel McCrea, from Henry Smith Leiper—15
Chancellery of the University Curator, to the Lecturers of the University of Berlin—14
Chancellery of the University Curator, to the Lecturers of the University of Berlin—14
Cover Letter
Questionnaire
Church Chancellery of the German Evangelical Church, from—12
Church Chancellery of the German Evangelical Church,
from Election Committee of the German Evangelical Churches of Sydenham and St. Paul—12
Church Chancellery of the German Evangelical Church, to—12
Church Foreign Office, from the German Evangelical Pastors in London—13
Colleges and Seminaries in the United States,
Letter of Recommendation from Paul Lehmann—15
Congregation of St. Paul's German Reformed Church in London, to—14
Consistory, from—9, 10
Consistory, to—10
Consistory of the Mark Brandenburg, from Emil Karow—13
Corbach, Karl-Heinz, from—15
Council of Brethren of the Confessing Church Berlin-Brandenburg, Education Office, to (Reference for Christoph Harhausen)—14
Council of Brethren of the Confessing Church Berlin-Brandenburg, Education Office, to (Reference for Alexander von der Marwitz)—14
Council of Brethren of the Old Prussian Union, from the Finkenwalde Preachers' Seminary—14

Council of Brethren of the Old Prussian Union, to—15
Council of the Evangelical Church of the Old Prussian Union, from the Provisional Administration of the German Evangelical Church—14
Cromwell, Ernst, to—14, 17 (for *DBWE* 13)
Cromwell, Philipp, from—17 (for *DBWE* 13)
Cromwell, Philipp, to—14
Cromwell Family, to—14
Czeppan, Richard, from—9
Czeppan, Richard, to—9
Czeppan, Richard and Maria, to—10

de Boor, Werner, and Gerhard Saß, to the "Brotherhood of Young Theologians" in Pomerania—15
Decker, Mr., to—11
de Félice, Théodore, from—12, 13
de Félice, Théodore, from Jürgen Winterhager—13
de Félice, Théodore, to—12, 13
Deißmann, Adolf, from—11, 12
Deißmann, Adolf, from Caius Fabricius—12
Deißmann, Adolf, from the Provisional Bureau for Ecumenical Youth Work—12
Deißmann, Adolf, Letter of Recommendation from—10
Deißmann, Adolf, to—10, 12
Deißmann, Adolf, to the Junior Teaching Faculty of Systematic Theology, Berlin—12
de Quervain, Alfred, to—16
Dibelius, Otto, from—10
Diestel, Max, from—10, 11
Diestel, Max, Letter of Recommendation from—10
Diestel, Max, to—10, 12, 13, 14, 16
Dietrich, Bishop, from Bishop Heckel—13
Dietze, Constantin von, to His Wife—16
Distler, Waltraut, to—16
Doebert, Heinz, from—15
Dohnanyi, Christine von, from—16
Dohnanyi, Christine von, from Hans von Dohnanyi—16
Dohnanyi, Christine von, to—13, 16
Dohnanyi, Christoph von, from—8
Dohnanyi, Hans von, "Camouflage Letter" to—16
Dohnanyi, Hans von, from—8

Dohnanyi, Hans von, to—8, 9
Dohnanyi, Hans von, to (Excerpt from File)—16
Dohnanyi, Hans von, to Christine von Dohnanyi—16
Dohnanyi, Hans von, to the Munich Military Intelligence Office (Excerpt from File)—16
Dohnanyi, Hans von, to the Schlawe District Military Recruiting Station (Excerpt from File)—16
Dreier, Wilhelm, from—9
Dreß, Margarethe, to—9
Dreß, Susanne, from—8
Dreß, Susanne, to—14, 15
Dreß, Susanne and Walter, to—14, 15
Dreß, Walter, to—9, 10, 13
Dreß, Walter and Ilse, from Paula Bonhoeffer—9
Dudzus, Otto, from—15

Ecumenical Youth Commission, Memorandum from—13
Ecumenical Youth Conference, to Ove Valdemar Ammundsen—13
Eden, Anthony, from George K. A. Bell—16
Eden, Anthony, to George K. A. Bell—16
Editor of *The Round Table*, from George Bell—13
Editor of *The Round Table*, from Lancelot Mason—13
Editors of *Die Tägliche Rundschau*, to—11
Ehrenström, Nils, to—12
Eichholz, Georg, from—15, 16
Eichholz, Georg, to—15, 16
Eidem, Erling, from—14
Eidem, Erling, from George K. A. Bell—16
Eidem, Erling, to—14, 16
Election Committee of the German Evangelical Churches of Sydenham and St. Paul, to the Church Chancellery of the German Evangelical Church—12
Ern, Richard, to—10, 11
Ern Family, to—10
"Ernst," to—13
Espy, Edwin, from—14
Evangelical Consistory of the Mark Brandenburg, from—11
Executive Committee of the City Synod in Berlin, from—11

Fabricius, Caius, to Adolf Deißmann—12
Families of Finkenwalde Brothers Drafted into the Armed Forces, to—15

Finkenwalde Brothers, to—15
Finkenwalde Brothers, to—15
Bonhoeffer's Circular Letter
Finkenwalde Brothers, to—15
Bonhoeffer's Circular Letter
Report by One Participant about the Zingst Retreat
Finkenwalde Brothers, to Gerritdina Stokmann—15
[Finkenwalde] First and Second Sessions, Circular Letter to the Brothers of—14
[Finkenwalde] First Session, Brothers of, from Albrecht Schönherr—14
[Finkenwalde] First Session, Brothers of, to—14
[Finkenwalde] First Session, Members of, from the House of Brethren—14
[Finkenwalde] First Two Sessions, Brothers of, to—14
Finkenwalde Preachers' Seminary, to the Council of Brethren of the Old Prussian Union—14
[Finkenwalde] Second Session, Brothers of, to—14
Fischer, Hans, to—11
Fischer, Martin, to—15
Foreign Office, to the German Legation in Stockholm—14
Foreign Office in Berlin, to—14
Forell, Birger, from George Bell—14
Fox, Henry Watson, from—13
Fricke, H., to—13
Friends and Supporters of the Seminary, from the House of Brethren—14
Fries, Willy, from—12

Gadow, Hartmut, from—15
Gandhi, Mahatma, from—13
Gandhi, Mahatma, from George Bell—13
Georgii, Wolf, to—14
German Congregations and Pastors Abroad, from Theodor Heckel—13
German Embassy in London, to the Ministry of Foreign Affairs—13
German Evangelical Congregations in Great Britain, from Theodor Heckel—13
German Evangelical Pastors Abroad, from Theodor Heckel—13
German Evangelical Pastors Abroad, from Helmut Rößler—13
German Evangelical Pastors Association, to All Pastors Abroad—13
German Evangelical Pastors in London, to the Church Foreign Office—13
German Evangelical Pastors in London, to the President of the German Reich—13

German Evangelical Pastors in London, to the Reich Church Government—13
German Legation in Stockholm, from the Foreign Office—14
German Pastors in London, to August Mararhens and Hans Meiser—13
German Section of the World Alliance for Promoting International Friendship through the Churches, from Wilhelm Stählin—11
Gerstenmaier, Eugen, from Hans Schönfeld—14
Gerullis, Georg, from Wilhelm Lütgert—12
Goes, Helmut, to—14
Grimme, Adolf, from Wilhelm Lütgert—10
Grunow, Richard, to—16

Hammelsbeck, Oskar, from—16
Hancock, Eric Gray, from—13
Harder, Günther, from—14
Harder, Günther, to—14
Harnack, Adolf von, from—10
Harnack, Adolf von, to—10
Hase, Hans Christoph von, from—10
Hase, Hans Christoph von, to—9, 10
Heckel, Bishop, to Bishop Dietrich—13
Heckel, Theodor, from Baron Bruno Schröder—13
Heckel, Theodor, Memorandum from—12
Heckel, Theodor, to—11, 12, 13
Heckel, Theodor, to Baron Bruno Schröder—13
Heckel, Theodor, to Friedrich Singer—12
Heckel, Theodor, to the Association of Congregations in London—13
  Cover Letter to the Chairman, Baron Bruno Schröder
  To the Association of Congregations
Heckel, Theodor, to the German Congregations and Pastors Abroad—13
Heckel, Theodor, to the German Evangelical Congregations in Great Britain—13
Heckel, Theodor, to the German Pastors Abroad—13
Heckel, Theodor, to the Ministry of Foreign Affairs—13
Heckel, Theodor, to the Regional Church Committee—14
Heckel, Theodor, to Friedrich Wehrhan—13
Held, Robert, from—9
Hellman, Gerhard, from—15
Henriod, Henry Louis, from—11, 12, 13, 14
Henriod, Henry Louis, to—11, 12, 13, 14
Hermann, Rudolf, from Wilhelm Lütgert—14

Hildebrandt, Franz, from—10, 13
Hildebrandt, Franz, from Martin Niemöller—13
Hildebrandt, Franz, to—15
Hildebrandt, Franz, to Karl Koch—13
Hildebrandt, Franz, and Bonhoeffer, to Martin Niemöller—13
Hildebrandt, Franz, and Bonhoeffer, to Erich Seeberg—13
Hodgson, Leonard, from—14, 15
Hodgson, Leonard, to—14, 15
Hofmann, Hans, from—15
Horn, Maria, to—9
Hosemann, Johannes, to the Members of the Provisional Bureau—11
House of Brethren, to Friends and Supporters of the Seminary—14
House of Brethren, to Members of the [Finkenwalde] First Session—14

Jannasch, Wilhelm, to—16
Jannasch, Wilhelm, to the Executive Committee of the Pastors' Emergency League—16
Jehle, Herbert, from—16
Jehle, Herbert, to—12
Jensen, Hans-Werner, to—16
Jensen, Paul Theodor, from—12
Johansson, Harry, from George K. A. Bell—18
Jordan, Richard, to—12
Junior Teaching Faculty of Systematic Theology, Berlin, from Adolf Deißmann—12

Kanitz, Joachim, to—12
Karlström, Nils, from—14
Karlström, Nils, to—14
Karow, Emil, from—11, 12
Karow, Emil, to Berlin Church Consistory—12
Karow, Emil, to the Consistory of the Mark Brandenburg—13
Kerrl, Reich Church Minister Hanns, from the Office of the Gestapo—15
Kirschbaum, Charlotte von, from—16
Kirschbaum, Charlotte von, from Dr. Sch[. . .]—16
Kirschbaum, Charlotte von, to—16
Kirschbaum, Charlotte von, to Paul Vogt—16
Kistner, Otto, from—15
Klapproth, Erich, from—15
Kleist-Retzow, Ruth von, from—15, 16
Kleist-Retzow, Ruth von, to Eberhard Bethge—15, 16

Kleist-Retzow, Ruth von, to Eberhard Bethge and Bonhoeffer—16
Koch, Karl, from Franz Hildebrandt—13
Koch, Karl, from Friedrich Wehrhan—13
Koch, Karl, to—13, 14
Koch, Karl, and Friedrich Müller, to—15
Koch, Werner, to—11, 14
Koch, Werner, to—15
  Letter
  Telegram
Koechlin, Alphons, from Wilhelm Rott—16
Koechlin, Alphons, to—16
Köller, Walter, to—14
Königsberg SD Regional Headquarters, to the Reich Central Security Office—16
Korporal, Master Builder, to—15
Kramm, Hans Herbert, from—14
Kramm, Hans Herbert, to—14
Krause, Gerhard, from—15
Krause, Reinhold, to—11
Krause, Winfried, to—16
Krencker, Daniel, to—11
Kunert, Erwin, to—14
Künneth, Walter, from—11
Künneth, Walter, to—11
Künneth, Walter, to the Theological Faculty—12

Lämmerhirdt, Hildegard, to—13
Lasserre, Jean, from—15
Lasserre, Jean, to an Unknown Woman—16
Lebrecht, Heinrich, from—14
Lebrecht, Heinrich, to—13, 14
Lecturers of the University of Berlin, from the Chancellery of the University Curator—14
Lehmann, Paul, from—15
Lehmann, Paul, from—16
  For Bonhoeffer
  To Erwin Sutz
Lehmann, Paul, from Reinhold Niebuhr—15
Lehmann, Paul, from Erwin Sutz—16
Lehmann, Paul, Letter of Recommendation to Colleges and Seminaries in the United States—15

Lehmann, Paul, to—11, 12, 14, 15, 16
Lehmann, Paul, to Timothy Lehmann—15
Lehmann, Paul, to Reinhold Niebuhr—15
Lehmann, Timothy, to Paul Lehmann—15
Lehne, Gerhard, from—15
Leibholz, Christiane, to—15
Leibholz, Gerhard, from George K. A. Bell—16
Leibholz, Gerhard, to—13
Leibholz, Gerhard, to Karl and Paula Bonhoeffer—16
Leibholz, Sabine, from—15
Leibholz, Sabine, to—10, 15, 16
Leibholz, Sabine and Gerhard, from—15
Leibholz, Sabine and Gerhard, to—10, 11, 13, 15
Leibholz Family, to—16
Leiper, Henry Smith, from—15
Leiper, Henry Smith, to—15
Leiper, Henry Smith, to Samuel McCrea Cavert—15
Leiper, Henry Smith, to Reinhold Niebuhr—15
Lempp, Albert, from—16
Lepsius, Renate, from—11, 12
Lepsius, Renate, to—12
Lerche, Otto-Karl, and Paul Henheik, from—15
Liedtke, Herbert, from—15
"Life and Work," Members of, from George Bell—13
Litt, Theodor, to—15
London Pastors, to Martin Niemöller—13
Lütgert, Wilhelm, from—10
Lütgert, Wilhelm, from Prussian Ministry for Education and Cultural Affairs—12
Lütgert, Wilhelm, Letter of Recommendation from—10
Lütgert, Wilhelm, to Georg Gerullis—12
Lütgert, Wilhelm, to Adolf Grimme—10
Lütgert, Wilhelm, to Rudolf Hermann—14
Lütgert,Wilhelm, to Adolf Schlatter—13, 17 (for *DBWE* 12)
Lynker, Grete, to—16
Lynker, Rudolf, from—15

Maechler, Winfried, to—16
Mararhens, August, and Hans Meiser, from German Pastors in London—13
Martin, Hugh, from George K. A. Bell—16

Martin, Hugh, from Willem A. Visser 't Hooft—16
Mason, Lancelot, to the Editor of *The Round Table*—13
Mayor of Biesenthal, to—11
MBK Publishers, from—16
Mebes, Max, to—15
Meiser, Hans, and August Mararhens, from German Pastors in London—13
Meiser, Hans, to—16
Mehnert, Klaus, to August Wilhelm Schreiber—10
Ministry of Foreign Affairs, from the German Embassy in London—13
Ministry of Foreign Affairs, from Theodor Heckel—13
Moberly, Walter, to—15
Müller, Ludwig, from Baron Bruno Schröder—13
Mumm, Reinhard, from—10
Munich Military Intelligence Office, from Hans von Dohnanyi (Excerpt from File)—16

Neurath, Baron Konstantin von, to Friedrich Wehrhan—13
Niebuhr, Reinhold, from Paul Lehmann—15
Niebuhr, Reinhold, from Henry Smith Leiper—15
Niebuhr, Reinhold, to—12, 13, 15
Niebuhr, Reinhold, to Paul Lehmann—15
Niemöller, Else, to—15
Niemöller, Martin, from—14
Niemöller, Martin, from Bonhoeffer and Franz Hildebrandt—13
Niemöller, Martin, from London Pastors—13
Niemöller, Martin, to—14
Niemöller, Martin, to Franz Hildebrandt—13
Niesel, Wilhelm, to—15
Nithack, Ulrich, from—15
Nørregaard, Jens, to—14
Nygren, Anders, to—14, 16

Office of the German Section of the World Alliance for Promoting International Friendship through the Churches, to—11
Office of the Gestapo, Berlin, to Reich Church Minister Hanns Kerrl—15
Office of the Reich President, to Friedrich Wehrhan—13
Office of the Secret State Police, from the *Reichsführer* SS and Chief of the German Police—14
Office of the World Alliance for Promoting International Friendship through the Churches, to—11

Olbricht, Fritz, from—10
Oldham, Joseph H., to—13
Onnasch, Friedrich (*also* Fritz), from—15
Onnasch, Friedrich, from Eberhard Baumann—16
Onnasch, Fritz, to—14, 15
Onnasch, Margret, to—16

Pastors' Emergency League, from Wilhelm Jannasch—16
Pauli, Mr., to—11
Pestalozzi, Gerty, to—16
Pfisterer, Franz Ernst, from—15
Pfizer, Theodor, from—9
Piper, Otto, to—13
Preachers' Seminary, to the Provisional Administration of the German Evangelical Church—14
President of the German Reich, from the German Evangelical Pastors in London—13
President of the Reich War Court, from Karl Bonhoeffer—8
Priebe, Hermann, Church Letter of Reference—10
Protestant Church Federation Office, from Wilhelm Stählin—11
Provisional Administration of the German Evangelical Church, from—14
Provisional Administration of the German Evangelical Church, from the Preachers' Seminary—14
Provisional Administration of the German Evangelical Church, to the Council of the Evangelical Church of the Old Prussian Union—14
Provisional Bureau, Members of, from Johannes Hosemann—11
Provisional Bureau for Ecumenical Youth Work, to Adolf Deißmann—12
Provisional Church Administration, to—13
Prussian Ministry for Education and Cultural Affairs, to Wilhelm Lütgert—12

Radtke, Johannes, to—15
Radtke, Johannes, to—15
Application for Army and Military Hospital Chaplaincy
Enclosure: Curriculum Vitae
Rector of the University of Berlin, from the Reich and Prussian Minister of Science, Training, and Public Education—14
Regional Church Committee, from Theodor Heckel—14
Reich and Prussian Minister of Church Affairs, to the Reich and Prussian Minister of Science, Training, and Public Education—14

Reich and Prussian Minister for Church Affairs, to the Reich Church Committee—14
Reich and Prussian Minister of Science, Training, and Public Education, from the Reich and Prussian Minister of Church Affairs—14
Reich and Prussian Minister of Science, Training, and Public Education, to—14
Reich and Prussian Minister of Science, Training, and Public Education, to the Rector of the University of Berlin—14
Reich Central Security Office, from the Königsberg SD Regional Headquarters—16
Reich Central Security Office, to—16
Reich Chamber of Literature, from—16
Reich Chamber of Literature, to—16
Reich Church Committee, from the Reich and Prussian Minister for Church Affairs—14
Reich Church Government in Berlin, from the German Evangelical Pastors in London—13
Reich Church Government in Berlin, from Friedrich Wehrhan—13
Reich Church Government in Berlin, to—13
Reichsführer SS and Chief of the German Police, to the Office of the Secret State Police—14
Rieger, Julius, to—14, 15
Rieger, Julius, and Franz Hildebrandt, to—14
Rohrer, Kurt, to—9
Röhrsheim, Ludwig, from—10
Röhrsheim, Ludwig, to—10
Rößler, Helmut, from—10, 13
Rößler, Helmut, to—10, 11, 12, 13
Rößler, Helmut, to the German Evangelical Pastors Abroad—13
Rott, Wilhelm, from—15
Rott, Wilhelm, to—15
Rott, Wilhelm, to Alphons Koechlin—16
Ryder, Mr. (Office of Baron Bruno Schröder), to—13

Salomon, Otto, from Karl Barth—16
Sandegren, Paul, to—11
Sander, Erwin, from—16
Sasse, Hermann, from—11, 12
Saunders, G. H., from—13
Sch[. . .], Dr., to Charlotte von Kirschbaum—16
Schauer, Friedrich, to—14

Schlatter, Adolf, from Wilhelm Lütgert—13, 17 (for *DBWE* 12)
Schlawe District Military Recruiting Station, from Hans von Dohnanyi (Excerpt from File)—16
Schlawe District Military Recruiting Station, to (Excerpt from File)—16
Schleicher, Hans-Walter, to—8, 16
Schleicher, Renate, from Eberhard Bethge—16
Schleicher, Rüdiger, from—8
Schleicher, Rüdiger, to—10, 14
Schleicher, Rüdiger, to Paula, Karl, and Dietrich Bonhoeffer—16
Schleicher, Ursula, from—8
Schleicher, Ursula, to—8, 15
Schleicher, Ursula and Rüdiger, to—10
Schleicher Family, from—15
Schlunk, Wolfgang, from—12
Schmid, Ernst Fritz, from—17 (for *DBWE* 9)
Schmid, Ernst Fritz, to—17 (for *DBWE* 9)
Schmidt, Karl Ludwig, from—14
Schmidt, Walter, to—16
Schneidemesser, Johannes von, to—12
Schnurmann, Anneliese, to—12, 16
Schönfeld, Hans, from—13
Schönfeld, Hans, to—12, 13
Schönfeld, Hans, to George K. A. Bell—16
Schönfeld, Hans, to Eugen Gerstenmaier—14
Schönherr, Albrecht, to Several Finkenwalde Brothers—15
Schönherr, Albrecht, to the Brothers of the First Session—14
Schönherr, Albrecht, to the Participants of the Theological Society in Pomerania—15
Schreiber, August Wilhelm, from—11
Schreiber, August Wilhelm, from Klaus Mehnert—10
Schreiber, August Wilhelm, from Wilhelm Stählin—11
Schreiber, August Wilhelm, to—11, 12
Schreiber, August Wilhelm, to Wilhelm Stählin—11
Schröder, Baron Bruno, from—13, 14
Schröder, Baron Bruno, from Theodor Heckel—13
Schröder, Baron Bruno, to—13, 14
Schröder, Baron Bruno, to Theodor Heckel—13
Schröder, Baron Bruno, to Ludwig Müller—13
Schröder, Baron Bruno, to Friedrich Wehrhan—13
Schröder, Baron Bruno, and Friedrich Wehrhan, to the Church Foreign Office—13

Schröter, Friedrich-Ernst, to—15
Schubring, Wilhelm, from—10
Schutz, Erwin, to—16
Schutz, Wiltrud, to—16
Seeberg, Erich, from—10, 12, 13
Seeberg, Erich, from Bonhoeffer and Franz Hildebrandt—13
Seeberg, Erich, to—10, 12, 13
Seeberg, Reinhold, from—10
Seeberg, Reinhold, from Karl Bonhoeffer—9
Seeberg, Reinhold, to—10
Seeler, Richard, to—14
Senior Reich Military Prosecutor, from—8
Senior Reich Military Prosecutor, from Karl Bonhoeffer—8
Senior Reich Military Prosecutor, to Karl Bonhoeffer—8
Several Finkenwalde Brothers, from Albrecht Schönherr—15
Seydel, Gustav, to—16
Siegmund-Schultze, Friedrich, from—11, 12, 13
Siegmund-Schultze, Friedrich, to—11, 12, 13, 16
Singer, Friedrich, from—12
Singer, Friedrich, from Theodor Heckel—12
Singer, Friedrich, to—12
Söhlmann, Fritz, from—11, 14
Staemmler, Wolfgang, from Eberhard Bethge—14
Staemmler, Wolfgang, to—14
Staewen, Gertrud, from—12
Stahlberg, Ruth Roberta, to—16
Stählin, Wilhelm, from—11, 12
Stählin, Wilhelm, from Erich Stange—11
Stählin, Wilhelm, to—11, 12
Stählin, Wilhelm, to the Church Federation Office—11
Stählin, Wilhelm, to the German Section of the World Alliance for Promoting International Friendship through the Churches—11
Stählin, Wilhelm, to the Protestant Church Federation Office—11
Stange, Erich, to Wilhelm Stählin—11
Steele, Pierre H., from—11
Steele, Pierre H., to—11
Stokmann, Gerritdina, from the Finkenwalde Brothers—15
Stolzenburg, Arnold, from—12
Strege, Martin, to—15

Strege, Martin, to—14
Bonhoeffer's Letter
Enclosure "Working Meeting on Congregational Development and Church Discipline"
Strege, Martin, to—15
Letter
Telegram
Sutz, Erwin, from George K. A. Bell—16
Sutz, Erwin, to—10, 11, 12, 13, 14, 15, 16
Sutz, Erwin, to Paul Lehmann—16

Talbot, Edward Keble, from George Bell—13
Temple, William, from Willem A. Visser 't Hooft—16
Theological Committee of the Confessing Church in Pomerania, Members of, to—15
Theological Faculty, from Walter Künneth—12
Theological Faculty, to—9
Theological Society in Pomerania, Participants of, from Albrecht Schönherr—15
Thimme, Hans, from—14
Thimme, Hans, to—14
Thumm, Hermann, from—10
Thumm, Hermann, to—10
Toureille, Pierre C., to—11
Trowitsch Publishers, to—10
Tryon, Harold H., to—10
Tübben, Ludwig, to—12
Two Student Fraternities, to—11

Unknown Recipients, to—13
Unknown Woman, from Jean Lasserre—16
Utsugi, Tamotsu, from—12

Vibrans, Elisabeth, to—16
Vibrans, Gerhard, from—14
Vibrans, Gerhard, to—14
Vibrans, Karl, to—16
Visser 't Hooft, Willem A., to George K. A. Bell—16
Visser 't Hooft, Willem A., to Hugh Martin—16
Visser 't Hooft, Willem A., to William Temple—16
Vogt, Paul, from Charlotte von Kirschbaum—16

Wahl, Hans (on Behalf of Theodor Heckel), to—13
Weckerling, Rudolf, to—16
Wedemeyer, Maria von, to—16
Wedemeyer, Maria von, to Ruth von Wedemeyer—8
Wedemeyer, Maximilian von, to—16
Wedemeyer, Ruth von, from Maria von Wedemeyer—8
Wedemeyer, Ruth von, to—8, 16
Wehrhan, Friedrich, from Theodor Heckel—13
Wehrhan, Friedrich, from Karl Koch—13
Wehrhan, Friedrich, from Baron Konstantin von Neurath—13
Wehrhan, Friedrich, from Office of the Reich President—13
Wehrhan, Friedrich, to the Reich Church Government—13
Wehrhan, Friedrich, from Baron Bruno Schröder—13
Widmann, Richard, from—9
Wienstein, Richard, to—12
Wingolf Fraternity, to—11
Winterhager, Jürgen, from—11
Winterhager, Jürgen, to—13
Winterhager, Jürgen, to Théodore de Félice—13
Wolf, Ernst, from—13, 16
Wolf, Ernst, to—13, 16

Yorck von Wartenburg, Helene, to—9
Young Brothers in Pomerania, to—15

Zielinski, Kurt, from—12
Zinn, Elisabeth, to—14
Zippel, Hans-Henning, from—14
Zippel, Hans-Henning, to—14
Zoellner, Wilhelm, to—12

Other Documentation under Correspondence

Abitur Report Card—9
American Diary—15
Appeal from the Berlin Pastors—12
Appeal from the Young Reformation Movement—12
Application for Admission to the Second Theological Exam—10
    Application
    Enclosure 1: Addition the Curriculum Vitae

Application for a Fellowship from the German Academic Exchange Service—10
Application for Leave of Absence from the Probationary Year—10
Application for Travel Visa—16
Munich Military Intelligence Office to Munich Military Intelligence Office
Munich Military Intelligence Office to Munich Police Headquarters
Visa Issued by Munich Police Headquarters
Application from Max Diestel to the German Evangelical Church Committee regarding Bonhoeffer's Ordination—10
Application from the Consistory to Excuse Bonhoeffer from Attending the Preachers' Seminary—10
Appointment as Assistant Pastor—11
Arrangements for Delegation of Work before Departure for the United States—15
Appointment of the Executor of Bonhoeffer's Estate
Directions for Successor
Transfer of Motorcycle Title
Assessment by Hans Schönfeld for the Ecumenical Advisory Committee of the Provisional Church Administration—14
Assistantship Contract—11

Bell, George K. A.: Diary Notes—16
Bell, George K. A.: Memorandum of Conversations—16
Bell, George K. A.: Notebook Entry—16
Bonhoeffer Inscription at Union Theological Seminary—11
Book Inscription to Herbert Jehle—17 (for *DBWE* 13)

Calendar Notes—16
Candidates' Poem Requesting Support for Their New Preachers' Seminary—14
Certificate Attesting to Bonhoeffer's Inclusion in the List of Candidates Approved for Ordination—9
Certificate Attesting to Participation in the Life of the Church—9
Certificate for Franz Hildebrandt—13
Certificate of the First Theological Examination—9
Christmas Letter—8
Circular Letter of the Provisional Bureau—11
Circular Letter of the Provisional Bureau for Ecumenical Youth Work—11
Circular Letter of the Working Group of Theologians and Economists—11

Circular Letter to Colleagues and Friends—12
Circular Letter to "Members and Friends of the Young Reformation Movement"—12
Circular Letter to Various Student Fraternities—11
Communication from the Department of Theology to the Ministry for Science, Art, and Public Education—10
  Cover letter from Erich Seeberg
  Enclosures: Curriculum Vitae and Bibliography
Conference with Representatives of the Reich Church Government—13
  Baron Bruno Schröder to Theodor Heckel
  Declaration by Theodor Heckel
  Declaration by the Pastors in Great Britain
  Declaration by the Pastors in London
  Minutes Recorded by Benjamin Locher
Confirmation Certificate—9
Courier Identification Card from the Ministry of Foreign Affairs—16
Curriculum Vitae—9

Death Notice for Julie Bonhoeffer—14
Declaration of the Berlin Pastors—12
Decree of the Senior Reich Military Prosecutor—16
Deportation Reports—16
  Report on the Evacuation of "Non-Aryans"
  Report on the Mass Deportation of Jewish Citizens
Diary Entry concerning Fritz Olbricht—10
Dietze, Constantin von: Discussion Notes—16
Doctoral Diploma—9
Draft for a Petition to the National Synod of the German Evangelical Church—12
Draft for a "Statement from Opposition Pastors"—12
Draft Guide for Candidates Preparing for the Pastoral Office—14
Draft of a Letter to the Church Foreign Office—13
  Bonhoeffer's Draft
  Introductory Statement by Edward Crüsemann
Draft Submission to the Department of Theology in Halle concerning the Dehn Case—11
  Cover Letter
  Theses

Ehrenström, Nils: Calendar Notes—16
Entry in the Guest Book of Otto Salomon—16

Entry in the Guest Book of the Lasserre Family—11
Entry in the Vibrans Family Guestbook—14
Evaluation of Bonhoeffer's Catechesis by Karl Meumann—10

Fictitious Diary Fragments—16
File Z—16
  Note No. 1
  Note No. 2
  Note No. 3
Finkenwalde Circular Letters—14 (*see* "[Finkenwalde] First and Second Sessions, Circular Letter to the Brothers of" above), 15 (*see* "Finkenwalde Brothers, to" above), 16
First Drafts of Letters by Bonhoeffer for His Interrogations—16
  To Manfred Roeder (June 10, 1943)
  To Manfred Roeder (June 12, 1943)
Foreign Office: Minutes of Proceedings—16
Foreign Office: Minutes of Proceedings—16
  Answer to the Bishop of Chichester
  On Peace Moves from Germany
  On the Bishop of Chichester's Trip to Sweden
Formal Request to Be Admitted to the First Theological Examination—9
Further Drafts of Letters by Bonhoeffer regarding His Interrogations—16
  To Manfred Roeder (6 Letters)

Gemeindebote, [Excerpts] from—13
General Decree of the Reich Central Security Office—16

Henriod, Henry Louis, Circular Letter to the Youth Secretaries of the World Alliance for Promoting International Friendship through the Churches—11

Indictment against Constantin von Dietze—16
Indictment against Hans von Dohnanyi and Hans Oster: Reproduction of Excerpts from Letters from—16
  Hans Oster to the Munich Military Intelligence Office
  Hans von Dohnanyi to Wilhelm Schmidhuber
Indictment against Klaus Bonhoeffer, Rüdiger Schleicher, Hans John, Friedrich Justus Perels, and Hans Kloß—16
Indictment Files against Bonhoeffer—16
  Indictment by the Reich War Court
  Indictment by the Senior Reich Military Prosecutor

Indictment Files against Hans von Dohnanyi and Hans Oster—16
Indictment by the Reich War Court
Indictment by the Senior Reich Military Prosecutor
Inscription in the Copy of *Discipleship* for Martin Niemöller—15
Inscription to Henry Sloan Coffin in *Nachfolge* [*Discipleship*]—15
Interrogation Protocol concerning the Worship Service on June 2, 1935—14
Invitation from the Provisional Bureau for Ecumenical Youth Work—12
Invitation from the Provisional Bureau to the Theological Conference of April 29–30, 1932—11
Invitation to an Intercession for the Preachers' Seminary of Finkenwalde, from the Council of Brethren of the Confessing Congregation in Neuruppin—14
Invitation to a Retreat for Theology Students—14
Italian Diary—9

Koch, Werner: Report on the Journey to Sweden—14
Cover Letter to the Ministry of Foreign Affairs
Report

Last Will and Testament (Tegel)—8
Lehmann, Paul, Circular Letter to Colleges and Seminaries in the United States—15
List of Documents Appended to the Petition—9
Lütgert, Wilhelm, Report on *Act and Being*—10

Manifesto of the Seminary Brotherhood of the Confessing Church—14
Manifesto "To Our Brothers in the Ministry"—14
Memorandum concerning an Ecumenical Exchange of Young Theologians—14
Ministry of Foreign Affairs, Report from the German Legation in Sofia—12
Ministry of Foreign Affairs on the Presentation by Bonhoeffer and Gustav Schönberger—13
Minutes Book of St. Paul's Church, [Excerpt] from—13
Minutes of a Discussion between London Pastors and the Leadership of the Confessing Synod in Berlin—13
Minutes of a Meeting of the Congregational Council—13
Minutes of a Meeting of the Congregational Council of St. Paul's Church—13

Minutes of a Meeting of the Congregational Council
of the Sydenham Church—13
Minutes of an Extraordinary Meeting of the Congregational Councils
of St. Paul's and Sydenham Churches—13
Minutes of Congregational Council Meetings—13
St. Paul's Church
Sydenham Church
Minutes of Meeting "The Struggle for the Church"—12
Minutes of Proceedings of an Interrogation of Wilhelm Canaris—16
Minutes of the Meeting of the Ecumenical Advisory Council
with the Provisional Administration—14
Minutes of the Session of the Reich Council of Brethren,
[Excerpt] from—13
Miscellaneous Notes—8
Moltke, Helmuth von, [Excerpts] from His Letters to Freya
von Moltke—16
Monthly Budget—14

Note of Excuse—11
Notes I—8
Notes II—8
Notes at the Conclusion of the Diary—15
Notes from the Time as Assistant—11
Notice Posted at the Technical College—12

Olbricht, Fritz, Excerpt from Report on the German Evangelical
Church Committee—10
Olbricht, Fritz, Report on the German Evangelical Church
Committee—10
Order from the Berlin Consistory regarding an Extension
of Bonhoeffer's Leave of Absence—10
Order from the Evangelical High Church Council concerning
Assignment as Vicar—10
Copy for Bonhoeffer
Cover Letter to Fritz Olbricht
Order of the Evangelical Consistory of the Mark Brandenburg—11
Ordination—10
Outline for a Book—8

Pastors' Conference in Bradford—13
Cover Letter by Friedrich Wehrhan
Declaration to the Reich Church Government
Notes Taken by Julius Rieger
Peschke, Kurt: Defense of Hans von Dohnanyi—16
Cover Letter
Defense Brief for Hans von Dohnanyi
Petition to the Armed Forces—16
Preparations for the Conference with Theodor Heckel—13
Friedrich Wehrhan to Baron Bruno Schröder
Memorandum from the Pastors in London
Preparations for the Freiburg Memorandum—16
Constantin von Dietze: Discussion Notes
Discussion Notes
Printed Thank-You Card—11
Proceedings of Interrogations of Hans von Dohnanyi—16
Interrogation on April 16, 1943
Interrogation on May 5, 1943
Pulpit Announcement—14
Draft for a 1936 Pentecost Statement
Pentecost Statement of the Provisional Administration

Reich Chancellery Memorandum—12
Report of the Pomeranian Members of the Preachers' Seminary—14
Report on His Year of Study Prepared for the Church Federation Office—10
Report on His Second Semester—10
Report on the Christmas Celebration at the London Seamen's Mission—13
Report on the Fifth International Youth Conference, Fanø, [Excerpt] from—13
Report on the Year 1936—14
Report to the Berlin Consistory—12
Request to the Gestapo—15
Response of the Evangelical High Church Council to the Application for Bonhoeffer's Early Ordination—10
Response to the Application to Excuse Bonhoeffer from Attending the Preachers' Seminary—10
Results of the Second Theological Examination—10
Certificate
Cover Letter from the Consistory

Evaluation of the Catechetical Examination
Evaluation of the Sermon
Results of the Second Theological Examination
Rieger, Julius, [Excerpt] from the Diary of—13

Schönfeld, Hans: Statement by a German Pastor—16
Secession of the German Evangelical Congregations in Great Britain from the Reich Church—13
Minutes Taken on Behalf of St. Paul's Church
Minutes Taken on Behalf of the Association of Congregations
Security Service of the Reichsführer SS, Regional Division North, Report to the Main Headquarters of the Security Service—14
Seeberg, Reinhold: Evaluation of Bonhoeffer's Dissertation—9
Spanish Diary—10
Statement by the Executive Committee of the World Alliance for Promoting International Friendship through the Churches—12
Statement of the Berlin Pastors "To the National Synod of the German Evangelical Church"—12
Statements of Bonhoeffer regarding Assertions by Bishop Bell on English Politics—16
Chief of the Security Police and the SD to the Foreign Office
Notes for the Presentation by Inland II B to the Reich Foreign Minister

Tegel Notes—8
Tegel Notes I—8
Tegel Notes II—8
Theses by the Student Members of the Young Reformation Movement at the University of Berlin—12

Visser 't Hooft, Willem A.: Notes on the State of the Church in Europe—16
Vote to Call Bonhoeffer as Pastor—13
From the Minute Book of the Sydenham Church
Letter from the Congregation to the Church Chancellery

"War and Peace," Excerpt from a Report on the Theme of the World Church Conference in Oxford, 1937—14

Academic Lectures

Inaugural Lecture: The Anthropological Question in Contemporary Philosophy and Theology—10

Lecture: "Christ and Peace"—12
Lecture: "Church Constitution"—14
  Bonhoeffer's Preparatory Manuscript on Confession
  Lecture Section on Ministry (Student Notes)
Lecture: "Concrete Ethics in Paul"—14
  Bonhoeffer's Notes on the Catalogs of Vices
  Excerpt from Lecture on the Catalogs of Vices (Transcription)
  Lecture Sections on Acts 2:43–47 and on the Actions of Christians ἐν Χρίστῳ (Student Notes)
Lecture: "Congregational Development and Church Discipline in the New Testament." Lecture Sections concerning the Space of Proclamation and the Space of the Pastoral Offices (Student Notes)—14
Lecture: "New Life in Paul"—14
  Bonhoeffer's Lecture Fragment on Death and Justification
  Bonhoeffer's Notes on Conduct, Growth, and Fruit
  Bonhoeffer's Preparatory Notes: Good Works
  Continuation of Lecture on Death and Justification (Student Notes)
  Lecture Section on Coming to Participate in Being in Christ (Student Notes)
  Lecture Section on Good Works (Student Notes)
  Lecture Sections on New Life and Discipleship (Student Notes)
Lecture: "Review and Discussion of New Publications in Systematic Theology"—12
Lecture: "The Visible Church in the New Testament"—14
  Bonhoeffer's Manuscript: The Space of the Pastoral Offices and Gifts and of Christian Life
  Bonhoeffer's Preparatory Sheet: Indwelling of the Trinity
  Distributed Copy of the Beginning of the Lecture according to Bonhoeffer's Manuscript
  Lecture Excerpt on the Church's Space (Student Notes)
  Lecture Section on False Teaching (Student Notes)
  Lecture Section on Holy Spirit and Church-Community (Student Notes)
  Lecture Section on Service to God and Service to One Another (Student Notes)

Lecture Course: The History of Twentieth-Century Systematic Theology (Student Notes)—11
Lecture Course: The Nature of the Church (Student Notes)—11
Lecture on Catechesis—14
"Catechesis" (1935–1936 Student Notes)
Concluding Section to the Lecture on Catechesis in the First Session (1935 Student Notes)
Lecture on Confirmation Instruction—14
Bonhoeffer's Outline for "Confirmation—History"
"Goal and Structure of Confirmation Instruction"
Lecture on Homiletics—14
Expansions of the Lecture on Homiletics
1. "The Word, the Preaching Office, and the Pastoral Office" (1936 Transcription)
2. "Questions That Reached Him" (1936 Student Notes)
3. "The Pastor and the Bible" (1936–1937 Transcription)
4. "On the Theme 'Evangelization'" (1936–1937 Transcription)
5. "The Pastor and the Worship Service" (1936–1937 Transcription)
6. "Historical Considerations" (1937 Student Notes)
7. "The Witness" (1937 Student Notes)
"Homiletics" (1935–1936 Student Notes)
Lecture Course on Lutheran Confessional Writings—14
Bonhoeffer's Notes on Law
Lecture Section on Augsburg Confession XVI (Student Notes)
Lecture on Marriage—15
Lecture on Pastoral Care—14
Expansion of the Lecture on Pastoral Care (1936 Student Notes)
"Pastoral Care" (1935–1936 Student Notes)
Lecture on Pastoral Counseling—15
Lectures on Personal Confession—14
"Personal Confession and Lord's Supper" (Theses)
"Personal Confession (according to the Large Catechism)" (Student Notes)

Seminar: Is There a Christian Ethic?—11
Excerpts from Student Notes
Fragment from Student Notes
Seminar Paper on 1 Clement—9
Seminar Paper on Job—9
Seminar Paper on Luther's Feelings about His Work—9
Seminar Paper on the Holy Spirit according to Luther—9

Seminar Paper on the Theology of Crisis and Its Attitude toward Philosophy and Science—10
Seminar Presentation on Church and Eschatology—9
Seminar Presentation on Early Lutheran Eschatology—9
Seminar Presentation on Germany's Situation before World War I—9
Seminar Presentation on the Historical and Pneumatological Interpretation of Scripture—9
Seminar Presentation on John and Paul—9
Seminar Presentation on Reason and Revelation—9
Seminar Presentation on Spirit and Grace in Frank—9

Bible Studies, Exercises, Lectures, Essays, Reports

1933–1934 Annual Report of the German Evangelical Church of Sydenham, London—13
1934–1935 Annual Report of the German Evangelical Church of Sydenham, London—13

Address in Gland—11
Address to the Fanø Conference—13
"After Ten Years": An Account at the Turn of the Year 1942–1943—8

Basic Questions of a Christian Ethic—10
Bethel Confession (First Draft and August Version)—12
Bible Study: King David—14
Bible Study Class on Fundamental New Testament Concepts—14
  Bonhoeffer's Notes on Holy Spirit
  On the Doctrine of the Holy Spirit
Bible Study on Ezra and Nehemiah: The Reconstruction of Jerusalem—14
Bible Study on Temptation—15
Bible Study on the Letters of Timothy (Student Notes)—14
Biblical Study Seminars on Basic New Testament Concepts—15
  Notes on Death
  Notes on the Concept of "Abstinence"
  Notes on the Concept of "Gratitude"
  Notes on the Concept of "Joy"
  Notes on the Concept of "Patience"
  Notes on the Concept of "Peace"
  Notes on the Concept of "Probation"
  Notes on the Concept of "Sin"
  Notes on the Concept of "Temptation"

Bonhoeffer's Lecture Concept for Confirmation Instruction—14
Bonhoeffer's Sketch for His Statement "From Barmen to Oeynhausen"—14

Catechetical Outlines—14
Appendix: On the Sixth Commandment (Student Notes)
"Catechetical Outline of a First Confirmation Class" (Student Notes)
"Conscience" (Student Notes)
"Outline on Christ the Lord" (Student Notes)
"Righteousness" (Student Notes)
Conference of the Central Office, Preliminary Report on—11
Conference of the Central Office, Primary Report on—11
Course Paper: "The Character and Ethical Consequences of Religious Determinism"—10
Course Paper: "The Religious Experience of Grace and the Ethical Life"—10

Discussion Paper for the Ecumenical Conference in Dassel—12
Disputation on Preaching the Law—14
Bonhoeffer's Queries (Student Notes)
Theses of Gerhard Ebeling
Doctrinal Examination on the Certainty of Salvation—9
Dogmatic Exercises on "Theological Anthropology"—12
Draft of a Lecture on the Theme of "Glory"—16
Draft Proposal for a Reorganization of the Church after the "End of the Church Struggle"—16

Essay: "Protestantism without Reformation"—15
Essay: "On the Question of Church Communion"—14
Bonhoeffer's Essay on Church Communion
Bonhoeffer's Questions concerning the Essay Discussion
Helmut Gollwitzer's Response to Bonhoeffer's Essay
Essay: "Concerning the Christian Idea of God"—10
Essay: "On Karl Heim's *Glaube und Denken*"—12
Essay: "On the Confessing Church and the Ecumenical Movement"—14
Essay: "Pastoral Care for Protestant Students at the Technical College"—11
Essay: "The Best Physician"—16
Essay: "The Church and the Jewish Question"—12
Essay: "The Younger Generation's Altered View of the Concept of Führer"—12

Essay: "Thy Kingdom Come! The Prayer of the Church-Community for God's Kingdom on Earth"—12
Essay: "What Is Church?"—12
Essay: "What Should a Student of Theology Do Today?"—12
Eulogy for Adolf von Harnack—10
Examination Paper: "The Meaning and Choice of a Biblical Text for the Sermon in the Worship of the Congregation"—10
Examination Paper: "What Is Paul's View on Earthly Suffering?"—10
Excerpt from Welcoming Address in Ciernohorské Kúpele (Transcription)—11
Exercises in the Pastoral Epistles (Fragment)—15
Expert Opinion on "False Teaching" in the Confessing Church—14

Fragment of an Essay: "What Does It Mean to Tell the Truth?"—16

Graduation Theses—9
Greetings to American Students—10

Homiletical Exercises—14
- Bonhoeffer's Sermon Outline on Isaiah 11:1–9 (Student Notes)
- On Luke 21:25–26
- On Memorial Day on Reminiscere Sunday, and on John 15:13–14 and Romans 5:6–8, 10a
- On Revelation 22:1–5

Homiletical Exercises—14
- Bonhoeffer's Outline on Exodus 20:2–3 (Student Notes) as a Sermon for Trinity Sunday
- Bonhoeffer's Sermon Outline on the Fourth Commandment Exodus 20:12 (Student Notes)
- On Acts 1:1–11
- On Luke 18:1–8
- On Matthew 17:1–9
- On Numbers 21:4–9
- On Revelation 1:9–20

Homiletical Exercises—14
- Bonhoeffer's Sermon Draft on Isaiah 60:1–6
- On Psalm 50:1–5

Initial Report on Youth Conferences of the World Alliance—11
Invitation to the "Thursday Circle"—9

Jesus Christ and the Essence of Christianity—10
"Joy" in Early Christianity: A Commemorative Paper
for Adolf von Harnack—9

Lecture: "The Führer and the Individual in the Younger Generation"—12
Lecture: "The Right to Self-Assertion"—11
Lecture and Discussion on the Power of the Keys and Church
Discipline—14
Bonhoeffer's Lecture on the Power of the Keys and Church Discipline
Discussion of the Lecture "The Power of the Keys and Church
Discipline in the New Testament and among the Reformers"
(Student Notes)
Theses regarding the Lecture in Finkenwalde (Transcription)
Lecture in Ciernohorské Kúpele: On the Theological Foundation
of the Work of the World Alliance—11
Lecture on Christ in the Psalms—14
Bonhoeffer's Notes
Conclusion of the Lecture (Student Notes)
Lecture on Contemporizing New Testament Texts—14
Bonhoeffer's Lecture Manuscript
Concluding Section of the Lecture (Student Notes)
Lecture on the Path of the Young Illegal Theologians
of the Confessing Church—15
Lecture on the Theology of Karl Barth and the Situation in Germany—13
Lecture on War—10
Lecture Outline: Theology and the Congregation—16
Lectures on Christology—12
Literary Attempt on the Theme of "Death"—11
Literary Attempt on the Theme of "Vocation"—11

Matriculation Essay on Catullus and Horace—9
Memorandum: "The Jewish-Christian Question as Status
Confessionis"—12
Memorandum: "The 'Social Gospel' (Soziale Evangelium)"—12

New Testament Examination on Baptism—9
Note on Luther's Lectures on the Letter to the Romans—9
Notes on Karl Barth's *Die Christliche Dogmatik im Entwurf*—9

Old Testament Examination on Amos—9
On Euripides' Philosophy—17 (for *DBWE* 9)

Paper on "The Catholic Church" for the "Thursday Circle"—9
Pastoral Duties—14
"Baptismal Homilies" (Student Notes)
"Funeral Homilies" (Student Notes)
Perels, Friedrich Justus: Draft of a Church Constitution following the Coup—16
Practical Exercises in Homiletics—14
Bonhoeffer's Sermon Outline on Isaiah 53 (Student Notes)
Bonhoeffer's Sermon Outline on Romans 6:1–11 (Student Notes)
Criteria and Mistakes (Student Notes)
On 1 Corinthians 1:18
On 1 Corinthians 15:12–19
On 1 Corinthians 15:20–28
On 2 Corinthians 5:19–21
On Galatians 3:10–13
On Galatians 6:14
On Hebrews 4:15–16
On Mark 4:26–29
On Romans 3:23–26
Prayers for Prisoners: Evening Prayer—8
Prayers for Prisoners: Morning Prayer—8
Prayers for Prisoners: Prayer in Particular Need—8
Preliminary Report on a Conference of the Provisional Bureau—11
Presentation on the History of the Protestant Hymn (Student Notes)—14
Primary Report on the Conference of the Provisional Bureau—11

Reading Notes for the Seminar "Ethical Interpretations of Current Events"—10
Bank Situation and the Court Corruption
First Page of Notes for the Course "Ethical Interpretations" of Current Events
Forced Exports in Russia
The German-Austrian Customs Union
Germany—Poland—Russia
The Power Utility Issue: Muscle Shoals
The Report of the Federal Council of Churches on Birth Control Situation in India
Unemployment
The Wickersham Report on Prohibition
Reading Notes for the Seminar "Ethical Viewpoints in Modern Literature"—10

Ernst Toller; Karel Čapek
Ibsen
Ludwig Lewisohn
Negro Literature
Sinclair Lewis
Theodore Dreiser
War Literature
Reflection: On Gratitude among Christians—16
Reflection on Easter: Resurrection—16
Reflection on the Ascension—16
Report on a Conference of the World Alliance in Cambridge—11
Report on a Meeting of the Provisional Bureau for Ecumenical Youth Work—11
Report on Experiences during Alarms—8
Report on Prison Life after One Year in Tegel—8
Report on the Theological Conference in Bruay-en-Artois—13
Report on the Youth Conference of the World Alliance in Epsom—11
Review of C. Cordes, *Der Gemeinschaftsbegriff*—11
Review of Friedrich Parpert, *Das Mönchtum und die evangelische Kirche*—10
Review of Robert Jelke, *Vernunft und Offenbarung*—12

Second Report on Youth Conferences of the World Alliance—11
Short Report on William James, *Varieties of Religious Experience*—10
Sketch for a Lecture by Eberhard Bethge: "The Significance of Mission to Non-Christians for the Church Renewal Movement"—16
Sketch of a Bible Study on 1 Corinthians 3—16
Study on "Personal" and "Objective" Ethics—16

Theological Position Paper on the *Primus Usus Legis*—16
Theological Position Paper on the Question of Baptism—16
Theological Position Paper on State and Church—16
Theses: The Discernible Nature of the Order of Creation—11
Theses for the Lecture in Ciernohorské Kúpele—11
Theses on "The Aryan Paragraph in the Church"—12
Theses Paper for the Fanø Conference: The Church and the Peoples of the World —13
Thesis Fragment: What Do We Learn from the Mission to Non-Christians?—16
Thesis Fragment about M. Heidegger and E. Grisebach—11
Thoughts on the Day of Baptism of Dietrich Wilhelm Rüdiger Bethge—8
Thoughts on William Paton's Book *The Church and the New Order*—16

Tragedy of the Prophetic and Its Lasting Meaning, The—10
Two Notes on Schleiermacher's Speeches on Religion—9

Unfinished Draft of a Pulpit Pronouncement following the Coup—16

Visser 't Hooft, Willem A.: On William Paton's Book *The Church and the New Order*—16

Poems

"By Powers of Good"—8
"Christians and Heathens"—8
"The Death of Moses"—8
"Fortune and Calamity"—8
"The Friend"—8
"Jonah"—8
"Night Voices"—8
"The Past"—8
"Stations on the Way to Freedom"—8
"Who Am I?"—8

Sermons and Meditations

Address on Jeremiah 27–28—9
Address on John 19—9
Address on Luke 12:35ff.—9
Address on Matthew 21:28–31—9
Address on the Decalogue—9
Address on the First Commandment—9

Baptismal Homily on Joshua 24:15—13
Baptism Sermon on 1 John 4:16—11
Baptism Sermon on Ephesians 5:14—11
Bible Reading and Prayer on 1 Corinthians 4:20—13
Biblical Reflection: Morning—14

Catechesis in the Second Theological Examination on the Fifth Petition of the Lord's Prayer—10
Catechetical Examination on Matthew 8:5–13—9
Catechetical Outline concerning the Second Article of Faith—9
Children's Address on Psalm 24:7—9

Communion Homily on 1 Corinthians 15:55—15
Confession Homily on Micah 4:9—15
Confirmation—15
  Confirmation Question
  Confirmation Sermon on Mark 9:24
  Confirmation Verses

Devotional Aids for the Moravian *Daily Texts*—16
  Daily Text Meditation for June 7 and 8, 1944
  Daily Text Meditation for Pentecost 1944
Devotions on John 8:31–32—11
Devotions on Luke 4:3–4—11
Devotions on Luke 4:5–8—11
Draft for a Catechism: As You Believe, So You Receive—11
Draft for a Liturgy, Remembrance Sunday—10
Draft for a Liturgy, Reminiscere (Memorial Day)—10
  Opening Liturgy
  Prayer
Draft for Worship Service on 2 Corinthians 2:14; 6:10; 6:1—15

Exegesis and Catechetical Lesson on Luke 9:57–62—9
Exegesis and Sermon on James 1:21–25—9
Exposition on Romans 9–11 (Student Notes)—14
Exposition on the First Table of the Ten Words of God—16

Fragment of a Wedding Sermon—13
Funeral Address on Luke 2:29–30—13
Funeral Liturgy and Homily on Proverbs 23:26 for Hans-Friedrich von Kleist-Retzow—16

Guide to Scriptural Meditation—14

Homily for the Children's Service—10
Homily on Daniel 10:1, 8, 16–19—12

Liturgy for a Seminar Worship Service—12
Liturgy Fragment for Christmas—15

Marriage Sermon on Ruth 1:16–17—13
Meditation and Catechetical Lesson on "Honor"—9

Meditation and Sermon on Luke 9:51–56 for the Theological Examination—9
Meditation on Luke 9:57–62—13
Meditation on Psalm 119—15
Bonhoeffer's Meditation (Fragment)
Two Structural Outlines of Psalm 119

Notes for a Young Man—10

Outline for a Homily for Personal Confession on Proverbs 28:13—14
Outline on Proverbs 3:27–33—14

Recommended Devotions on Jeremiah 16:21 and Ephesians 1:22–23—16

Sermon for Evening Worship Service on 2 Corinthians 12:9—13
Sermon for Evening Worship Service on Proverbs 16:9—13
Sermon for the Lector on Matthew 2:13–23—15
Sermon for the Second Theological Examination on 1 Thessalonians 5:16–18—10
Sermon (Fragment) on Deuteronomy 32:48–52—10
Sermon (Fragment) on Luke 12:49—10
Sermon (Fragment) on Matthew 7:1—10
Sermon (Fragment) on Song of Solomon 8:6b—10
Sermon Meditation on Isaiah 9:6–7—16
Sermon Meditation on Revelation 2:1–7—14
Sermon Meditations—15
Sermon Meditation on John 3:16–21 for the Second Day of Pentecost
Sermon Meditation on John 10:11–16 for Misericordias Domini Sunday
Sermon Meditation on John 14:23–31 for the First Day of Pentecost
Sermon Meditations on John 20:19–31 for Quasimodogeniti Sunday
Sermon on 1 Corinthians 2:7–10—13
Sermon on 1 Corinthians 12:27, 26—10
Sermon on 1 Corinthians 13:1–3—13
Sermon on 1 Corinthians 13:4–7—13
Sermon on 1 Corinthians 13:8–12—13
Sermon on 1 Corinthians 13:13—13
Sermon on 1 Corinthians 15:17—10
Pulpit Notes
Sermon
Sermon on 1 John 2:17—10
Sermon on 1 John 4:16—10, 11

Sermon on 1 Peter 1:7b–9—12
Sermon on 2 Chronicles 20:12—11
Sermon on 2 Corinthians 5:10—13
Sermon on 2 Corinthians 5:20—13
Sermon on 2 Corinthians 12:9—10
Sermon on Colossians 3:1–4—11
Sermon on Genesis 32:25–32; 33:10—11
Sermon on Exodus 32:1–8, 15–16, 18–20, 30–35—12
Sermon on Jeremiah 20:7—13
Sermon on John 8:32—11
Sermon on Judges 6:15–16; 7:2; 8:23—12
Sermon on Luke 1:39–56—14
Sermon on Luke 1:46–55
Sermon on Luke 12:35–40—11
Sermon on Luke 13:1–5—13
Sermon on Luke 16:19–31—11
Sermon on Luke 17:7–10—9
Sermon on Luke 17:33—10
Sermon on Luke 21:28—13
Sermon on Mark 9:23–24—13
Sermon on Matthew 5:8—10
Sermon on Matthew 8:23–27—12
Sermon on Matthew 11:28–30—13
Sermon on Matthew 16:13–18—12
Sermon on Matthew 18:21–35—14
Sermon on Matthew 24:6–14—11
Sermon on Matthew 26:45b–50—14
Sermon on Matthew 28:20—10
Sermon on Philippians 4:7—10
Sermon on Psalm 42—14
Sermon on Psalm 58—14
Sermon on Psalm 62:2—10
Sermon on Psalm 63:3—11
Sermon on Psalm 90—14
Sermon on Psalm 98:1—13
Sermon on Psalm 127:1—9
Sermon on Revelation 2:4–5, 7—12
Sermon on Revelation 3:20—10
Sermon on Revelation 14:6–13—14
Sermon on Romans 5:1–5—15
Sermon on Romans 11:6—10

Sermon on Romans 12:11c—10
Sermon on Romans 12:17–21—15
Sermon on Wisdom 3:3—13
Sermon on Zechariah 3:1–5—14
Supplements to the Monthly Letters from the Confessing Church Council of Brethren in Pomerania to Its Pastors—15
Meditation on Christmas
Meditation on Epiphany
Theological Reflection on the Lord's Supper

Wedding Sermon from the Prison Cell—8
Wedding Sermon on 1 Thessalonians 5:16–18—14
Wedding Sermon on John 13:34—14

Other Documents

Concerning the History of the Bethel Confession, by Carsten Nicolaisen—12
Theses on Youth Work in the Church—12
"Turning Away from the Phraseological to the Real": A Personal Recollection, by Hans Christoph von Hase—10

Master Indexes

Master Index of Scriptural References

OLD TESTAMENT

Genesis

Generally	9:217
1	1:60; 2:95; 3:74; 16:550, 602
1–3	1:4, 60–61, 63, 65; 3:1–5, 147–49; 4:29, 282; 6:300–301; 14:734, 771
1:1	3:158; 6:131; 11:150; 14:797
1:1–2	7:230
1:2	3:41; 6:392; 9:413
1:3	12:319
1:4–5	14:864
1:4ff.	3:161
1:5	3:42
1:9	3:50
1:11	3:50
1:22	16:519
1:26	3:61, 64; 9:534
1:26–27	3:162
1:27	4:31, 281; 6:210; 10:376; 14:540, 567, 728
1:27–28	14:791
1:28	6:210; 14:759; 16:519
1:31	6:53
1:31a	12:208
2	1:60; 16:550
2:1–3	8:537
2:3	3:155
2:4–3:14	3:157
2:4–3:24	3:74, 83
2:4b–25	3:95
2:6	3:38
2:7	3:160, 163, 164; 15:544
2:8–17	3:31, 165, 166; 15:387
2:9	6:309
2:14	14:453
2:15	6:70
2:16ff.	1:113
2:17	3:117, 125; 14:772

2:18	1:60; 6:210; 14:791; 16:629
2:18–25	3:12
2:20	3:42; 8:84; 16:387
2:23–24	6:210
2:24	3:171; 4:249; 6:304; 8:85
3	3:125, 171; 8:72; 4:171; 10:363; 14:377, 728, 733; 15:345–46; 16:602
3:1	3:169; 4:71; 6:311; 12:262; 13:307; 14:586; 15:391
3:1–3	3:102; 16:605
3:1–7	6:301
3:1–13	11:293
3:3	14:772
3:4	14:793
3:4–5	14:793, 960; 15:467
3:5	3:170; 4:7, 264, 282; 5:111; 6:277; 14:362, 545, 793
3:7	3:171; 6:304
3:7–11	14:771
3:9	9:499
3:13	12:288; 16:602
3:14–19	3:103; 14:362
3:15	14:535
3:16	8:87
3:17	9:255; 11:261; 12:384; 16:644
3:17–18	12:288
3:17–19	6:70; 13:371
3:19	8:87; 9:458; 10:518, 556; 14:794
3:20	3:97, 171
3:21	7:203; 8:215; 14:751
3:22	6:301–2; 7:58; 8:71
3:22a	3:93
3:22–24	7:229
3:24	6:302; 11:461; 14:596, 794
3:28	3:97
4ff.	6:389
4:1	7:230
4:1–16	15:467
4:8	9:458
4:9	5:104
4:10	6:138
4:10–11	14:790
4:12	14:793
4:15	14:771
4:17	6:71; 8:386
4:17ff.	6:70, 389; 16:520
4:17–24	6:71
4:20	6:71
4:21	6:71
4:22	6:71
4:22ff.	6:72
4:23–24	6:71
5	3:32; 4:171
6	9:485
6:4	7:165
6:5–8	14:724
6:14	4:260
6:19	14:724
8:2	1:109
8:21	12:516; 14:792
8:21–9:17	14:797

8:22 6:168; 14:767
9:5 9:241
9:6 14:790
9:20–23 14:729
9:20–28 9:459
10 16:521
11 9:473; 11:352; 16:521
11:1–9 11:352; 12:159; 14:399, 902
12:1 4:97, 251; 14:808
12:1ff. 4:91
12:10–20 15:70
13 16:602
14 9:168
15:5 4:97, 98
15:6 9:431; 10:385
15:15 15:378
17:1 10:484; 12:222; 13:395; 14:784, 796
18:15 16:602
18:20 4:192
18:22–23 11:55
18:23–33 16:496
18:32 1:120
19:4–5 4:192
19:27 5:52; 14:864–65
19:30–35 14:729
20:1–18 15:70
21:1 9:431
21:12 14:868
22 14:392; 16:602
22:1 15:348, 400
22:1–19 4:97
22:3 5:52
22:7 9:218
23:4 9:242; 15:521
25:8 8:397; 15:378
25:29–34 14:191, 587
25:33 4:34, 125
27 16:602
29:35 15:379
31 16:602
32:10 15:237
32:22–29 12:296
32:24–31 11:25, 428–33
32:24ff. 7:76
32:25–32 10:585; 14:596
32:26 9:427; 10:527
32:26b 12:8
32/33 11:428
33:10 10:585; 11:428–33
34 16:602
35:1 15:412
37 16:602
37:35 8:447
38 6:210
38:6–10 6:210
39:23 8:400, 441, 492; 16:628
41:52 8:326
43:33 9:241
44 16:602
45:1ff. 4:138
47:9 15:521
50:19 14:798
50:20 14:797–98

Exodus

Generally 9:217
1:1 16:602
1:11 8:533
1:19–20 16:602
1:39 3:121
3:14 1:47
3:18 16:499, 602

4:10 9:229; 13:380
7–9 15:339
7:11, 22 15:339
8:16 5:52
9:13 5:52
13:18 8:533, 534
13:21 8:533
13:21–22 8:534; 15:504
14:21–22 8:533; 15:40
14:31 9:229
15:1–18 15:168
15:1–21 5:65
15:2 15:246
15:11–13 4:17, 254
15:20–21 13:342
15:26 15:319; 16:126, 500
16 4:162; 15:477
16:4 15:348, 400
16:7 14:864
16:7–8 8:533
16:13–14 14:864
17:10–13 14:1041
19:5–6 12:417
19:12 16:633
19:18 8:535
20:1–7 11:335
20:2 14:784; 15:499; 16:634
20:2–3 12:475; 14:34, 153, 635, 788
20:2–11 16:24
20:2–17 6:358; 14:788
20:3 16:637
20:4 16:639
20:4–10 6:358
20:5 1:110; 4:54; 14:888
20:7 9:361; 16:640
20:7, 12–17 15:483
20:8 16:642
20:8–11 16:594
20:10 16:643
20:12 4:60; 6:381; 8:86; 14:645; 16:594
20:13 10:370; 11:367; 12:260; 14:730
20:13–15 6:382
20:14 14:728
20:16 14:689
20:17 14:734
20:18 16:633
20:32–33 9:459
21:10 6:210
21:24 6:144
22:10 4:128
22:20 15:521
23:4–5 4:138
23:7 6:196, 422, 454; 16:119, 680
24:4 5:52; 14:865
24:11 5:73
25:22 15:503
30:35 4:111
31:18 14:655; 15:503; 16:633
32 12:140, 472
32:1–8 8:533; 12:472–76, 517
32:11–14 10:509
32:15–16 12:472–76, 517; 14:655; 16:633
32:18–20 12:472–76, 517
32:30–32 16:497
32:30–35 12:472–76, 517
32:32 1:184; 11:322
33:7 3:96
33:9 3:42
33:11 8:535

33:26 3:96
33:29 3:96
34:6 9:228
34:10 8:242
34:33 14:855
34:35 14:855
36:9 3:44
38:21 15:503

Leviticus
Generally 9:217
1:8 14:729
1:12 14:729
3:3–4 14:729
7:22–27 14:729
10:1ff. 15:430
11ff. 15:332
11:44–45 9:495
16:10 4:88
16:16–17 4:254
16:21–22 4:88
18:3 9:232
18:5 14:355; 15:499
19:2 4:254, 260; 9:495; 10:337, 566; 14:725, 785, 794
19:18 4:74
19:33–34 12:389
19:34 12:389
20:7 9:495
20:25 9:232
20:26 9:495
21:8 4:254; 260
22:30 14:864
23:43 14:922
24:20 4:131; 6:144
24:22 12:389
25:23 15:521
26:6 8:139; 15:365

Numbers
Generally 9:217
5:16 12:389
6:1–21 14:729, 734
6:2–3 14:720, 734
6:24–26 16:632
6:27 14:784
9:15 15:503
11:16 14:823
11:23 8:511
12:2 15:430
12:3 8:536
12:7 9:229, 238
12:8 8:535; 9:229
14:18 9:229
14:36 (37) 8:533
15:22ff. 15:513
16 8:533
16:3 15:431
16:11 15:431
16:49 8:533
17:14 8:533
18:20 9:224
18:27 9:223
20:12 8:534
20:13 8:593
21:4–9 8:533; 14:650
21:5 14:652
21:6 8:533
21:8 14:653
27:12–13 8:532
27:14 8:534
32:5–6 15:427
32:16–24 15:427
34:2 9:224

Deuteronomy
Generally 9:217
1:37 8:532
4:2 16:636

4:6	16:636
4:6–10	15:499
4:7	16:636
4:8–9	16:636
4:13	16:633
4:34	9:223
5:6–21	11:335
5:9	4:54; 14:792, 888
5:14	6:278
5:15	15:499
5:16	8:86
5:19	16:634
5:22	16:633
6:4–5	15:309; 16:640
6:5	4:74
6:6	15:220
6:12	15:518
6:13	4:128; 11:419
6:16	15:409
6:20–23	15:498
6:20–25	15:498
6:24	15:498
7:7–11	12:417; 15:499
7:18	15:499
8:2	15:400, 499
8:16	15:503
9:10	16:633
10:4	16:633
10:18–19	8:538
10:20	4:128
12:10–11	14:882
14:2	9:223
18:15	14:799
18:18	9:340
21:23	14:358
24:14	12:388
27:9	15:500
27:26	14:355, 357, 793; 15:526
28:25	5:28
30:11ff.	15:437
32:1–14	15:168
32:6–7	15:379
32:7–18	15:499
32:8	9:223
32:15–47	15:168
32:35	12:419; 14:967
32:48–52	7:37; 10:585–89, 631, 640
32:49	8:532
32:49–50	8:532
32:51	8:534
33:1	8:532
33:3	15:499
34:1	8:531
34:4	8:532
34:10	8:242, 535

Joshua

Generally	9:217
1:8	15:437
2:11	15:502
3:1	5:52
6:12	5:52
22:3–4	15:427
24:15	13:364

Judges

2:22	15:400, 408
4, 5	13:342
5	14:906
5:20	9:225
5:31	5:49
6–8	14:166
6:15–16	12:23, 461–67, 520
7:2	12:23, 461–67, 520; 13:309
8:22–23	14:378

8:23 12:23, 461–67, 520
9:22 9:225
9:54 15:376

Ruth
1:16–17 13:358–59
2:11–12 8:376

1 Samuel
Generally 9:217, 221
2:1 15:361
2:1–10 14:906; 15:168
2:6 15:401
2:10 8:292
3:10 5:80; 10:502; 14:787
5 10:511
10:6 6:295
10:7 6:295
15:22 9:168; 15:432
16:1 14:875
16:7 6:284; 7:79; 14:792
16:11 14:875
16:13 14:875
16:14 14:875
16:23 5:158; 14:875
17:28 14:876
17:33 14:876
17:37 14:876
17:39 14:876
17:42–43 14:876
17:47 14:876
18:1 14:877
18:1–5 7:115
18:3 14:877
18:4 14:878
18:11 14:877
19:10 14:877
20 7:115
20:17 14:877
21:11–16 14:877
22:2 14:878
22:3 14:878
23:2–5 14:880
23:17 14:878
24:6 14:878
24:7 4:138; 14:878
24:18 14:877, 879
25 14:879
25:32 14:879
26:8 14:879, 891
26:10–11 14:879
26:19 9:224
26:21 14:877
26:21–25 14:879
27:1–12 14:877
28 15:375, 378
28:3–25 15:432
31 8:511, 582
31:4 6:199; 8:508, 582; 15:376
31:4–5 15:411

2 Samuel
Generally 9:221
1:26 14:877
2:4 14:880, 893
3:28–37 14:880
3:33 15:378
5:3 14:880, 893
5:8 14:880
5:12 14:880
6 14:892
6:2 14:880
6:7 14:881
6:8 14:881
6:14 14:881
6:22 14:881

7	13:218; 14:448, 922
7:1	14:881
7:5	4:11–14, 223; 14:448, 883
7:6	14:881
7:11	14:883
7:11–14	14:448
7:12	14:883
7:13	14:872, 883
7:14	14:884, 883–84
7:15	14:884
7:16	14:883–84
7:18	14:884
7:19	14:885
7:23	14:884
7:23–29	14:885, 893
11:1	14:886
11:5	14:886
11:6	14:886
11:8–13	14:886
11:27	14:886
12:7	14:887
12:8	14:887
12:9	14:887
12:10	14:887
12:11	14:887
12:13	14:888
12:15	14:888
12:16	14:888
12:20	14:889
12:24–25	14:889
12:29	14:890
12:30–31	14:890
14:14	15:378
15:23	14:890
15:25	14:891
15:26	14:891
16:7	14:891
16:9	14:891
16:10	14:891
16:21	14:890
16:22	14:890
17:23	6:200; 15:376
19:14–15	14:891
19:36 (35)	14:733
21:10	15:378
22:32	9:225
22:36	9:230
23:1	14:892
23:2	14:873, 875, 892
23:2–3	5:159
23:3	14:892
23:4	14:892
23:5	14:892
23:6	14:892
23:7	14:892
23:8–39	14:892
24	14:892
24:1	9:431; 15:348, 400, 402
24:1–15	14:659
24:14	14:966
24:18	14:892

1 Kings

Generally	9:217, 221
1	13:218
1:1–4	14:893
2:1–4	14:893
2:2–3	15:275
2:5–9	14:893
5:3	14:882
5:5 (4:25)	14:729
5:17	14:882
5:18 (5:4)	14:882
8:20	14:884
12:25–33	15:432
16:18	15:376

19	14:303
19:4	13:39
19:5	14:1011
19:7	14:1011
19:10	14:869
19:14	14:869
19:18	14:869
19:20	9:479
22:8	15:365

2 Kings

Generally	9:221
2:11	12:286
5:18	16:639
6:22	4:138
17	10:339
18:13–19:37	13:135
19	10:339; 13:217
24:10–12	9:515

1 Chronicles

Generally	9:221
17:14	14:883
21:1	9:431
22:8	14:882
25:2	5:160
28:3	14:882
29:15	9:242

2 Chronicles

Generally	9:217, 221
16:12	16:499
20:12	4:61; 6:412; 8:38; 10:36; 11:121, 362, 384, 434–40, 478, 497; 12:42, 213; 13:24
25:22–27	9:515
32:31	15:348, 510

Ezra

1	14:721
1:1	14:919
1:3	14:919
1:5	14:919
1:6	14:921
1:8	14:922
2:1–61	14:920
2:2	14:856, 922
2:64	14:919
2:68–69	14:921
3:1	14:919
3:1–4	14:922
3:2	14:922
3:5	14:921
3:6	14:922
3:8	14:922
3:9	14:920
3:11	14:923
3:12	14:923
3:13	14:923
4:1–2	14:923
4:2	14:923–24, 926
4:3	14:922, 924
4:7–16	14:925
4:17–22	14:925
4:23	14:925
5	14:927
5:1–5	14:926
5:2	14:922
6	14:927
6:16	14:927
6:21–22	14:927
8:22	14:920
8:31–32	14:920
10	14:921, 930

Nehemiah

2:18	14:921
2:19	14:926
3:34	14:926

3:38 (4:6) 14:926
4:2 14:926
4:6 14:926
4:8 14:926
4:10 14:926
4:11 14:926
4:14 14:926
4:15 14:926
5:10–12 14:921
6:15–16 14:927, 931
6:16 14:927, 931
8:1ff. 14:928
8:8–9 14:928
8:9–12 14:929
8:10 14:180
8:30 14:929
9:34 15:503
10:31 (30) 14:930

Esther

Generally 9:217
8:13 9:226
9:23 9:250

Job

Generally 8:81, 302; 9:217, 420–36
1 8:302
1:1 9:421
1:4 9:421
1:5 14:865
1:6–12 14:793
1:9–11 15:398
1:21 8:266; 14:739
2:10 9:423
2:11 9:423
3 9:428
3–31 9:421, 423, 429, 431, 432, 433, 434
3ff. 10:386
3:11 9:423
3:20 9:423
4:17 9:424
5:7 9:424
5:8 9:225
5:12–13 16:486
5:13 16:484
5:17 9:424
6:2 9:424
6:19 9:421
6:24 9:424
7:1 7:214; 8:388
7:8 9:424
7:13 9:424
7:17 9:424; 10:389
7:21 9:424
8 9:424
9 9:430, 431
9:1 9:424
9:3 9:424
9:4 9:424
9:17 9:425, 430
9:23 9:425
9:29 9:425
10:2 9:425
10:20 9:425
11:6 9:425
12:4 9:425
12:6 6:356; 9:425
12:9 9:425
12:10 9:425
12:14 9:424
13 9:429
13:3 9:425
13:7 9:425
13:10 9:425
13:15 6:356; 9:425
13:16 9:429
13:25 9:429
14:3ff. 9:424
14:10ff. 9:426

14:14 1:109; 9:239
14:15–17 9:426
14:18–22 9:426
16 9:429
16:2 9:423
16:5 9:423
16:6–16 9:426
16:8 9:426
16:10 9:421
16:17 9:426
16:20ff. 9:426
19 9:426–27, 429; 16:163
19:3 9:421
19:20 9:421
19:25–27 9:427
19:25ff. 9:432
19:27 9:429
20:6–7 9:427
21 9:427
22:23 9:246
23 9:427
23:12 15:515
25:4 15:346
26:7 9:432
27:12 8:407
28 9:433
28ff. 10:386
28:23 9:235
28:25 9:255
29 9:427
29:7 9:421
30:1 9:421
31 9:429
31:21 9:421
31:33 9:424
31:40 9:427, 429
32 9:432
32–37 10:386
33:17 9:429
35:10 13:357
36:9 9:429
36:15 9:429
38 9:430, 433; 14:796
38:1 9:429
38:4 3:29
38:6 9:432
38:7 5:65
38:26ff. 9:429, 432
40:2–4 6:256
40:8–14 9:429, 431, 432
40:10 9:429
41:11 15:235
42:2 14:796
42:3, 6 15:406
42:5 9:427
42:7 8:407; 9:432; 15:406
42:7ff. 8:266
42:10 9:423, 426
42:10a 9:423
42:17 15:378

Psalms

Generally 8:24, 63, 81, 180, 187, 269, 269, 336, 369, 431; 9:217, 224
1 5:160, 164; 14:320; 15:25, 85; 16:387
1:1 9:272
1:2 12:433; 14:654
2 5:160, 166, 176
2:7 9:491
2:7–8 14:884
2:9 10:336; 12:462
2:11 15:516
3 5:149; 8:81
4:4 5:100
5 5:57, 172, 174

5:4	5:51
5:5	14:794
5:11	10:381
6	5:171
6:6	15:379, 380
7	5:172, 174
7:1	9:431
7:2	14:784
7:18	15:380
8	5:163; 10:389
8:3	16:555
8:5	12:220
8:6	9:534; 14:797
8:7	14:797
9	5:172, 174
9:2	15:379
9:10	14:791
9:16	6:162
9:17	6:162
9:19–20	8:361
10	5:174
11:7	9:427; 10:88
11:19	12:213
12	12:223
13	5:150, 169; 8:80
13:1	8:80, 582
13:5–6	15:223
14	1:109; 5:171
14:1	9:277
15	5:167, 171
15:1–3	14:791
16	5:172, 174; 9:167; 15:277
16:6	15:499
16:9	5:176
17	5:172
17:3	5:173
17:3ff.	9:431
17:5	9:427
17:14–15	5:176
17:26	9:431
18:24	5:172
18:30 (29)	8:235, 236
19	5:163, 164; 14:797; 15:502, 507
19:2–5	14:595
19:3	10:552
20	5:166
20:5	15:24
20:8	8:485
21	5:166, 174
21:19	15:354
22	5:166; 14:392, 393
22:1	4:90; 7:165; 10:357, 523
22:2	5:162; 10:465; 14:873; 15:395, 413
22:4	14:1011
22:9	5:166
22:12	8:269
22:16	14:873
22:19	5:166
22:23	5:166; 14:872
23	5:168, 171, 174; 14:796; 15:277, 505
23:1	8:485
23:1, 2, 4	15:59
23:2	4:184
23:4	5:171
24:1	4:262; 14:791
24:7	9:6, 509–14; 10:545
25	5:171
25:5	15:322
25:6–10	14:760, 764
25:10	15:23
25:17	8:269
26	5:172

27	5:168
27:4	8:231
27:9	15:322, 392
27:10–11	14:738
27:14	16:284
28	5:174
28:2	9:255
28:7	15:218
29	5:163
30:5	8:389
30:6 (5)	5:112; 15:388
30:6	14:864
30:10	15:380
31	5:150, 169, 171, 174; 8:80; 15:277
31:6	5:162; 8:196, 342; 14:873
31:15	8:72, 73, 80, 196, 582; 10:530
32	15:278, 314, 317
32:1ff.	14:810
32:5	9:300
32:7	8:269
33:5	15:551
33:9	9:559; 12:462; 14:797
33:18	9:230
33:20	3:96
34	5:176; 9:590; 15:277
34:11	15:501
34:12	14:784
34:13	15:501
34:19	8:409; 16:631
34:20	8:493
35	5:169, 170, 171, 174
36	5:174
36:9	3:42, 44; 15:118
37	5:168, 171
37:3	8:415
37:3–4	5:168
37:4	15:501
37:5	8:164; 14:281, 797;15:169, 212
37:7	15:501, 502
37:9	15:502
37:11	15:502
37:15	6:199
37:16	5:168; 15:501
37:18	9:224
37:25	15:501
37:37	15:501
38	5:170, 171
38:5	8:422
38:10	15:387, 404, 506
38:11	15:387
38:22	15:392
39	5:171, 176
39:4	10:519
39:5	11:449
39:13	15:522
40	5:171, 174; 9:590
40:4	15:381
40:7–9	14:872
41	5:169, 171, 172, 174
41:5	5:173; 15:21
41:14	12:355
42	5:167, 178; 14:845–54, 1012–13, 1015; 15:275, 277
42:2	10:512; 14:1012
42:3	15:14, 275
42:5	5:28
42:6	8:475; 9:44; 14:1012

42:12 14:1012
43 15:277
43:1 5:173
44 5:169, 170, 172, 174
44:21 15:218
44:35 5:176
45 5:167; 14:453
45:10 5:167
45:11 14:453
46 5:167; 9:167
46:5 5:51, 146
46:6 5:51; 14:864
46:9 14:764
47 5:149; 8:81, 187
48 5:167
48:7 8:269
49 11:324
49:8–9 1:187; 5:106; 11:324
49:16 5:176
50 5:167, 168; 8:276; 9:91; 10:337
50:1 14:595
50:1–5 14:368, 595
50:1–6 14:368, 595
50:2 14:595
50:3 14:595
50:4 14:595
50:5 14:595
50:6 14:595
50:13–14 14:595
50:14 15:379
50:14–23 15:509
50:15 8:276
50:19 9:246
50:20–21 5:95
50:22–23 14:595
50:23 5:168; 15:379, 412; 16:492
51 5:171; 12:220
51:3 14:795
51:5ff. 9:300
51:6 4:256
51:7 1:110; 14:727, 737, 793
51:10 4:12, 107; 10:515
51:12–14 14:810
51:12–19 14:813
51:13 9:235; 14:477
51:17 4:45; 14:529
51:19 14:813
52 5:174
54 5:169, 174
54:4 8:409; 16:629
55 5:169, 174
55:18 14:864
56 5:169
56:8 14:955
56:9 14:848, 955
56:14 5:176
57:5 14:864
57:8–9 5:51, 146
58 5:54, 174; 8:361; 14:963–70, 1011
58:5 1:109
58:11 8:361
59 5:172, 174
59:17 15:100
60 8:150; 14:392
60:2 8:150
60:12 8:236
60:14 8:236
61 5:169
61:7–8 5:167
62 15:277
62:2 4:158; 8:475; 10:6, 127, 500–505, 637

62:13	14:610
63	5:167, 171
63:2	5:51
63:4	5:169; 11:401–8; 15:502
63:5–9	5:78
63:12	5:167
64:4	15:389
65	5:169
65:1	5:81
65:2	5:81
65:3	8:282
66	5:172
66:10	15:400
67	5:161
68	5:172, 174; 8:60
68:19	8:66
68:20	8:66, 195
69	5:166, 172, 174; 14:393; 15:352
69:6	5:166, 173
69:7–8	4:87
69:28	14:610
69:31	15:379
70	5:149, 174; 8:60, 81, 187
70:5	3:96
71	5:174
71:9	15:392
71:18	15:24, 392
72	5:166
72:20	5:160
73	5:171, 172; 9:167; 15:278
73:14	14:864
73:23ff.	9:427
73:24	5:176
73:25–26	5:169; 15:481
74	5:148, 169; 15:3, 84, 574
74:8	15:573
74:9–10	5:148
74:16	5:80
75	15:85
75:1	16:640
75:2	15:226
77:13, 19–20	15:505
77:38	9:228
78	5:160, 165
78:2	14:427
78:68–72	14:882
78:69	14:875
79	5:169, 170
80	9:396
80:4	14:738
81	5:167
81:7	8:534
84	5:167
84:6	15:385
85	13:199; 15:278
85:9	13:12, 201, 307; 14:412
85:15	9:228
86	5:169, 172
86:11	9:460; 14:600, 604, 784, 789
87	5:167
87:1	12:481; 13:189
87:5 (4–6)	14:453
88	5:169
88:11	15:380
88:12	15:379
88:14	5:51, 146
90	5:176; 8:246; 14:127; 16:284
90:4	12:458; 15:25
90:12	7:28; 13:59
90:14	8:381
91	5:173; 8:417
91:7	16:58
91:11	8:417, 549; 16:631

94	9:409
94:11	16:484
94:12	16:627
94:12–13	8:400
94:12–13a	16:627
94:13a	16:627
95:7–8	4:191; 8:201
95:11	3:70
95:27–28	3:70
96	5:176
96:1	5:65
97	5:176
98	5:176
98:1	5:65; 8:374; 13:353–57; 14:710
99	4:254
100:2	15:147; 16:377
100:4	15:380
102	5:169, 171, 176
102:8	9:228
102:18–19	15:381
102:22	15:381
103	9:226
103:2	15:412
103:8–10	14:794
103:13	14:796
103:15	10:520
103:16	14:635
104	5:163; 14:797
104:2	14:638
104:13–14	15:22
104:23	5:74
104:29–30	12:462; 14:797
104:30	14:797
105	5:165, 169
105:1	15:379
106	5:165
106:2	15:379
106:32–33	8:534
106:47	15:381
107:1–3	15:379
107:16	5:110; 6:16–17
107:22	15:379
108:4	15:379
109	5:28
109:4	4:139
110	4:40; 5:28, 166, 176; 14:392
110:2	4:139, 244; 14:361, 884; 15:469
110:2b	4:40
110:3	12:370
111:9	14:789
111:10	8:44; 14:784
112	15:502
115:1	14:784
115:3	14:796
115:9–11	3:96
116:13	12:450
116:16	15:379
118	5:180
118:15	5:176
118:15–16	2:95
118:17	14:893; 15:103
118:21	15:380
119	5:57, 58, 120, 156, 164, 178, 180; 8:431, 550; 12:220; 14:184, 570, 625; 15:28, 132, 133, 238, 296, 496ff., 500, 506, 513, 527; 16:5, 637
119:1	15:496–502
119:1–21	6:387
119:2	15:503–4
119:3	15:504–5

119:4 15:505
119:5 14:787; 15:506–7
119:6 15:507–8
119:7 14:787; 15:508–9
119:8 15:392, 509–11
119:9 6:187; 14:570; 15:511–12
119:10 15:512–13
119:11 15:513–14
119:12 14:784; 15:514
119:13 15:515
119:14 15:515–17
119:15 15:517–18
119:16 15:518–19
119:17 15:519–20
119:18 14:787; 15:520–21
119:19 5:164; 6:58; 11:362; 12:213; 14:787, 808; 15:521–24
119:20 15:524–25
119:21 15:526
119:32 16:637
119:45 4:59; 14:219
119:48 14:654
119:54 9:242
119:62 15:380
119:71 15:238, 246
119:89 14:229
119:92 16:636
119:94 8:475; 14:784
119:96 14:794
119:99 14:570; 15:511
119:100 14:570; 15:511
119:105 14:655; 15:225
119:120 14:386
119:147 5:51, 146; 14:864
119:147–48 14:784, 932
119:164 14:811, 932
119:176 15:497
120–122 14:310
120:5 9:242
121 5:71
121:1 14:638
121:1–2 3:96
121:3 15:505
121:4 5:79
121:6 8:448
121:7 5:80
123–25 14:310
124:8 3:96; 14:789
126 5:167; 14:918
126:3 14:689
126:5–6 10:536
126–28 14:310
127:1 9:316; 462, 47
127:1–2 4:166; 16:643
127:2 5:52, 73; 14:865
127:3 8:86
129–31 14:310
130 4:44; 5:171; 14:810
130:3 13:329
132–34 14:310
133:1 5:27; 8:453
137 5:167, 174; 14:918
137:1 12:480; 15:578
139 11:319; 14:389
139:1–2 14:792
139:1–3 14:797–98
139:1–10 14:377
139:5 8:549
139:6 12:450
139:7–8 2:95
139:11–12 14:1011
139:12 13:328; 14:856
139:21 4:138

139:23 15:350
143 5:171; 15:346
143:2 14:610; 15:346
144:1 7:214; 8:388
145:15–16 5:77
145:18 14:784
147 16:255
147:20 16:636
148 16:547
148–50 5:176

Proverbs

Generally 8:521; 9:217, 225, 230
1 15:290
1:2 9:231
1:7 8:44; 9:230, 231, 238
1:29 9:230, 231
2:5 9:230
3 15:290
3:4 9:232
3:5 14:861
3:11 9:231
3:12 9:231
3:19 9:235
3:27–33 14:860–62
4:1 14:790
4:13 4:314
4:18 8:379, 390
4:23 8:387
6:20–22 8:385
7:3 9:232
8 15:290
8:1 9:235
8:13 9:230
8:17 15:554
8:22 9:235
9:10 9:230
9:13 8:86
12:4 8:86
13:1 14:790
14 15:290
14:15 9:248
14:31 16:491
14:34 16:524
16:4 9:231
16:9 13:397–400
17:6 14:790
18 15:290
18:10 16:640
18:24 8:234, 388
19:17 14:791
21:25 15:506
22:11–12 8:367
23:26 5:108; 8:379; 14:784, 813, 1042; 15:476, 481; 16:617, 621
24 8:105; 9:233
24:10 8:73, 105
24:11–12 8:367
24:12 9:233
24:21 4:140
25:2 8:521
25:21–22 4:138; 15:470
28 15:290, 314, 317
28:13 5:112; 14:813, 862
30:7–9 8:386
30:8 8:386; 14:791
30:9 8:386
30:17 14:790
31 8:73
31:8 4:237; 12:44; 13:83, 217; 14:433
31:10 8:86
31:11–13 8:85
31:15 8:85

31:20 8:85
31:25 8:73, 85
31:28–29 8:85

Ecclesiastes

Generally 8:521; 9:230
1:2 10:517
2:24–25 6:187; 10:101
2:25 5:73; 6:187
3 6:365; 8:229
3:1 13:93
3:1–8 6:366; 8:72
3:1–4:11 15:389
3:4–5 8:229
3:7 5:84; 8:229; 13:93
3:11 8:229
3:12 6:187
3:13 6:365
3:15 8:229, 230, 385, 575
4:10 5:102
5:1 4:155
5:2 3:151; 8:521
5:2–3 8: 521
5:18 12:257
7:8 5:97
7:15 16:288
7:24 16:608
8:15 5:73
9:4–11 6:187
9:7 5:73
9:7–8 6:187
9:10 6:295; 9:499
9:12 15:389
11:9 6:187; 15:512
11:10 12:516
12:1 15:511, 512
12:12 10:101; 14:517; 15:91

Song of Solomon

Generally 3:173; 8:24, 410, 521
7:6 8:394
8:6 10:6, 152, 357, 537–38, 638; 13:378

Isaiah

Generally 9:217
2:2–4 4:112; 14:760, 764
2:3 16:633
2:3–4 14:777
2:12 10:338
2:14–17 10:338
3:5 9:232; 12:516
5:11 14:734, 864
5:25 8:276
6 10:337
6:1–8 14:193
6:3 13:357; 15:276; 14:796
6:5 1:116; 12:450
6:9 10:329
6:11 10:329
7:9 10:339; 13:127
7:14 4:217, 258; 14:799
8:18 8:371, 381, 396
9 6:394
9:3–4 6:394
9:5, 6 15:85
9:5–6 14:799
9:5–7 12:450
9:6 16:614
9:6–7 14:299; 16:106, 611–15
9:7 14:873
9:11 8:276

9:11–10:4 8:276
9:16 8:276
9:20 8:276
10:4 8:276
11:1 14:873; 15:494
11:1–2 12:449; 14:799
11:1–9 14:753–55; 15:494
11:2 9:248
12 15:168
12:1 15:379
12:2 9:230; 12:449
17 2:42
20 10:331
21:11 14:369
21:11–12 14:219
22:4 10:330
22:12–14 10:338
22:13 9:506
22:22 16:613
23 14:727
23:1–14 14:727
23:18 14:727
23:23 2:95
25:8 1:289; 15:487
26 9:167
26:9 14:864
26:20 8:389
28:1 14:729
28:7 14:729
28:16 10:339; 15:231
28:21 14:339
28:29 15:275
31:3 10:339
33:6 9:248
35:10 12:471; 15:235; 16:377
36–37 10:339
36–38 13:135
37 13:217
38:9–20 15:168
38:18 8:447; 15:378
38:20 10:262; 15:381
40 15:385
40:1 1:119
40:3 6:164; 9:460
40:3–5 6:161
40:4 6:161
40:6 9:159
40:6–8 14:764
40:7 13:322
40:8 14:655; 15:25
40:12–25 14:796
40:25 14:789
40:31 9:460; 15:370
41:4 10:495
41:9 15:218
41:10 8:475; 13:350; 14:789
42 14:156
42:3 4:54; 16:569
42:8 14:789
42:16 8:264
43:1 8:475; 10:525; 11:426; 13:330, 350; 14:735; 15:136
43:18–19 3:21
43:24 4:190; 14:592
45:6 15:275
45:7 15:275
45:9 14:835
45:19 15:227
49 14:156
49:8 15:486
49:14ff. 15:519
50:4 14:864–65
51:7 4:258
53 5:101; 8:218, 480, 481; 9:433;

14:34, 39, 156, 168, 359–61, 804, 869
53:1 8:481
53:2 11:347; 14:88; 15:537
53:2–3 14:360
53:3 14:360, 584, 873
53:4 4:5, 215; 5:101, 170; 8:479; 14:584; 15:318, 407
53:4–5 5:101; 8:480; 14:360
53:5 9:521
53:6 12:399
53:7 8:481; 9:218, 222; 14:360
53:8 14:360; 15:409
53:11 4:12, 190; 14:361
53:12 9:521; 14:752
54 14:156
54:7 4:258; 14:872–73; 15:387
55 9:363
55:3 14:872
55:6 15:274
55:8 10:483, 525
55:8–9 12:458; 14:168
55:11 1:232, 234, 269, 271, 280; 9:315, 528; 12:406
56:10 8:466
57:18 8:400; 16:626
58:3 9:246
58:7 5:74; 6:163
59:11 13:92
59:20–21 14:635
60:1–6 14:597–99
60:6 14:599
62:5 15:516
63:10 9:235
63:16 14:796
64:1 11:413
64:5 15:346
65:1 10:127; 12:423; 14:784
65:17 8:464; 11:381
65:19 15:363
66:1 9:462
66:8 14:760, 764
66:12–13 1:228
66:13 13:333, 336
66:22 8:464; 11:381
66:26 1:228

Jeremiah

Generally 9:217
1:4–8 15:431
1:5 13:350
1:6 12:516
1:6–8 12:450
2 9:396
2:2 9:246
2:19 15:407
3:15 15:432
4:18 15:407
6:14 7:172; 10:329; 13:351
8:11 7:172; 10:329
9:9–10 10:340
9:20–22 10:340
12:1 9:420
13:23 9:514
13:23–25 10:339
14:7–9 16:497
14:19–22 16:497
15:10 10:334
15:19 12:450; 15:437
16:21 16:625–26, 625

17:5	14:145; 15:507
17:8	16:387
17:9	8:79; 14:225
17:10	16:256
18:1–11	9:462
18:6	14:835
18:14	9:255
20:7	4:85, 294; 7:27, 223; 13:347–53; 14:966; 15:485
20:7–10	10:332
20:8	9:298
20:14	9:423, 514
20:14–15	10:333
20:14–18	11:253
20:18	10:333
20:24	9:423
23:5–6	14:799
23:9–15	10:329
23:21	15:430
23:32	15:430
23:35	16:213
25:3	9:514
25:15–29	11:455
25:15ff.	15:275
26:1	9:515
26:4	9:232
27:1–22	9:516
27:3	9:516
27:4	9:516
27:9–11	9:517
27:11	8:389
27–28	9:514–19; 10:331
28	9:516; 15:365
28:1–17	9:518
28:12–17	9:519
29:7	8:389
29:11	15:365
30:9	14:873
30:10	9:230
30:21	14:873
31	9:493
31:3	8:475
31:15	15:493
31:26	8:184
31:29	1:110; 9:515
31:33	9:490, 491
31:35–36	15:507
32:15	8:50; 14:873; 15:25
33:9	8:390
33:15–23	14:610
33:16	4:258
33:25–26	15:507
35:6	14:734
36	14:655
38	10:340
39:1–2	14:928
45	4:308; 8:486; 10:3, 631
45:4–5	4:308; 8:150, 387, 486; 10:631
45:5	5:37; 8:361
51:6	13:161
51:6ff.	8:386
51:9	8:386

Lamentations

Generally	9:90
2:19	9:255
3:12–13	13:350
3:22–23	6:321
3:23	5:51, 146; 14:864; 16:59
3:26	15:222
3:27	8:388
3:37ff.	15:275

Ezekiel

Generally	9:217
3:1–3	8:208
3:17–19	16:524
3:18	5:104
5:6	9:232
7	14:919
11:19	10:499; 13:379
14:14	9:423
16:4	4:111
16:6	15:23
16:63	6:306
18:2	1:110
18:20	1:110
29	14:220
33:2–7	15:428
33:11	14:794
33:32	9:492
34	4:185
34:11	16:212
34:23–24	14:873
36:26	13:379
36:31	6:306
36:31–32	6:306

Daniel

Generally	9:217, 248
3	16:638–39
4:5	9:235
4:6	9:235
4:15	9:235
5:11	9:235
7:9–27	14:644
10:1, 8, 16–19	12:446–48, 519
12	9:167
12:3	14:41, 468

Hosea

1:2	14:732
2:2ff.	1:259
3:1ff.	1:259
3:5	14:873
6:2	14:459
6:6	9:168
11:1	15:492
12:8	14:864
13:14	15:487
14:3	15:381

Joel

3:1–5	14:440
4:13	14:368

Amos

2:1	14:742
2:6–8	10:337
3:1	9:448
3:2	1:148; 10:335; 14:596
3:4–8	10:328
3:6	15:276
3:8	9:298, 514
4:4	14:864
4:12	16:635
5:8	14:864
5:24	10:337
6:4–6	10:338
7	9:448
7:1–9	10:329
8:1	9:515
8:11	11:457; 15:431
9:7	10:336
9:11–15	9:448

Jonah

1:1–16	15:431
1:4–15	8:547
2:1	14:459
2:3	8:447
2:10	15:381
4:5–11	13:39; 14:303

Micah

2:13	6:161
4:1–3	4:112
4:4	14:729
4:9	15:482–84
5:1	14:799
6:6	6:287
6:8	4:74; 6:287; 9:168; 10:337; 14:787; 16:239

Nahum

3:16	10:264

Habakkuk

Generally	9:217
1–3	15:61
2:20	12:449
3	15:168
3:18	15:322

Zephaniah

1–3	15:61
3:5	14:864
3:17	15:516

Haggai

1	15:25
1:2–4	15:33
2	15:25
2:8	14:791

Zechariah

2:8	15:3, 23, 84, 574
2:8, 12	5:148
3:1–5	14:134, 854–60
3:10	14:729
7:9	15:217
8:23	14:457
10:8–9	5:28
10:9	5:28
12:8–12	14:873

Malachi

Generally	9:217
1	15:25
2	15:25
2:17	15:410
3	15:25
3:1	15:22
3:3	15:229
3:15	15:410
3:20	5:49
4:2	5:49

OLD TESTAMENT APOCRYPHA

Tobit

1:3	9:252
2:13	15:380
4:20	15:380
12:22	15:380

Judith

Generally	9:217
8–16	13:342

Wisdom of Solomon

Generally	9:217
1:5	9:235
1:16	7:58, 230; 15:376
3:1–3	7:181; 14:908; 16:618
3:1ff.	13:42; 15:374
3:3	13:331–36; 14:908
3:9	16:618
4:7	16:618

4:10 16:618
4:14 16:618
5:15 16:618
5:16a 16:618
6:5 9:232
6:7 9:225
7:22 9:226, 235
8:3 9:225
8:7 9:254
9:17 9:235
10 9:235
10:7 9:238
10:10 9:252
11:26 9:225
12:10 9:248, 250
16:28 5:51
16:28–29 15:380
16:29 15:380
17:10 9:238
19:10 9:242
19:14 9:226

Prologue to Sirach
1:20 9:231
3 9:231

Sirach/Ecclesiasticus
Generally 9:217, 230
1:11 9:230
1:18 9:230
1:26 9:230, 235
1:27 9:230, 231
1:30 9:230
2:10 9:239
2:11 9:228
3:18 9:246
3:20 14:594
3:23 14:593
4:2 5:74
4:27–28 14:318
5:7 15:389
7:12 9:246
7:17 9:246
8:16 15:370
9:10 7:100
9:15 14:93; 16:223
10:13 14:593
10:13–14 5:111
10:28a 12:233
10:31 14:867, 934
11:20–21 4:244
13:11–12 8:545
13:14 8:545
15:1 9:235
16 9:233
16:12 9:233
16:14 9:233
16:18 9:255
17:9 6:240
17:11 6:240; 9:235
18:21 15:511, 512
19:20 9:235, 244
19:21 14:517
19:30 14:172
23:1 9:225
24:8 9:225
26:15 15:370
28:3 9:255
31:8 9:246
36:1 9:225
39:5 5:51
40 15:376
40:1b 3:76; 12:289
40:27 8:521
44:15 9:248
44:16 9:238
45:5 9:235
50:24–26 14:320; 15:25
59:3 9:255

1 Maccabees

2:67 9:492

2 Maccabees

Generally 9:225
1:24 9:225
4:2 9:226
4:11 9:225
6:28 9:255
7:23 9:225
10:13 15:376
14:335 9:227

2 Esdras

Generally 9:228, 233
7 9:381, 382
7:90–99 9:383

3 Maccabees

Generally 9:225
2:9 9:227
3:19 9:225

4 Maccabees

Generally 9:225
5:25 9:225
6:28 9:255
7:4 9:227
11:5 9:225
14:7 9:227

NEW TESTAMENT

Matthew

1 14:871
1:1 14:871
1:6 14:889
1:18 14:477, 481
1:18–25 15:534
1:20 14:477
1:22 4:86
2:1 16:612
2:1–12 8:481; 15:524
2:2 8:481
2:4–6 15:537
2:10 15:360
2:11 16:612
2:13–23 15:490–95; 16:13
2:16–18 15:23
2:23 15:494
3 14:477
3:1 6:164
3:1–3 6:164
3:10 14:481
3:11 4:209; 9:445; 11:455; 14:476–77, 481
3:11–15 14:906
3:13–17 15:536
3:15 1:147; 14:803; 15:536
3:16 14:477
3:17 14:796; 15:536
4:1–11 4:135; 6:311; 14:365, 793; 15:348, 392
4:4 14:714, 806
4:6 16:631
4:7 14:714; 15:409
4:8–10 10:357; 14:400
4:9 10:61, 70
4:10 14:563, 714, 789
4:11 15:372, 395
4:12 3:110
4:16 15:378
4:17 4:188; 9:498; 14:802; 15:324
4:18–22 4:79
4:23 14:802

4:33–37 16:602
5 4:100–145; 9:489; 14:472, 725, 734
5–7 10:385
5:1 4:183; 9:524
5:1–12 14:802
5:1–14 14:1010
5:2 4:101
5:3 4:105, 115, 251; 11:444; 14:802; 16:553
5:3–10 13:321
5:3–11 4:251
5:3–12 12:259; 15:268
5:4 10:479
5:5 4:132; 14:310; 15:502
5:6 5:32; 10:587; 11:445; 14:618
5:7 15:217; 16:252
5:8 2:46; 4:126, 276, 286; 7:49; 9:381; 10:7, 127–28, 511–16, 554, 638; 13:391; 14:715
5:9 4:108; 15:277
5:10 4:115; 6:346; 7:182; 14:802
5:10–11 4:109; 9:383
5:11 4:251, 258; 9:402
5:12 15:145, 361, 516
5:13 4:150, 212, 258; 14:297, 552, 737
5:13–14 4:226
5:13–16 4:110, 225; 14:439
5:14 4:150, 261; 14:89, 439, 432, 624
5:14–16 14:690, 785
5:15 13:94; 14:474
5:16 4:113, 149, 279; 14:614–15
5:17 4:115, 119; 14:776, 787, 803
5:17–18 14:473
5:17–19 11:449
5:17–20 4:115
5:17–48 8:456
5:17ff. 15:28
5:18 4:115
5:20 4:119; 12:84
5:21–22 10:370; 14:790
5:21–26 4:121
5:21–48 4:82
5:22 12:358
5:22–24 14:863
5:23 14:474, 749; 15:485
5:23–24 4:123; 5:117; 14:474
5:24 4:66, 121; 13:392; 15:485
5:27–28 14:791
5:27–32 4:125; 14:734, 737
5:29 4:45; 6:213; 7:123
5:29–30 10:348; 14:802
5:33–37 4:128; 6:280; 14:789; 16:642
5:34 15:45
5:34–35 15:45
5:37 4:129
5:38 4:102, 136; 6:72
5:38–42 4:132; 9:537, 540

5:38ff. 9:524
5:39 4:79, 136, 243, 290, 302; 6:243; 14:623
5:39–41 10:370
5:39ff. 4:289; 9:530, 537
5:40 4:133
5:43–48 4:137
5:43 4:138
5:43–45 10:370
5:44 1:186; 9:530, 540; 12:260; 14:624, 790
5:44–46 10:364
5:45 9:473; 10:386; 14:389
5:46 4:143
5:46–47 11:368
5:47 4:144, 145; 14:472
5:48 4:142, 145, 278, 300; 8:278, 456; 14:792
6 4:146–68; 8:73
6:1–4 4:146, 306; 6:314
6:1–18 14:949
6:2–3 4:279
6:3 4:251, 266; 6:318, 324; 7:225; 8:491; 14:132, 614, 629, 905; 15:427
6:3–4 4:311; 6:317
6:4 6:284
6:5–8 4:152; 14:811
6:6 4:146; 6:305; 14:109
6:8 4:167; 15:22
6:9 14:789; 16:640, 642
6:9–13 4:155; 5:157
6:9–15 4:155
6:10 3:46; 6:236; 9:312; 10:374, 377; 12:455; 14:802; 16:644
6:11 5:73; 10:375
6:12 4:269; 15:345
6:13 3:87; 10:375; 15:347, 350, 386
6:14 5:118
6:16 14:476; 15:370, 371
6:16–18 4:158
6:17 12:233; 15:361
6:18 4:146
6:19 4:78; 14:727
6:19–21 4:248
6:19–24 4:161
6:21 4:78; 14:789
6:22 4:278; 6:78, 319; 10:613
6:22–23 7:123
6:24 7:57, 230; 9:464; 14:72, 378, 789, 791; 15:478; 16:635
6:25 3:89; 4:79, 249; 9:464
6:25–26 16:643
6:25–34 4:165; 15:23, 131
6:26 14:796, 809
6:26–29 14:809
6:26–32 4:190
6:27 4:165
6:29 9:384
6:30 13:322

6:32	6:361; 15:437
6:33	4:79; 6:354, 361; 14:914
6:34	8:50, 72, 217; 14:864; 16:529
7	4:169–82: 6:326; 9:489; 15:277
7:1	4:241; 6:313; 10:7, 498–99, 637; 11:329, 367; 13:369; 14:791
7:1–5	14:401
7:1–12	4:169, 297
7:6	4:45, 269; 8:373; 14:520, 555, 574, 827; 15:318; 16:641
7:7	4:45; 9:534; 14:847
7:9	13:322
7:12	4:175
7:13	4:14, 162; 10:348; 16:55, 66
7:13–14	9:460
7:13–23	4:175; 16:66, 76
7:15	3:107; 4:184; 14:926
7:15–20	4:176–78
7:17	4:63; 6:51; 9:345, 497
7:21	4:178–79, 277; 6:331; 8:387; 9:469; 14:616; 15:277; 16:559
7:22	4:179–81; 6:331
7:23	4:180; 6:332; 15:549
7:24–29	4:181; 6:326
7:26	7:68; 9:492
7:26–27	9:497; 12:479
8:1–13	9:180
8:5–13	8:481; 9:552–61; 14:802
8:7	12:345
8:9	9:557
8:10	9:554, 560
8:11–12	9:552, 553, 560
8:12	9:552; 15:369
8:13	16:559
8:15–17	4:215
8:17	5:170; 8:479, 480, 481; 14:584; 15:406
8:19	9:477
8:19–22	9:476
8:20	14:877; 15:556
8:21	9:447
8:23–27	8:279; 12:454–61, 519; 14:113, 752, 803, 851; 15:30
8:23ff.	8:279
8:24–33	14:793
8:26	14:757
8:26–27	8:279
8:28ff.	14:803
9:1–8	10:58, 637
9:2	12:358; 16:559
9:3	5:118
9:9–13	4:107; 14:803
9:10–11	4:40, 284
9:11	6:279; 8:481
9:12	11:456
9:13	6:349; 8:415; 14:802
9:14–15	15:371
9:15–17	15:371
9:18–19	8:481
9:20	10:550

9:23–26	8:481
9:32–33	13:380
9:35	4:186
9:35–38	4:183; 14:89; 15:121
9:36	4:183; 7:41, 70
9:37	16:69
9:38	14:308; 15:430
9:40	6:343
10	4:183–98; 14:817, 821; 15:432
10:1	4:186, 191; 14:822
10:1–4	4:186
10:1–8	14:959
10:5–6	4:187; 10:275; 12:418; 15:431
10:5–25	15:549
10:6	4:100
10:7–8	4:188
10:8	4:249; 14:816–17
10:9–10	4:189
10:11–15	4:191
10:12	4:191
10:13	4:192; 15:369; 16:553, 560
10:13–14	4:173, 192; 14:214
10:13–28 par.	13:190
10:14	14:201, 520
10:14–15	4:173
10:16	6:78, 82; 14:808, 924
10:16–25	4:101, 193
10:16–42	14:468
10:20	14:479, 481
10:22	9:403; 15:354, 356
10:22–23	4:195, 247
10:23	4:173, 243; 13:161, 253, 268
10:24	4:89, 106
10:26	4:151, 243
10:26–39	4:196
10:27	14:806
10:28	9:387; 15:374
10:29	7:95; 8:227
10:30	14:797
10:30–31	14:798
10:32	15:425
10:32–33	14:630
10:33	14:475
10:34	12:261; 15:365, 366, 367
10:34ff.	9:478; 10:348
10:35	13:266
10:36	14:930
10:37	13:308; 16:594
10:39	11:455; 13:395; 15:263
10:40	14:468, 822
10:40–42	4:198; 14:468
10:41	14:822
11	14:802
11:2–6	14:802
11:5	9:312; 10:347
11:6	10:348, 465; 12:360; 14:544
11:11	9:312
11:12	11:329; 13:127
11:12–13	9:312
11:15	14:956
11:18–19	14:729
11:19	11:263; 15:369, 536
11:20	16:560
11:21	16:560
11:21ff.	1:284
11:23	14:743

11:27 14:795
11:28 4:38; 9:482; 14:580; 16:554
11:28–29 10:549; 14:802
11:28–30 4:39, 40; 7:41; 13:371–75
11:30 4:45, 91, 208; 14:230, 622; 15:24, 32, 437, 521; 16:636
12 14:483, 485
12:1ff. 6:311
12:18 9:312
12:20 4:54
12:22–30 14:803
12:24 14:567
12:28 9:312; 10:347; 14:478, 802
12:30 6:153, 342–43; 10:347; 14:580, 674, 682
12:31 14:480, 484; 15:413
12:31–32 4:52; 14:484, 612
12:32 14:480, 484, 486; 15:394, 413
12:33 14:612
12:34 15:317
12:36 14:791
12:38 6:343
12:39 14:757
12:40 14:459
12:46–50 6:333
12:48, 50 12:427
12:49 16:550
12:50 15:277
13 1:219; 9:319; 14:431, 802; 15:337
13:1–9 16:191
13:3–9 14:521
13:8 15:225
13:11–15 11:456
13:12 15:513
13:16 6:330
13:18 16:191
13:18–23 14:521
13:23 16:191
13:24–30 9:316; 11:329; 14:212, 657, 681; 15:141; 16:568
13:31–32 14:714
13:35 14:427
13:36–43 11:329; 16:568
13:43 13:341; 14:956
13:44 3:23; 4:44; 6:159; 14:349; 15:145, 361, 364, 515
13:44–46 10:348; 14:431, 749
13:45 10:511
13:45–46 4:45
13:47–50 9:316; 16:568
13:52 5:63; 15:555
14:1–12 15:376
14:4 16:598
14:13–21 5:74
14:19 15:381
14:22–33 14:227, 803
14:28–29 4:66
14:28–31 12:479
14:29 4:63, 69, 77; 7:171
15 9:395–404
15:1–9 9:479
15:1–20 4:38
15:5 14:474
15:21–28 14:802

15:21ff. 11:263
15:24 4:111; 12:397
15:29–31 14:760, 764
15:30 16:500
16 14:440
16:3 10:275
16:4 14:459
16:13 4:84
16:13–18 12:26, 477–81, 523
16:13–21 14:803
16:13ff. 4:46
16:15–20 10:347
16:16 4:128; 14:440, 630
16:16–26 14:802
16:17 9:293; 10:466; 12:419
16:18 1:153, 265; 4:187; 9:84; 11:299; 12:22, 140, 481; 14:457
16:18–19 15:317
16:19 4:270; 5:109; 14:825; 15:57, 544
16:21–26 14:808
16:21–28 4:84
16:22–23 4:85
16:23 3:110; 12:479
16:24 4:46, 87; 10:386; 11:257; 15:437
16:24–26 14:802
16:25 1:262; 3:89
16:26 10:370; 14:934; 15:374
16:27 4:277; 14:614–15, 792
16:28 15:375, 378
17:1–9 14:637; 15:537
17:2 12:345
17:4 14:639
17:5 4:204
17:20 14:714
17:23 15:361, 517
18:1 16:555
18:2–3 10:351, 553; 16:555
18:3 6:478
18:4 1:176
18:6 6:353; 10:351
18:7 15:400
18:11 8:407; 14:803
18:13 15:364
18:15 4:272; 14:833
18:15–16 4:273; 14:833
18:15–20 14:839
18:15ff. 6:316
18:16 15:400
18:17 4:273, 274; 14:834
18:17–20 11:299
18:18 4:270; 5:109; 11:325; 14:746, 813, 825–26; 15:544
18:18ff. 4:269; 14:834
18:19 1:226; 14:696
18:20 1:228, 280; 12:345, 481; 14:834; 15:277, 578
18:21 5:118
18:21–22 5:109
18:21–35 14:894–99, 1011
18:21ff. 4:269
18:23–25 10:570
18:31–34 14:899
18:35 5:118
19 15:310, 314, 345

19:1, 2, 13–24 12:158
19:1–12 14:734
19:5 8:85
19:6 8:84; 14:791
19:8 4:11–10, 127
19:10 14:729
19:11 14:729, 803; 15:346
19:12 14:729; 15:379, 371
19:13–15 15:345
19:14 10:351; 14:802
19:16 16:65
19:16–22 4:69, 116, 182; 6:359; 11:450; 13:372; 14:566; 15:310
19:16–26 15:345
19:16–30 14:802
19:17 4:117; 6:275; 14:421
19:18 4:71
19:21 4:64, 77; 6:275; 8:503; 14:622, 624
19:22 4:78; 15:145, 361, 517
19:23–26 4:83
19:26 4:99
19:28 4:186
20:16 12:373
20:26–28 10:275
20:28 14:801, 880
21:1–9 10:351
21:1–11 14:803
21:15 10:351
21:15–16 16:555
21:28–31 9:450, 466–70
21:28ff. 16:191
21:31 6:347; 7:41; 8:451; 9:469; 10:352, 466; 11:263, 380; 14:802; 15:277
21:31–32 14:582, 802
21:39–40 9:522
22 6:311, 354
22:1–14 14:802
22:2–14 13:47
22:11–13 10:588
22:15 6:354
22:15–22 6:311
22:21 4:243; 10:275, 496; 13:275; 14:84, 809, 973
22:23–33 6:311
22:30 14:791
22:31–32 9:221
22:34–40 6:311
22:35 10:364
22:36–40 4:175
22:37 9:464
22:37–39 10:364; 12:258
22:42 14:871
22:43 14:873, 875
23:3 6:314
23:5 6:314
23:8 5:107; 9:241; 13:93; 14:784
23:12 1:176
23:13–33 6:314
23:28 6:329
24 14:393; 15:363
24–25 6:163
24:1–14 14:320; 15:85
24:6 8:361; 11:426
24:6–14 11:419–27; 14:760–62, 764
24:12 15:356

24:13	4:151; 15:83
24:14	14:531
24:15–28	14:320
24:29–41	14:320
24:31	5:28; 15:375
24:36	12:445; 14:421
24:42–50	14:320
24:43–51	11:376
24:43ff.	16:481
25	7:225; 8:491; 9:513; 11:304
25:1–13	8:286; 10:588; 14:760
25:21	9:322, 456; 11:458; 15:146, 361
25:23	9:322; 15:361
25:25	12:295
25:30	11:458
25:31–45	7:225
25:31–46	4:277; 6:163; 15:434
25:31ff.	6:319; 14:614
25:32–40	10:545
25:33	9:322
25:34	12:295
25:35	11:304
25:36	8:324
25:37	5:74
25:37–40	8:491
25:40	6:137, 140, 253; 10:495; 12:295
25:41	15:549
25:42	11:304
25:42–43	9:513
25:45	9:513
26–28	8:60
26:20–25	14:957
26:22	14:958; 15:361
26:24	14:888, 958
26:26	12:346
26:26–29	15:266
26:31	12:360
26:33ff.	16:559
26:34–35	15:477
26:36–46	8:269, 550
26:37	15:361
26:39	4:42, 90, 133; 5:170; 8:550
26:39–42	14:622
26:39–44	15:394
26:40	8:480, 486; 14:957
26:41	4:159; 9:271; 15:348, 350, 396, 403
26:42	4:90, 133; 14:360
26:45–50	6:227; 14:490, 870, 957
26:47–50	8:494
26:48–49	12:307
26:49	15:363
26:52	4:170; 14:790
26:55	14:876
26:56	14:957
26:63	4:128
26:63–64	14:803
26:65	4:118
26:69–75	6:150; 9:480; 12:479
26:71	8:153
26:74	4:86
26:75	12:480; 15:477
27:3–5	14:962
27:3–10	15:411
27:5	6:200; 12:480; 15:376
27:25	9:520
27:29	12:307; 15:363
27:34	4:87
27:43	9:521

27:45	14:595, 598, 757
27:46	4:90, 106; 5:162, 170; 9:522; 10:357; 11:295, 425; 14:365, 757, 873; 15:395, 411, 470, 480
27:48	4:87
27:51	14:900
27:52	15:373
27:52–53	15:374
27:57–60	8:482
27:61	8:482
28:8	15:360, 364, 516
28:10	11:426
28:11ff.	16:475
28:16–20	8:269
28:18	6:401; 14:180, 378; 16:479, 511, 598
28:18–19	16:478
28:18–20	4:111, 188; 13:325; 14:478, 489, 821
28:18ff.	15:140
28:19	4:207; 14:459, 483, 631, 784, 796; 16:552
28:19–20	9:445
28:20	4:234; 8:275; 10:68, 127, 490–95, 637; 11:426; 14:180; 15:431
28:30	15:373
29:20	16:479

Mark

1:1–8	14:596
1:8	9:445; 14:476
1:9	14:875
1:9–11	15:534
1:10	14:756
1:15	8:481; 14:802
1:16–17	4:77
1:16–18	4:62, 64
1:16–20	4:45
1:17	4:46
1:18	4:48
1:21–39	14:803
1:29	14:576; 15:317
1:35	5:52; 14:864
1:44	14:555
2:5	4:201, 204
2:7	5:118
2:11–12	4:201
2:13–14	14:594, 802
2:14	4:57, 62, 77, 201, 207; 14:622
2:17	8:415
2:18ff.	15:361
2:19	15:145, 360
2:23	6:312
2:23–28	6:279; 7:75; 16:594
2:23ff.	14:803
2:27–28	14:790
2:28	7:78
3:1–5	6:312
3:1–6	16:594
3:8	9:445
3:22–23	6:156
3:24–25	16:34
3:29	14:380, 480, 484, 587; 15:394
3:30	14:475

3:31–35	10:349; 16:594
4:1–2	9:320
4:3ff.	1:222
4:9	12:27, 478; 14:956
4:11ff.	14:426
4:12	14:426, 967
4:17 (18)	15:363
4:23	14:956
4:26–29	14:368–70
4:26ff.	9:320
4:28	14:368
4:35–41	8:468
5:8	16:500
5:9	14:563
5:22–24	8:481; 15:374
5:34	15:369
5:35–43	8:481
5:36	11:426; 14:607
6:8–9	4:189
6:10	14:576; 15:317
6:56	14:320
7:11	14:474
7:21	5:39
7:21–22	4:264; 14:727, 731
7:22	727
7:32	16:554
7:34	14:554; 16:554
7:37	14:276
8:22	16:554
8:22–23	16:500
8:22ff.	15:520
8:31	4:84; 8:361
8:31–33	6:279; 14:957
8:31–38	4:84
8:33	3:110; 6:147; 16:554
8:34	4:48; 11:257; 14:621
8:36–37	4:84
9:1	9:313; 15:378
9:1ff.	15:373
9:23	12:443; 13:303; 16:559
9:23–24	13:404–8
9:24	2:154; 4:67; 10:459; 14:591, 784; 15:42, 198; 16:53, 558, 667
9:29	4:160; 7:165; 13:306; 14:817, 889; 15:370, 371
9:30–32	14:957
9:35	9:446
9:36	16:554
9:37	16:555
9:39	6:342
9:40	6:342–44; 14:674, 682
9:42	10:351
9:47	4:45
9:50	15:369
10	16:65
10:13	16:563
10:13–14	4:184
10:13–16	16:554
10:13ff.	11:263
10:14	14:631
10:14–15	16:552
10:14–16	8:481
10:17–22	14:992
10:17–31	14:802
10:17ff.	4:71
10:18	4:255; 11:263; 14:757
10:18b	3:59
10:20	6:359
10:21	4:72; 6:169; 8:482
10:25	14:550

10:27 6:147; 15:418
10:28 4:46, 135, 212, 237
10:28–30 14:802
10:28–31 4:99, 226; 14:738, 802, 808
10:29–30 14:432
10:29–31 15:502
10:30 4:125, 156, 210; 10:283
10:32 4:99
10:32–34 14:957
10:39 4:208
10:42–45 4:240; 14:472
10:42ff. 1:60
10:43 5:106; 14:472
10:45 4:240; 14:803
10:46 16:500
10:46ff. 25:520
10:48 4:184
10:51 5:114; 8:491
10:51–52 10:275
11:9 4:233; 14:872, 881
11:10 12:387; 14:803, 872
11:22 14:607
11:24–25 15:330
12 10:385
12:28–31 15:309
12:29–31 14:787
13 9:312; 15:363
13:12 6:177
13:13 9:402
13:24–37 14:757
13:33 15:377
13:36 13:127
14:11 15:364
14:22 15:539
14:22–24 15:266
14:22ff. 1:150
14:23–25 14:729
14:25 14:734
14:32–42 8:269
14:32ff. 11:263
14:33 12:440
14:35–36 8:269
14:43–45 8:494
15 6:228
15:13–14 4:233
15:14 12:387
15:20 4:79
15:33 5:78
15:34 5:162; 6:279; 7:165; 8:448, 479; 10:357, 465, 466, 523, 631; 11:263; 14:757, 800, 803; 15:372, 395, 413; 16:474
15:38 14:900
15:39 10:466
15:42–46 8:482
15:43 8:482
15:47 8:482
16:1 8:482
16:1–6 5:49
16:2–6 14:864
16:5–6 16:474
16:9 14:790
16:9–20 9:445; 16:477
16:15 14:520; 16:478
16:16 9:445; 14:631
18:26 15:355

Luke

1–2 9:91
1:1–25 14:320
1:1ff. 9:297

1:14	15:363
1:15	16:554
1:16	14:508
1:25–26	14:481
1:25–27	14:477
1:26–38	14:320; 15:278
1:28	14:906; 15:363
1:32	14:872
1:38	13:344
1:39–56	14:320, 906–7
1:41	16:554
1:46–55	5:65; 13:342–47; 14:906–7; 15:321
1:47	15:322, 361
1:48–53	11:449
1:51	9:300; 15:321
1:51–52	16:613
1:52	6:161; 16:555, 597
1:57–80	14:320
1:58	15:364
1:68–79	12:452
1:69	14:872
1:79	15:378
2	14:799
2:1–2	6:228
2:1–21	15:534
2:4	14:885
2:7	4:225; 6:63
2:8	16:612
2:9–14	14:595, 597
2:10	11:425; 15:145, 360, 516; 16:554
2:10–11, 14	12:453
2:11	8:242
2:13	14:756
2:14	10:543, 546; 12:447; 13:307; 15:85, 365, 366, 367
2:15–16	8:481
2:15–17	16:612
2:15–20	15:546
2:17	8:241
2:19	3:153; 5:88; 14:167, 495, 519, 933; 15:514
2:21–40	14:320; 15:25
2:25	4:104; 16:612
2:25–26	14:481
2:25–27	14:477
2:28	16:554, 612
2:29	9:225; 15:376
2:29–30	13:409–10; 14:739
2:30–31	16:554
2:37	4:160
2:41–52	10:263; 14:790
2:42–52	15:412
2:48–50	6:279
2:49	5:167
2:51	14:519
3	14:871
3:1	6:228
3:4–6	6:161
3:5	6:162
3:8b	3:57
3:16	14:476
3:22	9:491
4:2	4:160
4:3–4	11:416–17
4:5–8	11:418–19
4:6	10:61
4:13	14:364
4:16–21	14:655
4:18	14:875
4:19	4:215
4:28–30	14:958

5:1–11 8:472
5:21 5:118
5:32 8:415
5:39 6:297
5:39–6:9 6:297
6:5 6:297
6:15 4:187
6:20 4:102; 11:447
6:20–23 11:444
6:20–26 11:449
6:21 11:448
6:23 15:361
6:25 11:445
6:28–29 4:137
6:36 9:228
6:37 5:118
6:46 10:461
7 8:481
7:1–7 9:553
7:1–10 8:481
7:11 15:374
7:11ff. 14:803
7:22 11:445, 446, 447
7:36 14:576
7:36–50 6:150, 350; 14:577
7:36ff. 11:263
7:37–38 8:481
7:37–47 10:352
7:44–46 8:481
7:50 15:369
8:2 6:150
8:5 9:479
8:7 14:573
8:8 14:956
8:11ff. 15:514
8:13 15:351, 415
8:14 4:162; 6:408; 14:573
8:15 6:330; 14:90; 15:83, 354, 356
8:17 14:791–92
8:29 16:500
8:41–42 8:481
8:48 15:369
8:49–55 14:803
8:49–56 8:481
8:56 15:36
9 9:478
9:3 4:189
9:23 11:257
9:24 3:89
9:27 15:378
9:31 14:638
9:40–56 9:476
9:46 5:93
9:46–56 9:477
9:49–50 16:560
9:50 16:560
9:51–56 9:180, 540–51
9:53 9:541
9:54 16:315
9:55b 9:541
9:56a 9:541, 542
9:56b 9:541
9:57 4:207; 9:477
9:57–58 9:477
9:57–60 9:476
9:57–62 4:60, 298; 9:465, 476–88, 592; 13:347–49
9:57ff. 4:116; 10:386; 14:802; 16:559
9:59 3:170; 9:477, 478, 479; 13:127
9:60 9:476–79; 10:348

9:61	3:109, 170; 4:298, 311; 9:479
9:61–62	14:751
9:62	4:104; 9:479; 10:348
10	9:479; 14:468, 822
10:1	9:476; 14:516, 521, 822
10:2	9:479
10:5	4:5–6, 191
10:5–6	15:369
10:7	14:817
10:16	14:516, 698, 701–2, 822
10:17	15:361, 364
10:18	3:105; 9:312; 10:347; 14:802
10:20	14:743, 783; 15:361, 364
10:21	15:363
10:25	4:182; 6:311
10:25–29	4:75, 116; 14:566
10:25–37	11:442, 450; 14:423
10:25ff.	1:168
10:27	4:203; 9:459
10:29	12:101
10:31	5:99
10:36–37	10:531
10:38–42	14:787
10:38ff.	6:330
10:39	6:330
10:40	6:330
10:41	6:330
11:1	5:155
11:1ff.	1:201, 276
11:2–4	5:157
11:3	5:73

11:13	14:423, 456, 480, 486, 796
11:27–28	10:348
11:29	14:757
12:4	15:372
12:6	7:95
12:10	14:612; 15:394
12:13	6:354
12:15	14:701, 727, 791
12:16–21	14:580
12:19	14:495
12:20	15:361, 364; 15:377
12:30	14:612
12:32	4:176; 9:509; 11:426; 12:481; 14:371, 803; 15:437
12:35	10:587
12:35–40	11:376, 408–15; 12:471
12:35ff.	9:502–9; 15:377
12:37	13:318; 14:125; 15:371
12:45	16:544
12:45–48	14:303
12:47–48	15:348
12:49	10:127, 349, 495–98, 637
12:50	4:208
12:51	15:366
12:56	15:358, 364
13:1–5	13:365–70; 14:1012
13:6–9	15:151
13:10–13	6:312
13:17	15:361, 364
14:14	15:375
14:15	4:106; 5:74
14:16–24	14:802

14:19 15:360
14:24ff. 9:478
14:26 4:92, 127; 10:348; 11:263; 13:308; 14:612, 622, 646, 790
14:27 14:475; 15:352
14:28 14:925
14:28ff. 15:434
14:33 15:435
14:35 14:956
15 6:228; 14:228; 15:146, 231, 365
15:1ff. 11:263
15:2 4:215
15:4–6 4:185
15:6 15:146, 364
15:7 5:118; 11:456; 15:361, 364, 516
15:9 15:146, 364
15:10 15:361, 516
15:11–32 2:161; 6:169; 10:352, 568; 15:314
15:18–21 12:480
15:23 15:146
15:24 9:478, 484; 15:377
15:29 15:364
15:32 15:146, 361, 364
16:1–12 14:89, 954
16:8 15:369
16:10 6:295–96
16:19 3:82
16:19–26 6:150
16:19–31 8:271; 11:443–50; 14:740
16:19–32 15:373, 374
16:20–21 6:193
16:22 11:444; 14:791
16:23 15:374
16:25 11:444
17 9:592; 10:254; 15:382
17:2 15:400
17:5 12:459
17:7–10 9:451–61, 592
17:10 6:177; 9:499, 528; 10:484; 12:241
17:11 15:381
17:11ff. 15:381; 16:491
17:12 16:500
17:20–21 10:347; 14:802
17:20–37 14:647
17:21 1:138, 141, 208; 9:312; 12:295
17:33 1:176; 10:532–35
18 6:317
18:1–8 14:647
18:6 14:647
18:7 15:355
18:8 14:649
18:9–14 10:567; 14:795
18:9ff. 15:381; 16:491
18:10–14 10:352
18:11 6:310, 314; 13:369; 15:381, 509
18:11–12 6:317
18:12 15:371
18:13 9:456; 13:369; 14:795
18:14 14:730
18:15 16:554, 560
18:16 16:560
18:30 10:283
18:41 5:114

19:1–8	8:481
19:1–9	9:592
19:2–10	6:350
19:5	14:576
19:6	15:364, 516
19:9	8:385; 14:868
19:10	8:407; 14:803
19:12	15:85
19:17	6:296
19:36	15:365
19:37	15:361, 364
19:38	9:554; 15:369
19:42	15:368
20:36	13:336; 15:369
21:15	4:194
21:16	6:177–78
21:25–26	14:755
21:25–36	14:758–60
21:28	13:316, 337–41; 14:648, 758–59; 15:361
21:29	14:755
21:32	14:757–58, 759
21:34	14:756
22–24	8:60
22:5	15:364
22:14–20	15:266
22:25	9:226
22:28	14:364
22:28–29	15:348, 349, 396, 414, 415
22:30	15:375
22:31	15:349, 414
22:32	15:414
22:35	4:168; 5:168; 8:492; 15:501
22:40–46	8:269
22:43	15:348, 374, 395
22:44	15:378
22:48	14:961
22:61	6:147; 9:335
22:62	12:480
23:4	1:186
23:8	15:364
23:11	16:475
23:32	9:480
23:32ff.	4:40
23:34	4:88; 5:175; 9:521, 552; 10:86; 13:376, 386; 14:969; 15:325, 376, 469, 470
23:35	15:376
23:39–43	9:522
23:40–43	6:150
23:42	14:802; 15:145, 375
23:43	13:334; 15:145, 375
23:45	14:900
23:46	5:162; 9:522; 14:873; 16:474
23:50–53	8:482
23:55–56	8:482
24	14:805
24:12	4:216
24:14	14:532
24:29	5:78
24:30–31	5:72
24:41	15:145, 360, 364, 516
24:44	5:159, 166; 14:785
24:44–45	5:159
24:44–49	8:269
24:48	14:531, 533
24:50	16:632
24:50–53	16:477

24:52	15:145, 360, 364, 516; 16:481
27:12	8:407

John

1:1	9:293; 12:315; 14:803; 16:56
1:1–2	3:29
1:1–3	13:170
1:1–14	14:798
1:1–18	14:320; 15:25
1:1ff.	4:214
1:3	4:94; 6:259; 16:510, 595
1:3–4	6:344
1:4	6:250, 259; 9:372
1:5	9:373; 15:344
1:7	3:44; 14:531
1:10	6:68
1:11	4:225; 6:165; 16:548
1:14	4:214, 226; 6:290; 8:373; 9:294, 381, 497; 10:159, 638; 12:301, 359; 14:457, 639; 16:550, 566, 614
1:16	15:88
1:16–23	15:518
1:18	16:550
1:29	5:170; 8:481; 9:348; 14:510, 516, 611
1:31ff.	15:536
1:32–34	15:534
1:33	14:476
1:36	8:481; 14:516
1:46	13:180; 15:494
1:47	8:482
2	15:237; 16:123
2:1–11	14:425; 15:196, 537
2:3–10	14:734
2:11	15:196, 537
2:17	6:66
2:19	14:884
2:20–22	14:448
2:20ff.	4:223
2:21	14:884
3	9:316; 12:315
3:1–21	15:561
3:3	1:228; 14:479, 722
3:5	4:209; 9:316, 446; 14:479, 631, 735, 737
3:5–6	14:484
3:6	14:737, 800; 15:344
3:8	1:234; 9:336; 10:248; 13:343; 14:479, 484, 486
3:16	4:96, 164; 6:63, 155, 233, 316; 9:372; 14:765, 803, 808; 16:543, 568, 570–71, 598
3:16–20	15:88
3:16–21	15:557ff.
3:16–36	15:88
3:17	6:314, 316
3:17–19	6:316
3:18	6:316; 14:803
3:19	6:316; 14:613; 15:344
3:21	15:277, 420

3:22 9:445
3:29 9:371, 373; 15:52, 361, 364
3:30 9:159; 10:526
3:33 14:722
4:2 9:445
4:5–42 15:52
4:7–8 15:550
4:14 3:146
4:20 15:550
4:22 14:753, 785, 799
4:24 14:789
4:33 6:312
4:34 6:313
4:35 9:381, 479; 14:607; 15:52
4:36ff. 9:371, 377, 381
5:1–29 15:52
5:10 14:689
5:14 14:689
5:16 14:612
5:17b 3:69
5:23 9:530
5:24 9:478; 14:803; 15:373, 378
5:24–29 15:278
5:25 12:422
5:28 15:52
5:28–29 14:810
5:29 14:792
5:35 9:371, 373; 15:88, 363, 364
5:39 3:153; 14:172, 654, 785, 936
5:44 4:163; 5:97
5:46 14:785
6:1–69 15:52
6:6 15:350
6:27 14:722
6:28 15:277
6:29 14:607
6:35 4:106; 14:803; 15:265, 280; 16:618
6:37–39 16:618
6:41 6:313
6:44 12:382
6:54–56 14:453
6:63 9:398; 14:480, 486
6:68–69 14:798
6:70 14:959
7:16 9:272
7:17 14:784, 802, 950; 15:277, 421
7:37 14:848
7:38 14:848; 15:52, 88
7:39 14:438, 476, 481
7:42 14:871
8:1–11 15:314
8:1–36 15:52
8:2–11 6:150, 350
8:11 14:611
8:12 4:112; 9:372; 15:344; 16:617
8:24 15:372
8:31 14:807
8:31–32 11:433–34
8:31b–32 10:366
8:32 2:161; 11:465–72
8:34ff. 15:345
8:36 10:366
8:44 14:586; 15:345, 398; 16:607
8:46 15:345
8:49 9:530
8:51, 52 15:52, 373, 378

8:54 9:375
8:56 9:371, 373; 15:364
9:1–41 15:41
9:3 14:584
9:4 15:96, 377
9:40–41 15:521
9:41 14:484; 15:347
9:56 9:371
10 4:185; 9:501
10:4 4:11, 100
10:11 9:501; 16:212
10:11–13 15:547–49
10:11–16 15:547ff.
10:12–13 14:303
10:12ff. 9:441
10:14 8:485
10:14–15 15:550
10:15 9:501
10:16 14:400, 405; 15:550–51
10:19–20 15:369
10:28 9:372, 399; 14:783
10:30 14:454, 478; 16:615
11 4:201; 11:327; 15:52, 374
11:1 15:373
11:1–45 15:52
11:1–46 14:803
11:4 9:375; 14:549
11:14 9:371
11:15 9:371, 375
11:15–19 9:378
11:16 15:545
11:25 6:249; 9:372; 10:520; 13:334
11:25–26 15:88
11:25ff. 14:803
11:27 6:249
11:51 14:477
11:52 5:28, 29
12:6 14:959
12:11–12 9:378
12:19 9:402
12:23 9:375
12:24 15:354
12:26 15:218
12:28 14:789
12:28–31 14:476
12:31 9:402; 15:344, 388
12:32 14:805
12:35 9:402
12:35–36 9:372
12:36 15:369
12:46 15:344
12:47 10:498
13 16:315
13:1–15 14:801
13:10 9:398
13:15 1:183; 4:287
13:18 9:403
13:23 4:187; 16:315
13:26–30 14:960
13:31–32 9:375
13:34 4:287; 6:68; 14:720, 936–38; 16:519
13:34–35 1:183; 4:268
14 14:476
14–16 14:479, 483
14–17 9:371
14:1 14:607
14:2–3 12:469
14:5 15:545
14:6 4:176; 6:249, 313, 390; 9:378; 12:302, 317,

	382; 14:795, 800, 803; 15:420, 505
14:7	9:403
14:9	9:500; 16:615
14:12	11:447
14:13	9:379
14:13–14	14:388
14:16	14:478, 800, 802; 16:480, 630
14:17	14:479, 483
14:19	13:334
14:22	15:552
14:23	14:457, 478, 483, 622
14:23–24	15:552–53
14:23–31	15:551ff.
14:25–26	15:554–55
14:26	4:209; 12:383; 14:479
14:27	9:373, 397; 10:550; 12:261; 14:258; 15:366, 367, 368
14:27–31	15:555–56
14:28	9:371, 373; 15:364
14:31	15:552
15	9:395–404; 14:476, 620
15:1	9:395–96
15:1ff.	15:544
15:1–8	14:729
15:1–17	9:395, 398
15:2	9:399
15:2–8	14:620
15:3	9:398; 15:512
15:4–6	9:399
15:5	6:327; 15:277
15:7	9:374, 376, 399; 14:811
15:8	9:377, 400
15:9	9:400
15:10	14:623
15:11	9:371, 374; 15:146, 361, 516
15:11–13	15:253, 363
15:12	4:287
15:13	4:125; 9:401; 12:262; 14:475; 16:315
15:13–14	14:760, 764
15:14	14:623
15:15	9:401
15:16	1:125, 136, 142; 8:102; 9:401; 14:620; 15:384
15:16a	9:377
15:16b	9:374, 376
15:18–19	15:344
15:18–25	9:403; 14:808
15:19	9:402
15:20	9:401
15:22	15:347
15:24–27	9:395
15:25	9:403
15:26	9:403, 410; 12:383; 14:477, 482–83
15:26–27	14:479
15:27	14:531
16	14:476
16:1–4	14:808
16:7	4:104; 14:477, 481
16:7ff.	1:195
16:8	14:478, 483
16:8–11	14:479
16:8ff.	15:180
16:12	9:401

16:12–13	4:210
16:13	4:209; 14:478, 483, 805, 950
16:13–15	14:478
16:14	14:478, 482
16:14–15	14:483, 795
16:16–33	15:167
16:20	8:96; 9:371, 400; 15:145, 364
16:20–23	9:374
16:20–24	9:379
16:20ff.	15:361
16:21	9:371
16:22	9:371; 15:361, 362, 364, 516
16:23ff.	9:374, 376
16:24	9:376; 15:146, 361, 363, 364
16:25	9:371
16:33	6:93; 9:371, 373, 397; 12:457; 14:764; 15:366, 367, 368; 16:627
17	8:62, 76; 15:425
17:1–5	9:375
17:1–13	15:167
17:2	15:41, 196
17:9	15:344
17:9–13	14:388
17:12	14:723
17:13	9:371, 374, 400; 15:41, 146, 361
17:14	14:639, 690
17:14–26	15:167
17:15	14:723
17:17–20	14:400
17:17–21	14:388
17:20–21	10:583
17:21	1:203; 14:71
17:22–23	9:375
17:23	1:231
17:24	14:805
18:1	14:890
18:1–40	15:41
18:4–6	14:958
18:18	16:511
18:23	4:136, 302; 5:97
18:33–37	9:520
18:36	4:247; 10:357; 15:344; 16:597
18:37	14:532
18:38	16:511
18:40	12:387
19	9:519–23
19:1–42	15:41
19:2	9:520
19:5	9:520
19:11	6:390; 16:511
19:12	9:510
19:15	9:510
19:25	8:461
19:25–30	9:521
19:26	16:314
19:28	1:150; 5:78; 14:873
19:28–29	9:522
19:30	8:469; 9:52; 16:208
19:34	4:35, 216; 9:446; 14:818
19:35	9:446
19:38	8:482; 9:554
20	15:317; 16:314
20:1–31	15:41
20:2	16:314
20:2–8	4:216
20:17	15:546; 16:478
20:19	1:153; 14:237; 15:145

20:19–20 4:284
20:19–31 15:542ff.
20:20 15:41, 364, 516
20:21–23 14:489, 749; 15:552
20:22 14:477, 481, 483, 822
20:22–23 1:195; 14:746, 813
20:22ff. 16:478
20:23 1:189; 4:270; 5:109; 11:325; 14:825
20:24–29 15:553–56; 16:478
20:28 2:158
20:29 13:393
20:30, 31 15:556–57
21 15:41; 16:308, 315
21:4 14:864
21:15 4:185
21:15–17 6:396
21:15ff. 1:153
21:16 14:468
21:20 4:187; 9:371
21:22 4:46
21:23 15:373, 378

Acts of the Apostles

1 14:438, 805
1:1–11 14:34, 152, 632–34
1:3 14:633; 16:478
1:4–8 14:438
1:4–12 16:477
1:5 14:476, 478, 481
1:6–8 8:269
1:7ff. 1:195
1:8 14:179, 303, 476, 479, 533; 16:478
1:14–2:1 1:151
1:18 15:376
1:20 14:469
1:21–22 14:822
1:23 15:429
1:23–26 14:467
1:24–25 14:467
2 11:311; 14:434, 438–41, 458, 477, 479–81, 486, 985
2:1–2 15:553
2:1–13 8:105
2:1–28 15:552
2:1–41 4:218
2:2 14:757, 816
2:4 1:195; 14:476,481
2:14 14:479
2:14–36 14:479
2:15 14:484
2:17 16:554
2:17–21 14:440
2:22ff. 14:179
2:24 15:372, 378
2:30 14:872, 875
2:30–31 5:159
2:31 14:872
2:32 14:533
2:32ff. 4:232
2:33 16:478
2:35 9:479
2:36 14:378
2:37 14:440
2:38 9:445; 14:441, 479, 829; 16:554, 557
2:38–39 12:418; 14:829

2:40 14:441; 16:554
2:41 16:558
2:42 4:226, 232; 7:74; 14:441, 445–46, 501, 784, 988
2:42–47 4:226, 233; 14:317, 434, 443, 805
2:42ff. 4:232; 16:497
2:43 14:719
2:43–44 4:232
2:43–47 445, 718–22
2:44 14:720
2:44–45 4:268; 14:720
2:45 4:47, 233
2:46 14:532, 720–21; 15:516
2:47 14:443, 721–22, 921
3 14:458
3:11 14:816
3:17 15:325
3:19–26 12:418
3:21 16:478–79
4 14:479
4:12 11:331; 14:800, 803
4:24 9:225
4:29 16:96
4:31 14:458, 479, 487
4:32 14:791
4:32–33 12:443
4:32–35 4:233; 14:443, 988
4:36 15:369
5 4:274; 14:224, 479, 492, 834
5:1–11 14:720, 723
5:3 14:278, 480, 482, 484–85; 15:349, 410
5:6 15:376
5:9 14:478; 15:349, 410
5:12 14:816
5:17–33 14:630
5:25 14:816
5:29 12:183; 13:275, 313; 14:492, 789, 810; 16:594
5:29–32 14:630
5:31 2:95
5:32 14:456, 478, 483
5:38–39 9:474
5:41 14:785; 15:364
6 12:285; 14:823
6:1–3 14:470
6:3–6 14:467
6:4 14:518, 817, 866, 932
6:5 14:464, 470, 700, 820, 838; 15:429
6:6 9:445
6:7 14:458
6:8–7:59 14:470
7 14:458; 15:347
7:14 15:363
7:38 16:634
7:42–43 6:247
7:48 9:515
7:54–60 4:89
7:55 16:624
7:56 16:478
7:56ff. 15:376
7:59 15:374
7:60 15:373

8	8:482; 14:487
8:3	6:150
8:5	14:531
8:5–40	14:470
8:8	15:361
8:13–17	14:626
8:16	9:445; 14:480
8:17	14:468, 822
8:26–40	8:482; 14:631
8:29	14:477
8:35	14:829
8:36	9:446
8:36–37	14:459, 551
8:37	9:445; 14:459; 16:558
8:38	9:446
9:1	6:150
9:3–6	16:478
9:5	13:374; 16:478
9:11	14:817
9:15–16	15:352
9:17	14:479
9:20	14:531, 816
10	8:482; 15:332
10:2	14:631
10:20	14:458
10:24	14:631
10:34	1:204
10:36	15:365, 368
10:38	14:477
10:40	16:475
10:41	16:475, 478
10:42	16:478
10:44	14:479, 487
10:44ff.	14:480
10:47	4:209
10:47–48	14:631
11:1	14:458
11:14	14:576
11:15	14:479, 487; 16:553
11:28	14:468, 822
11:30	14:465, 469, 823
12:2	15:376
12:6	15:373
12:23	15:376
12:24	14:458
12:25	14:469, 823
13	14:458, 943; 15:339
13:1–3	14:521
13:2	4:230; 14:464, 820, 838
13:3	9:445; 15:439
13:5	14:816
13:8	14:458
13:14	14:816
13:15	14:816
13:26	14:458
13:31	16:478
13:33	16:471, 473
13:34	14:872
13:36	14:373
13:42	14:816
13:46	14:458
13:48	15:361
13:48–49	14:458
13:52	15:364
14	14:816, 943; 15:339
14:1	14:816
14:4	14:467, 469, 823; 16:598
14:14	14:822
14:15	15:372, 378
14:16	14:345
14:17	15:363
14:23	14:467, 469, 823
15	12:128; 14:469, 483

15:1–29 12:368, 487; 15:425
15:2 14:469, 823
15:4 14:469, 823
15:6 14:469, 823
15:8 1:204
15:22 14:469, 823
15:23 14:469, 823
15:28 14:478, 483
15:32 14:468
15:36–37 14:458
15:40 15:220
16 14:473; 16:544
16:1 15:334
16:1–2 14:942
16:1ff. 15:323
16:3 14:473, 942
16:4 14:469
16:6 14:477; 15:431
16:9–10 11:381
16:15 4:33, 211; 14:631; 16:553
16:21 14:473
16:25 5:65
16:25–26 10:509
16:31 14:576
16:33 16:553
16:36 15:369
16:40 16:553
17 12:421; 14:458
17:1–2 14:816
17:2 14:816
17:7 12:28
17:11 6:397; 14:458, 654, 785; 16:495
17:17 14:816
17:19 14:816
17:23 14:847; 16:551
17:24 4:262
17:24–25 14:789
17:26 11:262; 12:388
17:27 2:95
17:30 14:345
18 15:323
18:1ff. 4:243
18:2 4:243
18:4–8 14:816
18:6 14:816
18:8 4:211; 14:816; 16:553
18:9 16:478
18:18 15:341
18:19 15:437
18:24ff. 15:323; 16:484
18:25 14:817
18:25, 26 15:504
18:26 16:495
19 15:323
19:1 14:487; 16:484
19:1–6 14:631
19:2 14:480
19:2ff. 9:445
19:5 4:210
19:9 14:816; 15:504
19:10 14:458, 816
19:13 15:431
19:14ff. 15:323
19:17 15:226
19:20 14:458
19:22 15:341
19:24ff. 15:323
20 15:323
20:4 15:323, 341
20:7 14:790, 816
20:17 14:469, 823; 15:342
20:17–32 14:239
20:19 15:415
20:28 4:230, 275; 14:464, 468–69, 700, 820,

	823, 837–38; 15:342, 429
20:32	14:458
20:34	14:458
20:35	4:140
20:37	15:363
21	14:473
21:8	14:469
21:9	14:470, 824
21:10	14:468
21:18	14:469
21:18–26	14:473
21:20	15:427
21:23–26	14:729
21:26	9:479; 14:817
22:4	15:504
22:5	9:241
22:6–11	16:478
22:15	14:531
22:16	16:556, 558, 559
22:17	16:478
22:17–18	16:478
22:25–29	5:97; 6:106
22:28	16:503
23:1	15:334
23:6	15:334
23:11	14:531
23:24	16:511
23:26	16:511
24:2–27	16:511
24:7	16:511
24:14	15:334, 504
24:14ff.	16:544, 598
24:16	15:334
24:22	16:511
24:25	15:370
25:1–26:32	16:511
25:9ff.	16:598
25:10ff.	6:106
25:13–26:32	16:511
25:14	16:511
26	14:458
26:1	16:544
26:1ff.	16:598
26:12–18	16:478
26:14	13:374
26:16	14:531
26:20	14:613
26:25	16:96
28:23	14:785

Romans

Generally	9:156, 159, 217, 301, 316, 397, 496
1	14:730
1:1	9:229, 401
1:3	14:459, 871; 16:478
1:3–4	16:478
1:4	16:471, 473
1:7	4:253; 8:222; 15:72
1:8	15:381, 382
1:9	4:128; 14:534; 15:334
1:9–10	15:225
1:11	1:227
1:13	9:399
1:16	9:39, 491; 15:232
1:16–17	10:248
1:17	4:67; 14:345, 608
1:17–18	1:192; 14:608
1:18	4:141
1:18ff.	10:386
1:19–20	15:346

1:19ff. 15:402
1:20 9:403; 14:680
1:21 15:382; 16:492
1:22–25 14:789
1:24 14:727, 731
1:24–32 16:593
1:24ff. 14:726, 731
1:28 14:730; 15:358
1:29 4:265; 14:728
1:29ff. 14:731
1:30 15:345
1:32 4:264; 14:727, 731; 15:372, 378
2:1–2 14:617–18
2:1ff. 15:277
2:4 9:248; 14:345, 763; 15:355; 16:490
2:6 14:614–15
2:6–7 14:617
2:6ff. 4:277
2:7 15:354, 356
2:7–10 14:792
2:10 15:369
2:11 4:277
2:12 4:217
2:13 4:277; 9:492; 14:614, 617, 725; 15:277
2:14 14:765
2:14ff. 9:490
2:15 9:307; 14:380
2:16 15:325
2:18 6:320; 15:358, 360
2:20 9:244
2:23 15:345
2:26 12:207
3 14:606
3:3 14:607
3:4 4:256; 9:300, 455; 15:337
3:5 9:300
3:12–13 14:792, 793
3:12–20 14:608
3:17 15:368
3:19 4:217
3:20 14:614
3:21 4:21ff., 254–55; 14:608
3:21–5:21 6:147
3:21ff. 14:608
3:22 14:346
3:23 1:204; 9:453; 10:581; 14:609; 15:345, 346
3:23–26 14:345–48, 804, 968
3:24 1:109; 4:50; 14:345
3:24ff. 8:373
3:25 4:254–55; 14:88, 347, 352, 608, 609
3:26 4:254–55, 256; 10:283; 14:607, 608, 609; 15:355; 16:558
3:27 9:493; 15:345, 346
3:28 4:50; 6:147, 289; 14:614
3:28–31 4:278; 14:615
3:31 4:278; 9:349; 14:614, 803
4:2 14:614, 698; 15:345
4:4 4:50
4:4–5 14:614

4:5	14:607, 609, 614
4:6	14:614
4:11	14:722; 16:554
4:15	9:403
4:16	14:607
4:17	3:43
4:17–21	14:607
4:18	1:124; 4:98; 9:276
4:25	14:608; 16:474
5	9:159
5:1	15:365, 368, 543
5:1–2	15:311
5:1–5	15:39, 355, 359
5:1–11	4:218
5:2	15:559
5:2ff.	1:124; 10:387
5:3	15:353, 357, 359
5:4	15:358
5:5	1:168, 171; 4:221; 8:116; 10:387, 446; 13:394; 14:456, 479, 805
5:6	15:372
5:6–8	14:760–66
5:7	14:756, 765
5:8	4:10, 263; 14:612; 15:372
5:9	15:367; 16:568
5:10	9:401; 14:760–66; 15:469
5:11	15:559
5:12	14:793, 794; 15:345, 346, 372, 377, 378
5:12–14	2:136
5:12–19	6:137
5:12ff.	1:110–11, 138, 146, 154; 10:386; 15:345
5:13	9:403
5:14	15:372, 378
5:16	14:608
15:17	15:372, 378
5:18ff.	4:217
5:19	4:215; 14:612
5:19–20	1:138
5:21	14:611; 15:372, 378
5–6	4:208
6	2:157; 14:447, 479, 483, 606, 818; 15:337
6:1	9:244
6:1ff.	14:366–67, 475, 826; 15:373
6:2	1:123; 14:829
6:3	4:207, 208, 216, 258; 14:367, 610, 818; 15:378
6:3–4	14:631; 16:53, 54
6:3–5	8:448
6:3ff.	4:209, 228; 9:446
6:4	4:152, 217; 14:619; 15:378; 16:557
6:4–5	4:285; 16:557
6:5	4:217; 14:472; 15:378
6:6	4:152, 217; 9:401; 14:367
6:7	4:209; 14:475, 610
6:7–9	1:123
6:8	4:217; 14:475, 606; 16:557

6:9	14:367, 479, 728, 734; 15:378
6:10	3:47; 4:210, 211; 14:367, 610
6:11	4:210, 255, 258, 271; 14:610–11; 15:377; 16:557
6:12	14:611; 15:372, 378
6:13	1:136, 139; 2:111; 11:302; 15:373
6:14	14:611; 15:345
6:14a	4:263
6:16	9:401; 15:372, 378
6:16–21	14:724
6:16–23	14:724
6:16ff.	15:345
6:17	14:611, 618; 15:381; 16:490
6:18	14:460, 611, 618
6:19	1:136, 139; 2:111; 14:725, 727, 731, 734
6:19–22	4:253
6:20	14:611
6:21	15:378
6:22	14:611, 724
6:23	1:146; 14:793, 890; 15:372, 377, 378
7	12:220, 257; 14:454, 618; 15:61, 345, 346
7:5	4:217; 15:372
7:6	9:349
7:7	15:346
7:8	9:403
7:10	15:372, 378
7:12	9:349; 14:794; 15:325
7:13	15:378
7:14	9:327; 14:618
7:14–18	4:221
7:14ff.	14:810
7:16	15:325
7:18	14:792, 793
7:19	1:124
7:23	12:357
7:24	10:512; 14:966; 15:372, 378
7:24–25	14:801
7:25	9:342; 15:381; 16:489
8	10:385; 14:310, 484; 15:61
8:1	4:210, 267–68; 5:172; 14:309, 619; 15:378
8:1–2	9:397
8:1–26	14:479
8:2	9:493; 15:345, 378
8:2–3	4:283; 14:612
8:3	4:214, 217; 12:313, 356; 14:510, 799, 889; 15:372
8:3–9	8:429
8:4	4:210; 12:207; 14:619
8:5ff.	14:810; 15:344
8:6	10:401; 14:458; 15:365, 367, 372, 378
8:7	15:346
8:8	4:9, 217
8:9	14:457, 478
8:9–11	4:209

8:10	4:221; 9:397; 15:373, 378
8:11	15:373, 378
8:12–13	14:611, 793
8:12–16	15:40
8:13	15:3, 84, 372, 378
8:14	1:136, 139
8:14ff.	4:209
8:15	9:401; 14:456, 478; 16:558
8:15–16	14:812
8:15–17	14:800
8:15ff.	14:800
8:16	4:210; 9:410; 14:457, 478, 805
8:17	10:387–88
8:17ff.	16:52, 677
8:18	6:95
8:18ff.	14:584; 15:373
8:19	6:260
8:19–21	14:755
8:19–22	14:584, 759
8:19ff.	2:153
8:20–21	10:366
8:20ff.	1:124
8:21	6:260
8:22	9:401
8:23	9:350; 14:483
8:25	15:353, 355
8:26	4:154; 5:70; 8:491; 9:399, 403; 14:263, 478–79, 936; 15:506
8:26–27	16:558
8:28	7:226; 8:195; 10:387; 11:261; 14:797, 798, 852; 15:285; 16:487
8:28–29	14:310
8:29	1:136; 4:281; 6:94; 12:315; 16:550
8:31	8:485; 11:433; 12:8, 440
8:32	4:165, 168; 10:262; 16:489
8:34	14:805; 16:480
8:35	9:464; 10:388
8:35ff.	4:222
8:38	9:401
9	11:322, 323
9–11	12:418; 14:561, 868–50, 961
9:1–2	10:385
9:1–3	11:322
9:1–5	14:868; 16:497
9:3	4:275; 14:607, 836, 868
9:4	14:868
9:4–5	5:148; 15:3, 84, 574
9:5	14:868
9:6	14:614
9:6–13	14:868
9:7	14:868
9:7–9	14:614, 868
9:8	14:868
9:11	9:291
9:11ff.	1:184
9:12	14:869
9:14ff.	14:869
9:16	14:614
9:17	14:869
9:18	14:869
9:19–23	13:407
9:20	9:434, 435

9:20ff. 9:435
9:21 10:353
9:21–23 14:835
9:21–29 9:462
9:22 15:355
9:27 14:869
9:30–10:3 14:869
9:33 14:607
10:1 16:497
10:2 15:334
10:3 4:257–58; 14:608, 869
10:4 4:73, 115; 12:372; 14:775, 803
10:4–8 14:869
10:6 9:221
10:7 15:375
10:8 14:531
10:9 457, 459
10:10 9:398
10:11 14:869
10:14 14:606, 806
10:15 15:139, 368, 430
10:17 1:228; 6:166; 9:398; 14:457, 458, 607, 806, 812; 15:139; 16:494, 559
10:44 14:487
11 9:300
11:1 11:322; 14:869
11:1–2 14:961
11:2–4 14:869
11:6 10:64, 74, 76, 88, 127, 480–85, 627–28; 14:614
11:7 14:869
11:11 14:869
11:11–15 5:148; 15:3, 84, 574
11:11–16 14:961
11:15 9:402; 14:870
11:17 14:870
11:17–21 5:90
11:18 15:345
11.20 15:403
11:21–13:7 15:40
11:22 5:104; 6:105, 423; 14:870
11:24 14:870
11:25 14:870
11:25–27 14:753, 870
11:25–32 14:961
11:25ff. 9:390
11:26 1:101
11:28 14:870
11:29–36 5:90
11:33–35 10:516
11:34 9:300
11:36 2:95; 9:413; 15:235
11:38 9:401
12 15:62
12:1 6:370; 9:228; 15:340
12:2 3:61; 4:103, 247, 281, 283; 6:93–94, 296, 320, 322–23; 14:474, 738, 764; 15:344, 353, 358, 360, 361, 363
12:3 5:96
12:4–8 14:451
12:4–21 14:829
12:4ff. 1:136, 139, 183; 2:111

12:5 4:218, 220, 229; 6:67; 9:396; 14:451, 465
12:5–6 10:385
12:5ff. 1:141, 193; 14:808
12:6 1:227; 14:468, 822
12:7 14:468, 822
12:8 6:319; 14:470, 822, 823
12:10 14:473, 791
12:11 1:233, 272; 8:321; 14:473
12:11c 10:527–31, 608, 638
12:12 4:250; 14:811; 15:353, 357, 361
12:13 15:363
12:14 1:186; 15:361
12:14–21 5:90
12:15 8:405
12:16 5:96; 15:426
12:17 5:96; 9:538, 540
12:17–21 15:465–71
12:18 14:297; 15:40, 365, 369
12:19 5:175; 6:144; 14:967
12:20 4:140; 15:470
12:21 4:108, 136, 243; 10:183; 14:790
12:21–13:7 4:238
12ff.(–15) 14:606
13 6:427; 11:336; 14:432, 492; 15:62, 363; 16:59, 422, 516
13:1 6:73, 120; 9:535; 12:359; 13:275; 14:261; 16:503, 505, 513
13:1a–1c 4:240
13:1–7 14:492; 16:731
13:1–8 14:337
13:1ff. 4:240, 243; 10:385
13:2–3 4:241
13:2–4 16:592
13:3a 4:242
13:3–4 14:790
13:4 4:241; 16:513
13:5 4:242; 16:516
13:6 4:243; 16:550
13:7 16:516
13:8 9:400; 14:803
13:10 9:400; 14:776
13:11–12 10:285
13:12 9:478, 490; 14:613; 15:344
13:13 14:726, 728–29, 731, 734
13:14 1:137, 140; 2:112; 9:440, 446; 11:302; 14:447
13:22 3:61
14 4:55; 9:271; 11:336; 12:127; 14:334; 15:62, 150
14:1 15:56
14:1–15 5:71
14:4 15:167
14:6 12:431; 15:381
14:6–8 14:735
14:7 9:403
14:7–9 14:735, 783

14:7ff. 15:373
14:8 15:23
14:9 15:369
14:10–12 14:615
14:10ff. 14:614
14:15 15:56
14:17 9:380, 400; 15:365, 368
14:18 15:357, 360, 365
14:21 15:56
14:22 15:358
14:23 9:275, 527; 14:92; 15:56, 344, 346, 419; 16:594
15 8:87
15:1 15:352
15:1–33 62
15:4 13:654, 785; 15:352, 353
15:5 6:229; 15:82, 83, 352, 355, 356, 426
15:5–13 12:495
15:6 5:67; 16:550
15:7 5:24; 8:78, 87; 14:938
15:13 15:368
15:20 1:136
15:28 14:722
15:30 4:221; 14:456
15:33 15:366, 368
16:1 14:470, 823, 824
16:1–27 15:62
16:2 4:9, 12, 234
16:3 15:341
16:4 15:381
16:5 14:470
16:7 14:467, 821–22
16:10 15:358, 360
16:17 4:272; 14:832
16:18 4:266; 14:460, 729, 734
16:20 15:366, 367, 368
16:21 14:943
16:23 15:341
16:26 15:322
18:37 9:403

1 Corinthians

Generally 8:336; 9:217
1 16:495
1:1 4:229; 15:424
1:2 1:135–36; 4:253, 259; 14:725; 15:424
1:3 8:422
1:4 15:381
1:4–9 16:155
1:5–6 4:265
1:6ff. 15:357
1:10 1:193; 14:461; 15:344, 426
1:10–17 14:818
1:11 14:460
1:11ff. 4:231
1:12 4:205
1:12–13 14:837
1:13 1:137, 140; 2:111; 9:272, 440; 11:302; 14:818
1:14ff. 4:229
1:16 16:553
1:17 348
1:18 9:491; 10:465; 14:88, 348–52; 15:345, 467

1:18–19 10:382
1:18, 23 13:315
1:18–25 8:472
1:20 9:402; 15:118
1:21 10:465
1:22–24 12:419
1:23 10:465; 12:313, 319; 14:531
1:24 14:466, 820
1:25 10:465
1:26–28 4:237
1:27 10:465
1:27–28 7:107
1:27–29 10:353
1:29 10:465
1:29ff. 15:346
1:30 1:137, 140; 2:111; 4:258, 275, 280; 11:302; 14:609, 724; 16:495
1:30–31 4:280
1:31 9:529, 534, 536, 540; 15:228
2 11:449; 12:215; 14:795
2:1–4 15:325
2:2 2:129, 132; 6:317; 9:529; 14:367
2:5 14:457, 607
2:6–7 14:466
2:6ff. 14:820
2:7–10 13:350–63; 14:941; 15:529
2:8 14:607; 15:50
2:9–10 14:483
2:9–13 14:478, 479, 483
2:10 4:209; 14:457
2:12 2:125, 132; 4:210; 14:479
2:12–13 9:520
2:14 14:513
2:15 6:316
3 1:246; 15:375; 16:482–87, 484, 494
3:2 10:128; 13:94; 15:50; 16:494
3:3 14:479
3:3–4 14:460
3:3–10 16:485
3:5 12:411
3:6 4:231
3:6–8 14:214
3:8 14:614, 615
3:9 16:485, 498
3:11 1:136; 4:224; 7:68; 14:807
3:11–20 16:486
3:13 6:153; 15:344, 358, 359
3:14 14:614, 615
3:15 9:399; 14:618
3:16 1:137–38, 140–41; 2:111; 4:224, 258; 9:536; 10:376; 11:302; 14:449, 456, 457, 483
3:16–17 14:478
3:18 9:300
3:19 16:484, 486
3:20 16:484, 486
3:21 16:487
3:22 16:495
3:22–23 8:102; 14:915
3:23 8:539; 16:482
4:1 14:464, 820, 944; 16:550

4:3–4 6:326; 12:220
4:4 6:326; 12:211, 233; 14:380
4:5 14:614, 615
4:6 14:467
4:7 15:323
4:9 14:467
4:10 4:222
4:13 15:323
4:14 15:323
4:14ff. 14:468, 822
4:17 14:943; 15:323
4:20 13:410
5 1:259; 9:398; 11:320; 14:461
5:1 14:732
5:1–2 14:728
5:1ff. 4:264, 265
5:2 4:276; 14:838
5:2–5 14:449
5:3–5 5:71
5:5 4:274; 6:316; 11:330; 14:834, 835
5:6 1:138, 141
5:9–10 14:728
5:9ff. 4:266
5:10 4:244, 248, 264; 14:726, 727, 730
5:10–11 14:726, 729, 730
5:11 4:272, 274; 14:612, 726, 272, 730, 832
5:12–13 14:730
5:13 14:449
6:1 15:348, 427
6:1–8 4:250
6:7 9:537
6:9 4:264; 14:726, 727, 730, 731; 15:370
6:9–10 14:726, 730
6:9–11 4:277
6:10 4:264; 14:727, 731
6:11 4:209, 259, 263; 9:445; 14:724, 810; 16:556
6:12 16:487
6:13–15 4:127
6:13–19 14:449
6:13ff. 4:265; 14:728, 732
6:15 1:136–37, 139–40, 200; 2:111; 6:137; 9:440; 11:302
6:17 14:449
6:18 15:150, 346, 405
6:19 1:138, 141; 4:224, 258; 14:449, 456, 791; 16:501
6:20 4:45; 14:735; 15:350, 518
7 8:62; 14:729, 734; 15:333
7:1, 7 12:144
7:2 4:265; 14:727, 732
7:3ff. 6:210
7:5 4:160, 249; 14:817; 15:350
7:6 6:387
7:7 4:248; 14:729, 756
7:9 15:370
7:10–11 4:126

7:14 1:257; 9:445; 16:555, 559
7:15 15:333, 365
7:17 6:289
7:17–24 6:289
7:20 6:289
7:20–24 4:237
7:21–22 6:164; 16:544
7:22 4:234
7:23 4:239, 250; 15:344, 346, 518; 16:636
7:25ff. 15:324
7:28 10:388
7:29 4:250; 14:791
7:29–30 11:262
7:29–31 4:301; 14:729
7:29–32a 4:248
7:29ff. 4:97; 14:472
7:30–31 4:78
7:31 14:472; 15:34, 346
7:32 15:56, 371
7:33–40 4:248; 14:756
7:39 4:234, 249; 15:57, 373
8 12:430
8:1 14:466, 821; 15:325
8:1–13 5:71
8:3 6:336; 15:550
8:6 4:94, 214; 14:459, 798; 16:510, 595
8:9–12 15:56, 426
8:10 15:334
8:10–11 14:466
9:1 14:468, 822
9:1ff. 14:822
9:2 14:468, 722, 822
9:3 6:256
9:5–6 14:467
9:9 9:221
9:12 14:816
9:15 4:248; 14:816
9:16 9:298; 13:324, 352; 14:842; 16:498
9:17ff. 14:473
9:18–21 10:383
9:19–21 14:473
9:20 10:383; 12:412
9:21 10:383; 14:473; 15:325
9:23 14:472; 15:334
9:24 15:371
9:25 15:370, 371
9:25ff. 15:348, 371
9:27 14:333; 15:350, 359, 371
10 14:429; 15:350
10:7 4:265; 14:732
10:7[–8] 4:264
10:7–10 14:728, 732
10:8 14:728
10:9 15:344
10:10 15:348
10:11 15:348, 350, 351
10:12 6:77; 12:444
10:12–13 15:348, 403
10:13 8:195; 15:346, 415
10:14 15:405
10:16 8:492; 14:830
10:16–17 4:216; 14:819
10:17 4:218; 5:74
10:17ff. 4:229
10:24 15:266
10:30 15:382

10:31 9:530, 540; 14:784
10:32 1:135
10:33 16:487
11 14:818
11:1 15:427
11:3 16:487
11:3ff. 14:470, 824
11:5 14:470
11:19 14:460; 15:358
11:23–25 15:266
11:24 4:222; 14:830; 15:146, 533
11:26 1:243; 4:228; 14:818
11:28 14:830; 15:358, 360
11:29 4:279; 14:490, 830; 15:34
11:30 8:492; 15:373
11:32 15:345
12 1:138; 9:251; 10:385; 14:484
12–14 9:160
12:1 13:253
12:2ff. 1:136, 138–391
12:3 4:178, 221; 9:446; 12:382; 14:457, 459, 484, 795, 805; 16:558, 620
12:3–4 14:479
12:4 4:6–7, 230
12:4–6 14:465
12:4–10 14:465
12:4–11 14:820
12:4ff. 1:138, 193, 227
12:5ff. 14:808
12:6 14:465, 820
12:7 1:184; 11:322; 14:465, 820
12:8 14:466, 820, 821, 822
12:8–10 14:466, 820
12:9 14:466
12:10 14:73, 466
12:11 14:465, 478, 483, 820
12:11–13 1:138
12:12 2:111; 4:217–18; 9:396, 440; 11:302; 14:448, 451
12:12–26 4:234; 14:451
12:12–27 14:404, 690
12:12–30 12:323; 14:829
12:12ff. 1:136–37, 140–41, 183; 4:220, 229; 14:451
12:13 1:136, 193; 4:209, 210, 213, 216, 218; 9:446
12:18 9:401
12:25 15:277, 426
12:26 10:388, 505, 510; 11:299; 13:64; 15:146, 364, 426
12:26–27 10:127, 638
12:27 1:141; 2:159; 6:96; 10:505–11
12:28 4:28ff., 230; 9:401; 11:273; 15:429
12:31 1:169
13 1:172; 4:304; 5:42; 9:362, 492; 10:385; 12:333; 14:569, 617, 803; 15:140

13:1–3 13:375–81; 14:948
13:2 5:42; 13:394; 14:466, 821
13:2–3 4:180; 6:332
13:3 5:42; 14:948
13:4 10:417, 499
13:4–7 10:584; 13:382–87; 15:354
13:4–8 5:42
13:4ff. 4:180
13:5 15:353, 357, 466, 467
13:5–8 13:358
13:6 6:333; 15:363, 364
13:7 4:172; 6:155; 10:499; 11:442; 13:373; 14:569; 15:119; 16:487
13:8 11:442
13:8–12 4:151, 180; 13:387–91
13:12 2:81, 92; 4:108; 6:48; 8:296; 9:323; 10:515; 12:471; 14:767, 848; 15:218
13:13 4:121, 239, 256; 13:392–96
14 14:672, 822
14:1–31 14:468
14:3–5 14:456
14:5 14:468
14:6 14:466
14:14–17 12:224
14:23 1:205; 14:532
14:24 14:457
14:25 14:457
14:26 14:456, 468, 704, 822, 838; 15:140
14:31–33 14:456
14:32 14:466
14:32–33 4:230; 14:466
14:33 14:466, 824; 15:367
14:34 4:253; 12:429; 15:427
14:34–35 14:479
15 9:499; 14:88, 810; 15:377; 16:500
15:1 16:478
15:1ff. (3–5) 14:459
15:2–3 14:785
15:3 14:804
15:4 14:459
15:5 1:153
15:6 15:373
15:6–7 14:822
15:7 14:467, 468, 822
15:8 15:373; 16:478
15:9 1:135
15:10 15:119
15:12 14:370
14:12–19 14:370–72
15:13 14:370
15:14 14:370, 371
15:14–17 10:127
15:14–19 14:371
15:15 9:322; 14:370
15:16 14:370
15:17 10:485, 637; 12:312, 328; 14:30; 16:474, 487

15:17ff. 10:88
15:18 14:370; 15:345, 373
15:19 10:485, 489; 14:370
15:20 15:373
15:20–23 16:474
15:20–28 14:370, 374
15:20ff. 1:136
15:21–22 15:372, 378
15:22 1:110, 124, 138; 2:136; 4:217; 14:374, 799
15:23 1:137, 140; 9:440; 11:302
15:23–24 15:375
15:24 1:154, 289; 14:374; 16:512, 597
15:24–28 12:296
15:25 8:361
15:26 7:232; 8:333; 15:378
15:27 1:136; 14:374; 16:487
15:28 9:323, 324
15:29 4:208; 9:446; 16:557, 560
15:31 4:128, 159, 209, 211, 221, 251, 258, 267; 6:95; 7:27; 14:475, 611; 15:373, 378, 415; 16:208
15:33 14:532
15:33–57 16:474
15:35ff. 15:374
15:36 15:320, 378
15:44 16:479
15:45 1:136, 138; 2:136; 4:47, 215, 219
15:47 14:447
15:49 4:286
15:50 14:793
15:51 15:141, 373
15:52 15:375
15:53 15:372, 378
15:55 9:230, 320, 383; 15:320, 373, 378, 487–89
15:55–57 14:801
15:56 15:372
15:58 4:234; 14:619
16:1 1:135
16:3 15:358, 360
16:9 15:141
16:10 14:943
16:10–11 14:521
16:11 15:369
16:12 16:484
16:13 2:122; 8:515
16:15 14:470
16:21 5:30
16:22 4:232, 275; 5:176; 9:475; 14:405, 836, 461

2 Corinthians

Generally 3:107; 8:336; 9:411
1:1 1:135; 14:943; 15:323
1:2 8:422
1:3 9:228
1:5 10:388; 15:362, 363
1:5–7 4:222

1:6	15:353, 357
1:6ff.	15:356
1:10	15:378
1:12	14:381; 15:151
1:14	14:608; 15:361
1:15	15:361
1:20	8:511, 514, 515; 14:722
1:21	14:722
1:22	4:260; 9:445; 14:722
1:23	4:128
1:24	2:122; 9:382; 15:343
2:2	15:364
2:3	15:364
2:6–10	14:834
2:6ff.	4:273
2:9	15:358, 359
2:10	4:273; 14:612
2:12	15:141
2:14	8:313; 15:381, 484–86
2:17	4:234
3:2	14:486
3:2–11	16:201
3:5	9:262, 399
3:6	10:368; 14:457, 480; 15:555
3:8	14:480
3:13–16	14:855
3:17	4:209, 221; 9:411; 10:366; 14:454, 478, 483, 486
3:18	4:108, 131, 283, 286, 288; 6:94, 322; 7:49; 14:596
4:1	14:475, 515, 583
4:3	1:124
4:6	4:267; 15:344; 16:141, 144
4:7	9:261; 15:118
4:7ff.	10:387
4:8	15:363
4:10	4:222; 14:475; 15:373, 378
4:10–12	4:222
4:11	15:372, 373, 378
4:12	15:362, 373, 378
4:14	2:132
4:15	15:382
4:16	1:228; 4:267; 14:486, 611
4:20	10:387
5:1	2:132; 4:1ff., 219
5:1–4	6:306; 14:448
5:1ff.	15:373, 374
5:2	4:4, 219; 14:447
5:2ff.	6:306
5:7	1:191, 222, 264, 279; 9:412; 11:246
5:8	15:374
5:9	15:374
5:10	2:144, 147; 4:277; 11:309, 320; 13:326–31; 14:593, 614, 615, 792, 856
5:11–19	12:411
5:12–13	15:345
5:13	14:475
5:14	4:217
5:14, 15	15:271, 373
5:14–16	14:761, 764
5:16	4:205

5:17 1:123, 137, 140; 4:98, 115, 207; 5:112; 6:158, 405; 8:231; 11:302; 14:352, 441, 450
5:18 14:806; 16:473
5:19 4:19ff., 257; 6:63, 82; 9:492, 500; 14:352–53; 16:543
5:19–21 14:88, 352–53
5:20 4:222, 257; 10:548; 13:303, 321–26
5:21 4:214, 217, 257; 5:181; 12:357; 14:353, 608; 15:372
6:1 8:313; 15:484–86
6:1–10 8:13; 15:484
6:2 6:151; 15:274
6:8 15:230
6:9 15:97, 373, 378
6:10 8:313; 15:145, 484–86; 16:487
6:13 15:323
6:14 15:433
6:14ff. 4:266
6:15 13:253
6:16 1:137, 138, 140–41; 2:111; 11:302; 14:457, 478
7:1 14:724, 727, 732
7:2 14:732
7:3 4:217
7:4ff. 15:364
7:6–16 15:342
7:9 15:361
7:10 14:586, 594; 15:320, 378
7:13 9:381
8:2 6:319; 9:382, 400; 15:358, 359
8:8 15:358, 359
8:9 4:214; 14:799
8:22 15:358, 360
8:23 14:467, 821
9:7 14:530
9:11 6:319; 15:382
9:12 15:381
9:13 6:319; 15:358, 359
10:3 4:217
10:4–5 8:224
10:5 2:132; 14:586, 777
10:6 15:427
10:7 14:817; 16:484
10:12 2:144
10:18 15:360
11–12 14:793, 926
11:13–15 14:817
11:14 3:107; 6:77; 8:38; 12:217; 14:793, 926; 15:393; 16:531
11:16ff. 15:345
11:19 15:355
11:21ff. 15:334
11:23 15:378
11:23–25 4:243
11:26ff. 10:387
12 10:388; 15:411
12:2 14:822
12:4 3:147: 5:65; 8:365
12:5–9 10:522

12:7 589; 15:349, 413
12:7–9 14:589
12:8 9:400
12:9 9:221; 10:139, 334, 521–27, 586, 638; 12:43, 466, 467; 13:187, 316, 393, 401–4; 14:711; 15:313, 321, 413
12:12 11:413; 14:468; 15:354
12:19 6:255
12:20–21 14:726
12:21 4:265; 14:727, 728, 731, 732
13:3 15:358
13:3ff. 15:359
13:4 4:234
13:5 1:137; 2:111; 4:221; 6:317, 320, 325–26; 11:302; 14:607, 807; 15:350, 358, 360
13:5–8 13:358
13:7 15:357
13:8 6:326; 13:315
13:9 4:222
13:10 15:428
13:11 15:366, 368, 369, 426
13:13 1:136, 139; 4:221; 14:456, 459, 478, 479, 483, 484, 530, 635, 796

Galatians

1–4 12:368
1:1 14:467
1:2 1:135; 9:399
1:4 4:217; 9:402; 10:386, 518; 15:344
1:6–7 15:122
1:8 4:232; 14:405, 461
1:8–9 4:275; 14:836
1:8–10 5:176
1:9 4:276; 14:838
1:10 9:229, 401
1:13 1:135
1:13–14 4:121; 6:150
1:15 9:402; 15:334
1:19 14:467, 822
2:1 15:342
2:1–10 12:368; 15:425
2:2 9:397
2:3 15:342
2:3ff. 15:434
2:5 1:204; 12:431
2:11 14:704
2:11–21 14:473
2:14 12:431
2:15 4:17, 263
2:16 14:606, 607, 614; 16:558
2:19 4:285; 15:378
2:20 1:136; 2:122, 147, 150; 4:152, 221, 267, 287; 6:149; 9:397, 407; 14:451, 457, 606, 611; 16:558
2:21 3:119
2:22 9:401
3:1–14 6:147

3:2 14:456, 614
3:3 4:160; 14:191
3:5 14:478, 614
3:10 10:387; 14:355, 614, 793
3:10–12 14:356
3:10–13 14:88, 355–57
3:11 14:355
3:12 14:356, 792
3:13 4:217; 12:288; 14:356, 358, 612; 15:372
3:16 9:221
3:22 14:607; 16:558
3:23 4:260; 14:723; 15:369; 16:558
3:24 12:126; 14:456; 15:302; 16:587, 596
3:25 16:558
3:26 14:607
3:26–27 14:631
3:26ff. 16:557
3:27 1:137, 140; 2:112; 4:207, 216, 219; 9:440, 446; 14:447, 818, 859
3:27–28 4:210, 236; 14:812, 829
3:28 1:137, 140, 192, 205, 231; 2:111; 3:97; 4:218, 237; 6:164, 290; 7:107, 220; 9:159, 440; 10:388, 580; 11:302; 14:395, 447, 450, 809, 920
3:29 9:224
4 14:787
4:4 1:147; 4:214; 14:799
4:6 8:400; 9:403, 407, 410; 16:426
4:7 9:401
4:8 11:302
4:8–11, 21–31 12:368
4:9 2:92; 6:93; 8:296; 14:459; 15:549
4:13 14:467, 822
4:14 15:350, 351
4:19 4:222; 6:322; 8:475; 15:323
4:22 9:221
4:26 14:453
5 11:320
5:1 10:366; 11:236
5:3 4:264
5:4 14:459
5:13 15:370
5:14 9:400
5:16 4:210; 14:619; 15:346
5:16–25 14:479, 810
5:16ff. 15:344
5:17 4:160, 267; 15:351
5:18 4:210
5:19 4:263, 264, 266; 14:613, 727, 728, 731; 15:372
5:19–21 4:263–64, 266; 14:726; 15:346; 16:593
5:19–23 14:620, 730, 735

5:19ff.	4:266; 14:730
5:20	14:726; 15:367
5:21	4:264; 14:727, 729
5:22	4:24, 127, 267; 9:399; 14:606, 613, 620; 15:325, 255, 267
5:22–23	8:400; 16:627
5:23	15:325, 370
5:24	10:387; 14:611
5:25	4:210; 14:606, 619
5:25–26	10:385
6:1	5:102; 6:316; 14:696; 15:347, 370
6:2	1:180, 188; 4:88, 120; 5:100; 9:493; 10:510; 12:398
6:4	6:325; 15:345
6:5	11:320
6:6	14:468
6:7	12:463; 13:346; 14:731, 968
6:7–8	14:794
6:8	14:191
6:10	4:250; 12:365
6:11	5:30
6:12–13	14:361
6:14	4:163, 285; 14:361–64, 608, 804; 15:344
6:15	1:137; 8:231, 365; 14:441, 450
6:16	15:323, 350
6:17	4:222; 10:387; 14:475; 15:352

Ephesians

Generally	9:217, 251
1:3	14:725
1:3–14	15:88
1:3ff.	14:722
1:4	4:214, 253, 276; 9:402; 10:388; 14:724
1:4ff.	1:136–37, 142, 165, 218
1:5	10:388
1:5–6	14:800
1:5–9	14:800
1:7	8:422
1:8	14:466, 820
1:9	2:132; 4:210
1:10	8:230; 14:464, 820; 16:543
1:11	1:142
1:12	8:82, 87
1:12–14	4:261
1:13	14:722
1:14	4:260; 14:722, 723
1:15	14:607
1:16	15:381
1:17–19	14:607
1:19–21	16:479
1:20	16:479
1:21	16:597
1:22	1:136; 14:450
1:22–23	4:220; 6:96; 16:625–26
1:23	1:136–37, 139–40; 2:111; 6:75; 10:388; 11:302; 14:450; 16:480
1:26	10:388
2	12:417, 426; 14:620

2:1 9:478, 484; 15:372, 377
2:2 14:113, 619
2:4 10:385
2:5 4:217; 9:440, 478, 484; 15:372
2:6 16:481
2:8 6:147
2:8–10 4:278
2:9 14:614; 15:345
2:10 4:163; 12:402; 14:613, 614, 615
2:12 9:399; 16:503
2:14 2:111; 5:32; 6:88; 11:379, 423, 426; 12:417, 426; 14:297, 808; 15:311, 366, 367, 489, 544
2:14–15 15:367
2:14–16 4:108
2:14ff. 15:365
2:15 1:136–37, 138, 192; 4:218; 14:442, 446, 721
2:16 15:367
2:18 1:136; 15:365
2:19–22 14:193
2:20 4:224, 227, 230; 14:239, 444, 448, 467, 468
2:20ff. 1:136, 246
2:21 1:246; 4:224; 14:448, 619
2:22 1:136, 139; 4:221; 14:455, 456
3:2 14:464, 820
3:3 15:346
3:3–4 8:32
3:5 14:822
3:6 4:216; 14:472
3:9 14:464, 820
3:13–21 16:155
3:15 1:263
3:15–21 14:796
3:16–17 4:209
3:17 4:221; 14:456, 457, 458; 15:554
3:18 5:87
3:18–19 10:283
3:19 4:220; 12:450; 14:450
3:20–21 15:237
4 10:385
4:1 4:262; 14:725
4:1–4 16:155
4:2 5:102; 15:355
4:3 1:193; 4:221; 14:456, 479, 484; 15:138, 365
4:4–5 10:581; 14:818
4:4–6 4:174
4:4ff. 1:136, 138, 183, 193
4:5 1:200; 9:446; 14:818; 15:425
4:5–6 14:405
4:7–16 9:160
4:8 9:440; 11:302
4:8–10 15:375
4:8ff. 1:137, 140; 16:480
4:10 15:139; 16:479
4:11 4:230; 11:273; 14:464, 468,

	469, 700, 820, 822, 838; 15:139
4:12	4:221; 14:456
4:12ff.	1:183
4:13	1:137, 247; 14:80, 131, 619, 677, 818
4:15	12:435; 13:380; 15:167, 422, 423
4:15–16	1:136, 139, 247; 2:111
4:16	1:138; 14:619
4:17	15:324
4:19	4:264; 14:727, 728
4:22	4:263; 9:490
4:22–32	16:155
4:24	1:137, 140; 2:112; 4:218, 219, 287; 9:440; 11:302; 14:447
4:24–32	14:447
4:25	746, 791
4:26	5:79
4:28	4:248; 14:791
4:29	5:95
4:30	4:260; 9:445; 14:480, 484, 722, 723; 15:146, 218; 16:557
4:31	14:726
4:32	4:269; 5:109; 14:612, 746
5	8:410; 9:396; 10:385
5:1	4:288
5:2	4:287; 14:619
5:3	4:3–4, 264; 14:727, 730, 731
5:3–4	14:726
5:3–8	15:346
5:3ff.	14:730
5:4	3:77; 14:730
5:4–5	14:725
5:5	4:264; 9:314; 14:727, 731
5:8	4:263; 6:320; 15:344
5:9	4:266; 6:322; 14:479, 619, 620
5:9–10	6:296, 320
5:10	6:296, 320, 323; 15:358
5:11	4:263; 9:487; 14:613; 15:344
5:14	2:149; 3:77, 154, 163; 5:52; 9:478; 11:473–75; 14:812; 16:557
5:15	14:619
5:15–21	6:324, 463
5:16	8:311
5:17	6:320, 324
5:18	5:53, 66; 6:324; 14:729, 734
5:19	5:53, 66
5:20	10:578; 15:382; 16:487, 490
5:21–35	16:550
5:22	14:453
5:22–24	14:453
5:22–32	4:249; 14:819
5:22–33	4:220; 8:410; 13:410; 14:452, 453
5:22–6:9	16:598

5:23 8:86; 14:725
5:23–32 12:323
5:23ff. 1:136
5:25 1:136, 139
5:25–27 4:276
5:25–33 14:453
5:26 9:398; 10:388; 16:557
5:27 1:219; 4:253; 13:189
5:28 8:85
5:30 1:138, 141; 10:388; 11:302
5:30–32 3:99, 101; 4:249; 8:86, 410
5:30–33 14:452
5:31–32 6:71
5:32 1:137; 4:220, 249; 14:453
5:33 14:453
6:1 16:555
6:2 14:790
6:2–3 8:86
6:4 9:231
6:5 16:544
6:9 6:391
6:10 8:515
6:12 4:108; 7:165; 13:306; 15:398
6:11 14:793
6:12 14:793
6:14 2:122
6:14–17 14:760
6:15 15:365
6:16–17 15:415
6:17 14:457, 479
6:19 8:32
6:21 15:341
6:23 15:366, 368

Philippians

1:1 9:229; 14:469, 470, 823, 943
1:4 15:362
1:5 15:381
1:6 4:279; 14:614, 615
1:7 6:255
1:8 4:128; 14:534
1:9–10 6:320, 322
1:10 6:320–21; 15:358, 360
1:11 9:399, 400; 14:620
1:13 4:234
1:14 5:34; 15:337
1:16 6:255
1:17 6:255
1:18 10:262–63; 12:429; 13:301; 15:362
1:20 4:222
1:21 1:136; 4:287; 6:95, 250, 253; 7:49; 16:624
1:21ff. 15:361
1:22 9:399, 403
1:23 4:234; 8:342; 14:135; 15:340
1:23–24 14:739; 15:374
1:25 15:349, 361, 362, 364
1:27 4:262; 14:725
1:27ff. 15:362
1:29 4:222; 9:403; 10:387; 14:607; 15:408
1:30 15:351
2 11:328; 12:46; 15:364

2:1 1:136, 139; 4:234; 9:228
2:1–4 15:141
2:2 15:362
2:2–3:16 1:193
2:5 4:239, 287; 9:400
2:5–8 14:475
2:5–10 14:459
2:5ff. 4:283
2:6 6:332; 14:730
2:6–7 14:799
2:6ff. 4:214
2:7 4:239; 10:136; 12:347
2:8 4:107
2:9 14:359
2:10 6:317; 14:459
2:11 14:459
2:12 9:499; 10:588; 13:400; 14:841
2:13 16:58
2:17 4:222; 10:387; 15:145, 146, 340, 362, 364
2:18 15:364
2:21 15:346
2:22 15:323, 360
2:27 15:362
2:28 15:362
2:29 15:362
2:30 9:403; 15:362
3:1 15:362, 363
3:5 15:335
3:9 4:257–58; 6:147; 14:607, 608; 16:558
3:10 4:285; 6:94; 10:387; 13:208; 15:378
3:10ff. 15:373
3:12 14:619
3:13 14:619
3:19 4:266; 9:464; 14:729, 734
3:20 1:137, 140; 9:440; 11:302; 14:450, 808; 15:373; 16:481, 503
3:20–4:4 15:361
4:1 15:146, 361, 362
4:1–9 15:85, 361
4:3 14:743
4:4 4:234, 250; 9:249, 380, 400; 12:450; 15:145, 361, 362
4:5 4:250
4:6 4:249; 15:362, 382
4:7 1:192; 10:546–51, 584, 638; 13:364; 14:723; 15:268, 366, 368, 369
4:8 4:250
4:9 15:368
4:10 14:817; 15:362
4:12–13 4:249
4:13 4:234; 12:130; 13:405; 15:385; 16:487
4:14 10:388
4:15–18 14:817
4:18 16:487

Colossians

1 16:531
1:1–29 15:290
1:3 15:381

1:4 14:607
1:8 4:221; 14:456
1:9 14:450, 466, 820
1:10 4:262; 14:613, 614, 615, 619, 725
1:11 15:355, 364
1:12 15:382
1:13 14:441, 818; 15:344
1:15 1:136; 6:399
1:15–18 16:550
1:15ff. 6:399
1:16 4:214; 6:68, 402; 14:777, 809; 16:510, 511, 531
1:16–17 6:344, 361
1:17 6:54; 16:510, 511, 531, 543
1:18 1:136, 139; 2:111; 4:220; 6:96; 12:315; 16:510, 543
1:19 6:75; 14:450, 457, 611
1:20 6:75; 15:365, 367, 369; 16:479
1:21 14:613
1:22 4:253, 276; 14:724, 725
1:24 4:222; 6:96; 10:388; 13:93; 14:475; 15:355, 364
1:24–25 15:355
1:25 14:464
1:26–27 8:32
1:27 15:322
2 15:290
2:1 15:351
2:3 5:61; 14:466, 820
2:5 14:607
2:7 4:221; 14:456
2:9 3:96; 4:220; 6:74–75; 11:264; 14:450, 457
2:10 14:450; 16:597
2:11 16:553
2:12 4:209, 217; 9:445, 446; 14:818; 15:373; 16:481, 557
2:13 9:445
2:14–15 4:243
2:15 14:777; 15:485; 16:512
2:16 12:431; 14:448
2:17 1:137, 140; 2:111; 4:223–24; 11:302; 14:448
2:18 15:60
2:18–19 14:807
2:19 1:136, 138, 246; 4:220; 9:160; 14:619
2:22 4:249
2:23 14:466
3 8:84; 15:384
3:1 14:805; 16:481
3:1–2 16:481
3:1–4 11:450–57; 15:522
3:1–25 15:390
3:2 6:95
3:2–4 4:251

3:3 6:95; 14:348, 479
3:3–4 4:251, 252
3:3ff. 15:373
3:4 6:250
3:5 4:8, 264; 14:726, 727, 730, 731; 15:373
3:7 14:619
3:8 9:490; 14:726, 730
3:8–4:1 16:598
3:9 1:137; 9:446; 14:442, 447
3:10 4:218–19, 287; 9:440; 14:447
3:10–11 1:137, 140; 2:111, 112; 9:440
3:11 1:137, 140; 2:111; 4:236
3:12 9:228; 15:355
3:13 4:287; 5:102; 14:612; 15:355
3:15 1:183; 15:366, 368, 369
3:16 4:271; 5:48, 53; 9:399; 11:302; 14:90, 458, 520, 806, 832
3:16–17 13:95
3:17 5:76
3:18–19 8:84
3:18–4:1 4:236
3:20 14:790; 16:503, 555
3:23 5:76; 16:636
4 15:290
4:1 16:544
4:2 15:382; 16:213
4:2–4 10:388
4:3 8:32; 15:141
4:5 14:466, 619, 820; 16:234
4:7 15:341
4:10 15:340
4:12 9:229
4:14 15:340

1 Thessalonians

1–5 15:85
1:1 14:467; 15:323
1:2 15:381
1:3 15:353, 356
1:5 14:607
1:6 15:363, 364
2:4 15:358
2:5 14:534, 727
2:7 14:467, 822
2:7–8 14:468
2:11–12 15:323
2:12 4:262; 14:619, 725
2:13 4:227; 14:458
2:14 1:135
2:17 14:818
2:19 14:743; 15:146
2:19–20 10:579; 15:361
3:2 14:943
3:5 15:350
3:8 2:122
3:9 15:361
3:10 5:29
3:13 14:725
4 11:302
4:3 14:791, 810
4:3–4 14:732
4:3–7 4:264
4:4 14:725
4:4–7 14:727
4:4ff. 4:264

4:5 14:728, 732
4:6 4:249; 14:728
4:6–8 14:480
4:7 14:725
4:9–10 5:33
4:11 4:250
4:11–12 4:248; 14:809
4:12 4:248; 14:619
4:13 14:738; 15:373
4:13–5:11 14:265
4:14 15:373
4:15 15:373
4:15–18 11:302
4:16 1:137, 140; 9:440; 15:373, 375
5 11:302
5:1–4 11:302
5:3 15:366
5:4 15:344
5:5 15:369
5:10 4:217
5:11 4:14, 271; 14:832
5:12 14:470, 823
5:12–28 14:265
5:13 15:369
5:14 8:179; 14:26; 15:354
5:15 9:538
5:16 15:361, 363, 364
5:16–18 10:140, 226, 572, 573–79; 14:916
5:17 5:76; 10:127, 637; 14:811, 915
5:18 15:382
5:19 15:335
5:20 14:468, 822
5:21 6:317; 15:358, 360
5:23 4:260, 277; 8:409; 14:723, 739; 15:366, 368; 16:629

2 Thessalonians

1 14:265
1:1 14:467; 15:323
1:3 14:619; 15:381
1:4 14:608; 15:353, 355
1:7 9:440
1:7ff. 15:375
1:8 6:153
1:11 14:725
2 14:265
2:3–8 14:966
2:4 14:673
2:4–12 14:666
2:6–7 6:131
2:7 6:131
2:11 14:460
2:13 1:136–37; 14:724
2:17 14:614, 615
2:25–26 4:272
3 14:265
3:5 15:352, 356
3:6 4:272; 14:833
3:7–12 14:809
3:8 4:248; 14:816
3:10 4:190; 5:77
3:11–12 4:248
3:12 4:250
3:14 4:272, 273; 14:832, 833, 834
3:15 4:272; 14:833

3:16	15:368
3:17	5:30

1 Timothy

Generally	9:241
1:1	8:105; 15:322
1:2	5:29; 14:939; 15:322, 323
1:3	4:276; 14:837, 944, 947; 15:322–23, 324
1:4	6:104; 14:464; 15:323, 324, 330
1:5	14:950; 15:324
1:6	15:324–25, 332
1:7	15:324–25, 332
1:8	14:731
1:8–10	15:325
1:9	14:461, 731
1:9–10	14:726, 733, 949
1:10	4:231; 14:460, 461
1:11	15:325
1:12	15:381
1:12–17	15:325
1:13	6:349; 8:358; 14:480, 484, 485, 629; 15:334
1:14	14:607
1:15	4:264; 5:97; 6:136; 9:260; 14:453, 612; 15:327, 334, 341
1:16	14:607; 15:355
1:18	14:784, 946; 15:323, 326, 341
1:18–19	14:950
1:19	14:946, 947; 15:332, 341
1:19–20	14:950
1:20	4:274; 14:834, 835; 15:327, 337, 341
2:1	1:186; 4:250; 14:809; 15:323
2:1–2	11:324
2:1–3	14:810
2:2	14:197, 530, 919; 15:342; 16:239, 521
2:2ff.	10:385
2:3	9:232; 15:322, 329
2:4	11:331; 14:794; 16:568, 598
2:5	4:59; 14:799; 15:341
2:5ff.	15:329
2:8	15:330
2:9	15:330; 16:96
2:10	14:613, 614, 615, 947
2:11	10:387; 16:470
2:15	14:947; 16:96
2:22	15:348
3:1	14:308, 467, 469
3:1–7	5:106; 14:592
3:1–13	14:823
3:2	4:275; 14:469, 823, 836; 15:431
3:2ff.	15:431
3:2–7	14:469
3:3	14:727
3:4	14:470, 576

3:5 6:296
3:8 14:470
3:8–9 14:947
3:9 14:381; 15:325
3:10 15:358, 360, 431
3:11 14:470, 823
3:13 14:607
3:14–15 14:940
3:15 14:832, 941
3:15–20 14:947
3:16 14:459, 941; 15:326, 341
4:1 15:331
4:2 4:75; 14:948; 15:314, 331
4:3 14:948; 15:314, 331, 382, 502
4:3–5 5:164
4:4 4:249; 14:727, 809; 15:332, 382; 16:490
4:5 9:387; 15:332–33
4:6 14:940; 15:333
4:7 14:784, 949; 15:324, 333
4:8 15:324, 341
4:10 14:952; 15:322, 333
4:12 14:945, 952; 15:333, 335, 341; 16:498
4:13 4:13–14, 275; 5:58; 14:837; 15:333
4:13–16 4:275; 14:837
4:14 15:325, 326, 241
4:15 15:326
4:16 4:231, 275; 6:255; 14:532, 837, 952; 15:334; 16:486
4:16a 4:275
5:1–2 14:953
5:3–16 14:470
5:4 9:232
5:6 9:478; 15:372, 378
5:10 14:613, 614, 615
5:13 15:324
5:17 14:469, 470, 823; 15:342
5:19 14:469, 823, 834
5:19–21 4:273
5:20 14:834
5:21 14:834, 947, 953
5:22 4:275; 14:464, 700, 835, 836, 838, 947, 952; 15:431
5:22–23 14:820
5:23 14:729, 734, 952; 15:371
5:24 4:271; 14:832
6:1 4:231; 9:535; 14:461
6:1–3 14:460, 462
6:3 14:950; 15:501
6:4 14:948, 949
6:4–5 4:75, 276; 14:837, 949
6:5 4:231, 272; 14:460, 832, 837, 949; 15:358
6:6 15:338
6:6–7 8:386

6:6–9 4:249
6:8 8:386; 15:501
6:9 15:350
6:9–10 14:727
6:10 14:791
6:11 15:339
6:12 14:532, 687, 946, 951; 15:358
6:13 14:459, 532, 534, 953
6:13–21 14:945
6:14 14:953
6:16 6:290
6:18 14:947
6:20 4:231; 14:460, 837, 949, 951; 15:324

2 Timothy

Generally 9:241; 15:427
1 8:105
1:1 15:334
1:2 15:323, 334
1:3 6:349; 8:358; 14:944, 947; 15:324, 334, 340, 381
1:3–5 15:340
1:4 5:29; 14:521, 944; 15:323, 335
1:5 14:942, 946; 15:323, 335
1:6 14:944, 945; 15:335, 340
1:7 4:140; 8:105; 14:180, 456, 945; 15:335, 340
1:8 10:387; 14:945; 15:340, 341
1:9 1:142; 14:614; 15:340, 341
1:9ff. 15:340
1:10 15:340, 372
1:12 4:163; 15:230
1:13 14:607, 950
1:13–14 15:340
1:14 14:456, 457, 945
1:15 15:340, 341
1:16 15:341
1:16ff. 15:341
2:1 8:358, 379, 515; 15:275, 323, 336, 339
2:2 4:275; 12:516; 14:806, 836, 950; 15:323, 431
2:3 14:784, 808, 952; 15:336, 341
2:4 15:336
2:5 15:336
2:6 9:479; 15:336
2:7 15:336
2:8 14:532, 871, 940; 15:323, 336, 518
2:8–13 15:323, 341
2:9 10:387; 14:946, 951; 15:336–37
2:10 14:460; 15:145, 337, 353
2:11 4:217; 10:387; 14:475, 952; 15:373
2:11–12 14:808

2:11ff. 15:337
2:12 14:615; 15:83, 354, 356, 375
2:13 14:886
2:14 4:276; 14:837; 15:337
2:15 4:275; 14:837; 15:337, 358, 360
2:16 4:213; 14:837
2:16ff. 15:337
2:17 4:231, 274; 14:835, 948, 950
2:18 15:337
2:19 1:233; 12:309; 14:660; 15:337, 549
2:20 14:835; 15:337
2:21 4:278; 14:614, 615, 835, 947
2:22 15:365, 369, 504, 512
2:22–24 15:341
2:24 4:275; 14:476, 836, 952
2:25–26 4:272; 14:833
2:26 15:338
3:1–5 15:338
3:2 14:727; 15:345
3:2–5 14:726, 731
3:5 4:75, 231, 272; 14:832, 948, 949; 15:338
3:5ff. 4:75
3:6 14:949; 15:338, 433
3:6–7 4:276; 14:837
3:7 4:75, 231; 14:460, 575, 726, 948; 15:433
3:7–8 14:837
3:7–9 15:339
3:8 4:231; 14:460; 15:358
3:10 4:275; 14:462, 837; 15:354
3:10–11 14:943
3:10–12 15:339
3:11 14:943
3:13 4:177; 15:339
3:14 4:275; 14:837
3:14–15 15:339
3:15 5:63; 14:607, 655, 784, 942
3:16 9:231; 14:654; 15:339
3:16–17 14:786
3:17 4:278; 14:614, 615, 947
4:1 14:459; 15:339, 375
4:2 4:271, 275; 10:248; 14:832, 837, 951; 15:339, 375
4:3 4:231; 14:460, 950, 951
4:3–5 15:340
4:4 14:951; 15:323
4:5 14:469, 951
4:6 14:952; 15:340
4:7 15:334, 340
4:7–8 14:953
4:8 8:196; 15:334
4:9 14:521, 944; 15:335
4:9–11 15:335
4:10 15:341, 344

4:13 15:341
4:14–15 15:341
4:15 4:274; 14:835
4:16 6:255; 15:335, 341
4:16–17 15:341
4:18 15:341
4:19–20 15:341
4:21 14:521, 944; 15:232, 335, 341

Titus

1:1–3 15:342
1:3 15:322, 342
1:4 15:323
1:5 14:464, 467, 469, 700, 820, 838; 15:342
1:6 15:342
1:7 14:464, 729, 734, 820; 15:342
1:7–9 14:172, 469
1:8 15:370
1:9 4:231, 275; 14:460, 469, 836, 837, 950; 15:343
1:10 4:13, 231; 14:837; 15:324
1:10–11 15:343
1:11 14:817
1:12–14 15:343
1:13 14:460
1:14 6:105; 15:324
1:15 14:727, 731; 15:343; 16:487
1:16 4:278; 14:614, 615; 15:343, 358
2:1 4:231; 14:460, 950
2:3 14:729, 734
2:10 15:322
2:12 9:247
2:13 15:341
2:14 4:217; 14:801, 947
3 14:484
3:1 4:278; 14:614
3:3 14:619
3:4 4:40, 285; 15:322
3:4–7 1:179
3:5 9:239, 445; 14:479, 614; 16:556
3:7 6:147; 9:445
3:8 4:231, 275, 278; 14:460, 614, 615, 837
3:9 15:324
3:10 4:232, 276; 14:834, 837; 15:433
3:11 4:273; 14:834
3:12 15:342
3:14 4:278; 14:614, 615

Philemon

Generally 15:323
2–8 14:265
4 15:382
5 14:607
8–9 8:62
8–18 4:235
10 15:323
15 14:743, 818
16 4:235, 236; 14:818, 947

21	4:235
22	10:388
14	15:340

Hebrews

Generally	9:217, 229; 15:168
1:1ff.	4:214
1:2	4:94; 9:236, 293; 16:510, 595
1:3	9:236, 237; 12:397
1:5	15:392
1:6	1:136
2:6	9:220
2:11	4:107; 16:550
2:12	5:159, 166; 14:393, 872, 885
2:14	14:801; 15:372, 378
2:15	15:372, 378
2:17	4:107, 123, 284
2:18	14:799; 15:397
3:2	9:238
3:5	9:229, 238
3:7	5:159
3:9	15:358
3:13	15:398
3:15	14:486
4	15:369
4:2	14:607
4:6	9:220
4:7	4:191; 8:201
4:9	3:70; 8:537; 14:790
4:10	14:790
4:12	12:315; 14:842
4:12–13	14:792
4:14	14:364; 16:479–81
4:15	4:214; 6:157; 13:330; 14:364, 388; 15:378, 392, 479, 545
4:15–16	14:88, 364–66
4:16	348
5:7	14:388
6	16:494
6:1	14:614
6:1–3	16:494
6:4	14:456, 480, 611
6:4–6	14:485, 561, 612
6:4ff.	4:210
6:5–6	4:258
6:6	14:480, 484; 15:325, 412
6:12	9:224
6:15	15:355
7:1–3	15:366
7:2	15:368
7:26	16:479
8:2	9:222
8:5	4:223–24; 9:222; 14:873
8:10	9:490
8:13	4:115
9	16:53
9:11ff.	4:210
9:14	4:124; 14:613; 15:372
9:24	16:479–80
9:27	15:372, 378
10:1	4:223–24; 9:222; 14:448
10:5	5:159; 14:872
10:10	3:47; 9:489

10:21–25 12:222
10:22 8:235
10:23–25 14:807
10:24 14:613
10:26 14:611; 15:325, 347, 413
10:26–27 4:258
10:26–29 14:480
10:26–30 14:485
10:27 15:413
10:28 9:228
10:29 12:398, 419; 14:725
10:30 12:419
10:31 9:498
10:32 15:145, 353
10:34 15:363
10:36 15:353, 356
10:36ff. 15:358
11 8:235; 10:17
11:1 9:311
11:3 14:797
11:5 9:238
11:7 9:238
11:8 4:98
11:9 9:224; 15:521
11:10 16:504
11:13 4:251; 14:433, 764
11:17 4:98
11:39, 40 15:358
12 12:397
12:1 1:248; 10:17, 24, 261, 385, 612, 631; 14:542, 612; 15:351, 353, 356, 358
12:2 1:136; 14:765; 15:83, 351, 356, 358, 361, 363
12:3 15:351, 356
12:4 6:138; 13:135
12:4–11 15:348
12:5 9:231
12:7 9:231
12:11 9:231; 15:363
12:12–13 13:40
12:14 4:276; 14:725; 15:365
12:14–17 14:485
12:15 14:469
12:16 4:125, 265; 14:728, 732
12:16–17 14:611
12:17 9:250, 512; 14:612
12:18 15:344, 369
12:22 16:504
13 10:385; 15:364
13:2 14:577
13:4 4:265; 14:728, 732
13:5 14:727
13:7 14:468, 822
13:8 6:132; 10:495; 14:738; 15:243
13:9 8:213; 15:511
13:12 14:890
13:12–13 4:88, 114, 124
13:12–14 14:221
13:14 4:251; 12:471; 15:282; 16:504
13:17 14:468, 822
13:20 14:468; 15:366–68
13:22 15:355
13:24 14:468, 822

James

Generally 9:383
1 15:277
1:1 9:488; 15:363

1:2	15:348, 353, 363, 364
1:2–4	15:401
1:3	15:83, 354, 359
1:4	4:8, 278; 6:81; 14:617; 15:83, 354, 356, 500
1:5	6:319; 14:466
1:6	6:319; 15:330
1:7	6:319
1:8	6:81, 319; 8:278; 14:617; 15:500
1:12	15:349, 353, 358, 359, 415
1:13	15:350, 351
1:13–15	14:793; 15:399
1:14	15:346, 352, 415
1:15	15:346, 372, 378
1:17	4:157
1:18	9:491
1:19–20	9:490
1:20	9:490
1:21	9:490; 14:727, 732
1:21–25	9:488–99
1:22	6:328–29; 9:492; 14:495
1:23	9:492
1:24	6:329; 9:492
1:25	4:181; 6:329; 9:492; 10:366
1:26ff.	9:493
1:27	14:728, 734; 15:345
2:1	9:488
2:1–10	13:322
2:2–6	14:791
2:12	10:366
2:13–17	13:410–11
2:14ff.	14:614
2:15	14:474
2:15–16	5:74
2:16	15:369
2:17ff.	4:278; 14:615
2:19	9:495; 14:617
2:23	9:401
2:25	9:401
3:1	14:468, 489, 822; 15:431
3:2	14:617; 15:500
3:2–12	14:791
3:3–12	5:94
3:13	14:466
3:15	14:466
3:17	14:620
3:18	15:365, 369
4:1–2	4:266; 15:277
4:1ff.	6:137
4:4	6:66; 14:728, 732, 734; 15:346
4:8	6:81
4:9	15:363, 364
4:11	6:327
4:11–12	5:95; 15:277
4:12	6:327
4:13–5:6	14:220
4:14	14:864
4:15	8:183, 275, 384; 14:269; 15:282; 16:529
4:17	14:209
5	15:317
5:7–20	14:220
5:7ff.	15:355
5:11	9:423; 15:349, 352, 357, 414
5:12	9:228, 423
5:13	15:363

5:14 14:469, 470, 823
5:15–16 1:187
5:15ff. 14:612
5:16 5:108, 109, 118; 14:612, 746, 813, 817, 826
5:20 5:106

1 Peter
1:1 4:251; 9:242; 14:472, 808
1:2 14:724, 725; 15:366
1:3–5 14:723
1:4 15:412
1:5 4:260; 14:723
1:6 15:415
1:6–8 15:362
1:7 15:357, 358, 359
1:7b–9 12:468–71, 521
1:8 15:145, 361
1:12 8:361; 9:410; 14:457
1:13 14:85, 219
1:15 10:337
1:15–16 10:566
1:16 14:725, 785
1:17 9:233, 242; 14:472; 15:128, 227
1:20 1:218
1:21 16:481
1:23 9:398
1:25 14:655
2:2 10:490; 14:619; 15:547
2:4 1:136
2:5 4:5ff., 224; 14:441
2:8 13:315
2:9 9:241, 259
2:9–10 14:472
2:11 14:808
2:12 14:785
2:12–17 14:809
2:13 16:516
2:14 16:515
2:16 14:195
2:17 9:535; 16:516
2:18 15:428
2:18–20 14:810
2:20 6:346; 8:180; 15:352
2:21 4:287; 15:352
2:24 4:255, 257; 14:610, 611
2:25 14:468, 469
3:4 15:481
3:7 6:210
3:9 8:409, 493; 9:538; 16:631
3:10 14:791; 15:355
3:11 15:290, 365, 367
3:14 6:210; 8:180
3:15 6:255
3:17 6:210
3:18ff. 15:375
3:20 14:620
3:20–21 14:724
3:22 8:371; 16:597
4 15:363
4:1 4:22; 8:185; 14:475, 808; 15:349, 407
4:2 15:348
4:3 14:619, 728, 729, 732, 734
4:4 14:472
4:4–6 15:375

4:10 14:464, 944
4:12 14:472; 15:400, 408
4:12–17 15:349, 363, 408
4:12–19 14:808
4:13ff. 15:145
4:14 14:785; 15:363
4:15 6:296; 14:489
4:16 15:408
4:17 14:596, 841; 15:400, 401, 501
4:18 15:409
4:19 9:225; 15:349, 409
5:1 14:469, 470
5:1–2 14:823
5:1–11 15:85
5:2 14:469, 817
5:2–3 14:469
5:4 15:548
5:5 12:465, 516; 15:526
5:6 8:292; 9:495
5:7 14:796
5:8 14:535, 793; 15:403
5:9 9:241
5:12 2:122
5:19 9:241

2 Peter

1:1–7 15:597
1:4 9:279; 15:344, 348, 405
1:6 15:83, 354, 357, 370
1:7 4:250
1:10 9:355
1:16 15:324
2:1 9:225
2:4 14:723
2:7 14:728, 732
2:8 14:613
2:9 14:723; 15:349, 415
2:18 14:728, 732
3:7 14:723
3:9 15:355
3:10–13 8:464
3:12 4:156; 14:304
3:13 6:224; 10:536; 12:295; 14:304
3:14 15:365
3:15 15:355, 414
3:18 14:619

1 John

1ff. 14:531
1:1 4:227; 14:534
1:1–2:6 15:41
1:1ff. 14:531
1:2 14:533
1:3b 9:377
1:4 9:376, 377
1:5 5:39; 6:302; 13:328; 15:344
1:7 5:29; 12:344; 14:619
1:8 14:453, 481, 612, 792; 15:346, 505
1:8–2:1 4:269
1:8ff. 9:300
1:9 14:612; 15:505
1:10 14:481; 15:345
1:15–17 14:808
2:1 14:478, 612, 805; 15:345; 16:480
2:2 14:612

2:6	4:287
2:7–17	15:41
2:12	16:555
2:12ff.	4:211
2:14	8:515; 16:555
2:15	4:96, 164; 6:66
2:15–17	14:808
2:16	10:519; 14:731
2:16–17	14:760
2:17	6:156; 10:516–21, 638; 14:230; 15:283; 16:571
2:18–19	14:666
2:19	14:807
2:20	6:316
2:22	14:333; 16:607
2:28	9:376
2:29	14:611
3:1	14:784
3:2	4:286; 12:422
3:4	15:344, 346, 505
3:5	14:611
3:5ff.	15:345
3:6	10:140; 14:481, 611; 15:345
3:8	14:801; 15:345
3:9	4:263, 267; 6:147; 11:217; 14:453, 611; 15:345, 505
3:10	1:183
3:12	16:555
3:13–18	6:334; 14:761, 764
3:14	8:400; 16:555
3:15	14:790
3:16	1:243; 4:287; 6:334; 14:474, 765
3:18	4:140, 181
3:21	9:376, 378
3:24	14:456; 16:628
4:1	12:434; 14:59; 15:460
4:1–3	14:401
4:2–3	14:333
4:3	4:229–30; 14:461
4:4	12:262; 14:179
4:7ff.	6:334
4:8	10:454
4:9	6:334
4:10	6:334; 14:788; 16:315
4:13	14:805
4:13–14	14:796
4:15	4:221
4:16	6:334; 9:460; 11:440–42; 13:358, 395; 16:315
4:16b	10:341, 580–84, 640
4:17	9:376; 15:180
4:18	4:140
4:19	6:336; 14:788; 16:315
4:20	4:124; 10:417; 14:474
4:20–21	14:788
5	14:220
5:2	14:462
5:3	4:39; 5:164; 9:546; 14:784
5:4	13:306, 396; 15:51
5:6	9:446; 14:534
5:7	14:478, 483
5:9	14:534

5:11 14:533
5:13–14 9:376
5:15 9:374, 376
5:16 1:171, 187; 14:480, 484, 485, 612; 15:413
5:17 15:378, 413
5:18 14:485
5:19 6:65; 16:597

2 John

1 14:469
2 14:602
3 15:323
4 9:376, 377; 15:146, 364
6 14:602, 619
7–11 14:602, 696
8 15:48
9 14:838; 15:433
9–10 4:276
10 14:838
10–11 9:377, 378; 14:462; 15:369
10ff. 4:232
11 14:835
12 5:29; 9:376, 377; 15:47

3 John

1 14:469
2 15:48
3 9:376, 377, 378
4 5:44; 9:377; 15:146, 361, 364
6 14:725
8 14:462

Jude

Generally 9:225; 15:52
1 14:723
2 15:323
4 14:728, 732; 15:349
15 14:613
24 15:363
25 15:322

Revelation

Generally 8:180
1:5 1:136; 14:534, 535
1:8 3:29; 6:48–49; 9:321; 10:495; 12:302; 14:789
1:9 14:641, 642; 15:83, 352, 356
1:9–10 8:104
1:9–20 14:640–45
1:10 5:28
1:10–11 14:641
1:11 10:495; 14:655
1:12–16 14:641
1:14 14:644; 16:240, 256
1:17 10:495
1:17–20 14:641
1:18 15:372
1:19 14:643, 645, 655
2 1:120, 384
2:1–7 14:954–56
2:1–11 14:220
2:1ff. 8:429
2:2 15:350, 353
2:3 15:352
2:4 8:429
2:4–5 14:954

2:4–5, 7 12:22, 423, 439–46, 519
2:5 14:191, 929
2:6 4:15ff., 231; 13:93; 14:837, 956
2:7 1:120; 14:855, 954
2:10 10:479; 13:303; 15:373
2:11 15:377, 378
2:13 15:373
2:14 14:461
2:15 14:837
2:20 14:461
3 1:120, 284
3:1–13 14:220
3:5 14:743
3:6 1:120
3:7–12 15:85
3:7ff. 15:437
3:8 15:352
3:10 1:284; 14:723; 15:349, 351, 352, 353, 354, 415
3:11 15:223, 415
3:14 14:534, 535
3:14–22 13:94; 14:220
3:16 1:284
3:20 4:110; 9:505, 511, 551; 10:542–46, 638; 11:413; 12:448
3:22 14:178
4 10:513
4:4 14:460
4:7 14:741
4:8 9:226
4:10 14:470
5:5 14:470
5:8 15:596
5:12 14:466
6 15:374
6:8 15:372, 377, 378
6:10 9:225
7:1–8 10:349
7:4–5 14:722
7:11 14:470
7:12 1:289; 14:466
7:12–17 14:810
7:13 14:470
7:13–14 4:110
7:14 5:56, 173
7:16–17 4:110
7:17 10:556
8:13 14:761
9:6 14:740
10 8:71; 14:654
10:6 8:72
10:9–10 8:208
11:14ff. 9:378
11:15 12:453; 16:550
11:16 14:470
11:17 9:226
12:1 8:404
12:2 8:537
12:9–10 6:84
12:10 12:453; 14:793
12:11 9:378; 15:349
12:12 9:378; 15:363
13 16:545, 597–98
13:1 16:526
13:1–10 14:273
13:7 16:517
13:10 15:353, 356
13:18 14:466; 16:149
14 15:363
14:1–3 10:349
14:2–3 13:357

14:3 5:65; 14:470
14:6 4:196; 9:378
14:6–13 4:179, 196; 14:134, 899–906
14:9 14:904
14:10–11 14:904
14:12 14:607; 15:354, 356
14:13 9:379; 10:479; 15:373
14:13b 3:70
15:2 5:65
15:2–4 14:711
15:3 5:65; 9:226
16:7 9:226
18 5:176
18:2 9:378
18:20 14:822; 15:363
19 5:176
19:1–7 13:357
19:4 14:470
19:7 9:378; 14:453; 15:363
20:1–6 15:375
20:1–10 14:376
20:4 12:424; 15:374
20:6 9:378; 15:377, 378
20:8 13:93
20:11 5:176
20:12 13:328
20:13 15:378
20:14 15:372, 377, 378
21 15:112; 16:512
21:1 6:224; 12:295; 15:238
21:1–3 4:110
21:2 4:105; 6:71; 14:453; 15:22; 16:504, 550
21:3 4:219; 10:491; 14:457
21:4 1:289; 10:540, 556; 12:296, 423; 16:618
21:4–5 14:908
21:5 3:154; 6:158; 10:546; 14:170
21:8 15:377, 378
21:12 4:14, 186
21:18–21 6:71; 9:507
21:21 10:515
21:22 1:289; 4:224; 9:226, 323; 14:448
21:23 16:617
22 14:344; 15:112
22:1 3:146; 14:770
22:1–3 14:769
22:1–5 3:146; 14:767–73; 15:355
22:2 3:146; 14:770, 956
22:3 14:770, 771
22:3–5 14:769
22:4 14:771, 784
22:5 14:771
22:9 14:822
22:11 6:136; 14:724
22:13 6:48–49
22:16 14:873
22:17 14:453
22:20 9:475, 551; 10:546; 15:25

Master Biographical Index of Names

This index lists people mentioned in the sixteen volumes of this edition, including authors and editors of literature cited in the notes. It also includes names referenced in this index volume in the retrospective by Clifford Green, the afterword by Wolfgang Huber, the new documents, and the chronology. It provides brief profiles of the people listed and differs from the German edition by also including information about those whose work began after 1945, as well as additional information of interest to readers of the English edition. It does not include personal names that appear in book titles or only in the bibliography. When possible, dates of birth and death have been provided.

"FP" (fictional person) indicates a character in *Fiction from Tegel Prison.*

Aalen, Leiv: prominent Lutheran dogmatician in Norway and member of the confessional movement (allied with Germany's Confessing Church) during the Nazi era—16

Aaron: biblical character—5, 10, 12, 15

Abegg, Lily (1901–74): Swiss journalist and author; 1936–43, Far Eastern correspondent for the *Frankfurter Zeitung* in Japan; from 1954, for the *Frankfurter Allgemeine Zeitung*—6

Abel: biblical character—2, 6

Abelard, Peter (1079–1142): French philosopher and theologian—1

Abernathy, B. S.: 1934, represented Columbia University at the Fanø youth conference—13

Abigail: biblical character—14

Abimelech: biblical character—15

Abiram: biblical character—15

Abishag: biblical character—14

Abishai: biblical character—14

Abner: biblical character—14

About, Edmond (1828–85): French author—8

Abraham: biblical character—1, 4, 5, 6, 8, 9, 10, 11, 12, 14, 15, 16

Abrahamson, Ernst: until 1919, fellow student of Dietrich Bonhoeffer at the Friedrich Werder Gymnasium, Berlin-Grunewald—7

Abromeit, Christoph (1873–1956): 1909–44, pastor in the Evangelical Lutheran Free church in Rucken/Memel with pulpit duties in Tilsit and Memel; acquainted with the Confessing Church pastors in that area; after 1945, retired, Klettbach near Erfurt—16

Abromeit, Hans-Jürgen: German Lutheran bishop and Bonhoeffer scholar —8, 12, 15

Absalom: biblical character—14

Achelis, Ernst Christian (1838–1912): Reformed theologian; university preacher and professor of practical theology, Marburg—14

Adam: biblical character—1, 2, 3, 4, 5, 6, 7, 8, 10, 11, 12, 14, 15

Adam, Alfred: German professor of dogmatics—15

Adam, Karl (1876–1966): 1917, Catholic professor of moral theology, Strasbourg; 1919, professor of dogmatics, Tübingen—1, 9, 11

Adam, Uwe Dietrich: German historian; author of works on the Third Reich —12, 15

Adams, Frank T.: author of biography of James Dombrowski—10

Adams, James Luther (1901–93): prominent U.S. Unitarian theologian and ethicist—2, 15

Adler, Alfred (1870–1937): Viennese physician and psychotherapist; after being temporarily associated with Sigmund Freud, broke with Freud and founded the practice of individual psychology—14

Admetus: in Greek mythology, king of Pharae; dies in Euripides's play *Alcestis* —17 (for vol. 9)

Adonijah: biblical character; fourth son of David—14

Adorno, Theodor W. (1903–69): German sociologist; leading member of the Frankfurt school of critical theory—2

Aeschylus (ca. 525–456 B.C.E.): Greek tragedian—6, 17 (for vol. 9)

Agabus: biblical character; Christian prophet in Jerusalem—14

Agamemnon: character in Greek mythology—6

Agesander (first century C.E.): Greek sculptor of marble statues; famous for his marble presentation of Laocoön and his sons—9

Agnes: character in Ibsen's *Brand*—10
Agricola, Johann (ca. 1494–1566): originally Johann Schneider; Lutheran theologian, reformer—14, 15, 16
Agrippa, Menenius (Herod Agrippa II): biblical character—4, 14, 16
Aguti, Andrea: Italian professor of the philosophy of religion—8
Ahab: biblical character—15
Ahasuerus: biblical and legendary character—10, 12
Ahithophel: biblical character—6, 15
Ahlbenstiel, Miss (1936): active in the Confessing Church in Pomerania; mentioned in June 1936 Gestapo report—14
Ahlfeld, Friedrich (1810–84): German Protestant theologian; 1851, prominent preacher, Leipzig; author of folktales, devotional books, and sermon collections—10
Aion: Phoenician god of time—15
Akiba-ben-Joseph (ca. 50/55–135 C.E.): rabbi and kabbalist; sayings can be found in the Midrash *Sifra*—9
Aland, Kurt (1915–94): Protestant theologian, exegete, historian, and textual critic; associated especially with editions of the Greek New Testament (known as Nestle-Aland)—10, 16
Alber, Erasmus (1500–1553): student of Martin Luther; follower of the Reformation and pastor, Hesse—5
Albers, Detlef (1902–60): teacher of history, geography, and German at the German Protestant school, Barcelona; 1931, married Katharina, née Rupprich—10
Albertz, Martin (1883–1956): 1921, director of the preachers' seminary at Johannesstift, Berlin-Spandau; 1923, pastor, Stettin-Kückenmühle; 1931–53, pastor and superintendent at St. Nicholas, Berlin-Spandau; 1933, member of the Berlin Confessing Church Council of Brethren; responsible for the assistant pastors and vicars, Berlin-Brandenburg; 1935–41, after dismissal from office, directed the Confessing Church theological examination board, Berlin-Brandenburg; 1936–45, chair, second Provisional Church Administration; 1940, arrested; 1941, sentenced to eighteen months in prison in the collective trial against the Confessing Church examination board; 1945, professor of Reformed theology (university) and of New Testament (seminary), Berlin; 1949, moderator of the Reformed Alliance—8, 14, 15, 16, 17
Albrecht, Johannes (1901–73): Benedictine brother at the Ettal monastery, upper Bavaria; 1940–41, acquainted with Bonhoeffer during the latter's stay in Ettal—6, 16
Albrecht, Karoline: Erwin Sutz's godmother—11

Albrecht von Mainz (Albert of Mainz) (1490–1545): margrave of Brandenburg; 1513, archbishop of Magdeburg; 1514, archbishop of Mainz; 1518, cardinal; powerful opponent of the Reformation; denounced by Luther as *organum Satanae singularissimum* (Satan's unique tool)—9

Alcibiades (ca. 450–404 B.C.E.): Athenian statesman, military commander —8

Alcmaeon in Corinth: in Greek mythology, son of Amphiaraus and Eriphyle; subject of Euripides's play *Alcmaeon in Corinth*—17 (for vol. 9)

Alemany, José: Spanish Bonhoeffer scholar—4

Alexander, Horace: British Quaker from Selly Oak, Birmingham; 1934, recommended to Dietrich Bonhoeffer as a contact to Gandhi and the Indian peace movement; member of the Friends Service Committee in England during the war; spring 1940, with the concurrence of British foreign minister, established contacts with Friedrich Siegmund-Schultze and others in Switzerland—13, 16

Alexander (the coppersmith): biblical character (2 Tim. 4:14–5)—4, 15

Alexander the Great (356–323 B.C.E.): king of Macedonia and military leader—9

Alexis, Willibald (1798–1871): German author of Prussian historical novels —9

Alfonso XIII (1886–1941): king of Spain; 1931, in Roman exile—10

Alivisatos, Hamilcar Spyridonos (1887–1969): Greek Orthodox theologian and ecumenist; 1919, professor of church law, Athens; 1931, secretary of the Orthodox group of the Universal Christian Council for Life and Work; September 1933, delegate (like Dietrich Bonhoeffer) at the conference of the World Alliance for Promoting International Friendship through the Churches, Sofia; 1936, general secretary of the First Congress of Orthodox Theology, Athens; 1948, member of the World Council of Churches; 1951, general secretary of the pan-ecclesiastical apostle Paul celebrations—11, 12, 16

Alla: *see* Stahlberg, Alexander

Alston, Wallace: U.S. Presbyterian minister; 1996–2005, director of the Center of Theological Inquiry, Princeton—11, 14, 15

Altaner, Berthold: German Catholic professor of church history and patristics—12

Altdorfer, Albrecht (ca. 1480–1538): southern German painter and graphic artist—8, 15

Altenähr, Albert: German Benedictine abbot and theologian—2, 4, 8

Althaus, Paul (1888–1966): German Lutheran theologian, especially influenced by Schlatter and Holl; 1920s and early 1930s, considered the

nation, understood as a unity constituted by blood relations, to be an order of creation—a concept eagerly adopted by the German Christians and strictly rejected by Dietrich Bonhoeffer; 1919, professor of systematic and New Testament theology, Rostock; 1925–56, Erlangen; 1933–38, defended the German Christians and National Socialism; 1934, member of the Lutheran Council; 1947, temporarily dismissed by the military government during the denazification proceedings for his early support of National Socialism; 1926–64, president of the Luther Society—1, 2, 3, 4, 6, 8, 9, 10, 11, 12, 13, 14, 15, 16

Althusius (Johannes Althaus) (1557–1638): Dutch jurist and Calvinist philosopher—8

Alvarez de la Campa: one of Bonhoeffer's acquaintances in Barcelona—10

Amann, Max (1891–1957): head of a Munich publishing house; 1922, director of the central publishing house of the NSDAP; 1933, president of the Reich Press Guild—16

Amaziah: biblical character—9

Ambrose of Milan (ca. 340–97): Latin church teacher; bishop of Milan—1, 5, 6

Ambrosius Catharinus (1386–1439): Italian humanist and abbot of the Camaldul monastery, Florence—1

Amelung, Eberhard: studied Protestant theology and economics in Marburg, Bethel, Basel, University of Chicago, and Harvard University; 1954, ThD; 1962, ThD (Harvard); 1969, postdoctoral lecturing qualification in social ethics, Marburg; 1971, professor of social ethics, Marburg; from 1975, professor at the University of the Armed Forces, Munich; publications include *Die Gestalt der Liebe* (1972); *Ethisches Denken in der Medizin* (ed.) (1992); various essays on ethics and medical ethics; coeditor, *DBW* 11, Ökumene-Universität-Pfarramt 1931–32—11

Ames, Edward Scribner (1870–1958): professor and Disciples of Christ pastor, Chicago; prominent pragmatist philosopher—12, 15

Ammermann, Jackie: theological librarian, assisted with *DBWE* 1—1

Ammundsen, Esther (1906–92): daughter of Ove Valdemar Ammundsen —12, 13

Ammundsen, Ove Valdemar (1875–1936): 1901–23, professor of church and dogmatic history, Copenhagen; 1923–36, bishop of Hadersleben, Denmark; member of the Universal Christian Council for Life and Work; from 1919, member, and after 1935, president of the World Alliance for Promoting International Friendship through the Churches—11, 12, 13, 14

Amnon: biblical character—14

Amos: biblical character; shepherd and prophet; preached against social injustice—9, 10

Amsdorf, Nicholas von (1483–1565): theologian and follower of Luther; prepared the way for Lutheran orthodoxy—9

Ananias: biblical character; with his wife, Sapphira, held back part of a gift to the church and lied about it; they were rebuked by Peter and fell dead (Acts 5:1–11)—9, 14, 15

Anaxagoras (510–428 B.C.E.): Greek philosopher—17 (for vol. 9)

Andersen, Dorothea, née Vibrans (Dorli): oldest sister of Gerhard Vibrans; organist and parish aide; 1934, parish aide at St. Gertrud's church, Lübeck; 1939, married Johannes Andersen—4, 8, 15, 17

Andersen, Hans-Christian (1805–75): Danish author and teller of fairy tales—10, 13, 15

Andersen, Johannes: 1938, pastor, Viöl, district of Husum; 1948–78, at the Church of the Cross, Hamburg-Ottensen; 1939, married Dorothea (Dorli), née Vibrans—15

Andler, Erich: 1926, pastor, Schönberg, district of Calau; 1929, Buckow, district of Müncheberg; 1940, arrested—15

Andrae, Tor Julius Efraim (1885–1947): Swedish theologian; 1927, professor of comparative religions, Stockholm; 1929, Uppsala; 1936, minister for church affairs; 1936, bishop of Linköping—15

Andrea del Sarto (1486–1531): Florentine painter of the High Renaissance —9

Andreae, Ursula-Ruth (1904–87): author and publisher; niece of Walther Rathenau; held theological doctorate; Bonhoeffer's classmate; later married Hans von Mangoldt-Reiboldt, author and publisher—9

Andreas, Willy (1884–1967): professor of modern history, Berlin and Heidelberg—8

Andres: member of Bonhoeffer's congregation in Barcelona—10

Andrew: biblical character—4

Andrews, Charles Freer (1871–1940): British Anglican priest and publicist; 1913, joined Tagore's Institute Santinitekan, Bengal, later becoming vice president; 1913–14, supported Gandhi's work in South Africa; 1932, first met Bonhoeffer at joint conference of Life and Work and the World Alliance at Gland, Switzerland—11, 13, 14, 16

Andrich: 1931–32, participant in Bonhoeffer's seminar on "The Idea of Philosophy and Protestant Theology"—11

Andromeda: in Greek mythology, daughter of King Cepheus—17 (for vol. 9)

Andronicus: biblical character—14

Angelico, Fra (Guido di Pietro; as a monk, Fra Giovanni da Fiesole) (ca. 1400–1455): Florentine Italian painter; Dominican monk; outstanding painter of early Renaissance—8, 15

Angell, James Waterhouse (1898–1986): professor of economics, Columbia University, New York—10

Angelus, Silesius: *see* Scheffler, Johann

Anna (FP): character in the drama; *see* the mother—7

Anna (FP): character in the novel; *see* Sophie von Bremer—7

Anna: cook in the Bonhoeffer home—9

Anne (Saint): mother of Mary; patron saint of those in distress; invoked by Luther during his famous experience during a thunderstorm—8

Annie (FP): character in the drama, deceased daughter—7

Anschütz, Gerhard (1867–1948): 1899, professor of civil law, Tübingen; 1900, Heidelberg; 1908, Berlin; 1916–33, again in Heidelberg—9

Anschütz, Liselotte (Lilo): daughter of Gerhard Anschütz—9

Anselm of Canterbury (ca. 1033–1109): scholastic theologian; 1060, monk; 1093, archbishop of Canterbury—1, 2, 6, 11, 12, 14

Antaeus: character in Greek mythology; son of Poseidon and Gaia; defeated and killed by Hercules—6, 7, 8, 10, 14

Anthony (Saint) (1195–1231): Portuguese nobleman who became a Franciscan; patron saint of travelers, the poor and oppressed—10

Antigone: character in Greek mythology—6

Antiope: in Greek mythology, sister of Hippolyte—17 (for vol. 9)

Antonescu: spring 1943, mentioned as a Romanian ecumenist in Dietrich Bonhoeffer's "camouflage letter"—16

Antoni, Wilhelm Karl (1897–1960): from 1930, pastor, Berlin-Kölln—12

Anz, Johannes: pastor, Lebusa; member of the provincial Saxon Council of Brethren—14, 15

Anzinger, Herbert: studied Protestant theology, German philology, and philosophy at the Universities of Mainz and Heidelberg; 1984, ThD, Heidelberg; 1984–93, editor for *DBW*; 1993, minister, Protestant congregation of Heidelberg-Rohrbach—6, 13, 14, 17

Anzinger, Waltraud: Herbert Anzinger's wife—14

Apelles: second-century gnostic in Rome—12

Aphrodite: Greek goddess of feminine beauty and love—8

Apollinarius of Laodicea (ca. 310–390): bishop of Laodicea; defended Nicene Trinitarian doctrine—12

Apollo: Greek god of music, harmony, and order; son of Zeus and Leto, brother of Artemis; master of Delphi—2, 8

Apollos: biblical character—4, 14, 15, 16

Appius Claudius: 307 B.C.E., Roman consul—13

Aquila: biblical character—15
Aquinas, Thomas: *see* Thomas Aquinas
Arad, Yitzhak: Lithuanian-born Israeli historian; Holocaust survivor—15
Archelaus: biblical character; son of Herod the Great—15
Archimedes (ca. 285–212 B.C.E.): Greek mathematician, inventor, and physicist—7, 8, 10
Arenales, Augustine: Spanish Protestant pastor whom Dietrich Bonhoeffer met during his time as a vicar in Barcelona; member of the World Alliance for Promoting International Friendship through the Churches, Spanish section—15
Arendt, Hannah (1906–73): German-born political scientist and philosopher: 1933, emigrated to France; 1940, to America; after 1963, professor, Chicago; after 1967, New York—7
Aristion (first century): allegedly a primary authority, with the Presbyter John, for the traditions about Jesus—9
Aristophanes (446–386 B.C.E.): Greek comic playwright—3
Aristotle (384–322 B.C.E.): Greek philosopher; student of Plato; tutor of Alexander the Great—1, 2, 3, 4, 6, 7, 8, 10, 11, 12, 14, 15
Arius (ca. 250–ca. 336): presbyter in Alexandria; founder of Arianism, which denied the true divinity of Jesus Christ—12, 15
Armin (Hermann) the Cheruskian—7
Arminius, Jacobus (1560–1609): Dutch reformed theologian, critic of the central Calvinist doctrine of predestination—8
Arnauld, Antoine (1612–94): French Catholic philosopher and theologian —1
Arndt, Elmer Jakob Frederick: 1930–31, resident fellow at Union Theological Seminary, New York; 1931, participated in the summer semester with Karl Barth; 1931–41, assistant professor for social ethics and philosophy of religion at Eden Theological Seminary, Missouri; 1941–69, professor there for historical theology and Christian ethics—11
Arndt, Ernst-Moritz (1769–1860): German writer of pro-Prussian political pieces, propaganda, and travelogues—10, 12
Arnd(t), Johann (1555–1621): Lutheran theologian and mystical writer —10, 14
Arnim-Lützlow, Wilhelm von (1879–1943): estate owner in Lützlow with a residence in Berlin-Wannsee; member of the Council of Brethren and of the Council of the Evangelical Church of the Old Prussian Union; 1934–36, member in the Confessing synods; 1943, killed during an air attack in Berlin—15
Arnold, Eberhard (1883–1935): German Protestant revivalist; 1920s, founder of Bruderhof pacifist community—6, 10, 13

Arnold, Friedrich Julius: author of a popular hymn concordance—14

Arnold, Fritz Werner: from 1927, Berlin attorney and notary; 1933, threatened with dismissal as a "non-Aryan"; 1938, permitted to work as a Jewish legal consultant; 1939, head of the legal section in the "Grüber Office," the Berlin church office that helped Jews and others affected by the racial laws leave Germany; 1941–42, spokesperson for the group "Operation 7," with whom he, his wife, and daughter were able to emigrate to Switzerland at the end of September 1942—15, 16

Arnold, Gottfried (pseudonym for Christophorus Irenaeus) (1666–1714): church historian, hymnist and mystic; most prominent advocate of the so-called radical pietism movement—4

Arnold, Hardy (1912–87): son of Eberhard Arnold and member of the Bruderhof community in England; 1934, student at Birmingham University in England; met with Bonhoeffer in London, and wrote letters and published a report about the meetings; 1939, wrote famous pacifist statement *The Call of the Hour*—6, 10, 13, 14

Arnold, Talitha: pastor, United Church of Sante Fe, New Mexico—12

Arper, Karl (1864–1936): 1892, pastor, Weimar; 1919, superintendent in Eisenach and member of the regional church council in Weimar—14, 15

Arsenev, Nicholaus: Russian religious historian who believed Russian Orthodox Christianity was called to save Western Christianity—1

Arsenio: one of Bonhoeffer's acquaintances on the *Columbus*—10

Artaxerxes: biblical character—14

Asaph: biblical character—5

Asbeck, Baron Frederick Mari van: Dutch expert in constitutional law, professor of international law, University of Leiden—16

Aschenfeldt, Christoph (1792–1856): hymnist—15

Aschoff, Elisabeth von: from Melsungen in Hesse-Kassel; studied at University of Jena November 25, 1925–April 26, 1926; studied German in Berlin; member of Harnack's seminar—9

Asmussen, Hans Christian (1898–1968): 1923, pastor, Flensburg; 1925, Albersdorf, Dithmarschen; 1932, Hamburg-Altona; 1933, suspension; 1934, forced retirement; active in the leadership committees of the Confessing Church; head of the theological section of the administrative committee of the Confessing synod in Bad Oeynhausen; 1934, member of the Reich Confessing Church Council of Brethren; 1935–36, director and lecturer at the seminaries in Berlin and Elberfeld; 1936, pastor, Berlin-Lichterfelde; 1941, arrested and convicted in the collective trial of the examination board of the Old Prussian Union Council of Brethren; 1943, assistant pastor, Württemberg; 1945, president of the chancellery

of the Evangelical Church of Germany; 1948, provost, Kiel; 1955, retired —6, 8, 12, 13, 14, 15, 16

Astruc, Jean (1684–1766): French founder of modern Pentateuch criticism —3

Athanas: *see* Kalff, Athanasius

Athanasius (ca. 296–373): bishop of Alexandria—6, 12

Athenodorus (first century C.E.): according to Pliny, one of the sculptors of the marble statue of Laocoön and his sons—9

Atkinson, Henry A. (1877–1960): U.S. sociologist and pastor in the Congregationalist church; head of the Church Peace Union; until 1932, general secretary, then until 1946, international secretary of the World Alliance for Promoting International Friendship through the Churches; 1928, general secretary of the Universal Christian Council for Life and Work; September 1933, participated in the conference of the World Alliance for Promoting International Friendship through the Churches, Sofia —12, 13

Attis: Phrygian god, consort of Cybele—10

Aubrey, Melbourn Evans (1885–1957): 1926–51, general secretary of the Baptist Union of Great Britain and Ireland; one of the Free Church leaders most active in ecumenical work—16 (this is a correction to the entry in *DBWE* 16, listed as "Aubrey, Edwin Ewart")

August, Reinhold Wilhelm (1910–43 [killed in action]): from Posen; winter 1936–37, participated in the fourth Finkenwalde session; 1937, pastoral administrator in Kirchohmfeld, Worbis—8, 15

Augustin: *see* Keßler, Augustin

Augustine, Aurelius (354–430): Latin church father; after 395, bishop of Hippo—1, 3, 4, 5, 6, 8, 9, 10, 11, 12, 14, 15, 16

Augustus (63 B.C.E.–14 C.E.): first Roman emperor—6

Aulén, Gustav Emanuel Hildebrand (1879–1977): Swedish theologian; 1910, professor of dogmatics, Uppsala; 1913–33, of systematic theology, Lund; 1933–52, bishop of Strängnäs—14, 16

Aurifaber, Johannes (1519–75): editor of Luther's letters, sermons, and "table talk"—11

Austad, Torleiv: professor of systematic theology at the Theological Congregational Seminary, Oslo—16

Averroes (Ibn Rushd) (1126–98): Islamic philosopher—1

Ayer, Joseph C. (1866–1944): American clergyman and theologian—12

Azariah, Vedanaya Samuel (Dornakal) (1874–1945): bishop of the diocese Dornakal, Hyderabad, India—16

Baader, Franz von (1765–1841): representative of an unorthodox theosophical mysticism—1
Babick, Albert: from 1921, pastor, Berlin—12
Babs: not otherwise identified—9
Bach, Carl Philipp Emanuel (1714–88): German composer and musician; son of J. S. Bach—7, 16
Bach, Etienne: French officer; head of the "Chevaliers de la Paix"; 1928, member of the youth commission of the World Alliance for Promoting International Friendship through the Churches—12
Bach, Johann Sebastian (1685–1750): German church musician and composer—1, 7, 8, 9, 10, 13, 14, 15, 16
Bach, Wilhelm Friedemann (1710–84): German composer; son of J. S. Bach—16
Bachmann, Wilhelm: inspector of studies at the seminary, Ilsenburg; 1935–37, worked in Bishop Theodor Heckel's Church Foreign Office; 1940, in Heckel's evangelical relief organization for (civilian) internees and prisoners of war; 1944, arrested by the Gestapo; close friend of Eugen Gerstenmaier—8, 14
Backe: one of Bonhoeffer's acquaintances from Barcelona—10
Backhaus, Erich (1886–1946): from 1928, pastor, Berlin—12
Bacon, I. C.: 1931, organizer of youth camping trips in Cambridge and director of the Cambridge youth conference—11
Bacon, Lord Francis (1561–1626): British philosopher, author, and politician—8, 14
Badoglio, Pietro (1871–1956): Italian marshal; July 1943–June 1944, minister president after Mussolini's arrest; September 3, 1943, signed the cease-fire between Italy and the Allies—8
Baedeker: bookseller family; known since 1827 for its travel guides—8
Baedeker, Karl (1801–59): publisher of famous travel guides in Europe—9
Baelz, Reinhardt: February 11, 1935, Bonhoeffer officiated at his funeral—13
Baer, Heinrich von: 1927, pastor in Neuwarp, Pomerania—12
Bahr, Pastor: not otherwise identified—10
Bailey, Cyril (1871–1957): British classical scholar—1
Baillie, Florence: wife of John Baillie—15
Baillie, Jan: son of John Baillie—15
Baillie, John (1886–1960): Scottish Reformed theologian and ecumenist; 1934, professor of theology, Edinburgh; 1943, moderator of the General Assembly of the Church of Scotland; 1954, president of the World Council of Churches; also professor at Union Theological Seminary, New York, and in Canada—6, 10, 11, 13, 15, 16

Baird, Albert C.: U.S. theologian and expert on rhetoric and speech—6
Balaam: biblical character—14
Balanos, Dimitrios S.: Greek theologian; 1923–48, professor of church history, Athens; member of the Greek section of the World Alliance for Promoting International Friendship through the Churches; 1935–36 and 1945, minister of education and cultural affairs—16
Baldwin, Roger Nash (1884–1981): U.S. Unitarian; one of the founders of the American Civil Liberties Union—12
Baldwin, Stanley (1867–1947): British politician; May 1923–January 1924, prime minister with a Conservative cabinet; January 1924, Labor Party came to power, and change in administration led to some détente with Germany; November 1924–June 1929, second Baldwin cabinet; March 1935, demand for a program of defense; June 7, 1935–May 28, 1937, prime minister of a Conservative government until his resignation; 1937, knighted as the First Earl Baldwin of Bewdley—6
Ballanche, Pierre Simon (1776–1847): French philosopher; precursor of liberal Catholicism—1
Balthasar, Hans Urs von (1905–88): Swiss Catholic theologian; until 1948, Jesuit; freelance writer in Basel—4, 5, 16
Balzac, Honoré de (1799–1850): French author—6
Bamm, Peter (pseudonym for Curt Emmerich) (1897–1975): physician (ship's doctor, later surgeon in Berlin) and author—8
Bangs, Carl (1922–2002): theologian and Reformation scholar—8
Barabbas: biblical character—9, 12
Barbey d'Aurevilly, Jules (1808–89): French novelist—11
Bargen, Fritz Adolf von (1896–1966): from 1925, pastor, Berlin—12
Barié, Helmut: German Protestant church leader, regional church of Baden—14
Barker, H. Gaylon: U.S. Evangelical Lutheran Church in America pastor and professor; president of the International Bonhoeffer Society–English Language Section—14
Barnabas: biblical character—12, 14, 15
Barnes, Kenneth: U.S. professor of German history; author of works on Nazi Germany—16
Barnett, Victoria: U.S. scholar on the churches and the Holocaust; one of the general editors of the *Dietrich Bonhoeffer Works*, English edition; director, programs on religion, ethics and the Holocaust, U.S. Holocaust Memorial Museum—6, 7, 8, 9, 10, 12, 13, 14, 16, 17
Barteczko-Schwedler, Bärbel: author of work on Gossner mission—16
Barth, Emmy: historian of the Woodcrest Bruderhof in Rifton, New York—13

Barth, Heinrich: brother of Karl Barth; professor of philosophy and Kierkegaard scholar, Basel—1

Barth, Karl (1886–1968): Swiss Reformed theologian; 1911, pastor in Safenwil/Aargau, Switzerland; 1921, professor of Reformed theology in Göttingen; cofounder of dialectical theology and, in 1922, of the periodical *Zwischen den Zeiten*; 1925, professor of dogmatics and New Testament exegesis, Münster; 1930, of systematic theology, Bonn; October 1934, member of the Reich Council of Brethren and the Advisory Council of the German Evangelical Church; 1935, dismissed for political reasons by the National Socialist Reich Minister of Culture; 1935–62, professor of systematic theology, Basel; early in his career, a leading voice of dialectical theology; later authored the highly influential *Church Dogmatics*; leading figure in the Confessing Church; exercised considerable influence on Dietrich Bonhoeffer and the pastors in his circle—all volumes

Barth, Markus: son of Karl Barth—14, 15

Barth, Paul (1857–1922): German philosopher and sociologist; Hegel scholar—1

Bartholomew (disciple): biblical character—4

Bartimaeus: biblical character—5, 15

Bartl, Klaus: German pastor—8

Bartmann, Bernhard (1860–1938): German Catholic priest, theologian, and professor of dogmatics—1, 2, 3, 11

Barton, John M. T.: author of work on penance—5

Barzillai: biblical character—14

Basilides: second-century Syrian gnostic—12

Bastert, Christiane: author of work on the Stuttgart Declaration of Guilt—6

Bastian, Hans-Dieter: professor (retired) of religious pedagogy, University of Bonn—14

Bastian, Max (1883–1958): career military; 1935–38, head of the General Office of the Navy; 1938, admiral; 1939, managing president of the military high court; 1940, president; November 30, 1944, dismissed—8, 16

Bathsheba: biblical character—14

Batocki, Otto von (1914–40): from Berlin; June 9, 1940, killed in action as a first lieutenant along the Aisne River in France—16

Battenberg, Victoria Eugénie von: *see* Victoria Eugénie von Battenberg

Baucis: character in Greek mythology—10

Bauer, Bruno (1809–82): Protestant theologian; student of Hegel—11

Bauer, Friedrich (1885–1969): 1925, pastor, Nuremberg; 1933–53, Munich—12

Bauer, Karl-Adolf (1874–1939): Reformed pastor and church historian—8

Bauer, Walter (1877–1960): professor of New Testament, Göttingen; initiator of *A Greek-English Lexicon of the New Testament and Other Early Christian Literature*—9, 13, 15

Bauer, Walter (1901–68): businessman; 1924, employed in the Berlin headquarters of the Petschek company (brown coal); 1928, member of the board of directors; until 1938, sales manager; from 1938, had his own company; lived in Fulda after the war; active member of the Confessing Church; 1942, participated in the Freiburg circle; October 15, 1944, arrested; April 21, 1945, released from the prison on Lehrter Strasse in Berlin; after 1945, member of the Synod of the Evangelical Church of Germany and of the Diaconate Council of the Evangelical Church of Germany—16, 17

Bauke, Hermann: twentieth-century German scholar of Calvin and Christology—12

Baum, Mr. and Mrs.: members of the congregation in Barcelona—10

Baumann, Eberhard (1871–1956): 1923–43, superintendent and Reformed consistory official in Stettin; 1934, member of the Pomeranian Council of Brethren and deputy president of the Pomeranian Confessing Synod; 1935, deputy member of the Reich Council of Brethren; deputy moderator of the Reformed Alliance—5, 14, 15, 16

Baumdicker, Siegfried: from Allenstein, East Prussia; studied theology in Königsberg; July 1940, participated with Dietrich Bonhoeffer in the weekend retreat in Blöstau—16

Bäumer, Gertrud (1873–1954): early German feminist and conservative nationalist politician; she withdrew from the political sphere and became a novelist during the Nazi years—8, 16

Baumgärtel, Friedrich (1888–1981): 1922, professor of Old Testament, Rostock; 1928, Greifswald; 1937, Göttingen; 1941–56, Erlangen—5, 14

Baumgärtel-Fleischmann, Renate: director, Museum of the Bamberg Diocese—14

Baumgarten, Alexander Gottlieb (1714–62): philosopher and founder of "aesthetics" as a philosophical discipline—3

Baumgarten, Otto (1858–1934): German theologian; after 1894, professor, Kiel; 1912–21, chair of the Protestant Social Congress; 1919, member of the German peace delegation at Versailles—6, 8

Baumgarten, Siegmund Jacob (1706–57): follower of Christian Wolff; he applied Wolff's demonstrative method to dogmatics—9

Baumgartner, Hieronymus (1498–1565): student of Martin Luther and supporter of the Reformation in Nuremberg—14

Baumgärtner, Raimund: German historian of the Third Reich—15

Baumgartner, Walter: 1929, professor of Old Testament, Basel—14

Baur, Ferdinand Christian (1792–1860): from 1826, professor of historical theology, Tübingen; founder of the Tübingen school of theology—14

Bax, Douglas: South African pastor; translator of *DBWE* 3—3, 14

Bayer, Barbara, née von Dohnanyi: daughter of Hans and Christine von Dohnanyi; married Wilhelm Friedrich Bayer—8, 10, 12, 13, 16

Baynes, Norman Hepburn (1877–1961): twentieth-century British historian—12, 14

Bazzi, Giovanni (artistic name: Sodoma) (1477–1549): Italian Renaissance painter of the Siena school; influenced by Leonardo da Vinci and Raphael—9

Beaverbrook, Lord William Maxwell Aitken (1879–1964): British statesman and newspaper publisher; 1918, minister of information; during World War II, was for a time minister for airplane manufacturing; 1941, head of the British delegation to the Alliance Conference in Moscow—16

Beck, Johann Tobias (1804–78): pastor and professor of systematic theology, Tübingen—9

Beck, Ludwig (1880–1944): career military officer; during World War I, general staff officer; 1933–35, head of the General Army Office; 1935–38, chief of the Army General Staff; August 1938, resignation following the Sudeten crisis, dismissed as colonel general; shortly thereafter began participating as a central military figure in the military resistance against Hitler; was designated to be the head of state after Hitler's removal; July 20, 1944, forced to commit suicide after the failed coup attempt—8, 13, 15, 16, 17

Becker, Carl Heinrich (1876–1933): German orientalist; worked in the ministry of culture under the Weimar Republic—1

Beckhaus, Johann Heinrich Konrad: church superintendent; 1874, conducted the funeral for the writer Hoffmann von Fallersleben—14

Beckmann, Gottfried (1909–80): summer 1935, participated in the first Zingst/Finkenwalde session; nickname was "Excellency"; October 28, 1934, cosigner of the letter from the Wittenberg preachers' seminary; 1936, pastor, Rottelsdorf; 1937, incarcerated in Magdeburg; 1945–74, pastor, Calvörde—8, 14

Beckmann, Joachim (1901–86): 1923, doctorate; 1926, pastor, Wiesbaden; 1928, pastor, Westphalian Church Women's Association, Soest; 1932, manager of the Protestant Men's Services, Westphalia; June 1933, founder of the Rhineland Pastors' Brotherhood; 1934, head of the theological office of the Confessing Church in the Rhineland; February 1934, temporarily dismissed; until 1945, member of the Rhineland, Prussian, and Reich councils of brethren; 1945, member of the Rhineland church

administration and lecturer at the seminary in Wuppertal; 1951, professor there; 1958–71, president of the Evangelical Church of the Rhineland—6, 13, 14, 15, 16

Beckmann, Leopold (1886–1946): Confessing Church pastor at the Ponarth church, Königsberg; 1938, placed on leave by the consistory, after which time he held worship services in the Löbenichts community hall; 1942, head of the East Prussian Council of Brethren; 1945, remained in Königsberg after Germany's surrender; 1946, presumably murdered—16

Becks, Miss: school friend of Paula Bonhoeffer in Königsberg; 1940, Dietrich Bonhoeffer stayed with her briefly—16

Beelzebub: biblical designation for Satan—15

Beese, Dieter: Protestant church superintendent and scholar of police ethics and German chaplains during World War II—8

Beesk, Gottfried: German Protestant pastor and prison chaplain—8

Beethoven, Ludwig van (1770–1827): German composer—7, 8, 9, 10, 13, 16

Behrends: (London) not otherwise identified—15

Behrens, Dr.: colleague of Hans Schönfeld in Geneva—13

Bekes: (Lagendorf) not otherwise identified—15

Bela, Mr.: 1932, representative of the Hungarian section of the World Alliance for Promoting International Friendship through the Churches and of the Universal Christian Council for Life and Work at the Gland youth conference—11

Beljin, Jelena: graduate, University of Flensburg; did work on Bonhoeffer—14

Bell, George Kennedy Allen (1883–1958): Anglican priest and bishop; 1907, assistant priest in Leeds; 1910, taught at Oxford; 1914–24, residential chaplain with the archbishop of Canterbury, assigned particularly to international relations; 1924, dean of Canterbury; 1925, coauthored the statement of the Stockholm Church Conference; 1929–57, bishop of Chichester; 1932, head of the British section and executive committee of the Universal Christian Council for Life and Work; 1933, first contact with Bonhoeffer; 1934, head of the Ecumenical Council of Life and Work; 1937, member of the House of Lords; 1942, met with Bonhoeffer and Hans Schönfeld in Sweden to learn about German resistance plans; struggled to gain support from the British and U.S. governments for the German resistance; after 1945, one of the architects of the World Council of Churches; 1945, chair of the Council for Foreign Relations of the Church of England; 1948, head of the central and executive committee of the World Council of Churches; 1954, honorary president of the World Council of Churches; married to Henrietta Millicent, née Livingstone—4, 5, 6, 8, 10, 11, 12, 13, 14, 15, 16, 17

Bell, Henrietta Millicent Grace, née Livingstone: wife of George K. A. Bell —12, 13, 15, 16

Bellarmine, Roberto (1542–1621): Jesuit theologian, cardinal, and archbishop of Capua—9, 11

Bellerophon: in Greek mythology, mortal hero—17 (for vol. 9)

Bellini, Giovanni (1430–1516): Venetian Renaissance painter; teacher of Titian; worked with his father and brother in Padua—9

Below, Georg von (1858–1927): German constitutional and legal historian —1

Belteshazzar: biblical character—12

Benckert, Heinrich (1907–68): Confessing pastor, Striche/Grenzmark—14

Benedict of Nursia (d. ca. 547 C.E.): Italian monk; founder of the monastery of Monte Cassino and of the Benedictine monastic order—5, 9

Benedix, Julius Roderich (1811–73): actor and writer—13

Bengel, Johann Albrecht (1687–1752): Württemberg theologian; "father of Swabian pietism"; associated astrology with redemption history; known for his commentaries and for text-critical works on the New Testament—4, 9, 15, 16

Ben Israel, Hedva: Israeli-born historian; specialist on World War II and nationalism—16

Benktson, Benkt-Erik: Swedish professor and Kierkegaard scholar—8

Benn, Gottfried (1886–1956): German poet, dramatist, literary critic—10, 11

Benson, R. M.: 1865, founder of the Anglican community Society of St. John the Evangelist in Oxford—14, 15

Bentham, Jeremy (1748–1832): British lawyer and philosopher—6

Bentinck: *see* Cavendish-Bentinck, Victor Frederick William

Benz, Richard (1884–1966): literary, musical, and cultural historian—8

Benz, Wolfgang: German historian, director of the Center for Research on Anti-Semitism, Berlin—15

Berdyaev, Nikolai (1874–1948): Russian religious philosopher; 1917, professor, Moscow; 1922, expelled; 1922, Berlin; 1924, Paris; active in the ecumenical movement and in the Christian student movement—13

Berendts, Otto: 1936–37, participated in the fourth Finkenwalde session; until 1945, pastor in Schermeisel, Neumark; October 1945–March 1949, Berlin-Marzahn; from April 1949, in Berlin-Wittenau and superintendent for the French sector of Berlin; 1969–76, senior church officer in the Church Foreign Office, Frankfurt am Main—14, 17

Berg (FP): character in Bonhoeffer's story "Lance Corporal Berg" (*DBWE* 7) —7, 8

Berg, Hans Georg: from Bielefeld; 1935–36, participated in the second Finkenwalde session; thereafter pastor, Kolberg and in the district Belgard, Pomerania; 1950, pastor, Damme/Oldenburg; 1967, Lüdenscheid—14, 15

Berg, Paal: president of the Supreme Court in Oslo; 1940–45, head of the Norwegian resistance—16

Bergemann, Arnold: from 1916, pastor, Berlin-Lichterfelde—12

Bergen, Doris: Wolff Professor of German History, University of Toronto; also taught at Notre Dame; authority on the German Christians—6, 11, 12, 14

Bergengruen, Werner (1892–1964): German novelist, short-story author, and lyric poet—8

Berggrav, Eivind Josef (1884–1959): Norwegian theologian; 1925, bishop of Tromsö; 1937–51, bishop of Oslo; 1939, chair of the executive committee of the World Alliance for Promoting International Friendship through the Churches; 1941–45, leading participant in the resistance of the Norwegian church against the German occupation, in which capacity he came into contact with Helmut von Moltke and Theodor Steltzer of the Kreisau circle; 1950–54, member of the administrative committee of the World Council of Churches—16

Bergkamp, Will: publisher and managing director of Fortress Press—17

Bergmann, Claudia D.: U.S. scholar and ordained pastor in the Evangelical Lutheran Church in America; cotranslator of *DBWE* 15—15

Bergson, Henri (1859–1941): French philosopher and essayist; 1927, Nobel Prize in Literature—10, 11, 14

Berkelbach van der Sprenkel, Simon F. H. J.: Dutch theologian; from 1935, professor of Protestant theology and dogmatics; from 1952, professor of ecumenical studies, Utrecht—16

Berlig, P.: editor of a newsletter, *Der Krankentrost* (Comfort for the sick) —14

Berlowitz, Kurt: head of the Republican Student Association (Republikanischen Studentenverein); 1933 or 1934, emigrated from Germany —13

Bernadotte, Count Folke (1895–1948): nephew of King Gustav V Adolf of Sweden; 1943, vice president, and, in 1946, president of the Swedish Red Cross; sought to rescue Jewish refugees from German concentration camps during World War II; 1945, approached by the SS leadership as a mediator for peace negotiations; September 17, 1948, assassinated by militant Zionist group in Jerusalem—16, 17

Bernadotte, Prince Eugen: son of King Oskar II of Sweden—14

Bernadotte, Prince Oskar (1859–1953): son of King Oskar II of Sweden and brother of Gustav V—14

Bernanos, Georges (1888–1948): French author and representative of the Catholic renewal movement—6, 7, 10, 12, 15, 16

Bernard of Clairvaux (ca. 1090–1153): influential Christian mystic and preacher; founder of the Cistercian Order—1, 9, 15

Bernd, Clifford A.: Germanist; expert on German poetry—8

Berndt: 1932, state counselor—11

Bernheim, Ernst (1850–1942): historian and professor, Greifswald—9

Bernini, Giovanni Lorenzo (Gianlorenzo) (1598–1680): Italian sculptor and architect; dominant figure of the Italian baroque—9

Berns (in Sacrow): not otherwise identified—8

Bertheau, Carl (1836–1910): German theologian and religious historian —15

Bertholet, Alfred (1868–1951): professor of Old Testament theology, Berlin —10

Bertram, Georg: lecturer in New Testament, Berlin—9

Bertram, Robert W.: professor emeritus of historical and systematic theology at the Lutheran School of Theology at Chicago—14

Besch, Günter: Confessing Church pastor in Pomerania—14, 15

Besier, Gerhard: German professor of historical theology; director of the Hannah-Arendt-Institute for Research on Totalitarianism, Dresden—10, 15

Besig, Hans (1873–1941): lawyer; senior consistory official in the Church Federation office; 1934, in the Church Foreign Office; 1939, retired—10, 11, 13

Best, Isabel: translator of *DBWE* 13; cotranslator for *DBWE* 8, 11, and 12—10, 12, 13, 14

Best, Sigmund Payne: captain in the British secret service; November 1939, kidnapped in Venlo, Holland, by the German security service SD; April 1945, in the same prisoner transport as Dietrich Bonhoeffer—8, 13, 16, 17

Beste, Niklot (1901–87): 1933–45, pastor in Neubukow; 1936, in the Advisory Council of the Lutheran Church of Germany; 1946–71, bishop of Mecklenburg; 1968–71, presiding bishop of the United Evangelical Lutheran Church of the German Democratic Republic—14

Bethge, Christoph: Eberhard Bethge's youngest brother; married Gerhard Vibrans's widow Elisabeth Trebesius—6, 8, 14, 16

Bethge, Dietrich Wilhelm Rüdiger: son of Eberhard and Renate Bethge; from 1953, in London; studied law at Oxford (Christ Church); cellist (coprincipal in the English Chamber Orchestra)—7, 8, 13, 15, 17

Bethge, Eberhard (1909–2000): pastor, educator, theologian and biographer of Dietrich Bonhoeffer; friend of Bonhoeffer; 1920–29, attended

the Humanities Gymnasium, Monastery of Our Good Lady in Magdeburg; October 1934, expelled from the preachers' seminary in Wittenberg at the behest of the Reich bishop; after 1934–35, assistant pastor under Confessing Church pastor Paul Henheik; 1935–37, participated in the preachers' seminary in Zingst/Finkenwalde (also member of the House of Brethren) led by Bonhoeffer; 1937–40, inspector of studies at one of the two Pomeranian collective pastoral training programs (Groß-Schlönwitz and Sigurdshof) led by Bonhoeffer that prepared ministers for the Confessing Church; 1940–44, missions inspector at the Gossner Mission in Berlin; 1943, married Bonhoeffer's niece Renate Schleicher; 1943, military service; October 1944, arrested in Italy and deported to Berlin as a political prisoner in connection with July 20, 1944; April 25, 1945, freed from Lehrter Strasse Prison; after the end of the war, assistant to Bishop Otto Dibelius; 1946–53, student chaplain at the Humboldt University, Berlin; 1953–61, overseas pastor in London; 1961–75, director of the pastoral college of the Rhineland church, Rengsdorf; 1969, honorary professor of practical theology, Bonn; 1976, emeritus; during retirement, active in lecturing, conferences, publications, particularly devoted to Christian-Jewish relations and above all as part of the editorial board producing the critical edition of Bonhoeffer's works, *DBW*; last lived in Wachtberg-Villiprott near Bonn—all volumes

Bethge, Elisabeth (Aunt Else), née Nietzschmann (1879–1964): Eberhard Bethge's mother; widowed since 1923; lived in Kade, district of Ziesar—8, 15, 16

Bethge, Hans (1905–92): Eberhard Bethge's older brother; engineer—8, 14, 15

Bethge, Helene (Aunt Lene) (1882–1969): youngest sister of Eberhard Bethge's father; lived together with Elisabeth Bethge in Kade—16

Bethge, Margret: *see* Onnasch, Margret

Bethge, Renate Ursula Gertrud Paula: daughter of Rüdiger Schleicher and Ursula, née Bonhoeffer; Dietrich Bonhoeffer's niece; grew up in Berlin; March 17, 1940, confirmation; studied music and psychology; May 15, 1943, married Eberhard Bethge; has written essays on the Bonhoeffer family and on contemporary history during the Third Reich; honorary doctorate from Lynchburg College, Lynchburg, Virginia—4, 5, 6, 7, 8, 10, 13, 14, 15, 16, 17

Bethge, Wilhelm (1867–1923): Eberhard Bethge's father; pastor in Warchau and Zitz/Ziesar—8

Bethge-Vibrans, Elisabeth, née Trebesius: wife of Gerhard Vibrans; in second marriage, wife of Christoph Bethge—14, 16

Bethmann-Hollweg, Theobald von (1856–1921): conservative politician; German chancellor; 1909, succeeded Bernhard von Bülow; overthrown by Ludendorff and Hindenburg in response to his attitude of conciliation at the end of World War I—9

Bettenson, Henry: U.S. patristics scholar—6, 8

Betts, George Herbert (1868–1934): prominent U.S. expert on religious education—15

Bewer, Julius A. (1877–1953): professor at Union Theological Seminary, New York—15

Beyer, Hermann Wolfgang (1898–1942): 1926, professor of church history and Christian archaeology, Greifswald; September 27, 1933, synod representative at the Wittenberg national synod; 1936, of New Testament, Leipzig; end 1933–beginning 1934, member, Clerical Ministry; 1942, killed in action—13

Beyschlag, Willibald (1823–1900): New Testament scholar—1

Bezzel, Hermann (1861–1917): 1891–1909, rector of the deaconesses' institute in Neuendettelsau; 1909–17, president of the high consistory in Munich, head of the Bavarian Lutheran Church—14

Biedermann, Alois Emanuel (1819–85): Swiss Reformed theologian; 1850, professor of systematic theology and dogmatics, Zürich; representative of critical speculative rationalism and of Hegelian influenced religious liberalism in Switzerland—1, 9, 11, 12, 16

Biehl, Michael: director of the Missionsakademie, University of Hamburg, and author of work on Indian mystic Sadhu Sundar Singh—10

Bieritz, Karl-Heinrich: professor of practical theology and religious pedagogy, Rostock—15

Biesental, Günter (1913–43): from Berlin-Charlottenburg; 1938–39, participated in the collective pastorate in Köslin; ordination and ministry in Fürstenwalde; November 22, 1941, wounded on the eastern front; 1943, killed in action—16

Bigi, Mrs.: widow of a German professor living in Rome; rented a room to Bonhoeffer—9

Bildad: biblical character—9

Bildt, Eva: daughter of the Berlin actor Paul Bildt; trained in the women's seminar, Burckhardt House; engaged to Pastor Helmut Gollwitzer; 1945, committed suicide during the final battles in Berlin—16

Bildt, Paul (1885–1957): Berlin actor; member of the Confessing Church in Dahlem—16

Binder, Wolfgang: Swiss Germanist and Hölderlin scholar, University of Zürich—11

Binding, Karl (1841–1920): German professor of criminal law, Freiburg; early advocate of euthanasia—6, 9

Binding, Rudolf G. (1867–1938): Swiss author of German descent; commanded an independent squadron of reconnaissance dragoons in World War I; published diary and letters on his war experiences—8

Birk, Hellmuth (1913–84): from Berlin; 1939–40, participated in the collective pastorate in Sigurdshof; assistant pastor, Berlin-Charlottenburg; 1941–45, military service; after the war, pastor in Göttingen and Berlin, finally superintendent in Berlin Tempelhof; 1980, retired—15

Birkenhauer, Renate: German linguist and translator, author of work on nazified German—12

Birnbaum, Walter (1893–1987): 1922, pastor, Radeberg, Saxony; 1924, director of the Wichern Association for the Awakening of Christian Folk Life, Hamburg; 1934, senior church official in Berlin; August 1934, participated in the conference in Fanø; 1935, professor of practical theology, Göttingen; 1945, dismissed—13

Bismarck, Hans-Otto von (1919–40): son of Herbert von Bismarck of Lasbeck; killed in action in the campaign in France—16

Bismarck, Hans von (1943–90): son of Klaus and Ruth-Alice von Bismarck —8

Bismarck, Herbert von (1884–1955): estate owner in Lasbeck, district of Regenwalde; grand nephew of Reich chancellor Otto von Bismarck; husband of Maria, née von Kleist-Retzow; 1918–31, regional representative, Regenwalde district; 1930–33, member of the national parliament (representing the German National People's Party); end of 1932, state secretary in the Prussian Ministry of the Interior; 1945, cofounder and first speaker of the Association of Pomeranians—8, 16

Bismarck, Jürgen Philipp Robert Karl Herbert von: son of Herbert von Bismarck; engineer—8, 15, 16

Bismarck, Karl Ernst Günther: authorized signatory (*Prokurist*), Pomerania —8

Bismarck, Klaus von: mechanical (machine fitter) and agricultural training; 1939–45, military service; 1949–61, leader of the social office of the West Palatinate Church in Villigst House; 1961–76, director of West German Radio; 1976–89, president of the Goethe Institute—7

Bismarck, Luitgarde von: granddaughter of Ruth von Kleist-Retzow and wife of resistance figure Fabian von Schlabrendorff—16

Bismarck, Maria von, née von Kleist-Retzow (1893–1979): wife of Herbert von Bismarck—16

Bismarck, Otto Christian, Third Prince von (1897–1975): 1923–27, representative (German National People's Party) in the national parliament;

1927, in the Ministry of Foreign Affairs, legation officer in Stockholm; 1928–37, legation and embassy officer in London; 1940, envoy in Rome; from autumn 1944, administrator in Friedrichsruh; 1953, member of parliament (Christian Democratic Union)—13

Bismarck, Otto Edward Leopold von (1815–98): Prussian statesman, began his career as a monarchist; 1871–90, chancellor of the (second) German Empire; 1890, became Duke of Lauenburg—6, 9, 10, 11, 12, 16

Bismarck, Ruth-Alice von, née von Wedemeyer: daughter of Hans and Ruth von Wedemeyer, sister of Maria von Wedemeyer, editor of the latter's correspondence with Dietrich Bonhoeffer; July 15, 1939, married Klaus von Bismarck in Pätzig—7, 8, 12, 16

Bismarck, Spes von: *see* Pompe, Spes

Bissinger, Fritz: 1920–78, published and director of the Chr. Kaiser Verlag; 1937, published Bonhoeffer's *Nachfolge* (*Discipleship*); 1939, published Bonhoeffer's *Gemeinsames Leben* (*Life Together*); after World War II, publisher of editions of Bonhoeffer's works—17

Bitter, Wilhelm (1886–1964): owner of the Paulus Verlag publishing company in Recklinghausen; prior to 1933, member (Center Party) of the national parliament; after 1933, reprimanded as a Catholic publisher; traveled as a secret agent for the Catholic Bishops' Conference; 1938, Johannes Neuhäusler distributed his brochure "How can I raise my child in the Christian faith?"; together with Dr. Josef Himmelreich, prepared a Catholic memorandum addressed to Hitler—16

Bitzius, Albert (the younger; 1835–82): son of Jeremias Gotthelf; popular preacher—14

Bizer, Christoph: professor of religious pedagogy, Göttingen—14

Bizer, Ernst: German Protestant church historian—10, 11, 12

Bizet, Georges (1838–75): French composer—10

Björkquist, Manfred (1884–1985): Swedish theologian and ecumenist; 1910, director of the adult evening school, Hampness; founder of the Young Church Movement in Sweden; 1917, director of the Sigtuna Foundation; 1942–54, bishop of Stockholm; from 1943, court chaplain—14, 16

Blackman, Edwin Cyril: church historian; August 1934, British participant at the Fanø youth conference and subsequent Bruay conference—13

Blake, William (1757–1827): English poet, visionary, and artist—10

Blakely, Paul, S. J. (1880–1943): U.S. Jesuit journalist—10

Blanck, Ottonie, née Lubarsch (1899–1976): parish assistant for Martin Niemöller in Berlin-Dahlem; extremely active on behalf of the Confessing Church, she allowed the illegal Berlin church seminary to hold its seminars in her home after 1937 and was among those tried in 1941—15

Blanck-Lubarsch, Hans-Jürgen: son of Ottonie Blanck, active in the work of Action Reconciliation—15

Blankenburg, Walter: German musicologist—17 (for vol. 9)

Blaschke, Olaf: German historian of the Catholic Church—17 (for vol. 12)

Blasquez, Niceto: author of a work on church doctrine on suicide—6

Blau, Paul (1861–1944): 1911, general superintendent, Posen; after 1918, spiritual head of the (German-speaking) United Evangelical Church in Poland—16

Bloch, Ernst (1885–1977): German philosopher, heir to the nineteenth-century dialectical tradition of Hegel and Marx; 1933–48, in exile; returned and became professor in Leipzig; 1957, left East Germany; 1961, became professor in Tübingen—10

Block, Eduard (1886–1970): superintendent in Schlawe, Pomerania; 1938, enabled Dietrich Bonhoeffer to establish the collective pastorate in Schlawe; after the war, worked in the foreign office of the Evangelical Church of Germany in Frankfurt—8, 15, 16, 17

Block, Elfriede: wife of Eduard Block—16

Block, Ernst: 1933, theology student in Berlin—12

Block, Irmgard, née Lütgert: wife of Klaus Block—13

Block, Klaus (1910–53): from Berlin-Lichterfelde; 1936, participated in the third Finkenwalde session; ministry in Brandenburg-Görden; military service; after 1945, consistory official in Berlin—13, 15

Bloesch, Daniel W.: translator, *DBWE* 5—5

Blomberg, Werner von (1878–1946): from 1933, Reich Minister of the Armed Forces; 1935–38, Reich war minister and commander in chief of the armed forces; 1936, general field marshal; February 4, 1938, resigned; died in U.S. custody—15

Bloth, Peter Constantin: German professor of practical theology—14

Bluhm, Heinz (1910–67): 1937–38, participated in the collective pastorate in Groß-Schlönwitz; assistant pastor in Templin; 1939, pastor, Frankfurt an der Oder; 1943, Luckenwalde; 1946, pastor and administrator for the superintendent office, Luckenwalde—14, 15

Blumenberg-Lampe, Christine: author of work on Freiburg circle; chair of the July 20 research association (Forschungsgemeinschaft 20. Juli)—16

Blumenstock, C.: member of the congregational council, German Reformed St. Paul's Church in London—13

Blumhardt, Johann Christoph ("the elder") (1805–80): 1838–52, pastor, Möttlingen near Calw; 1852, moved to Bad Boll—14, 15

Blumhardt, Johann Christoph Friedrich ("the younger") (1842–1919): German Protestant theologian and politician; pastor, Bad Boll; 1900–1906,

representative in the Württemberg parliament; religious socialist—9, 11, 12, 15

Boberach, Heinz: German historian and archivist; member of the Commission for the History of the Church Struggle and of the Protestant Committee for Contemporary Church History—6

Bobert-Stützel, Sabine: professor of practical theology, Kiel; author of work on Bonhoeffer's pastoral theology—1, 4, 8, 14, 15

Bobrik, Rudolf: German diplomat; 1937, in Spain; embassy counselor in Copenhagen; legation officer in Foreign Ministry; 1944, contact person there for the Reich Central Security Office—16

Bock, Fedor von (1880–1945): career military; 1940, general field marshal; 1941, commander in chief of the Center Army Group in Russia; 1942, of the Army Group South—16

Bode, Wilhelm (1845–1929): professor of art history, Berlin, where the museum he founded now bears his name—9

Bodelschwingh, Friedrich von (1831–1910): pastor, founder of the Bethel institutions for epileptics, alcoholics, and the homeless—9, 14

Bodelschwingh, Friedrich von (the younger; 1877–1946): German pastor and after 1910, director of what after 1921 became the Bodelschwingh institutions, including Bethel in Westphalia; May 27–June 24, 1933, briefly elected as Reich bishop by the church opposition to the German Christian movement; 1940, opposed the Nazi euthanasia measures—6, 12, 13, 14, 16, 17

Bodelschwingh, Gustav von (1872–1944): missionary and sympathizer (though not member) of the German Christians; brother of Friedrich von Bodelschwingh—14

Bodenstein, Andreas (called Karlstadt) (1480–1541): Reformation theologian—15

Bodenstein, Walter: German theologian; author of work on Karl Holl—9

Bodin, Jean (1530–96): French jurist and prominent political theoretician; opponent of Machiavelli; developed the concept of sovereignty—6, 8

Boeckheler, Konstantin: pastor; dean in Küntzelsau; friend of Bonhoeffer's grandparents—9

Boeckheler (Böckheler), Martin: 1933–35, navy chaplain and pastor of the German Lutheran church, Hull, England; from April 1935, Bonhoeffer's representative and later (1936) successor in London (St. Paul's and the United congregation in Sydenham); interned at the beginning of the war; 1940–45, camp chaplain in British and Canadian internment camps; 1945, pastor in Stuttgart, Alpirsbach, and Ulm; 1970, retired—13, 14, 15

Boeckheler, Nathaniel (d. 1923): son of Konstantin Boeckheler; dean in Küntzelsau—9

Boegner, Marc (1881–1970): French theologian and ecumenist; 1911, pastor of the Parisian Mission Society; 1918–54, pastor, Passy; 1929–61, president of the Fédération des Églises Protestantes de France (Federation of Protestant Churches in France); 1939–50, also president of the National Council of Reformed Churches in France; 1949–54, member of the administrative committee of the World Council of Churches; member of the Academie Française—13, 16

Boér, Alexis de: Hungarian lawyer; September 1933, like Dietrich Bonhoeffer, delegate to the conference of the World Alliance for Promoting International Friendship through the Churches in Sofia—12, 16

Boericke, Irma and Harold: distant relatives (Tafel side of the family) of the Bonhoeffer family in Philadelphia; children: Ray, Betty, and Binkie—10, 12, 15

Boeselager, Baron Georg von (1915–44): career military; 1942, lieutenant colonel, tactical instructor for Romanian troops; January 1943, with the staff of the Center Army Group on the eastern front, where he established the Central Cavalry Regiment, which for a time was planned as a strike force in the event of a coup; 1944, in close contact with Count Stauffenberg; August 27, 1944, killed in action on the eastern front—16

Boeters (Böters), Ernst: 1936, regional consistory official, Stettin—15, 16

Bohle, Ernst-Wilhelm: 1932, joined NSDAP; 1933, head of the party's overseas organization headquartered in Hamburg, also regional Nazi party leader (*Gauleiter*) and member of the national parliament; 1937–41, head of the National Socialist foreign department in the Ministry of Foreign Affairs; 1943, SS-*Obergruppenführer*; 1949, sentenced at Nuremberg to five years in prison—13

Böhm, Franz (1895–1977): 1933, private lecturer, Freiburg; 1938, teaching appointment for civil and labor law, Jena; 1940, removed from office for opposing National Socialist policies against the Jews; 1942–43, participant in the Freiburg memorandum; 1945, deputy vice-chancellor, Freiburg; 1947, professor, Frankfurt am Main; 1953–65, member of parliament (representing the Christian Democratic Union)—16

Böhm, Hans Adolf August Hugo (1899–1962): 1935, responsible for foreign affairs in the Provisional Church Administration; 1936, member of the Provisional Church Administration of the German Evangelical Church; 1941, convicted in the collective trial of the examination board of the Old Prussian Union Council of Brethren; after July 20, 1944, arrested, held in the prison of the Reich Central Security Office; 1945–59, church provost

of Berlin; senior church official in the consistory of Berlin-Brandenburg; vice president of the Synod of the Evangelical Church of Germany—8, 14, 15, 16, 17

Böhme, Kurt: 1923, assistant with the German section of the World Alliance for Promoting International Friendship through the Churches; 1924–45, pastor and editor with the Protestant Press Association for Germany, Berlin—11, 12

Bohne, Gerhard: German pedagogical scholar, influenced by Barth; emphasized the importance of religious faith and education—14

Bohren, Rudolf: Swiss professor of practical theology; founder of the sermon research institute (*Predigtforschungsstelle*), University of Heidelberg—14

Bojack, Konrad (1910–41): from Brieg, Silesia; 1935, participated in the first Zingst/Finkenwalde session; ministry in Lyck, East Prussia; according to the Finkenwalde newsletter of August 15, 1941, killed in action on the eastern front—8, 14, 16

Böker (Arnold), Edith: Hardy Arnold's fiancée at the time of Arnold's encounter with Bonhoeffer—13

Bölke, Mr. and Mrs.: made Bonhoeffer's acquaintance on his journey to Barcelona—10

Bölke, Mrs. (uncertain reading): (Lagendorf) not otherwise identified—15

Böll, Heinrich (1917–85): German writer; 1972, Nobel Prize in Literature—15

Bölte, G.: 1932, student of Bonhoeffer in Berlin—12

Boltermann, Dr.: headmaster of the Bismarck Gymnasium, Berlin—9

Bonald, Viscount Louis Gabriel Ambroise de (1754–1840): French Catholic philosopher and monarchist—1

Bonaventura, Johannes Fidanza (1221–74): Franciscan theologian—9

Bonde, Baron Knut: Swedish diplomat—16

Bonhoeff, Henrik van den: Dutch ancestor of Bonhoeffer—11

Bonhoeffer, Christine (Christel): *see* Dohnanyi, Christine von

Bonhoeffer, Cornelie Sabine Julie Elisabeth: daughter of Klaus and Emmi Bonhoeffer—8

Bonhoeffer, Dietrich (1906–45): the sixth of eight children, born in Breslau; after 1912, grew up in Berlin; 1921–24, studied theology, Tübingen, and 1924–27, Berlin; 1927, graduated with doctorate from Berlin; 1928–29, vicar in Barcelona; 1930, qualified as lecturer, Berlin; 1930–31, studied in New York; 1931–33, lecturer, theology department, Berlin University; 1933–35, London pastorate; 1935–37, directed theological education at the Finkenwalde preachers' seminary for the Confessing Church; 1937–39, after Finkenwalde's closure by the Gestapo, led two underground col-

lective pastoral training programs in rural Pomerania; 1940, connected with the resistance group in the Military Intelligence Office (*Abwehr*), under whose orders, during 1941–42, he made trips to Switzerland and Scandinavia; January 1943, engaged to Maria von Wedemeyer; April 5, 1943, arrested in Berlin; April 9, 1945, hanged in Flossenbürg concentration camp—all volumes

Bonhoeffer, Emilie (Emmi) Amalie Charlotte Henriette, née Delbrück (1905–91): daughter of the historian Hans Delbrück and his wife, Lina, née Thiersch; 1930, married Klaus Bonhoeffer—7, 8, 9, 10, 11, 15, 16, 17

Bonhoeffer, Eugen (1852–1938): pastor and teacher; director of the upper-level commercial school in Stuttgart—13

Bonhoeffer, Friedrich (1828–1907): Dietrich Bonhoeffer's grandfather; son of Sophianas Bonhoeffer and Luise, née Haspel; October 6, 1863, married Julie, née Tafel; father of Otto, Gustav Adolf (who died early), Karl, and Walter; president of the assize court and of the state court in Ravensburg and Ulm—7, 8, 10, 11, 15

Bonhoeffer, Fritz: son of Otto and Hedwig Bonhoeffer—10

Bonhoeffer, Hedwig: wife of Otto Bonhoeffer—10

Bonhoeffer, Johann Friedrich: son of Karl-Friedrich and Margarete Bonhoeffer—8

Bonhoeffer, Julie, née Tafel (1842–1936): Dietrich Bonhoeffer's grandmother—6, 7, 9, 10, 11, 12, 13, 14, 17

Bonhoeffer, Karl-Friedrich (1899–1957): Dietrich Bonhoeffer's eldest brother; physicist; March 22, 1930, married Margarethe, née von Dohnanyi; father of Karl, Friedrich, Martin, and Katharina (married name Schmidt); 1930, professor of physical chemistry, Frankfurt am Main; 1934–46, Leipzig; 1947, Berlin; 1949, director, Max-Planck Institute for Physical Chemistry, Göttingen—2, 3, 5, 6, 7, 8, 9, 10, 11, 12, 13, 14, 15, 16, 17

Bonhoeffer, Karl Ludwig (1868–1948): Dietrich Bonhoeffer's father; son of Friedrich and Julie Bonhoeffer; March 5, 1898, married Paula, née von Hase; 1903, professor of psychiatry, Königsberg; 1904, Heidelberg, that same year called to Breslau; 1908, appointed Privy Medical Counselor; professor of psychiatry and neurology, Berlin; 1912, director of the university neurological clinic at the Charité hospital, Berlin; retired in 1936, but remained in office until 1938; father of Karl-Friedrich, Walter, Klaus, Ursula (married name Schleicher), Christine (married name von Dohnanyi), Dietrich, Sabine (married name Leibholz), and Susanne (married name Dreß)—1, 2, 5, 6, 7, 8, 9, 10, 11, 12, 13, 14, 15, 16, 17

Bonhoeffer, Karl Walter Paul: son of Karl-Friedrich and Margarete Bonhoeffer—8, 10, 11

Bonhoeffer, Katharina Elisabeth Pauline: daughter of Karl-Friedrich and Margarete Bonhoeffer—8

Bonhoeffer, Klaus (1901–45): Dietrich Bonhoeffer's brother; lawyer; studied international law in Geneva, Amsterdam, and England; 1930, married Emmi Delbrück; corporate lawyer with Lufthansa; member of the resistance conspiracy against the National Socialist regime; February 1945, sentenced to death; April 23, 1945, executed by SS firing squad in Berlin—6, 7, 8, 9, 10, 11, 12, 13, 15, 16, 17

Bonhoeffer, Lola, née Schattenmann (1898–1971 in Starnberg): married to Lothar Bonhoeffer; language teacher—9

Bonhoeffer, Lothar (1893–1971): son of Otto Bonhoeffer and Hedwig B., née Meyer; married to Lola, née Schattenmann; father of Friedrich Otto, Gerhard, Ilse (married name Quest), Burkart, and Berhild (married name Lippl); August 9, 1914, wounded and almost blinded; later director of the Behring Factory (IG Farben) in Munich—9

Bonhoeffer, Margarete (Grete) Maria Anna, née von Dohnanyi (1903–92): daughter of the composer Ernst von Dohnanyi; sister of Hans von Dohnanyi; 1930, married Karl-Friedrich Bonhoeffer—8, 9, 10, 11, 12, 13, 14, 17

Bonhoeffer, Martin Klaus Anton (1935–89): son of Karl-Friedrich and Margarete Bonhoeffer—8

Bonhoeffer, Otto (1864–1932): son of Friedrich and Julie Bonhoeffer; married Hedwig B., née Meyer; brother of Karl Bonhoeffer; father of Fritz, Lothar, Gertrud, and Werner; Fritz and Werner died in World War I; German industrialist; chemist at Bayer Leverkusen; chair of the Rhineland-Westphalia employers' association—7, 8, 9, 10, 14

Bonhoeffer, Pauline (Paula), née von Hase (1876–1951): Dietrich Bonhoeffer's mother; daughter of Karl Alfred von Hase and Klara, née Countess Kalckreuth; March 5, 1898, married Karl Bonhoeffer—7, 8, 9, 10, 11, 12, 13, 14, 15, 16

Bonhoeffer, Sabine: *see* Leibholz, Sabine

Bonhoeffer, Susanne: *see* Dreß, Susanne

Bonhoeffer, Thomas: son of Klaus and Emilie Bonhoeffer—8, 11, 15, 17

Bonhoeffer, Ursula: *see* Schleicher, Ursula

Bonhoeffer, Walter: son of Klaus and Emilie Bonhoeffer; lawyer—8

Bonhoeffer, Walter (1899–1918): Dietrich Bonhoeffer's brother; April 28, 1918, died in a field hospital from injuries received on April 23 at the front in France—1, 2, 6, 7, 8, 9, 10, 16

Bonhoeffer, Werner: son of Otto and Hedwig Bonhoeffer—10

Bonhöffer, Eugen (1852–1938): son of Adolf Bonhöffer and Christiane, née Pistorius; fourth cousin of Karl Bonhoeffer; September 7, 1882, married

Eugenie, née Höring; father of Gertrud (married name Zeller), Hildegard Bonhöffer, Hedwig (married name John), and Elisabeth (married name Nägele); pastor and teacher; director of the upper-level commercial school in Stuttgart; did genealogical research—9

Bonhöffer, Sophonias Franz (1797–1872): Bonhoeffer's great-grandfather; pastor in various Württemberg parishes; born and died in Schwäbisch Hall—13

Boniface (ca. 675–754): the "apostle of Germany"; 740, entrusted with reformation of Frankish church—10

Boniface VIII (1235–1303): from 1294, pope; renewed the thesis of the supremacy of spiritual power over worldly power; his death was followed by a long decline in papal power—6

Bonnevie-Svendsen, Conrad (1889–1963): Norwegian theologian; 1933–63, pastor in Norwegian parishes; during the war, member of the Norwegian *Heimatfront* (a resistance group); 1945, consultant state counselor on church affairs to the Norwegian government—16

Bonnus, Hermann (1504–58) (actually van Bunnen): hymnist—14

Boor, Werner de (1899–1976): 1924, pastor, Bobeck, Thuringia; 1928, Kordeshagen, district of Köslin; 1932, Stolp; 1945, Lübtheen; 1946–56, senior church official, Schwerin; 1957–65, head of the Evangelical Conference in the German Democratic Republic—8, 15

Booth, Irmgard: cotranslator of early edition of *The Cost of Discipleship*—2, 4

Bordone, Paris (1500–1577): Venetian painter—9

Borg, Daniel R.: author of study on the Old Prussian Union Church during the Weimar Republic—11

Bori, Pier Cesare: professor of theology, University of Bologna; author of study in Italian on Bonhoeffer and von Harnack—8

Bormann, Eugenie: physician, psychiatrist, student of Karl Bonhoeffer; she and her sister maintained contact with the Bonhoeffer family—8

Bormann, Martin (1900–1945): agriculturist; 1933, chief of staff in the office of the Deputy to the führer; 1941, head of the party chancellery; 1943, secretary to the führer; 1944, appointed Reich minister; April 1945, disappeared during the final battles in Berlin—15, 16, 17

Born, Ann R.: translator of Kierkegaard—15

Bornhäuser, Karl (1868–1947): Protestant theologian; professor of systematic theology, Breslau, later Frankfurt am Main—4, 11

Borning, Walther (1888–1949): from 1930, pastor, Berlin—12

Bornitz, Gerhard: a schoolmate of Hans von Dohnanyi—9

Bornkamm, Elisabeth, née Zinn (1908–95): Dietrich Bonhoeffer's third cousin; German theologian; 1932, doctorate, Berlin; served as vicar under Confessing pastor Gerhard Jacobi; 1933, vicar and member of the

Confessing Church; 1938, married the New Testament scholar Günther Bornkamm—3, 4, 6, 7, 10, 12, 13, 14, 15

Bornkamm, Heinrich (1901–77): church historian and Luther scholar, University of Giessen; 1933, briefly a member of the German Christians—13

Borromini, Francesco (1599–1667): Italian baroque architect—9

Borthwick, Jane (1813–97): Scottish translator of German hymns

Bosanquet, Mary: British writer; author of an early biography of Bonhoeffer—9

Bosc, Jean (1910–69): studied theology in France and Germany; 1934, one of the French delegates (who were unable to attend) to the conference in Bruay, France; 1935–44, general secretary of the French Christian Student Federation; 1944–55, Reformed pastor, Meaux; 1952, professor of dogmatics, Paris—13

Bosch, Robert (1861–1942): industrialist (electronics)—8

Böse, Miss: Toni Volkmann's friend—9

Botterwerk, G. Johannes: coeditor of *Theologisches Wörterbuch zum Alten Testament*—15

Botticelli, Sandro (Alessandro di Mariano Filipepi) (1444–1510): Florentine Renaissance painter of the Renaissance—9

Boudaille, George: French art historian and critic—10

Bousset, Wilhelm (1865–1920): German theologian, professor of theology and early church history and doctrine, Göttingen; one of the founders of the history of religions school—1, 6, 11

Bouvier, André: Swiss Reformed pastor; September 1933, participated in the meeting of the executive committee of the Ecumenical Council for Life and Work in Novi Sad and in the conference of the World Alliance for Promoting International Friendship through the Churches in Sofia; 1934, spoke at the plenary session of the Ecumenical Council for Life and Work in Fanø—12, 13

Boveri, Margret (1900–1975): German journalist; author of works on the German resistance and the German experience under Hitler—16

Bowden, John: British publisher and translator—2, 7, 8

Boy, Johannes: from 1930, pastor in Berlin—12

Boyens, Armin: German Protestant minister, church historian, and ecumenist—6, 12, 13, 14, 16

Bracher, Dorothee, née Schleicher: daughter of Rüdiger and Ursula Schleicher; May 3, 1951, married the historian Karl Dietrich Bracher—8, 10, 15, 16

Bracher, Karl Dietrich: German historian of the Nazi period; lecturer, Berlin, and professor of history, Bonn; fellow of the Center for Advanced Study at Princeton—8, 11

Bracht, Franz (1877–1933): 1923, state secretary in the Reich chancellery; 1932, representative of the Reich commissioner in Prussia—12

Brackmann, Karl-Heinz: author of work (with Renate Birkenhauer) on nazified German language—12

Bracks, Heinz: 1940, studied philosophy, Königsberg; secret agent for the security service (SD) in Königsberg—16

Brahms, Johannes (1833–97): German composer—7, 8, 9, 13

Brake (FP: family in the novel): 7
  Christoph
  Ekkehard (Little Brother)
  Franz
  Hans (father; physician, professor)
  Josias (cathedral provost)
  Karoline (grandmother)
  Klara
  Maria (mother)
  Martin
  Theodor (uncle)

Brakelmann, Günter: German church historian of the Church Struggle—11

Brand: Norwegian pastor, the title character of Henrik Ibsen's play about religion and personal freedom—6, 10

Brandenburg, Hans: pastor, Lübeck; 1930, missions inspector in the City Mission in Berlin; 1932, head of the "Free Youth" of Paul Le Seur; 1949, missions inspector for evangelism—11

Brandenburg, Johannes: 1922, city missions inspector in Berlin; 1934, pastor, Salem House for Deaconesses, Berlin-Lichtenrade—12

Brandenburg, Kurt: head physician, Virchow Clinic (part of the Charité), Berlin—16

Brandenburg, Willi (Willy) Max Hermann (1909–42): from Berlin; 1932–33, among the circle of students around Bonhoeffer; 1934, participated in the Fanø youth conference; 1936–37, participated in the fourth Finkenwalde session; 1938, ordained; ministry in Pätzig/Neudamm (Neumark); 1942, killed in action on the eastern front—4, 13, 14, 16

Brandt, Günther: 1939–45, Confessing Church pastor, Potsdam; 1945–49, pastor, Werder/Havel; 1949–54, Potsdam; 1954–60, Berlin-Siemensstadt; 1960–71, pastor and superintendent, Spandau; retired, Müllheim-Feldberg—15

Brandt, Irene: friend of Ursula Bonhoeffer; after 1933, forced to emigrate because of National Socialist race laws—9

Brandt, Karl (1904–48): 1934–44, Hitler's personal physician; 1948, executed —13

Brandt, Klaus: occasional private tutor of Klaus Bonhoeffer; after 1933, forced to emigrate because of National Socialist race laws—9
Brandt, Willy (1913–92): German Social Democrat politician; 1957–66, mayor of West Berlin; 1966–69, foreign minister and vice-chancellor; 1969–74, chancellor; 1971, awarded Nobel Peace Prize—8
Brandts, Franz (1834–1914): manufacturer; pioneer for the factory welfare system and for social labor politics; 1890, cofounder and until his death head of the People's Association for Catholic Germany—11
Brauchitsch, Walter von (1881–1948): career military; 1938–41, commander in chief of the army; 1940, general field marshal; December 1941, dismissed by Hitler—16, 17
Brauer: 1931–32, participant in Bonhoeffer's seminar on "The Idea of Philosophy and Protestant Theology"—11
Bräuer, Ernst: husband of Johanna (Hanni) Bräuer, née Delbrück—9
Bräuer, Johanna (Hanni), née Delbrück: wife of Dr. Ernst Bräuer—9
Braun, Hannelore: staff member, Institute for Contemporary German History, Munich—12
Braun, Hermann: 1933, pastor, Argenbruck (formerly Neu-Argeningken) near Tilsit; 1937, Confessing Church district pastor, represented Tilsit in the East Prussian Council of Brethren; June 18, 1940, Dietrich Bonhoeffer visited him—16
Braun, Walter (1892–1973): from 1926, missions inspector for the Berlin Mission Society; 1947–63, general superintendent, Old Prussian province of Mark Brandenburg (Kurmark)—12
Braun, Werner: from 1939, pastor, Greater Tychow, Pomerania; member of the German Christians—16
Braune, Paul Gerhard (1887–1954): German Protestant pastor and director of Lobetal, an institution for the disabled; vice president of the executive committee of the Inner Mission; outspoken opponent of the euthanasia measures; August–November 1940, imprisoned by the Gestapo; 1945, president of the Inner Mission in the eastern German territories and member of the Berlin-Brandenburg church administration—6, 16, 17
Breazeale, Daniel: U.S. professor of German philosophy—1
Brecht, Bertolt (1898–1956): German dramatist, lyricist, poet, and producer; 1933, emigrated from Nazi Germany; 1945, returned to the German Theater in Berlin—7
Brecht, Martin: German scholar of Luther—10, 16
Breit, Thomas (1880–1966): 1914–18, military chaplain; 1925, church dean, Hof, Bavaria; 1933–45, senior church official in Munich and representative of Bavarian bishop Hans Meiser; 1934–36, member of the Reich

Council of Brethren and of the council of the German Evangelical Church —13, 14

Breithaupt, Martin: 1912, pastor in Berlin—12

Bremer (FP: family in the novel)—7

Georg von

Harald von (father, major)

Harald von (deceased son)

Johannes von

Renate von

Sophie von (mother)

Brendel, Maria, née Weigert: daughter of the director of the state court, Dr. Erich Weigert; later studied archaeology; married to Dr. Otto Brendel; had to emigrate because of National Socialist race laws; lived next door to Bonhoeffer; first girl to study at a boys' Prussian Gymnasium—9, 10

Brenner, G. (died toward the end of 1933): baker, member of the congregational council, St. Paul's Church in London; Bonhoeffer officiated at his funeral—13

Brenner, Harro: first class legation officer, office of the Reich foreign minister—16

Brenz, Johannes (1499–1570): Swabian reformer; 1518, took Luther's side at the Heidelberg Disputation; from 1522, worked on behalf of the Reformation in Schwäbisch Hall; 1559, church administrator, Württemberg—2, 12, 14

Breyhan, Christian (1903–77): law student and member of the Hedgehogs since the 1921–22 winter semester; later became a senior government finance president—17 (for vol. 9)

Briand, Aristide (1862–1932): French statesman, lawyer, socialist; 1925–29, foreign minister; 1928, chief architect of the Kellogg-Briand pact; prominent in the League of Nations; 1926, Nobel Prize Peace Prize (together with Gustav Stresemann)—9, 10

Brieger, Ernst: Berlin physician; married Käthe, née Friedenthal; emigrated to England as a "non-Aryan"—16

Brightman, Edgar Sheffield (1884–1953): U.S. Methodist philosopher and theologian; taught at Boston University—10

Brilioth, Yngve (1891–1959): Swedish theologian and ecumenist; 1925, professor of practical theology and 1928, cathedral provost in Lund; 1937, bishop of Vasjö; 1950–58, archbishop of Uppsala; 1920, participated in the first Conference for Faith and Order; 1947–56, chair of this commission; member of the central and executive committees of the World Council of Churches—14, 16

Brinkel, Karl: German scholar of Luther—16

Brocker, Mark: U.S. Lutheran pastor; member of editorial board, *DBWE*; editor of *DBWE* 16; coeditor of *DBWE* 11 and *DBWE* 14—1, 2, 4, 6, 11, 14, 16

Brodersen, Arvid (1904–96): Norwegian social scientist; June–September 1940, secretary of the Storting administrative committee at the Reich council negotiations with Reich commissar Terboven; from autumn 1940, contact person for the Norwegian home front with the German resistance, especially with Theodor Steltzer; 1945, played a significant role in rescuing Steltzer from a death sentence; 1946, adviser with UNESCO in Paris, later professor of social research, New York—16

Brodersen, Peter (1913–42): from Flensburg; 1939–40, city vicar and deputy student chaplain, Munich; February 1942, killed in action on the eastern front—16

Bronisch, Gotthelf: assessor of Bonhoeffer's sermon for his first theological exam; church superintendent, Züllichau—9

Bronisch-Holtze, Ernst Oskar Paul (1890–1944): 1919, ordination; 1927, pastor at the Trinity Church and student chaplain, Friedrich Wilhelm University; 1930, founder of the working group of Protestant students; 1942, cathedral pastor and city superintendent, Königsberg; June 1944, arrested for listening to "enemy broadcasts"; presumably committed suicide in prison—11, 12, 17

Bronzino II (Agnolo di Cosimo di Mariano) (1503–72): Florentine mannerist painter—9

Brorson, Hans Adolf (1694–1764): Danish hymnist and bishop of Ribe—15

Brouwer, Luitzen Egbertus Jan (1881–1966): Dutch mathematician; 1912–51, professor, Amsterdam—1

Brown, A.: member of the congregational council, German congregation, Sydenham, London—13

Brown, Maurice J. E.: coauthor of work on Schubert—8

Brown, Peter: Irish-born historian; author of study of Augustine—11

Brown, William Adams (1865–1943): leading figure in the North American Church Federation; 1919–30, president of the Committee of Educational Policy, Yale; 1933, participated in the conference of the World Alliance for Promoting International Friendship through the Churches in Sofia; 1937, U.S. president of the ecumenical conference in Oxford—6, 10, 12, 13, 15, 16

Browning, Robert (1812–99): British poet and playwright—10

Browning, Robert M.: editor of German poetry—10

Brownjohn, John: British translator—17

Bruckner, Anton (1823–96): composer—8

Brückner, Karl (1851–1938): civil servant; married Margarethe (Gretchen), née Domrich, a cousin of Karl August von Hase; father of Elizabeth (married name Hansen), Konstantin, and Helene (Leni)—9

Bruder, Otto: *see* Salomon, Otto

Brueghel, Pieter (ca. 1525/30–1569): Dutch Renaissance painter—8

Brüning, Heinrich (1885–1970): centrist German politician; March 1930–May 1932, German Reich chancellor—11, 12, 17

Brunner, Emil (1889–1966): Swiss Reformed theologian, one of the founders of dialectical theology; 1924–53, professor of systematic and practical theology, Zürich; also taught in the United States and Japan—1, 2, 3, 4, 6, 8, 10, 11, 12, 13, 14, 15, 16

Brunner, Peter (1900–1981): 1927, private lecturer in systematic theology, Giessen; 1932, pastor, Ranstadt, Upper Hesse; 1933, teaching appointment in Giessen withdrawn for political reasons; March–May 1935, imprisoned in the Dachau concentration camp; 1936, *venia legendi* (authorization to teach at university after postdoctoral lecturing qualification) at the university in Giessen withdrawn; 1936–40 and 1945–47, lecturer in Lutheran dogmatics at the Confessing Church seminary in Elberfeld and (after the war) at the seminary in Wuppertal; 1940–47, pastor of the Lutheran Confessing Church in Elberfeld; 1947–68, professor of systematic theology, Heidelberg—14, 15

Brunner, Theodor: Swiss psychiatrist; founder and head of the private Brunner Neurological Institute, Küsnacht; medical services colonel in the Swiss army, assigned to General Guisan at army headquarters during the war; member of the exchange commission of the Red Cross for the seriously wounded—16

Bruno, Giordano (1548–1600): Italian philosopher, burned at the stake during the Inquisition—8

Brunotte, Heinz: prominent Lutheran and critic of the Confessing Church; senior lawyer for the Evangelical Consistory in Berlin—16

Bruns, Professor: chair of the Academic Exchange Service committee that approved Bonhoeffer's fellowship at Union—10

Brunstäd, Friedrich (1883–1944): German theologian and philosopher; offered a critical explication of Hegelian idealism; 1917, professor of philosophy, Erlangen; 1925, professor of systematic theology, Rostock; 1922–34, head of the Protestant Social School, Spandau; 1934, member of the Lutheran Council—1, 2, 3, 6, 8, 10, 12, 14, 16

Brutus (Marcus Junius Brutus) (ca. 85–42 B.C.E.): along with Caius Cassius Longinus, principal assassin of Julius Caesar—9

Bryce, James (1838–1922): British statesman, jurist—6

Buber, Martin (1878–1965): 1923–33, professor of Jewish religious philosophy, Frankfurt University; 1933, dismissed by government; 1938, emigrated to Palestine and ultimately became professor of sociology at the Hebrew University in Jerusalem, where he researched Hasidic literature and translated the Hebrew Bible into German with Franz Rosenzweig —1, 2, 5, 10, 11, 12, 14

Bubnoff, Nicolai von: professor of philosophy, Heidelberg—11

Bucer, Martin (1491–1551): Reformer from Strasbourg; 1518, took Luther's side at the Heidelberg Disputation; father of Protestant confirmation—9, 14

Buchholz, Fritz (1877–1960): from 1918, pastor, Berlin-Friedenau—12

Buchman, Frank (1878–1961): U.S. theologian of German-Swiss descent; 1908, following a conversion he helped found the Oxford Group movement (after 1938, became the Moral Rearmament movement; after 1945, called the Caux movement)—4, 6, 10, 11, 13, 14

Buchmann, Adolf Herbert Johannes (1914–77): from Bernau near Berlin; 1936, vicar, Biesental; 1937, Blankenburg; 1938, Pforten; 1938, predicant, Havelsberg-Wilsnack; 1938, participated in the collective pastorate in Groß-Schlönwitz; listed as a lieutenant in Bonhoeffer's address book during the war; 1947, pastor, Heilbronn; 1949, Berlin-Moabit; 1975, retired—15, 16

Büchmann, Georg (1822–84): German philologist—3, 4, 8, 12, 13

Büchner, Ludwig (1824–99): German physician, brother of the dramatist Georg Büchner; advocated a popular, unlimited materialism and promoted Darwinism—6

Büchsel, Hans-Jakob (1909–43): from Köslin, Pomerania; 1935–36, participated in the second Finkenwalde session; pastor, Pomerania; 1943, missing in action at Stalingrad—15

Büchsel, Karl (1803–1889): jurist and administrative director of the Friedrich Wilhelm University, Berlin—11, 14

Budde, Karl Ferdinand Reinhardt (1850–1935): 1900–1921, professor of Old Testament, Marburg—9

Buddha (Siddhartha Gautama) (ca. 563–ca. 483 B.C.E.): founder of Buddhism—1, 10, 12

Bugenhagen, Johann (1485–1558): 1509, consecrated as priest without having studied theology; from 1521, at Wittenberg University, studied Luther's theological lectures; from 1523, city pastor of Wittenberg; creator of various church administrative structures—14

Bühler, Karl: language theoretician—14

Buhre, Gunnar (1889–1965): from 1932, pastor, Berlin—12

Bull, Paul: Anglican priest at Mirfield monastery in England—14

Bullinger, Heinrich (1504–75): Swiss humanist and Reformer; pastor; author of about twelve thousand letters; 1531, Zwingli's successor in Zürich —9, 14

Bülow, Bernhard von (1885–1936): 1930, state secretary in the Foreign Ministry—12

Bülow, Gabriele von (1802–87): daughter of Wilhelm von Humboldt—8

Bultmann, Peter: 1937, Confessing Church pastor in Pomerania—14, 15

Bultmann, Rudolf (1884–1976): German theologian; 1916, professor of New Testament theology, Breslau; 1920, Giessen; 1921–61, professor of New Testament, Marburg; member of the Academies of Science in Heidelberg, Göttingen, and Oslo; 1933, member of the Pastors' Emergency League; advocate of demythologization and an existentialist interpretation of the New Testament—1, 2, 4, 6, 8, 9, 10, 11, 12, 16, 17

Bünger, Wilhelm (1870–1937): lawyer; July 1929–February 1930, Saxon minister president (German National People's Party); president of the senate—8

Bunke, Adolf: brother of Hermann Bunke; attorney in Glogau/Silesia; member of the Silesian Provincial Council of Brethren; 1936, held in preventive detention; 1937, released from the Buchenwald concentration camp and expelled from Silesia; company lawyer and later manager of the East Prussian Council of Brethren; 1940, member of the Confessing Church council, Blöstau—8, 16

Bunke, Ernst (1866–1944): 1912, director of the Johannes institutions, Berlin-Spandau—12

Bunke, Hermann (1895–1969): deputy Protestant military chaplain in defense district III (Berlin-Brandenburg)—8, 12

Bunners, Christian: German theologian; member, historical commission for research on pietism—10

Buoninsegna, Duccio di (1278–1319): early Italian artist; first leading representative of the Sienese school—9

Burckhardt, Carl Jacob (1891–1974): Swiss; 1932, professor of history, Geneva; later in Zürich; 1937–39, high commissioner of the League of Nations for Danzig; vice president of the International Red Cross during the war and its president from 1944 to 1948—12, 16

Burckhardt, Jacob Ludwig (1818–97): Swiss cultural and art historian—6, 7, 8, 9

Burdach, Colonel: not otherwise identified—15

Buren, Paul van (1924–98): U.S. theologian; educated at Harvard University and Episcopal Theological School; ThD, University of Basel; ordained in the Episcopal Church, United States; best known for his theology of the post-Holocaust relationship between Christianity and Judaism—8

Burge, Evan: classics scholar and professor; 1974–97, warden of Trinity College, University of Melbourne—6, 9

Burger, Ewald (1905–42): theology student and Bonhoeffer's fraternity brother in Tübingen—9

Burgess, Joseph: professor in Philadelphia; owner of one of Bonhoeffer's original letters to Otto Piper—13

Burggraf, Julius (1853–1912): German Protestant theologian; 1883, pastor, Bremen; delivered poetic sermons of a nationalist idealist nature—10

Burghart, Georg (1865–1954): 1891–1917, assistant pastor and pastor in Berlin, Düsseldorf, and Barmen; 1917, privy counselor and full-time member, High Church Consistory; 1921, general superintendent of Berlin; 1927–33, clerical vice president, Protestant High Church Consistory, and senior court preacher; president of the German section of the World Alliance for Promoting International Friendship through the Churches; 1927–49, head of the Evangelical Central Bible Society in Berlin; member of the German Evangelical Church Committee; 1933, retired—10, 12, 13, 15

Burgwitz, Martin (1899–1957): 1925, pastor in Lugau, district of Luckau; 1936, at the Bethany diaconate house, Stettin; from 1938, deputy chair of the Pomeranian Confessing Church Council of Brethren, Pomerania; 1941–42, deputy head of the Old Prussian Confessing Synod; 1942, dismissed by the consistory; 1943, drafted into the military; 1946, pastor, Bitterfeld; from 1954, Berlin—15, 16

Burlage, Wilhelm: physician, specialist in nervous diseases; 1931–35, at the Clinic for Psychiatric and Nervous Diseases of the Charité hospital; assistant to Karl Bonhoeffer—8

Burlingham, Rev. R. E.: member of the working committee of the World Alliance for Promoting International Friendship through the Churches—12, 13

Burn, Andrew Ewbank: British patristics scholar—1

Burroughs, Edward Arthur (1882–1934): 1909, examining chaplain for the bishop of Liverpool; 1917, also for the bishop of Exeter; 1926, lord bishop of Ripon; 1928, head of the youth commission of the World Alliance for Promoting International Friendship through the Churches—11, 12

Burrowes-Cromwell, Toni: daughter-in-law of Ernst Cromwell—14

Bursche, Julius (1862–1942): 1889, pastor, Warsaw; 1905, general superintendent; 1937, bishop of the Evangelical Augsburg Church in Poland; from 1939, imprisoned in concentration camps—12

Burtness, James (1929–2006): U.S. Lutheran professor of systematic theology; author of works on Bonhoeffer—2, 5, 6, 8

Busch, Benedikt: German historian of Catholic cloisters and monasteries —16

Busch, Eberhard: German professor of reformed theology; biographer of Karl Barth—11, 12, 13, 15, 16

Busch, Joseph Hubert: author of work on original sin—1

Busch, Wilhelm (1832–1908): graphic artist, poet, painter—8, 11

Busch, Wilhelm (1897–1966): Westphalian pastor; 1931–62, youth pastor in Essen; popular evangelist and author—16

Büsing, Erika: wife of Wolfgang Büsing—15

Büsing, Wolfgang Paul (1910–94): 1933, member of Bonhoeffer's circle of students in Berlin; 1935–36, seminarian at the second Finkenwalde session and member of the House of Brethren; 1936, emigration, assistant pastor at the German Evangelical St. George's Church, London; 1940, pastor at the German Christ Church, London; from 1938, commissioned by Bishop Bell to work with German refugees (Church of England Committee for Non-Aryan Christians); 1949, emigrated to Canada; 1951, joined the Anglican Church and was active in various congregations around Quebec and in Montreal; pastor in Ottawa until 1988—13, 14, 15

Busse, Margarete, née Nietzschmann (1877–1963): oldest sister of Eberhard Bethge's mother—8, 16

Butler, Harold: director of the Nuffield College, Oxford—16

Buxton, Dorothy F. (Bonhoeffer also spells her name "Dorothee"): British Quaker activist; helped refugees from Nazi Germany—16

Buxton, Lord Noel: bishop of Willesden; brother-in-law of the British Quaker Dorothy Buxton; spring 1943, Dietrich Bonhoeffer mentions him in the "camouflage letter"—16

Cable, Mr.: staff member, Society of Friends of Foreigners in Distress in Great Britain—13

Cadogan, Sir Alexander George Montagu (1884–1968): British diplomat; 1938–46, permanent undersecretary in the British Foreign Office; expert in Near Eastern affairs—16

Caesar, Caius Julius (ca. 102–44 B.C.E.): Roman statesman, ruler, and military leader; assassinated by political opponents—9

Caesar, Octavian (Augustus) (63 B.C.E.–14 C.E.): grandnephew and adopted heir of Julius Caesar—9

Cain: biblical character—2, 5, 6, 8, 10, 11, 14, 15

Caiphas: biblical character—9

Calderón de la Barca, Pedro (1600–1681): Spanish dramatist—8

Calixtus, Georg (also: Calixt; 1586–1656): German theologian who extended the influence of Philipp Melanchthon—9, 11

Calov (Kalau), Abraham (1612–86): Lutheran Orthodox theologian; professor and pastor, Danzig and Wittenberg—3, 9

Calvin, John (1509–64): French Protestant reformer and formative theologian of Reformed Protestantism—1, 2, 4, 6, 8, 9, 11, 12, 13, 14, 15, 16

Cambon, Jules Martin (1845–1935): French diplomat; chaired the group responsible for overseeing the enforcement of the Treaty of Versailles—9

Cameron, Ruth Tonkiss: archivist, Union Theological Seminary, New York —10, 11

Canapero: owner of the hotel Albergo Piemonte in Rome (mentioned by Richard Czeppan)—9

Canaris, Wilhelm (1887–1945): career military/navy; 1924–28, on the staff of the Chief of the Navy in the Reich Armed Forces Ministry; 1935, rear admiral and head of the Military Intelligence Office in the Ministry of Defense; later in the Armed Forces High Command; February 1944, dismissed from office; July 23, 1944, arrested; April 9, 1945, executed in the Flossenbürg concentration camp—6, 8, 16, 17

Cancik, Hubert: professor of Latin, Tübingen—10

Canterbury (archbishop of): *see* Lang, Cosmo Gordon (1928–42); and Temple, William (1942–44)—13

Cantor, Georg (1845–1918): German mathematician—3

Čapek, Karel (1890–1938): Czech writer, author of naturalistic novellas and novels; advocate of socially critical science fiction—10

Caracalla (Marcus Aurelius Antoninus) (188–217): Roman emperor—9

Caravaggio, Michelangelo Merisi da (Amerigi da Caravaggio) (1573–1610): revolutionary and realistic Italian painter—9

Cardanus (Cardano), Jerome (1501–76): Italian mathematician, physician, philosopher, and astrologer—8

Carlson: (U.S.) not otherwise identified—15

Carlyle, Thomas (1795–1881): Scottish historian and essayist—6

Carneades (214–129 B.C.E.): Greek philosopher; 155 B.C.E., Athenian ambassador to Rome—6

Carter, Dan T.: U.S. historian; wrote on the Scottsboro trial—6, 10

Carter, Guy Christopher: U.S. Lutheran historical theologian and Bonhoeffer scholar; author of study on Bethel confession—6, 12

Carter, Keyna: British participant in the Fanø youth conference—13

Casel, Odo (Johannes) (1886–1948): Benedictine, liturgical scholar, one of the founders of the "theology of mystery"—10

Caspar, Horst (1913–52): German stage and film actor—16

Caspari, Walter (1847–1923): professor of pastoral theology, Berlin—9, 14

Cassel, Gustav (1866–1945): Swedish national economist—9

Cassius (Caius Cassius Longinus) (d. 45 B.C.E.): one of the principal assassins of Julius Caesar—9

Castor: Greek mythological character; twin of Pollux—7

Catchpool, Corder: British Quaker; 1933, already active in the Berlin secretariat of the Quakers; member of the Friends Service Committee in England during the war—16

Catharinus, Ambrosius (real name: Lancelotto Politi) (1483–1553): Italian canon lawyer—1

Catullus, Gaius Valerius (84–ca. 54 B.C.E.): Roman lyric poet—9

Cauer: family in Bad Kreuznach; over three generations, this family produced a series of famous sculptors; the wife of Dietrich Bonhoeffer's great-grandfather Count Stanislaus of Kalckreuth also came from this family—16

Cauer, Hanna: Bonhoeffer's maternal third cousin; painter and a sculptor; occasional visitor to the Bonhoeffer home—8, 9

Cavendish-Bentinck, Victor Frederick William: from 1940, incumbent counselor in the Central Department of the British Foreign Office—16

Cavert, Samuel McCrea (1888–1976): U.S. pastor and ecumenist; 1921, general secretary of the Federal Council of the Churches of Christ in the United States; May–June 1939, involved in efforts to have Dietrich Bonhoeffer come to the United States; 1946, contact person between the World Council of Churches, the Evangelical Church of Germany, and the Office of Military Government for Germany, United States; 1954, managing secretary in the New York office of the World Council of Churches—15, 16

Cedergren, Elsa: daughter of Prince Oskar Bernadotte; niece of the Swedish king; wife of Hugo Cedergren; member of the "Ekumeniska Nämnden"—8, 16

Cedergren, Hugo (1891–1971): nephew by marriage to King Gustav V of Sweden; general secretary of the Swedish YMCA—8, 16

Cervantes Saavedra, Miguel de (1547–1616): Spanish novelist, dramatist, and poet; author of *Don Quixote*—6, 7, 8, 10

Chafee, Zechariah, Jr. (1885–1957): U.S. legal scholar and professor, Harvard Law School; influential expert on freedom of speech and other civil liberties—10

Chaise, Père François de la (1624–1709): Jesuit priest; confessor of Louis XIV—10

Chamberlain, Arthur Neville (1869–1940): British statesman, successful in domestic politics; 1937–40, prime minister after Baldwin's resignation; to avoid war, sought negotiations with Hitler and Mussolini; 1938, signed the Munich agreement with Hitler—6, 15, 17

Chamberlain, Houston Stewart (1855–1927): British writer; from 1885, in Dresden, Vienna, and Bayreuth; admirer of German intellectuals, particularly Richard Wagner; married Wagner's daughter; prepared the way for National Socialist racial ideology—10

Chamberlain, William Henry: conservative U.S. political commentator and editor—10

Chambers, Oswald: a Scottish minister—14

Chamisso, Adalbert von (de Boncourt, Louis Charles Adélaïde) (1781–1838): Franco-German author and natural scientist—6

Chantré: Gestapo official—15

Chapman, G. Clarke Jr.: 1963, PhD, Boston University, systematic theology; from 1963, professor of systematic theology at Moravian College; research and writing on liberation theology, Jürgen Moltmann's theology of hope, Bonhoeffer studies, and theological ethics in a nuclear age; author of *Facing the Nuclear Heresy* (Brethren Press, 1986)—9, 10, 13, 16

Charlemagne (742–814): king of the Franks; 772–804, subjugated the Saxons; 800, first emperor of the Holy Roman Empire—4, 6, 10, 13, 14, 15

Charles V (1500–1558): Duke of Burgundy and the king of Spain and Germany; 1519, elected Holy Roman emperor; political and religious opponent of the Lutheran Reformation; 1556, stepped down as emperor to retire to a monastery; lived there in seclusion until his death in 1558; was the last German emperor of the Holy Roman Empire to be crowned by the pope; presided over the Diet of Worms and the Diet of Augsburg—1, 14, 15

Charlesworth, James H.: George L. Collord Professor of New Testament Language and Literature and director of the Dead Sea Scrolls Project at Princeton—14

Chase, Stuart (1888–1985): U.S. economist, engineer, and journalist—10

Chemnitz, Martin (1522–86): student of Melanchthon; superintendent in Brunswick (Braunschweig)—12

Cherbury: *see* Herbert, Edward Lord of Cherbury—8

Chichester: *see* Bell, George

Child, Clifton: British intelligence expert during World War II—16

Childs, Brevard S. (1923–2007): Presbyterian theologian; 1950, B.D., Princeton; 1955, ThD, Basel; 1958, assistant professor of Old Testament, Yale University Divinity School; 1961, associate professor; 1966, full professor; 1992, named Sterling Professor of Divinity; interests in Old Testament interpretation, criticism, and theology, and in Judaica; honorary degrees from the University of Aberdeen and from the University of Glasgow; 1994, named a fellow of the American Academy of Arts and Sciences—3

Chilon: sixth-century Spartan ephor (ca. 550 B.C.E.): ranked as one of the Seven Sages, or Seven Wise Men of Greece; one of the alleged authors of the inscription "know thyself" in Delphi—2

Chlodwig (466–511): Frankish king—14

Chomjakov, Alexej Stepanowitsch (1804–60): Russian poet, dramatist, and essayist—11

Chowaniec, Elisabeth: German historian of the German resistance—8, 14, 16

Christ, Günther (1912–41): from Berlin; 1935, predicant, Goßmar, district of Luckau; 1936, participated in the third Finkenwalde session; ministry in Müncheberg near Fürstenwalde and Kyritz near Havelberg; August 8, 1941, killed in action at the eastern front—16

Christ, Lukas (1881–1958): 1911–48, pastor, Pratteln-Augst, Switzerland —11, 14

Christoph (FP): character in Bonhoeffer's fragmentary prison drama and novel who most resembles Bonhoeffer himself; cf. Brake—6, 7

Christopher (Saint): third-century martyr and patron saint of travelers—10

Chrysippus (280–207 B.C.E.): Greek Stoic philosopher—17 (for vol. 9)

Chrysostom, John (ca. 347–407): Greek church father and theologian of the Antioch school; patriarch of Constantinople—3, 4, 6, 8, 10, 14

Churchill, Sir Winston Spencer (1874–1965): British statesman; 1940, became prime minister after the start of the German western offensive; June 1945, resigned after defeat at the polls; 1951–55, served as prime minister after Conservatives won power—6, 8, 16, 17

Cicero, Marcus Tullius (106–43 B.C.E.): Roman statesman, author, orator —1, 6, 8, 9, 14

Cisar, Alexandre (1880–1954): archbishop of Bucharest—16

Clark, Frank: cotranslator of first edition of *Letters and Papers from Prison*—2, 8

Clarkson, John F., S. J.: patristics scholar—14

Claß, Gottfried: worked on scholarly apparatus for *DBW* 3—8

Claudius, Matthias (1740–1815; called himself Asmus): German poet and father of German popular journalism; 1771–76, editor of the newspaper *Der Wandsbecker Bote* (The Wandsbeck messenger)—4, 6, 8, 10, 13, 14, 15, 16

Claudius, Tiberius (10 B.C.E.–54 C.E.): Roman emperor—4, 15

Cledney, I. U.: during World War II, official in the British Foreign Office—16

Clegg, Aaron: assisted with *DBWE* 7—7

Clemen, Otto (1871–1946): German theologian and philologist—11

Clement of Alexandria (Titus Flavius Clemens) (ca. 150–215): Greek church father; teacher of Origin; ca. 180–201, head of the catechetical school in Alexandria—9, 10, 11, 14

Clement of Rome (d. ca. 97 C.E.): third bishop of Rome after Peter; author of historically and theologically significant letter to the church at Corinth —4, 9

Clements, Keith: British Baptist minister and ecumenist; 1997–2005, General Secretary of the Conference of European Churches in Geneva; editor of *DBWE* 13—2, 4, 8, 12, 13, 14, 16

Cleopatra (69–30 B.C.E.): 53–30 B.C.E., queen of Egypt—9

Clodius, Carl: 1933, worked with the German legation in Sofia—12

Clytemnestra: character in Greek mythology—6

Coccejus, Johannes (actually: Coch) (1603–69): 1630, professor of theology, Bremen, later in Franeker; 1650, Leiden; first great representative of covenant theology—14

Coch, Friedrich (1887–1945): 1914, pastor, Saxony; 1916, military chaplain; 1931, joined the NSDAP; 1932, joined the German Christians; district adviser for church affairs; 1933–45, bishop of the Evangelical Lutheran Church of Saxony—13

Cochrane, Arthur C.: author of work on the Church Struggle—6

Cochrane, Charles Norris (1889–1945): Canadian historian and philosopher —1

Cocks, John Sebastian Somers: 1942, official in the Northern Department of the British Foreign Office—16

Coffin, Henry Sloane (1877–1954): U.S. Protestant theologian; 1904–54, professor of practical theology, Union Theological Seminary, New York; 1926–45, president of Union Theological Seminary; 1943–44, moderator, Presbyterian Church, United States—10, 15, 16

Cohen, Hermann (1842–1918): German neo-Kantian philosopher; professor of philosophy, Marburg school; founder of the Marburg school—2, 9, 10, 11

Cohn, Leopold: German Philo scholar—9

Collmer, Paul (1907–79): economist from Stuttgart; 1931, head of the Tübingen office for students; official in the Reich Ministry of Labor; 1940, civilian adviser, Dutch Ministry for Social Affairs; arranged contacts between the Dutch and German resistance movements; 1946, vice president of the main office of the Inner Mission and of the relief organization of the Evangelical Church of Germany; founder and head of the Evangelical Verlagswerk (publishing house) in Stuttgart—16

Colman, Ruth: daughter of Frank and Doris Goetz, whose marriage service Bonhoeffer conducted at St. Paul's Church, London, May 3, 1934—13

Colvin, Harold: acquaintance of Bonhoeffer's in New York; not otherwise identified—15

Comba, Ernesto (1880–1959): professor of systematic theology, Facoltà veldese di Teologia, Rome; president of the Italian section, World Alliance for Promoting International Friendship through the Churches; 1925, representative of the Waldensian Church at the Stockholm Ecumenical Conference; 1927, in Lausanne; 1937, at the Life and Work conference, Oxford, and Faith and Order, Edinburgh; spring 1943, mentioned by Dietrich Bonhoeffer in the "camouflage letter" as an Italian ecumenist—8, 16

Compton, C.: member of the congregation at the German Reformed St. Paul's Church, London—13

Comte, Auguste (1798–1857): student of Saint-Simon; 1824, broke with his teacher; founder of positivism and of modern sociology; friend of J. S. Mill and George Grote—1, 9

Condillac, Etienne Bonnot de (1715–80): French priest and philosopher—1

Conrad, Paul (1865–1927): from 1925, vice president of the Consistory of the Protestant Church of the Old Prussian Union; senior court preacher; head of the cathedral seminary—9, 14

Constantine (the Great) (ca. 285–337): 306–37, Roman emperor; legalized the Christian church as *religio licita*; after 324, sole emperor of Rome; made Byzantium the capital (renamed Constantinople)—9, 10, 14, 15

Conway, John: British-born historian of European history; professor emeritus, University of British Columbia; author of one of the first studies of the German Church Struggle—11, 12, 16

Conway, Martin: British ecumenist, linguist, and Bonhoeffer scholar—13

Conze, Peter (1860–1939): undersecretary in the Reich Colonial Office; head of the Evangelical Press Association for Germany; 1925, member of the executive committee of the Evangelical Federation—9

Cooper, Alfred Duff (1890–1954): British politician and historian—8

Coote, Edward Osborne (1894–1948): from 1939, first secretary in the Central Department of the British Foreign Office—16

Corbach, Karl-Heinz: from Berlin-Friedenau; 1937, participated in the fifth Finkenwalde session; pastor in Buckow; 1938, married the theologian Ursula Duckstein; after 1945, youth chaplain for Brandenburg in Potsdam —15

Corbach, Ursula, née Duckstein: theologian; wife of Karl-Heinz Corbach —15

Cordes, Cord: Confessing Church pastor; author of dissertation on Protestant and Catholic understandings of community as well as history of the social ministry in the Hannover church—10, 11

Cornehl, Peter: professor emeritus of practical theology and homiletics, University of Hamburg—14

Cornelius: biblical character—8, 14

Cornelius Nepos (ca. 100–25 B.C.E.): Roman historian, chronicler, biographer—9

Cornelius, Peter (1824–74): composer, author on musical topics—8

Cornog, Mary: assisted with *DBWE* 1—1

Coulon, Wilhelm Daniel Albert (1865–1945): 1891, ordination; 1921, clergy inspector of the French Reformed church in Mark Brandenburg, pastor at the French Hospital church, Berlin-Niederschönhausen; 1923, consistory official; 1936–38, responsible for a senior council position in the Berlin consistory—9, 10, 11

Courvoisier, Jacques: Swiss theologian and ecumenist; 1939–69, professor of church history, Geneva; during the war, chair of the ecumenical relief organization for prisoners of war, World Council of Churches; 1941, introduced to Dietrich Bonhoeffer by Visser 't Hooft; 1955, president of the Ecumenical Institute of Bossey near Geneva—16, 17

Cox, Harvey G.: U.S. theologian; Hollis Professor of Divinity emeritus, Harvard University—6

Cragg, R. H.: chaplain at the British embassy in Berlin; later bishop of Durham—13

Craig, Gordon Alexander: Scottish-born historian of European diplomatic and military history and modern German history; professor emeritus of history, Stanford University—13, 15

Craske, Frederick William Thomas (1901–71): 1928, pastor, Manchester; 1931, appointed one of the three youth secretaries of the World Alliance for Promoting International Friendship through the Churches; 1950–53, British Council of Churches representative to Germany; 1953–59, bishop of Gibraltar; 1961, assistant bishop in London—11, 12, 13, 14

Cremer, Hermann (1834–1903): professor of biblical theology, Greifswald —1, 9, 11, 16

Creon: character in Greek mythology—6

Crescens: biblical character—15

Cresswell, Amos: past president of the Methodist Conference in England; coauthor of book on Franz Hildebrandt—10

Crinis, Max de: psychiatrist and SS physician; 1938, successor of Karl Bonhoeffer as director of the psychiatric clinic in the Charité hospital—8, 16, 17

Cripps, Sir Stafford (1889–1952): British statesman and diplomat; 1940–42, ambassador in Moscow; 1942, Lord Privy Seal, minister for airplane manufacture, and head of the House of Commons—16, 17

Crispus: biblical character—14
Crites, Steven: professor of religion, Wesleyan University—1
Cromwell, Ernst: 1935, one of Bonhoeffer's confirmands in London—13, 14
Cromwell, Lotte: wife of Philipp Cromwell, mother of Ernst—14
Cromwell, Luise: sister of Ernst Cromwell—14
Cromwell, Oliver (1599–1658): British politician; a strict Puritan from youth; 1653–58, Lord Protector of England, Scotland and Ireland during the brief period of the Commonwealth of England—6, 7
Cromwell, Philipp: lawyer; father of Ernst Cromwell—13, 14, 15
Cromwell, Thomas: brother of Ernst Cromwell—14
Cross, Dr.: British church leader who worked with George Bell—13
Crossman, Richard: British journalist and politician; 1934, member of the British delegation to Fanø; 1938–55, deputy editor in chief of the journal *New Statesman and Nation*; during the war, head of the office of psychological warfare—16
Cruciger, Caspar (1504–48): professor, Wittenberg; student and colleague of Luther; especially involved with Luther's translation of the Bible—9
Crüsemann, Edward: lawyer; member of the German congregation, Sydenham, London—13, 15
Crüsemann (Cruesemann), Gerhard Edward and Ingrid Elisabeth: confirmed by Bonhoeffer on Palm Sunday 1934—13, 17 (for vol. 13)
Cullen, Countee (1903–46): African American writer—10, 15
Cullmann, Oscar (1902–99): New Testament scholar; studied classical philology and theology at Strasbourg seminary; 1926, assistant professor at the Thomas Seminary, a position previously held by Albert Schweitzer; 1930, professor of New Testament; 1936, also professor of early church history; 1938, professor at Basel Reformed Seminary; 1948, in Paris and Basel; 1972, retired; became a member of the Institute of France, where he continued his theological writing; leading ecumenical figure, influential in establishing dialogue between Catholics and Lutherans; his studies on New Testament eschatology and Christology focus on redemptive history—16
Culmann, Theodor (1824–63): German theologian and ethicist; author of *Die christliche Ethik*—11
Curry, John F.: 1929–34, leader of Tammany Hall, the Democratic Party political machine that dominated New York City politics from 1854 to 1934—10
Curti, Theodor (1848–1914): Swiss journalist and politician—12
Curtis, Lionel: British politician and writer; 1919, member of the British delegation at the Versailles peace conference in Paris; initiated the founding of the Royal Institute of Foreign Affairs (Chatham House);

1924, fellow of All Souls College in Oxford; from 1935, acquainted with Helmut von Moltke—16

Curtius, Julius (1877–1948): 1929–31, foreign minister of Germany—10

Cusa: *see* Nicholas of Cusa

Cyprian, Thascius Caecilius (ca. 210/15–258): ecclesiastical author, church father; from about 248–49 until his martyrdom he was bishop of Carthage; his involvement in the North African schism led to significant writings on ecclesiology; maintained that the Roman bishop could not claim judicial authority over other bishops; September 14, 258, martyred—1, 8, 9, 10, 11, 14

Cyril of Jerusalem (315–387): bishop of Jerusalem—1, 9, 14

Cyril (376–444): 412, bishop of Alexandria; church father, born in Alexandria; a persecutor of Nestorius, who became patriarch of Alexandria; known for his homilies, apologetics, and defense of the doctrine of the Trinity at the Council of Ephesus in 431—12

Cyrus: biblical character—12, 14

Czeppan, Inge: Bonhoeffer's godchild; baptized on March 24, 1928—10

Czeppan, Maria, née Horn (nickname: Hörnchen) (1884–1967): sister of Käthe Horn; member of the Herrnhut community of Moravian Brethren; 1906–23, governess in the Bonhoeffer family; her piety, characteristic of the Herrenhuter brotherhood, influenced the development of the younger Bonhoeffer children; 1923, married Richard Czeppan—7, 8, 9, 10, 11

Czeppan, Richard (1883–1945): teacher of ancient languages, Friedrich Werder Gymnasium, Berlin-Grunewald; teacher of Klaus Bonhoeffer and, until 1919, of Dietrich Bonhoeffer; 1923, married Maria Horn; a conservative, later block warden of the Nazi party; nonetheless criticized Nazi actions like *Kristallnacht*—9, 10

Czerny, Adalbert (1863–1941): German doctor, one of the founders of modern pediatrics, professor in Breslau and Strasbourg; 1919–32, worked in Berlin—7

Daase, Albert (1907–84): from 1935, pastor, Seckenburg/East Prussia; 1937, on the East Prussian Council of Brethren for the district of Niederung; June 7, 1940, Dietrich Bonhoeffer visited him; after the war, pastor, Rheydt-Mönchengladbach, 1960–69, Hamm/Sieg—16

Dach, Simon (1605–59): German lyric poet, schoolmaster, professor of poetry in Königsberg; representative of the Königsberg school of poetry; wrote for special occasions (weddings, funerals, christenings) to supplement his income—8

Dahill, Lisa E.: associate professor of worship and Christian spirituality at Trinity Lutheran Seminary; translator of *DBWE* 16 and part of *DBWE* 8 —8, 16

Dahn, Felix (1834–1912): jurist, historian, author; leading representative of nineteenth-century historicism—8, 9

Daix, Pierre: French cultural and art historian—10

Dalcho, Frederick (1770–1836): physician, editor, and active Anglican, South Carolina—15

Damaschke, D.: signator of Bonhoeffer's 1933 petition in Berlin; not otherwise identified—12

Damerow: pastor at St. Matthew's, Berlin—11

Dammeier, Anna: domestic in the Schleicher family—8

Danicke, Wolfhard (1913–44): 1935, participated in the first Zingst/Finkenwalde session; killed in action during the war—14

Daniel: biblical character—12, 14

Dannenbaum, Hans (1895–1956): 1926, chaplain in the Berlin City Mission; 1945, its director; from September 3, 1939, chaplain assigned to the military detention prisons in Tegel and on Lehrter Strasse; 1947, head of the missionary office of the regional Lutheran church of Hannover—8, 12

Dante Alighieri (1265–1321): Italian poet—8

Darwin, Charles Robert (1809–82): British biologist (theory of evolution) —3, 8, 12

Dathan: biblical character—15

D'Aubigné, Jeanne Merle: member of the French Protestant organization Cimade (a resistance organization that also helped prisoners); from 1941, organized ecumenical camp services in Gurs, a Nazi internment camp in the south of France—16

Daumier, Honoré (1808–79): French painter and caricaturist—8

Davey, Francis Noel: British Anglican New Testament scholar—8

David: biblical character; Israelite king; successor of Saul—4, 5, 7, 9, 10, 12, 14, 15

David, Christian (1690–1751): one of the founders of the Moravian church (Herrnhüter)—4, 5

David, Lydia: student at the German school in Barcelona—10

Davies, Ruth: U.S. author—15

Day, Thomas: Canadian-born pastor; author of works on Bonhoeffer—2, 4, 6

Deborah: biblical character—13, 14

Decatur, Stephen (1779–1820): U.S. naval officer—16

Decke-Cornell: German fellowship student in the United States the same year as Bonhoeffer—10

Decker, Mr.: unidentified; recipient of letter 53—11
Deechy: case worker for Max-Peter Meyer; not otherwise identified—15
de Gruchy, John W.: South African theologian, author and editor of numerous works on Bonhoeffer—2, 3, 4, 6, 8, 13, 16
de Gruchy, Steve: South African theologian and pastor—13
Dehn, Günther Karl (1882–1970): 1911, pastor in Berlin-Moabit; 1916, joined the religious socialists; 1923, head of the Berlin Neuwerk circle; 1928–33, attacked by right-wing Germans after delivering a pacifist lecture; until 1930, pastor, Berlin; 1931–33, professor of practical theology, Halle; 1933, dismissed as a socialist and pacifist ("Dehn affair"); 1933, assistant with the Berlin Council of Brethren and Confessing Church; 1936–41, lecturer at the seminary in Berlin; 1941, arrested and convicted in the collective trial against the examination board of the Old Prussian Union Council of Brethren; 1942–45, parish curate in Ravensburg; 1946–53, professor of practical theology, Bonn—6, 8, 10, 11, 12, 14, 15, 16, 17
Deißmann (Deissmann), Gustav Adolf (1866–1937): 1895, pastor and lecturer, preachers' seminary, Herborn; professor of New Testament theology, Marburg; from 1897, Heidelberg; after 1908, Berlin; founder and for many years chair of the German section of the World Alliance for Promoting International Friendship through the Churches; member of the Ecumenical Council for Life and Work; 1930, head of the latter's commission for "ecumenical cooperation between professors of theology"; member of the Prussian General Synod—1, 9, 10, 11, 12, 13, 14
Deißner, Pastor: mentioned in June 1936 Gestapo report—14
DeJonge, Michael: Bonhoeffer scholar and graduate director of religious studies, University of South Florida—11
de Kruif, Paul Henry (1890–1971): U.S. bacteriologist, author—7, 8
de Lange, Frits: Dutch theologian and ethicist, author of several works on Bonhoeffer—7
Delbrück, Emmi: *see* Bonhoeffer, Emilie
Delbrück, Hans (1848–1929): historian; the Delbrücks were friends and neighbors of the Bonhoeffers in Berlin; daughter Emmi Delbrück married Klaus Bonhoeffer—8, 9
Delbrück, Johanna: *see* Bräuer, Johanna
Delbrück, Justus (1902–45): son of Hans Delbrück; brother of Klaus Bonhoeffer's wife, Emmi; childhood friend of the Bonhoeffer children; after studying law, was employed in various governmental offices; from 1940, worked in the Canaris office and was part of the conspiracy with Oster, Dohnanyi, and Klaus Bonhoeffer; August 1944, arrested; April 1945,

released but picked up by the Soviets two weeks later; October 1945, contracted diphtheria and died in a Soviet internment camp in Niederlausitz —8, 9, 16, 17

Delbrück, Lene (1898–1980): daughter of Hans Delbrück; married name Lene Hobe—9

Delbrück, Max (1906–71): son of the historian Hans Delbrück; brother of Emmi Bonhoeffer; professor of biophysics; 1937, emigrated to the United States, where he taught at California Institute of Technology and Vanderbilt University; 1969, Nobel Prize in Medicine—9, 13, 16

Delekat, Friedrich (1892–1970): 1925–29, academic head of the Religious Pedagogical Institute, Berlin; 1929, professor of religious studies, Technical College, Dresden; 1937, forced retirement; 1946–60, professor of systematic theology, philosophy, and pedagogy, Mainz—14, 16

Delgehausen, Ann: editor and publishing consultant for *DBWE*—17

Delitzsch, Franz (1813–90): German Protestant theologian; broadly educated, focused largely on redemptive history; 1844, professor, Leipzig; 1846, Rostock; 1850, Erlangen; 1867, Leipzig—1, 2, 5, 10, 14

Dell, Wolfgang (1910–79): 1935, participated in the first Zingst/Finkenwalde session (one of four students from Saxony); October 28, 1934, cosigner of the letter from the preachers' seminary in Wittenberg; 1936–78, pastor, Eichsfeld and near Gardelegen—14

Delp, Luise: August 6, 1934, Bonhoeffer officiated at her funeral—13

Demant, Vigo Auguste (1893–1983): British Anglican canon; historian of the Anglican church—16

Demas: biblical character; Paul's colleague in Rome—15

Demetrius: biblical character—15

Democritus (ca. 450 B.C.E.): universally learned Greek philosopher and scholar; contemporary of Socrates—1

Denck, Hans (or Denk) (1495–1527): schoolmaster in Nuremberg; 1523, turned to spiritualism; expelled from city for his Anabaptist beliefs; settled in Basel, where he participated in various religious controversies; 1527, with L. Hätzer, made an excellent translation of the Hebrew prophets, known as the *Wormser Propheten*—14

Denzinger, Heinrich (1819–83): German Catholic priest, scholar of dogmatics and patristics—1, 2, 6, 14

Derrida, Jacques (1930–2004): French philosopher—2

Derschau, Alexander von (1906–82): 1935–46, pastor in Zezenow/Stolp; married to Irmgard Onnasch—8

Descartes, René (Renatus Cartesius) (1596–1650): French philosopher and mathematician—1, 2, 6, 8, 15

D'Espine, Henri (1895–1982): Swiss theologian; 1937, professor of practical theology, Geneva; 1954, president of the Swiss Church Federation; member of the central committee of the World Council of Churches—16, 17

Detmering, Mrs.: director of Protestant women's organization, Mecklenburg —14

Detten, Hermann von (1879–1954): officer, estate owner; July 1935–July 1936, ministerial director in the Reich Ministry for Church Affairs—14

Deutsch, Harold C.: U.S. historian of the German resistance—16

Dewey, John (1859–1952): U.S. philosopher and educator; professor, Chicago and New York; influenced initially by Hegel; influential advocate of pragmatism as a result of his acquaintance with William James—6, 10, 15

Dibbers: not otherwise identified—12

Dibelius, Martin (1883–1947): 1910, professor of New Testament, Berlin; 1915, professor of New Testament, Heidelberg; 1928, Bonn; 1946, Berlin; from 1927, active in the ecumenical movement, including Faith and Order and Life and Work; pioneer of form criticism—9, 10, 11, 12, 13, 14

Dibelius, Otto (1880–1967): German pastor and church leader; 1921, senior consistory counselor and member of the high consistory responsible for school affairs; 1925, general superintendent of the Old Prussian province of Mark Brandenburg (Kurmark); active leader in the Confessing Church; 1933, placed on forced leave by German Christian church authorities; assigned by the Confessing Church's Provisional Church Administration to work on the Freiburg memorandum; 1937, arrested briefly and released; 1945, one of the signers of the Stuttgart Declaration of Guilt; 1945–66, bishop of Berlin-Brandenburg; 1949–61, chair of the governing council of the Evangelical Church of Germany; 1954, one of presidents of World Council of Churches—6, 8, 9, 10, 11, 12, 13, 14, 15, 16

Dickens, C.: member of the congregational council, St. Paul's congregation, London—13

Dickens, Charles (1812–70): British novelist—9

Dickens, Doris: *see* Goetz, Frank and Doris

Dickinson, Sir Willoughby Hyett (1859–1943): British parliamentarian and ecumenist; 1914, cofounder and executive secretary, World Alliance for Promoting International Friendship through the Churches; 1931–35, president of its International Council; September 1933, participant, World Alliance meeting in Sofia; 1934, participant, plenary session of the Ecumenical Council for Life and Work, Fanø—11, 12, 13, 16

Diedrich, Karlheinz: author of work on Belgian-German relations—16

Diekamp, Franz (1864–1943): studied Roman Catholic theology in Münster and at the Episcopal institute of higher education, Eichstsätt; 1887,

ordained priest; 1889, director of studies at the Collegium Borromaeum of Münster; 1895, ThD; 1898, postdoctoral lecturing qualification at the Catholic Academy of Münster; 1902, assistant professor, 1904, professor of patristics, history of Christian doctrine, and church history; 1906, professor of dogmatics, University of Münster; 1923, private papal prelate, 1924, canon; major publications include *Katholische Dogmatik*, 3 vols., 1912–14; Latin translation, *Theologiae dogmaticae manuale*, 4 vols., 1932–34—6

Diels, Hermann (1848–1922): from 1882, professor of classical philosophy, Berlin—2, 9, 10, 17 (for vol. 9)

Diels, Rudolf (1900–1957): 1933, head of the Gestapo, Berlin; 1934, governmental president, Cologne; 1936–43, Hannover; 1944, imprisoned temporarily by the Gestapo—12, 13, 17

Diem, Gudrun: daughter of Carl and Liselotte Diem; friend of Christine Schleicher—8

Diem, Hermann (1900–1975): 1934–56, pastor, Ebersbach, and head of the Württemberg Ecclesiastical-Theological Society, which had ties to the Confessing Church; 1957, professor of systematic theology, Tübingen—2, 6, 9, 12, 13, 14, 15, 16

Diem, Liselotte: wife of Carl Diem; Carl Diem was the secretary general of the preparation committee of the Olympic Games in Berlin 1936 and director of the International Olympic Institute—16

Diener, Hermann (1897–1955): German violinist and conductor—7

Dierks, Margarete: German philosopher; author of book on Jacob Hauer, controversial because of the apologetic stance she shared with Hauer regarding Nazism—6

Diest, Gerhart von (1909–41): brother of Maria von Kleist-Retzow; killed in action on the eastern front—16

Diest, Heinrich von (1889–1939): brother of Maria von Kleist-Retzow; killed in action in the campaign in Poland—16

Diest, Mrs. von: youngest sister of Baron Bruno Schröder from Liebenzell; active in the mission society there—13

Diestel, Karl Julius Max (1872–1949): German theologian, ecumenist; 1903, pastor, Dettingen/Hohenzollern; 1914, Berlin; from 1925, church district superintendent, Berlin-Lichterfelde (which included the Grunewald parish); 1927, assigned by Otto Dibelius to build an ecumenical youth program; 1931, governing secretary, German section of the World Alliance for Promoting International Friendship through the Churches; after 1933, member, Confessing Church Council of Brethren, Berlin-Brandenburg; 1946–48, general superintendent, Berlin, and pastor, Kaiser Wilhelm Memorial Church, Berlin—6, 8, 9, 10, 11, 12, 13, 14, 15, 16

Diestel, Ludwig (1825–78): professor of Old Testament, Greifswald, Jena, and Tübingen—9

Diestel, Renate: daughter of Max Diestel—10

Dieterich, Albrecht (1866–1908): classical philologist and historian of religion; professor, Giessen and Heidelberg—3, 9

Dieterich, Theodor: second cousin of the Bonhoeffer children on the father's side—9, 10

Dieterle, Wilhelm (William) (1893–1972): German actor and film director; from 1932, in Hollywood; later returned to Germany—15

Dietrich, Ernst Ludwig (1897–1974): prominent German Christian; 1934–36, bishop of Hessen-Nassau (appointed by Reich Bishop Müller); 1936, removed from office by Minister of Church Affairs Hans Kerrl—13

Dietrich, Fritz (1905–45): 1931–34, assistant at the music institute, Heidelberg; 1935, postdoctoral lecturing qualification, though for political reasons denied any further university career; worked at the Bärenreiter publishing house in Kassel as a composer and editor; 1945, disappeared—14

Dietrich, Veit (Theodoricus) (1506–49): German Protestant theologian; student and colleague of Luther; his German prayers associated with gospel interpretations are viewed as the Reformation version of the Medieval Latin form of the collection—6, 9, 14

Dietz, Otto: German Protestant liturgical scholar; member of the "Luther renaissance"—14

Dietze, Constantin von (1891–1973): economist; 1927–33, professor of agricultural and trade sciences, Jena; 1933–37, Berlin; 1937, prohibited from teaching; in the same year, professor, Freiburg im Breisgau; 1937, arrested because of his activity in the Confessing Church; contacts with Goerdeler and with the Kreisau circle; 1942, significant contributor to the Freiburg memorandum; 1944, arrested as a result; imprisoned in the prison on Lehrter Strasse; April 1945, liberated; after 1945, member of the Baden synod and of the Council of the Evangelical Church of Germany; 1948, delegate to World Council of Churches meeting in Amsterdam, 1955, in Evanston; 1955–61, president of the Evangelical Church of Germany—8, 16, 17

Dietzfelbinger, Hermann (1908–84): 1939, assistant consultant in the regional church office, Munich; 1945, rector of the preachers' seminaries in Erlangen and Nuremberg; 1953, rector of the deaconesses' institute, Neuendettelsau; 1955–75, bishop of Bavaria—16

Dike: Greek goddess of justice—17 (for vol. 9)

Dillmann, August (1823–94): theologian and Orientalist; 1851, private lecturer, and 1853, professor in Tübingen; 1854, Kiel; 1860, professor

of oriental languages, Kiel; 1864, professor of Old Testament exegesis, Giessen; 1869, successor of Ernst Wilhelm Hengstenberg, Berlin; 1881, president of the International Congress of Orientalists, Berlin; specialist in the Ethiopian language; reestablished Ethiopian philology—3

Dilschneider, Otto Alexander (1904–91): German theologian and pastor; after 1951, professor of systematic theology at the seminary, Berlin—6, 16

Dilthey, Wilhelm (1833–1911): philosopher who helped form the modern study of hermeneutics and the philosophy of history; from 1866, professor in Basel, Kiel, and Breslau; 1882–1905, professor, Berlin—1, 2, 8, 9, 11, 12, 16

Dimel, Grete: friend of Ruth von Wedemeyer—8

Dinger, Jörg: German theologian and pastor, author of publications on Bonhoeffer: 6, 8

Dinglinger, Wolfgang: German musicologist—17 (for vol. 9)

Dinkler, Erich (1909–81): German theologian, church historian, and philosopher; scholar of Christian antiquity—2, 13

Dinkler-von Schubert, Erika (1904–2002); scholar of Christian antiquity; honorary professor, Heidelberg—13

Dio Chrysostom (ca. 40–112): Greek rhetorician in Rome; 82–96, banished by Diocletian, during which time he turned to cynic philosophy—4

Diocletian (240–313): 284–305, Roman emperor who persecuted Christians —15

Diogenes of Sinope (ca. 400–329/323 B.C.E.): Greek philosopher, itinerant teacher, advocated a lifestyle focused on satisfying only the simplest needs —8

Dionysios the Pseudo-Areopagite (first century): Christian Neoplatonist writer; exerted lasting influence on scholasticism and Western mysticism —9

Dionysus: Greek god of wine; son of Zeus and Semele—8, 10

Dipper, Christoph: German historian of the Nazi era—16

Distler, Hugo (1908–42): church musician and composer; 1931, organist, Lübeck; 1933, composition and organ instructor at the music conservatory, Stuttgart; 1940, professor of composition and organ at the music conservatory, director of the state and cathedral choir and head of the conservatory choir, Berlin; November 1, 1942, committed suicide—7, 8, 14, 16

Distler, Waltraud: widow of Hugo Distler—6, 7, 16

Dittrich, Ottmar (1865–1951): German-speaking ethicist and linguist; from 1912, professor of philosophy, Leipzig; April 1, 1933, retired—6

Dittus, Gottlieben: young woman parishioner of Johann Christoph Blumhardt from whom he supposedly cast out demons—15

Döblin, Alfred (1878–1957): German writer; 1914–18, medical officer; after the war, practiced in the slums of East Berlin; became politically active as a Social Democrat; August 1933, endangered as a Jew and socialist, emigrated to France; 1940, to the United States; converted to Roman Catholicism; 1945, returned to Germany; 1951, settled in Paris—10

Dobrick, Heinz: 1938–39, participated in the collective pastorate in Groß-Schlönwitz—15

Doctor (FP): proposed character for drama—7

Doebert, Heinz: from Berlin-Brandenburg; 1939, participated in the collective pastorate in Sigurdshof; ministry in Berlin-Zehlendorf and Teltow; 1964, hospital chaplain, Frankfurt—15

Doehring, Bruno (1879–1961): professor of practical theology; court chaplain—10

Doerne, Martin (1900–1970): 1927, director of the preachers' seminary, Lückendorf, Saxony; 1934, professor of practical theology, Leipzig; 1947, professor of systematic theology, Rostock; 1952, Halle; 1954, professor of practical theology, Göttingen—12, 14

Doerr, Karin: Germanist; professor, Concordia University, Montreal—6

Dohnanyi, Barbara von: *see* Bayer, Barbara

Dohnanyi, Christine (Christel) von (1903–65): Dietrich Bonhoeffer's sister; 1925, married Hans von Dohnanyi; member of the resistance movement against the National Socialist regime; 1943, briefly arrested and imprisoned—7, 8, 9, 10, 11, 12, 13, 14, 15, 16, 17

Dohnanyi, Christoph von: conductor emeritus, Cleveland Symphony; son of Hans and Christine von Dohnanyi; Dietrich Bonhoeffer's nephew and godson; 1957, married Renate Zillesen; second marriage to the singer Anja Silja—6, 8, 16

Dohnanyi, Elisabeth (Elsa) von, née Kunwald (1877–1946): mother of Hans and Grete von Dohnanyi; divorced from Ernst von Dohnanyi; pianist—8, 13

Dohnanyi, Ernst von (1877–1960): Hungarian composer, pianist, and conductor; father of Hans von Dohnanyi—9

Dohnanyi, Hans von (1902–45): son of the composer Ernst von Dohnanyi; February 12, 1925, married Christine, née Bonhoeffer; father of Barbara (married name Bayer), Klaus, and Christoph; from 1929, consultant in the Reich Ministry of Justice; 1932, lawyer, Hamburg; 1933, consultant to the president of the Reich Court; 1934, personal consultant to Reich Minister of Justice Franz Gürtner; 1938, Reich court councilor in Leipzig; August 25, 1939, appointed to the Central Division in the

Military Intelligence Office of the Armed Forces High Command; head of the political department in Major General Hans Oster's office; with General Oster one of the leaders of the conspiracy against Hitler; April 5, 1943, arrested; executed in 1945 in the Sachsenhausen concentration camp—4, 5, 6, 7, 8, 9, 10, 11, 12, 13, 14, 15, 16, 17

Dohnanyi, Klaus von: lawyer and politician; son of Hans and Christine von Dohnanyi; 1949, received his doctorate after studying law; 1953, graduate study, Yale University; 1954, trainee at the Ford plant; 1960, partner in Infratest in Munich; federal minister; until 1988, first mayor of Hamburg; married Renée Illing in 1951; second marriage to Christa Groß —8, 10, 16

Dohnanyi, Margarete von (Grete): daughter of the composer Ernst von Dohnanyi; sister of Hans von Dohnanyi; *see* Bonhoeffer, Margarete—9

Döhring, Bruno (1879–1961): court and cathedral preacher in Berlin—8

Dohrmann, Franz (1881–1969): 1920, military district pastor, Stettin; 1934–45, Protestant bishop of the military forces; 1945, interned in the Benedictine monastery Niederaltaich—8, 15, 16, 17

Dolivo, Catherine (orig. Käthe), née Meyer (1892–1961): married Dr. Dimitri Dolivo, who was born in Berlin of a Russian family; 1918, Heidelberg; from 1920, Lausanne—16

Dollfuss (Dolfuß), Engelbert (1892–1934): Austrian politician; 1932, federal chancellor; May 25, 1934, shot to death during a National Socialist coup —13, 17

Dombrowski, James: U.S. religious socialist; 1930–31, studied with Bonhoeffer at Union Theological Seminary, New York—10, 12, 15

Domitian (Titus Flavius Domitianus) (51–96): Roman emperor; son of Vespasian—9

Don José: famous Spanish tenor—10

Don Juan: central character in the classic Spanish play of the same name —10

Don Quixote: title character in Cervantes's novel—6, 7, 8, 10

Donaldson, Mara: professor of religious studies, Dickinson College—2

Donatus (d. 355): bishop of Carthage—14

Donkan, Rupert: *see* Zischka, Anton

Döpke, Mrs.: from 1938, wife of the estate administrator in Pätzig—8

Doré, Gustave (1833–83): French painter and graphic artist—16

Dornakal: *see* Azariah, Vedanaya

Dorner, August Johannes (1846–1920): German theologian, son of Isaak Dorner—1

Dorner, Isaak August (1809–84): professor of theology, Berlin—9

Dörner, Klaus: German historian—6

Dörr, Max: 1932, pastor, Rodebach (formerly Enzuhnen), district of Ebenrode (formerly Stallupönen)/East Prussia; 1937, member of the East Prussian Council of Brethren as district pastor; June 1940, Dietrich Bonhoeffer visited him—16

Dostoyevsky, Fyodor Mikhaylovich (1821–81): Russian novelist—6, 7, 8, 9, 10, 11, 12, 14, 15

Dottermann (uncertain reading; perhaps "Boltermann"): 1922, headmaster of the Bismarck Gymnasium, Berlin—9

Douglas, Charles Malcolm: U.S. Episcopal priest—10

Dove, John: editor of the British periodical *The Round Table*—13

Draeger, Kurt (1897–1978): from 1926, pastor in Berlin-Spandau—12

Dreier, Wilhelm (1905–77): law student and Bonhoeffer's fraternity brother in Tübingen—9, 17 (for vol. 9)

Dreiser, Theodore (1871–1945): U.S. writer; wrote novels critical of society—10

Dreist, Walter: author of introductory guide for medical personnel—8

Drescher, Hans-Georg (1929–2008): German theologian; biographer of Troeltsch—11

Dreß, Andreas: youngest son of Susanne and Walter Dreß; professor of mathematics, Bielefeld University—8, 13, 15, 16

Dreß, Ilse (1907–93): sister of Walter Dreß—8, 9

Dreß, Margarethe, née Vogt (1882–1969): mother of Walter Dreß—8, 9

Dreß, Michael Johannes (1935–75): son of Walter and Susanne Dreß; musician, dancer—8, 14

Dreß, Ruprecht: grandson of Susanne and Walter Dreß—15

Dreß, Susanne (Susi, Suse), née Bonhoeffer (1909–91): Dietrich Bonhoeffer's sister; 1929, married Walter Dreß; mother of Michael and Andreas—1, 7, 8, 9, 10, 11, 12, 13, 14, 15, 16

Dreß, Walter (1904–79): 1929, married Susanne, née Bonhoeffer; father of Michael and Andreas; 1938, Confessing Church pastor, Berlin-Dahlem, and lecturer at the seminary, Berlin; professor of church history, Berlin—1, 7, 8, 9, 10, 13, 14, 15, 16

Drewes, Hans-Anton: Barth scholar and director, Karl Barth-Archiv, Basel, Switzerland—16

Drews, Arthur (1865–1935): German philosopher; author of controversial book on "the Christ myth"—10, 11

Drews, Paul (1858–1912): pastor and professor of theology, Giessen and Halle; specialist in the history of the Reformation and of liturgy—1, 6, 9, 11, 14

Driesch, Hans (1867–1941): German biologist and philosopher—6

Droste-Hülshoff, Annette von (1797–1848): German poet—14

Drummond, Henry (1851–97): Scottish evangelist and inspirational author —15

Drummond, William Hamilton: secretary of the World Alliance for Promoting International Friendship through the Churches; September 1933, participated in that organization's conference in Sofia—12

Drüsedau, Walter (1892–1961): from 1924, pastor, Berlin—12

Dryander, Ernst von (1843–1922): vice president of the high consistory of the German Protestant Church of the Old Prussian Union; senior court preacher—9

DuBois, William Edward Burghardt (1868–1963): American-Ghanaian philosopher and writer—10

Duchrow, Ulrich: German pastor, professor of theology, and ecumenist—6, 16

Duckstein, Ursula: *see* Corbach, Ursula

Duckwitz, Georg Ferdinand (1904–73): German diplomat; after studying law and economics, worked in business; 1939, appointed to the German legation in Copenhagen as a shipping expert; 1943, member of the initiative to rescue over seven thousand Danish Jews; from 1950 in the service of the Foreign Ministry; 1955, German ambassador in Copenhagen; 1958, head of the eastern section in the Foreign Ministry; 1961, ambassador to India; 1967, secretary of state in the Foreign Ministry; 1970, retired —16, 17

Dudzus, Otto (1912–2000): one of Dietrich Bonhoeffer's students; studied theology, initially in Bonn; also studied in Rostock; summer semester 1933, attended Bonhoeffer's lectures on Christology; 1934, participated in the Fanø youth conference; 1936–37, participated in the fourth Finkenwalde session; summer 1937, participated in the fifth Finkenwalde session; 1937–38, (illegal) vicar with Günther Harder in Fehrbellin; from 1938, pastor of the Confessing Church in Wilhelmshorst near Potsdam; January 1942, military service; 1946, pastor, Berlin, and student chaplain at the Technical College; 1948–54, academic inspector at the seminary; 1954–80, pastor, Cologne—2, 4, 5, 8, 11, 12, 13, 14, 15, 16, 17

Dudzus, Wilhelm: brother of Otto Dudzus—14

Duensing, Friedrich (1889–1944): 1930, city youth chaplain, Hannover—14

Dufft, Heinz (1911–43): 1935, participated in the first Zingst/Finkenwalde session; pastor in Pomerania; missing in action at Stalingrad—14, 15

Duhm, Bernhard (1847–1928): 1877, professor of Old Testament, Göttingen; 1888, Basel—9, 10, 14

Dujarier, Michel: French Catholic priest and missionary; author of work on history of the catechumenate—14

Duke, David Nelson (1950–2000): professor of religion, William Jewell College, Missouri; Bonhoeffer scholar and author of works on the Bible and Christian ethics and on Harry F. Ward—10

Dulles, Allen Welsh (1893–1969): U.S. governmental official; 1916, entered diplomatic service; 1922, chief of the State Department's Division of Near Eastern Affairs; 1926, resigned to practice law; during World War II, prominent member of the Office of Strategic Services; 1951, returned to government service as deputy director of the Central Intelligence Agency; 1953, director; 1961, resigned—16

Dumas, André: French Reformed theologian; Cimade representative at the Rivesaltes concentration camp; author of book on Bonhoeffer's theology—2, 3, 4, 8, 10

Dumschat, Arno: from 1934, pastor, Herdenau (formerly Kallningken) in East Prussia; 1944–45, Rauschken, district of Osterode; 1945–73, Schmalförden, district of Diepholz; from 1973, retired—16

Duns Scotus, Johannes (1265–1308): scholastic philosopher and theologian—1, 2, 3, 9, 10, 11

Dürer, Albrecht (1471–1528): German Renaissance painter, engraver, and theoretician—1, 8, 9, 10, 14, 15, 16

Düring, Ingemar: Swedish scholar of Aristotle—16

Düring, Walter: German Catholic scholar, author of works on Catholic ecclesiology and theology—15

Durkheim, Émile (1858–1917): French sociologist—1, 6, 12

Dusen, Henry Pitney van: *see* Van Dusen, Henry Pitney

Duske, Johannes (1866–1929): 1925, vice president of the Evangelical High Church Council—10

Düsterberg, Theodor (1875–1950): German nationalist and political leader—11

Dybwad, Carmen: worked at Union Theological Seminary, New York—10

Ebel: 1933, pastor in Berlin—12

Ebeling, Cometa: Swiss concert violinist; wife of Gerhard Ebeling—16

Ebeling, Gerhard (1912–2001): from Berlin; German theologian; 1936–37, participated in the fourth Finkenwalde session; 1938–39, pastor; after 1946, professor of church history, Tübingen; 1954, professor of systematic theology; after 1956, professor of systematic theology, history of dogmatics, and hermeneutics, Zürich—6, 8, 10, 14, 15, 16

Eber, Paul (1511–69): German theologian and hymnist—5

Eberhard, Otto (1875–1966): theologian and educator; school inspector in Hohen-Neuendorf near Berlin; ca. 1920, introduced the notion of "voca-

tional education" (as opposed to merely "receptive" education and with a decided emphasis on character development) into Protestant religious instruction—11, 14

Eberhardt: not otherwise identified (1923)—9

Ebermann, Bernhard: historian of the Redemptorist movement—16

Ebert, Friedrich (1871–1925): Social Democratic Party politician; from 1912, member of the national parliament; succeeded August Bebel as party chair; October 11, 1918, after the proclamation of the Republic, succeeded Hugo Haase as head of the Assembly of the People's Delegates; November 2, 1919, elected Reich president by the National Assembly at Weimar; remained in this office until his death—9

Echternach, Helmut (1907–88): lecturer in systematic theology and philosophy, Greifswald; member of the Nazi party; 1934, became pastor in Goddentow, Pomerania—14

Eckardt: 1933, doctoral student in Berlin—12

Eckart-Bäcker, Ursula: German musicologist—17 (for vol. 9)

Eckermann, Johann Peter (1792–1854): German poet and essayist; best known as Goethe's companion and secretary in the last years of Goethe's life; assisted Goethe in the preparation of the definitive edition of Goethe's works and published *Conversations with Goethe*, a valuable biographical source—9

Eckert, Alfred: German theologian; author of catechetical studies—10

Eckert, Otto (1891–1940): 1919, pastor, Groß-Ziescht, district of Baruth; 1931, Zossen; military chaplain; 1933, provost of Neumark; 1934, president of the provincial synod Brandenburg; leading member of the German Christians—13

Eddy, George Sherwood (1871–1963): 1896, national secretary of the YMCA for India; 1911, for Asia—12

Edelhoff: 1933, student from Westphalia—12

Eden, Anthony, Earl of Avon (1897–1977): British statesman; 1935, foreign minister; 1938, resigned; 1940, minister of war and foreign minister in Churchill's cabinet; 1955, prime minister; 1957, resigned—16, 17

Eder, Hildegard: German novelist—8

Edward VII [Bonhoeffer has "VIII"] (1841–1910): 1901–10, king of Great Britain and Ireland—9

Edwards, Jonathan (1703–58): U.S. theologian; 1734, his penitential sermons inaugurated the "great awakening"—15

Edwards, Mark: U.S. Reformation historian; president (emeritus), St. Olaf College, Minnesota—6

Egelhaaf, Gottlob (1848–1934): historian, Stuttgart—9

Eger, Johannes (1873–1954): 1929–34, general superintendent, Magdeburg; 1933, early retirement; October 1935–37, chair (appointed by Hanns Kerrl) of the Old Prussian Union regional church committee—12, 14, 17

Eger, Karl (1864–1945): German professor of practical theology—14

Ehemann: 1940, employed in the security service (SD) headquarters, Königsberg—16

Ehlers, Hermann (1904–54): 1931, legal specialist, Emergency Organization of the Inner Mission; 1934–40, lawyer, Confessing Church Council of Brethren of the Old Prussian Union; 1936, judge; 1939, dismissed from civil service; from 1941, military service; 1945, member of the high church council in Oldenburg; member of the advisory council of the Evangelical Church of Germany; 1949–54, member of parliament (representing the Christian Democratic Union); 1950, parliamentary president—13, 14, 17

Ehrenberg, Hans (1883–1958): 1910, lecturer in philosophy, Heidelberg; 1918, professor; 1920, studied theology; 1925, pastor, Bochum; 1937, forced to resign because of his "non-Aryan" descent; 1938, imprisoned, Sachsenhausen concentration camp; 1939–47, emigrated to Great Britain; 1947–54, return to Germany, active in the Westphalian *Volksmission* —11, 12, 14

Ehrenforth, Gerhard: author of work on the Church Struggle in Silesia—14

Ehrenreich, Barbara: U.S. writer, feminist, and social activist—10

Ehrenström, Nils (1903–84): Swedish theologian and ecumenist; 1930, staff member, ecumenical research department; 1934, assistant director, 1940, codirector, 1946–54, director of the academic section of the World Council of Churches; 1940–42, director of the Nordic Ecumenical Institute, Sigtuna; 1955–69, professor of ecumenical studies, Boston—6, 12, 13, 14, 15, 17

Ehrhardt, Arthur: right-wing German political leader; helped form the SA; head of the secret organization responsible for the assassination of Walther Rathenau—9

Ehrich, Johannes: from 1924, pastor in Berlin-Lankwitz—12

Ehrlich, Walter: author of *Kant und Husserl* (1923)—2

Eichendorff, Joseph Baron von (1788–1857): German poet and novelist, associated with the Romantic period—10

Eichholz, Georg (1909–73): 1933, doctorate in theology; pastor in the Confessing Church in the Rhineland; 1935, lecturer, seminary of the Rhineland Mission Society, Wuppertal; 1945, lecturer, New Testament and systematic theology, seminary in Wuppertal; 1961, professor of New Testament there—15, 16

Eichhorn, Albert (1856–1926): Protestant church historian—11

Eichhorn, Johann Gottfried (1753–1827): German Protestant biblical scholar—3

Eichmann, Adolf (1906–62): high commander of the SS Assault Battalion; 1939, after the beginning of the war, directed the Division on Jews in Office V (the Gestapo) of the Reich Security Central Office; organized the "final solution to the Jewish question" planned in January 1942 (Wannsee Conference), namely, the delivery of the majority of the Jews in countries controlled by National Socialism to mass extermination camps; after the end of the war, escaped from a U.S. prison camp via Italy to Argentina; 1960, brought to Israel by the Israeli Secret Service; April 2–December 5, 1961, public trial in Jerusalem; December 15, 1961, sentenced to death; June 1, 1962, executed—7

Eichners: acquaintances of Bonhoeffer's parents—10

Eichrodt, Walther (1890–1978): 1934, professor of Old Testament, Basel —14

Eidem, Erling (1880–1972): Swedish theologian and ecumenist; 1913, lecturer in New Testament, Lund; 1924, pastor, Gårdstånga; 1928, professor of New Testament, Lund; 1931–50, archbishop of Uppsala; 1940–59, upper court chaplain; 1948–50, member of the governing council of the World Council of Churches, also one of that organization's presidents —12, 13, 14, 16, 17

Einhart, Albert: "Auch Einer" (Someone too), title character of a novel by F. T. Vischer—6

Einstein, Albert (1879–1955): German physicist; 1921, Nobel Prize in Physics; 1933, emigrated to United States; taught at Princeton—10, 12

Eisemann, G.: member of the congregational council, the German Reformed St. Paul's Church, London—13

Eisenhuth, Heinz Erich (1903–83): professor of systematic theology, Jena —2

Eisenmenger: chair of congregational council, Barcelona—10

Ekk, Nicolai: Russian film director—11

Ekkehard: *see* Little Brother in the novel, and under Brake—7

Elert, Werner (1885–1954): German theologian; 1919, director of the Old Lutheran Theological Seminar, Breslau; 1923–54, professor of historical theology, Erlangen; after 1932, also professor of systematic theology; 1934, member of the Lutheran Council—4, 6, 12, 14, 16

Elfriede (FP): character in novel—7

El Greco (Doménikos Theotokópoulos) (ca. 1541–1614): Greek painter in Spain; leading exponent of Spanish mysticism in painting—9, 10, 15

Eliab: biblical character—14

Elihu: biblical character—9, 10

Elijah: biblical character—10, 12, 13, 14

Eliot, Sir Thomas Stearn (1888–1965): U.S.-born English poet and literary critic; from 1914, lived in London; 1927, became a British citizen; 1948, awarded the Nobel Prize in Literature—7, 16

Eliphaz: biblical character—8, 9

Elisha: biblical character—9

Elizabeth: biblical character—14

Elliger, Karl (1901–77): brother of Walter Elliger; 1929, private lecturer, Münster; 1934, Kiel; 1937, special professor, and 1948, regular professor of Old Testament, Tübingen—14

Elliger, Walter (1903–85): professor of church history and Christian archaeology; 1934, Kiel; 1936, Greifswald; 1950, Berlin; 1963, Bochum—14, 16

Elliot, Harrison Sacket (1882–1951): 1925, professor of practical theology, Union Theological Seminary, New York—10

Elliot, Roland: active in U.S. refugee aid during World War II; later director of Church World Service—15

Ellwood, Charles Abraham (1873–1946): U.S. sociologist; founder of social psychology—12

Else: domestic in the Bonhoeffer family who took care of appointment schedules and other chores—8, 16

Elser, Johann Georg (1903–45): cabinetmaker; November 8, 1939, attempted to assassinate Hitler in the Munich Bürgerbräukeller; imprisoned in a concentration camp; April 9, 1945, executed in Dachau concentration camp—15, 17

Elshtain, Jean Bethke (1941–2013): U.S. ethicist and political philosopher —2, 4

Emerson, Ralph Waldo (1803–82): U.S. philosopher, author, and poet—10, 15

Emilie ("Aunt"): not otherwise identified—9

Emmanuel: housing manager at Union Theological Seminary, New York —15

Emmerich, Heinz (1910–46): from Berlin; 1937, vicar for Günther Harder in Fehrbellin; vicar, Berlin-Lichterfelde; 1938–39, participated in the collective pastorate, Groß-Schlönwitz; 1939, ordination, drafted into military service; 1946, died in the military hospital in Svadovo, Russia—15, 16

Empedocles (490–430 B.C.E.): itinerant physician, sage, prophet, miracle worker, and philosopher of nature; author of didactic poem, *Nature*—2, 14

Emsmann, Dr. (uncertain reading: perhaps "Erdmann"): not otherwise identified—11
Ende, Werner: German scholar of Islam and director of the Oriental Institute, University of Freiburg—6
Enders, Ernst Ludwig (1833–1906): pastor; editor of the Erlangen edition of Luther's works—2, 4, 9
"Engel" (real name: Holzendorf): photographer; member of the guard staff in Tegel, helped Bonhoeffer with illegal correspondence; January 1944, killed during an air raid; Bonhoeffer disguised his name in the prison letters—8, 16, 17
Engel, Ingrid: author of study of Friedrich Naumann—16
Engelberg, Ernst: German historian and biographer of Bismarck—11
Engelke, Johannes: Confessing Church pastor in Königshorst, eventually served as pastor in Lobetal—14, 16
Engelmann, Wilhelm: Westphalian pastor, official in the Inner Mission—11
Engels, Friedrich (1820–95): German-born businessman, economist, socialist writer; with Karl Marx one of the founders of modern communism —6, 11
Engler: musician in Barcelona—10
Engler, Edgar (1911–41): from Stolp, Pomerania; 1937–38, participated in the collective pastorate, Groß-Schlönwitz; 1938, ordination; student chaplain, Greifswald; assistant preacher, Köslin; 1941, killed in action in Dünaburg—16
Engler, Wolfgang: pastor, Zion Church in Berlin (after 1945)—11
Enoch: biblical character—9
Enslin, Morton Scott (1897–1980): professor of New Testament, Crozer Seminary; one of Martin Luther King Jr.'s professors there—10
Enterlein, Hilde: *see* Schönherr, Hilde
Epicharmus (540–450 B.C.E.): Greek philosopher and dramatist—(17, for vol. 9)
Epictetus (ca. 50–138): Phrygian stoic philosopher—4, 9
Epicurus (314–271 B.C.E.): Greek philosopher; based his ethics on spiritualized pleasure—1, 7
Episcopius, Simon (1583–1643): Dutch theologian, follower of the Arminians—8
Eppenstein, Rudolf: confirmed by Bonhoeffer in Sydenham, London—13
Eras, Bernard: Dutch Catholic theologian; 1930–52, rector of the Dutch theological college, Rome—16
Erasmus of Rotterdam, Desiderius (1466–1536): Dutch humanist and theologian; scholar of classics, patristics, and the New Testament, of which

he published an important Greek edition; inclined to church reforms, he separated from the Reformation after a debate with Luther on the freedom of the will—2, 6, 9, 10, 12

Erastus: biblical character—15

Erastus, Thomas (Thomas Lüber) (1524–83): Swiss theologian and physician—12

Erdmann, Karl Dietrich: German historian, professor emeritus, University of Erlangen—10, 15

Erich (FP): character in novel—7

Ericksen, Robert P.: U.S. historian; author of works on German Protestant theologians under Nazism—3, 6, 11, 12, 14, 16

Erikson, Erik H. (1902–94): German-born psychologist; later professor of psychology, Harvard; father of developmental psychology—8

Ern, Louise: Richard Ern's sister—10

Ern, Richard: young friend of Bonhoeffer in the United States; met on the *Columbus*—10, 11

Erna: domestic in the Dreß family—8

Ernst, Paul (1866–1933): German novelist, poet, critic, and essayist—6

Erzberger, Matthias (1875–1921): 1903, Center Party delegate to the German parliament; leader of the German Armistice Commission; 1919–20, finance minister; murdered by two former German naval officers—9

Eschenbach: *see* Wolfram (von Eschenbach)

Eschenburg, Theodor (1904–99): German professor of political science, Tübingen—9

Eschweiler, Karl (1886–1936): 1926, professor of dogmatics, Braunsberg —12

Espinas, Alfred Victor (1844–1922): French philosopher and sociologist; influenced Durkheim's thought—1

Espy, Edwin (1909–93): U.S. ecumenist; 1935, became secretary of the youth section of the World Alliance for Promoting International Friendship through the Churches—14

Esschen, Johannes van (d. 1523) (Johannes Esch): one of Luther's Augustinian brothers in Antwerp; burned at the stake for his Protestant leanings —14

Ethan: hymnist of Psalm 89—5

Etzien, Walter: representative of the Reich Association of Protestant Young Men's Associations in the Provisional Bureau for Ecumenical Youth Work—11

Eucken, Rudolf (1846–1926): German philosopher; 1874, professor, Jena —11

Eucken, Walter (1891–1950): economist; 1925, professor, Tübingen; 1927, Freiburg; founder of the Freiburg School; 1942, participated in the Freiburg circle—16

Eugene IV (Gabriel Condulmaro) (ca. 1383–1447): 1431–47, pope—11

Eunice: biblical character—15

Euripides (ca. 485–ca. 406 B.C.E.): Greek tragic poet and dramatist—6, 8, 9, 17 (for vol. 9)

Eusebius: name of the verger at St. Peter's when Bonhoeffer visited Rome—9

Eusebius of Caesarea (Eusebius Pamphili) (ca. 263–339): Greek apologist and church historian; bishop of Caesarea—6, 9, 10

Euthymius (377–473): monk; exercised a formative influence on Palestinian monasticism—4

Eutyches of Constantinople (ca. 378–451): presbyter and archimandrite of Constantinople—12

Evans, Richard J.: Regius Professor of History and president of Wolfson College, University of Cambridge; author of works on the Third Reich—14

Eve: biblical character—6, 7, 9, 10, 11, 14, 15

Evelein, Johannes: professor at Trinity College, Hartford, Connecticut—7

Ewald, Pastor Dr.: pastor of the Zion church, Berlin—11

Eyck, Erich: historian in England; expert on Bismarck—16

Eyden, René van: professor emeritus of theology, Catholic University, Utrecht—6

Ezekiel: biblical character—8, 9

Ezra: biblical character—5, 14

Fabinyi, E.: 1934, participant from Budapest in the Fanø youth conference —13

Fabriano, Gentile da (Niccolo di Giovanni di Massio) (ca. 1370–1422): Italian painter; first great representative of Umbrian school; exponent of Gothic style—9, 16

Fabricius, Caius (1884–1950): 1921, professor of systematic theology, Berlin; 1927, worked with Faith and Order; 1935–43, professor of systematic theology and general religious studies, Breslau; member of the German Christians—10, 12, 13

Fabricius ("Smith"), Jakob (1593–1654): hymnist from Pomerania—14

Fabry, Heinz-Josef: coeditor of *Theologisches Wörterbuch zum Alten Testament* —15

Fahland, Paul: pastor, Berlin-Lichtenberg; member of the examination committee for Bonhoeffer's first theological exam; assessor of Bonhoeffer's catechetical work for his second theological exam—9, 10

Fahle, Doris: friend of Maria von Wedemeyer—8
Faißt (also: Feist), Hans: superintendent—14
Falcke, Heino: theologian and church leader, influential in the church in the German Democratic Republic; church provost (emeritus), Erfurt—13
Falk, Johannes Daniel (1768–1826): hymnist—14
Falkenhausen, Baron Alexander von (1878–1966): career military; 1935–38, military adviser in China; commanding officer in Military District IV (Dresden); 1940–44, commanding officer in Belgium and northern France; after July 20, 1944, arrested; released at the end of the war—16, 17
Falkenhorst, Nikolaus von (1885–1968): career military; 1940, colonel general; 1942–44, commanding officer in Norway—16
Fallersleben, Hoffmann von: *see* Hoffmann (von Fallersleben), August Heinrich
Fangen, Ronald (1895–1946): member of Norwegian confessional movement —16
Fant, Clyde: U.S. scholar of biblical studies and archaeology—10
Farrar, Frederic W. (1831–1903): Anglican clergyman and author—3
Farrera, Beth Orling: consultant for *DBWE* 2 and 5—2, 5
Fascius, Friedrich: coauthor of work on the Bundesarchiv—8
Father (FP): character in drama; *see* Hans (FP); also Brake (FP)—7
Faulhaber, Michael Cardinal (1869–1952): Catholic theologian; 1903, professor of Old Testament, Strasbourg; 1911, bishop of Speyer; 1917, archbishop of Munich and Freising; 1921, cardinal—15, 16
Fauser: unidentified discussion partner of Robert Held and Dietrich Bonhoeffer—9
Faust: character in Goethe's poem—7, 10, 12
Feder, Alfred Leonhard (1872–1927): German religious historian; wrote works on Justin Martyr, Jerome, Hilary of Poitiers, Ignatius Loyola, and historical methodology—9
Feil, Ernst (1932–2013): 1952–60, studied theology, Greek philology, and philosophy, Münster, Innsbruck, and Munich; 1963–71, assistant, Catholic Ecumenical Institute of the University of Münster, also taught religious education at secondary schools; assistant at the Fundamental Theology Seminar of the Catholic theological faculty, University of Münster; 1970, ThD; 1971–75, professor of Catholic theology at the Pädagogische Hochschule (Teachers College) Ruhr, Dortmund department; 1975, professor of Catholic theology, University of Munich; member of the editorial board, *DBW*—2, 4, 5, 6, 8, 10, 11, 12, 14, 15, 17
Feine, Paul (1859–1933): German professor of New Testament, known for mediating between critical and conservative theology—1

Feirefiz: brother of Parsifal—8
Felber, Stefan: author of work on Wilhelm Vischer—17 (for vol. 12)
Félice, Théodore de (1904–2005): studied theology in Strasbourg and Paris; 1929–30, Reformed pastor, Mars (Ardèche); 1930–36, secretary of the International Committee of Christian Youth Associations, Geneva; 1933–36, secretary of the youth commission of the Ecumenical Council for Life and Work and of the World Alliance for Promoting International Friendship through the Churches; 1934–45, president of the Alliance of Religious Socialists, Romance language section; 1936–41, studied law and international relations, Lyon and Geneva; 1939–70, general secretary of the International League against Slavery (FAI); 1945–70, representative in the Great Council in the Canton of Geneva—12, 13, 14
Felix, Antonius: procurator or governor of Judea; in the New Testament, Paul was tried before him at Caesarea—16
Fendt, Leonhard (1881–1957): 1915, professor of Catholic theology, Dillingen; 1917, Halle; 1918, converted to Protestantism; 1927, pastor, Heilsbronnen church, Berlin; 1931, postdoctoral lecturing qualification, private lecturer (like Bonhoeffer); 1934–45, professor of practical theology, Berlin; university preacher, Berlin-Wilmersdorf; 1945, instructor at the mission school, Liebenzell—9, 10, 11, 12, 14
Fentress-Williams, Judith: U.S. Hebrew Bible scholar—1
Ferber, Gertrud: from Danzig; 1910–13, teacher, Danzig; from October 10, 1913, taught the history of religion, French, and German, University of Berlin; 1924, received her doctorate in Hamburg with the dissertation "Structures of Work and the Values of Education in Bertold Otto's Teaching Methodology"—9, 15
Fest, Joachim C.: German historian and journalist, biographer of Hitler—15
Festus, Porcius: succeeded Felix as governor of Judea; in the New Testament, heard Paul's defense—16
Feuerbach, Ludwig (1804–72): German philosopher, critic of religion; 1828, lecturer, Erlangen University; 1832, resigned because of his unorthodox views on religion; most influential work was *Das Wesen des Christentums* (The essence of Christianity) (1841)—3, 7, 8, 10, 11, 12
Fezer, Karl (1891–1960): 1920, city pastor, Tübingen; 1926, professor of practical theology, Tübingen; 1930, full professor of practical theology and supervisor, Protestant seminary, Tübingen; May–September 1933, member of the German Christians; July–September 1933, member of the provisional leadership of the German Evangelical Church; 1956–59, professor, Tübingen—11, 13, 14
Fiancée (FP): character in drama; *see* Renate (FP)—7

Ficht, Nikolaus (Niko): career military; colonel general; from May 1942, head of the Military Intelligence Office VII in Munich—16

Fichte, Johann Gottlieb (1762–1814): philosopher of German idealism—1, 2, 3, 6, 8, 9, 10, 11, 12

Ficino, Marsilio (1433–99): Italian humanist and philosopher—10

Fick, Rudolf (1866–1936): professor of anatomy; 1892–1905, Leipzig; 1909, Innsbruck; 1917–34, Berlin—9

Ficker, Johannes (1861–1944): church historian, Luther scholar; 1900, professor, Strasbourg; 1919, Halle—1, 2, 9, 14

Fiedler, Eberhard (1898–1947): 1934, lawyer with the Reich Court in Leipzig; May 1934, member of the Reich Council of Brethren; October 1934, of the Advisory Council of the German Evangelical Church; summer 1934, director of the legal section, Confessing Church central office, Bad Oeynhausen; November 1934, legal member and director of the church chancellery of the first Provisional Church Administration; 1936, resigned for health reasons; after 1945, official of the upper regional court in Gera—13

Field, David N.: coordinator for Theological Education, Office of the United Methodist Bishop of Central and Southern Europe—12

Figur, Fritz: 1930, pastor, Segenskirche (Church of the Blessing), Berlin; later superintendent and president, provincial synod Berlin-Brandenburg (east); 1966–67, bishop's duties in Berlin-Brandenburg; 1967–84, president, German Evangelical Church Convention (Kirchentag), East Germany—10, 11, 12

Filser, Hubert: German professor of Catholic theology and philosophy, Munich—15

Finefrock (FP): character in the novel, pastor; see Schönrock—7

Fink, Barbara: assisted with the International Bonhoeffer Bibliography—17

Finndorf, Adolf: Bonhoeffer's successor as vicar in Barcelona—10

Finney, Ruth (1898–1979): muckracking U.S. journalist; first woman nominated for a Pulitzer Prize—10

Fischer, Alfred (1874–1940): 1930, consistory officer and member of the Evangelical High Church Council—9, 10

Fischer, Franz: religious educator and professor, Vienna; secretary, Austrian section of the World Alliance for Promoting International Friendship through the Churches; 1932, led the Austrian participants at the Gland youth conference; September 1933, participated in the conference of the World Alliance for Promoting International Friendship through the Churches in Sofia—11, 12

Fischer, Fritz (1908–99): German historian; author of work on World War I that was controversial since it attributed the cause of that war to Germany—10

Fischer, Ilse: wife of Martin Fischer—15

Fischer, J. H. R. (Hans) (1906–70): student of Karl Barth in Münster and acquaintance of Bonhoeffer; 1931, Berlin; 1933, assistant pastor, Bochum-Weitmar; participated in work on the Bethel Confession; 1934, dismissed by the German Christian leadership; June 1934, pastor of the German Reformed church (Hervormde Kerk), Amsterdam; 1940, pastor of the German overseas church in Rotterdam (under the Church Foreign Office); worked with refugees during the war; later revived the German Seamen's Mission in Rotterdam—11, 12, 13, 17

Fischer, Martin (1911–82): 1937–45, directed the office for student affairs of the Confessing Church; member of the second Provisional Church Administration; 1945, lecturer, and 1949, professor of practical theology at the seminary in Berlin—15, 16

Fisher, Albert Franklin (Frank) (1908–60): 1930–31, African American friend of Bonhoeffer at Union Theological Seminary, New York—10, 11, 15

Fiske, John (1842–1901): American philosopher and historian, was responsible for applying the Darwinian theory of evolution to philosophical and historical studies in the United States—15

Fjellmo, Astrid: sent by Swedish church to Finkenwalde to arrange for their 1936 trip to Sweden—14

Flacius (Vlacich) Illyricus, Matthias (1520–75): orthodox Lutheran and defender of Luther's doctrines; 1544, professor of Hebrew, Wittenberg, where he was supported by Luther; became alienated from the Wittenberg establishment; 1557, professor, Jena; 1562, left Jena—1, 2, 10, 14, 15

Flasch, Kurt: German professor emeritus of philosophy, University of Bochum—11

Flechtner, Hans-Joachim (1901–80): German physicist—8

Flecken, Mr. von: factory director in Barcelona; acquaintance of Otto Bonhoeffer—10

Fleisch, Paul (1878–1962): German Protestant theologian—11

Fleischhack, Heinz (1913–88): from Magdeburg; 1937–38, member of the collective pastorate, Groß-Schlönwitz; attended the Silesian seminary in Halle; 1937, predicant, Groß-Santersleben; predicant, Eisleben and Arnswalde; 1939, assistant pastor, Eisleben; 1940, civilian service at an Eisleben factory; 1942, drafted into military service; prisoner of war;

1950, pastor, Eisleben; 1956, church official, Magdeburg; 1958, provost, Magdeburg; 1978, retired—4, 8, 15, 16

Fleming, Daniel: professor of missions, Union Theological Seminary; former missionary to India—10

Fletcher, John C.: first translator of *Creation and Fall*—2, 3

Flex, Walter (1887–1917): poet and writer; studied at Erlangen and Strasbourg; tutored the Bismarck children; World War I, killed in action; his popularity rested largely on his military career and death in battle; most widely read work was the 1916 war book *Der Wanderer zwischen beiden Welten* (The wanderer between two worlds); also published two volumes of poems; after 1945, his mystical, quasi-religious praise of war and of sacrificial death diminished in popularity—4, 10

Fliedner, Fritz (1845–1901): viewed as the initiator of evangelization in Spain; ultimately organized the Spanish Protestant churches into the Iglesia Evangelica Espanola—10

Fliedner, Juan: Spanish Protestant pastor, Madrid; member and treasurer of the Spanish section of the World Alliance for Promoting International Friendship through the Churches—16

Flor, Wilhelm (1882–1938): church lawyer; 1923–31, upper regional court official and honorary member of the Evangelical Consistory, Oldenburg; 1931, Reich court official, Leipzig; member of the Saxon Council of Brethren; October 1934, member of the Reich Council of Brethren of the first Provisional Church Administration (because he was prohibited by the state from practicing law, he was represented by Eberhard Fiedler); 1937, head of the Saxony Confessing Synod—13

Florian, Saint (d. 304): martyr, patron saint of Poland; his conversion to Christianity as a Roman officer led to his execution by drowning—8

Flöter, Hans Hinrich: religious historian; 1932–33, attended Bonhoeffer's Berlin lectures—3

Floyd, Wayne Whitson, Jr.: theologian and educator; author and editor of numerous works on Bonhoeffer; one of the general editors of the *DBWE* series—1, 2, 3, 4, 5, 6, 7, 8, 9, 10, 16, 17

Fock, Gorch (pseudonym of Hans Kinau) (1880–1916): deep-sea fisherman's son; author of a number of stories and collections concerned with the sea—14

Foertsch, Karl (1883–1952): 1929, pastor, Berlin-Friedenau; 1932, consistory official, Stettin; 1934, pastor, Halle—12

Fontane, Theodor (1819–98): German novelist of Huguenot descent—6, 7, 8, 9, 10, 14

Forck, Bernhard Heinrich (1893–1963): 1926, pastor, Hamburg; 1936, member of the Provisional Church Administration of the German Evangelical Church; 1950, superintendent, Luckenwalde—14, 15

Forde, Gerhard (1927–2005): U.S. Lutheran theologian and Reformation expert—14

Forel, Oscar: Swiss psychiatrist and director of the sanitarium "La Materie" near Nyon; a friend of Karl Bonhoeffer—9

Forell, Birger (1893–1958): Swedish pastor; 1930–42, attached to the Swedish embassy as pastor for the Swedish congregation, Berlin; sent information abroad concerning the Church Struggle in Germany; 1942, senior pastor, Borås; 1944–54, chaplain in Britain for German prisoners of war; 1948, helped Ernst Wilm establish a refugee settlement, Espelkamp, Westphalia; 1951–58, director of German-Swedish refugee relief, Cologne-Nippes—12, 13, 14, 16

Forell, Friedrich: German pastor; 1916, ordained; social ministry in Silesia; 1933, forced into early retirement because of his "non-Aryan" ancestry; 1933–38, worked for the Swedish Israel-Mission, Vienna; helped "non-Aryan" refugees in France with the aid of the World Council of Churches in Geneva; autumn 1940, after temporary internment emigrated to the United States with the help of ecumenical contacts; founded two relief committees in the United States for refugee relief—16

Forli: *see* Melozzo da Forli

Fornaçon, Siegfried Paul Karl Gottlieb (1910–87): 1940, ministry in Groß Friedrichsdorf, East Prussia; June 14, 1940, Dietrich Bonhoeffer visited him; 1942, drafted into military service—16

Fornoff: two brothers in Bonhoeffer's children's worship group in Barcelona—10

Forstmann (family): members of the congregation in Barcelona—10

Fortlage, Karl (1806–81): German philosopher—6

Fosdick, Harry Emerson (1878–1969): prominent Baptist theologian and preacher; 1915–46, professor of practical theology, Union Theological Seminary, New York; 1930–46, pastor, Riverside Church, New York—10, 12, 15

Fox, Henry Watson (1872–1941): Church of England minister; general secretary of the British section of the World Alliance for Promoting International Friendship through the Churches in England—11, 13

Fox, Richard Wightman: biographer of Reinhold Niebuhr—11, 15

Fra Angelico: *see* Angelico, Fra

Fraenkel, Heinrich (1915–73): German-born journalist; went into exile during Nazism; cofounder of the "Free German Movement" in England—16

Francfordia, Johannes de (1330–1440)—theologian and rector, University of Heidelberg, 2

Francis of Assisi (ca. 1181–1226): founder of the mendicant Franciscan order—3, 10, 13, 14

Franck, Johann (1618–77): hymnist—12, 14, 15

Franck von Wörd, Sebastian (1499–ca. 1542): from Donauwörth; associated with Anabaptist groups and spiritualists; 1540, condemned by the assembly at Smalcald—14

Francke, August Hermann (1663–1727): German pietist and educator—16

Franco Bahamonde, Francisco ("Caudillo") (1892–1975): Spanish general and politician; 1939–74, dictator of Spain—14, 17

Frank, Franz Hermann Reinhold von (1827–94): from 1857, Protestant theologian and professor of systematic theology, Erlangen; leading representative of the "Erlangen school" of Lutheran theology; teacher of Reinhold Seeberg—1, 6, 9, 11, 12

Frank, Walter (1905–45): German historian, sympathetic to Nazism; president of the Reich Institute for the History of the New Germany—12

Franke, Martin: young theologian from Pomerania; 1941, killed in action on the eastern front; August 15, 1941, mentioned in the Finkenwalde newsletter—16

Fraser, Colin: in possession of *DBWE* 11 document from Karl-Friedrich Bonhoeffer—11

Frederick II ("the Great") (1712–86): 1740–86, king of Prussia—6, 8, 9, 14, 17 (for *DBWE* 9)

Frederking, Alexander: pastor, Berlin-Charlottenburg—10

Freeman, Kathleen (1897–1959): British classicist and translator—17

Freisler, Roland (1893–1945): lawyer and judge under the Nazi regime; 1932, Prussian member of regional parliament (representing the NSDAP); 1934, state secretary in the Reich Ministry of Justice; 1942, president of the People's Court; February 3, 1945, killed during an air raid on Berlin—8, 16, 17

Freitag, Albert (1880–1959): 1913, pastor at Trinity Church, Berlin-Charlottenburg; 1933, Reich press secretary for the German Christians—10

Frenssen, Gustav (1863–1945): pastor (until 1903) and writer; his *Village Sermons 1899–1903* went into several editions; also wrote novels (*Jörn Uhl*, 1901; *Hilligenlei*, 1905)—14

Frere, Walter Howard (1863–1938): British Anglican bishop; cofounder and former superior of the Mirfield monastery—17 (for vol. 13)

Frettlöh, Magdalena L.: German theologian—8

Freud, Sigmund (1856–1939): Viennese neurologist and psychotherapist; founder of psychoanalysis—12, 14, 15

Freudenberg, Adolf (1894–1977): German diplomat and pastor; 1922–35, in the Foreign Ministry, ultimately as legation officer; 1935, dismissed because of his wife's Jewish ancestry; studied Protestant theology and was ordained by the Confessing Church in Berlin-Dahlem; 1939, because of his wife's Jewish ancestry, emigrated to England, where he became secretary for refugee relief in the provisional World Council of Churches in London and Geneva; during the war, cordial contacts with Bonhoeffer during the latter's visits to Switzerland; 1947, pastor in the refugee settlement Heilsberg/Bad Vilbel near Frankfurt am Main—8, 13, 15, 16, 17

Frey, Arthur (1897–1955): head of the Evangelical Press Service in Switzerland and owner of the Zollikon publishing house near Zürich—16

Frey, Christopher: studied theology, philosophy, and sociology in Berlin, Tübingen, Chicago, Göttingen, Heidelberg, and Paris; doctoral dissertation on the theology of French Catholic reform, 1967; postdoctoral dissertation on Hegel, 1972; church service in Stuttgart and Reutlingen; university teacher in Heidelberg and Erlangen; professor of systematic theology and social ethics at the University of Bochum—2, 7

Freybe, Hermann: from 1917, pastor, Berlin—12

Freyer, Hans (1887–1969): German philosopher of culture and sociologist; 1938–44, visiting professor, Budapest—1, 7, 10

Freylinghausen, Johann Anastasius (1670–1739): German pietist and hymnist—16

Frick, Heinrich (1893–1952): 1924, professor of general religious history, Giessen; 1929, professor of practical theology, Marburg—12

Frick, Peter: professor of New Testament, University of Waterloo; member of *DBWE* editorial board and cotranslator for *DBWE* 15—2, 8, 10, 12, 16

Frick, Wilhelm (1877–1946): Nazi government official; member of the national parliament (representing the NSDAP); 1930–31, Reich Minister of the Interior and of Public Education in Thuringia; 1933–43, Reich Interior Minister; 1943–45, Reich Protector of Bohemia and Moravia; 1946, executed after the Nuremberg trials—13, 14, 16, 17

Fricke, H.: member of the German congregation, Sydenham, London—13

Fricke, Paul (1896–1961): from 1932, pastor, Berlin; member of Young Reformation movement—12

Fridrichsen, Anton Johnson (1888–1953): Swedish theologian; 1928, professor of New Testament, Uppsala—16

Friedenthal, Charlotte (1892–1973): daughter of a Berlin bank director; trained as a social worker; 1935–36, acting director of the Evangelical Welfare Office, Berlin-Zehlendorf; from 1935, employed by the Provisional Church Administration; from October 1937, personal secretary to Berlin church superintendent Martin Albertz; from 1939, registered

for emigration to the United States; September 4, 1942, left Germany for Switzerland as part of the "Operation 7" rescue; after the war, again active in church work in Berlin—16, 17

Friedenthal, Ernst: brother of Charlotte Friedenthal—16

Friedländer, Max J. (1867–1958): prominent German art historian—15

Friedrich, Karl Josef: German art historian—4, 15

"Friend" (FP): character in the drama; *see* Ulrich (FP)—7

Fries, Jakob Friedrich (1773–1843): philosopher and physicist—11

Fries, Willy (1907–80): Swiss painter and sculptor; 1929, studied art and literary history, University of Zürich; 1930–34, further study, including in Berlin; 1947, president of the Swiss Art Commission—12

Frik: unidentified member of Harnack's seminar—9

Frik, Lotte: *see* Kühn, Lotte

Fritsch, Paul: 1927, pastor, Brandenburg; 1933, Berlin-Pankow—12

Fritsch, Werner Baron von (1880–1939): German colonel general; 1934–38, head of the army leadership; from 1935, commander in chief of the army; February 1938, defamed and dismissed from office—15

Fritz, Frede: mentioned in letter from Gertrud Staewen; not otherwise identified—12

Fromm, Friedrich (1888–1945): career military; 1939–44, ultimately colonel general and commander in chief of the reserve army; after July 20, 1944, arrested despite speaking out against the Stauffenberg group; executed after being convicted by the People's Court—16

Frör, Kurt (1905–80): German Protestant theologian, author of works on theological differences between Protestantism and Catholicism—14

Fuglsang-Damgaard, Hans (1890–1975): Danish theologian; 1934–60, bishop of Copenhagen and primate of the Danish church—16

Fuller, Reginald H.: New Testament scholar; translator of the first edition of *Letters and Papers from Prison*—2, 4, 8

Füllkrug, Gerhard (1870–1948): German theologian, active in the Protestant Inner Mission—14

Funke, Gotthold (1901–75): member of the German ecumenical working committee; 1934, pastor, Betsche, district of Meseritz—12

Furtwängler, Wilhelm (1886–1954): German musical conductor—8

Gabriel, Walther (1887–1983): from 1923, pastor, St. Laurentius church, Halle/Saale; member of the Young Reformation movement; 1933, member of the Pastors' Emergency League; 1934, chair of the district Council of Brethren; Inner Mission representative in the Confessing Church; 1941–43, in Dachau concentration camp; 1962, retired—16

Gad: biblical character—15
Gadow, Hartmut: 1936, vicar, Berlin-Schöneberg; 1937, participated in the fifth Finkenwalde session; pastor of the Confessing congregation, Berlin-Friedrichsfelde; 1944, pastor, Zühlsdorf, Arnswalde; 1945, Leopoldshagen-Anklam; after 1946, Berlin, and later, Kaiserswerth; 1984, retired—15
Gadow, Hellmut: summer semester 1933, attended Bonhoeffer's lectures on Christology—12
Gaedecke, Albert: Hitler Youth group leader (in connection with the transfer of the Biesenthal hut to the Hitler Youth)—12
Gaedertz, Alma: 1931, assistant lecturer (unpaid) in ophthalmology, University of Berlin—16
Gaia (Ge; Gaea): the earth, conceived as a vaguely personal goddess; mother and wife of Uranos (the heavens)—10
Gailus, Manfred: historian of the German churches under National Socialism—15
Galen, Clemens August Count von (1878–1946): German Catholic priest; 1906, priest, Berlin; 1919, head of the Berlin Apprentice Labor Association; 1929, priest, St. Lamberti Church, Münster; after 1933, bishop of Münster; became known for his pastoral letters and sermons against National Socialist ideology and outspoken opposition to the euthanasia measures; 1946, cardinal—16
Galeota, Gustavo: Italian Jesuit historian—11
Gallas, Alberto: Italian professor of the history of theology, Milan; editor of the *Dietrich Bonhoeffer Works*, Italian edition—6, 8, 17
Gallego sisters: Bonhoeffer's landladies in Barcelona—10
Galling, Kurt (1900–1987): German theologian—10
Gamaliel II (ca. 80–115): influential rabbi and patriarch in Yavneh; 70, presided over the national-religious restoration after the destruction of the temple and Jerusalem by the Romans—9
Gandhi, Mohandas Karamchand (Mahatma) (1869–1948): Indian statesman and philosopher; Hindu nationalist leader and advocate of nonviolent political resistance; studied law, London; lawyer, India; 1893, went to South Africa, where he worked as political leader of the Indian immigrants; 1914, returned to India; initiated nonviolent resistance against British rule; arrested twenty times; repeated hunger strikes in prison; 1947, attained Indian independence; 1948, assassinated—4, 5, 6, 9, 10, 11, 12, 13, 14, 16, 17
Garrod, Heathcote William (1878–1960): British classics scholar; 1923–28, Oxford professor of poetry—15

Garvie, Alfred Ernest (1861–1945): British pastor and church leader; 1903, professor of religious philosophy, London; 1920, head of the Congregational Union; 1924, president of the Free Church Federal Council—16

Gates, Henry Louis: W. E. B. Du Bois Professor of Humanities and chair of the Department of African and African American Studies at Harvard—10

Gaudig, Hugo (1860–1923): German educator, representative of the vocational education movement—14

Gauger, Joachim: compiled three-volume documentation on the German Church Struggle—11, 12, 13, 16

Gauguin, Paul (1848–1903): French painter—8

Gaulle, Charles de (1890–1970): initially career military; 1940, brigadier general and commander of a tank division; after France's surrender, leader of the French resistance from London; 1945, minister president; 1958–69, French state president—16, 17

Gaupp, Robert (1870–1953): student friend of Karl Bonhoeffer; 1906–36, professor of psychiatry, Tübingen—9

Gauwald (uncertain reading; perhaps "Hauwald"): friend of Karl-Friedrich Bonhoeffer—9

Gawlick, Günter: German religious philosopher—8

Gay, Cesare: Italian attorney and ecumenist; cofounder of the Italian section of the World Alliance for Promoting International Friendship through the Churches; represented the Waldensians on the World Alliance executive committee; September 1933, participated in the World Alliance conference in Sofia; spring 1943, Dietrich Bonhoeffer mentions him in the "camouflage letter"—8, 12, 16

Gebhardt, Otto von (1844–1906): German New Testament and patristics scholar; colleague of Adolf von Harnack—9

Gehlen, Arnold (1904–76): German philosopher and sociologist—8

Gehlhoff, Gerhard (1896–1954): 1934–45, pastor, Lupow/Stolp, Pomerania; member of the Pomeranian Confessing Church Council of Brethren; later worked in ministry for refugees in Westphalia—8, 15

Gehloff, Mrs.: wife of Pastor Gerhard Gehlhoff—15

Gehre, Ludwig (1895–1945): lawyer; initially manager in the construction industry; 1939, drafted into military service in the Military Intelligence Office III; member of the inner circle of the Oster and Dohnanyi resistance group; January 1944, escaped capture; November 1944, arrested after a suicide attempt; April 9, 1945, executed in the Flossenbürg concentration camp—16, 17

Geiger, Theodor (1891–1952): German sociologist—1

Geismar, Eduard: prominent Danish Kierkegaard scholar—8, 15

"Gelbstiefel" (Yellowboots) (FP): *see* Kruse (FP)

Gellately, Robert: U.S. historian and professor of Holocaust studies—6

Gellert, Christian Fürchtegott (1715–69): German poet, dramatist, and novelist; professor of poetry, rhetoric, and ethics, Leipzig; best known for his verse fables—12, 14

Genizi, Haim: Israeli historian; author of several works on international rescue efforts during the Holocaust—15

Gennrich, P. W.: 1929, took doctoral exams in theology; Bonhoeffer one of his questioners—10

Gensen: not otherwise identified—10

Gentile da Fabriano: see Fabriano, Gentile da

Georg: student in Barcelona—10

George, David Lloyd: *see* Lloyd George

George, Heinrich (1893–1945): German stage and film actor—16

George, Stefan (1868–1933): German poet; after Hitler's appointment as chancellor, George was offered the presidency of the new Poets Academy, which he declined; soon afterward, he moved to Switzerland—7, 12

Georgii, Hans-Otto (1911–41): from Berlin; 1936, assistant pastor, Schloßkirche, Altlandsberg; 1937, Buckow; 1937–38, participated in the collective pastorate; June 26, 1941, killed in action on the eastern front —15, 16

Georgii, Wolfgang (1913–44): from Berlin; 1937–38, participated in the collective pastorate; 1939, assistant pastor, Confessing congregations, Havelberg and Stöbritz, district of Calau; 1944, missing in action at the Narew River—15, 16

Gerber: German fellowship student in the United States the same year as Bonhoeffer—10

Gerber, Hans: author of works on state philosophy and Luther—16

Gerbrandy, Pieter S.: minister president of the Dutch exile government in London—16

Gerd: character in Ibsen's *Brand*—10

Gerhard, Johann (1582–1637): leader of German Lutheran orthodoxy—9, 12

Gerhardt, Paul (1607–76): German theologian and hymnist; 1651, provost, Mittenwalde; 1657, pastor, Nicholas Church, Berlin; an aggressive representative of Lutheran orthodoxy, he lost his pastorate because of his refusal to follow the royal prohibition on anti-Reform polemics, and was without a position for some time; 1669, archdeacon, Lübben—1, 5, 7, 8, 9, 10, 11, 12, 13, 14, 15, 16

Gerlach, Paul (1893–1945): from 1928, pastor, Berlin—12

Gerlach, Wolfgang: German pastor; author of work on the Confessing Church and the Jews—12, 15

Gerlach-Praetorius, Angelika: author of work on the churches and the July 20th conspiracy—15

Germanos, Lukas Panteleimon (1872–1951): Orthodox archbishop based in London; president of the Orthodox section of Life and Work; member of the World Council of Churches—16

Gerok, Karl (1815–90): preacher, religious poet, and hymnologist—14

Gerrens, Uwe: German pastor and theologian; author of publications on Karl Bonhoeffer and Dietrich Bonhoeffer in relation to the Reichstag fire, forced sterilization, and "euthanasia"—6, 8, 16

Gerritsen, S. M. C.: Dutch delegate at the Fanø youth conference—13

Gersdorff, Maria: wife of Baron Heinz von Gersdorff, who worked in the office of General Paul von Hase, military commandant of Berlin—15

Gersdorff, Rudolf-Christoph Baron von (1905–80): Silesian career military, ultimately general major; 1941, military intelligence officer with the general staff of the Center Army Group on the eastern front; member of Major General von Treskow's resistance group there; March 1943, volunteered to carry out an assassination attempt against Hitler; 1944, chief of the general staff of an army in the west—16, 17

Gerson, Johannes (Jean Charlier aus Gerson) (1363–1429): French theologian and church politician—10

Gerstenberg, Walter (1904–88): German musicologist—17 (for vol. 9)

Gerstenmaier, Eugen (1906–86): 1936–44, officer in Bishop Theodor Heckel's Church Foreign Office; 1939–40, special assignments in the information section of the Ministry of Foreign Affairs; 1942, became member of the Kreisau circle through contact with Helmut von Moltke; July 24, 1944, arrested and sentenced by the People's Court to seven years' imprisonment; April 14, 1945, liberated from the Bayreuth penitentiary; 1945–51, head of the relief organization of the Evangelical Church of Germany, Stuttgart; 1949–69, member of German parliament (representing the CDU) in Bonn; 1954–69, president of the German parliament—8, 10, 14, 15, 16, 17

Gerth, Hans: German-born sociologist; later professor, Columbia University, New York—6

Gertz, Bernhard: German theologian—2

Gerullis, Georg (1888–1945): 1919, postdoctoral degree for Baltic philology, Königsberg; 1922, professor, Leipzig; 1931, joined the NSDAP; 1933, minister director of the Prussian Ministry of Culture; May–October, 1934, continued after this ministry was combined with the Reich Ministry of Education; 1936, rector, Königsberg; 1937, professor, Berlin—12, 13

Gesell, Silvio (1862–1930): Belgian-born German merchant and economist; advocated paper currency as a medium of exchange—9

Geß, Ernst: from 1928, pastor, Berlin-Zehlendorf—12
Geß, Wolfgang Friedrich (1819–91): representative of a kenotic theology —12
Geyer, Christian (1862–1929): 1887, pastor; 1902, senior pastor, Sebaldus Church, Nuremberg; worked closely with Rittelmeyer (two books of sermons), but ceased after the latter's turn to anthroposophy—14
Geyser, Joseph (1869–1948): German philosopher—2 (incorrectly listed there as Johannes)
Geyser, Paul (1824–82): Reformed pastor, Elberfeld; critic of the state church and of the Kulturkampf (the 1871 conflict in the German Empire between the state and the Roman Catholic Church)—14, 15
Giacometti, Zacharias (1893–1970): professor of international law, University of Zürich—16
Gibson, Edmund (1669–1748): from 1713, bishop of London; worried about opposition to missionary work among black slaves; author of 1727 pastoral letter "To the Masters and Mistresses of Families in the English Plantations abroad"—15
Gibson, W. R. Boyce—2
Gideon: biblical character—12, 13, 14
Gierke, Anna von (1874–1945): German early childhood educator; 1910–33, led a home for youth, Berlin-Charlottenburg—7
Gierke, Otto Friedrich von (1841–1921): prominent legal scholar; father of Anna von Gierke—1
Giersch, Helmut (1907–44): academic inspector for the Silesian seminary, Halle; later pastor, Altherzberg; missing in action—14
Giese, Kurt: from Berlin-Brandenburg; 1936–37, participated in the fourth Finkenwalde session—15
Gieseking, Walter (1895–1956): German-born pianist—8
Giessler, Lydia: 1933, theological student, Berlin—12
Gilbert, Felix: historian; school friend of the Bonhoeffer children and descendant of Felix Mendelssohn-Bartholdy, lived in Berlin with grandmother Mendelssohn; later emigrated to the United States—9, 15
Gilbert, Mary: sister of Felix Gilbert; friend of Ursula Bonhoeffer—9
Gildemeister, C. H.: author of work on Johann Georg Hamann—11
Gildemeister, Martin (1876–1943): from 1924, director of the physiological institute at the university, Leipzig—8
Giles of Rome (ca. 1243–1316): archbishop of Bourges; wrote commentary on Aristotle—1
Gilfond, Duff: U.S. journalist—10
Gill, Ruthann: staff member, Conference of European Churches—13

Gill, Theodore (1920–2005): 1939, met Bonhoeffer during the latter's stay at Union Theological Seminary; later became president of San Francisco Theological Seminary—15

Gilli, Mario: engineer; captain in the technical corps of the Italian air force; October 1943–August 1944, prisoner of war in Tegel—8

Gioberti, Vincenzo (1801–52): Italian philosopher and politician; ordained Roman Catholic priest; attacked Cartesianism and developed a philosophy called ontologism—2

Giotto di Bondone (1276–1337): Florentine painter, architect, and sculptor —9

Girbig, Werner: German author of works about World War II—8

Girgensohn, Karl (1875–1925): Lutheran theologian, organist; wrote on the psychology of religion; lived in Berlin—9

Gisevius, Hans Bernd (1904–74): from 1933, government official in the Prussian Ministry of the Interior; from 1939, special officer in the Military Intelligence Office; 1941, vice-consul and local representative of the Military Intelligence Office at the German consulate, Zürich; on July 20, 1944, in Berlin; January 1945, fled to Switzerland; after the war, publicist —8, 16, 17

Gisevius, Johannes (1880–1995): 1925, senior consistory officer on the Evangelical High Church Council and in the Church Federation Office, Berlin; later in the chancellery of the German Evangelical Church—10, 12

Gladen, Paulgerhard: author of works on German fraternities (including right-wing groups)—11

Gladstone, William Ewart (1809–98): British statesman—6

Glasenapp, Helmut von: German professor of Indology and comparative religion—12

Glen-Doepel, William: one of the translators of the first English edition of Bethge's biography of Bonhoeffer—2

Glenthøj, Jørgen Johannes (1922–96): Danish theologian; during World War II, member of the Danish resistance; studied theology after the war; 1949, ordination and assistant pastorate at the Esajaskirke, Copenhagen; 1951, pastor, Hassing-Villerslev; 1964, Borum-Lynbgy; 1966–73, taught at the theological seminary, Aarhus, 1974–82, on the congregational faculty, 1983–84, on the department of theology there; 1980–86 member, executive committee, theological commission of the World Evangelical Fellowship; 1990, retired; author of numerous works on church history, the Church Struggle, and Dietrich Bonhoeffer—3, 4, 10, 11, 12, 13, 14, 15, 16, 17

Gloege, Gerhard (1901–70): 1933–38, director of the preachers' seminary (from 1934, connected to the Confessing Church), Naumburg am Queis;

1935, dismissed from office; 1938, expelled; 1939, copastor with Bernhard Riemer, Erfurt; 1946, professor of systematic theology, Jena; 1961–68, Bonn—14

Gloel, Johannes Eduard (1852–91): professor of New Testament, Halle and Erlangen—1

Glondys, Viktor (1882–1949): 1932–40, bishop of the German Evangelical Church, Romania—13

Gloucester: *see* Headlam, Arthur Cayley

Gneisenau, August Neithardt Count von (1760–1831): Prussian military leader who led reforms in the military—10

Godsey, John D. (1922–2010): U.S. professor of systematic theology; author of works on Bonhoeffer, including the first published monograph on Bonhoeffer's theology; member of *DBWE* editorial board; coeditor of *DBWE* 4—3, 4, 5, 6, 7, 8, 13, 16

Goebbels, Joseph (1897–1945): National Socialist politician and publicist; 1933–45, Reich Minister of Public Information and Propaganda; 1945, committed suicide—4, 6, 8, 12, 13, 14, 15, 16, 17

Goebel, Johannes (1910–89): 1935, participated in the first session at Zingst/Finkenwalde; 1949, pastor, Brandenburg/Havel—14

Goedeking, Hans: studied Protestant theology in Wuppertal, Heidelberg, Chicago, and Göttingen; 1963, doctoral degree, Münster, dissertation on "The Understanding of Modern Technology. Its Development and Incorporation into Protestant Theology"; 1963–64, pastor, Rödinghausen near Herford; 1964–67, pastor, Düsseldorf; 1974–84, lecturer at the Ecumenical Institute of Bossey near Geneva; from 1984, pastor, Wuppertal; author of publications on ecumenical questions and on ethical questions associated with modern technology; one of editors of *DBW* 13—13

Goerdeler, Carl Friedrich (1884–1945): lawyer and government official; 1920–30, vice mayor of Königsberg; 1930–37, mayor of Leipzig; 1931–32 and 1934–35, Reich commissar of price controls; spring 1937, resigned in protest over the removal of the Mendelssohn-Bartholdy monument; 1937–39, foreign trips for the Krupp and Bosch companies; from 1939, leading figure, along with Colonel General Beck, in the civilian resistance movement; August 12, 1944, arrested; September 1944, sentenced to death; February 2, 1945, executed—8, 13, 16, 17

Goertz, Hans-Jürgen: Mennonite theologian and historian—15

Goes, Albrecht (1908–2000): German Lutheran pastor, poet, and writer, Württemberg; 1939–45, army chaplain; until 1953, parish pastor—14

Goes, Helmut: from Langenbeutingen in Württemberg; brother of the poet Albrecht Goes; 1924–28, studied theology in Tübingen, Berlin, and Bonn; 1925–26, studied in Berlin; was a member of Harnack's seminar;

one of the founders of the Württemberg Ecclesiastical-Theological Society, which was aligned with the Confessing Church; 1935–50, pastor, Ohmden; from 1950, Stuttgart-Uhlbach—2, 9, 10, 14

Goes, Markus: son of Pastor Helmut Goes—9, 14

Goethe, Johann Wolfgang von (1749–1832): German poet, dramatist, novelist, and scientist—1, 2, 3, 4, 6, 7, 8, 9, 10, 11, 12, 13, 14, 15

Goetz, Frank and Doris, née Dickens: May 3, 1934, Bonhoeffer officiated at their wedding at St. Paul's in London—13

Goetz, Fritz: 1933, doctoral candidate in theology, Berlin; 1935, pastor, Großsteinhausen near Zweibrücken—12

Goetz, L.: member of the congregational council, German Reformed St. Paul's Church, London—13

Gogarten, Friedrich (1887–1967): German theologian, pastor, and professor of theology; representative of dialectical theology; 1922, cofounder of the periodical *Zwischen den Zeiten*; 1925, lecturer in systematic theology, Jena; 1931–35, professor of systematic theology, Breslau; 1933, favored German Christians, break with Karl Barth; 1935–53, professor, Göttingen—1, 2, 3, 4, 6, 9, 10, 11, 12, 13, 14, 16

Gogh, Vincent van (1853–90): Dutch painter—11

Goldschmidt, Mr.: German refugee in Great Britain, mentioned in letter to Ernst Cromwell—14

Goldschmidt, Victor: 1931, student and member of Bonhoeffer's "Thursday circle" in Berlin—10

Goliath: biblical character—14

Gollwitzer, Helmut (1908–93): studied theology in Bonn with Karl Barth; 1936–38, active in the Council of Brethren of the Old Prussian Union; 1938, pastor, Berlin-Dahlem as Niemöller's replacement after Niemöller's arrest; after 1940, military service; 1945–49, prisoner of war in Russia; 1950, professor of systematic theology, Bonn; from 1957, professor, Free University and college of theological studies, Berlin; 1973, retired—8, 11, 14, 15, 16, 17

Goltz, Georg Konrad, Count von der (1902–85): son of Rüdiger and Hanna von der Goltz; 1925, married Wanda, née Hjort; father of Lilian (married name Müller-Elmau, later von Nerée), Conrad, Karin, Viktoria (married name Wegner), and Gottfried—9, 15

Goltz, Hannah Caroline Helene Marie Countess von der, née von Hase (1873–1941): sister of Bonhoeffer's mother, daughter of Karl Alfred and Clara von Hase; twin sister of Hans von Hase; wife of Rüdiger von der Goltz; mother of Georg Conrad von der Goltz—8, 9, 13, 16

Goltz, Rüdiger Count von der (1894–1976): justice official and defense attorney in important political trials; Nazi party member; son of Rüdiger and Hannah von der Goltz; Bonhoeffer's cousin; September 1933, Prussian state official (representing the NSDAP); June 1933–April 1934, "work trustee"; 1943, Bonhoeffer's and Dohnanyi's defense lawyer—8, 12, 13, 16, 17

Goltz, Rüdiger Count von der ("Uncle Rudi" was the Bonhoeffers' code name for the war) (1865–1946): married Hannah, née von Hase; father of Rüdiger, Hans, and Georg Conrad; brother-in-law of Bonhoeffer's mother; Prussian career military officer; in World War I, major general and commander of the Baltic Division; 1918, liberated Finland from Soviet troops; after the war, engaged in efforts to unite German patriotic associations; 1932, cofounder of the Harzburg Front—8, 9, 10, 15, 16

Goltz, Wanda, Countess von der, née Hjort (1902–1983): married to Georg Conrad von der Goltz—9

Goosmann, Max: from 1929, pastor, Berlin-Adlershof—12

Gordon, Ernst Heinrich (anglicized in 1940: Ernest Henry) (1909–91): 1932–33, one of Bonhoeffer's first students in Berlin; 1933–34, participated in the preachers' seminary, Wittenberg; October 1933, member of the Pastors' Emergency League; December 1934, ordination; by summer 1937, expelled from four congregations because of his Jewish ancestry; November 1937, fled to Switzerland; January 1939, flight to England; joined Anglican Church; 1940, ordination as priest; 1977, retired—13, 14

Gordon, J. King (1900–1989): 1920s and 1930s, prominent Canadian Christian Socialist; 1930–31, met Bonhoeffer during his time at Union Seminary; son of Charles Gordon, one of the founders of the United Church of Christ in Canada—10, 11

Gore, Charles: founder of the Community of the Resurrection, Mirfield—17 (for vol. 13)

Gore, Richard S.: official in the British Foreign Office—16

Göring, Wilhelm Hermann (1893–1946): National Socialist politician; aviator in World War I; 1922, joined the National Socialist Party and assumed leadership of the SA (the armed and uniformed section of the NSDAP); November 9, 1923, seriously wounded in front of the Munich Feldherrnhalle; 1928, member of the national parliament; 1932, president of parliament; 1933, Prussian minister president; January 30, 1933, prominent role in forming Hitler's government; occupied various ministerial offices; 1935, Reich Minister of Aviation and commander in chief of the air force; 1940, Reich Marshal; April 23, 1945, removed from office and

the Nazi party by Hitler; after World War II, condemned to death at the Nuremberg trials; 1946, committed suicide before execution—6, 13, 16

Görnandt, Werner (1893–1969): from 1920, pastor, Potsdam and elsewhere; 1931, superintendent, Potsdam; 1934–60, senior pastor, St. Peter's, Copenhagen—12, 14

Gorski, Siegfried: freelance editor for medical publishing houses—6

Gotthelf, Jeremias (pseudonym of Albert Bitzius the elder) (1797–1854): Swiss theologian, pastor, and novelist; after 1831, pastor, Lützeflüh in the Emmental Valley; 1837, publication of first novel, *Jeremias Gotthelf*, from which his pseudonym, based on the title character, was taken—6, 7, 8, 14, 16

Götz von Olenhusen, Irmtraud: author of works on youth and education during the Third Reich—12

Goya y Lucientes, Francisco José (1746–1828): Spanish painter, etcher, and lithographer—10

Goysen, Jan van (1596–1656): Dutch painter; best known for his landscapes and river scenes—11

Grabbe, Christian Dietrich (1801–36): German dramatist—7

Grädler, Hans: inspector in the passport office of Munich police headquarters—16

Graf, Friedrich Wilhelm: German professor of Protestant theology, history, and philosophy—6, 11

Graf, Karl Heinrich (1815–69): German Old Testament scholar—3

Grafe, Hugald: professor, Hildesheim; author of works on mission history and world religions—14

Graff, Gerti: coeditor of work about the Dahlem parish during the Third Reich—15

Graham, Eric (1888–1964): 1929, principal, Cuddesdon College near Oxford; 1944, bishop of Brechen—13

Graml, Hermann: German historian of Nazi era—16

Gramlow, Georg (1894–1973): superintendent, church district in Arnswalde/Neumark—14

Gramm, Erich: German pastor—9

Grandet, Eugénie: title character of novel by Balzac—6

Grandmother (FP): character in drama; *see* Brake (FP), Karoline—7

Grandyot, V. (or P.): member of the congregational council, St. Paul's Church, London—13

Granier, Gerhard: coauthor of work on the Bundesarchiv—8

Grant, Michael (1914–2004): British classicist and historian—8

Grassi, Orazio (1583–1654): Italian architect of the baroque period—9

Graue: 1933, pastor in Berlin—12

Grauer, Elisabeth: German theology student; 1931, participated in the Cambridge conference; later active in the Confessing Church as vicar and member of the Confessing Church theological examination board—11

Graves, Robert (1895–1985): British poet, novelist, and critic; 1961–66, professor of poetry at Oxford; best known for his historical novels and his coming-of-age novel about his experiences in World War I, *Goodbye to All That*—10

Greco (Doménikos Theotokópoulos) (ca. 1541–1614): Greek painter in Spain; leading exponent of Spanish mysticism in painting; *see* El Greco —9

Green, Barbara: U.S. Presbyterian pastor; 1977–81, National Council of Churches liaison to the German Democratic Federation of Protestant Churches; 1983–98, policy advocate for the Washington Office of the Presbyterian Church; 1998–2010, executive director, Churches' Center for Theology and Public Policy; cotranslator, *DBWE* 4—2, 4

Green, Clifford J.: Australian-born U.S. theologian; author and editor of numerous works on Bonhoeffer; executive director, *DBWE*—1, 2, 3, 4, 5, 6, 7, 8, 9, 10, 12, 14, 16, 17

Gregor: *see* Rümmelein, Gregor

Gregor, Christian (1723–1801): poet, songwriter, and from 1789, bishop of the Moravian (Herrnhut) community—5, 13, 14, 15

Gregorovius, Ferdinand: (1821–91): German historian and philosopher; expert on Italy—16

Gregory I (the Great) (540–604): from 590, pope—14, 15

Gregory VII (Hildebrand): (ca. 1021–85): from 1073–85, pope—6, 8

Greiser, Arthur Karl (1897–1946): National Socialist politician; 1934, president of the Danzig senate; 1939, regional Nazi party leader and Reich governor of the Reich district Wartheland; SS *Obergruppenführer*; June 20, 1946, executed in Posen—16, 17

Gremmels, Christian: studied theology in Berlin, Marburg, and Göttingen; 1970, doctorate in theology, Marburg; 1976, postdoctoral work in systematic theology, Marburg; 1979–81, professor of social ethics, department of Protestant theology, Philipps University, Marburg; after 1981, professor of Protestant theology, Gesamthochschule Kassel; from 1985, chair of West German section of the International Bonhoeffer Society; from 1992, chair of the International Bonhoeffer Society, German section—2, 4, 5, 7, 8, 9, 10, 12, 13, 16, 17

Greschat, Martin: German professor of church history and contemporary church history—6, 14, 15

Greßler, Dr.: major; head of the Central Trading Company East (Zentralhandelsgesellschaft Ost) in the Military Intelligence Office of the Armed Forces High Command—16

Greßmann, Hugo (1877–1927): professor of Old Testament theology, Berlin —9

Grey, Sir Edward (1862–1933): British statesman; third baronet and Viscount Grey of Fallodon—9

Griebel, Minna: editor and translator of works by Walter Rauschenbusch —12

Grieg, Edvard Hagerup (1843–1907): Norwegian composer—8

Griffith: canon (England)—15

Grillmeier, Alois (1910–98): German Jesuit professor of dogmatics and history of dogmatics—8

Grimm, Hans (1875–1959): German author; salesman in South Africa for many years—7, 10

Grimme, Adolf (1889–1963): German Social Democrat politician; 1930–33, Prussian minister of culture; member of a resistance group against Nazism —10

Grisebach, Eberhard (1880–1945): German philosopher and educator; 1913–30, teaching responsibilities, Jena; 1931, professor of philosophy and pedagogy, Zürich—1, 2, 3, 10, 11, 12

Gritschke: SS major [*Sturmbannführer*]; 1940, leader of the security service (SD) section, Königsberg—16

Groener, Wilhelm (1867–1939): German politician and military leader—11, 17

Gröger, Mrs: 1931, owner of a parcel of land leased by Bonhoeffer and his students—11

Groos, Karl (1861–1957): professor of philosophy, Basel, Giessen, and Tübingen, where Bonhoeffer studied with him—2, 9

Grosch, Götz (1912–43 [killed in action]): summer 1936, participated in the third Finkenwalde session; 1934–35, headed the Brotherhood of Young Theologians of the Confessing Church, Berlin-Brandenburg; April 1940, drafted into the military—8, 15

Grosch, Rudolf (1875–1959): father of Götz Grosch; secondary school teacher; 1906–37, teacher at the Realgymnasium, Grunewald—8

Groscurth (Großcurth), Heinrich (1898–1943): career military; colonel in the general staff; 1939–40, head of the section for Military Affairs of the Armed Forces High Command; 1942, chief of the general staff of the 11th Army Corps; captured at Stalingrad; March 1943, died there—16

Groß, Wilhelm (1883–1974): Berlin sculptor and painter; student of Otto Lessing in Berlin; from 1906, exhibited in Munich, Berlin, Bremen,

Mannheim, and elsewhere; member of the Berlin-Brandenburg Council of Brethren—12, 14

Grosse, Dr. Aristid von: 1929, Bonhoeffer's fellow traveler on the trip to the United States; nuclear scientist; professor, Columbia University, New York—10

Grosse, Heinrich W.: German Protestant ethicist; professor at the Pastoral Sociological Institute, Hannover—8

Grossmann: pastor of the church in Berlin-Steglitz—12

Grosz, George (1893–1959): anti-Nazi painter and graphic artist; 1932, emigrated to the United States; his work was banned by the Nazis as "degenerate art"—12, 14

Grot, Elisabeth von: from 1934, employed full-time in the business office of the East Prussian Confessing Church, Königsberg; June 1937, temporarily arrested; until December 1947, remained in East Prussia—16

Grote, Wolfgang: lawyer; former assistant to Gerhard Leibholz in Göttingen; took care of financial matters after the Leibholzes' emigration—15, 16

Grotefeld, Stefan: author of work on Friedrich Siegmund-Schultze—12, 16

Grotius, Hugo (1583–1645): Dutch scholar of international law; main work: *De iure belli ac pacis libri tres* (1625)—5, 8

Grubb, Sir Kenneth George, (1900–1980): British theologian, publicist, and ecumenist; 1923, missionary, South America; 1941–46, controller in the British Ministry of Information; 1946, chair of the Church Commission for Internal Affairs, World Council of Churches—16

Gruber, Franz (1787–1863): Austrian composer of the Christmas song "Silent Night" (1818)—10

Grüber, Heinrich Karl Ernst (1891–1975): 1934, pastor, Berlin-Kaulsdorf, and of the Dutch congregation in Berlin; 1933, member of the Pastors' Emergency League; 1937, founder and head of the Protestant relief service for "non-Aryan" Christians ("Grüber office"); 1940, arrested and taken to Sachsenhausen concentration camp and later to Dachau; 1945, church provost, East Berlin; 1949, authorized representative of the council of the Evangelical Church of Germany to the government of the German Democratic Republic—16

Gruchmann, Lothar: German historian of World War II—16

Grude, Gottfried: 1937, pastor, Magdeburg—14

Grude, Werner: Confessing Church pastor, Pomerania—15

Grude-Onnasch, Margret: *see* Onnasch, Margret

Gruehn, Werner Georg Alexander (1887–1961): German theologian and psychologist of religion—12

Gruhl: 1933, senior consistory officer, Berlin—11
Gründel, Ernst Günther (1903–46): German historian and cultural philosopher—12
Gründer, Horst: German ecumenical historian—11
Grundherr, Dr. von: envoy in the Foreign Ministry, political section VI—16
Grundmann, Walter (1906–76): professor of New Testament, Jena; 1939–45, director of the Institute for the Study and Eradication of Jewish Influence on German Religious Life, Eisenach—16
Grüneisen, Karl (1871–1941): Confessing pastor, Berlin-Lichterfelde—12
Grünewald, Matthias (Mathis Nithardt) (ca. 1470–1528): German painter; most famous work was the Isenheim Altar in Colmar—8, 9
Grunow, Richard (1908–68): German pastor and editor; 1935, participated in the first Zingst/Finkenwalde session; 1937, ordination; 1940, pastor, Danzig; after the war, publishing house editor; 1957, editor of *Der Sonntag*, Braunschweig—6, 9, 14, 16
Gruschke: 1933, doctoral student in theology, Berlin—12
Grußendorff, Miss: Bonhoeffer family piano teacher—9
Guardini, Romano (1885–1968): German Catholic theologian and religious philosopher; 1939, under Nazism lost his teaching position in Breslau; after 1945, professor, Tübingen—6, 7, 11
Guddas, Paul: 1926, pastor, Nülten, district of Lötzen/East Prussia, and in Silberbach, district of Mohrungen, from which the police expelled him; 1939–44, worked in the administration of the secretariat of the Pomeranian provincial Council of Brethren, Stettin—16
Guido da Siena: thirteenth-century Italian painter, Sienese school—9
Guillon, Charles François (1883–1965): French Reformed pastor and ecumenist; from 1921, in the French border town Le Chambon-sur-Lignon; from 1931, also mayor there; from 1927, reporting member in the central office of the YMCA in Geneva; in close contact with the Swiss refugee aid organization and the French Cimade (a resistance organization that also helped prisoners); March and September 1941, took part in discussions with Dietrich Bonhoeffer in Geneva—16, 17
Gulbranssen, Trygve (1894–1962): Norwegian novelist—14
Güldenberg, Otto: secondary school teacher, Halle an der Saale—11
Gumprecht, Miss: fiancée of Hermann Thumm—10
Gundert, E.: author of a study of 1 Clement—9
Gunkel, Hermann (1862–1932): professor of Old Testament theology; 1888, received the first of his many graduate degrees from Göttingen; taught in Göttingen, Halle, and Berlin; 1907–20, Giessen; 1920–27, again in Halle; published numerous books and articles and was the first editor of *Die Religion in Geschichte und Gegenwart*; known as the founder of form

criticism; his works on Genesis and Psalms remain definitive works for biblical scholars in those specialties—3, 4, 10, 11, 14, 15

Günther: government counselor and SS major [*Sturmbannführer*] in the Reich Central Security Office; member of the "July 20 special commission" —16

Günther, Georg: German musicologist—17 (for vol. 9)

Günther, Hans Friedrich Karl (1891–1968): German racial theoretician and social anthropologist; 1930, professor, Jena; 1935, Berlin—10

Günther, Walter: author of study of Bonhoeffer's relevance in the Moravian church—5

Gürtler, Paul: author of study on the Church Struggle—16

Gürtner, Franz (1881–1941): lawyer; 1932–41, Reich minister of justice; some in the *Abwehr* resistance circle perceived him to be a sympathetic ally; 1941, died suddenly—6, 13, 14, 15, 16, 17

Gustafson, James M.: U.S. Christian ethicist—6

Gustav, Adolf, crown prince of Sweden (1882–1973): married Louise, née Mountbatten (1889–1965); from 1950, King Gustav VI Adolf of Sweden —16

Güstrow, Dietrich: author of work on Manfred Roeder—8

Guthke: 1932, Berlin pastor—12

Guthrie, William Norman: rector of the Manhattan Episcopal Church St. Mark's in the Bouwerie, 1911–37—10

Gutjahr, Herbert: radio announcer—12

Gutman, Israel: Polish-born historian of the Holocaust—15

Gutmann, Bruno (1876–1966): 1902–38, missionary for the Leipzig Mission among the Chagga at Mount Kilimanjaro—11, 12

Gütt, Arthur (1891–1949): German physician; National Socialist expert on populations and leading advocate of eugenics—6

Guttenberg, Baron Karl Ludwig von and zu (1902–45): estate owner, Salzburg near Neustadt/Saale; editor of the *Weiße Blätter*; September 1939, colleague of Hans von Dohnanyi in the Military Intelligence Office's *Zentralabteilung* (the department that handled foreign policy reports); 1943, transferred for his own protection to Agram, on the staff of General Glaise von Horstenau, the general in charge of Croatia; after July 20, 1944, arrested; April 23/24, 1945, shot to death by the SS—16, 17

"Gypsy" (FP): proposed character in drama—7

Haack (Haag): businessman; one of Bonhoeffer's neighbors at the Barcelona pension—10

Haag, Erich: from winter semester 1919–20, studied philosophy and was a member of the Hedgehog fraternity, Tübingen—9

Haan, Baron von: 1931, delegate from the International Labor Office in Geneva to the conference of the World Alliance for Promoting International Friendship through the Churches in Cambridge—11

Haas, August de: 1931, Reformed pastor, Riffenhausen near Göttingen; 1936, Dresden; 1931, member of the German youth delegation of the World Alliance for Promoting International Friendship through the Churches in Cambridge—11, 12

Haase, Norbert: German military historian—16

Haber, Fritz (1868–1934): professor of physical chemistry, Berlin—10

Habicht, Karl (1868–1937): from 1905, pastor, Berlin—12

Hadrian (Publius Aelius Hadrianus) (117–138 C.E.): Roman emperor; nephew of Trajan—9

Hadrian I, Pope (d. 795 C.E.): 772, elected pope—9

Haeckel, Ernst (1834–1919): zoologist and philosopher of nature—11

Haeften, Hans-Bernd von (1905–44): brother of Werner and Elizabeth von Haeften; confirmed with Bonhoeffer; 1930–33, manager of the Stresemann foundation; from 1933, member of the Confessing Church; 1933, joined the Foreign Ministry; cultural attaché in Copenhagen (renewed contact with Bonhoeffer); 1935, in Vienna; 1937, legation secretary, Bucharest; 1940, reporting legation officer in the cultural section of the Foreign Ministry, Berlin; from 1941, active member of the Kreisau circle; 1943, deputy head of the information section, later of the cultural section in the Foreign Ministry; participated with his brother Werner with preparations for July 20, 1944; arrested immediately after the failed coup; August 15, 1944, executed in Plötzensee—8, 9, 13, 14, 16, 17

Haeften, Werner von (1908–44): brother of Hans Bernd von Haeften; corporate attorney with a Hamburg bank; stationed on the eastern front as a first lieutenant; after receiving a serious wound, became adjutant for Count Stauffenberg with the commander of the reserve army; July 20, 1944, shot to death with Stauffenberg in the courtyard on Bendlerstrasse—9, 16, 17

Haemmerling, Knut: resident manager of the Bonhoeffer Haus, Berlin—11

Haenchen, Ernst (1894–1975): 1927, lecturer, Tübingen; professor of systematic theology, Giessen; November 1933, left the German Christians after the Sports Palace rally; winter 1933–34, worked with Hermann Beyer when the latter was clerical adviser to the Reich Ministry for Church Affairs; 1939–46, professor of New Testament, Münster—13

Haendler, Gustav (1863–1938): 1911–33, general superintendent, Berlin; provost at the St. Nicholas church—10

Haese, Bruno: pastor, Michendorf near Potsdam—15

Häfele, Walter (1900–1935): 1926, pastor, Emmendingen/Baden; vicar for urban ministry; from 1930, pastor, Berlin—12, 13

Hafenreffer, Matthias (1561–1619): representative of post-Concordian Lutheran orthodoxy; university chancellor, Tübingen—9, 12

Hagen, Rosemarie von der, née von Hase: daughter of Hans Karl von Hase —9

Haggai: biblical character—14

Hahn, Hugo (1886–1957): German pastor and church official; 1910, Estonia; 1919 (after expulsion), pastor in Germany; 1930, superintendent, Dresden; 1933, member, Council of Brethren of the Pastors' Emergency League and Reich Council of Brethren; 1934, dismissed from office; 1934, head, Saxon Council of Brethren, member of the Reich Council of Brethren and of the Lutheran Council; 1936, member, council of the Evangelical Lutheran Church of Germany; 1938, expulsion from Saxony; 1939, pastor, Stuttgart; 1947–53, Lutheran bishop of Saxony—14

Hahn, Kurt (1886–1974): 1922–33, influential German educator emphasizing experiential education, founder of the Salem School in Germany until his dismissal from office because of "non-Aryan" lineage; later educator in Scotland—14, 17 (for vol. 13)

Hahn, Otto (1879–1968): prominent German-born chemist—6

Hahn, Traugott (1875–1919): German seminary student shot by Communists in Estonia during the revolution—10

Haldane of Cloan, Richard Burdon, Viscount (1856–1928): during World War I, British statesman—9

Haldeman, Isaac Massey (1845–1933): pastor from 1884–1933, First Baptist Church, Broadway and West 79th, New York City—10

Halder, Franz (1884–1972): career military; 1940, general; 1938–42, chief of the general staff, Army High Command; 1942, dismissed by Hitler; after July 20, 1944, imprisoned in a concentration camp; 1945, liberated from Dachau concentration camp—15, 16, 17

Halem, Nikolaus von (1905–44): businessman; 1938, left legal service and entered business; February 1942, arrested on suspicion of conspiratorial contacts; October 9, 1944, executed—16

Halifax, Lord Edward (Edward Lindley Wood; 1881–1959): British statesman; 1925–34, known as Lord Edward Irwin; 1926–31, viceroy of India; 1938–40, foreign minister and ambassador to the United States—10 (referred to in that volume as Lord Irwin), 15, 16

Halkenhäuser, Johannes: German church historian—5

Hall, Thomas Cuming (1858–1936): 1898, professor of Christian ethics, Union Theological Seminary, New York; 1921, professor, Göttingen—10, 15

Hallesby, Ole (1879–1961): member of Norwegian confessional movement —16

Ham: biblical character—12

Hamann, Johann Georg (1730–88): German religious thinker; one of the fathers of the German *Sturm und Drang* movement; proponent of religious immediacy, attacked the religious rationalism of the Enlightenment; called the "Magus in the North"—1, 11

Hamel, Johannes: member of the brotherhood of assistant pastors and vicars of the province of Saxony, Confessing Church; academic assistant with Wolfgang Staemmler; 1946–53, student chaplain, Halle; lecturer and later rector of the theological institute and catechetical higher seminary, Naumburg—14, 15

Hamilton, William: U.S. theologian—6

Hammelsbeck, Oskar (1899–1975): religious educator and theologian; 1927, director of the adult education center, Saarbrücken; 1934, dismissed for political reasons; 1937, head of the catechetical seminar of the Confessing Church, Berlin, and consultant on religious education in the Council of the Old Prussian Confessing Church; 1942–43, worked with Dietrich Bonhoeffer on the "*primus usus legis*" committee of the Old Prussian Council of Brethren; 1944, ordination and pastor, Falkenhagen (Lippe); 1946–59, professor and rector of the Pedagogical Academy, Wuppertal; also lecturer at the Wuppertal seminary; chair of the Association for Education and Instruction in the Council of the Evangelical Church of Germany; advocate of the unity of a person's lifelong "religious instruction"—14, 15, 16, 17

Hammersen, Nicolai: author of work on German resistance—12

Hammerstein-Equord, Baron Kurt von (1878–1943): career military; general; 1930–34, chief of the army command staff; 1939, commander in chief of the army section A in the West; participated in plans for a military coup—16

Hampe, Johann Christoph: German author of work on Bonhoeffer's poetry —8

Hananiah: biblical character—9

Hancock, Eric Gray: 1934, at the behest of Jürgen Winterhager, sent Bonhoeffer a pacifist book for his birthday—13

Hancock, Sir Patrick Francis (1914–74): British diplomat; from January 1942, second secretary in the Central Department of the British Foreign Office—16

Handel, Georg Friedrich (1685–1759): composer—8

Handy, Robert T. (1918–2009): professor emeritus of church history, Union Theological Seminary, New York—10

Haniel, Franz (1779–1868): founder of the Rhine Iron Works, which later expanded into a consortium that included companies that refined and manufactured steel, as well as several companies involved with trade and shipping—9

Hannah: biblical character—14

Hans (FP): character in the drama, father and doctor; *see also* Brake (FP), Hans—7

Hansen, Conrad (1906–2002): renowned German pianist; taught at the Berlin Conservatory during the 1930s—8

Hansen, Elisabeth, née Brückner (1883–1941): Dietrich Bonhoeffer's second cousin, daughter of Karl and Margarethe Brückner; September 26, 1903, married Lieutenant General Karl Hansen; mother of Ottomar and Klaus—9

Hansen, Wilhelm: 1928, ordained, Rehme/Oeynhausen-South; 1930, German pastor in Manchester, England; 1934, Bradford—13

Hanstein, Joachim-Hans: from Krumpe, district of Halle; 1938–39, participated in the collective pastorate in Groß-Schlönwitz—15

Harbsmeier, Götz (1910–79): pastor, Hannover regional church—8

Hardegen, Agnes-Marie: fiancée of Wolfgang Georgii—15

Hardeland, Otto (1853–1926): author of the 1913 catechetical work *Luthers Katechismusgedanken in ihrer Entwicklung bis zum Jahre 1529* (The development of Luther's understanding of the catechism until 1529)—10

Hardenberg, Baron Friedrich von (pen name: Novalis) (1772–1801): poet of early Romanticism—8

Hardenberg, Prince Karl-August von (1750–1822): Prussian statesman, government official, ultimately foreign minister and, in 1810, chancellor; pursued policy of social reform, including the emancipation of the serfs and the Jews in 1812; Prussian representative at the Congress of Vienna—10

Harder, Günther Heinrich Reinhold (1902–72): pastor, Fehrbellin; 1933, cofounder of the Pastors' Emergency League; 1936–72, lecturer and professor of New Testament at the Confessing seminary, Berlin; 1941, convicted in collective trial against the examination board of the Old Prussian Union Council of Brethren; 1942–43, together with Dietrich Bonhoeffer on the "*primus usus legis*" committee of the Old Prussian Council of Brethren—8, 14

Harder, Hans Adolf: lawyer—15

Harder, Hartmut: son of Hans Adolf Harder—15

Harding, Inge: 1933, theology student, Berlin—12

Hardy, Edward: patristics scholar; author of works on Christology—6

Harhausen, Christoph Rudolf Constantin (1909–41): from Berlin-Brandenburg; 1932–33, theology student, Berlin, member of the circle of students around Bonhoeffer; 1935, vicar, Dahme/Mark; 1935–36, participated in the second Finkenwalde session; Confessing Church pastor, Guben; August 26, 1941, killed in action on the eastern front—12, 14, 15, 16

Häring: son of the Tübingen theology professor Dr. Theodor Häring—17 (for vol. 9)

Häring, Theodor (1848–1928): 1895, professor of systematic theology. Tübingen—1, 14, 16

Harkness, Georgia (1891–1974): U.S. Methodist theologian and ecumenist —15

Harleß, Adolf von (1806–79): German (Bavarian) Lutheran theologian—6

Harling, Otto von (1866–1954): one of the leading German Protestants in the mission to convert Jews to Christianity—12

Harms, Hans Heinrich: 1934, theology student, Göttingen; 1960–67, senior pastor, Hamburg; 1967, bishop, Oldenburg—13

Harms, Ludwig (1808–65): 1849, pastor, Hermannsburg—14

Harnack, Adolf von (1851–1930): German Protestant theologian; son of Theodosius Harnack; 1876, professor of church history, Leipzig; 1879, Giessen; 1886, Marburg; from 1888, Berlin; 1890, member of the Prussian Academy of Science; 1892, involved in a dispute (initiated against Harnack) concerning the Apostles' Creed; 1905–21, general director of the Prussian State Library; 1911, cofounder and first president of the Kaiser Wilhelm Society for the Advancement of the Sciences; 1914, ennobled; researched the history and doctrines of the early church; influential church historian and liberal theologian; Bonhoeffer already knew Harnack as a neighbor in Grunewald, attended his seminar, and delivered the student eulogy at the memorial after Harnack's death—1, 2, 3, 4, 6, 7, 8, 9, 10, 11, 12, 13, 14, 15, 16

Harnack, Axel von (1895–1974): son of Adolf von Harnack and friend of Dietrich Bonhoeffer; library official at the Prussian National Library, Berlin; from 1944, Tübingen; from 1947, lecturer in library science—9

Harnack, Theodosius (1817–89): father of Adolf von Harnack; 1848, professor of practical and, later, systematic theology, Dorpat; 1853, Erlangen; 1856, Dorpat—12, 14, 15

Harnack, Wolf Alexander Oskar Ernst von (1888–1945): lawyer; son of Adolf von Harnack; 1919, joined the Social Democrat Party; government president of Merseburg; 1933, dismissed; worked as a textile representative; ultimately worked in registration of the graves of famous persons in Berlin cemeteries; contacts with Beck, Goerdeler, Leber, and Klaus Bonhoeffer; after July 20, 1944, arrested; March 5, 1945, executed—16

Harnisch, Wilhelm (1887–1960): from 1931, pastor at the Samaritan church, Berlin-Friedrichshain; member of the Berlin Council of Brethren—12

Harris, Erdman: professor, Union Theological Seminary, New York—15

Harris, Henry Silton (1926–2007): British-born Hegel scholar; professor of philosophy, York University, Canada—11

Harrison, Geoffrey Wedgwood (1908–90): private secretary in Parliament; undersecretary of state, British Foreign Office—16, 17

Harteck, Paul (1902–85): chemist; friend of Karl-Friedrich Bonhoeffer; 1934, professor of physical chemistry, Hamburg; after 1951, in the United States—8, 10

Hartenstein, Karl (1894–1952): Württemberg theologian; 1926, director, Basel Mission Society; 1941, seminary preacher and prelate, Stuttgart; 1948, member, Council of the Evangelical Church of Germany—16

Hartl, Albert: 1933, Catholic religious educator; 1934, as a relative of Himmler, receives research position in the central SS headquarters; SS major (*Sturmbannführer*) and leader of the group IV B (ideological and racial opponents), Reich Central Security Office; 1941–42, head of an SD strike force, Kiev; after 1945, interned in the Hammelburg prison camp—16

Hartmann, Eduard von (1842–1906): German philosopher, founder of the contemporary science of vitalism—6, 11

Hartmann, Friedrich (1880–1958): from 1926, pastor in Berlin—12

Hartmann, Hans: German pastor; advocate of socialism and pacifism during the 1920s—12

Hartmann, Nicolai (1882–1950): from 1931, German philosopher and professor, Berlin; after 1946, Göttingen; representative of "realistic ontology" —2, 6, 8, 10, 16

Hartmann, Paul (1889–1977): German stage and film actor—16

Harttmann, Karl Friedrich (1743–1815): German hymnist and theologian; Schiller's teacher—6

Hase, Ada Amalie von, née Schwarz (1881–1956): married to Hans von Hase —9

Hase, Benedikt Karl August von (Uncle Bubi) (1890–1979): son of Karl Alfred and Clara von Hase; painter, artisan, etcher; youngest brother of Paula Bonhoeffer; 1914–19, French prisoner of war; required psychiatric care and was supported financially by his siblings—8, 9, 16

Hase, Carl: *see* Hase, Karl August von

Hase, Dorothea von (1911–63): Bonhoeffer's cousin; daughter of Hans and Ada von Hase; married name Schröter—9, 10

Hase, Elisabeth von (1872–1945): Bonhoeffer's aunt, sister of Paula Bonhoeffer, daughter of Karl Alfred and Klara von Hase; missing after the February 1945 bombing of Dresden—8, 9, 10, 14, 15, 16

Hase, Frieda von (1849–1943): married to chief staff physician Paul von Hase (1840–1918); mother of Karl Paul Immanuel von Hase—8

Hase, Georg von (1878–1971): publisher and bookseller—10

Hase, Hans Christoph Karl Eduard von (1907–2005): Bonhoeffer's cousin; son of Hans and Ada von Hase; from 1930, Dietrich Bonhoeffer's successor as academic assistant to Wilhelm Lütgert; 1933–34, fellowship, Union Theological Seminary, New York; 1934, pastor, Berlin-Wilmersdorf; 1934–37, military chaplain, Jüterborg; 1937, Rostock; September 23, 1943, married Clara, née Schwalfenberg; 1947, pastor, Marburg; 1954, Herford; 1957–73, head of the central office, Diaconical Welfare and Social Agency of the Evangelical Church of Germany, Stuttgart; December 15, 1983, married Agnes, née Carrière; father of Christoph, Hans Michael, Ragnhild (married name Fiebig), Wolf Rüdiger, Ulrike (married name Siberski-von Hase), and Dietrich; coeditor of *DBW* 10—2, 4, 7, 8, 9, 10, 11, 12, 13, 15, 16

Hase, Hans Karl Paul Stanislaus von (1873–1958): son of Karl Alfred and Clara von Hase; brother of Paula Bonhoeffer; uncle and godfather of Dietrich Bonhoeffer; April 30, 1906, married Ada, née Schwarz; father of Hans Christoph, Klara (married name Pernice), Dorothea (married name Schröter), Renate (married name Ruhenstroth-Bauer), Rosemarie (married name von der Hagen), Traute (married name de Vasconcellos), and Walter; pastor and superintendent in Großwandriß, in Waldau, district of Liegnitz (today Legnical); from 1925, Frankfurt an der Oder—8, 9, 10

Hase, Hans-Jürgen von: second cousin of Dietrich Bonhoeffer; mid-January 1933, emigrated to southwest Africa, where he was at first a civil servant; 1940–46, interned in camps in South Africa; 1947–75, farmer in Namibia —7

Hase, Johann Georg von (1926–1957): son of Benedikt von Hase; technician of high-frequency physics—8

Hase, Karl Alfred von (1842–1914): German theologian, son of Karl August and Paula von Hase; grandfather of Dietrich Bonhoeffer; July 19, 1871, married Clara, née Countess Kalckreuth; father of Elisabeth, Hans, Hannah (married name Countess von der Goltz), Paula (married name Bonhoeffer), Gottfried, and Benedikt; 1889, court preacher, Potsdam; 1894, high consistory council and professor of theology, Breslau; wrote a history of the von Hase family, *Unsre Hauschronik*—7, 9

Hase, Karl August (von) (1800–1890): father of Karl Alfred von Hase; German theologian and church historian; as a dueling club fraternity member, incarcerated for eleven months on the Hohenasperg; after 1830,

professor of church history, Jena; knighted in 1833 but never used the title; Real Privy Councilor (an honorary title)—1, 3, 6, 7, 8, 9, 10, 14, 16

Hase, Klara von: daughter of Hans Karl von Hase; married name Pernice —9

Hase, Klara von: wife of Hans Christoph von Hase—15

Hase, Klara von, née Countess von Kalckreuth (1851–1903): daughter of the (painter) Stanislaus Count von Kalckreuth and Anna Eleonore, née Cauer; sister of Pauline Countess von Kalckreuth and Helene Countess Yorck von Wartenburg; married to Karl Alfred von Hase—10

Hase, Margarete (Deta) von, née von Funck (1898–1968): wife of Major General Paul von Hase—8, 16, 17

Hase, Paul (Karl Paul Immanuel) von (1885–1944): career military officer; cousin of Paula Bonhoeffer; 1940, major general and military commander of Berlin; 1944, general; July 20, 1944, participated in the attempted coup; August 8, 1944, executed in Plotzensee—8, 16, 17

Hase, Pauline von: *see* Bonhoeffer, Pauline

Hase, Pine von: married Benedikt von Hase, the brother of Bonhoeffer's mother—13

Hase, Renate von: *see* Ruhenstroth, Renate

Hase, Rosemarie von: *see* Hagen, Rosemarie von der

Hase, Traute von: *see* Vasconcellos, Traute de

Hase, Walter von: younger brother of Hans Christoph von Hase; killed in action in World War II—11

Haser, Annie: *see* Oster, Annie

Häsler, Alfred A.: Swiss Protestant official who worked with refugees—16

Hasse (or Hesse), Otto: one of Bonhoeffer's Berlin confirmands—13

Hassell, Ulrich von (1881–1944): government official and diplomat; 1932, German ambassador, Rome; 1938, ambassador for special duty; with Goerdeler, leading participant in the civilian resistance; July 29, 1944, arrested; September 8, 1944, executed—16, 17

Hauck, Albert (1845–1918): professor of church history, Erlangen and Leipzig—9

Hauer, Jakob Wilhelm (1881–1962): German religious scholar; 1906–11, missionary for the Basel Mission, India; 1925, professor of Indology and religious studies, Marburg; 1927–49, Tübingen; 1933–36, cofounder and head until his resignation of the German Faith movement, a neopagan coalition of various groups committed to Germanic or "Aryan" ideologies; controversial because of his postwar apologetics for Nazism—6, 9, 14

Hauff, Wilhelm (1802–27): German author of historical and satirical novels, fairy tales, stories, poems—8, 13

Hauptmann, Gerhart (1862–1946): German novelist, dramatist, and poet—8, 9, 12

Hausamann, Hans: officer in the news service of the Swiss army; September 1940, initiated the founding of the "national resistance action"—16

Hauschild, Wolf-Dieter: professor of patristics and church history, Münster—15

Hausmann, Julie von (1825–1901): hymnist—10, 14

Hausmann, Manfred (1898–1986): writer—16

Hauwald, Mr.: *see* Gauwald

Havaz, Andrea: staff member, Conference of European Churches—13

Havenstein, Martin (1871–1945): Bonhoeffer's philosophy teacher; his best-known work was on Nietzsche as educator—9

Haydn, Franz Joseph (1732–1809): Austrian composer—7, 9

Headlam, Arthur Cayley (1862–1947): 1923–45, bishop of Gloucester; 1922–45, head of the Council on Foreign Relations of the Church of England; leading member of Faith and Order—13

Headlam-Morley, Sir James-Wycliffe (1863–1929): British political historian; student of Treitschke and Hans Delbrück; wrote history of the World War I peace settlement—9

Hechler, Hermann (1885–1977): Confessing Church pastor, Heppenheim—14

Hecht, Siegfried: 1931, pastor, Dorschhymmen (East Prussia); member of the Thuringian German Christians—16

Heckel, Theodor (1894–1967): pastor and church official; 1922, pastor, Munich-Solln; 1925, secondary school teacher, Erlangen; 1928, senior consistory officer, German Evangelical Church Federation office, Berlin; 1933, cofounder, Young Reformation movement; February 21, 1934, appointed bishop and director (until 1945) of the newly instituted Church Foreign Office of the German Evangelical Church; 1939–45, director of the Protestant relief organization for internees and prisoners of war; 1950–64, church dean, Munich—8, 11, 12, 13, 14, 16, 17

Heckscher, Ruth Roberta (Raba): daughter of Walter and Spes Stahlberg; author of various publications; wife of the physician Helmut Ripke in Schreiberhau/Silesia; 1986, emigration to Israel; 1989, conversion to Judaism, taking the name of her great-grandfather Wilhelm Moritz Heckscher, son of a rabbi and Hamburg delegate in the Frankfurt Church of St. Paul in 1848—8, 16

Hecuba: in Greek mythology, queen and wife of King Priam—17 (for vol. 9)

Hedin, Sven (1865–1952): Swedish scholar of Asiatic studies; sympathetic to "Aryan" ideologies—8

Hedinger, Ulrich: German Protestant theologian, author of works on Barth and dogmatics—8

Heermann, Johann (1585–1647): German hymnist—5, 14

Hegel, Georg Wilhelm Friedrich (1770–1831): German idealist philosopher; professor of philosophy at a number of German universities, including Jena, Heidelberg and Berlin—1, 2, 3, 4, 5, 6, 8, 9, 10, 11, 12, 14, 15, 16, 17

Heide, Mrs.: Bonhoeffer's landlady in Berlin when he was at Zion Church —11

Heidegger, Martin (1889–1976): German existentialist philosopher; 1923, professor of philosophy, Marburg; 1928–45, professor, Freiburg; after 1933, first National Socialist rector of Freiburg university; 1945–51, dismissed and forbidden to teach by the Allied occupation forces—2, 3, 4, 6, 7, 8, 10, 11, 12, 15, 16

Heideking, Jürgen: German historian of the Third Reich—16

Heidelmeyer, Wolfgang: German legal scholar and expert on human rights —6

Heidenhain, Else ("Hainchen"): close acquaintance of the Bonhoeffer family; sister of Martin Heidenhein, one of Karl Bonhoeffer's colleagues in Breslau whose son, who died young, was an assistant to Karl Bonhoeffer —8, 13

Heidenhain, Hilde: daughter of Martin Heidenhain—9

Heidenhain, Martin (1864–1949): professor of anatomy, Breslau; 1907, professor, Tübingen; Bonhoeffer family friend—8, 9

Heidmann: June 18, 1940, mentioned by Dietrich Bonhoeffer during a visitation in Pokraken, district of Tilsit; not otherwise identified—16

Heienbrock, Mr.: secondary school teacher, Berlin-Steglitz; head of the religious educational working group of the German section of the World Alliance for Promoting International Friendship through the Churches; leading contributor to the periodical *Die evangelische Pädagogik*—11

Heiler, Friedrich (1892–1967): professor of the comparative history of religions, Marburg; originally Catholic; 1919, converted to Protestantism in Sweden under the influence of Nathan Söderblom—1, 9, 10, 11, 16

Heim, Ernst Ludwig (Old Heim) (1747–1834): Berlin physician—8

Heim, Karl (1874–1958): 1899–1903, secretary, German Christian Student Association; 1914, professor of systematic theology, Münster; 1916–18, student chaplain for soldiers, prisoners of war, and the wounded; 1920–39, professor, Tübingen; 1948, Evangelical Academy of Bad Boll—1, 2, 6, 8, 9, 10, 11, 12, 14, 15, 16

Heimann, Eduard (1889–1967): 1925, professor of economics, Hamburg; 1933, emigrated to the United States—12

Heimbucher, Martin: studied Protestant theology in Göttingen and Mainz; research on the Protestant Church Struggle; from 1988, pastor in the regional church of Lippe; 1992, doctorate, Göttingen, with a dissertation on Dietrich Bonhoeffer; publications on Bonhoeffer, peace issues, and theological perspectives on ecology; one of the editors of *DBW* 13—12, 13

Heine, Heinrich (1797–1856): German poet; 1825, converted from Judaism to Christianity; 1831, left Germany for Paris—7, 11, 12, 14

Heine, Leopold: professor of medicine, Breslau; Dietrich Bonhoeffer's godfather—9

Heinecke, Karl (1872–1945): from 1914, pastor, Berlin—12

Heinemann, Gustav: Confessing Church lawyer; politician; 1969–74, president of the Federal Republic of Germany—9

Heiniger, Mr.: teacher in Berlin; on the examination board for secondary schools—9

Heinrich (FP): character in the drama written by Bonhoeffer and published in *Fiction from Tegel Prison*—6, 7

Heinrich II: Count Palatine of the Rheinish Franks—11

Heinrich IV (Henry IV) (1050–1106): from 1054, German king and Holy Roman emperor—6, 8

Heinrich V (1081–1125): 1105–25, German king; 1111–25, Holy Roman emperor—9

Heinrich VI (1165–97): Holy Roman emperor and German king; father of Friedrich II—9

Heinrich von Laufenberg (ca. 1390–1458): medieval spiritual poet—8

Heintze, Johannes: from 1928, pastor, Paul Gerhardt foundation, Berlin-Adlershof—12

Heinz: involved with financial matters related to the Leibholz family and their emigration; not otherwise identified—16

Heise, Hans-Wilhelm (1909–41): 1934, Wittenberg preachers' seminary; October 28, 1934, one of the signers of the protest letter from the preachers' seminary in Wittenberg to Reich Bishop Müller; leading member of the Brotherhood of Assistant Pastors and Vicars in the province of Saxony; Confessing Church pastor, Burg near Magdeburg; 1941, killed in action on the eastern front—16

Heisenberg, Werner Karl (1901–76): German physicist; 1927–41, professor, Leipzig; 1941–45, director, Kaiser Wilhelm Institute; 1945–76, director, Max Planck Institute; known especially for development of quantum mechanics and the principle of indeterminacy (1927); 1932, Nobel Prize in Physics—15

Heitmann, Ludwig (1880–1953): leading figure in the Berneuchen movement and coauthor of the Berneuchen Book—11, 17 (for vol. 13)

Heitmüller, Wilhelm (1869–1926): 1908, professor of New Testament theology, Marburg; 1920, Bonn; 1923, Tübingen; with Johannes Weiß and Paul Wernle, one of the leading representatives of the history of religions school—9, 11

Helbig, Georg: Luther and New Testament scholar—14

Helbig, Heinrich: 1931, pastor, Stralsund—14

Helbing, Lothar (pseudonym of Wolfgang Frommel) (1902–86): German theologian and writer whose books were banned under Nazism; member of the Stefan George literary circle—6

Held, Heinrich (1897–1957): 1930–46, pastor, Essen-Rüttenscheid; cofounder of the Rhineland Confessing Church; member of the council of the Evangelical Church of the Old Prussian Union; temporary chair of the Old Prussian Council of Brethren; 1946, superintendent and High Church Council member; 1948–57, president of the Rhineland Church—15, 16

Held, Robert: lawyer and tax consultant; studied law, Tübingen and Berlin; 1924–25, in Berlin during winter semester and summer semester 1925—9, 10, 17 (for vol. 9)

Helen (of Troy): character in Greek mythology; daughter of Zeus and Leda, and wife of Menelaus—8, 17 (for vol. 9)

Helfferich, Karl (1872–1924): German economist; after 1920, president of the German National Peoples' Party (DVNP); leading member of the conservative opposition in the Weimar Republic; after World War I, opposed all attempts to come to a peaceful understanding between Germany and the Allies—9

Hellbardt, Hans (1910–44): April 1935, inspector at the preachers' seminary and lecturer in Old Testament at the seminary, Elberfeld; 1935–38, lecturer at the seminary, Wuppertal; December 1939, military service; died while a prisoner of war in southern France—14

Hellmann, Gerhard: from Berlin; 1935, participated in the first Zingst/Finkenwalde session; pastor, Wustermark/Osthavelland—15

Hello, Ernest (1828–85): French author, mystic—5, 6, 15

Hellpach, Willy (1877–1955): psychologist and politician; 1911, professor, Karlsruhe; member of the board of directors of the German Democratic Party; 1922, government minister, Baden; 1924, governmental president of Baden; 1925, candidate for Reich president of Germany—9

Hellwig: businessman in Skaisgirren, East Prussia; June 20, 1940, Dietrich Bonhoeffer visited him—16

Helmbold, Ludwig (1532–98): wrote Latin poetry and hymns in German —15

Helmlinger: 1934, designated as a French delegate to the Bruay conference —13

Helmreich, Ernst Christian: U.S. church historian and professor; author of work on Church Struggle—6, 11, 12, 14, 15, 16

Heman: hymnist of Psalm 88—5

Hemingway, Ernest (1899–1961): U.S. author—16

Hengstenberg, Ernst Wilhelm (1802–69): Protestant theologian; 1824, post-doctoral lecturing qualification in humanities; 1826, professor of theology, Berlin; from 1827, editor of the *Evangelische Kirchenzeitung*—11, 14

Henheik, Paul: Confessing Church pastor, Lagendorf near Salzwedel; Eberhard Bethge served as his vicar—14, 15, 16

Henke, Josef: coauthor of work on the Bundesarchiv—8

Henkys, Jürgen: Protestant theologian; studied in Wuppertal, Göttingen, Heidelberg, and Bonn; 1954, assistant pastor, Gross Mehßow, Niederlausitz; 1956–65, assistant pastor, director of studies and instructor, preachers' seminary, Havel, Brandenburg, and pastor at the cathedral there; 1965, doctorate in practical theology; professor of practical theology, Protestant theological institute, Berlin-Brandenburg; 1991, professor, Humboldt University; publications on practical theology, Bible study, hymnody, and Bonhoeffer's prison poetry; editor, *DBW* 14—7, 8, 13, 14, 15

Henne, Eugen (ca. 1890–1970): butcher; member of the congregational council, German Reformed St. Paul's Church, London; board member of the German Seamen's Mission in Great Britain; trustee of the Dietrich Bonhoeffer Church; awarded the Bundesverdienstkreuz (the highest German governmental honor for civilians) for his engagement on behalf of German Jewish refugees during the Third Reich—13

Henne, Gottlieb (1887–1956): 1920–56, leading member, St. Paul's German Reformed Church, London; 1933, member of the parish election committee—8, 12, 13, 14, 15

Henne, Miss: not otherwise identified—15

Hennecke, Edgar (1865–1951): 1895–1935, pastor, Betheln near Hannover; editor of New Testament apocryphal writings—4, 10, 14

Henrici: mentioned in 1933 letter from Théodore de Félice; not otherwise identified—12

Henriod, Henry-Louis (1887–1970): Swiss Reformed theologian; studied theology in Neuchatel, Marburg, and Basel; 1915, foreign secretary, British Student Christian Federation; 1920, general secretary, World Student Christian Federation, World Alliance for Promoting International

Friendship through the Churches, and Life and Work; 1931, after the Cambridge conference, secretary of the World Alliance's ecumenical youth commission (whose three secretaries included Bonhoeffer); from 1932, general secretary of the World Alliance and until 1938 of the Ecumenical Council for Life and Work; September 1933, participated in the Sofia conference; 1946–51, managing director, Ecumenical Institute of Bossey near Geneva—4, 11, 12, 13, 14, 16, 17

Henry V: *see* Heinrich V

Henry VI: *see* Heinrich VI

Henry VIII (1491–1547): from 1509, English king; 1534, severed England from the Roman Catholic Church by declaring himself head of the English church; papal bull of excommunication led the king to join Protestantism—6

Hensel, Rudolf (1911–42): seminarian from Pomerania; 1937, participated in the fifth Finkenwalde session; 1938, "legalized"; 1942, missing in action in Russia—15

Heppe, Heinrich (1820–79): theologian; defender of the Reformed confession in Hesse against Vilmar (A. F. C. Vilmar) Lutheranism—14, 16

Hera: Greek goddess; spouse of Zeus—8

Heracles: in Greek mythology, divine hero—17 (for vol. 9)

Heraclitus (also Heracleitus) (ca. 535–455 B.C.E.): Greek philosopher—10, 17 (for vol. 9)

Herbart, Johann Friedrich (1767–1841): philosopher and educator—14

Herberg: chair, congregational council, and head of the German club in Barcelona—10

Herberger, Valerius (1562–1627): schoolmaster and pastor, Fraustadt; author of Protestant hymns—16

Herbert, A. G.: Old Testament scholar—17 (for vol. 13)

Herbert, Edward Lord of Cherbury (1583–1648): British philosopher, founder of a religious philosophy not dependent on Christianity—8, 11

Herbert, Karl: German author of work on the Church Struggle—15

Herbst, Wilhelm (1891–1957): from 1929, pastor, Elisabeth Deaconess Home, Berlin—12

Hercules: character in Greek mythology—6, 7

Herder, Johann Gottfried von (1744–1803): theologian, philosopher, writer —3, 8, 14

Herman, Nikolaus (1500–1561): schoolmaster and cantor, Joachimsthal; author of two collections of hymns with tunes he composed that were intended for household use in replacement of profane songs—15

Hermann, Rudolf (1887–1962): 1923, professor of systematic theology, Breslau; 1926, Greifswald; 1953, Humboldt University, Berlin—12, 14

Hermas (second century C.E.): Christian author of a penitential sermon in the form of an apocalypse, *The Shepherd of Hermas*—9

Hermelink, Heinrich: German church historian—16

Hermes: Greek god of travelers—8

Hermle, Siegfried: German church historian—17 (for vol. 12)

Hermogenes: biblical character—15

Herntrich, Volkmar (1908–58): 1932, pastor and university instructor, Kiel; 1934, withdrawal of the *venia legendi* (authorization to teach at university after postdoctoral lecturing qualification); 1934–39, lecturer in Old Testament, theological college in Bethel (until its closure); 1940, head of the Burckhardt House, Berlin-Dahlem; 1942, senior pastor; 1949, professor of Old Testament, seminary in Hamburg; 1956–58, bishop of Hamburg; 1958, killed in an accident—14

Herod: biblical character—14, 15, 16

Herod Agrippa: biblical character—15

Herrenbrück, Walter: regional church superintendent, Reformed Church; council member, Evangelical Church of Germany—6, 8

Herrmann, Johannes Hugo: German pastor; 1919, ordination; 1920, pastor, Groß-Nossin, Pomerania; 1925, pastor, Johannesburg, South Africa; 1955, retired—13

Herrmann, Wilhelm (1846–1922): German Protestant theologian; 1879–1917, professor of systematic theology, Marburg; teacher of Rudolf Bultmann, Karl Barth, and others—2, 4, 6, 10, 11, 12, 16

Hertzler, Joyce Oramel (1895–1975): professor of sociology, University of Nebraska—12

Herwegen, Ildefons (1874–1946): Benedictine monk and liturgical scholar —10

Herzlieb, Minna (Wilhelmine; nicknamed "Minchen") (1789–1865): adopted daughter of the Jena publisher Friedrich Frommann; in 1807, Goethe was for a time passionately attracted to her; model for Ottilie in Goethe's novel *Elective Affinities*—8

Herzog, Ernst: from 1927, pastor, Berlin—12

Heschel, Susannah: Eli Black Professor of Jewish Studies, Dartmouth College —15, 16

Hess, Rudolf Walter Richard (1894–1987): National Socialist politician; 1924, Hitler's secretary; 1933, Reich minister; 1935, head of the party chancellery in Munich and "representative of the führer"; 1941, prisoner of war after voluntary flight to England; 1946, sentenced in Nuremberg to life in prison—14, 16

Hesse, Helmut (1916–43): son of the Elberfeld pastor Hermann Hesse; 1935, studied theology; ordained to the ministry in Barmen; 1943, arrested (as was his father); died in the Dachau concentration camp—16

Hesse, Hermann (1877–1962): German poet and novelist; 1943, blacklisted by National Socialists; 1946, Nobel Laureate in Literature—9, 10

Hesse, Hermann Albert (1877–1957): 1902, pastor, Duisburg; 1909, Bremen; 1916–46, Wuppertal-Elberfeld; from 1929, director of the Reformed preachers' seminary there; April–June 1933, Reformed representative of the German Evangelical Church Federation ("Kapler committee" for reforming the German Evangelical Church); 1934, member, Reich Council of Brethren; 1934–46, moderator of the Reformed Alliance; 1943, imprisoned in the Dachau concentration camp—12, 13, 14, 15, 16, 17

Hesselbacher, Karl (1871–1943): pastor, author of several volumes of sermons; representative of what was known as the "village sermon"—14

Hettler, Friedrich Hermann: biographer of Josef Müller—8

Heuner, Fritz: 1919–35, pastor, Eichlinghofen; 1935–61, superintendent, Dortmund; member, Westphalian Council of Brethren; arrested several times—15

Heusen: New York acquaintance of Bonhoeffer and Richard Ern—10

Heuß, Theodor (1884–1963): German statesman; early member of the Friedrich Naumann circle; 1920–33, lecturer, Institute for Politics, Berlin; forbidden to publish under the National Socialist regime; 1946, cofounder of the Free Democratic Party (FDP), helped draft the basic constitution of the Federal Republic of Germany; 1949–59, federal president of Germany—6, 12

Heussi, Karl (1879–1961): German church historian, Jena; his textbook on church history remains in use today—9, 10

Heyde, Werner (1902–64): German physician and, under Nazism, SS physician; 1939, professor of neurology and psychiatry, Würzburg; 1939–42, directed the "euthanasia" program; 1946, escaped en route to interrogation in Nuremberg; medical and consulting practice in Flensburg under a pseudonym, "Dr. Fritz Sawade"; November 1959, surrendered to a Frankfurt court; February 1964, as the main defendant in the largest postwar "euthanasia" trial, hanged himself in his cell five days before the trial began—6

Heydorn, Adolf Frederick: church council member of the Sydenham congregation in London—12, 13

Heydrich, Reinhard (1904–42): National Socialist politician; 1931, joined the NSDAP and the SS; July 1932, head of the Security Service of the SS;

1936, also head of the Security Police (Gestapo and criminal police); 1933, head of the political section, Munich police administration; head of the political police, Reich Ministry of the Interior; 1939, director, Reich Central Security Office; 1941, commissioned by Göring with the "final solution to the Jewish question"; autumn 1941, acting Reich Protector in Bohemia and Moravia; June 4, 1942, assassinated in Prague—14, 15, 16, 17

Heyse: young theologian from Saxony; 1941, killed in action on the eastern front; August 15, 1941, mentioned in the Finkenwalde newsletter—16

Hezekiah: biblical character—15

Hielscher, Friedrich (1902–90): unorthodox German conservative nationalist, influenced by Nietzsche—12

Hieronymus: *see* Jerome

Higgins, David: U.S. translator; translated part of *DBWE* 12—12

Hilberg, Raul (1926–2007): professor emeritus of political science, University of Vermont; author of numerous works on the Holocaust—15

Hilbert, Gerhard (1868–1936): pastor and professor of practical theology; lost his pastorate under the German Christian church government in Saxony—1

Hilde (FP): character in the novel—7

Hildebrand, Klaus: German historian; author of works on the Third Reich—12, 15

Hildebrand, Walther (1892–1975): 1924–48, pastor in Berlin-Lichterfelde—12

Hildebrandt, Bärbel: *see* Kempner, Bärbel

Hildebrandt, Franz (1909–85): German pastor and close friend of Dietrich Bonhoeffer; 1927, met Dietrich Bonhoeffer; 1931, doctoral work and vicar assignment; 1933, assistant pastor, Klein-Machnow, Berlin; September 1933, resigned after the "Brown Synod"; until January 1934, with Dietrich Bonhoeffer in the parsonage, London; 1934, assistant to Martin Niemöller, Berlin-Dahlem; 1935–37, lecturer at the Confessing seminary, Berlin; 1937, emigrated to England after brief imprisonment; 1938, assistant pastor, St. George's, London; 1939–46, pastor to German Protestant refugees in Cambridge; 1946–51, Methodist minister, Cambridge; 1953, professor of theology, Drew University, Madison, New Jersey; 1968, left the Methodist conference; 1969–83, chaplain, Marie Curie Fairmile Nursing Home, Edinburgh, Scotland—4, 6, 7, 8, 10, 11, 12, 13, 14, 15, 16

Hildebrandt, Helmut: 1932, assistant pastor, 1933, pastor, Klein Kessel, district of Johannisburg (East Prussia); temporarily in Gestapo custody in Allenstein; 1938–45, Confessing pastor, Königsberg-Ponarth; after the war, settled in Berlin—16

Hildebrandt, Horst: German constitutional historian—11, 12

Hillel, Rabbi (surnamed Ha-babli, "the Babylonian" and Ha-zaken, "the Elder") (dates uncertain, ca. 60 B.C.E.–15 C.E.): Jewish rabbi and distinguished interpreter of the Jewish law; founder of the moderate Pharisaic school of the law, the Hillelites; writings can be found in the Mishnah and Talmud—9, 10

Hiller, Johann: 1933, chief political inspector, Munich police headquarters; 1942, in section II/1 (passport office)—16

Hiller, Philipp Friedrich (1699–1769): hymnist—15

Hillerbrand, Hans Joachim: German-born Reformation historian; professor, Duke University—14

Himmelreich, Josef: press adviser for the Reich governor of Bavaria, Munich; made multiple attempts to influence Catholic circles; editor of the journal *Der Rufer* (The voice calling); after the war, lived by the Lake of Thun in Switzerland, where he also died—16

Himmler, Heinrich (1900–1945): agriculturist and National Socialist politician; 1929–45, *Reichsführer* of the SS; 1933, head of the political police in Bavaria and the other German states; 1934, participated in the murders associated with the Röhm coup; 1935, chief of the German police; June 1936, also became head of the German police in the Reich Ministry of the Interior; one of the organizers of the Holocaust; August 1943, Reich interior minister; 1944–45, commander of the reserve army; May 23, 1945, committed suicide—4, 8, 14, 15, 16, 17

Hindemith, Paul (1895–1963): composer—11

Hindenburg, Paul von Beneckendorff (1847–1934): general field marshal; 1916, head of the highest army command; 1925–34, president of Germany—3, 8, 9, 11, 12, 13, 15, 17

Hinderer, August (1877–1945): 1918–45, director of the Evangelical Press Association for Germany in Berlin; June 24, 1933, temporarily dismissed from office—12

Hinsley, Arthur (1865–1943): Catholic archbishop of Westminster; cardinal; worked with Protestant ecumenical leaders—16

Hippolytus (ca. 170–236): ecclesiastical writer—4, 16

Hippolytus: in Greek mythology, son of Theseus; subject of Euripides play—17 (for vol. 9)

Hirsch, Emanuel (1888–1972): German Protestant theologian; studied theology in Berlin under Karl Holl and Adolf von Harnack; broad theological-philosophical interests, especially in Luther and Kierkegaard; 1921–45, professor of church history, Göttingen; after 1936, professor of systematic theology; 1933, National Socialist sympathizer, supporting member of the SS, and preeminent theological adviser to the German

Christians; 1934–43, editor of the German Christian periodical *Deutsche Theologie*; after 1937, NSDAP member; 1950–61, translator and editor of the works of Kierkegaard—1, 2, 3, 4, 5, 6, 9, 10, 11, 12, 13, 14, 16

Hirsch, H.: member of the congregational council, German Reformed St. Paul's congregation, London—13

Hirschfeld, Ottwig von: January 1920, attempted to murder Matthias Erzberger as he left the Moabit County Court following a lawsuit summons against Dr. Karl Helfferich—9

Hirtle, Rudi: son of a colleague of Karl Bonhoeffer from Breslau—9

His, Wilhelm (1863–1934): professor of internal medicine, Berlin—10

Hitler, Adolf (1889–1945): National Socialist politician, German dictator; 1920, founded the National Socialist Workers' Party (NSDAP); 1933, became Reich chancellor and führer; 1938, became commander in chief of the armed forces; 1941, also commander in chief of the army; April 30, 1945, committed suicide in Berlin—all volumes

Hitze, Franz (1851–1921): 1878, ordained as priest; 1884–1921, member of parliament; 1890, cofounder of the People's Association for Catholic Germany; 1893–1920, professor of Christian social thought, Münster—11

Hitzer, Arnold (1902–77): Confessing Church pastor; 1930–40, Rösnitz, district of Leobschütz/Silesia; 1937, expelled from Silesia; 1937–38, in prison; 1940, pastor, Rehhof/West Prussia; 1941–42, wrote his "Notes concerning baptism"; December 1941, drafted into military service in Marienwerder; 1944–48, in British prisoner of war camp; from 1949, head of the free *Christengemeinde* (anthroposophical congregation), Kiel; 1960–77, Munich—16

Hitzigrath, Hellmut (1891–1950): from 1926, pastor, Berlin—12

Hjort, Wanda: *see* Goltz, Wanda

Hoare, Sir Samuel (1880–1959): British statesman; 1938–40, minister of aviation; ambassador in Madrid—16

Hobbes, Thomas (1588–1679): British philosopher—1, 12, 14

Hobe, Lene: *see* Delbrück, Lene

Hoche, Alfred Erich (1865–1943): German psychiatrist; opponent of Freudian psychoanalysis and early advocate of euthanasia and sterilization; professor, Freiburg im Breisgau; 1920, author with Karl Binding of influential tract on the "elimination" of "life unworthy of life"—6, 9

Höck, Michael: Catholic priest and publicist; editor in chief of the Munich Catholic church newspaper; after the newspaper was banned, he was a pastor at St. Benno in Munich; May 23, 1941, arrested; initially sent to the Sachsenhausen concentration camp, from July 1941, in Dachau with Neuhäusler and Niemöller; April 5, 1945, liberated; after the war, prelate and regent at the priests' seminary in Freising, Upper Bavaria—16

Hockenos, Matthew: U.S. professor of history; expert on the German churches—15

Hodgkin, Henry Theodore (1877–1933): British Quaker; 1914, cofounder with Friedrich Sigmund-Schultze of the International Fellowship of Reconciliation—10

Hodgson, Leonard (1889–1969): 1931, cathedral canon of Winchester; general secretary of Faith and Order; 1938–59, professor of theology, Oxford; secretary of Faith and Order, England—12, 13, 14, 15, 17

Hodgson, Peter: U.S. professor of theology, Vanderbilt University; authority on Hegel—6

Hoefer, Elmer (1903–2003): housemate of Franz Hildebrandt in Tübingen; emigrated to the United States; served churches in New York, Illinois, and Missouri—10

Hoesch, Leopold von (1881–1936): from 1907, held various diplomatic posts for Germany; 1924, ambassador in Paris; 1932, in London—13

Höfer, Joseph: German Catholic priest—4

Hofer, Walther: German-born historian, author of works on National Socialism, human rights and historical theory—15

Hoff, Walter: 1930, pastor, Berlin-Charlottenburg; 1933, head of the Student Fighting Association of German Christians (*Studentenkampfbundes*); member, Reich leadership of German Christians and assistant to Joachim Hossenfelder; 1934, consistory official, Berlin; 1936, provost, St. Peter's, Berlin; military service, during which he was involved in killing Jews in Russia and later confessed to these; 1946, released from British internment camp to Schleswig-Holstein; 1949, dismissed from service and right to practice as a minister revoked; 1957, reinstallation of these privileges—12

Hoffer, Margarete: 1932, participated in the ecumenical youth conference in Ciernohorské Kúpele; 1934, Austrian delegate at the Fanø youth conference; representative of the Austrian section of the World Alliance for Promoting International Friendship through the Churches—11, 13

Hoffmann: pastor in London—12

Hoffmann, Adele: 1932, student of Bonhoeffer in Berlin—12

Hoffmann, Heinrich: renowned preacher in Halle—11

Hoffmann, Peter: German-born historian, professor of history (emeritus), McGill University; expert on the German resistance—6, 12, 16

Hoffmann (von Fallersleben), August Heinrich (1798–1874): generally known as Hoffmann von Fallersleben; professor of German language and literature; poet; later librarian at Schloß Corvey; notable collector and publisher of folk songs; lyricist of the German national anthem, "Deutschland, Deutschland über alles"—14

Hofmann, Hans (1911–43): from Pomerania; 1936–37, participated in the fourth Finkenwalde session; assistant pastor in Lupow, Pomerania; 1943, killed in action at Leningrad—15

Hofmann, Johann Christian Konrad von (1810–77): professor, Rostock; 1845–77, professor, Erlangen; leading representative of the Erlangen school and the interpretation of the Bible as salvation history; constant critic of rationalism—1, 9, 11, 12, 15

Hofmann, Klaus: director, Johann-Sebastian-Bach-Institut, Göttingen—16

Hofmann, Melchior (1500–1543): lay preacher and popular writer; from May 1533, incarcerated in Strasbourg and prohibited from writing—14

Hofmannsthal, Hugo von (1874–1929): Austrian poet—11, 15

Hofmeister: military prosecutor with the military high court—16

Hofmeister, Alexander Corbinian (1891–1966): abbot of the Benedictine monastery, Metten, Lower Bavaria; already an acquaintance of Josef Müller before the war; traveled with Müller to various neighboring countries and to Rome on church business; during the war, Müller introduced him to the Military Intelligence Office; April 1943, arrested and taken to the Dachau concentration camp; April 1945, liberated—16

Hohenlohe-Langenburg, Prince Max Egon zu (1897–1969): Sudeten German noble; 1938, involved in contacts between Konrad Henlein and Lord Runciman; secret agent of the Military Intelligence Office, also close to the SS leadership and the Foreign Ministry—16

Hohlwein, Hans: 1929, pastor, Eilenburg; 1934, head of the Protestant preachers' seminary, Eisenach, Thuringia; 1939, high consistory official; 1939, officer; 1951, senior teacher, Solingen—11

Höhne, Heinz: biographer of Canaris—16

Holbein, Hans (the Younger) (ca. 1497–1543): German painter and draftsman —6

Holder, John J.: Sanskrit scholar; professor of philosophy, St. Norbert's College—11

Hölderlin, Friedrich (1770–1843): German poet—8, 11

Holl, Karl (1866–1926): German Protestant theologian and Luther scholar; 1900, professor of church history, Tübingen; 1906–26, professor of church history, Berlin; 1915, member of the Prussian Academy of Science—1, 2, 3, 4, 5, 6, 7, 8, 9, 10, 11, 12, 13, 14, 15, 16

Holl, Karl: professor emeritus of contemporary history, Bremen—10

Hollatz (also Hollaz), David (1648–1713): Lutheran dogmatician and pastor; studied in Erfurt and Wittenberg; most famous work, *Examen theologicum acroamaticum, Rostochhii* (later *Homiae*) *et Lipsiae* (1707); rector of the Lyceum in Colberg—1, 2, 3, 9, 14, 16

Hollenberg, Wilhelm: author of a Hebrew language schoolbook in the mid-1980s—9

Hollmann, Georg: from 1909, pastor, Berlin-Nikolassee—9, 12

Hollweg, Johannes (1886–1976): from 1930, pastor, Berlin—12

Holmes, John Haynes (1879–1964): Unitarian minister and social activist, pacifist, and promoter of Gandhi's nonviolent activism; pastor Community Church, New York City, 1919–49; close friend of Rabbi Stephen Wise—10

Holstein, Günther (1892–1931): 1924, professor of public law and church law, Greifswald; 1930, Kiel—10

Holstein, Horst (1894–1945): Berlin lawyer and notary; had a law office in Berlin-Kohlhasenbrück; church elder, Trinity Church, Berlin; delegate to several Confessing Church synods; 1936, member of the constitutional committee of the Provisional Church Administration; defense attorney for Confessing Church members at several civil and criminal trials; 1940, officer at the front, but for health reasons soon reassigned to Berlin; 1945, died of a heart attack—8, 14, 16

Holsten, Walter (1908–82): 1932, pastor, Hannover regional church; worked with the Gossner Mission Society, Berlin; 1947, professor of religious studies and mission studies, Mainz—16

Holtzmann, Heinrich Julius (1832–1910): Protestant theologian, biblical critic, New Testament scholar; 1854–57, professor, Heidelberg; 1858–74, Strasbourg; leading representative of the historical-critical study of the Bible; one of the founders of the *Handkommentar zum Neuen Testament*, a very influential publication series of New Testament commentaries; prolific scholar—1, 9

Hölzel, Christoph: dissertation on Grotius's legal philosophy—8

Holzendorf: *see* "Engel"

Holzner, Richard: reference for Max-Peter Meyer's immigration application —15

Homer (lived between 750 and 650 B.C.E.): Greek poet; the epics, the *Odyssey* and the *Iliad,* are attributed to him—4, 7, 8, 14

Honecker, Martin: German professor of social ethics and systematic theology —6, 9

Hong, Edna H. (1913–2007): renowned U.S. writer and Kierkegaard translator —2

Hong, Howard V. (1912–2010): renowned U.S. Kierkegaard scholar; general editor of his works in English translation—2

Hoogstraten, Hans Dirk van: Dutch professor of social ethics—6

Hoover, Herbert Clark (1874–1964): 1929–33, thirty-first president of the United States; 1931, initiated a one-year moratorium on German reparation payments—10

Hope, Nicholas: professor, University of Glasgow; author of work on European Protestantism—14

Hopf: 1937, predicant, Striche; was on Confessing intercessory lists—14

Horace (Quintus Horatius Flaccus) (65–8 B.C.E.): Roman lyric poet and satirist—8, 9

Horn, Elisabeth: sister of Katharina and Maria Horn Czeppan—10

Horn, Katharina (Käthe) (1893–1977): sister of Maria Czeppan, née Horn; educator in Hamburg and Berlin; taught the Bonhoeffer twins for many years; later became an elementary school teacher in Havana, Cuba, where Bonhoeffer visited in 1930—9, 10, 11

Horn, Maria: *see* Czeppan, Maria

Hörnchen: *see* Czeppan, Maria

Horstmeier, Marie: secondary school teacher, Berlin-Friedenau—11

Hort, Fenton John Anthony (1828–92): British professor of New Testament, Cambridge and elsewhere—4, 6

Horton, Myles (1905–90): U.S. educator, founder in 1932 and director of the Highlander Folk School dedicated to training labor union and civil rights activists; 1930–31, knew Bonhoeffer as a student at Union Theological Seminary—10

Horton, Walter Marshall: professor, Oberlin College—10, 15

Hosea: biblical character—1

Hosemann, Johannes (1881–1947): high consistory official; 1924–33, director of the Church Federation Office, council member of Life and Work, head of the Philosophical Association of the Wingolf Alliance in Berlin; 1936–46, church consistory president, Breslau—11, 12

Hoskin, Marilyn: 1995–2009, dean, University of New Hampshire; since 2009, dean of social science, City College of New York—7

Hoskyns, Edwyn Clement (1884–1947): British theologian—2, 8

Hoßbach, Friedrich Wilhelm Ludwig (1894–1980): general; 1934–38, military adjutant with Hitler—15

Hossenfelder, Joachim (1899–1976): 1919, member of the *Freikorps* (paramilitary groups of World War I veterans); 1925, pastor, Upper Silesia; 1929, member of the NSDAP; 1931, pastor, Berlin; 1932, cofounder and Reich leader of the German Christian faith movement; September 1933, bishop of Brandenburg; September–November 1933, ministerial adviser in the Reich Church Administration; December 1933, provisional leave; 1939–45, pastor, Potsdam; 1945, placed on provisional leave; given

administrative assignment overseeing church placements; 1954–69, pastor, Ratekau/Eutin near Lübeck—12, 13, 14, 17 (for vol. 13)

Hovel, Dr. von: worked with the Christian Social Services—11

Howard, Molly: assisted with *DBWE* 7—7

Howe, Günther: German professor of mathematics and physics, Protestant Institute for Interdisciplinary Research (FEST), Heidelberg—6

Hoyland, John S. (Jack) (1887–1957): 1912, school director, Hoshangabad, India; 1919, lecturer, Nagpur; 1928, at Woodbrooke College, Birmingham, U.K.; member of the Royal Historical Society—13

Hoyle, Richard Birch (1875–1939): author of work on Barth—17 (for vol. 12)

Hrabanus: *see* Rabanus Maurus

Hromádka, Josef L. (1889–1969): Czech Protestant theologian; from 1912, pastor; 1928, professor of systematic theology, Prague; 1939, emigrated to the United States by way of Switzerland; professor of ethics, Princeton; 1947, returned to Prague, where he founded the Christian Peace Conference—15, 17

Hübbe: 1937, estate owner—14

Hübener, Otto: businessman; co-owner of the insurance firm Jauch & Hübner in Hamburg; during the war, had special contact with Colonel Oster and Hans von Dohnanyi; his loan to Dohnanyi for the construction of Dohnanyi's house in Sacrow was investigated by the military high court—16

Huber: acquaintance of the Bonhoeffer family in Madrid—10

Huber, Ernst Rudolf (1903–90): author of work on church and state in Germany—1, 12, 14

Huber, Wolfgang: studied theology at Heidelberg, Göttingen, and Tübingen; 1966, ThD, Tübingen; assistant minister and minister at the established Protestant church of Württemberg; 1968–80, colleague, member of the governing board, and vice chairperson of the Forschungsstätte der Evangelischen Studiengemeinschaft (FEST, a Protestant institute for interdisciplinary research), Heidelberg; 1972, postdoctoral lecturing qualification, Heidelberg; 1980, professor of social ethics, Marburg; 1984, professor of systematic theology (concentrating on ethics), Heidelberg; 1983–85, president of the Kirchentag; 1989, Lilly Visiting Professor, Emory University, Atlanta; member and, from 1990, chair of the editorial board of *DBW*; 1994, bishop of the Evangelical Church of Berlin-Brandenburg; honorary professor at the universities of Berlin and Heidelberg; 1997, member of the council of the Evangelical Church in Germany—1, 2, 4, 5, 6, 8, 12, 13, 14, 16, 17

Hubert, Konrad (1507–77): hymnist—15
Huch, Ricarda (1864–1947): German writer and literary scholar—16
Hughes, Langston (1902–67): African American writer; directed a theater company in Harlem—10
Huhn, Martin J.: from 1928, pastor, Berlin—12
Hührling, Miss: acquaintance in Barcelona—10
Hülle, Johannes: from 1931, pastor, Berlin—12
Hülst, Friedrich (Frieder) von (1922–43): brother of Marie Luise von Hülst; September 1943, killed in action; September 25, 1943, Maria von Wedemeyer describes the memorial service in a letter—16
Hülst, Marie-Luise von (1921–84): daughter of the estate owner von Hülst in Rohrbeck (Neumark); acquaintance of the von Wedemeyer family in Pätzig; 1941, lived with Ruth von Kleist-Retzow in Stettin; after the war, lived in Essen, married name Schlemmer—16
Hultsch, Friedrich (1833–1906): German philologist and classicist—10
Humboldt, Baron Wilhelm von (1767–1835): German scholar and statesman —1, 6, 8
Humburg, Paul (1878–1945): 1906, pastor, Dhünn, Rhineland; 1909, Elberfeld; 1919, general secretary of the German Student Christian Federation; 1921, national overseer of the German Young Men's Association; 1929–43, pastor of the Reformed congregation, Barmen-Gemarke; 1934–43, head of the Evangelical Confessing Church Synod in the Rhineland; 1934–January 1936, member of the first Provisional Church Administration; 1936, of the Reich Council of Brethren—13, 14
Hume, David (1711–76): British philosopher and historian—6, 11
Hume, Theodore: Congregational pastor from the United States; sent to Europe to work for the World Council of Churches; autumn 1944, killed when his plane was shot down by the Luftwaffe on its flight from London to Stockholm—16
Humperdinck, Engelbert (1854–1921): German composer—8
Humphrey, Nicolas S.: assistant professor of German and the humanities at St. Norbert College; translated part of *DBWE* 11—11
Hundt, Anton Adolf: career military; 1940–42, major and head of the Military Intelligence Office VII in Munich; 1943, colonel—16
Hundt, Ernst, D. (1877–1945): 1916, privy consistory official and member of the Evangelical High Church Council, Berlin; 1929, vice president, German Evangelical Church; 1933, deputy head of the Church Chancellery of the German Evangelical Church—10
Hunsche, Klara (1900–1979): winter semester 1932–33, attended Bonhoeffer's lectures on contemporary systematic theology; summer semester 1933, attended his lectures on Christology; 1937, vicar, Berlin; 1938–

43, worked in the Evangelical Relief Office for non-Aryan Christians (Grüber office); 1946–48, adviser in the Church Educational Committee for Berlin; 1948–60, provincial pastor, Berlin—12

Hunsinger, George: U.S. Barth scholar; professor, Princeton Theological Seminary—11

Huntemann, Georg: German professor of theological ethics—6

Huppenkothen, Walter (1907–79): governmental attorney; 1933, joined the SS, ultimately attaining the rank of unit leader; 1944, director; group leader section IV E in the Reich Central Security Office; after the reorganization, sectional leader in section IV A3; leading member of the "July 20 special commission"; from February 12, 1945, deputy leader of group IV A; oversaw the summary courts in the concentration camps Sachsenhausen (April 6, 1945) and Flossenbürg (April 8, 1945) that condemned Hans von Dohnanyi and Dietrich Bonhoeffer to death—16

Huss, John (Jan Hus) (1369–1415): Bohemian theologian and reformer; 1400, priest and teacher at the university, Prague; 1415, at the Council in Constance, expelled from the clerical office as a heretic; July 6, 1415, burned at the stake—1, 11, 13, 14

Husserl, Edmund (1859–1938): phenomenologist, professor of philosophy, Göttingen and Freiburg—1, 2, 8, 9, 10, 11

Hutcheson, Francis (1694–1746): British philosopher—6

Hutten, Kurt: author of article on "God-believers"—10

Hutter, Leonhard (1563–1616): Lutheran theologian and professor, Wittenberg; honored in his time as *Lutherus redonatus*—1, 9

Huxley, Aldous (1894–1963): British-American author—6

Huxley, Thomas Henry: Royal Navy doctor; lecturer at the Royal School of Mines; outspoken advocate of the theory of evolution—15

Hymenaeus: biblical character—4, 15

Hymmen, Johannes (1878–1951): 1926, church official, Münster; 1932, senior church official on the Evangelical Central Council, Münster; 1936, vice president of the Evangelical High Church Council; 1940–45, member of the Confidential Council of Clerical Advisors of the German Evangelical Church; 1946, retired—8, 15, 16, 17

Hyperius, Andreas (1511–64): 1542, professor of theology, Marburg; founder of practical theology as a theological discipline—14

Ibn Saud (Abd al-Aziz ibn Saud) (ca. 1880–1953): 1932–53, king of Saudi Arabia—6

Ibsen, Henrik (1828–1906): Norwegian poet and dramatist—6, 10, 11, 16

Ickradt, Heinrich Wilhelm (Heinz)(1897–1954): businessman; secretary in the Portuguese consulate, Munich; captain in the reserves; assigned

to the Munich Military Intelligence Office VII as head of the office I/Aviation; acquainted with Wilhelm Schmidhuber; 1942, implicated and arrested with Schmidhuber in the currency affair ("*Depositenkasse*" affair)—8, 16, 17

Ignatius of Antioch (Theophorus) (ca. 35–ca. 107 C.E.): bishop of Antioch in Syria; died as a Christian martyr in Rome; author of several letters to churches in Asia Minor and Rome—1, 9, 14

Ignatius of Loyola: *see* Loyola, Ignatius

Ihde, Wilhelm: publicist; 1937, secretary, Reich Writers' Guild; SS lieutenant (*Obersturmführer*)—16

Ihmels, Ludwig (1858–1933): 1898, professor of systematic theology, Erlangen; 1902, Leipzig; 1922–33, bishop of Saxony; advocate of the theology of revelation—9, 11

Ilse: aunt of Bonhoeffer, not otherwise identified—10

Imholz, Friedrich: 1936, journalist—14

Immer, Karl (junior) (1916–84): 1941, first theological examination before the Rhineland Council of Brethren; 1971–81, president of the Evangelical Church in the Rhineland—14

Immer, Karl (senior) (1888–1944): German Reformed theologian; 1914–25, pastor, Rysum, East Frisia; 1914–18, military chaplain; 1925–27, director of the Educational Association, Neukirchen; 1927–44, pastor, (Wuppertal) Barmen-Gemarke; March 1934, compulsory temporary retirement; founder of the Assembly of Reformed Preachers; cofounder of the Rhineland Confessing Church; May 1934, member of the Confessing Church Council of Brethren of the Old Prussian Union and of the Reich Council of Brethren; 1937, imprisoned for several months; leading member of the Confessing Church; cofounder of the seminary in Wuppertal—13, 14, 15

Immermann, Karl Leberecht (1796–1840): German writer; from 1818, Prussian civil service; later in Magdeburg and Düsseldorf; author of novels and plays, including comedies; his late novels, especially *Münchhausen* (1838–39), employ both fantasy and realism with irony as the link between the two—8

Innocence III (ca. 1160–1216): from 1198, pope—14

Insull, Martin J.: U.S. industrialist; president, Middle West Utilities Company—10

Iolaus: in Greek mythology, divine hero and friend of Hercules—17 (for vol. 9)

Iphigenia: character in Greek mythology—6, 17 (for vol. 9)

Irenaei: from 1919, Orthodox bishop of Novi Sad, Yugoslavia; secretary of the Yugoslavian section of the World Alliance for Promoting Inter-

national Friendship through the Churches; spring 1943, mentioned in Dietrich Bonhoeffer's "camouflage letter" as the "most influential and popular church leader there"—16

Irenaeus of Lyons (ca. 125–202): Greek prelate; after ca. 177, bishop of Lyons; early systematizer of Christian tradition and doctrine; known for his writings against gnosticism—1, 4, 6, 8, 9, 14, 16

Irving, Edward (1792–1834): Scottish clergyman—12

Irwin, Lord Edward—*see* Halifax, Lord Edward

Isaac: biblical character—4, 5, 8, 9, 14, 15

Isaacson, Walter: U.S. author of biography of Einstein—12

Isaiah: biblical character—1, 5, 9, 10, 13

Iserland, Prof. I.: member of the International Missionary Council—13

Iserloh, Erwin: German scholar of Reformation history—5

Ishmael: biblical character—14

Iwand, Hans-Joachim (1899–1960): 1927, private lecturer in systematic theology, Königsberg; 1935, withdrawal of the *venia legendi* (authorization to teach at university after postdoctoral lecturing qualification); 1935–37, director of the preachers' seminary of the Confessing Church of the Old Prussian Union, Blöstau, East Prussia; 1936, member, Reich Council of Brethren; 1937, after this seminary was closed, pastor in Dortmund; 1938–39, imprisoned; 1945, professor of systematic theology, Göttingen; 1952, Bonn—14, 15, 16, 17

Iyer, Pushpa: Indian scholar of conflict resolution—13

Jackson, Eleanor M.: historian of the ecumenical movement—16

Jacob: biblical character, renamed Israel in Genesis 32:28—5, 6, 7, 8, 9, 11, 12, 15

Jacob, Günter (1906–93): 1932, pastor, Noßdorf near Forst; 1933, cofounder of the Pastors' Emergency League; 1946, general superintendent of the Neumark; 1949–72, pastor, Cottbus; 1963–67, administrator of the bishop's office for the Regional Synod East of the Berlin-Brandenburg church—2, 12

Jacobi, Friedrich (1743–1819): German philosopher—12

Jacobi, Gerhard (1891–1971): 1914–19, military service; 1921–23, secretary of prison chaplains for the Province of Saxony-Anhalt; also prison chaplain, Halle; 1923, pastor, St. Paul's, Halle; 1927, cathedral preacher, Magdeburg; 1930–54, pastor, Kaiser Wilhelm Memorial Church, Berlin; 1933, leading member of the Young Reformation movement and of the Pastors' Emergency League; 1934–39, president of the Confessing synod, Berlin; 1934, member of the Old Prussian Union and the Reich Council of Brethren; repeatedly imprisoned; 1939–40, military service; 1941,

acquitted in the collective trial against the examination board of the Old Prussian Union Council of Brethren; 1946, superintendent, Berlin (West) Sprengel I; 1954–67, bishop of Oldenburg—4, 6, 8, 10, 11, 12, 13, 14, 15, 16, 17

Jacobsen, Hans-Adolf: German historian; author of works on the German resistance—8

Jacobsen, Inge (1915–42): daughter of a "non-Aryan" Berlin physician; business training; employed by the Kaiser Wilhelm Memorial Church; 1938, secretary in the "Grüber office"; 1941, unable to emigrate to the United States, although she had an affidavit; eventually died in a concentration camp—16, 17

Jaeger, Werner (1888–1961): German classical philologist; 1914, professor, Basel; 1915, Kiel; 1921, Berlin; 1936, emigrated to the United States—6

Jaenicke, Walther: author of article on Karl Bonhoeffer—8

Jaensch, D.: urged that Walter Müller be invited to the Fanø youth conference in 1934—13

Jäger, August (1887–1949): 1921, councilor in the regional court, Wiesbaden; June 1933, head of the church section in the Prussian Ministry of Culture; June 24–July 14, 1933, state commissioner for all Protestant Prussian regional churches; April–October 1934, member and legal administrator of the Clerical Ministry (Geistliches Ministerium) for the Reich Church government; 1936, senate president in the supreme court in Berlin; 1939, deputy head of the German civil administration, Warthegau; later administrative president and general representative of the Reich governor there; 1949, sentenced to death and executed for war crimes in Poland—12, 13, 15, 16, 17

Jäger, Miss: Bonhoeffer's landlady in Tübingen—9

Jagow, H.: author of 1931 work on the church's social task—11

Jahn, Ernst: author of works on religion and psychology—14

Jairus: biblical character—8

Jakoby: not identified; mentioned in 1934 Bruay report—13

Jakoby, L. S.: author of work on Methodist church—14

James: brother of Jesus; traditional author of the Letter of James; leader of the Jerusalem church; Christian martyr—4, 8, 9, 11, 12

James, son of Alphaeus (disciple)—4

James, son of Zebedee (disciple): biblical character; one of the twelve disciples, called James the Greater; brother of John—1, 4, 9, 14, 15, 16

James, William (1842–1910): U.S. psychologist and philosopher; often considered the founder of pragmatism; from 1872, instructor in anatomy and physiology, Harvard University; 1876–1907, professor of psychology and philosophy—6, 10, 11, 12, 15

Jan, Julius von (1897–1964): 1925, pastor, Herrentierbach; 1928, Brettach; 1935–40, Confessing pastor, Oberlenningen, Württemberg, where he preached against the Nazis after Kristallnacht and was imprisoned—15

Jänicke, Johannes (1900–1979): 1929, pastor at the St. Ulrich Church, Halle; 1935, Palmnicken/East Prussia; member of the East Prussian Council of Brethren; 1945–47, remained in East Prussia; 1947, pastor, Berlin-Schlachtensee; 1949, provost of Magdeburg and Merseburg; 1955–68, bishop of the church province of Saxony—16

Jänicke, Theo: 1933–34, inspector of studies, preachers' seminary, Naumburg/Queis; 1934–49, pastor, Buckow, Brandenburg; 1949–58, director of the Burckhardt House, Berlin; 1958, pastor, Berlin-Dahlem—12

Janitsch, Prof.: September 1933, Yugoslavian participant at the conference of the World Alliance for Promoting International Friendship through the Churches in Sofia—12

Jannasch, Hans Peter: son of Wilhelm Jannasch—16

Jannasch, Wilhelm (1888–1966): 1922, senior pastor, Lübeck; 1934, forced to retire; 1933–45, worked for the Confessing Church; 1936, member of the Provisional Church Administration; 1937, secretary of the Pastors' Emergency League; 1946, professor of practical theology, Mainz; 1956, retired—8, 16

Jansen, Ernst (1903–78): Confessing pastor, Lübeck—11

Jansen, Nikolaus (1880–1965): monsignor of the Aachen Cathedral; August 1941, arrested; December 1941, taken to Dachau concentration camp; April 29, 1945, liberated—16

Japheth: biblical character—12

Jäschke (also spelled Jeschke), Richard: from 1932, pastor, Laptau, East Prussia; belonged to the Thuringian German Christians; mentioned in Dietrich Bonhoeffer's calendar in connection with Elbing—16

Jason: character in Greek mythology—6

Jasper, Ronald C. D.: Anglican liturgical scholar; dean of York; authorized biographer of George Bell—8

Jaspers, Karl (1888–1969): German philosopher; one of the primary advocates of the philosophy of existentialism; began as a psychiatrist at the University of Heidelberg; from 1916, professor of psychology; from 1921, professor of philosophy; 1937, removed from office; 1945, reinstatement; 1948–61, professor of philosophy, University of Basel—6, 7, 16

Jaspert, Bernd: author of study on Bonhoeffer's 1931 lectures on twentieth-century systematic theology—11

Jaurés, Jean (1859–1914): French Socialist leader and historian—9

Jean Paul (Johann Paul Friedrich Richter) (1783–1825): storyteller, novelist —8

Jeep, Walter (1878–1964): 1922, chaplain for Inner Mission, Brunswick (Braunschweig); 1933, director of the executive committee for Inner Mission, Berlin; 1934, pastor, Bremen—12

Jehle, Herbert (1907–83): Quaker and pacifist; mathematician and physicist from Stuttgart; 1932–33, belonged to the Berlin Bonhoeffer circle; 1933–34, studied in Cambridge, England; 1936, visited Finkenwalde; 1937–38, research assistantship, Southampton; then Brussels; 1941, emigrated to the United States following internment in the French camp of Gurs; 1942–46, Harvard; 1947–49, University of Pennsylvania; 1949–59, University of Nebraska; 1959–72, professor of physics, George Washington University—6, 8, 10, 12, 13, 14, 15, 16

Jelke, Robert (1882–1952): German Protestant theologian and religious philosopher—10, 12

Jellinek, Georg (1851–1911): German expert on constitutional law—6

Jellinghaus, Theodor (1841–1913): Protestant pastor—11

Jenny, Markus (1923–2001): Swiss Reformed liturgist and hymnist—14

Jensen, Hans-Werner (1912–83): from Kiel; 1937–38, vicar, Hamburg-Altona; 1938–39, participated in the collective pastorate in Groß-Schlönwitz; 1939, pastor, Buchholz, district of Fürstenwalde; temporarily incarcerated in Frankfurt an der Oder; assistant pastor, Langengrassau, Saxony; 1940–45, military service; 1945, consultant to the Evangelical Church of Germany chancellery; 1946, pastor, Gelting, Schleswig; 1950, Kiel; 1966, high regional church official and head of the catechetical office, Kiel; 1970, retired—6, 8, 14, 15, 16

Jensen, Paul Theodor (1870–1938): 1919, member of the German Unity Board of the Moravian (Herrnhuter) Church; 1920–30, that organization's head; 1922–35, bishop; 1935–38, hospital chaplain at the deaconesses' institute, Kaiserwerth; head of the German section of the continuing Committee of Faith and Order—12

Jenson, Robert W.: U.S. Lutheran and ecumenical theologian—14

Jeremiah: biblical prophet—7, 8, 9, 10, 11, 12, 13, 15

Jeremias, Alfred (1864–1935): German pastor and theologian—11

Jeremias, Joachim (1900–1979): 1928, professor and director of the Institutum Judaicum, Berlin; 1929, professor of New Testament, Greifswald; 1935, Göttingen; 1968, retired; member of the Confessing Church—8, 16

Jeroboam: biblical character—15

Jerome (347–419/420): Latin church author, biblical scholar; studied at Rome; greatest achievement was his translation of most of the Bible into

Latin from the original languages (Vulgate); also wrote many biblical commentaries—1, 5, 15
Jervell, Jacob: German New Testament scholar—9
Jeshua: *see* Joshua
Jesse: biblical character—12
Jessen, Otto: professor of geography, Tübingen; later in Cologne—9
Jesus Christ (Jesus of Nazareth) (ca. 4 B.C.E.–ca. 30 C.E): *see* subject index
Jesus Sirach (Jeshua ben Eleazer ben Sira): author/book in the Apocrypha —5, 9
Jezebel: biblical character—14
Jézéquel, Anne: wife of Jules Jézéquel—11
Jézéquel, Jules (1870–1963): French Reformed pastor and ecumenist; 1933, secretary of both the French section and the international office of the World Alliance for Promoting International Friendship through the Churches; September 1933, participated in the conference in Sofia—11, 12, 16
Jhering, Rudolf von (1818–92): German legal scholar and author, founder of the modern philosophical-historical school of law—6
Joab: biblical character—14
Joachim: not otherwise identified—16
Job: biblical character—6, 8, 9, 10, 15
Jocca, Signora: German acquaintance who lived with her husband in Rome; Dietrich and Klaus Bonhoeffer met her during their trip to Rome—9
Jochimsen, Jutta—16
Johann Friedrich von Saxony, the Magnanimous (1503–54): 1532–47, Elector of Saxony, alongside Philipp of Hesse, one of the leaders in the Smalcald Alliance; 1547–52, in imperial custody; refused to yield in matters of faith—14
Johannes: *see* Albrecht, Johannes
Johannes de Francfordia—*see* Francfordia
Johannsen, Heinz: 1936–37, member of the fourth Finkenwalde session—15
Johansson, J. S. Harry: Swedish theologian; 1930, secretary of the Swedish Student Christian Movement; 1937, assistant with the Sigtuna Foundation; 1943, director of the Nordic Ecumenical Institute, Sigtuna—16, 17
John: biblical character; son of Zebedee; brother of James; one of the original twelve disciples—4, 5, 9, 14
John (epistle author)—5
John, Hans (1911–45): lawyer; 1939, academic assistant, Institute for Aviation Law, Berlin University, where he served for a time as a legal assistant

for Rüdiger Schleicher; 1940–43, military service associated with the Military Intelligence Office; participated in preparations for the assassination of Hitler; after July 20, 1944, arrested on the charge of conspiratorial contacts with Klaus Bonhoeffer and others; imprisoned in the Berlin prison on Lehrter Strasse; April 23, 1945, shot to death—8, 16

John, Otto (1909–97): lawyer; 1937–44, like Klaus Bonhoeffer, corporate lawyer in the central administration of German Lufthansa in Berlin; after July 20, 1944, fled to England by way of Spain; worked in the British military's "Calais Soldiers Broadcast"; after the war, worked with German prisoners of war in England; 1950–54, chief of the Federal Office for the Protection of the Constitution in Cologne; July 1954, abducted to the east sector of Berlin; December 1955, escaped back to West Berlin; 1956, in custody, sentenced to four years in prison; 1958, released from prison—8, 16

John Chrysostom: *see* Chrysostom, John

John of Damascus (ca. 675–ca. 749): Greek theologian and doctor of the church; his most important work, the *Fount of Wisdom*, deals with philosophy, heresies, and the orthodox faith—3

John of Patmos: biblical character—5, 8

John of Salisbury (ca. 1120–80): medieval humanist; studied in France; secretary to the archbishops of Canterbury; 1176, bishop of Chartres—10

Johnson, Alex (1910–89): Norwegian theologian; 1935, secretary of the Norwegian Student Christian Movement; 1939–46, chair; during the German occupation, member of the coordinating committee of the Norwegian home front; 1961, rector of the practical theological seminary; 1964–74, bishop of Hamar—16

Johnson, Donald Oskar: U.S. author of work on American Civil Liberties Union—12

Johnson, James Weldon (1871–1938): African American writer, lawyer, and diplomat—10

Johnson, Marshall: New Testament scholar; former editorial director of Fortress Press—2, 5, 9

Johnson, Roger A.: U.S. theologian; intellectual historian; authority on Bultmann; professor of religion, Wellesley College—6, 10

John the Baptist: biblical character—4, 6, 8, 9, 10, 12, 14, 15, 16

John the Evangelist: biblical character—4, 8, 9, 10, 12, 13, 14, 15, 16

Jonah: biblical character—8, 9, 12, 13, 14, 15

Jonas, Hans (1903–93): studied in Freiburg under Husserl and Heidegger, in Berlin, and in Marburg under Bultmann and Heidegger; 1928, doctoral dissertation on the concept of gnosticism; 1933, emigration to Lon-

don, 1934 to Jerusalem; 1940–45, soldier in the British Army (Jewish Brigade); 1943, married Lore, née Weiner; 1949, emigration to Canada; professor in Montreal and Ottawa; 1955, moved to New York, professor at the New School for Social Research; known especially for his work on gnosticism in both English and German—3, 10
Jonas, Justus (1493–1555): Reformation theologian—14, 15
Jonas-Corrieri, Waltraut: German musicologist—17 (for vol. 9)
Jonathan: biblical character—7, 14
Jone, Heribert (1885–1967): German theologian—6
Jones, Andrea: staff member, Hartford Seminary Library, Connecticut—6, 10
Jones, Clemens Harold: from 1939, British legation chaplain, Stockholm —16
Jones, Dick: member of the British intelligence service; Bonhoeffer's fellow prisoner in Tegel—8
Jones, Eli Stanley (1884–1973): U.S. theologian—12, 15
Jordahn, Bruno: German liturgical scholar—14
Jordan, Richard Theodor: member of the Evangelical Church of Brethren; 1921, ordination; worked with the social working group in east Berlin; 1925, chaplain, Berlin; 1925, with the German section of the World Alliance for Promoting International Friendship through the Churches; 1928, pastor, Wachow, church district of Brandenburg; 1929, secretary of the German section of the World Alliance for Promoting International Friendship through the Churches—11, 12
Jörgensen, Alfred Theodor: German theologian—1
Joseph: biblical character—8, 10, 14, 15
Joseph of Arimathea: biblical character—8
Josephus, Flavius (37–ca. 97 C.E.): Jewish historian and soldier—9
Joshua (also Jeshua): biblical character—5, 14
Jost, Adolf: German theorist who supported euthanasia—7
Jost, Wilhelm (1903–88): colleague of Karl-Friedrich Bonhoeffer; 1938–44, professor of physical chemistry, Leipzig—8
Joyce, James (1872–1941): British writer of Irish background—12
Juarez, Benito Pablo (1806–72): 1861–72, president of Mexico—15
Judah: biblical character—15
Judas: biblical character; prophet—14
Judas Iscariot: biblical character—1, 2, 4, 6, 8, 9, 12, 14, 15, 16
Jude: biblical character—12
Judith: biblical (apocrypha) character—13

Julian the Apostate (Flavius Claudius Julianus) (ca. 331–363 C.E.): 361–63, Roman emperor and cousin of Constantine I; nephew of Constantine the Great; successor of Constantius II; attempted unsuccessfully to restore paganism to the Roman Empire—4, 7, 9

Jülicher, Adolf (1857–1938): professor of New Testament and church history, Marburg; introduced the *tertium comparationist* into New Testament exegesis for the interpretation of the parables; virtually blind after 1925—9, 14

Julius III (John Maria del Monte) (1487–1555): pope—9

Juncker, Alfred (1865–1945): German Protestant theologian and New Testament scholar—17 (for vol. 12)

Jung, Carl Gustav (1875–1961): Swiss physician and psychologist—5, 14

Jüngel, Eberhard: German theologian, influenced by Barth—2, 6, 8, 16

Jungmann, Josef (1899–1975): Austrian professor of pastoral theology; leader in "kerygmatic renewal"—5

Junias: biblical character—14

Jupiter: Roman deity—12

Jüssen, Klaudius: German Roman Catholic professor of dogmatics, patrology, and theology—6

Just, Mr.: German consul in Casablanca during the crisis of 1905–6—9

Justin Martyr (ca. 100–165): saint and church father, the most significant of the early Christian apologists; 165, martyred in Rome—6, 14

Justinian (483–565): 527–65, Byzantine emperor—6

Kabisch, Richard (1868–1914): theologian and educator; one of the successful opponents of Herbart—14

Kabitz, Ulrich: studied history and literature at Regensburg; 1945–60, consultant for cultural questions of the Protestant youth movement, first for the Protestant Bavarian youth ministry at Nuremberg, and after 1952, for the youth department of the Evangelical Church of Germany, Stuttgart; 1960–84, senior editor at Chr. Kaiser Verlag, Munich; specialist on literature of and about Bonhoeffer; coeditor, *DBW* 16; 1992, coeditor with Ruth-Alice von Bismarck, *Brautbriefe Zelle 92: Dietrich Bonhoeffer-Maria von Wedemeyer 1943–1945*, for which he received the Christopher Award in 1996—6, 8, 12, 13, 16, 17

Kafka, Franz (1883–1924): German novelist and short-story writer—7

Kaftan, Julius Wilhelm (1848–1926): Protestant theologian, philosopher of history; 1874, professor of systematic theology, Basel; 1881, Leipzig; 1883, Berlin; 1921, vice president of the Old Prussian Church; cofounder of the Evangelical-Social Congress—1, 9, 11, 14, 16

Kahl, Werner—German theologian and professor of mission and ecumenical history—14

Kähler, Martin (1835–1912): Protestant theologian; 1860, professor of New Testament theology, Halle; 1864–67, professor in Bonn and Halle—11, 12, 14

Kahn, Emanuel (1910–39): from Berlin-Lankwitz; 1937–38, participated in the collective pastorate in Groß-Schlönwitz; pastor in Sternberg; December 2, 1939, while a soldier, died as a result of a fatal accident—15, 16

Kahr, Gustav Ritter von: monarchist; September 26, 1923, named general state commissar—9

Kailuweit: farmer and head of the church board of directors in Groß Friedrichsdorf, East Prussia—16

Kain, August: secondary school headmaster, Berlin—11

Kaiser, Hermann J.: German musicologist—17 (for vol. 9)

Kaiser, Jakob (1888–1961): Catholic labor leader; 1924, member of the national parliament (representing the Center Party); 1938, temporarily in prison; before July 20, 1944, designated as a member of the new government; survived the end of the war; cofounder of the Christian Democratic Union (CDU) political party; 1949, member of parliament; 1949–57, Minister for All-German Affairs—16, 17

Kaiser, Jochen-Christoph: German Protestant theologian and church historian—16

Kalbfleisch, George (1910–66): 1933, studied under Paul Lehmann at Elmhurst College; pastor in the Evangelical Synod of North America; August 1939, delegate at the World Conference of Christian Youth, Amsterdam; afterward visited the collective pastorate, Groß-Schlönwitz; during the war, military chaplain with the U.S. Navy; chaplain at Dartmouth College, Hanover, New Hampshire—15, 16

Kalckreuth, Christine Countess von (Ninne) (1898–1984): daughter of Berta and Leopold von Kalckreuth; cousin of Paula Bonhoeffer; painter and graphic artist, Munich-Schwabing—8, 15, 16, 17

Kalckreuth, Friedrich Adolf Count von (1737–1818): Prussian field marshal; during the Seven Years War, adjutant to Prince Heinrich; 1807, conducted the negotiations for the cease-fire with Napoleon; 1810, governor of Berlin—16

Kalckreuth, Johannes Count von (1893–1956): composer, music writer, and critic in Munich—7, 16

Kalckreuth, Leopold, Count von (1855–1928): Bonhoeffer's maternal great-uncle; painter and graphic artist; 1885–90, instructor at the art academy, Weimar; 1895–99, at the art academy, Karlsruhe; 1899–1905 (temporarily

also director), Stuttgart; 1903, president of the German Artists Federation; married Berta Yorck, née Countess Yorck von Wartenburg; children: Wolf, Anna (married name Koenigs), Johannes, Berta (married name Koenigs), Christine—7, 8, 11, 15, 16

Kalckreuth, Pauline Countess von (1856–1928): wife of Leopold; daughter of Count Stanislaus von Kalckreuth and Anna Eleonore, née Cauer; sister of Clara von Hase and Countess Helene Yorck von Wartenburg; great-aunt of Dietrich Bonhoeffer; the young Bonhoeffer referred to her as Aunt Lina—9

Kalckreuth, Stanislaus, Count von (1820–94): painter; 1858–76, director of the art academy, Weimar; married to Anne, née Cauer, from Bad Kreuznach—8, 16

Kalckreuth, Wolf Count von (1887–1906): German poet; October 9, 1906, committed suicide; Rainer Maria Rilke wrote the *Requiem für Wolf Graf von Kalckreuth*—7

Kalff, Athanasius (formerly Walter) (1904–85): Benedictine and secondary school teacher in the Ettal monastery in Upper Bavaria—16

Kalin, Everett: professor emeritus of New Testament, Pacific Lutheran Theological Seminary—16

Kaltenborn, Carl-Jürgen (b. 1936): professor (emeritus) of ecumenics, Humboldt University, Berlin; 1969, doctoral dissertation on Harnack as teacher of Bonhoeffer; involved in the ecumenical activities of the Christian Peace Conference (Prague)—1, 2, 8, 9, 10, 11, 12

Kaltenbrunner, Ernst (1903–46): lawyer; 1935, leader of the illegal Austrian SS; 1942, SS *Obergruppenführer* of Vienna; 1943, succeeded Reinhard Heydrich as chief of the Reich Central Security Office; 1946, executed—16, 17

Kalthoff, Albert (1850–1906): Protestant pastor; 1906, cofounder and first director of the German Alliance of Monists—11

Kameke, Karl Otto von (1889–1959): 1927, president, German Protestant Railway Missions; 1927, minister director, Reich Ministry of the Interior; representative of the national Protestant Young Men's Association in Germany in the Provisional Bureau for Ecumenical Youth Work—11

Kamlah, Wilhelm (1905–76): German philosopher; from 1951, professor, Hannover; 1954, Erlangen—6, 7

Kampffmeyer, Karl: editor of work on preaching—14

Kandler: German fellowship student in the United States the same year as Bonhoeffer—10

Kanitz, Joachim Werner Archibald (Jochen) (1910–96): German theologian; 1931–33, student of Bonhoeffer in Berlin; 1935, participated in the first Zingst/Finkenwalde session; 1936, pastor, Klinkow, district of Prenz-

lau; 1937, Hohenseefeld near Dahme/Mark; cofounder of the Brotherhood of Young Theologians (affiliated with the Confessing Church), Berlin-Brandenburg; May 1939, conscripted into the military (auxiliary medical service); 1947–79, pastor, Berlin-Lichterfelde—4, 5, 6, 8, 10, 11, 12, 13, 14, 16, 17

Kannapin, Norbert: German military historian—16

Kant, Immanuel (1724–1804): German philosopher of transcendental or critical idealism; professor of logic and metaphysics, Königsberg, Prussia; his epistemology addressed the limits and conditions of human knowledge, and his moral philosophy the coordination of human intellect and conscience—1, 2, 3, 6, 8, 9, 10, 11, 12, 14, 16

Kapler, Hermann (1867–1941): 1925–33, president of the Evangelical High Church Council in Berlin and thus simultaneously president of the German Evangelical Church Council; from April until June 1933, representative of the German Evangelical Church Federation Office ("Kapler committee"); June 30, 1933, retired—10, 12, 17

Kappus, Carl: Bonhoeffer's Hebrew teacher—9

Karajan, Herbert von (1908–89): musical conductor—8

Karamazov, Ivan: character in Dostoyevsky's *The Brothers Karamazov*—6, 7

Karding, Inge: *see* Sembritzki, Inge

Karlstadt, Andreas Bodenstein von (ca. 1480–1541): church reformer—10, 12, 16

Karlström, Nils: 1933–39 and 1948–51, secretary of the Swedish Ecumenical Board; 1947–51, lecturer in church history, Uppsala—14

Karnatz, Bernhard (1882–1976): 1916, church consistory official; 1919, member and privy senior church councilor; 1929, legal director of the Evangelical High Church Council; 1933, forced leave of absence and retirement—10

Karow, Emil Albert Oswald (1871–1954): from 1899, pastor in various parishes, Mark Brandenburg; 1901, pastor, Wegun, district of Prenzlau; 1913, senior pastor and superintendent, Eberswalde; 1921, high consistory official and member of the Evangelical High Church Council in Berlin; 1928, general superintendent, Berlin; 1933, brief leave of absence; November 1, 1933, bishop of Berlin; July 31, 1934, requested retirement; member of the German Evangelical Church Council and of the council of the German Evangelical Church Federation Office; 1936, ordered to an assignment in Athens as substitute pastor—10, 11, 12, 13

Karrenberg, Friedrich (1907–66): industrialist and social ethicist, lived in Velbert; 1937, participated in preparations on behalf of the Confessing Church for the World Church Conference in Oxford; 1946, chair of the committee for social ethics of the Rhineland Church; member of the

synod and social committee of the Evangelical Church of Germany; 1961, honorary professor, Cologne—12, 16
Karstensen, Mrs. (FP): character in the novel, Ulrich's mother—7
Karstensen, Ulrich (FP): character in the novel—7
Karwehl, Richard: German theologian—1
Kasch, Christine: doctoral candidate in theology, Freiburg; consultant on *DBWE* 16—16
Kasten, Seth: reference librarian, Burke Library, Union Theological Seminary, New York—10
Kastl, Ludwig (1878–1969): manager of the Reich Association of German Industry; 1925, member of the Permanent Mandates Commission of the League of Nations—10
Käte: domestic in the house of Paula and Karl Bonhoeffer—11, 15
Katte, Hans-Hermann von (1704–30): Prussian lieutenant and friend of Crown Prince Frederick II of Prussia; executed for trying to help Frederick escape to England—14
Kattenbusch, Ferdinand (1851–1935): 1878, professor of systematic theology, Giessen; 1904, Göttingen; 1906, Halle—1, 2, 11
Kaufmann, Major General: not otherwise identified—15
Kaufmann, Walter A. (1921–80): U.S. philosopher, translator, and Nietzsche scholar—1, 2, 5, 10
Kaufmanns: not otherwise identified (London)—15
Kautsch, Emil (1841–1910): professor of Old Testament in Basel, Tübingen, and Halle—3, 9
Kautsky, Karl (1854–1938): socialist theorist; went into exile under Nazism—10
Kayser, Wolfgang (1904–44): law student; Bonhoeffer's fraternity brother in Tübingen—9
Keckermann, Bartholomäus (1571–1608): Reformed theologian—11
Kegel, Martin (1884–1959): consistory officer—10
Kehnscherper, Gerhard (1903–88): 1928, ordination and assistant pastorate; 1929, pastor, Zechlin/Brandenburg; 1931, member of the NSDAP; 1934, Diaconate Association of Berlin-Zehlendorf; 1935, expulsion from the NSDAP—10
Kehr, Pastor: pastor, Seelow—14
Kehrl, Dr.: 1937, held service at Finkenwalde; not otherwise identified—14
Kehrl, Rudolf (1890–1964): 1927–45, teacher at the cathedral academy in Kolberg; close ties to the Confessing Church—8
Keil: fellow student of Franz Hildebrandt—10
Keimann, Christian (1607–62): Protestant hymnist—8

Keitel, Wilhelm (1882–1946): career military; 1938–45, colonel general, chief of the High Military Command; 1940, general field marshal; May 8, 1945, signed the German surrender; 1946, executed—8, 16, 17

Keller (Mrs.): Silesian farm woman—8

Keller, Adolf (1872–1963): 1896–1928, pastor in Cairo and in Switzerland; 1920, cofounder and until 1940 first secretary of the Swiss Protestant Church Federation; 1921, private lecturer in social ethics, Zürich; 1922, founder and until 1945 general secretary of the European Headquarters for Church Relief Work; 1925, assistant secretary and member of the international executive committee of the Ecumenical Council for Life and Work in Stockholm; 1926–37, general secretary of the Ecumenical Institute of Bossey near Geneva; 1937, vice president of the Reformed World Federation—13, 15

Keller, Gottfried (1819–90): Swiss writer; initially a painter, settled in Munich; 1842, returned to Zürich; 1840s, developed as a writer (poetry); 1848–50, studied in Heidelberg, where the lectures of Ludwig Feuerbach undermined his belief in Christianity; 1854–55, published first novel, *Der grüne Heinrich*; 1856, published *Die Leute von Seldwyla,* his collection of extremely popular short stories; his literary range encompasses profound passion and grotesque comedy, political preaching and sensitive legends; one of the foremost representatives of poetic realism—7, 8, 14

Keller, Samuel (1856–1924): Swiss-born pastor and evangelist; became renowned evangelist in Germany; cofounded the Eisenbach Conference —11

Kellerman, James: U.S. Lutheran pastor and scholar—14

Kelly, Father Herbert: British Anglican, founder of Society of the Sacred Mission in England, visited by Bonhoeffer—17 (for vol. 13)

Kelley, James Patrick: U.S. theologian and Bonhoeffer scholar—2, 4, 6

Kellogg, Arthur: business manager of *The Survey*, a progressive journal that surveyed social conditions in the United States—10

Kelly, Geffrey B.: U.S. theologian; professor of theology, La Salle University, Philadelphia; author of numerous writings on Bonhoeffer; 1992–2000, president, International Bonhoeffer Society, English Language Section —2, 4, 5, 7, 8, 10, 15, 16

Kelly, John: translator of hymns—5, 12

Kempis, Thomas à: *see* Thomas à Kempis

Kempner, Bärbel, née Hildebrandt: Christine Bonhoeffer's best friend; forced to emigrate because of the National Socialist race laws—10

Kennedy, John F. (1917–63): 1960–63, thirty-fifth president of the United States—6

Kepler, Johannes (1571–1630): mathematician, astronomer—8

Keppel-Compton, Mrs.: Reinhold Niebuhr's mother-in-law—13

Kergel, Walter (1909–45): winter 1937–38, participated in the collective pastorate in Köslin—8

Kerlin, Bruno (1913–41): from Berlin-Weißensee; 1938–40, vicar, Pförten/Niederlausitz; 1939–40, participated in the collective pastorate in Sigurdshof; 1940, drafted into military service; 1941, killed in action on the eastern front—16

Kern, Dietrich (b. 1905): student, Tübingen and October 25, 1925– March 26, 1926, Berlin; member of Harnack's seminar—9

Kerr, Marquess of Lothian: *see* Lothian, Lord Philip Henry

Kerrl, Hanns (1887–1941): National Socialist justice official; April 1933–June 1934, Prussian Minister of Justice; July 1935, Reich and Prussian minister for church affairs—4, 13, 14, 15, 16, 17

Kerschensteiner, Georg (1854–1932): educator, representative of the vocational school movement—14

Kerschner, Frederick Doyle: Christian educator and dean of the School of Religion at Butler University—15

Kershaw, Ian: British historian of Germany; author of biography of Hitler —12

Kersting, Andreas: author of work on the Confessing Church—15

Kessel, Albrecht von (1902–76): German diplomat; legation officer in the Foreign Ministry; 1941, at the German consulate in Geneva; from 1943, at the German embassy in the Vatican—16

Kesselring, Albert (1885–1960): general field marshall of the German Air Force; December 1941–March 1945, commanding officer of German troops in Italy—8

Keßler, Augustin (formerly Franz): Benedictine monk and secondary school teacher in the Ettal monastery in Upper Bavaria—16

Kettenacker, Lothar: German historian—16

Keusch, Günther (1911–92): 1935, participated in the first Zingst/Finkenwalde session; 1936–69, pastor, forced to retire for health reasons; 1970–79, active in care for the elderly—14

Key, Ellen Karolina Sofia (1849–1926): Swedish educator and writer; author of numerous works on the feminist movement, child welfare, pacifism, and other topics—2

Keynes, John Maynard (1883–1946): British economist—10

Khomiakov, Alekse Stepanovich (1804–60): Russian lay theologian—1

Kiausch, Helmut (1912–89): from Pomerania; 1938, participated in the collective pastorate in Groß-Schlönwitz; he was then "legalized" and ordained;

1940, pastor, Arnshagen, Pomerania; after 1945, pastor, Burhave/ Oldenburg and Westerstede; 1979, retired—15

Kiderlen-Wächter, Alfred (1852–1912): German career diplomat and politician; before World War I, German undersecretary of foreign affairs; attempted to enlarge Germany's influence and economic presence in Africa—9

Kierkegaard, Søren (1813–55): Danish theologian, author, and philosopher; influenced the development of existentialism and modern philosophy—1, 2, 3, 4, 5, 6, 8, 9, 10, 11, 12, 13, 14, 15, 16

Kilborn, Mrs. E.: guest at Bruay conference September 1934—13

Kilborn, Trevor H. H.: British pastor and ecumenist; August 1934, participated in the Fanø youth conference—13

Killy, Walther: German literary critic; professor of German literature, Göttingen—7

Kinder, Christian (1897–1972): lawyer in Hamburg-Altona; 1925, worked for the regional church office in Kiel (Schleswig-Holstein); 1933, vice president of that regional church; 1937, its president; December 1933–September 1935, Reich leader of the German Christians; 1943–45, university trustee, Kiel; after 1945, businessman in Hamburg—13

Kindt, Karl Friedrich Wilhelm (1901–59): Protestant theologian, educator, philosopher—8

King, Martin Luther, Jr. (1929–68): U.S. Baptist pastor and civil rights leader—6, 10

Kingsley, Charles (1819–75): British writer, leading member of the Christian social movement—12

Kintzel, Elimar (1908–94): "illegal" Confessing Church pastor—13

Kipling, Rudyard (1865–1936): British writer; born in India, reared in England; 1907, Nobel Prize in Literature—14

Kircher, Athanasius (1602–80): Jesuit mathematician and music scholar—9

Kirchmann, Franz (1898–1945): 1926, pastor, Lossow; 1933, Berlin-Stralau—12

Kirchner, Timotheus (1533–87): German Lutheran theologian and pastor—2

Kirkpatrick, Matthew: professor of theology, Oxford; Kierkegaard scholar—14

Kirndorf: pastor, Lagendorf—15

Kirsch, Johann Peter (1861–1941): Catholic priest, church historian, and archaeologist—1

Kirschbaum, Charlotte von (1899–1975): 1929–66, private secretary to Karl Barth; general's daughter from Munich; graduated from the Munich

social women's school; from 1929, lived with Karl Barth as his private secretary; in the last years of the war, member of the Swiss group "Free Germany"—6, 12, 14, 16

Kisiel, Theodore: professor of philosophy; translator of and commentator on Heidegger's works—11

Kiss, Sandor: member of the Hungarian section of the World Alliance for Promoting International Friendship through the Churches—11

Kistiakowski, Theodor: Russian-born sociologist—1

Kistner, Otto (1907–96): "illegal" theologian in the Confessing Church from the Rhineland; 1937, participated in the fifth Finkenwalde session; 1947–70, pastor, Boppard am Rhein—15

Kittel, Gerhard (1868–1948): German New Testament scholar, sympathetic to National Socialism; 1917, private lecturer and, after 1921, professor in Leipzig; 1921, appointed professor, Greifswald; 1926, Tübingen; 1935, participated in the German Lutheran Day, Hannover; 1939–43, professor, Vienna and Tübingen; 1945, dismissed and arrested by the occupation authorities; 1946–48, diaspora pastor in Beuron; the term "Kittel" is also the abbreviation for the *Theological Dictionary of the New Testament* (*TDNT*), which he edited and which began appearing in 1932—2, 4, 12, 13, 14, 15, 16

Kittel, Helmuth (1902–84): 1930–36, lecturer and professor of religious education, Hamburg-Altona, Kiel, Lauenburg, Danzig; professor of New Testament and religious education, Münster; member of the German Christians until the November 1933 Sports Palace rally; 1946, professor, Celle; 1953, Osnabrück; 1963–70, Münster—10, 13

Kittlaus, Eduard: from 1922, pastor, Berlin—12

Klaas: (Lagendorf) not otherwise identified—15

Klaaßen, Mrs.: seamstress who sometimes took care of the Bonhoeffer house while they were away—17 (for *DBWE* 9)

Kläbisch: boy in Bonhoeffer's children's worship group in Barcelona—10

Klabund (pseudonym of Alfred Henschke) (1890–1928): German writer who published a number of novels on historical figures and wrote ecstatic expressionistic poetry; 1918, principal novel was about a vagabond named Bracke—15

Klages, Ludwig (1872–1956): German philosopher, psychologist—8, 11

Klamroth, Erich (1888–1970): 1927, pastor, Berlin-Neukölln; 1933–58, Berlin-Steglitz—12

Klän, Werner: author of study on the "illegal" pastors in the Confessing Church—13, 15, 16

Klappert, Bertold: professor of systematic theology, church seminary, Wuppertal—8

Klapproth, Erich (1912–43): Confessing Church theologian from Karlsruhe/Baden; 1932–33, member of Bonhoeffer's circle of students in Berlin; assistant pastorate, Berlin-Wilmersdorf and Ruppin; 1936–37, participated in the fourth Finkenwalde session; 1937, predicant, Neuruppin; 1938, Kölln-Land; 1938, head of the Brotherhood of Young Theologians of the Confessing Church of Berlin-Brandenburg; pastorate, Berlin-Friedenau; July 18, 1943, as a senior officer cadet, killed in action near Orel—3, 4, 8, 14, 15, 16

Klassen, A. J. (1926–2003): Mennonite theologian; editor of work on Bonhoeffer—4, 5

Klausener, Erich (1885–1934): German politician and head of Catholic Action, Berlin; murdered during the Röhm putsch—13

Klaveness, Frederik: Norwegian pastor; 1898, hospital chaplain, Bergen; until 1936, also senior pastor there; spring 1943, mentioned by Dietrich Bonhoeffer in the "camouflage letter"—16

Kleeberger: Berlin internist, cardiac specialist—8

Klein, William Guss: 1930–31, Bonhoeffer's fellow student at Union Theological Seminary, New York; later worked in Kentucky—10, 15

Kleinert, Paul (1839–1920): German professor of Old Testament and practical theology—14

Kleinschmidt: member of German Reformed St. Paul's church, London—13

Kleist, Dieter (Dennis) von (1893–1971): career military (ultimately colonel) and estate owner of Wendisch-Tychow (Pomerania); 1933, commander of the military district Stolp, also garrison senior officer; March 1945, dispatched as commandant to the defense of Stolp—15, 16

Kleist, Ewald von: estate owner of Wendisch-Tychow (from December 1937: Tychow)—15

Kleist, Heinrich von (1777–1811): German writer—8, 14

Kleist, Margarethe von: wife of Ewald von Kleist—15

Kleist-Retzow, Hans-Friedrich von (1923–41): son of Hans Jürgen and Maria von Kleist; April 1938, confirmed by Dietrich Bonhoeffer in Kieckow; July 1941, killed in action as senior officer cadet on the eastern front—8, 14, 15, 16, 17

Kleist-Retzow, Hans-Hugo von (1814–92): German politician; reflected the ultra-conservative, high church perspective of some Prussian conservatives—6, 8

Kleist-Retzow, Hans Jürgen von (1887–1969): estate owner in Kieckow/Pomerania; son of Ruth von Kleist-Retzow; husband of Maria, née von Diest; Dietrich Bonhoeffer often stayed at his home; after July 20, 1944, arrested; 1945, taken to the Soviet Union as prisoner of war; after return to Germany, secretary, Association of Evangelical Congregations in

Pomerania in Lippstadt; from 1954, in Bremen-Kattenesch, where he was the property owner of the newly founded Thomas community—8, 14, 15, 16, 17

Kleist-Retzow, Jürgen Christoph von (1921–41): son of Hans Jürgen von Kleist; August 5, 1941, killed in action as a lieutenant in a rifle regiment on the eastern front—8, 16, 17

Kleist-Retzow, Konstantin von (b. 1919): son of Hans Jürgen and Maria von Kleist-Retzow; 1936, confirmed by Martin Niemöller; after military service and being a prisoner of war, studied theology; 1951, missionary, South Africa; 1965, pastor, Kirchweye near Bremen; 1974, Hämelchenburg—8, 16

Kleist-Retzow, Maria von (Mieze), née von Diest (1893–1965): wife of the estate owner Hans-Jürgen von Kleist—8, 15, 16

Kleist-Retzow, Ruth von, née Countess von Zedlitz-Trützschler (1867–1945): grandmother of Maria von Wedemeyer; married Jürgen von Kleist; after 1897, following her husband's death, she owned the estate of Klein-Krössin near Kieckow; from 1935, attended the Confessing Church services in Finkenwalde; supporter of Dietrich Bonhoeffer—4, 6, 7, 8, 14, 15, 16, 17

Klemperer, Klemens von: *see* Von Klemperer, Klemens

Klemperer, Victor (1881–1960): scholar of Romance languages; from 1920, professor, Dresden; 1933, removed from office due to Nazi race laws; after 1951, professor, Humboldt University, Berlin—6, 8

Klepper, Jochen (1903–42): German poet, author, and hymnist; representative of the Christian historical novel; 1942, he, his Jewish wife, and her daughter committed suicide together—6, 16, 17

Kliefoth, Theodor (1810–95): 1840, pastor; 1844, church superintendent, Schwerin; 1848, leader of the Lutheran restoration in the new church administration, Schwerin; 1886, president, Evangelical High Church Council—1, 11, 14

Klingenberg: German fellowship student in the United States the same year as Bonhoeffer—10

Klinger, Max (1857–1920): German neoclassical painter, etcher, and sculptor—7, 9, 11

Kloppenburg, Heinz (1903–86): 1932, pastor, Wilhelmshaven; 1934, dismissed from office; 1934–45, head of the Confessing Church, Oldenburg; 1934 and 1936, member of the Reich Council of Brethren; 1945–53, senior church official, Oldenburg—14

Klopstock, Friedrich Gottlieb (1724–1803): German lyric poet; his religious epic poem, *Der Messias* (1748, final installment 1773), immediately established his national reputation as a poetic genius; also well known for his

odes; regarded as the originator of a new age in poetry in Germany—8, 14

Kloß, Hans (b. 1908): Viennese businessman; initially employed by the Austrian Aviation-AG; from 1933, worked in management of German Lufthansa; had professional as well as conspiratorial contact with Klaus Bonhoeffer; October 7, 1944, arrested; after February 2, 1945, following his trial before the People's Court, sentenced to four years in the Brandenburg prison—16

Klostermann, Erich (1870–1963): Protestant New Testament and patristics scholar—9, 14

Klotz, K.: member of the congregational council, German Reformed St. Paul's Church, London—13

Klotz, Leopold: publisher—13

Kluge, Hans Günther von (1882–1944): career military; 1941, general field marshal, leader of the Center Army Group in Russia; 1944, commander in chief in the West; after July 20, 1944, deposed by Hitler; August 19, 1944, committed suicide—16

Kluge, Pastor: recipient of Bonhoeffer's 1933 circular letter; not otherwise identified—12

Kluge, Ulrich: author of work on the Freiburg circle—16

Klügel, Eberhard (1901–66): 1929, assistant pastor; 1931, worked with the Berlin City Mission and as an adviser to the Evangelical Press Association for Germany; chaplain in the regional association for Inner Mission, Hannover; 1933, pastor, Bennigsen; 1933, member of the Council of Brethren of the Pastors' Emergency League; 1937–50, head of the preachers' seminary in Erichsburg; 1943–46, adviser to Bishop Marahrens; 1950, member of the regional church council in Hannover; 1959, church superintendent of Hannover—13

Klugkist-Hesse, Hermann: Confessing Church pastor of the Reformed church in Elberfeld; part of the leadership of the Coetus Reformed Preachers in the Rhineland—16

Klugmann, H.: member of the congregational council, German Reformed St. Paul's Church, London—13

Kluke, Paul: historian of twentieth-century Germany—12

Kluxen, Wolfgang: philosopher, author of works on Thomas Aquinas—16

Knackfuß, Hermann (1848–1915): German art historian, professor at the art academy, Düsseldorf—9

Knak, Gustav (1806–78): hymnist—14

Knak, Siegfried (1875–1955): 1901, pastor, Pomerania; 1910–20, inspector, Berlin Mission Society; 1921–49, director, Berlin Mission Society; 1933,

deputy head of the German Missionary Council; from 1950, professor of mission studies at the seminary, Berlin, and at the University of Halle—11, 12, 13, 16

Knight, Eric (1897–1943): British writer—16

Knittermeyer, Hinrich (1891–1958): German philosopher; director of the state library, Bremen—2, 10, 12

Knobloch: noncommissioned officer, member of the guard staff in Tegel; together with noncommissioned officer Helmut Linke helped convey the illegal correspondence between Bonhoeffer and Eberhard Bethge—8

Knolle, Theodor (1885–1955): Confessing Church pastor; later professor of practical theology—14

Knop, Miss (not otherwise identified): fellow student of Franz Hildebrandt—10

Knopf: assistant to Hermann von Soden during the latter's journey to Palestine—8

Knopf, Rudolf (1874–1920): professor of New Testament and historian of early Christian thought—9

Knorr, August (1900–1958): physician; 1932–45, head of internal medicine at the Deaconess Hospital in Köslin, Pomerania; extremely active there on behalf of the Confessing Church; member of the Pomeranian Council of Brethren; 1947, head of the Evangelical Academy, Tutzing, Upper Bavaria; 1950, director of the Palmenwald spa, Freudenstadt—8, 15, 16

Knudson, Albert Cornelius (1873–1953): U.S. theologian and philosopher; 1906, Boston—10

Knuth, Hans Christian: German Lutheran theologian—15

Knutson, David (1937–2004): professor of religion, Pacific Lutheran University—16

Koch, Annemarie: wife of the lawyer Hans Koch—16

Koch, Anton (1859–1915): Roman Catholic priest and professor of moral and pastoral theology, University of Tübingen; represented Reform Catholicism—6

Koch, Eduard Emil (1809–71): renowned Protestant hymnist—14

Koch, Hans (1893–1945): lawyer; 1927, attorney-at-law; 1933, notary, Berlin; member of the Confessing Church; 1938, defense attorney, with Horst Holstein and W. Hahn, in the Martin Niemöller trial; because he also had Jewish clients, temporarily held in a concentration camp; conspiratorial contact with Canaris, Oster, and Dohnanyi; in the event of a successful coup, Goerdeler had designated him as head of the German Supreme Court; January 21, 1945, arrested; April 24, 1945, executed—16, 17

Koch, Hans: professor, Königsberg; August 1934, participated in the Fanø conference—13

Koch, Hans Friedrich (1881–1942): church provost, Güstrow; member of Mecklenburg Council of Brethren—14

Koch, Ingeborg (Inge) (1914–76): from Merseburg; Confessing Church theologian in the church province of Saxony; married to Confessing pastor Hans Zippel; 1939–40, ministry, Merseburg; after Zippel was drafted into the military, she led the Brotherhood of Assistant Pastors and Vicars of the province of Saxony; performed compulsory wartime work in a factory; 1943, Zippel was killed in action; after the war, married name Anz—16

Koch, Karl (1876–1951): 1904, pastor, Westphalia; 1916–49, Bad Oeynhausen; 1919–33, representative in the Prussian parliament (German National People's Party); 1927, church superintendent in Vlotho and president of the Westphalian provincial synod; 1930–32, member of the national parliament; 1934, member of the Provisional Church Administration of the German Evangelical Church; 1934–43, president of the Old Prussian and Confessing Synods of the German Evangelical Church; 1945–49, president of the Westphalian regional church—13, 14, 15, 16, 17

Koch, Laurentius: author of works on Ettal—16

Koch, Rudolf (1876–1934): graphic artist and book designer in Offenbach; a master of art associated with religious scripts, books, and altars—8, 14, 15

Koch, Werner (1910–94): 1935–36, participated in the second Finkenwalde session; 1936, assistant pastor, Barmen, also accompanied Bonhoeffer to Switzerland; November 1936, arrested for having forwarded to foreign recipients the Provisional Church Administration memorandum to Hitler; February 1937–December 1938, in Sachsenhausen concentration camp; 1939, drafted into military service as a translator; 1945–46, prisoner of war and prison chaplain with the British; 1947, pastor, Berlin; 1952, Espelkamp; 1958, Netphen/Sieg; 1969, retired—8, 11, 14, 15, 16

Kochheim, Gustav (1893–1962): church deacon—12

Köckert, Christian: East German pastor; after 1989, politician—4

Kodalle, Klaus-Michael: professor of practical philosophy, University of Jena—11

Koebner, Thomas: professor of contemporary German literature and media studies, Philipps University, Marburg—12

Koechlin, Alphons (1885–1965): Swiss theologian and ecumenist; 1910, pastor, Stein/Rhein; 1921, Basel; 1923, head of the Basel Mission; 1936–59, its president; from 1925, member of the Universal Christian Council for Life and Work; 1926, vice president of the World Alliance of the YMCA; 1933, president of the Basel Church Council; 1933–54, church president; 1934, participated in the conference in Fanø; maintained close contact

with George Bell during the Church Struggle; 1940–54, member of the executive committee of the World Council of Churches; 1941–54, president of the Swiss Protestant Church Federation; October 1945, participated in the Stuttgart conference—13, 16

Koellreutter, Otto (1883–1972): German lawyer; 1938–39, represented Nazi Germany in Japan in a cultural exchange program between the two nations; 1940, professor of public law, University of Munich—6

Koenigs, Anna (Mucki), née Countess von Kalckreuth: wife of Franz Koenigs—15

Koenigs, Franz (1881–1941): banker and art collector in Amsterdam; husband of Anna, née Countess von Kalckreuth; autumn, 1940, temporarily imprisoned—15, 16

Koepp (Köpp), Wilhelm (1885–1965): from 1922, professor of systematic theology, Greifswald—10

Koffka, Otto: student in Tübingen; interested in the Hedgehog fraternity —9

Kohlbrügge, Hermann Friedrich (1803–75): pastor for thirty years in the Dutch Reformed church, Wuppertal-Elberfeld—2, 4, 10, 14, 15

Köhler: 1936, "neutral" pastor, Greifswald—14

Köhler, Johannes (b. 1895): from 1924, pastor in Berlin—12

Köhler, Jutta: friend of Ursula Schleicher—9

Köhler, Rudolf: author of 1932 article on Barth's approach to missions and theology—12

Köhler, Udo: winter semester 1932–33, attended Bonhoeffer's lectures on contemporary systematic theology—3, 12

Köhler, Wolfgang: Berlin gestalt psychologist; 1924–25, Bonhoeffer attended his course on gestalt theory at Berlin University—9

Kohlhaas, Michael: character in novel of the same name by Kleist—8

Koken, Mrs.: mentioned in letters from Tübingen—9

Kolb, Robert: Missions Professor of Systematic Theology and director of the Institute for Mission Studies at Concordia Seminary, Saint Louis—13, 15

Kolbe, Johannes: author of catechetical studies—10

Kolbenheyer, Erwin Guido (1878–1962): German writer—12

Koller, Martin (b. 1873): pastor, Stahnsdorf, between Teltow and Potsdam, belonging to the diocese of Kölln-Land, whose superintendent was Max Diestel—9

Köller, Walter: 1934, member of the Brotherhood of Assistant Pastors and Vicars of the province of Saxony, Confessing Church; 1943, killed in action—14

Kollmann, Hans: East Prussian theologian; 1940, lieutenant in heavy-artillery section 37; July 1940, participated in the weekend retreat in Blöstau—16
Köneren, Felix: stepfather of Karl-Heinz Köttgen—10
König, Stefan: author of work on lawyers during the Third Reich—8
Koonz, Claudia: U.S. historian, author of works on Nazi Germany and the Holocaust—12
Köpf, Ulrich: German church historian—14, 15
Koplin: off-duty officer (1935)—14
Köpp, Wilhelm—*see* Koepp, Wilhelm
Korah: biblical character—5, 15
Kordau, Mr.: member of the Hedgehog fraternity—9
Korenke, Christine Elisabeth, née Schleicher: daughter of Rüdiger and Ursula Schleicher; wife of Dr. Heinz-Dieter Korenke—8, 10, 15, 16
Korn, Elisabeth: writer on the German Youth Movement—9
Korporal: building contractor; father of Hinrich Korporal—15
Korporal, Hinrich: from the church province of Saxony; 1939, participated in the collective pastorate in Sigurdshof; 1942, pastor, Mehmke near Salzwedel; 1977, retired—15
Körte: 1936, pastor, Luckau—14
Körte, Wilhelm: German scholar of linguistics—8
Korth, Thomas: from 1927, editor of *Der Krankentrost*—14
Koschorke, Manfred (1908–85): 1937, vicar at the Corpus Christi Church, Königsberg; imprisoned for nine weeks after taking collections for the Confessing Church; pastor, Königsberg-Ließt; student chaplain, Königsberg, assigned by the Council of Brethren to the Löbenicht church; after the war, pastor in Aachen—16
Kossak, Dr.: director, Humboldt University archives—2
Köster, Peter: Nietzsche scholar—6
Köstlin, Julius (1826–1902): Protestant theologian and church historian; author of works on Luther—1, 9, 14, 15
Köttgen, Karl-Heinz: one of Bonhoeffer's remedial pupils in Barcelona; 1944, killed in action, Russia—10
Köttgen-Köneren, Wilma: mother of Karl-Heinz Köttgen—10
Kottwitz, Hans Ernst, Baron von (1757–1843): leading figure in the nineteenth-century Berlin revival movement—14
Kracauer, Siegfried: sociologist—1
Kracht, Moritz: from 1914, pastor, Berlin—12
Kraell, Alexander: from 1938, lawyer in the military justice system; 1943, senior lawyer in the military high court; head of legal staff of the military high court—16

Kraemer, Hendrik (1888–1965): Dutch theologian and ecumenist; 1922, missionary in Java; 1938, professor of religious history, Leyden; 1948, director of the Ecumenical Institute of Bossey near Geneva; 1956, retired —16

Kraemer, Wilhelm: 1938–39, participated in the collective pastorate in Groß-Schlönwitz—15

Kramer, Franz (1878–1967): senior assistant to Karl Bonhoeffer in Breslau and at the Charité hospital in Berlin; Jewish background; November 1933, withdrawal of his teaching permit; 1935, dismissal; 1938, emigration to Holland—15

Krämer, Sybille: lecturer in psychiatry, Technical University, Munich—8

Kramm, Hans Herbert (1910–55): vicar in Potsdam, Sweden, and Berlin (with Birger Forell); 1932–33, member of Bonhoeffer's circle of students in Berlin; 1934, participated in the ecumenical youth conference in Fanø, and 1935 in Chamby; from February 1935, ecumenical adviser with the Confessing Church; 1936, curate, London and Copenhagen; 1936, hospital chaplain, Berlin; 1938–39, fellowship at Oxford; 1941, pastor, German Lutheran St. Mary's Church, London; 1953, pastor, Lüneburg—13, 14, 16

Kramp, Erich: East Prussian Confessing Church pastor; brother of Willy Kramp; 1939, sent by the East Prussian Council of Brethren to Ebenrode (formerly Stallupönen); drafted into the military shortly thereafter—16

Kramp, Willy (1909–86): writer; until 1939, teacher and army psychologist; resided from 1936 with his brother in Margen on the Courland Bay; active in the East Prussian Confessing Church; 1943, drafted into military service; after returning from Russian prisoner of war camps, head of the Protestant student foundation, Villigst, Westphalia—8, 16

Kranz, Walther (1884–1960): Greek scholar; after 1919, Greek and Latin teacher of Bonhoeffer at the Friedrich Werder Gymnasium, Berlin-Grunewald; later professor in Halle, Istanbul, and Bonn; published on the history of Greek literature—2, 7, 9, 10, 17 (for vol. 9)

Krätschel(l), Eberhard: 1930, pastor, Berlin-Mahlsdorf; 1933, Berlin-Heinersdorf—12

Kraus, Hans-Joachim (1918–2000): Old Testament scholar; one of the founders of Christian-Jewish dialogue in postwar Germany—8

Kraus (also Krauß), Paul: Hedgehog member in Tübingen; later professor of medicine, Göppingen—9, 17 (for vol. 9)

Krause, Bruno (1880–1967): father of Winfried and Gerhard Krause; pastor in Ückermünde, Vilmnitz, Grimmen (1926–34, superintendent), Spantekow/Anklam—8

Krause, Gerhard (b. 1887): 1934, pastor in Zingst, church district of Barth —14

Krause, Gerhard (1912–82): German theologian; winter 1936–37, participated in the fourth Finkenwalde session; in contrast to Bonhoeffer, supported the "legalization" of Confessing Church clergy to allow them to obtain positions in the official German Evangelical Church; until 1955, prisoner of war in Russia; 1956, pastor, Bünde, Westphalia; from 1962, professor of practical theology and Reformation history, Bonn—2, 4, 6, 8, 13, 14, 15

Krause, Hans: engineer; 1913–19, fellow student of Dietrich Bonhoeffer in the Friedrich Werder Gymnasium, Berlin-Grunewald—7

Krause, Reinhold (1893–1980): 1922–33, academic assessor; 1932, joined the NSDAP; 1932–33, district head and spokesperson for Protestant church questions; 1932, head of the German Christians for Berlin; member of the provincial synod and of the Old Prussian General Synod (Mark Brandenburg); cofounder of the German National People's Party in Berlin-Pankow; after November 13, 1933, relieved as district head after his Sports Palace speech and dismissed from all church offices; 1934–45, deputy headmaster, Berlin; 1945–50, interned in Landsberg/Warthe and Buchenwald; 1951–58, secondary school teacher—11, 13

Krause, Sigrid: wife of Gerhard Krause—15

Krause, Winfried (1910–43): Gerhard Krause's brother; 1935, vicar in Stolp and Stettin; summer 1937, participated in the fifth Finkenwalde session; 1938, assistant pastor at St. Mary's, Köslin; September 1939, drafted into military service; 1943, died in the military hospital in Marburg from wounds suffered in Russia—8, 14, 15, 16

Krause, Wolfgang (1913–41): 1936, vicar in Köthen/Anhalt; 1937, participated in the fifth Finkenwalde session; afterward expelled from Anhalt; 1939, ministry in Breitau-Sontra near Dessau; September 10, 1941, killed in action near Smolensk—16

Krauß, Alfred: German theologian—1

Krauss, Reinhard: U.S. Presbyterian pastor, born and educated in Germany; doctorate on Barth; translator of several volumes in *DBWE*—1, 2, 6, 15

Krebs, Dr.: colleague of Otto Bonhoeffer in Barcelona—10

Kreck, Walter (1908–2002): 1935, lecturer at the Confessing Church preachers' seminary, Frankfurt am Main; 1937, pastor of the French Reformed congregation there; 1941, Oberfischbach; 1946, professor at the theological seminary, Herborn; 1952, professor of systematic and practical theology, Bonn—16

Krencker, Daniel (1874–1941): professor of architecture at the Technical College in Berlin-Charlottenburg—11

Kretschmar, Georg: author of work on the Barmen confession—12

Kretzer, Albert (formerly Karl) (1905–75): Benedictine monk and secondary school teacher in the Ettal monastery, Upper Bavaria—16

Kreutzer, Leonid (1884–1953): pianist; 1921–33, professor of piano at the state music academy in Berlin; 1933, emigrated to the United States—9

Krey, Peter: U.S. Lutheran pastor and Luther scholar; doctorate in early modern history of Christianity—12

Kriege, Johannes (1859–1937): diplomat; 1921–32, member of the Prussian parliament—14

Krivocheine, Basile (1900–1985): Russian-born Orthodox priest and scholar —1

Kroner, Richard (1884–1974): German philosopher; 1928, professor, Kiel; 1938, emigrated to England; 1940, emigrated to the United States; 1941, professor, New York—6

Kropatschek, Friedrich (1875–1917): German theologian—9

Kröpelin, Wilhelm: from 1919, pastor, Berlin—12

Kroppenstedt, Heinrich (1884–1958): from 1914, pastor, Berlin-Siemensstadt—12

Krötke, Wolf: German professor of systematic theology; 1958–65, studied theology, Leipzig (German Democratic Republic) and East Berlin; 1958–59, political prisoner in the Waldheim prison during his studies; 1967–70, pastor, Görschen, Naumberg/Saale; 1970–73, student chaplain, Halle/Saale; 1973–91, professor of systematic theology, Protestant theological institute, Humboldt University; 1976, honorary doctorate, University of Tübingen; 1990, recipient of the Karl Barth Prize of the Evangelical Church of the Union (EKU); 1991, postdoctoral lecturing qualification, Leipzig; from 1995, member of the European Academy of Sciences—7, 8, 12, 16

Krückmann, Emil (1865–1944): professor of ophthalmology; from 1912, director of the university hospital eye clinic, Berlin; father of Oluf und Püppi Krückmann—9

Krückmann, Oluf: son of Emil Krückmann—9

Krückmann, Püppi: son of Emil Krückmann—9

Krueger, Karl: since 2003, director of the Krauth Memorial Library, Lutheran Theological Seminary, Philadelphia—6

Kruger, Colleen: assisted with *DBWE* 1—1

Krüger, Hans Jürgen (1908–85): from Berlin; 1935, participated in the first Zingst/Finkenwalde session; 1936–78, pastor—14

Krüger, Heinz (1912–95): 1937, participated in the fifth Zingst/Finkenwalde session—14

Krukenberg: professor in Stettin—12

Krummacher, Friedrich Adolf: theologian, bishop, and ecumenist of the German Evangelical Church; played an important ecumenical role during the Church Struggle but was not always helpful to Bonhoeffer's cause; historian; author of work on Weimar Republic—9

Krummacher, Friedrich-Wilhelm (1901–74): 1928, pastor, Essen-Werden; 1934, high church official and bishop, Church Foreign Office, German Evangelical Church; high consistory official; 1939, military chaplain; 1943–45, prisoner of war in Russia, cofounder of the "National Committee Free Germany"; 1945, church superintendent, Berlin-Land and pastor, Berlin-Weißensee; 1946, general superintendent, Berlin; 1955–72, bishop of the Pomeranian church (after 1968, regional church of Greifswald); head of the Conference of Protestant Church Administrations, German Democratic Republic; 1961–69, member, advisory council, Evangelical Church of Germany—13, 14, 15

Krupp, Friedrich Alfred (1854–1902): founder of the Krupp steel industry, which also produced weapons—9

Kruse (FP): character in the novel; the forestry assistant called "Yellowboots"—7

Kruseberg: pastor; not otherwise identified—15

Krüss (Krüß), Hugo Andres (1879–1945): 1925–45, director, Prussian State Library, Berlin—10

Kübarth, Mrs.: one of Ruth von Kleist-Retzow's acquaintances in Stettin—16

Kube, Wilhelm (1887–1943): journalist and publicist; 1920, general secretary, German National People's Party; 1924–27, member of parliament (National Socialist Freedom Party); 1928, joined the NSDAP; 1932, cofounder of the German Christian faith movement in Prussia; 1933, regional Nazi party leader [Gauleiter] of the electorate of Mark Brandenburg [Kurmark] and, until 1936 (when he was dismissed), senior president of the province of Brandenburg; 1941, general commissar in Weissruthenia (Belarus)—11, 13

Küch, Mrs.: Bonhoeffer officiated at her funeral in London—13

Küchler, Georg von (b. 1881): career military; 1941, commander in chief of the Eighteenth Army Division; 1942, general field marshal, commander in chief of the Army Group North on the eastern front; January 1944, recalled and transferred to the führer reserves—16

Kuessner (Küßner), Theodor (1896–1984): 1925, lecturer in church history, theological college, Bethel; 1931, pastor, Lötzen, East Prussia, head of

the Mazurian deaconesses' home; 1933, founder of the East Prussian Pastors' Emergency League; head of the first East Prussian Confessing Synod; 1935, appointed to the executive committee of the Reich Church; after 1945, pastor, Quakenbrück—16

Kuhlmann, Gerhardt: German theologian—2

Kühlmann, Richard von (1872–1948): diplomat and writer; 1917, permanent secretary in the foreign office; 1918, forced to resign because of his policy of rapprochement—10

Kuhn (family): members of the congregation in Barcelona—10

Kühn, Lotte, née Frick: wife of Rudolf Kühn; participated in the Fanø youth conference—13

Kühn, Rudolf (1909–44): studied theology until 1935; 1932–33, member of Bonhoeffer's circle of students in Berlin; 1934, part of the German delegation to the Fanø youth conference; 1936, participated in the third Finkenwalde session; 1937, pastor, Berlin-Tempelhof; 1938, Potsdam; 1941, military service, ultimately as a sergeant first class; December 1944, killed in action near Saarlautern—13, 14, 15, 16

Kümmel, Werner Georg (1905–95): 1929, doctorate; 1931, member of the German youth delegation to the ecumenical meeting in Cambridge; 1932, professor of New Testament theology, Zürich; 1946, professor, Zürich; 1951, Mainz; 1952, Marburg—11

Kunert, Erwin (1910–94): summer 1935, participated in the first Zingst/Finkenwalde session; 1936–76, pastor—8, 14

Kunisch, Sigmund: storm trooper (SA) group leader; 1935, minister director, Reich and Prussian Ministry for Science, Training, and Public Education—14

Künkel, Friedrich (1892–1937): from 1931, pastor, Berlin-Schmargendorf—12

Künkel, Fritz (1889–1956): physician (psychotherapist) and characterologist in Berlin; worked with Alfred Adler but later broke with him; also conducted religio-psychological seminars for theologians; 1939, emigrated to the United States during a lecture tour—6, 14

Künneth, Walter (1901–97): 1923, doctorate; 1927, postdoctoral lecturing qualification and lecturer, Friedrich Wilhelm University, Berlin; 1927, head of the office on apologetics of the Johannes institutions, executive committee for Inner Mission, Berlin-Spandau; 1930, private lecturer in systematic theology, Berlin; 1933, cofounder of the Young Reformation movement; 1937, withdrawal of the *venia legendi* (authorization to teach at university after postdoctoral lecturing qualification) for political reasons and prohibition against public speaking and publishing; 1938, pastor, Starnberg, Upper Bavaria; 1944, dean, Erlangen; 1946, professor

honoris causa, Erlangen; 1953, professor of systematic theology, Erlangen —11, 12, 13, 14

Kunze, Dr.: SS *Obersturmführer*; adviser for church questions, Reich Central Security Office, section IV B; participated in Christine von Dohnanyi's interrogations regarding church contacts—16

Kunze, Johannes Gerhard (1892–1954): 1922, pastor, Leipzig-Gohlis; 1925, student chaplain, Leipzig, also a member of the Church Congregational Association; 1933, dismissed from office; representative of the Conference of Protestant Student Chaplains in the Headquarters for Ecumenical Youth Work; 1933–48, pastor, initially in Hannover-Bothfeld; 1946–48, city church superintendent, Hannover; 1950, director of the reopened preachers' seminary, Preetz, Holstein—1, 10, 11, 14

Kunze, Otto (1912–96): winter 1937–38, participated in the collective pastorate, Köslin; 1941–45, military chaplain—8

Kunzendorf: 1933, pastor, Berlin—12

Kunzler, Michael: author of work on liturgy—14

Kupfer, Angelus (1900–1950): Benedictine monk; 1933, abbot of the Ettal monastery in Upper Bavaria—15, 16

Kupisch, Karl (1903–82): German theologian and scholar of church history; studied in Berlin; 1939, doctorate; 1946–51, taught history and church history at the seminary, Berlin; 1955, professor *honoris causa* of general religious and intellectual history at the Technical College, Berlin; 1959–61, rector of the Berlin seminary; editor of the works of several prominent theologians, including K. Barth, K. Kautzky, and H. Vogel; contributed seventy articles to the encyclopedia *Religion in Geschichte und Gegenwart*, 3rd ed.; with Heinrich Albertz und Helmut Gollwitzer, one of the leading critical theologians in Berlin—9, 11

Kurtz, Adolf (1891–1975): 1922–62, pastor in Berlin; 1947, honorary cathedral canon of Brandenburg—12

Kuske, Martin (1940–95): studied theology, Rostock; 1965, assistant, Institute for Systematic Theology, University of Rostock (German Democratic Republic); 1968, ThD and ordination to the ministry; 1969, pastor, Rostock; 1973, director of studies, Protestant preachers' seminary, Gnadau (GDR); 1978, pastor, Teterow-Mecklenburg; 1981, secretary of the Bonhoeffer Committee, Alliance of Protestant Churches, GDR; 1992, after German reunification, second chairperson of the International Bonhoeffer Society, German section; publications include *Dietrich Bonhoeffers Wertung und Auslegung des Alten Testaments*, Berlin (GDR) 1970, Göttingen 1971, English edition, Philadelphia 1976; *Weltliches Christsein, Dietrich Bonhoeffers Vision nimmt Gestalt an*, Berlin (GDR) and Munich 1984; coeditor of *DBW* 4—3, 4, 5, 6, 8, 14, 17

Küstermann, Helene (Leni), née Brückner (1886–1960): daughter of Karl Brückner and Margarethe, née Domrich; often visited the Bonhoeffer home with her daughters—9

Kütemeyer, Wilhelm: Kierkegaard scholar—6, 14

Kutter, Hermann (1863–1931): Swiss Reformed theologian, philosopher, pastor, and social activist in Zürich; with Leonhard Ragaz, one of the founders and leaders of religious socialism in Switzerland; influenced by Christoph Blumhardt in Bad Boll—9, 11, 14, 16

Kutzner, Helmuth: officer in the military high court in Berlin; during the first half of 1944, conducted the investigations into activities involving Dohnanyi and Bonhoeffer—8, 16, 17

Kuyper, Abraham (1837–1920): Dutch Calvinist theologian and politician —3, 13

Lächele, Rainer: German church historian—17 (for vol. 12)

Lachmund, Heinrich (1875–1952): 1927, pastor, Blankenburg, Harz—12

Lactantius (260–330): patristic theologian—1, 6

Ladenig: military justice inspector with the military high court—8, 16

Laer, Friederike von, née von Wedemeyer (1884–1945): sister of Maria von Wedemeyer's father; lived on the Oberbehme estate in Westphalia—8

Lagarde, Paul Anton de (1827–91): born Paul Bötticher; German Orientalist, linguist, and cultural philosopher; professor, Göttingen; opponent of materialism; anti-Semite who advocated a supraconfessional national church and Germanic ethics—10, 11

Lahusen: 1920s, pastor of the German congregation in Madrid—10

Lalage: woman mentioned in Horace—9

La Mettrie, Julien Offray de (1709–51): French philosopher—6

Lämmerhirdt, Hildegard (1909–98): 1930, worked with a German youth organization, *Jungdeutschen Ordens*; 1933, in London; 1935, at Burckhardt House in Berlin-Dahlem; 1937, worked with German emigrants, Amsterdam; 1947–65, ecumenical adviser to the Westphalian regional church—13

Lammers, Hans-Heinrich (1879–1962): 1912, judge in Beuthen; from 1921, in the Reich Ministry of the Interior; 1922, legal counselor in that ministry; 1932, departmental police head; 1933–45, head of the Reich chancellery; 1933, state secretary; 1937, Reich minister; 1949, sentenced in the Nuremberg "Wilhelmstrasse" trial to twenty years in prison; 1951, sentence reduced to ten years; 1952, released in amnesty—12, 13

Lampe, Adolf (1897–1948): economist; from 1926, professor, Freiburg im Breisgau; member of the Confessing Church and of the Freiburg circle;

economic adviser to Goerdeler; 1942–43, worked on the Freiburg memorandum; September 8, 1944, arrested; April 25, 1945, released from the Lehrter Strasse prison in Berlin—8, 16, 17

Lampe, Gertrud (1904–97): Confessing Church member and member of Freiburg circle—16

Lamprecht, Gerhard (1897–1974): German film producer and director—10

Landshut, Siegfried (1897–1968): economist; 1932, lecturer, Hamburg; 1933, emigrated to Palestine because of Nazi race laws; lecturer at the University of Cairo; 1936–38, researcher, Hebrew University in Jerusalem; 1940–45, worked for the British Headquarters for Middle Eastern Affairs; 1945–48, appointed by the British Foreign Office to do cultural work with German prisoners of war in the Near East; 1948–51, conducted research in London; 1951, professor of political science, Hamburg—12

Lang, Alois (1872–1954): German-born master woodcarver, born in Oberammergau; specialized in the medieval art of ecclesiastical carving; 1890, emigrated to the United States—15

Lang, Anton: professor of German, Georgetown University; son of German potter Anton Lang who played Christ in the Oberammergau Passion Play and subsequently came into conflict with Nazi authorities—15

Lang, August (1867–1945): 1921, district superintendent, Reformed church of Halle; professor *honoris causa*, Halle—12

Lang, Cosmo Gordon (1864–1945): 1888, fellowship at All Souls College, Oxford; 1890, ordained; 1901, (suffragan) bishop of Stepney; 1908, archbishop of York; 1928–42, archbishop of Canterbury—13, 16, 17

Lang, Kurt (1904–82): fellow student of Franz Hildebrandt; Swiss pastor; 1930, ordained in Berlin; ministry in Bad Saarow; member of the Pastors' Emergency League; 1934, expelled; 1936, pastor in Montreux, where Eberhard Bethge visited him; 1941, Winterthur; 1961, institutional chaplain in the deaconesses' home, Bern—14, 16

Lang, Theodor (1870–1931): 1925, senior consistory official, Evangelical High Church Council; 1929, pastor, Berlin-Dahlem—10

Lang, Theodor (1890–1973): diplomat; chancellor of the German embassy in London; 1934, lived in Sydenham—8

Lang, Walter: signatory for the Trowitzsch publishing company—10

Langbehn, Carl (1901–44): lawyer; even before the war, active in the political opposition; conspiratorial contacts in foreign countries; contacts to Himmler, whom he hoped to win over to the resistance against Hitler; 1943, arrested; October 1944, executed—16

Lange, Frits de: *see* de Lange

Lange, R.: not otherwise identified—15

Lanz, Jakob—2

Laocoön: legendary Trojan prince, priest of Apollo and Poseidon; protested against the plan to draw the wooden horse into Troy because the gods wished the destruction of Troy; two serpents sent by Poseidon killed him and his two sons; their death agony was depicted in a marble group (ca. 50 B.C.E.) now in the Vatican—8, 16

Lapide, Pinchas (1922–97): Austrian-born Jewish philosopher; survived the concentration camps; after war, became Israeli diplomat to the Vatican and elsewhere; active supporter of Christian-Jewish dialogue—8

Laplace, Pierre Simon Marquis de (1749–1827): French mathematician and physicist—8

La Rochefoucauld, François VI, Duke of (1613–80): French writer—15

Larson, Erik: U.S. author—14

Laske, Paul: 1940, member of student parish, Königsberg; participated in Dietrich Bonhoeffer's weekend retreat in Blöstau—16

Lasker, Eduard (1868–1941): chess theoretician—8

Lasker-Schüler, Else (1869–1945): Jewish-German poet and member of avant-garde literary circles in Berlin during the 1920s; 1933, emigrated; 1939, settled in Jerusalem—10

Lassar (Mrs.): married to a Jewish attorney who committed suicide—8

Lasserre, Jean (1908–83): French Reformed theologian, pastor, and pacifist; 1926–30, student, Protestant theological faculty, Paris; 1930–31, fellowship at Union Theological Seminary, New York, where he was together with Dietrich Bonhoeffer and Erwin Sutz; after 1931, Reformed church pastor, Mauberge, France; 1961–69, secretary of the French-speaking section of the International Fellowship of Reconciliation, representing France, Belgium, and Switzerland—4, 6, 8, 10, 11, 12, 13, 14, 15, 16, 17

Lasson, Georg (1862–1932): German theologian and pastor, Berlin; from 1907, editor of the complete works of Hegel for the publishing house of Felix Meiner in Leipzig—2, 6, 8, 11

Latmiral, Gaëtano (1909–95): Italian engineer; professor of electromagnetic theory; during the war, reserve officer; 1943, member of an Italian military commission of radar technicians in Berlin, where they were surprised by the cease-fire between Italy and the Allies after the fall of Mussolini; its six members were arrested as persons cleared for access to secret information; from November 11, 1943, until Christmas 1944, prisoner in Tegel with Dietrich Bonhoeffer; after the war, professor in Naples —7, 8, 16

Lauerer, Hans (1884–1953): 1918, rector of the deaconesses' institute, Neuendettelsau; 1932, deputy head of the Kaiserwerth association; December 1933, appointed (although never took office) Lutheran clerical adviser

to the Reich Church government; June 1934, appointed to governing council of the Inner Mission, Bavaria; 1936, church council member; from 1949, taught at the Augustana Institute, Neuendettelsau—13

Laufenberg: *see* Heinrich von Laufenberg

Lauga, Pastor: delivered lecture at the Gland conference—11

Lauterbach, Anton: friend of Martin Luther; promoted the Reformation in Pirna, Saxony—9

Lautz, Ernst (1887–1979): lawyer from Wiesbaden; World War I, served as artillery officer; 1920, state attorney, Neuwied; 1930, in Berlin; 1936, general state attorney, Berlin Supreme Court; 1939, head Reich attorney, People's Court; 1944–45, prosecuting attorney in trials against members of the resistance; 1952, compulsory retirement; 1958, revocation of his right to title use and pension—16

Lawford, Valentine George: from 1939, second private secretary to the British Foreign Minister—16

Lazarus: biblical character—4, 6, 8, 11, 13, 15

Le Blanc, Max (1865–1943): predecessor of Karl-Friedrich Bonhoeffer as director of the Institute of Physical Chemistry, Leipzig University—8

Le Bon, Gustave (1841–1931): French psychologist—1

Leber, Annedore (1904–68): German publisher and Social Democrat politician; widow of resistance figure Julius Leber—8

Leber, Julius (1891–1945): German Social Democrat politician and journalist; 1921, editor of the *Lübecker Volksbote*; 1924–33, member of parliament; after incarceration in a concentration camp, worked as a coal merchant in Berlin; member of the July 20 resistance group; designated for a cabinet position as interior minister after the planned coup; October 24, 1944, sentenced to death; January 5, 1945, executed—6, 16, 17

Lebrecht, Heinrich (1901–45): "non-Aryan" Confessing Church pastor, Hesse; 1934, corresponded with Bonhoeffer about emigration to England; remained in Germany as pastor in Groß-Zimmern; 1944, ordered to forced labor in the Todt organization—13, 14

Lebrecht, Marianne: wife of Heinrich Lebrecht—13, 14

Lechner, Leonhard (1553–1606): German composer—17 (for vol. 9)

Leduc, Florence: indexer for *DBWE* 1—1

Leenhardt, Frantz J. (1902–90): Swiss theologian; 1932–67, professor of New Testament, Geneva—16, 17

Leenhardt, Henri: professor of theology, Montpellier, (southern) France —13

Leffler, Siegfried: German Christian leader, Thuringia; after 1939, at the Institute for the Study and Eradication of Jewish Influence on German Church Life, Eisenach—14

Lehel, Ferenc: winter semester 1932–33, attended Bonhoeffer's lectures on contemporary systematic theology; summer semester 1933, attended Bonhoeffer's lectures on Christology; 1952, Lutheran pastor, Szombathely, Hungary—2, 3, 4, 12

Lehmann, Marion: wife of Paul Lehmann—10, 12, 15

Lehmann, Paul Louis (1906–94): U.S. Reformed theologian; from 1927, studied at Union Theological Seminary, New York, where he met Bonhoeffer in 1930; 1936, doctorate; 1947, professor of practical theology and, after 1949, of ethics, Princeton; 1956, professor of divinity, Harvard; 1963–74, professor of systematic theology, Union Theological Seminary, New York; retired, 1974—4, 6, 8, 10, 11, 12, 14, 15, 16, 17

Lehmann, Rudolf: minister director and chief general staff judge in the military high court; chief of the armed forces legal section in the Armed Forces High Command—16

Lehmann, Timothy: Protestant pastor; 1928–48, president of Elmhurst College; father of Paul Lehmann—15, 16

Lehndorff, Hans Count von (1910–87): Confessing Church member in East Prussia—16

Lehne, Gerhard (1910–42): from Berlin-Lichterfelde; 1936, vicar, Beutnitz near Crossen; 1937–38, participated in the collective pastorate, Groß-Schlönwitz; 1938, predicant, Berlin-Lichterfelde; 1942, killed in action on the eastern front—15, 16

Leiber, Robert (1887–1967): Jesuit; from 1924, private secretary and close adviser of Eugenio Pacelli (Pius XII); professor of church history at the Gregoriana in Rome—8, 16, 17

Leibholz, Christiane Renate Elisabeth: daughter of Gerhard and Sabine Leibholz—10, 15, 16

Leibholz, Gerhard (Gert) (1901–82): German lawyer; 1926, married to Dietrich Bonhoeffer's twin sister, Sabine; 1929–31, professor of state law, Greifswald; 1931–33, Göttingen; 1935, forced to retire as a result of Nazi race laws; 1938, emigrated to England with his family; 1947, returned to Göttingen; 1951–71, judge in the federal constitutional court, Karlsruhe —4, 5, 6, 7, 8, 9, 10, 11, 12, 13, 14, 15, 16, 17

Leibholz, Hans: elder brother of Gerhard Leibholz; regional court official; emigrated to Holland; May 1940, committed suicide when German troops invaded Holland—15, 16

Leibholz, Marianne Regina Nanette Paula Ursula: daughter of Gerhard and Sabine Leibholz; Bonhoeffer's godchild; 1938, emigrated to England with her family; writer and editor—8, 10, 11, 13, 15, 16

Leibholz, Peter: youngest brother of Gerhard Leibholz; emigrated to Melbourne, Australia, where he became owner of the Sommerfeld linen factories—15, 16

Leibholz, Sabine (Bina), née Bonhoeffer (1906–99): Dietrich Bonhoeffer's twin sister; 1926, married Gerhard Leibholz; forced to emigrate to England because of her husband's Jewish ancestry; mother of Marianne and Christiane; 1947, returned to Göttingen—2, 4, 5, 7, 8, 9, 10, 11, 13, 14, 15, 16, 17

Leibholz, William: father of Gerhard Leibholz; Berlin manufacturer and local politician—13

Leibniz, Gottfried Wilhelm (1646–1716): German philosopher, mathematician, theologian, natural scientist, legal scholar, historian, linguistics scholar, and inventor; as president of the Berlin Academy of Science, sought to bring natural science and philosophy into dialogue; as a religious philosopher, sought to bring Catholics and Protestants into dialogue; advocate of the inductive scientific method—1, 2, 3, 8, 9, 10, 11

Leichtle: Bonhoeffer family friends; lived in Lenzfried- Kempten—11

Leidreiter, Erich (1890–1945): 1927, pastor, Groß Samrodt district, Mohrungen, East Prussia; from 1937, Confessing Church district pastor, Königsberg; June/July 1940, mentioned in Dietrich Bonhoeffer's calendar—16

Leiper, Henry Smith (1891–1975): U.S. theologian and ecumenist; 1929–45, ecumenical secretary of the Federal Council of Churches; 1938, associate general secretary of the nascent World Council of Churches—7, 8, 15, 16, 17

Leise: 1933, student chaplain, Berlin—12

Leith, John (1919–2002): U.S. Presbyterian theologian and scholar—4

Lejeune, Robert: author of work on Christoph Blumhardt—15

Lekszas, Horst (1910–45): 1935, participated in the first Zingst/Finkenwalde session; 1936, member of the House of Brethren; 1937, pastor; military service; February 1945, missing in action—4, 14, 15

Lemme, Ludwig (1847–1927): professor of theology—9

Lempp, Albert (1877–1943): bookseller and publisher; owner of the Chr. Kaiser Verlag, Munich; 1943, leader of a small resistance circle in Bavaria that issued a statement of solidarity on behalf of the Jews—3, 8, 12, 16, 17

Lenin, Vladimir Ilich Ulyanov (1870–1924): Russian Communist leader—4

Lenker, John Nicholas (1858–1929): U.S. Lutheran pastor and translator—1

Lenkitsch, Wilhelm (b. 1896): 1927, pastor, Königsberg; 1934, pastor, city church, Tilsit; beginning of 1942, drafted into the military; after the war, superintendent in Brandenburg/Havel—16

Lent, Joachim (1910–90): 1936, member of third Finkenwalde session—14
Lenz: secretary at the German consulate in Barcelona—10
Lenz, Mrs.: 1940–41, lived in Ettal/Upper Bavaria as a "bomb refugee"—16
Leo X (1475–1521): from 1513, pope—14
Leo XIII (Giacchino Pecci) (1810–1903): 1878–1903, pope—1, 9, 12
Leo, Heinrich (1799–1877): German historian and Prussian conservative—12
Leochares (fourth century B.C.E.): Greek sculptor; probably an Athenian—9
Leonardo da Vinci (1452–1519): Italian painter, sculptor, architect, musician, engineer, and scientist—9
Leonhardi, Gustav: editor of nineteenth-century study of German preaching—14
Lepsius, Johannes (1858–1926): Protestant theologian—11
Lepsius, Renate: worked with the social work group in East Berlin; secretary of Friedrich Siegmund-Schultze—11, 12, 13
Lerche, Otto-Karl (1910–45): summer 1936, participated in the third Finkenwalde session; assistant pastor in Lagendorf near Salzwedel; killed in action—8, 14, 15
Lesbia: woman mentioned in the poetry of Catullus—9
Le Seur (Le Soeur), Paul (1877–1963): German Protestant theologian; involved in social issues; 1925–33, head of the youth secondary school, Hainstein near Eisenach; from 1933, freelance evangelist—1, 12
Lesser, Jonas: author of work on German youth at the beginning of the Third Reich—12
Lessing, Eckhard: German church historian—12
Lessing, Gotthold Ephraim (1729–81): German poet, dramatist, literary critic, and philosopher—6, 8, 9, 10, 14
Leubuscher, Charlotte (Lotte Leu) (1888–1961): daughter of Georg Leubuscher and Elisabeth, née Vermehren, a great-granddaughter of Karl August von Hase; professor of colonial law, Berlin University; emigrated to England because of National Socialist race laws—9, 13, 16
Leuschner, Wilhelm (1888–1944): Social Democrat politician and labor union leader; 1928–33, Hessian interior minster; 1933–34, in a concentration camp; manufacturer in Berlin; member of the July 20 conspiracy and designated as member of the new government to follow the coup; 1944; arrested after the failed assassination attempt; September 29, 1944, executed—16, 17
Leutheuser, Julius: Thuringian German Christian, one of the early leaders of that movement—14
Levi the tax collector: biblical character—4

Levintoff: a Russian whom Bonhoeffer heard play the piano in his Italian pension—9

Lewis, Edwin (1881–1959): British-born American Methodist theologian; taught at Drew University—15

Lewis, Harry Sinclair (1885–1951): U.S. writer; 1930, Nobel Prize in Literature—10

Lewisohn, Ludwig (1882–1955): literary figure, critic, and translator; Zionist—10

Ley, Robert: head of Reich organizational matters for the NSDAP; head of the German Work Front—16

Lhotzky, Heinrich (1859–1930): until 1898, pastor; freelance writer—11

Lichtenberg, Georg Christoph (1742–99): German physicist and author of aphorisms—6, 8

Lichtenfeld, Manacnuc: author of article on the Bethel confession—12

Licinius (Caius Lincinius Macer Calvus) (82–ca. 47 B.C.E.): Roman poet and orator—9

Lidzbarski, Mark (1868–1928): German semiticist and palaeographist; professor, Greifswald and Göttingen—9

Liebeneiner, Wolfgang (1905–87): German actor and film director—16

Liedtke, Herbert (1910–44): 1937, participated in the fifth Finkenwalde session; assistant pastor; 1944, missing—15

Liefmann, Else (1881–1970): German Jewish doctor; deported to Gurs; survived—12

Lienhard, Marcus: author of article on France—16

Lietzmann, Hans (1875–1942): 1900, private lecturer in church history, Bonn; 1905, professor of New Testament and church history, Jena; 1924, successor to Adolf von Harnack, Berlin; winter semester 1927–28, became dean of the theological faculty, Berlin—9, 10, 12, 13, 14, 15

Lifton, Robert Jay: U.S. psychiatrist; author of work on the medical profession in Nazi Germany—4

Lightfoot, Joseph Barber (1828–89): bishop of Durham, England; British patristics scholar—9

Lilje, Johannes (Hanns) (1899–1977): German Protestant theologian; 1925, student chaplain, Hannover; 1924–34, general secretary of the German Student Christian Federation; 1928, on the executive committee of the World Student Christian Federation; from 1932–35, its vice president; 1933–36, editor of the Confessing Church periodical *Junge Kirche*; 1935–44, general secretary of the Lutheran World Convention; after July 20, 1944, arrested and imprisoned until the end of the war in Nuremberg; 1945, regional senior church official, 1947–71, bishop of Hannover and abbot of Loccum; from 1948, senior bishop of the United Evangelical

Lutheran Church of Germany; 1949, deputy council head; 1952–57, president of the Lutheran World Federation; 1955, presiding bishop of the United Evangelical Churches in Germany—3, 8, 10, 11, 12, 14, 16

Lina, Aunt: *see* Kalckreuth, Pauline

Lina: cook for the Leibholz family in Göttingen—15

Linck, Hugo (1890–1976): East Prussian Confessing Church pastor; 1930, pastor, Löbenicht church in Königsberg; until 1937, Confessing Church district pastor, Königsberg—16

Lincoln, Abraham (1809–65): 1861–65, sixteenth president of the United States—10

Lindauer, Miss: Dietrich Bonhoeffer's French teacher—9

Lindbergh, Charles (1902–74): U.S. aviator; 1927, first transatlantic solo flight—16

Lindenberg, Annelise: daughter of the regional chief administrative officer Karl Lindenberg, Kremli, district of Soldin (Neumark); 1941, resided with Ruth von Kleist-Retzow in Stettin; 1942, married the agriculturist Dietrich von Bonin—16

Lindenmeyer, Eduard (b. 1887): 1931, pastor, Berlin-Wilmersdorf—12

Lindenmeyer, Friedrich Wilhelm (1878–1954): 1919, chaplain, Reich association for inland boatmen in Germany—12

Linderholm, Johannes Emanuel (1872–1937): 1919, Swedish professor of church history (representing the history of religions school) and member of the cathedral chapter, Uppsala—14

Lindgren, Henrik: author of work on Adam von Trott—16

Lindsay, A. D.: Master of Balliol College, Oxford—15

Lindström, Erik Valter (b. 1907): 1932, representative of the Swedish section of the World Alliance for Promoting International Friendship through the Churches; 1933, theology student; 1943, lecturer in systematic theology, Lund; 1944, head of the Swedish Student Christian movement; 1947, professor of the academy, Åbo, Finland—11

Link, Herbert: from 1926, pastor in Berlin—12

Link, Wilhelm (1905–40): businessman in Düsseldorf; member of the Rhineland Council of Brethren; May 1934, of the Reich Council of Brethren—13

Linke, Helmut: noncommissioned officer; member of the guard staff in Tegel; together with noncommissioned officer Knobloch helped convey illegal correspondence between Bonhoeffer and Eberhard Bethge—8

Linus: biblical character—15

Linz, Friedrich: Confessing Church pastor in the Rhineland, where he directed the ministry for laymen—15, 16

Lipgens, Walter: historian of modern European history—16
Lipperheide, Franz, Baron von (1838–1906): German publisher—7
Lippi, Filippo (ca. 1457–1504): Florentine painter, son of Fra Filippo Lippi; studied under Botticelli—9
Lippi, Fra Filippo (ca. 1406–69): Florentine painter—8
Lippmann, Walter (1989–1974): prominent U.S. political journalist and commentator—15
Lipsius, Richard Adelbert (1830–92): Protestant theologian and professor, Vienna—1, 9
Liszt, Franz (1811–86): Hungarian pianist and composer—9
Litt, Theodor (1880–1962): German philosopher and educator; 1919, professor of philosophy, Bonn; 1920, Leipzig; 1937, emeritus; from 1947, professor, Bonn—1, 11, 15, 16
Littell, Franklin H. (1917–2009): U.S. Protestant theologian; active in Holocaust education; founder of the Annual Scholars Conference on the Holocaust and the Churches—14
Little Annie (FP): character in the drama—7
Little Brother (FP): character in the drama and the novel: see Brake (FP), Ekkehard—7
Livius (59 B.C.E.—17 C.E.): Roman historian—4
Ljostveit, Kr.: probably member of Norwegian confessional movement—16
Lloyd George, David, first Earl Lloyd-George of Dwyfor (1863–1945): British statesman; during World War I, chancellor of the exchequer and minister of war; at the end of the war, became prime minister; played an important role in shaping the Versailles treaty—9
Locher, Benjamin (1909–87): 1933–34, vicar, London; 1934, Bernhardi fellowship recipient, Utrecht; 1937, pastor, Amsterdam; 1937, inspector of studies at the preachers' seminary, Wuppertal; wartime military service; 1946, pastor, Wuppertal; 1958–72, director of the seminar for congregational care and catechetical studies; 1968–76, member of the executive committee of the World Council of Churches—13
Lochner, Stephan (d. 1451): Cologne painter and copper engraver—16
Locke, Alain Le Roy (1886–1954): U.S. educator, critic, writer; 1907–11, first African American Rhodes scholar; 1917–53, professor of philosopher, Howard University; leader and chief interpreter of the Harlem Renaissance; encouraged and promoted many African American writers, painters, and musicians—10
Locke, John (1632–1704): British philosopher; "father of liberalism"—11
Loemker, Leroy E. (1900–1985): scholar of the philosopher Gottfried Leibniz—2

Loerzer (Lörzer), Fritz (1893–1954): 1923, pastor in Falkenstein, Friedberg; 1928, Berlin; 1932, member of the NSDAP and of the German Christians; 1933, deputy Reich head of the German Christians; provost of the electorate of Mark-Brandenburg (Kurmark); 1935, deputy head of the German Christians; 1936–38, high consistory official, Magdeburg; 1939, in Berlin; wartime military service; 1945–48, worked as an unskilled laborer—13

Loewe, Johann Karl Gottfried (1796–1869): composer, regarded as the creator of the German ballad—14

Loewenfeld, Julius Ludwig Wilhelm von (1808–80): Prussian general; 1870–71, governor of Metz—8

Loewenich, Walther von (1903–92): church historian—4

Löhe, Wilhelm (1808–72): 1837, pastor, Neuendettelsau; 1841, founder of the Neuendettelsau Lutheran Mission; 1854, chaplain of the deaconesses' institute, Neuendettelsau—1, 11, 14, 15

Lohmann, Gerhard (1911–42): from Berlin-Lankwitz; 1935–36, participated in the second Finkenwalde session; 1937, assistant pastor at the Kaiser Wilhelm Memorial Church in Berlin; 1938, pastor, Naurod near Wiesbaden; 1942, died of pulmonary tuberculosis—14, 15, 16

Lohmeyer, Ernst (1890–1946): Protestant theologian and New Testament exegete; 1920, professor of New Testament, Breslau; 1930–31, rector of the university; 1935, forced transfer to Greifswald for anti–National Socialist sentiment (for having supported, among others, Martin Buber); during World War II, military service; 1943, returned to Greifswald; December 1945, professor of New Testament, Greifswald; August 1946, sentenced to death for alleged war crimes by a Soviet military tribunal; September 19, 1946, executed in Greifswald; August 15, 1996, full rehabilitation by the attorney general of the Russian federation—1, 9, 11, 16

Lohmeyer, Klara: representative of the Association of Protestant Societies for Working Women in Germany, Provisional Bureau for Ecumenical Youth Work—11

Lois: biblical character—15

Lokies, Hans Emanuel Christoph (1895–1982): 1922, pastor, East Prussia; 1927, inspector and director of the Gossner Mission Society, Berlin; 1933, member of the Pastors' Emergency League; 1934, director of the German Federation for Christian Evangelical Education in Homes and Schools; 1938–62, lecturer in missionary and religious studies at the seminary, Berlin; December 1941, convicted in the collective trial against the examination board of the Old Prussian Union Council of Brethren; 1945, head of the Church Education Committee, Berlin—8, 14, 15, 16, 17

Lombardus, Petrus (Peter Lombard) (ca. 1100–1164): Italian scholastic theologian and bishop of Paris; his work *Sentences* was the standard textbook of Catholic theology until the Reformation—9, 14

Loofs, Friedrich (1858–1928): from 1888, professor of church history, Halle —12

Lord Herbert of Cherbury: *see* Herbert, Edward Lord of Cherbury

Lorenz: 1933, political science student in Berlin—12

Lorenz, H.: member of the congregational council, German congregation, Sydenham, London—13

Lorrain, Claude (Claude Gellée; called Le Lorrain) (1600–1682): French landscape painter—8, 9

Loßberg, Bernhard von: career military officer from Berlin; 1942, colonel and first general staff officer for the military commander in Norway; 1944, general major and chief of the general staff of the "special commission Donau"; lived in Wiesbaden after the war—16

Lot: biblical character—9, 14

Lothian, Lord Philip Henry Kerr, Marquess of (1882–1940): British liberal politician; Christian Scientist; chairman of the Rhodes Trust and chief editor of *The Round Table*; 1939–40, British ambassador to Washington —13, 14, 16

Lotter, Karl: 1942, attorney with the military high court; 1943–44, investigated the *Depositenkasse* affair under Dr. Roeder; 1944, appointed head of the armed forces legal section; judge general—8, 16

Louis IX (Saint Louis) (1214–70): 1226–70 king of France (until 1234, under his mother's regency)—14

Louis XIV (1638–1715): from 1643, king of France; known as *le Roi Soleil*, "Sun King"—6, 10

Louis Ferdinand, Prince of Prussia (1907–94): second son of Crown Prince Wilhelm of Prussia; trainee at Ford Motor Company, United States; worked for the German Lufthansa airline, where he came into contact with Klaus Bonhoeffer and Otto John; from 1951, head of the house of Hohenzollern—16, 17

Lovin, Robin W.: U.S. theologian and ethicist; 1989–93, project director for the English translation of *DBWE*—2, 4, 6

Löw, Rudolf (1878–1948): Swiss artist and novelist—8

Lowe, Walter: professor of systematic theology, Candler School of Theology—2

Lowell, James Russell (1819–91): American poet, literary critic, and hymn writer—10

Löwith, Karl (1897–1973): German philosopher of Jewish background; 1935, National Socialists rescinded his right to teach; 1941, emigrated to the United States; 1949, professor, New School for Social Research, New York; 1952, returned to Germany; until 1964, professor in Heidelberg —2, 12

Loxley, Peter Noël (1905–45): from 1941, private secretary for the permanent undersecretary, British Foreign Office—16

Loyola, Ignatius (1491–1556): Spanish church leader; founder of the order of the Society of Jesus (Jesuits)—3, 4, 5, 6, 9, 14

Lubarsch, Otto (1860–1933): professor of pathology, Berlin—15

Lubbe, Marinus van der (1909–34): Dutch communist accused of setting the Reichstag afire; December 23, 1933, sentenced to death by the military high court for high treason; January 10, 1934, executed in Berlin—8

Lübeck, Vincent (1654–1740): composer of organ works and cantatas—8

Lucas, Dr.: 1929, one of Bonhoeffer's traveling companions on the trip to the United States—10

Luccock, Halford E. (1885–1960): 1928–53, professor of homiletics, Yale —15

Luce, Miss: secretary of Baron B. Schröder—13

Lucifer: *see* Satan

Lucke, Werner: gave a 1933 radio address in the same series in which Bonhoeffer gave his February 1933 radio talk—12

Lücking, Karl (1893–1976): 1922, pastor, Dortmund; from 1934, leading member of the Confessing Church; 1945–49, superintendent, Minden; 1949–60, theological vice president of the Westphalian regional church —12

Lucretia: character in Roman legend—6

Ludendorff, Erich (1865–1937): Prussian general, head of the overall land war effort; after World War I, participated in the German-*völkisch* liberation movement; November 1923, participated in the Hitler putsch; 1926, founded the anti-Semitic Tannenberg alliance against "supranational powers" such as Freemasons, Jews, Jesuits, Marxists, and with it the "Ludendorff movement"; 1933, Tannenberg alliance dissolved; he and his wife were advocates of a "Germanic" theology; 1961, the Ludendorff movement was banned in the Federal Republic of Germany—6, 9, 12, 14, 17

Ludendorff, Mathilde (1877–1966): wife of Erich Ludendorff—12

Lüder: (Lagendorf) not otherwise identified—15

Ludloff, Hanfried (1868–1951): physicist; friend of Karl-Friedrich Bonhoeffer from Breslau—9, 10

Ludlow, Peter: author of work on Pius XII and the German resistance—16

Ludwig, Emil (real name: Cohn) (1881–1948): German-Swiss writer and journalist; very popular in the 1920s and 1930s—10
Ludwig, Hartmut: German church historian; author of work on the Grüber office—10, 14, 15, 16
Ludwig, Renate (b. 1905): from Berlin-Schöneberg; history student in Berlin; member of Harnack's seminar—9
Luecken: German fellowship student in the United States (in Frankfort, Kentucky) the same year as Bonhoeffer—10
Luke: the evangelist; biblical character—4, 9, 10, 15
Lukens, Michael: professor emeritus of religious studies, St. Norbert's College; editor, *DBWE* 11; member of *DBWE* editorial board—2, 11
Lukens, Nancy: professor of German studies and women's studies, University of New Hampshire (Durham); cotranslator, *DBWE* 1; translator, *DBWE* 7; translator of the poems in *DBWE* 8—1, 2, 7, 8
Lull, Timothy (1943–2003): president, Pacific Lutheran Theological Seminary—16
Lunde, Wilhelm: from 1930, pastor, Berlin-Wilmersdorf—12
Luserke, Martin (1880–1968): German educator and writer—14
Lütgens, Gertrud: 1934, Bonhoeffer officiated at her funeral in London—13
Lütgert, Martha: wife of Wilhelm Lütgert—17 (for *DBWE* 12)
Lütgert, Wilhelm (1867–1938): 1895, professor of New Testament, Greifswald; 1901, Halle; 1902, professor of systematic theology, Halle; 1929, succeeded Reinhold Seeberg in the chair of systematic theology, Berlin; summer semester 1929–September 1930, held seminar for systematic theology, University of Berlin, for which Dietrich Bonhoeffer was registered as an assistant; acted as intermediary with the Bertelsmann publishing house for Bonhoeffer's postdoctoral dissertation, *Act and Being*; 1935, forbidden to lecture and retired—2, 6, 7, 10, 11, 12, 13, 16
Luthardt, Christoph Ernst (1823–1902): German theologian—6, 16
Luther, Katharina, née Bora (1499–1552): wife of Martin Luther—9, 10, 15
Luther, Magdalena (Lenchen) (1529–42): daughter of Katharina and Martin Luther; died at the age of thirteen; Lucas Cranach painted her before her death—9, 15
Luther, Martin (1483–1546): German biblical scholar and theologian; leading figure in the Reformation; author of seminal theological works, hymns, and commentaries; translator of the most famous edition of the German Bible—1, 2, 3, 4, 5, 6, 7, 8, 9, 10, 11, 12, 13, 14, 15, 16
Luther, Paul (1868–1954): pastor, Trinity Church, Berlin-Charlottenburg; editor of nationalistic German religious literature—10
Lütkemann, Wilhelm (1891–1973): 1925–37, consistory official, Berlin-Brandenburg; 1942–48, president of the regional church, Kassel—12

Lutschewitz, Gotthold Wilhelm Heinrich (1902–89): 1931–33, inspector of studies, preachers' seminary, Stettin; 1933–45, professor, Gross Dübsow (Pomerania)—8

Lutze, Hermann: pastor, Kleinich, district of Bernkastel; member of the Rhineland Council of Brethren—16

Luz, Ulrich: professor emeritus of New Testament, University of Bern, Switzerland—15

Lydia: biblical character—14, 16

Lydia: the woman to whom the poet Horace addresses his Ode IX—9

Lyman, Eugene William (1872–1948): U.S. theologian; studied in Halle, Berlin, Marburg, Heidelberg, and Jena; 1918, professor of philosophy of religion, Union Theological Seminary, New York—10, 11

Lynker, Grete: wife of Rudolf Lynker—16

Lynker, Rudolf (1912–42): from Schalksmühle/Westphalia; 1938, participated in the collective pastorate, Groß-Schlönwitz; 1939, assistant military chaplain; July 21, 1942, killed in action on the eastern front—15, 16

Lysias: biblical character—16

Lythgoe, Len: Canadian scholar of liturgical music—16

Maas, Hermann (1877–1970): from 1900, pastor; 1903–15, pastoral administrator and pastor, Lauffen/Sulzburg, Baden; 1914, cofounder and member of the World Alliance for Promoting International Friendship through the Churches in Constance; 1915–45, pastor in Heidelberg; 1918, two terms as a city councilor (German Democratic Party), Heidelberg; 1933–34, joined Pastors' Emergency League and the Baden Confessing Church; had maintained contact with Jewish circles since the time of his university theological studies; 1936, with Heinrich Grüber, founded the relief office of the Confessing Church for racially and religiously persecuted persons in Berlin; head of the Heidelberg section of that office; 1940, banned from preaching; attempted to obstruct the deportation of Heidelberg Jews; 1943, forced retirement; 1944, deported to France for forced labor; 1946–65, church district superintendent; 1956, prelate of the northern Baden regional church; 1948, participated in the founding World Council of Churches meeting, Amsterdam; 1950, first German to be invited to Israel after the war—11, 13, 14, 16

Maaß, Rudolf (1893–1945): career military; April 1942, lieutenant colonel; commander, of the Lehrter Strasse military interrogation prison, Berlin-Moabit—8

Maaß, Theodor (1911–39): from Stralsund; 1936, participated in the third Finkenwalde session; assistant pastor of the Confessing congregation, Podejuch; September 3, 1939, killed in action in Poland—15, 16

Macartney, Clarence E. (1879–1957): conservative Presbyterian pastor and author; leading fundamentalist in the fundamentalist-modernist controversy within Presbyterianism—15
Macbeth: character in Shakespeare's play—6
Macfarland, Charles Stedman (1866–1956): Congregationalist pastor in the United States; 1911–30, general secretary, Federal Council of the Churches of Christ in America—12, 13
Machen, John Gresham (1881–1937): British fundamentalist; 1929, professor of New Testament theology, Westminster Theological College—10
Machiavelli, Niccolo (1469–1527): Italian politician and political theorist —6, 8
Macholz, Waldemar (1876–1950): 1924–27, director of the preachers' seminary, Wittenberg; from 1927, professor of practical theology, Jena; 1938, forced retirement; 1938–45, professor emeritus of confessional studies and related areas, Jena—10, 14
Macintosh, Douglas Clyde (1877–1948): Canadian-born theologian; professor of theology, Yale Divinity School—10
Mackay, N.: 1934, Hungarian participant at the Fanø youth conference—13
Mackensen, August von (1849–1945): general field marshal; estate owner and church patron in Brüssow/Mark; used by Hitler to gain control of the armed forces—15, 16
Mackensen-Astfeld, Stephanie von (1894–1985): wife of the deputy president of Pomerania (who was the son of August von Mackensen); participated in Confessing Church synods in Barmen and Dahlem (1934), Augsburg (1935), and Bad Oeynhausen (1936); secretary, Pomeranian Council of Brethren in Stettin—14, 15
Mackenzie, Alexander Slidell: popular nineteenth-century U.S. author and naval officer—16
MacKinnon, Donald M.: Scottish Anglican theologian and philosopher—16
Mackworth-Young, Gerard (1884–1965): British administrator in India and archaeologist—8
Maclear, James F. (1923–99): professor, University of Minnesota; expert on Puritans—14, 15
MacMurray, John: British moral philosopher; 1922, at Balliol College in Oxford; 1928, London; 1944, Edinburgh—16
Macquarrie, John (1919–2007): Scottish-born systematic theologian and philosopher—2, 11
Macro, Anthony: assisted with *DBWE* 1—1
Macy, Paul: pastor with the Federal Council of the Churches of Christ in America—15
Maderna, Carlo (1556–1629): Italian architect—9

Mádr, Adolf: Czech pastor and ecumenist—11
Maecenas, Gaius Cilnius (ca. 73 B.C.E.–8 B.C.E.): Roman statesman and patron of letters—9
Maechler, Winfried Max (1910–2003): 1932–33, member of Bonhoeffer's circle of students in Berlin; 1934, participated in the Fanø youth conference; summer 1934, participated in Bruay conference; 1935, member of the first Finkenwalde session; member of the House of Brethren; November 1936, ministry, Berlin-Dahlem and in Schlawe, Pomerania; after 1945, pastor, Berlin-Charlottenburg and in Neu-Westend; 1961–68, pastor, London-Sydenham; 1968, pastor and head of studies at the Evangelical Academy in West Berlin; 1978, retired—5, 6, 8, 11, 12, 13, 14, 15, 16
Maetz, Walter: captain and commander of the Tegel military interrogation prison branch office on Seidelstrasse 39—8
Magerstädt, Johannes: from 1920, pastor, Berlin—12
Mähl, Otto H. W. (1884–1939): from 1927, pastor, Berlin—12
Mahling, Friedrich (1865–1933): 1892, director of the City Mission, Hamburg; 1904, pastor, Frankfurt; 1909, professor of practical theology, Berlin, and member of the Central Board of Home Missions—9, 10
Mahlmann, Theodor: German theologian; editor of some of the manuscripts in *DBW* 9—2, 9
Maier, Heinrich: Bonhoeffer's philosophy professor in Berlin—2, 9
Maier, Hermann (b. 1906): from the summer semester 1924, active in the Hedgehog fraternity; later director of a publishing house in Stuttgart—9
Mainz, Albrecht von (1490–1545): Margrave of Brandenburg; 1513, archbishop of Magdeburg; 1518, cardinal; decided opponent of the Reformation; Luther called him an *Organum Satanae singularissimum* (unique instrument of Satan)—9
Maisch, Herbert (1890–1974): German film director—16
Major (FP): character in the story—7; *see* also Bremer (FP), Harald von
Major, Georg (1502–74): 1537, court preacher; 1544, professor of theology, Wittenberg—14
Makarenko, Anton Semyonovich (1888–1939): Russian educational pioneer—11
Makins, Roger Mellor, Lord Sherfield: from 1940, counselor, British Foreign Office—16
Malebranche, Nicole (Nicolas) (1638–1715): French philosopher—2
Mallet, Victor: British diplomat; from 1940, diplomatic envoy, Stockholm—16
Maltusch, Johann Gottfried (Götz) (1911–80): from Berlin; 1938–39, participated in the collective pastorate, Köslin; 1945, regional youth pastor,

Oldenburg; 1954, worked with the Inner Mission, Hannover; 1959, director of that organization; 1966, bishop, Schaumburg-Lippe—15

Mangey, Thomas: Philo scholar and editor—9

Mann, Theophil (1872–1939): Methodist; member of the World Alliance for Promoting International Friendship through the Churches; from 1927, lecturer at the preachers' seminary of the Episcopal Methodist Church, Frankfurt am Main; secretary of the German section of the World Alliance for Promoting International Friendship through the Churches—13

Mann, Thomas (1875–1955): German author; 1929, Nobel Prize in Literature —10, 12, 15

Manning, William Thomas (1866–1949): bishop of the New York diocese of the Protestant Episcopal Church—10

Mansfeld, Counts of: Count Albrecht (1486–1560), Count Johann Georg (1532–79), and Count Philipp (1531–46); Johann Georg and Philipp were cousins of Albrecht; known for their support of Luther and the Reformation—9

Mansfeld, Johann Georg Count von: *see* Mansfeld, Counts of

Mansfeld, Philipp Count von: *see* Mansfeld, Counts of

Marahrens, August (1875–1950): 1925–47, bishop of Hannover; opposed German Christians but advocated course of compromise with Nazi authorities; April–July 1933, authorized Lutheran representative on the "Kapler committee" for reorganizing the German Evangelical Church; 1934–36, chair of the Provisional Church Administration; from 1934, member of the Lutheran Council; 1935, president of the Lutheran World Convention; 1939, member of the German Evangelical Church's Confidential Council of Clerical Advisers; 1941, approved the exclusion of "non-Aryan" Christians from German Evangelical Church parishes; 1947, resigned as bishop—8, 12, 13, 14, 15, 16, 17

Marbach, Johann: Lutheran theologian; 1561, participated in the Dispute of Strasbourg—2

Marchan: 1932, member of the French section of the World Alliance for Promoting International Friendship through the Churches—11

Marcion (85–160 C.E.): founder of a gnostic community during the early Christian period; decisively rejected the Old Testament and the Jewish roots of Christianity; 144, expelled from the Christian community in Rome—3, 4, 5, 10, 15

Marcks, Erich (1861–1938): prominent German historian, best known for his study of Bismarck—16

Marcus Aurelius Antoninus (Marcus Annius Verus) (121–180 C.E.): Roman emperor, stoic philosopher; opponent of Christianity—4, 9

Marczynski, Martin (1884–1954): 1926, pastor, Berlin; 1933, provost in Buenos Aires for the La Plata states; from 1936, provost for Brazil as well—12
Maresch, Martin P. W. (1880–1937): from 1911, pastor, Berlin-Pankow—12
Margaliot, Abraham: historian of the Holocaust—15
Marheineke, Phillip (1780–1846): German Protestant church leader; professor of philosophy; Hegel scholar—1, 11
Mariana, Juan de (1536–1624): 1554, Jesuit; studied the doctrine of tyrannicide (which was later forbidden by the Jesuit general)—14
Maritain, Jacques (1882–1973): French Catholic philosopher; 1945–48, French ambassador to the Vatican; from 1948, professor, Princeton University—6, 8, 15
Mark: biblical character—4, 15
Marks, Ivy: assistant secretary of Henri Henriod in London; 1932, secretary, World Alliance for Promoting International Friendship through the Churches and later at the World Council of Churches in Geneva—11, 13
Markusson, Andreas: Norwegian writer—16
Marmeladova, Sonya Semyonovna: character in Dostoyevsky's *Crime and Punishment*—11
Maron, Gottfried: German Protestant theologian—6
Marrus, Michael R.: Canadian historian; expert on the Holocaust and Vichy France—16
Marsh, Charles: U.S. professor of religious studies, University of Virginia; author of works on Bonhoeffer—1, 2, 4, 10
Marshall, Thomas (Tom) H. (1893–1981): professor, London School of Economics; during the war, head of the German section of the Foreign Research and Press Service; from 1943, head of the Foreign Office research department—16
Marten, George Henry (1876–1966): 1931, archdeacon of Kingston- on-Thames; participated in the Fanø conference; head of the British section of the World Alliance for Promoting International Friendship through the Churches—13
Martens, Mr.: member of St. Mary's congregational council, London—13
Martensen, Hans Lassen (1808–84): Danish theologian, taught in Berlin —16
Martha: biblical character—6
Marthinussen, Karl (1890–1965): Norwegian theologian; 1916, pastor, Bergen; 1932, Sandviken; 1949–60, bishop, Stavanger—12
Martin (FP): character in the novel; *see* also Brake (FP), Martin—7
Martin, Alfred von (1882–1979): German intellectual historian and sociologist; 1933, resigned his teaching position and began work as an author when the National Socialists seized power; March 1943, Gestapo confis-

cated his *Religion in Jacob Burckhardt's Life and Thought*; after 1946, taught at the Technical College, Munich—6, 7

Martin, Bernd: historian of German resistance—16

Martin, Ernst: dean, Magdeburg cathedral—12

Martin, Hugh: head of SCM Press in London; during the war, worked in the British Ministry of Information—16

Martin, Karl: author of 1904 work on the Gospels—11

Martin, Liutenant Colonel Lawrence: author of work on the sixteen peace treaties after World War I—11

Martinesque, J.: from Madagascar; 1934, participated in the Fanø youth conference (1934, noted as being from Paris)—13

Marwitz, Alexander von der (1910–42): 1933, theology student, Berlin; 1932–33, among the circle of students around Bonhoeffer; 1935–36, participated in the second Finkenwalde session; pastor in Hassendorf near Neuwedell, district of Arnswalde; Advent 1942, killed in action on the eastern front—12, 14, 15

Marx, Karl (1818–83): German social, political, and economic theorist; developed the theory of class struggle and the exploitation of the working class—2, 6, 8, 9, 11, 14

Mary: biblical character; mother of Jesus—5, 6, 9, 10, 11, 12, 13, 14, 15, 16

Mary: biblical character; sister of Martha—6

Mary Magdalene: biblical character—6

Marzahn, Wolfgang (1911–88): 1936, participant in third Finkenwalde session; until 1977, pastor—14

Mascall, Eric Lincoln (1905–93): Anglican theologian and priest; professor of historical theology, King's College, London—11

Maser, Peter: professor of church history and church art, Münster—14

Mason, Lancelot: chaplain; secretary of George Bell—13

Massie, Richard (1880–87): British translator of German hymns—14, 15

Matern, Gerhard (1907–43): East Prussian pastor; 1933–34, assistant to Professor Schniewind; 1934, member of the Confessing Church; 1937, temporarily imprisoned; pastor in Aulenbach near Insterburg; June 19, 1940, Dietrich Bonhoeffer visited him; killed in action as a first lieutenant on the eastern front—16

Matheny, Paul: pastor, ecumenist, professor, missionary, theologian, and editor; professor of systematic theology at Union Theological Seminary in the Philippines; member of the pastor-theologian program of the Center of Theological Inquiry, Princeton, and on the editorial board of the *DBWE* translation project; coeditor of *DBWE* 9—2, 9

Mathews, Shailer (1863–1941): U.S. Baptist; 1894–1933, professor of New Testament theology at the Divinity School, University of Chicago—1, 12

Matiwe, Hans: 1936, member of third Finkenwalde session—14
Matsuda, R.: Japanese participant at the Fanø youth conference; Tokushima Technical College, Japan—13
Matthew the Evangelist—4, 14
Matthew the tax collector: biblical character—4
Matthews, John W.: U.S. Lutheran pastor; 2005–11, president of the International Bonhoeffer Society's English Language Section—4, 8
Mau, Rudolf: German historian, specialist on Luther—16
Mauchamp: French doctor murdered in Morocco in the prelude to World War I—9
Maunder, John Henry (1858–1920): British composer—13
Maurenbrecher, Max (1874–1930): Protestant theologian and publicist—1, 12
Maurer, H.: not identified—16
Maurer, Wilhelm: German Protestant theologian—6
Maurice, Duke of Saxony (1521–53): cousin of Frederick the Wise; a Protestant who fought for Charles V in the Schmalkaldic war; 1552, turned against Charles V and forced him to conclude the Treaty of Passau—9
Maury, Pierre (1890–1956): French Reformed theologian and ecumenist; 1930, secretary, World Christian Student Federation; 1934, pastor, Paris; 1951–53, president of the National Council of Reformed Churches in France—16
Mausbach, Joseph (1861–1931): German theologian; from 1892, professor of moral theology and apologetics, Münster—6
Mauthner, Fritz (1849–1923): philosopher and author—1, 8
Maxentius I (Marcus Aurelius Velerius): Roman emperor; rival of Constantine the Great; 312, defeated by Constantine in battle at the Milvian Bridge—9
Maximilian I (1459–1519): known as "the last knight"; 1486–1519, king of Germany; 1493–1519, Holy Roman emperor; laid foundation for Habsburg dynasty—8
May, Georg Gerhard: Austrian Protestant bishop and ecumenist—8
May, Karl (1842–1912): German author of travelogues and popular adventure stories—8
Mayer, Rainer: German professor of systematic theology and religious education; author of several publications on Bonhoeffer—2, 6, 8, 13
Mayer, Rupert (1876–1945): German Jesuit; 1899, ordained to the priesthood; 1900, joined the Jesuits; from 1912, worked in Munich as a priest in pastoral care for men and in charitable services; World War I, army chaplain, seriously wounded; 1937, forbidden to preach and speak publicly;

1937–38, after trial and conviction, inmate in Stadelheim and Sachsenhausen; 1940–45, interned in the Ettal monastery; 1987, beatified—16

McComb, John H.: pastor, Broadway Presbyterian Church, New York—15

McCown, Chester Carlton: Methodist; 1914–47, professor of New Testament theology, Pacific School of Religion—12

McCulloh, Mark: professor of German, Davidson College—13

McDougall, William (1871–1938): social psychologist—1

McGiffert, A. C. (1861–1933): U.S. theologian and church historian—8

McGrath, Alister: British theologian—14

McNeil, Brian: translator of the centenary edition of *Dietrich Bonhoeffer: A Life in Pictures*—17

Mebes, Max (1913–45): from Berlin-Brandenburg; 1939–40, participated in the collective pastorate, Sigurdshof; assistant pastor, Berlin—15

Medea: character in Greek mythology—6, 17 (for vol. 9)

Meerscheidt-Hüllesem, Eberhard Sigismund Wolfgang Baron von (1870–1943): estate owner in Kuggen near Königsberg/East Prussia; retired major; royal Prussian chamberlain; member of the synodal committee of the East Prussian Confessing Church; put the neighboring estate house Blöstau at the disposal of the East Prussian Council of Brethren for use as a preachers' seminary; July 1940, hosted a student retreat led by Pastor Koschorke and Dietrich Bonhoeffer—16

Mehlhausen, Joachim (1936–2000): professor of church history and law, Tübingen—12

Mehnert, Klaus (1906–84): German publicist; 1929–30, secretary with the German Academic Exchange Service (DAAD)—10

Meier (FP): character in the story, sergeant major—7

Meier, Kurt: German historian of the churches during the Nazi era, particularly the German Christians—8, 10, 13, 14, 15, 16

Meier-Bothling, Hans-Peter; *see* Meyer-Bothling, Hans-Peter

Meinecke, Friedrich (1862–1954): German historian; 1914–28, professor, Berlin; 1947, first rector of the Free University, Berlin-Dahlem—6, 16

Meinzolt, Hans (1887–1967): regional governmental council member, Kirchheimbolanden; 1933, senior church official, Munich; 1935–45, vice president of the Bavarian regional church office; 1941, military service; 1945, state counselor, Bavarian Ministry of Culture; 1945–46, 1954–57, state secretary there; 1948, honorary professor of international and administrative law at the Technical College, Munich; 1947–59, president of the Bavarian synod—13

Meiser, Hans (1881–1956): 1911, chaplain with the Inner Mission, Nuremberg; 1915, pastor, Munich; 1922, director of the preachers' seminary,

Nuremberg; 1928, senior church official, Munich; 1933–55, bishop of Bavaria; 1933, head of the German Lutheran Bishops' Conference and of the United German Lutheran Churches; 1934, broke with Reich Bishop Ludwig Müller, became a member of the Reich Council of Brethren and, in 1936, of the Lutheran Council, becoming its chair in 1938; 1949–55, first senior bishop of the United Evangelical Lutheran Church of Germany; 1945–54, member of the council of the Evangelical Church of Germany, of the executive committee of the Lutheran World Federation, and of the executive committee of the World Council of Churches—12, 13, 14, 16, 17

Meissner, Otto (1880–1953): lawyer; 1920, head of the office of the Reich president; 1923, state secretary; 1934–45, head of Reich chancellery; 1949, acquitted at Nuremberg in the "Wilhelmstrasse" trial—13

Meitner, Lise (1878–1968): Austrian-Swedish physicist; first identified nuclear fission—6

Mejcher, Helmut: German scholar on the Middle East—6

Melanchthon, Philipp (1497–1560): German theologian, reformer, humanist; Luther's colleague in Wittenberg—1, 2, 4, 6, 9, 10, 12, 13, 14, 15

Melito of Sardes (d. ca. 170 C.E.): bishop of Sardis and theologian; antignostic—9

Melozzo da Forli (1438–94): Italian Renaissance painter—8

Melzel, Karl-Heinrich: author of work on the Confessing Church Confidential Council Clerical Advisors—16

Melzer, Paul (1892–1970): after 1930, pastor in Schloßbach (formerly Pillupönen), Ebenrode (formerly Stallupönen) district, East Prussia; June 17–18, 1940, visited by Bonhoeffer—16

Memling, Hans (1433–94): Dutch painter—15

Menacher, Mark D.: U.S. Lutheran pastor; author of article on Gerhard Ebeling—14

Mendelssohn, Arnold (1855–1933): composer; 1891, regional director for church music in Darmstadt—14

Mendelssohn, Franz von (1865–1935): prominent banker; member of the Academic Exchange Service committee that approved Bonhoeffer's fellowship at Union—10

Mendelssohn-Bartholdy, Felix (1809–47): German composer, pianist, and conductor; grandson of Moses Mendelssohn; added the name Bartholdy on inheritance from a maternal uncle—1, 9

Menelaus: brother of Agamemnon, king of Sparta—8

Menken, Gottfried (1768–1831): revivalist preacher in Bremen—12

Menn, Wilhelm (1888–1956): 1921, head of the pastoral social office of the Rhineland regional church; 1929, member of the ecumenical study

commission; 1934, pastor and superintendent, Andernach; 1946, helped establish and lead the central German ecumenical affairs office in Frankfurt am Main; 1950, director of the German ecumenical study committee —12, 13, 14

Mennel, Robert: character who is a conscientious objector in a book by Beverly Nichols—13

Mensing, Karl (1876–1953): lawyer in Wuppertal-Elberfeld; 1934, member of the council of the Rhineland Confessing Synod; 1936, member of a constitutional committee of the Provisional Church Administration; 1945, Rhineland delegate to the church conference in Treysa; member of the legal committee of the General Synod of the Evangelical Church of Germany established there—16

Mentzer, Balthasar (1565–1627): Lutheran theologian, Giessen—11, 12

Mephistopheles: character in Goethe's poem *Faust*—7

Merivale, John Herman (1779–1844): English barrister; translator of Schiller's poems—11

Merrill, William Pierson: pastor of the Brick Presbyterian Church; 1914, deputy head of the World Alliance for Promoting International Friendship through the Churches—12

Mertz von Quirnheim, Albrecht Ritter (1905–44): career military; acquainted with Count Stauffenberg from their training years together at the War Academy; ultimately colonel on the general staff and chief of staff, General Army Office; July 20, 1944, participated in the coup attempt; shot to death on the same day, as was Stauffenberg, in the Bendlerstrasse headquarters—16, 17

Merz, Georg (1892–1959): Protestant theologian; 1926, student chaplain and pastor, Munich; theological adviser to the Chr. Kaiser publishing house; 1930, lecturer, theological college, Bethel; 1922–33, managing editor of the periodical *Zwischen den Zeiten*; 1933, worked with Bonhoeffer on the Bethel confession; 1934, member of the Lutheran Council; 1936–39, head of the theological college, Bethel; 1939, pastor, Zion Church, Bethel, and head of the Confessing Church catechetical office in Westphalia; 1942, church dean, Würzburg; 1946, rector of the newly established pastoral college in Neuendettelsau; 1947, rector of the newly established Augustana Institute, Neuendettelsau; 1951–57, professor there; 1957, retired—3, 11, 12, 13, 14

Messerschmidt, Manfred: author of work on military chaplains—8

Messow, Werner Bruno Wilhelm (1888–1961): from 1929, pastor, Berlin-Steglitz—8, 12

Metella, Caecilia (ca. 50 B.C.E.): famous for her gravestone on the Via Appia in Rome—8

Metz, Brigitte: German pastor and author of works on the Church Struggle —8

Metzger, Paulus (formerly Max Josef) (1887–1944): Catholic priest from the Black Forest; 1917, cofounder and head of the Peace Alliance of German Catholics; 1921, first German at the International Peace Congress in Paris; 1938, founder of the Una Sancta movement; June 29, 1943, arrested; April 17, 1944, executed in Brandenburg—16

Meulemans, Connie J.: director, Interlibrary Loan Services, Miriam and James Mulva Library, St. Norbert College—11

Meumann, Karl (1888–1960): 1924, assistant pastor; from1925, pastor, Grunewald church, Berlin; 1925–27, under his supervision, Bonhoeffer conducted children's services there; 1928, accompanied Dietrich and Klaus Bonhoeffer on a tour of Spain—9, 10, 12

Meurer, Hans-Jürgen: with the Gütersloher/Chr. Kaiser publishing house —17

Meuß, Gisela: author of study of Bonhoeffer's *Arkandisziplin*—8

Meyding, Pastor: late nineteenth-century pastor in Cleversulzbach; later in Kichentellinsfurt; married Rosa Bonhoeffer, a sister of Bonhoeffer's grandfather—13

Meyer, Alice: author of work on Switzerland during the Nazi period—16

Meyer, Archibald (FP): character in the novel—7

Meyer, Conrad Ferdinand (1825–98): Swiss writer, representative of poetic realism; describes the secular and religious forces shaping history in relation to what he termed the human psyche; often presents his characters as enigmatic figures, torn by conflicting emotions and attitudes, whose actions determine, at times almost accidentally, the course of history—8, 10, 14

Meyer, Dietrich: coeditor with Eberhard Bethge of *Nachlass Dietrich Bonhoeffer*, the index to Bonhoeffer's literary estate—2, 11, 13, 14, 17

Meyer, Eduard (1855–1930): German historian—17 (for vol. 9)

Meyer, Hans Bernhard (1924–2002): Jesuit; professor of moral theology and sociology, Innsbrück—14

Meyer, Johannes: pastor and National Socialist, Ladelund (northern Germany)—14

Meyer, Max-Peter: German Jewish composer (converted to Catholicism); sought Bonhoeffer's help in emigrating to the United States—15

Meyer, Mrs. (FP): character in the novel—7

Meyer, Mrs.: mentioned in connection with Susi Bonhoeffer's gymnastics accident at school—9

Meyer, Theodor (1821–1913): Christian social ethicist—1

Meyer, Walter: from the Young Men's Christian Association in Barmen; representative of the National Federation of Young Men's Associations at the Provisional Bureau for Ecumenical Youth Work—11

Meyer, Winfried: German historian and expert on the "Operation 7" rescue—8, 16

Meyer-Bothling, Hans-Peter: German historian; author of work on Fritz Reuter—10

Meyer-Erlach, Wolf (1891–1982): 1933–45, professor of practical theology, Jena; 1935, rector of the University of Jena; leader of the German Christians in Bavaria; 1951–61, pastor, Hesse—14

Meyfart, Johann Matthäus (1590–1642): German hymnist—4, 14

Micaiah, son of Imlah: biblical character—15

Michael, Horst (1901–83): until his dismissal in 1933, senior assistant and lecturer, history department, University of Berlin; journalist; member of the Berlin-Brandenburg Council of Brethren; church correspondent with the Berlin newspaper *Tägliche Rundschau*; correspondent for British papers as well; publicist with the *Münchener Neueste Nachrichten*; 1950, converted to Catholicism; employed with the *Herder Correspondence*—12

Michael, Robert: U.S. historian; professor of European history, Dartmouth —6

Michaelis, Johann David (1717–91): professor of oriental languages and theology, Göttingen; scholar of biblical studies who wrote on both the Old and the New Testaments, on the Hebrew and Arabic languages, and on the early versions of the Bible; pioneer in the use of historical-critical methods of biblical interpretation—9

Michaelis, Wilhelm (1896–1965): from 1923, private lecturer in New Testament, Berlin; from 1930, professor, Bern—9

Michal: biblical character—14

Michel, Otto (1903–93): private lecturer in New Testament and student chaplain; led the student group of the Young Reformation movement in Halle; after the war, professor, Tübingen—16

Michelangelo Buonarotti (1475–1564): Italian Renaissance sculptor, painter, and architect—3, 8, 9, 10, 11

Michescu: *see* Mihlcescu, Joan

Micklem, Nathanael (1888–1976): British theologian; 1932–53, principal and professor of dogmatics at Mansfield College, Oxford—16

Mickley, Johannes: 1936–37, participated in the fourth Finkenwalde session; 1939–75, pastor—4, 14, 15

Middendorff, Friedrich: 1936, member of the Reich Council of Brethren —14

Migne, Jacques Paul (1800–1875): French Catholic cleric; editor of the collection of church fathers and authors, *Patrologiae Cursus completus*—5, 8

Mihlcescu (Mihalescu; Michescu), Joan: patriarch of Budapest; Romanian ecumenist; member of the Romanian section of the World Alliance for Promoting International Friendship through the Churches; September 15–20, 1933, like Dietrich Bonhoeffer, delegate at that organization's conference in Sofia, Bulgaria; spring 1943, apparently identical with "Prof. Michescu" mentioned in Bonhoeffer's "camouflage letter"; patriarch of Budapest—12, 16

Mikusch, Dagobert von (1874–1950): army major and author—6

Milch, Werner (1903–50): editor and German literary scholar; wrote under pseudonyms of Ferdinand Hallender and Hans Ibben; reported on Bonhoeffer's youthful opposition to anti-Semitism—9

Mill, John Stuart (1806–63): British philosopher, economist, and social reformer; developed utilitarian ethics—6

Miller, Francis (1895–1978): U.S. Protestant theologian—15

Mingazzini, Giovanni (1859–1929): leading Italian neurologist of his time; director of the clinic for mental and neurological illnesses in Rome—9

Minucius Felix (second or third century): author of *Octavius*; birthplace is believed to be in Africa; wrote a defense of Christianity—9

Mirbt, Carl (1860–1929): historian of Catholicism—16

Miriam: biblical character—13, 15

Mistacco, Vicki: professor of French, Wellesley College—13

Mithras: god of the ancient Roman mystery cult Mithraism (first to fourth centuries); typically portrayed killing a bull—10

Miyata, Mitsuo: Japanese political scientist; author of numerous publications in Japanese and German, including writings on Bonhoeffer—6

Moberly, Sir Walter: British vice president of the State Commission for Universities; 1937, participated in the ecumenical World Conference in Oxford—15, 16

Modersohn, Ernst (1870–1948): Protestant pastor and evangelist—11

Mödlhammer, Johann Matthäus: Austrian professor of theology and ecumenics—4

Moe, O.: probably member of the Norwegian confessional movement—16

Moehlmann, Conrad Henry: U.S. Baptist pastor—12

Moeller van dan Bruck, Arthur (1876–1925): German author; after World War I, active as a political and cultural publicist in Berlin; best-known political work was *Das Dritte Reich* (1923), which expressed antiliberal and antiparliamentary views and asserted what he called a revolutionary conservatism; due to the book he was regarded as one of the fathers of the NSDAP; committed suicide—10, 12

Mohammed (Muhammad, Mahomet) (570–632): Arab prophet and founder of the Islamic faith—9, 12

Mohler, Armin (1920–2003): Swiss journalist and novelist; self-proclaimed German nationalist who crossed the Swiss border to join the Waffen-SS in 1942—12

Möhler, Johann Adam (1796–1838): German Catholic theologian—11

Mohn, Heinrich (1885–1955): director of Bertelsmann publishing house—10

Mohr, Joseph (1792–1848): Austrian hymnist—15

Moinier, Charles: French general; 1911, entered Fez during second Morocco crisis—9

Mokrosch, Reinhold: professor of practical theology and religious pedagogy, Osnabrück—2, 14

Moldaenke, Theodor (1880–1947): from 1917, pastor, Berlin-Steglitz—12

Moleschott, Jacob (1822–93): Dutch physiologist, one of the most significant representatives of scientific and philosophical materialism; professor, Switzerland and Italy—6

Molesworth, William: editor, first edition of Thomas Hobbes's works—1

Molina, Luis (German: Ludwig) (1535–1600): Spanish social philosopher —2

Möller: fellow student of Franz Hildebrandt—10

Moller, Martin (1547–1606): hymnist—8, 14

Möller, Michael F. (1957–97): professor of Lutheran theology—2

Moloch: a Canaanite deity who demanded human sacrifice—6

Molotov, Vyacheslav Mikhaylovich (1890–1986): Soviet Russian political leader; 1930–41, minister president; 1939–49, Soviet commissar for foreign affairs; 1939, signed the nonaggression pact with Hitler—16

Moltke, Freya von, née Deichmann (1911–2010): 1931, married Helmut James von Moltke, after whose execution she rescued his "Kreisau papers" and correspondence; 1960, emigrated to the United States—8, 16

Moltke, Helmuth Count von (1800–1891): military commander and author; established an estate entailed to the Moltkes at Kreisau—8

Moltke, Helmuth James Count von (1907–45): German attorney for international law; his mother, Dorothy Rose Innes, was the daughter of one of the highest judges in the South African Union; traveled frequently to England; after 1939, administrative adviser in the Military Intelligence Office of the Armed Forces High Command, subsection VI for questions of international law; April 1942, traveled to Norway and Sweden with Dietrich Bonhoeffer; May 1942, founded the Kreisau circle (named for his estate in Silesia); January 1944, arrested in connection with the investigation of the Solf circle and taken to the Ravensbrück concentration

camp; end of September 1944, sent to the Tegel military detention center; January 23, 1945, executed in Berlin—6, 7, 8, 16, 17

Moltmann, Jürgen: German Protestant theologian and professor of systematic theology—2, 6, 8

Mommsen, Hans: German historian—16

Monica: mother of Augustine—3, 16

Monis, Antoine Emmanuel Ernest (1846–1929): French statesman; premier of France and minister of justice—9

Monod, Wilfried (1867–1943): pastor in the French Reformed Church; 1932, president of the French section of the World Alliance for Promoting International Friendship through the Churches—11

Montaigne, Michel Eyquem Seigneur de (1533–92): French philosopher; influential through his *Essays*, the most significant work in late French humanism—6, 8

Montenuova, Leonardo: title figure in play written by Karl Barth—11

Monteverdi, Claudio (1567–1643): Italian composer—8

Moor, Joe: referred to in *DBWE* 15; not otherwise identified; *see also* Moore, John Buchanan, and Moore, Karl Francis—10, 15

Moore, John Buchanan: student at Union Theological Seminary, 1928–30—10

Moore, Karl Francis: student at Union Theological Seminary, 1931—10

Moore, Scott A.: translator and ordained pastor in the Evangelical Lutheran Church in America; cotranslator of *DBWE* 15—15

Mordhorst, Adolf (1866–1951): 1924 to 1933, bishop of Holstein; September 12, 1933, dismissed from office—12

More, Sir Thomas (1478–1535): British statesman and humanist; 1532, resigned high state positions because of Henry VIII's antipapal policies; 1534, refused to take an oath repudiating papal supremacy over the English church in favor of royal supremacy; arrested; July 1535, beheaded; 1935, canonized—6, 7

Morgenstern, Christian (1871–1914): German poet, humorist; much of his lyric poetry was fundamentally religious, though not Christian—8

Möricke, Otto (1897–1978): Württemberg Confessing pastor; beaten and imprisoned for his protests against Nazism; became involved in the rescue of Jews—15

Mörike, Eduard (1804–75): German pastor, poet—8, 13

Morin, Germain (1861–1946): Belgian Benedictine patristics scholar—1

Moritz of Saxony (1521–53): 1541, duke of Saxony-Meissen; 1547, also prince elector of Saxony—14

Morrison, Charles Clayton (1874–1966): U.S. Disciples of Christ minister; editor and publisher of *The Christian Century* after 1908—15

Morsbach, Adolf (1890–1937): 1927–34, head of the German Academic Exchange Service (DAAD) in Berlin—10

Mosbacher, Eric (1903–98): British journalist and translator—17

Moser, Hans Joachim: biographer of Heinrich Schutz—16

Möser, Peter: German Protestant theologian and Bonhoeffer scholar—2, 6, 16

Moses: biblical character—1, 4, 5, 6, 7, 8, 9, 10, 11, 12, 14, 15, 16

Mosheim, Johann Lorenz von (1694–1755): German Protestant theologian, church historian, and pulpit orator; one of the founders of the University of Göttingen—1, 9

Mosse, George (1918–99): German exile and historian, author of numerous studies on National Socialism; at the end of his career, professor of Jewish Studies, University of Wisconsin—6

Mother (FP): character in the drama; *see* Anna

Moton, Robert R. (1867–1940): African American educator, successor to Booker T. Washington as president of Tuskegee Institute; author of a book owned by Bonhoeffer—10

Mott, John Raleigh (1865–1955): Methodist layman and pioneer of global ecumenical cooperation; 1895–1920, founder and general secretary, World Student Christian Federation; 1915–31, general secretary of the YMCA; 1942, honorary president, International Missionary Council; 1946, Nobel Peace Prize—10, 13

Mottu, Henry: French-Swiss theologian—14

Mozart, Wolfgang Amadeus (1756–91): Austrian composer—7, 8, 9, 16

Mücke, Franz (1819–63): composer and choral director; royal music director—10

Muhammed V (1354–91): sultan of Granada—10

Mühle, Hans: until 1933, head of Ulmenhof, the boarding school founded by Siegmund-Schultze—12

Mühlen, Patrik von zur: German social historian—13

Mühlenberg, Ekkehard: professor of patristics and church history, Göttingen—12

Mühlhausen, Rudolf: author of work on the Enthusiasts—11

Mühling, Andreas: Swiss historian of the Reformation—12, 14

Muhlphordt, Hieronymus: mayor of Zwickau, to whom Luther dedicated his treatise on Christian freedom—11

Mulert, Hermann (1879–1950): Protestant theologian, politician, and publicist; after 1918, one of the most important representatives of liberal Protestantism—1

Müller (FP): character in the story, Lance Corporal—7

Müller, Alfred Dedo (1890–1972): German theologian; professor of practical theology, Leipzig—6, 7, 16

Müller, Christine Ruth: German theologian; author of work on Bonhoeffer and the Jews—4, 8, 12, 13, 14, 16

Müller, Christof: German scholar on Augustine—15

Müller, D. Karl (1852–1940): professor of church history, Tübingen, influenced by Albrecht Ritschl and Adolf von Harnack—9

Müller, Eberhard (1906–89): 1932, traveling secretary for the German Student Christian Federation; 1934–38, general secretary of the organization; 1946–72, founder and head of the Evangelical Academy in Bad Boll —8, 12

Müller, Ernst: 1935–36, participated in the second Finkenwalde session—14

Müller, Friedrich (Fritz) (sometimes referred to as Müller-Dahlem) (1889–1942): 1924, pastor, Lautawerk; 1928, Berlin-Steglitz; from 1933, Berlin-Dahlem; cofounder of the Pastors' Emergency League; member of the council of the Evangelical Church of the Old Prussian Union, of the Reich Council of Brethren, and from 1936, chair of the second Provisional Church Administration of the Confessing Church; 1939, dismissed from office; military service; September 20, 1942, killed in action at Leningrad—12, 13, 14, 15, 16

Müller, Friedrich Max (1823–1900): scholar of religious studies—11

Müller, Gerhard: author of work on the doctrine of justification—10

Müller, Gerhard Ludwig: author of work on Bonhoeffer's theology—4, 5, 8

Müller, Gotthold: German systematic theologian—8

Müller, Hanfried (1925–2009): German professor of systematic theology; author of first German dissertation on Bonhoeffer—4, 5, 6, 7, 8

Müller, Hans Michael (1901–89): 1928, private lecturer, Jena; 1933, professor of systematic theology, Jena and Königsberg; June 24, 1933, temporary state commissioner of the Evangelical Press Association for Germany, Berlin; summer/autumn 1933, adjutant to Reich Bishop Ludwig Müller; 1934–45, professor of systematic theology, Königsberg—2, 10, 11, 12

Müller, Johannes (Elmau) (1864–1949): Protestant theologian and writer; founder of an undogmatic Christian community in Elmau, Bavaria—4, 11, 12

Müller, Johannes: 1933, doctoral candidate in theology and assistant pastor in Berlin—12

Müller, Johannes Franz Max (1869–1931): ordained in 1900; third pastor of the Zion Church, Berlin—11

Müller, Johannes Tobias (1804–84): German scholar of the Lutheran confessions—9

Müller, Josef (nickname: Ochsensepp) (1898–1979): Catholic attorney in Munich who knew Eugenio Pacelli (later Pius XII) from the 1920s; during the 1930s, active as legal adviser and attorney for Catholic institutions; in this capacity, became acquainted with later partners in the resistance, such as Monsignor Neuhäusler, and the abbots of Ettal and Metten, and with various persons in the Vatican; 1939, reserve first lieutenant in the Military Intelligence Office VII in Munich; from October 1939, visited the Vatican several times with Bonhoeffer to extend resistance peace feelers to the British government; from 1940, maintained contacts on behalf of the resistance with the Vatican and the Allies; April 5, 1943, arrested together with his wife, Marie; April 1945, liberated by U.S. forces; after the war, cofounder of the Bavarian Christlich-Soziale Union (CSU) political party; 1947–52, deputy Bavarian minister president and minister of justice—8, 16, 17

Müller, Julius (1801–78): German theologian—2, 11

Müller, Karl (1852–1940): professor of church history, Tübingen—12

Müller, Karl Ferdinand (1911–74): winter 1935–36, participated in the second Finkenwalde session; member of the House of Brethren; pastor, Greifenberg-Rega (Pomerania) and Karnitz (Pomerania)—8, 14

Müller, Ludwig (1883–1945): 1908, pastor, Rödinghausen, Westphalia; from 1914, military chaplain in various posts; 1920, pastor, Cuxhaven and Wilhelmshaven; 1926, military district chaplain, Königsberg; 1931, joined the NSDAP; 1932, leader of the German Christians in East Prussia; member of the Reich leadership of the German Christians (in charge of national questions); April 25, 1933, appointed by Hitler as confidential adviser and authorized representative for questions concerning the evangelical church; May–June 1933, participated in this capacity in discussions regarding the constitution of the German Evangelical Church; May 1933, patron of the German Christians; July 20–September 27, 1933, member of the temporary leadership of the German Evangelical Church; August 4, 1933, elected by the Old Prussian Church Senate to be president of the Evangelical High Church Council of Berlin with the designation of bishop; September 27, 1933, elected Reich bishop by the Wittenberg national synod; September 23, 1934, official installation in this office in the Berlin cathedral; October 1935, authority withdrawn by the Reich Church Committee appointed by the Reich Minister of the Church; July 1945, committed suicide—4, 6, 12, 13, 14, 16, 17

Müller, Major: major in the general staff of the military commander in Norway; mentioned in a letter from Helmuth von Moltke to Freya von Moltke—16

Müller, Marie, née Lochner (1909–96): wife of Josef Müller; from April 5–25, 1943, in Gestapo custody—8

Müller, Martin: 1936, member of third Finkenwalde session—14

Müller, Sebastian: son of Karl-Ferdinand Müller—8

Müller, Walther: August 1934, wanted to participate in the Fanø youth conference—13

Müller-Lyer, Franz (1857–1916): historian of social development—1

Müller-Schlomka, Johannes (1889–1942): from 1917, pastor, Berlin-Tempelhof—12

Müller-Schwefe, Hans Rudolf (1910–86): 1936–39, assistant to Karl Heim; 1947–52, pastor, Kassel, and director, Evangelical Academy Güntershausen; 1952–55, director of the Evangelical Academy Hofgeismar; 1955, professor of practical theology, Hamburg—12

Mumm, Reinhard (1873–1932): pastor, publicist, and social politician; 1912, member of the national parliament; 1920–32, member of the German National People's Party in parliament; general secretary of the Church Social Federation and chair of the German Evangelical Office for Social Concerns in Germany—10

Münchmeyer, August Friedrich Otto (1807–82): German theologian—1

Muni, Paul (1895–1967): Austrian-born actor—15

Müntzer, Thomas (ca. 1490–1525): German theologian representing the Anabaptist "left wing" of the Reformation; 1516, master in theology; 1525, from the Reich city Mühlhausen, organized the Peasant's War in Thuringia; May 15, 1525, beheaded after his peasant army was annihilated by the princes near Frankenhausen: 6, 9, 14, 15

Murakami, Hiroshi: Japanese ecumenist—16

Murphy, James J.: professor of English; medieval rhetoric scholar—14

Murr, Wilhelm (1888–1945): businessman and National Socialist politician; 1928, regional Nazi party leader; 1933, Reich governor of Württemberg; 1939, Reich defense commissar for military district V (Stuttgart); 1945, committed suicide—16

Musculus, Wolfgang (1497–1563): Reformed theologian of the Reformation—2

Mussolini, Benito (1883–1945): Italian dictator and leader *(Duce)* of the Fascist Party; 1945, shot to death by partisans at Lake Garda—8, 9, 13, 14, 15, 16, 17

Muste, Abraham Johannes (1885–1967): Dutch-born U.S. pacifist, labor leader, and social activist—15

Mybes, Fritz: pastor; author of various local church histories—14

Naaman: biblical character—16
Nabal: biblical character—14
Nagel, Gottfried (1876–1944): 1920–44, director of the high church council of the Evangelical Lutheran Church in Prussia (old Lutheran Free Church) in Breslau; head of the Union of Evangelical Lutheran Free Churches in Germany; lecturer at the Evangelical Lutheran Theological Seminary in Breslau—12
Nägelsbach: 1912, church official—14
Nägelsbach, Karl Friedrich von (1806–59): German educator and philologist—9
Nanny (FP): character in the novel—7
Naomi: biblical character—8
Napoleon (Bonaparte) (1769–1821): 1804–15, emperor of France—7, 8, 9, 11, 14
Naso, Eckart von (1888–1976): German author; wounded in World War I; 1918–45, producer and adviser in the Berlin state theater; from 1954–57, in Stuttgart; best known for the nationalistic historical novels *Seydlitz* (1932) and *Moltke* (1937)—8
Nathan: biblical character—9, 13, 14
Nathanael: biblical character—8
Natorp, Paul (1854–1924): philosopher and social educator; from 1885, professor, Marburg; with Hermann Cohen the primary representative of the Marburg School; 1903, publication of most famous work, *Platos Ideenlehre;* 1911, publication of *Die Philosophie, ihr Problem und ihre Probleme,* one of the best introductions to neo-Kantianism and to Cohen's teachings—1, 2, 8, 10, 11
Naumann, Friedrich (1860–1919): German pastor, theologian, and politician; representative of modern social liberalism and advocate of Christian responsibility and social justice; 1890, participant in the Protestant Social Congress; 1907–12 and 1913–18, member of the national parliament, represented the Progressive Peoples' Party; 1918, cofounder of the German Democratic Party; from 1919, its chair—6, 7, 8, 10, 11, 14, 16
Naumann, Kurt: theology student—11
Nawyn, William: author of work about American Protestant churches and refugees—15
Neale, John Mason (1818–66): British Anglican priest and hymnist—5
Neander, Joachim (1650–80): hymnist—15
Neander, Johann August Wilhelm (1789–1850): church historian; a Jew by birth, he was baptized in 1806 after coming under the influence of Schleiermacher; from 1813, professor of church history in Berlin—4

Nebe, Arthur (1894–1945): government lawyer; 1933, criminal and governmental adviser, Berlin police headquarters; 1937, Reich director of the criminal police; 1940, general major of the police and SS group leader (*Gruppenführer*); at the same time, in contact with Canaris, Oster, and Gisevius; January 16, 1945, arrested for his resistance contacts; March 21, 1945, executed—16, 17

Nebe, Mr.: acquaintance of Bonhoeffer and Walter Dreß (1928)—10

Nebel, Franz (1878–1966): from 1927, pastor, Berlin-Charlottenburg—12

Nebelsick, Mary C.: faculty member, Union Theological Seminary, the Philippines; member of the advisory committee to the *DBWE* editorial board —2, 9

Nebuchadnezzar II (d. 562 B.C.E.): biblical character—9

Nehemiah: biblical character—5, 14

Nehmiz, Hugo (1879–1967): from 1915, pastor, Berlin-Schmargendorf—12

Neiman, Susan: U.S. moral philosopher, cultural commentator, and essayist; has written extensively on the juncture of Enlightenment philosophy and politics—12

Neisser: acquaintance of Elisabeth von Hase—10

Nelson, F. Burton (1924–2004): U.S. professor of theology and ethics, North Park Seminary, Chicago; Bonhoeffer scholar—4, 5, 7, 8, 10

Nepos, Cornelius (100–ca. 25 B.C.E.): Roman historian; friend of Pomponius Atticus, Cicero, and Catullus—9

Nero (37–68 C.E.): 54–68, Roman emperor—15

Nestle, Eberhard (1851–1913): professor of ancient Semitic languages and Greek in Ulm and Tübingen; associated today with his Greek-German edition of the New Testament—4, 5, 9, 15

Nestle, Erwin: son of Eberhard Nestle; edited subsequent versions of the Nestle translation of the New Testament—6

Nestle, Wilhelm (1865–1959): German philologist and philosopher—17 (for vol. 9)

Nette: member of the congregational council, German Reformed St. Paul's Church, London—13

Neubert, G.: member of the congregational council, German Reformed St. Paul's Church, London—12, 13

Neubert, W.: member of the congregational council, German Reformed St. Paul's Church, London—13

Neuer, Werner: German Protestant theologian; expert on Adolf Schlatter—17 (for vol. 12)

Neufeld, Karl H.: Jesuit; professor of theology, Austria—11

Neuhäusler, Johannes, D. (1888–1971): Catholic priest; 1932, appointed monsignor by Cardinal Faulhaber; shortly thereafter, as prelate,

appointed to be Faulhaber's political adviser; had various secret contacts in resistance, including with Dr. Josef Müller and the Vatican; February 4, 1941, arrested; May 24, 1941, taken to Sachsenhausen concentration camp; July 12, 1941, to Dachau; April 24, 1945, released; 1947, suffragan bishop; 1955, cathedral provost of Munich—16, 17

Neumann, Johannes: psychotherapist—14

Neumann, Peter: German historian of the Church Struggle—8, 10

Neumann, Sigmund: prominent sociologist during the Weimar era; author of works on political parties in Germany—12

Neurath, Constantin (Konstantin) Baron von (1873–1956): German statesman; 1932–38, Reich foreign minister; 1939–43, Reich protector of Bohemia and Moravia; 1946, sentenced at the end of the Nuremberg trials to fifteen years in prison; 1954, released from prison—13, 14, 16

Newman, Cardinal John Henry (1801–90): British Anglican priest who converted to Catholicism and led the Oxford Movement—14

Newton, Isaac (1643–1727): British mathematician, physicist, astronomer —8

Niceta(s) of Aquileia (second half of fifth century): bishop of Aquileia—1

Niceta of Remesiana (fourth or fifth century): Greek prelate, theologian, and poet; ca. 366, bishop of Remesiana; major doctrinal work, *Six Books of Instructions for Baptismal Candidates*; apparently introduced expression "communion of saints"—1

Nicholas: biblical character—14

Nicholas of Cusa (1401–64): theologian; 1448, cardinal; 1450, prince bishop of Brixen—8

Nichols, Beverley (1898–1983): author of the 1933 political novel *Cry Havoc* —13

Niclaus: pastor (1936)—14

Nicodemus: biblical character—14, 15

Nicol, Martin: professor of practical theology, Erlangen—14

Nicolai, Philipp (1566–1608): German theologian and hymnist—8, 10, 16

Nicolaisen, Carsten: studied Protestant theology and German literature in Göttingen and Hamburg; 1966, doctorate in theology; secretary of the Protestant working group for contemporary church history and academic director at the Institute for Contemporary History, Munich; publications include *Der Weg nach Barmen: Die Entstehungsgeschichte der Theologischen Erklärung von 1934* (1985); edited several editions and published essays and articles in the field of contemporary church history; German coeditor, *DBW* 12—12

Nicolaus: biblical character—14

Nicolaus: young theologian from the Rhineland; August 15, 1941, announcement of his death at the front in the Finkenwalde newsletter—16
Nicole, Pierre (1625–95): French Catholic philosopher—1
Niebergall, Alfred: professor emeritus of practical theology, Marburg—11, 14
Niebergall, Friedrich (1866–1932): Protestant theologian—10, 11, 14
Niebuhr, Christopher: son of Reinhold Niebuhr—6
Niebuhr, Helmut Richard (1894–1962): U.S. Protestant theologian, brother of Reinhold Niebuhr—6, 10, 15
Niebuhr, Hulda: Reinhold Niebuhr's older sister—15
Niebuhr, Lydia: Reinhold Niebuhr's mother—11
Niebuhr, Reinhold (1892–1971): U.S. theologian and social ethicist; 1915–18, pastor, Detroit; 1928–30, professor of religious philosophy, Union Theological Seminary, New York; 1930–31, one of Bonhoeffer's professors there; 1930–60, professor of Christian ethics there—4, 6, 8, 10, 11, 12, 13, 15, 16, 17
Niebuhr, Ursula Mary, née Keppel-Compton: 1931, married Reinhold Niebuhr—11, 13, 15
Nieden, Ernst zur (1903–74): 1929, pastor, Offenbach; 1945, director, Evangelical Academy in Hesse-Nassau; 1950–69, provost of the visitation district of South Nassau—14
Niemeier, Gottfried (1906–84): 1933, pastor, Arnsberg; 1939, military service and prisoner of war; after war, theological adviser and vice president of the chancellery of the Evangelical Church of Germany—10
Niemöller, Else, née Bremer: 1919, married Martin Niemöller—15, 16
Niemöller, Gerhard: author of works on the Church Struggle—13
Niemöller, Jan: son of Else and Martin Niemöller—15
Niemöller, Martin (1892–1984): World War I naval officer and submarine captain; 1919–24, studied theology, though also member of the *Freikorps* (paramilitary groups of World War I veterans); 1924, headed the Inner Mission, Münster; after 1931, pastor, Berlin-Dahlem; May 1933, cofounder of the Young Reformation movement; September 1933, cofounder of the Pastors' Emergency League; 1937, arrested; 1938, acquitted, but taken to the Sachsenhausen concentration camp as "Hitler's personal prisoner," then to Dachau (until 1945); 1945, member of the advisory council of the Evangelical Church of Germany and head of the Church Foreign Office; 1947–64, president of the Protestant Church in Hesse-Nassau; 1957, president of the German Peace Society; 1961–68, one of the presidents of the World Council of Churches—4, 6, 7, 8, 12, 13, 14, 15, 16, 17
Niemöller, Wilhelm (1898–1983): 1915–18, military service; 1924, assistant pastor, Witten and Hattingen; 1925, pastor, Schlüsselburg/Weser;

1930–63, Bielefeld; during Church Struggle, member of the Westphalian Council of Brethren—13, 14, 16

Niesel, Wilhelm (1903–88): Reformed theologian from Berlin, leading member of the Confessing Church of the Old Prussian Union; 1930, pastor, Wuppertal-Elberfeld and academic inspector at the preachers' seminary there; 1934–45, member of the Council of Brethren of the Old Prussian Union, responsible for seminary education; 1935, lecturer in systematic theology at the seminary in Berlin; arrested several times by the Gestapo; 1940, expulsion from Berlin; prohibited from speaking publicly in the Reich; 1941, assistant pastor, Breslau; December 1941, convicted in the collective trial against the examination board of the Old Prussian Union Council of Brethren; 1943–46, curate in Reelkirchen, Lippe; 1945–72, member of the advisory council of the Evangelical Church of Germany; 1946, pastor in Schöller and professor at the seminary in Wuppertal; 1946–73, president and moderator of the World Alliance of Reformed Churches; 1947–63, member of the executive committee of the World Council of Churches; 1964–70, president of the World Presbyterian Alliance (which in 1970 became the World Alliance of Reformed Churches)—6, 8, 11, 13, 14, 15, 16, 17

Nietzsche: 1933, secondary school teacher in Berlin—12

Nietzsche, Friedrich Wilhelm (1844–1900): German philosopher, poet, and classical philologist; 1869–79, professor of classical philology, Basel—1, 2, 3, 6, 7, 8, 9, 10, 11, 12, 13, 14, 15, 16

Nimz, Kurt (1913–93): from Pomerania; 1938–39, participated in the collective pastorate in Köslin—15

Nipkow, Karl Ernst: professor in the departments of Protestant theology and of social and behavioral sciences, Tübingen—14, 15

Nissen, Johann: author of work on Luther catechism—10

Nithack, Ulrich (1913–41): from Berlin-Friedenau; 1936, vicar, Buckow and Schneidemühl; 1937, predicant, Küstrin; 1938, participated in the collective pastorate in Groß-Schlönwitz; 1939, assistant pastor, Elstal-Döberitz; July 14, 1941, killed in action on the eastern front—15, 16

Nitzsch, (Karl) Carl Immanuel (1787–1868): Protestant theologian, church leader and professor of practical theology—14

Niven, Miss: member of the World Alliance publications commission—12

Noah: biblical character—9, 14

Nobiling, Siegfried (b. 1891): 1928, pastor, Berlin-Friedenau; 1932, member (adviser for personnel questions) of the Reich leadership of the German Christian faith movement; 1933, high consistory official, Evangelical High Church Council, Berlin; 1934, in Stettin; 1939, in Berlin—12

Noble, Bernard: translator of early English edition of *Act and Being*—2

Noel-Buxton, Dorothee: *see* Buxton, Dorothy F.

Noel-Buxton, Lord: *see* Buxton, Lord Noel

Nohl, Herman (1879–1960): German philosopher, educational theorist, and social pedagogue; until 1904, student in Berlin, in the end as the amanuensis of Wilhelm Dilthey; 1915–18, soldier; 1919, founded the adult continuing education schools, or *Volkshochschulen*, in Jena and Thuringia; professor, Jena; 1933, Nohl's students were dismissed; 1937, dismissed from office; 1937, while working as an author in Karlshafen, visited by Dietrich Bonhoeffer and Eberhard Bethge, presumably at the suggestion of Gerhard Leibholz; 1945, resumed university teaching—6, 7, 16

Nold, Karl (1903–42): 1922–26, studied theology in Erlangen, Leipzig, Tübingen, and Göttingen (with Karl Barth); 1931, pastor, Nördlingen —11

Nolde (Hansen), Emil (1867–1956): German painter and graphic artist; prohibited from painting during the Third Reich—6

Noots, Hubert-Albert: Belgian general abbot of the Premonstratensian order in Rome; one of Josef Müller's confidential contacts at the Vatican —16

Norden, Eduard (1868–1937): German classical philologist—9

Norden, Günther van: German church historian, specialist on Church Struggle—12, 13, 14, 16

Nordmann, Walter: from 1935, pastor of the Bethlehem congregation, Berlin; 1949, professor at the vocational-pedagogical institute, Frankfurt am Main—16

Norman, Edward Robert: British church historian—16

Nørregaard, Jens Skousboe (1887–1953): 1923–49, professor of church history, Copenhagen—14

Norris, Clarence: one of the nine young black men convicted in the infamous 1931 Scottsboro trial that Bonhoeffer alluded to in *Ethics*—6

Norris, George William (1861–1944): liberal U.S. senator from Nebraska—10

Nossen, Annemarie: born in Berlin; studied history in Munich and Berlin; April 19–June 22, 1926, member of Harnack's seminar—9

Nostitz-Drzewiecki, Gottfried von (1902–76): German diplomat; 1934, counselor with the Viennese legation; 1938, worked in the Foreign Ministry; 1940, consul in Geneva—16

Noth, Martin (1902–68): German Old Testament scholar; studied at Erlangen, Rostock, and Leipzig; private lecturer at Greifswald and Leipzig; 1930–44, professor, Königsberg; 1945–65, Bonn—4

Nötzky, Mr.: academic assessor for secondary schools in Berlin—9

Novalis: see Hardenberg, Baron Friedrich von

Nowak, Kurt (1942–2001): professor of church history, Leipzig—10, 11, 12
Nübel, Hans Ulrich: author of article on the Freiburg circle—16
Nuding, Albrecht: German church historian—17 (for vol. 12)
Nygren, Anders (1890–1978): Swedish theologian and ecumenist; 1924–58, professor of systematic theology, Lund; 1949–58, bishop of Lund; 1947–52, first president of the Lutheran World Federation established in Lund —5, 14, 16

Obendiek, Harmannus (1894–1954): German Reformed theologian, member of Confessing Church; served on the governing council (with Karl Barth) of Alliance of Reformed Churches during the 1930s—16
Oberheid, Heinrich (1895–1977): 1914, studied theology; military service in World War I; 1919, studied economics; 1920, department head in the Mining Association in Essen (organized passive resistance); 1925, agriculturist; continued his study of theology; 1928, textile merchant; 1930, joined the NSDAP and the storm troopers; 1933, pastor, Asbach, Westerwald; October 1933, German Christian bishop of Cologne-Aachen; November 1933, worked closely with the Reich bishop; mid-1934, leave of absence from both offices; joined the Thuringian German Christians; 1936, pastor, Thuringia; military service and prisoner of war until the end of 1945; postwar, businessman in Düsseldorf—13
O'Brien, Father: superintendent general of the Society of St. John the Evangelist; 1931, in Oxford—13
Occam: *see* William of Occam
Ochs, Siegfried (1858–1929): 1920–28, director of the choir of the state academic high school for music in Berlin—17 (for vol. 9)
Octavian (Gaius Julius Caesar Octavianus Augustus) (63 B.C.E.– 14 C.E.): first Roman emperor; adopted son and heir of Julius Caesar; known as Caesar Augustus—9
Oecolampadius, Johannes (1482–1531): Swiss reformer—15
Oehler, Richard (1878–1948): Nietzsche scholar—10
Oehme, Werner: author of work on Christian resistance figures—16
Oepke, Albrecht (1881–1955): 1914, theological instructor at the mission seminary in Leipzig; 1920–22, editor of the *Evangelisch-Lutherisches Missionsblatt*; 1922, professor of New Testament, Leipzig; from 1933, member of the Confessing Church; 1946, founded the organization Mission in Israel; 1949, professor of New Testament, Leipzig—14, 16
Oertzen, Friedrich Wilhelm von (1898–1944): member of a German aristocratic family from Mecklenburg—6, 7
Oestreich: pastor (1935)—14

Oetinger (sometimes Ötinger), Friedrich Christoph von (1702–82): Lutheran theologian and adherent of theosophy—3, 5, 15

Oettingen, Alexander von (1827–1906): German theologian and moral statistician—6, 16

Ohly: pastor in Stockholm (1936)—14

Ohnesorge, Anna: from Silesia; secondary school vice principal, forced to retire; from spring 1938, lived in Bergen on the island of Rügen; member, Pomeranian Council of Brethren, assigned to oversee catechetical training—8, 16

Olbrich, Harald: German art historian—1

Olbricht, Frau: wife of Pastor Friedrich Olbricht—10

Olbricht, Friedrich (1874–1962): 1920–34, pastor of the German congregation in Barcelona and president of the German-Iberian Conference; Bonhoeffer's supervisory pastor in Barcelona—10

Olbricht, Friedrich (1888–1944): career military; general in the infantry; 1935, chief of staff of the Fourth Army Corps, Dresden; from March 1940, chief of the general army office and commander in chief of the reserve army; later belonged to the intimate circle around Count Stauffenberg, with whom he was executed by firing squad after the failed coup on July 20, 1944—16, 17

Olden, Peter H.: Bonhoeffer's fellow student at the Friedrich Werder Gymnasium, Berlin-Grunewald—10

Oldenhage, Klaus: German archivist and expert on contemporary archives—8

Oldham, Joseph Houldsworth (1874–1969): Scottish lay theologian; graduate of Oxford University; 1896–97, secretary of the Student Christian Movement and Missionary Volunteer Union in England; 1897–1900, secretary of the YMCA in Lahore, India; 1900–1904, studied in Edinburgh and Halle; organizing secretary of the 1910 World Missionary Conference, Edinburgh, and secretary of its continuation committee, 1910–20; founder and editor of the *International Review of Missions*; 1921–38, general secretary of the International Mission Council (founded 1921); author of seminal study *Christianity and the Race Problem* (1924) and numerous other writings; 1934–38, chair of the Research Commission of Life and Work (Universal Christian Council for Life and Work); 1939–45, editor of the *Christian News Letter*; 1942–47, founding head of the Christian Frontier Council; a chief architect of the World Council of Churches—13, 14, 16, 17

Olier, Jean Jacques (1608–57): 1633, priest; 1642, founded the St. Sulpice seminary, Paris—14

Oliver: title character in George Santayana's novel *The Last Puritan*, in whom Bonhoeffer recognized aspects of himself—6, 7

Olivier, Laurence (1907–89): British actor, director, and producer—10

Ollendorf, Friedrich (1889–1951): lawyer and social worker; 1920–27, head of the Central Welfare Agency in Berlin; ultimately upper magistrate councilor; 1927–34, director of the Central Welfare Agency of German Jews; organized international conferences on Jewish welfare work; 1934, emigrated to Palestine as a result of National Socialist race laws; engaged in social work there—12

Olson, Jeannine E.: professor of history, Rhode Island College—14

Onan: biblical character—6

Onesimus: biblical character—4

Onesiphorus: biblical character—15

Onnasch, Bernhard (1921–96): youngest brother of Friedrich (Fritz) Onnasch; wounded several times as an officer; from 1948, pastor in the Hannover regional church—8

Onnasch, Friedrich (1881–1945): father of Friedrich Onnasch (Fritz); 1922, pastor at St. Mary's and superintendent, Köslin; member of the Pomeranian Council of Brethren; from December 1937, Bonhoeffer's collective pastorate met in his home; arrested several times; September 1940, Reich prohibition against speaking in public (at the same time as Bonhoeffer) and travel restrictions for the province of Pomerania; September 1941, assigned to the pastorate Berlinchen/Neumark, from which he also participated in the visitation services of the Brandenburg Council of Brethren; from 1943, member of the Council of Brethren of the Old Prussian Union; February 17, 1945, shot to death by Russian soldiers in Berlinchen—8, 15, 16

Onnasch, Friedrich (Fritz) (1911–45): son of superintendent Friedrich Onnasch; 1935, participated in the first Zingst/Finkenwalde session; member of the House of Brethren; Confessing Church pastor in Stettin; 1937–39, academic inspector in Finkenwalde (until its closure in September 1937), then in the collective pastorate in Köslin; September 17, 1939, married Eberhard Bethge's sister Margret; like his father, shot to death in Köslin by Russian soldiers in 1945—8, 14, 15, 16

Onnasch, Kurt (1917–42): brother of Fritz Onnasch; studied theology in Marburg; 1942, killed in action on the eastern front—16

Onnasch, Margret, née Bethge: sister of Eberhard Bethge; September 17, 1939, married Friedrich (Fritz) Onnasch; second marriage to Gottfried Grude, pastor in Magdeburg—8, 15, 16

Onnasch, Maria: wife of (superintendent) Friedrich Onnasch—15

Onnasch, Martin: professor of church history, Greifswald—8

Opitz, Hans Georg (1905–41): 1933, private lecturer in church history, Berlin; 1939, professor, Vienna—13

Oppen, Dietrich von: professor of social ethics, Marburg—12

Oppenheimer, Franz (1864–1943): German economist and sociologist—1, 9

Orestes: in Greek mythology, son of Clytemnestra and Agamemnon—17 (for vol. 9)

Orff, Carl (1895–1982): composer, music educator; main work: *Carmina burana: Cantones profanae* (1937)—8

Origen (ca. 185–254): Alexandrian biblical critic, exegete, theologian, and spiritual writer—8, 14, 16

Orlow, Dietrich: professor emeritus of German history, Boston University —11

Ormerod, Mary: Quaker; director of the Refugees' Committee for Professional Workers—13

Orsenigo, Cesare (1873–1946): 1930–45, papal nuncio with the German Reich government in Berlin—16

Ortega y Gasset, José (1883–1955): Spanish cultural philosopher—6, 8

Orwell, George (1903–50): British author, journalist, and socialist—10

Osborn, Robert: U.S. professor of theology, Duke University—9

Osiander, Andreas (1498–1552): Nuremberg reformer; 1549, Königsberg —10

Osiris: Egyptian god; variously associated with death and resurrection—10

Ossietzky, Carl von (1889–1938): German journalist and pacifist; from 1927, editorial head of the *Weltbühne*; from 1933, incarcerated in concentration camps; 1936, Nobel Peace Prize—12

Oster, Annie, née Haser: secretary in Josef Müller's Munich law office; later married Hans Oster's son Achim—16, 17

Oster, Hans (1887–1945): career military officer; 1929, major in the Sixth Division in Münster; winter 1932–33, discharged; October 1933, began working as a civilian employee in the Military Intelligence Office; 1935, reactivated as a lieutenant colonel by Admiral Canaris; 1938, start of contacts with the resistance during the Fritsch affair, including with Ludwig Beck, Hans von Dohnanyi, Bonhoeffer, and others; September 1938, chief of section Z (Central Section) in the Military Intelligence Office; December 1942, major general; April 16, 1943, dismissed from service after Hans von Dohnanyi's arrest and transferred to the führer reserves; July 21, 1944, arrested; April 9, 1945, executed in Flossenbürg—6, 8, 16, 17

Ostermann, Christian: German author of a Latin exercise textbook—7

Ostermann, Joseph: U.S. Catholic priest; director during the 1930s of the Committee for Catholic Refugees from Germany—15

Ostwald, Carl Wilhelm Wolfgang (1883–1943): colleague of Karl-Friedrich Bonhoeffer; professor of colloid chemistry, Leipzig University—8

Ott, Heinrich: Swiss theologian and pastor—2, 4, 6, 8

Otto, Ernst (1891–1941): pastor in Eisenach; 1935, member of the Sydow Brethren and of the Reich Council of Brethren; chair of the Council of Brethren, Thuringia; 1936, member of the advisory council of the Evangelical Lutheran Church of Germany; 1938, withdrawn from prison chaplaincy—14

Otto, Rudolf (1869–1937): Protestant theologian and philosopher of religion; professor, Göttingen, Breslau, and Marburg; best known for his book *The Idea of the Holy*—9, 10, 11, 12, 14

Otto, Walter Friedrich (1874–1958): classical philologist; 1897, doctorate in Bonn; 1898, assistant research specialist for the *Thesaurus linguae latinae*; until 1911, editor and author for the *Onomasticum Latinum*; 1905, postdoctoral lecturing qualification; 1911, professor, Vienna; 1913, Basel; 1914, Frankfurt am Main; 1934, forced to move to Königsberg, which he had to flee in 1944, leaving behind his entire possessions; 1945, professor, Munich and Göttingen; 1946, Tübingen—8, 9

Overbeck, Franz Camille (1837–1905): German Protestant theologian; professor in Jena and in Basel; friend of Nietzsche; held that the gospel was wholly eschatological; influenced the young Barth—4, 9, 11

Ovid, Publius Ovidius Naso (43 B.C.E.–ca. 17 C.E.): Latin poet—14

Ovington, Mary White (1865–1951): U.S. Unitarian, active in social and political causes; cofounder of the NAACP—10

Owen, Lord David: prominent British Social Democrat politician—16

Pabst, Walter: Confessing Church pastor, Berlin; after 1945, active in the Protestant church in the German Democratic Republic—8

Pacelli, Eugenio: *see* Pius XII

Paeplow: participant in Bonhoeffer's seminar on "The Idea of Philosophy and Protestant Theology"—11

Page, Kirby (1890–1957): 1918, pastor, New York—12

Pagel, Karl: German author of works on the Church Struggle—8

Paissy: *see* Raikov, Alexander

Palestrina, Giovanni (1525–94): Italian composer, church musician—8

Palladius (ca. 364–425): bishop and historian of early monasticism; alleged author of the *Dialogue* on the life of Chrysostom—10, 14

Palmer, Larry: U.S. author of Distler biography—7

Palmer, Otmar (1873–1964): 1916–34, pastor, Blankenburg, Harz; 1935, church consistory official, Braunschweig—12

Palmström: character in Christian Morgenstern poems—8

Pamphili, Cardinal: *see* Pompilij, Basilio

Pan: Greek god; guardian of shepherds and their flocks—10

Pangritz, Andreas: German professor of systematic theology; author of numerous publications on Bonhoeffer and Barth—2, 4, 6, 8, 11, 12, 14, 16

Pank, Oskar (1838–1928): senior pastor of St. Thomas Church, Leipzig, and renowned sermon author—10

Pankow, Hermann: from 1911, pastor, Berlin-Pankow—12

Pannenberg, Wolfhart: studied theology in Berlin, also in Basel under Karl Barth, but sensed that Barth's stringent critique of natural theology was too radical; 1954, doctorate in Heidelberg; 1955, postdoctoral lecturing qualification; 1958–61, professor of systematic theology at the seminary in Wuppertal; 1961–68, in Mainz; from 1968, in Munich; until 1993, head of the Ecumenical Institute in Munich; keen theological interest in universal history as the locus where God is revealed, i.e., known indirectly; God conducts his self-disclosure through his decisive divine deeds, primarily those in the history of Israel and in the life, death, and resurrection of Jesus Christ—2

Pannwitz, Rudolf (1881–1969): German philosopher, cultural historian, and poet—12

Papamichael, Gregorios (1875–1956): Greek Orthodox theologian; from 1918, professor of apologetics and encyclopedia, Athens; member of the Greek section of the World Alliance for Promoting International Friendship through the Churches—16

Papen, Franz von (1879–1969): from 1921, member of the Prussian parliament (representing the Center Party); June–December 1932, German Reich chancellor; 1933, vice-chancellor under Hitler; 1936, ambassador in Vienna; 1939, in Ankara, Turkey; 1946, acquitted in the Nuremberg trials—11, 12, 17

Papias (second century C.E.): Christian bishop of Hierapolis in Phrygia; recorded early traditions about the origin of the Gospels—9

Pappus (ca. 320 C.E.): Alexandrian mathematician, author of commentaries on Euclid and Ptolemy, also of a universal geography based on the world map of Ptolemy; most important work is a handbook on the Greek mathematical sciences—8, 10

Paris: Character in Greek mythology whose elopement with Helen caused the Trojan War—8

Parks, Rosa Louise (1913–2005): African American civil rights activist and seamstress; her 1955 arrest for refusing to give up her seat sparked the Montgomery Bus Boycott; "Mother of the Civil Rights Movement"—10

Parpert, Friedrich: theologian and philologist—10

Parsifal: protagonist of Middle High German epic by Wolfram von Eschenbach concerning the quest for the Holy Grail—8

Pascal, Blaise (1623–62): French religious philosopher, mathematician, and physicist—4, 9, 12

Paschalis I (Paschal I) (d. 824): 817–24, pope—9

Pasewald, Elisabeth: from 1939, secretary for Rüdiger Schleicher—8

Pastor (FP): proposed character in drama—7

Patijn, C. L.: Dutch expert in constitutional law; director of the section for internal affairs in the Dutch Foreign Ministry; professor of international political relations, Utrecht—16

Paton, William (1886–1943): Scottish theologian; 1917, military chaplain in India, contact with Gandhi and Nehru; 1927–43, secretary, International Missionary Council in London; 1939–43, assistant general secretary of the provisional World Council of Churches; 1940, founded a British working group dedicated to peace—6, 7, 8, 16, 17

Patrick, Denzil: Scottish ecumenist; theological secretary of the British Student Christian Movement; secretary of the World Student Christian Federation and the international office of the YMCA, Geneva; 1941, mentioned by Visser 't Hooft as a dialogue partner—13, 16

Pätzold, Ernst (1891–1969): 1933, pastor, Berlin-St. Bartholomäus; 1940, superintendent; 1945–55, member of the Berlin-Brandenburg church government—12

Pauck, Marion: wife of Wilhelm Pauck; one of the translators for *DBWE* 11—11

Pauck, Wilhelm (William) (1901–81): theologian and historian in New York—15

Paul (FP): character in the novel—7

Paul: apostle, biblical character—1, 2, 4, 5, 6, 7, 8, 9, 10, 11, 12, 13, 14, 15, 16

Paul (Jean): *see* Jean Paul

Paul, Jonathan (1853–1931): Protestant pastor; from 1899, freelance evangelist and leader of the Pentecostal movement—11

Paul of Samosata: ca. 260–272, heretical bishop of Antioch; his deviant views involved the nature of the Godhead and of Christ—12, 15

Paul the Deacon (ca. 720–95): Lombard theologian in the court of Charlemagne; chronicler, known as the "Father of Italian History"; also lived in Monte Cassino—10

Pauli: official at the Friedrich Wilhelm University in Berlin—11

Paulsen, Anna (1893–1981): first woman to attain a doctorate in theology in Germany; 1926, director of the center for women's service to the church, Burckhardt House, Berlin-Dahlem; 1951–58, adviser for women's affairs in the chancellery of the Evangelical Church of Germany in Hannover—12, 16

Paulsen, Friedrich (1846–1908): German philosopher—15

Peachey, Paul: U.S. Mennonite theologian, pacifist, and historian—6

Pearsall, R. L. de: translator of hymns—12

Pecina, Johannes (1901–89): assistant pastor in the Confessing Church, Seelow; attracted overflowing crowds to his worship services; expelled; later arrested—4, 14

Peck, William J.: U.S. theologian; author of various articles on Bonhoeffer, with a special interest in Bonhoeffer and Judaism—4, 6, 7

Peirce, Charles Sanders (1839–1914): U.S. scientist, logician, and philosopher—11

Pejsa, Jane: U.S. author of work on Ruth von Kleist—8, 15, 16

Pelagius: theologian, exegete, and ascetic; scriptural teacher in Rome, later in Palestine; opponent of Augustine; ca. 399, accused of heresy, condemned by various councils; 417, excommunicated; Pelagianism was originally an ascetic movement that held that salvation can be reached by human efforts—2, 3, 10, 14

Pelikan, Herbert Rainer: author of book on Bonhoeffer—4, 6

Pelikan, Jaroslav (1923–2006): U.S. theologian and scholar of Christian history—14

Pepping, Ernst (1901–81): German church musician; from 1934, instructor at the church music academy in Berlin-Spandau; 1953–68, professor of composition at the Music Academy, Berlin—16

Perels, Christoph: studied German philology, history, and philosophy at the Universities of Erlangen, Kiel, Paris, and Göttingen; 1964–66, editor at S. Fischer publishers, Frankfurt am Main; 1969–80, assistant professor, Technical University, Braunschweig; 1980–84, professor of German literature; after 1983, director, Free German Foundation of the Goethe Museum in Frankfurt am Main; after 1987, honorary professor of German literature, Johann Wolfgang Goethe University, Frankfurt am Main—7

Perels, Emil Erwin Leopold (1875–1954): lawyer; 1907, lecturer, commercial secondary school, Mannheim; 1912, professor, Heidelberg; 1933, teaching permission withdrawn under Nazi race laws; 1940, interned in the southern French camp at Gurs; after the war, lived in Perigueux, France—16

Perels, Friedrich Justus (1910–45): Berlin lawyer; 1933, eligibility for civil service affected by the Nazi Aryan laws; 1936–40, lawyer for the Old Prussian Council of Brethren and for the Pastors' Emergency League; 1940–44, employed in the chancellery of the attorney Dr. Horst Holstein in Berlin; October 5, 1944, arrested and taken to the Lehrter Strasse prison; February 2, 1945, sentenced to death by the People's Court; April 23, 1945, executed by firing squad—4, 6, 7, 8, 14, 15, 16, 17

Perels, Hans (1918–41): brother of Friedrich Justus Perels; November 1941, killed in action in Africa—14

Perels, Helga, née Kellermann (b. 1915): wife of Friedrich Justus Perels; after receiving her secondary school diploma, attended the seminar on women's service to the church in Burckhardt House; 1938, secretary for the Old Prussian Council of Brethren; 1940, married; 1946, secretary for the Council of Brethren of the Evangelical Church of Germany, Schwäbisch Gmünd; 1952–56, employed in the headquarters for Protestant women's programs, Frankfurt am Main—16

Perels, Otto (1908–2003): from Berlin; 1933, ordained and until 1946 pastor in Rehfelde, district of Strausberg; member of the Confessing Church and of the Pastors' Emergency League; senior member, Berlin German Student Christian Federation; 1942, worked in medical services on the eastern front; 1947–69, pastor, Berlin; 1969–75, head of the pastoral college, Berlin-Brandenburg; 1975–78, pastor, Berlin—12, 16

Pernice, Klara: *see* Hase, Klara von

Perrone, Giovanni (1794–1876): Italian Jesuit theologian; contributed to the formulation of the doctrine of the immaculate conception—9

Perry, Ralph Barton (1876–1957): student of William James; 1913, professor, Harvard; theoretician of values—10

Perugino II (Pietro Vannucci) (1446–1523): Italian painter; the leading Umbrian master of early Renaissance; Raphael's teacher; among the painters who worked on the Sistine Chapel frescoes—9

Peruzzi, Baldassare (1481–1536): Italian architect and painter of the High Renaissance—9

Peschke, Kurt: attorney and notary, Berlin-Halensee; 1943–44, together with Dr. Graf von der Goltz, defense attorney for Hans von Dohnanyi before the military high court—16, 17

Pestalozzi, Gerty, née Eidenbenz: wife of Rudolf Pestalozzi—16

Pestalozzi, Johann Heinrich (1746–1827): Swiss educator and social reformer—8, 15

Pestalozzi, Rudolf: manufacturer in Zürich; close acquaintance of Karl Barth and Eduard Thurneysen; put his vacation home on the "Bergli"

in Oberrieden, Canton Zürich, at the disposal of the Barthian circle for their meetings—11, 15, 16, 17

Peter, Friedrich (1892–1960): 1914–18, military service; 1918, member of the *Freikorps* (paramilitary groups of World War I veterans); 1922, pastor, Jessen, Saxony; 1926, Berlin; 1929, member of the NSDAP and of the German Christians; from 1933, in the Reich leadership of the German Christian faith movement, with responsibility for youth issues; 1933–35, senior consistory official, Evangelical High Church Council, Berlin; bishop of Magdeburg; 1936–48, cathedral preacher, Berlin; 1948, dismissed; 1949, given leave assignment in the Westphalian church; 1953, pastor, Gronau, Westphalia—11, 12, 13, 14

Peter (Simon): biblical character; disciple of Jesus—1, 4, 6, 7, 9, 10, 11, 12, 14, 15, 16

Peters, Hans Helmut (1908–87): from Hannover; German pastor in Nice, France; 1939, appointed by the Church Foreign Office as secretary of the Evangelical Relief Service for Internees and Prisoners (EHIG); 1940, stationed in Paris; after the war, regional youth pastor, Hannover; 1954, superintendent and then regional superintendent, Celle—16

Peters, Tiemo Rainer: author of work on Bonhoeffer's political theology—2, 4, 5, 8

Petersdorff, Herman von (1864–1929): German historian and biographer —8

Petersen, Peter (1875–1957): Confessing pastor, Berlin-Lichterfelde—12

Petersmann-Borsdorff, Gertrud: coeditor with Rudolf Otto of book of sermons—10

Peterson, Erik (1890–1960): 1924, professor of New Testament theology and church history, Bonn; 1930, converted to Catholicism; 1934, professor of ancient Christian literature and general religious history, Papal Institute, Rome—1, 2, 11

Peterson, Otto: lecturer in German literature, New York—10

Petrarch (Francesco Petrarca) (1304–74): Italian poet and scholar—8, 13

Petras, Renate: German author—15

Petrick, Herbert: Baptist; secretary of the German section of the World Alliance for Promoting International Friendship through the Churches and Bonhoeffer's predecessor as secretary of the Provisional Bureau for Ecumenical Youth Work—11, 12

Petzina, Dietmar: German sociologist—11

Pfaff, Peter: Germanist; author of studies of Goethe—11

Pfannschmidt, Heinrich: church musician—14

Pfatteicher, Philip H.: U.S. Lutheran liturgical scholar—14

Pfeffer, Karl Heinz (1906–71): 1940–46, professor of sociology (folklore and regional studies), Berlin—8

Pfeifer, Hans Martin (1930–2011): theologian, teacher, pastor, and editor; 1964, doctorate in theology, Heidelberg, with a dissertation on Bonhoeffer's doctrine of the church; 1975–78, secretary of the International Bonhoeffer Society, West German section; from 1996, liaison for the *DBW* editorial board; author and editor of many works by and about Bonhoeffer, student chaplain, teacher of religion, and pastor until 1995—2, 4, 6, 7, 8, 9, 10, 12, 13, 15, 16, 17

Pfeiffer, Hilde: *see* Rannenberg, Hilde

Pfeiffer, Johannes (1897–1970): from 1930, pastor, Berlin-Friedenau—12

Pfeil, Christoph Karl Ludwig von (1712–84): hymnist—14

Pfister, Oskar (1873–1956): Swiss pastor; first person to apply Freud's psychoanalytical theories to education and pastoral care—14

Pfisterer, Franz-Ernst (1911–44): from Bochum; 1936–37, participated in the fourth Finkenwalde session; 1938–40, pastor, Siegen; August 3, 1944, killed in action on the eastern front—15, 16

Pfitzner, Hans Erich (1869–1949): composer, music author—8

Pfizer, Theodor (1904–92): studied law; Bonhoeffer's fraternity brother; later became mayor of Ulm—9, 10

Pfleiderer, Otto (1839–1908): pastor and professor of New Testament, Jena and Berlin—9

Pfuhlstein, Alexander von: career military; ultimately major general; 1943–44, commander of the Brandenburg Division—16, 17

Phaedra: in Greek mythology, wife of Theseus—17 (for vol. 9)

Philemon: biblical character—4

Philemon: character in Greek mythology—10

Philip: biblical character—4, 9, 14

Philip, André (1902–70): French lawyer and ecumenist; 1928, professor of political economy, Lyon; 1931, vice president of the Youth Commission of the World Alliance for Promoting International Friendship through the Churches; 1932, participant in the ecumenical youth conference in Gland; 1936, socialist representative in parliament; during the war, worked with de Gaulle in London; 1946–47, minister of finance; professor of law, Paris—11, 13, 16

Philip II (1529–98): king of Spain—10

Philipp of Hesse (the Magnanimous) (1504–67): 1509–67, Count of Hesse; 1524, won over to the Reformation and became one of its leaders in Germany—14

Philipp, Arthur Lothar: historian of Scotland Yard—8

Philipps, Wilhelm Karl Heinrich (1891–1982): 1922, provincial youth chaplain, Herdecke; 1926, pastor, Düsseldorf; 1932, head of the Johannes institutions, Berlin-Spandau; 1939, high church official, Münster—11, 12

Phillip, Lee Cato: 1930, acquaintance of Bonhoeffer at Howard University and source of a text that he kept; 1939, MTh Howard University; 40 years dean of chapel, Prairie View A&M University, Texas; retired 1969—10

Phillips, John Anthony: author of a dissertation on Bonhoeffer's Christology; student of Ronald Gregor Smith—3, 6

Philo of Alexandria (Philo Judaeus) (ca. 20 B.C.E.–50 C.E.): Hellenistic-Jewish philosopher of Alexandria; known as the "Jewish Plato"; interpreted Jewish history and law in Platonic categories—9

Phoebe: biblical character—14

Phygelus: biblical character—15

Picasso, Pablo (1881–1973): Spanish painter—10

Piccard, B.: 1922, professor of physics, Brussels—11

Picht, Georg (1913–82): German educator and religious philosopher; nephew of Ernst Robert Curtius; 1940, studied in Freiburg under Martin Heidegger; worked with the Patristics Commission of the Berlin Academy of Science; 1942, assistant in classics in Freiburg, attaining doctorate; after the war, founded a boarding school, researched various pedagogical questions; from 1958, head of the Protestant Institute for Interdisciplinary Research (FEST), Heidelberg—2

Pickens, William (1881–1954): African American linguist, author, and social activist—10

Piechowski, Paul Felix (1892–1966): 1919, pastor, Berlin-Neukölln; religious socialist, conscientious objector, and pacifist; 1927, cofounder and one of the heads of the Brotherhood of Socialist Theologians in Germany—10, 11, 14

Piekenbrock, Hans (1893–1959): chief of the *Abwehr* secret intelligence and espionage division, under Admiral Canaris—16

Pieper, Josef (1904–97): German Catholic philosopher; 1933, freelance writer; 1946, private lecturer; 1959, professor of philosophical anthropology, Münster; influential through his modernization of Thomist ethics —6, 8, 16

Pilate, Pontius (d. 39 C.E.): 26–36 C.E., Roman procurator of Judea—6, 9, 11, 12, 13, 14

Pinsk: pastor—12

Piper, Otto (1891–1982): German Protestant theologian; 1920, lecturer in systematic theology; 1928, professor of systematic theology, Göttingen; 1930, Münster; 1933, representative of the Young Protestant Movement; 1933, dismissed from civil service; emigrated to England; member of

the Association of Friends of *Die Christliche Welt* (The Christian world), a liberal Protestant periodical; various guest professorships; 1941, professor of New Testament theology, Princeton University; 1962, retired—1, 2, 6, 10, 11, 13, 14
Pirithous: in Greek mythology, king of the Lapiths—17 (for vol. 9)
Pisano, Giovanni (ca. 1250–1314): Italian Gothic sculptor; made sketch for the Palazzo Publico in Siena—9
Pisker, Lotte: domestic for many years in the Bonhoeffer family—8
Pius V (Antonio Ghislieri) (1504–72): from 1566, pope—14
Piux IX (Giovanni Maria Mastai-Ferretti) (1792–1878): from 1846, pope—1, 6, 14
Pius X (Giuseppe Melchiorre Sarto) (1835–1914): from 1903, pope—3, 6
Pius XI (Ambriogo Damiano Ratti) (1857–1939): 1922–39, pope—6, 9
Pius XII (Eugenio Pacelli) (1876–1958): 1920–29, nuncio in Berlin; 1930–39, cardinal state secretary; 1939–58, pope—8, 9, 16
Plag, Albrecht: German pastor—8
Planck, Heinrich: Luther scholar—9
Planck, Max (1858–1947): German physicist; founder of quantum theory —10
Plant, Stephen: dean and director of studies, Trinity Hall, Cambridge; author of works on Bonhoeffer—14
Plath, Friedrich (b. 1890): from 1931, pastor, Berlin—12
Plath, Georg (b. 1860): from 1907, pastor, Berlin-Biesdorf; also superintendent—12
Plathow, Michael: pastor and professor of systematic theology—8
Plato (427–347 B.C.E.): Greek philosopher; disciple of Socrates and teacher of Aristotle; ca. 387, founded the Academy in Athens—1, 2, 3, 4, 6, 7, 8, 9, 10, 13, 17 (for vol. 9)
Platon (Paul Kulbusch) (1869–1919): Russian Orthodox bishop, one of the "Baltic martyrs"—10
Platte-Platenius: Catholic seminarian who traveled briefly with Klaus and Dietrich Bonhoeffer during their Italian journey—9
Plutarch (ca. 46–ca. 120 C.E.): Greek philosopher and writer; ethicist and author of the lives of distinguished Greeks and Romans—8, 9, 10
Poelchau, Harald (1903–72): from 1933, prison chaplain, Berlin; member of the Kreisau circle; chaplain in Tegel to many of the imprisoned resistance members—8, 16
Pohl, Michael Joseph: German Latin scholar and publisher of Thomas à Kempis's *Imitation of Christ*—8
Pollard, Russell: librarian, Andover-Harvard Library, Harvard Divinity School—10

Pollmann, Klaus Erich: historian—11

Pollux: Greek mythological character; twin of Castor—7

Polte, Miss: seamstress who worked for the Bonhoeffers in Breslau and Berlin—9

Polycarp (69–155 C.E.): Christian bishop of Smyrna; martyred—1

Polydorus (first century C.E.): according to Pliny, one of the sculptors of the marble statue of Laocoön and His Sons—9, 17 (for vol. 9)

Pompe, Hans-Dietrich (1910–99): from Pomerania; 1935–36, participated in the second Finkenwalde session; 1937, assistant pastor, Pomerania; 1939–42, military service; 1942, second secretary of the Evangelical Relief Service for Internees and Prisoners of War; from April 1945, continued this work from Lübeck; 1946, head of the Lübeck section of the executive committee of Inner Mission; 1947–48, in Geneva to work with prisoners of war; 1949, pastor, Coblenz; 1961, Opladen; 1967, Essen-Holsterhausen; 1975, retired—8, 15, 16

Pompe, Spes, née von Bismarck: 1938, confirmed by Bonhoeffer in Kieckow; 1951, married Hans-Dietrich Pompe—15, 16

Pompilij, Basilio (1852–1931): cardinal and vicar of Rome at the time of Bonhoeffer's travels there—9

Pontoppidan, Erik (1698–1764): founder of the moderate pietist movement in Denmark and Norway—2

Popitz, Johannes (1884–1945): German lawyer; 1933–44, Prussian finance minister; active in Goerdeler's resistance circle—16

Popp, Philipp (1893–1945): 1931, bishop of the German Evangelical Christian Church in Yugoslavia; ecumenist—13

Portmann, Heinrich: Catholic priest and assistant to Bishop Graf von Galen from 1938–46; author of several works on von Galen—16

Poseidon: Greek mythological character; god of the sea; father of Antaeus —10

Posidonius (ca. 135–51 B.C.E.): Greek historian, scientist, and Stoic philosopher; works are extant only as fragments—9

Possidius of Calama (ca. 370–ca. 440): student and biographer of Augustine in the monastery at Hippo; 397, bishop of Calama in Numidia; helped Augustine in his struggle against Donatism and Pelagianism—10

Posth, Gustav: pastor in Stolpe; church consistory representative and member of the examination commission that evaluated Bonhoeffer's first theological exams—9

Potschka, Herbert (1906–88): 1935, Confessing Church pastor, Kaukehmen in East Prussia; June 9, 1940, Dietrich Bonhoeffer mentions him in connection with a visitation in Kuckerneese; after the war, pastor and instructor of religion, Kitzingen/Main—16

Pound, Ezra (1885–1972): American expatriate poet and critic—10

Poussin, Nicolas (1594–1665): French historical and landscape painter; known for scriptural and mythological subjects—9

Powell, Adam Clayton, Sr. (1865–1953): prominent African American pastor; pastor of Abyssinian Baptist Church, Harlem until 1936—10

Praetorius, Willy (1884–1973): 1910, pastor, Golsen, Brandenburg; 1914, Soest, Westphalia; 1918, Unterbarmen; 1930, Berlin-Lichterfelde; 1934, president of the Berlin-Brandenburg Council of Brethren until his arrest and expulsion in 1940; 1942–54, pastor, Ratingen near Düsseldorf—12, 15

Prenter, Regin: Danish theologian; author of works on Luther—8

Press, Samuel D.: 1919–41, president of Eden Theological Seminary in St. Louis—15

Pressel, Wilhelm (1895–1987): student of theology in Tübingen while Bonhoeffer was a student; member of the Hedgehog fraternity beginning in the winter semester 1913–14, and a friend of Rüdiger Schleicher; 1925, pastor; because he became a member of the Nazi party as early as 1933, he was chosen to be the chair of the Hedgehog fraternity; as the confidant of the bishop of Worms, he became a member of the high consistory in the fall of 1933; resigned as chair of the Hedgehog fraternity and, 1934, resigned from the fraternity; 1934, member of the Lutheran Council; 1935, expelled from the NSDAP for having criticized the führer; 1936, member of the advisory council of the Evangelical Lutheran Church of Germany and of the Reich Council of Brethren; 1945–50, head of the Evangelical Relief Foundation in Württemberg—9, 14

Preus, James S.: Old Testament scholar—14

Preuß, Adolf-Friedrich (1909–41): from Berlin-Wilmersdorf; 1935, participated in the first Zingst/Finkenwalde session; pastor, Landsberg Holländer (Neumark); July 29, 1941, killed in action—14, 16

Preuss, Horst Dietrich (1927–93): German professor of Old Testament—14

Preysing-Lichtenegg-Moos, Konrad Count von (1880–1950): Catholic priest; initially bishop of Eichstätt; from 1935, bishop of Berlin; founded an aid service in his office for politically and racially persecuted persons; in personal contact with Count Moltke—16, 17

Priebe, Hermann (1871–1961): pastor, Berlin-Grunewald; confirmed Dietrich Bonhoeffer—9, 10

Primo de Rivera y Orbaneja, Miguel (1870–1930): Spanish general; 1923, dictator; 1930, forced to resign after loss of army support—10

Pringle-Pattison, Andrew Seth (1856–1931): Scottish-born philosopher; from 1891, professor of logic and metaphysics, Edinburgh—15

Prisca: biblical character—15

Prisoner (FP): character in the story—7
Probst, Christopher: author of work on Luther and the Jews—14
Probsthain, Karl-Heinz: 1939–40, participated in the collective pastorate, Sigurdshof—15
Prodicus: Greek sophist, contemporary of Socrates—6
Prolingheuer, Hans: German historical journalist; author of numerous publications, including a study of Barth's expulsion from Germany in 1935—6, 12, 13
Prometheus: Greek mythological character—2, 9, 10, 12
Protagoras: Greek philosopher and mathematician—10, 17 (for vol. 9)
Przywara, Erich (1889–1972): writer and Catholic philosopher of religion; 1922, editor of the periodical *Stimmen der Zeit*—2, 3, 4, 9, 10, 11
Ptolemy: biblical character—15
Pückler, Eduard Count von (1853–1924): lawyer; cofounder of the German Student Christian Federation; 1895–1912, its head—11
Pugh, Jeffrey C.: U.S. Bonhoeffer scholar; professor of religious studies, Elon University—12
Putnam, Roger L.: 1938–43, mayor of Springfield, Massachusetts—15
Puttkammer, Gerhard: 1930–65, pastor, Teltow—12
Pylades: character in Greek mythology—6
Pythagoras (ca. 580–500 B.C.E.): Greek philosopher, mathematician, and physicist from Samos—3

Qoheleth: biblical character—5
Quaas, Lydia: staff member at the Luther Archives, Tübingen—6
Qualben, Lars P.: author of work on the Lutheran Church in colonial America—15
Qualmann, Mr.: owner of a boarding house in Boltenhagen—9
Quenstedt, Johann Andreas (1617–88): German Lutheran professor and theologian; leading figure of Lutheran orthodoxy—3, 9
Quervain, Alfred de (1896–1968): Swiss Reformed theologian; 1930, private lecturer, Basel; 1931, pastor of the Reformed congregation, Wuppertal-Elberfeld; 1935, lecturer in systematic theology and Reformed dogmatics at the seminary, Elberfeld; 1938, expelled from Germany; thereafter pastor in Laufen (Canton Bern), also lecturer and professor of systematic theology and social ethics, Basel and Bern; 1947–66, professor of Protestant ethics, Bern—2, 6, 12, 16
Quervain, Anne de: wife of Alfred de Quervain—16
Quirinius (d. 27 C.E.): Cyrenius in the Greek New Testament and the German Bible; 12 B.C.E., Roman consul; according to Luke 2:2, Roman

governor (procurator) of the province Syria, under whose census Mary and Joseph came to Bethlehem—6

Quisling, Vidkun (1887–1945): founder of the Nasjonal Samling, the Norwegian National Socialist Party; 1942, Norwegian head of state during the German occupation; October 24, 1945, executed—16, 17

Quitmann, Clive Ernst Otto: baptized by Bonhoeffer in Sydenham, London —13

Quittschau, Ewald F. (1888–1945): 1929, pastor, Berlin-Steglitz; 1934, cathedral pastor, Königsberg; 1938, forced by the consistory to take a leave of absence because of his Confessing Church membership; February 9, 1945, killed with a refugee transport on the torpedoed *Steuben*—12, 16

Quixote: *see* Don Quixote

Raabe, Wilhelm (1831–1910): German humorist and novelist—8, 9

Raack, Paul: 1904, superintendent and senior pastor, Paul Gerhardt Church, Berlin-Schöneberg—10

Rabanus (Hrabanus), Maurus (ca. 776–856): abbot of Fulda and archbishop of Mainz; known as Raban Maur or Magnentius; scholar, teacher, and Frankish theologian; helped to spread Romance learning in Germany; authored many commentaries, theological works, and pedagogical writings—9, 11

Rabenau, Eitel-Friedrich von (1884–1959): 1923–54, pastor, Church of the Apostle Paul, Berlin-Schöneberg; participated in the Confessing Church Synods; member of the Berlin Council of Brethren; 1936, member of the Provisional Church Administration—12, 14

Rabenau, Friedrich von (1884–1945): artillery general; 1939–43, head of the army archives; after July 20, 1944, arrested; April 12, 1945, executed in Flossenbürg—8, 16, 17

Rachel: biblical character—15

Rachmanova, Alia (Alexandra) (pseudonym for Galina Diuriagina) (1898–1991): Russian author; from 1926, in Austria; 1945, emigrated to Switzerland after the entry of Soviet troops; the German translations of her works were done by her husband, Arnulf von Hoyer—6

Rad, Gerhard von (1901–71): Old Testament scholar; acquainted with Dietrich Bonhoeffer from their youth; 1934, professor of Old Testament, Jena, Göttingen, and Heidelberg; member of the Confessing Church in Jena—4, 9, 16

Rade, Martin (1857–1940): founder and editor of the periodical *Die christliche Welt*; 1921, professor of systematic theology, Marburg—8, 10

Räder, Friedrich: (1815–72): hymnist—14

Rades, Jörg: at the University of St. Andrews, Scotland—2

Radtke, Johannes: head military chaplain in Berlin Spandau—8, 15

Raesfeld, Ferdinand Baron von (1855–1929: German naturalist and author —9

Raffray, Sándor (1866–1947): Hungarian theologian and ecumenist; 1896, professor, Preßburg; 1908, pastor, Budapest; 1918, bishop of the Montan district; 1945, retired—16

Ragaz, Clara, née Nadig (1874–1957): wife of Leonhard Ragaz; pacifist; important representative of the nascent women's movement; for over thirty years president of the Swiss section of the International Women's League for Peace and Freedom—12

Ragaz, Leonhard (1868–1945): 1908–21, professor, Zürich; with Hermann Kutter, cofounder of the religious social movement in Switzerland; social activist and pacifist—9, 12, 14, 16

Rahab: biblical character—9

Rahlwes, Ferdinand (1864–1947): 1919, dean, St. Peter's, Berlin; privy consistory councilor; member of the Evangelical High Church Council; 1927, clerical vice president; 1932, retired—10

Rahner, Karl (1904–84): German Jesuit theologian—4, 8, 14

Raikov, Alexander (1888–1973): Bulgarian Orthodox theologian and ecumenist; initially a lecturer at the theological seminary in Sofia; 1923, archimandrite ("Father Paissy") and suffragan bishop in the church administration; 1930, elected metropolitan of Vratsa; 1925, participated in the conference of Life and Work in Stockholm; 1930, at the Lambeth Conference, and in various other activities of the World Alliance for Promoting International Friendship through the Churches—16

Raina, Peter: biographer of George Kennedy Arthur Bell, bishop of Chichester—14

Rainalter, Josef (1907–96): attorney in Meran; served in the same military unit as Eberhard Bethge in Italy—8

Rajaobelina, P.: from Madagascar; 1934, Parisian participant at the Fanø youth conference—13

Ramsey, Arthur Michael (1904–88): British theologian; 1940–50, professor of divinity, Durham University, and canon of Durham Cathedral; 1950–52, Regius Professor of Divinity, Cambridge; 1961–74, archbishop of Canterbury—16

Ramsey, Paul: U.S. Christian ethicist—6

Rang, Martin: religious educator—14

Range, Otto (1909–76): 1939, ordination in Stettin; assistant pastor, Groß-Schlönwitz—8

Ranke, Leopold von (1795–1886): German historian and professor, Berlin —1, 6, 8, 9, 10

Rannenberg, Hilde, née Pfeiffer: winter semester 1932–33, attended Bonhoeffer's lectures on contemporary systematic theology and participated in the working group on "theological psychology"; summer semester 1933, attended Bonhoeffer's lectures on Christology—3, 12

Raphael (Raffaelo Santi) (1483–1520): Italian Renaissance painter—8, 9, 15, 16

Rasch, Wolfdietrich (1903–86): author, professor of literary history—8

Raskolnikov, Rodion Romanovich: protagonist of Dostoyevsky's *Crime and Punishment*—10, 11

Rasmussen, Larry L: U.S. Christian ethicist and author of several works on Bonhoeffer; 1970, PhD, Union Theological Seminary, New York, with a dissertation on Bonhoeffer's ethics and resistance; 1969–72, professor of religious studies, St. Olaf College; 1972–86, professor of Christian ethics, Wesley Theological Seminary, Washington, D.C.; 1986–2004, Reinhold Niebuhr Professor of Social Ethics, Union Theological Seminary, New York; retired; editor of *DBWE* 12—4, 6, 10, 13

Rath, Else: friend of Ruth von Wedemeyer—8

Rathenau, Walther (1867–1922): German industrialist and politician; one of the few German Jews to attain political prominence; from February 1922, Reich minister of foreign affairs; April 1922, concluded the Russo-German Rapallo Treaty during the World Economic Conference in Genoa; June 24, 1922, assassinated in Berlin by two members of a nationalist anti-Semitic organization—6, 9, 12

Ratschow, Carl Heinz (1911–99): professor of theology, Marburg—8

Ratter, Richard: from Ulm; studied in Tübingen and Berlin; May 25, 1925–March 26, 1926, member of Harnack's seminar—9

Rättig, Elfriede: senior employee in the MBK publishing house, Bad Salzuflen—16

Rau, Gerhard: editor of series on pastoral theology—14

Rau, Oskar Richard Arthur (1910–67): from Berlin-Charlottenburg; 1936–37, participated in the fourth Finkenwalde session; 1938, assistant pastor, Berlin-Charlottenburg; 1939, pastor, Reetz; 1942, Prädikow, district of Oberbarnim; 1945, Berlin-Spandau; 1965, retired—16

Rauschenbusch, Walter (1861–1918): U.S. Baptist theologian of German descent; 1902, professor at Rochester Theological Seminary; founder and early advocate of the "social gospel"—10, 12, 15

Rauschning, Hermann (1887–1982): German politician; after World War I, directed cultural affairs for ethnic Germans living in Posen (now Poznan),

when German-populated territories were ceded to Poland; 1933, elected president of the Danzig (now Gdansk) city senate after the National Socialist victory there; early confidant of Hitler; November 1934, broke with Hitler and resigned from the NSDAP; 1936, fled Germany—6, 7, 15

Rauth: *see* Rößler, Alice Jutta

Ready, Michael Joseph (1893–1957): U.S. Catholic prelate; worked for the National Catholic Welfare Conference during the 1930s—15

Reck-Malleczewen, Friedrich (1884–1945): German author; killed in Dachau —8

Reeves, Frederick: pastor of the Methodist church in Oxford—16

Reger, Max (1873–1916): composer—8

Rehmke, Johannes (1848–1930): German philosopher; 1885–1921, professor, Greifswald—2

Reich, Andreas: author of work on Schleiermacher—12

Reichel, Paul Gerhard (1874–1953): pastor and bishop of the Swiss Moravian (Herrnhut) church; offered refuge to Confessing Church members —14

Reichenau, Walter von (1884–1942): February 1933, head of the ministry of the Reich Armed Forces; January 1934, major general; head of the armed forces office in the Reich Ministry of War; 1940, general field marshal—14

Reichwein, Adolf, (1898–1944): educator; participated as a personal adviser on pedagogical reform to the Reich minister of culture; 1930, professor, pedagogical college, Halle; after 1933, dismissed and employed as a village school teacher; July 4, 1944, arrested as a member of the Kreisau circle; October 20, 1944, executed—16, 17

Reimarus, Elise (Margaretha Elisabeth Reimarus) (1735–1805): German author and translator; "the muse of Hamburg"—8

Reimer, Karl-Heinrich (1904–90): from 1930, pastor, Naseband, district of Belgard/Pomerania; Confessing Church member; member of the final Pomeranian Council of Brethren; 1934, arrested and expelled from Köslin; 1943, military service; 1947, return from prisoner of war camps in Russia; 1951–77, pastor, German Christ Church, London—8, 14, 15, 16

Reimers, Wilhelm: 1936, participated in third Finkenwalde session—14

Rein, Wilhelm (1847–1929): educator, representative of Johann Herbart's educational philosophy as applied by Tuiskon Ziller; from 1886, professor of pedagogy and director of the pedagogical department, University of Jena—14

Reinfandt, Karl-Heinz: German musicologist—17 (for vol. 9)

Reinhard, Franz Volkmar (1753–1812): Protestant theologian—11

Reinhardt, Walther (1871–1930): army general; 1919, last Prussian war minister; October 1919, chief of the army; resigned after putting down the Kapp riot; until 1925, commanding officer of the Fifth Army Corps, Stuttgart —9

Reinke, Elisabeth: 1933, translated one of Bishop Bell's books with Bonhoeffer and Bertha Schulze—13

Reischle, Max (1858–1905): Protestant theologian—11

Reist, Benjamin A.: professor (emeritus) of systematic theology, Graduate Theologian Union, Berkeley—3

Reitzenstein, Franz Baron von: Catholic journalist in Rome—16

Reitzenstein, Richard (1822–89): professor of classical philology, Göttingen and other German universities—9

Remarque, Erich Maria (pseudonym of Erich Paul Remark) (1898–1970): German-American writer; 1938, deprived of German citizenship; exiled in Switzerland and the United States; author of the antiwar novel *All Quiet on the Western Front*—10, 12

Rembrandt (Harmenszoon van Rijn) (1606–69): Dutch baroque painter and etcher; leading representative of the Dutch school of painting—1, 7, 8, 9, 10, 12, 13, 15

Renate (FP): character in the drama and the novel—7

Rendler, Alfred (1910–64): 1936–37, participated in the fourth Finkenwalde session—14

Rendtorff, Heinrich (1888–1960): 1919, pastor; 1921, missionary; 1924, director of the preachers' seminary, Preetz; 1926, professor of practical theology and New Testament, Kiel; 1930–33, bishop of Mecklenburg-Schwerin and honorary professor, Rostock; 1934, dismissed from office; 1934–45, pastor, Stettin-Braunsfelde; 1934, member of the Pomeranian Council of Brethren; 1945, professor, Kiel; 1956, retired—8, 11, 12, 14, 16

Rengstorf, Karl Heinrich: 1936, appointed professor of New Testament in Kiel, but ultimately dismissed; 1948, professor of New Testament, history and literature of Judaism, Münster—14

Reni, Guido (1575–1642): Italian painter of the early baroque period—9

Renkewitz, Heinz (1902–74): 1928, lecturer in church history at the theological seminary of the Herrnhut community; 1954, head of the Evangelical Academy Arnoldshain—12

Renn, Ludwig (1889–1979): German writer; 1928, joined the German Communist Party; 1929–30, visited the Soviet Union twice; commander in the Spanish civil war; 1939, exiled in Mexico; 1947, returned to (East) Germany —10

Reppin: 1933, doctoral candidate in theology in Berlin—12

Resa, Fritz: member of the commission that examined Bonhoeffer for his *Abitur* at the Friedrich Werder Gymnasium, Berlin-Grunewald—9

Resa, Manfred: not identified—9

Rese, Ludwig: 1933, gave a radio address in the same series in which Bonhoeffer spoke on the führer—12

Reuben: biblical character—15

Reuter, Fritz (1810–74): northern German dialect writer and poet; 1833, arrested for suspected sedition in connection with student attack on a military guardhouse in Frankfurt; detained for three years; 1837, condemned to death; sentence commuted to life imprisonment; 1840, released—8, 10, 14, 15

Reuter, Hans-Richard: German Protestant theologian and professor of systematic theology; after 1999, professor and director of the Institute for Christian Social Sciences at the Wilhelm University, Münster; editor of *DBW* 2—2, 6, 10, 13

Reuter, Luise (1817–94): wife of Fritz Reuter—10

Reventlow, Ernst Count zu (1869–1943): German journalist and pan-Germanist; World War I, staff writer for the influential newspaper *Deutsche Tageszeitung*; until 1936, member of the national parliament and of the NSDAP (when he left the party); leading member of the German faith movement—9

Reventlow, Henning Graf: biblical scholar and professor emeritus of theology, Bochum—11

Rexin, Manfred: historian—12

Rhode, Kurt (1908–42): Confessing Church theologian from Pomerania; 1935–36, participated in the second Finkenwalde session; pastor, Treblin, Pomerania; 1942, killed in action on the eastern front—14, 16

Rhoden, Wilhelm, von (1901–90): 1928, academic inspector at the preachers' seminary in Wittenberg; 1930, pastor, Rosian; member of the Saxon Council of Brethren; 1934, pastor, Eichenbarleben, district of Magdeburg; 1946, consistory official, Magdeburg; 1948, director, pastoral college, Ilsenburg; 1963, lecturer in New Testament, catechetical seminary, Naumburg; 1966, at the seminary, East Berlin—14

Ribbentrop, Joachim von (1893–1946): National Socialist politician and diplomat; 1936–38, ambassador in London; 1938–45, Reich foreign minister; sentenced at Nuremberg; executed in 1946—13, 14, 15, 16, 17

Ribera, José de (1588–1652): Spanish painter and etcher; one of the leading painters of the Neapolitan school—10

Richardson, Cyril (1909–76): professor of church history, Union Theological Seminary, New York—15

Richert, Miss: German art historian in Barcelona—10

Richter, Adrian Ludwig (1803–84): German painter and graphic artist during the Biedermeier period—15

Richter, Christian Friedrich (1676–1711): hymnist—4, 14

Richter, Friedrich: 1928, church superintendent, Berlin—12

Richter, Julius (1862–1940): 1913, professor of mission history, Berlin; member of the German Protestant mission board and of the World Alliance for Promoting International Friendship through the Churches; from 1928, professor of mission studies, Berlin; September 1933, participated with Bonhoeffer in the ecumenical conference in Sofia; 1934, in Fanø—9, 10, 11, 12, 13, 17

Richter, Lothar (1894–1948): 1918, governmental official; 1920, in the Berlin labor ministry; lecturer at the Johannes institutions, Berlin; 1933, emigrated to England as a "non-Aryan" (University of Leeds); 1934, moved to Halifax, Canada; professor at Dalhouse University—12, 13

Richter, M. Carol Ernst: author of an 1828 edition of the works of Philo—9

Richter, Werner: 1939, scheduled to teach at Elmhurst College, Illinois—15

Rickers, Folkert: director of the Institute for Interreligious Learning, Duisburg—14

Rickert, Heinrich (1863–1936): German philosopher; founder with Wilhelm Windelband of the southwest German school of neo-Kantianism and its philosophy of values—2, 6, 11

Ricoeur, J. P.: August 1934, French participant at the Fanø youth conference—13

Riebar (unclear reading): 1926, mentioned by Bonhoeffer in connection with a sermon—9

Riecker, Otto: 1927–35, pastor, Ahorn-Buch, Baden; 1936, Heidelberg; 1950, Eppingen-Adelshofen; 1935, published his dissertation, *The Evangelical Word: Pneumatology and Psychology of the Evangelical Movement*—15, 16

Riedesel, Erich: 1937, Confessing Church pastor, Lauth-Palmburg near Königsberg; 1938, Lyck, Masuria; 1940, St. John's Church, Memel; 1942, military service; after the war, pastor, Wuppertal; 1975, retired—16

Riefenstahl, Leni (1902–2003): German photographer and documentary filmmaker; best known for her film on the rise of Nazism, *The Triumph of the Will*, which the Nazis used for propaganda—6

Rieffert: private lecturer, Berlin University in 1925—2

Rieger, Gottfried: son of Julius Rieger—15

Rieger, Julius (1901–84): German pastor; 1927, inspector of studies, preachers' seminary, Naumburg/Queis; after 1933, pastor of the German Lutheran congregation of St. George's, London, where he worked with Dietrich Bonhoeffer; also assigned to the German Seaman's Mission

there; 1953, superintendent, Berlin-Schöneberg—6, 7, 10, 12, 13, 14, 15, 16

Riehl, Alois (1844–1924): German philosopher; precursor of Marburg neo-Kantianism—2, 10

Riehl, Wilhelm Heinrich (1823–97): cultural historian, novelist—8

Rieker, Karl (1857–1927): German Protestant scholar of church law; initially private lecturer in law, Leipzig; professor, Erlangen—16

Riemann, Heinrich: author of article on the use of Schiller's poetry and plays in musical compositions—9

Riemer, Annemarie, née Buchenau: 1936, married Bernhard Riemer—14

Riemer, Bernhard (1911–43): brother of Gerhard Riemer; friend and fellow student of Eberhard Bethge from their days at the secondary school in Magdeburg; called "Herr Zander" after a rendezvous with a woman named Zander from a dance class; October 28, 1934, signed the protest letter from the preachers' seminary in Wittenberg; 1935, at the preachers' seminary, Naumburg am Queis, under Gerhard Gloege; 1936, married Annemarie Buchenau (called "Gräfin"); 1937, in prison; 1943, killed in action on the eastern front—8, 14, 15

Riemer, Gerhard (1910–92): 1932–33, among the circle of students around Bonhoeffer; summer semester 1933, attended Bonhoeffer's lectures on Christology; 1935–36, participated in the second Finkenwalde session; 1937, assistant pastor, Berlin; 1957–77, pastor, Oldenburg—12, 14

Riemschneider, Ernst G.: German historian, author of work on Jochen Klepper—16

Riethmüller, Otto (1889–1938): 1928–38, chair and director of the Burckhardt House in Berlin-Dahlem and of the Protestant Reich Association of Young Women; hymnist; 1935, head of the youth board of the Provisional Church Administration; 1936, member of the Reich Council of Brethren—5, 8, 12, 14

Rietschel, Georg (1842–1914): German Protestant theologian, liturgist, and hymnologist—14

Rilke, Rainer Maria (1875–1926): German poet, born in Prague; best known for his *Duino Elegies* and *Sonnets to Orpheus*—7, 8, 11, 12

Rinckart, Martin (1586–1649): hymnist—10, 14

Ringer, Karlernst: professor, Bochum—16

Ringgren, Helmer: Swedish professor of theology; coeditor of *Theologisches Wörterbuch zum Alten Testament*—15

Ringshausen, Gerhard: German historian, author of works on German resistance—16

Ripon: *see* Burroughs, Edward Arthur

Rissi, Mathias: Swiss pastor, author—16

Rist, Johann (1607–67): 1635, pastor in Wedel, Holstein; song lyricist—3, 13, 15

Ritschl, Albrecht (1822–89): German Protestant church historian, systematic theologian, and New Testament scholar; 1852, professor, Bonn; 1864, Göttingen; founder of the Ritschlian school, which emphasized social ethics and an appreciation for the inner life of Christ—1, 2, 3, 4, 6, 9, 10, 11, 12, 14

Ritschl, Otto (1860–1944): professor of systematic theology, Bonn—11

Rittelmeyer, Friedrich (1872–1938): originally a Protestant pastor in Nuremberg; developed an interest in anthroposophy; 1922–38, cofounder and head of the Christengemeinschaft (religious society incorporating Christian and anthroposophical elements)—10, 11, 14, 16

Ritter, Adolf Martin: professor emeritus of patristics, Heidelberg—12, 15

Ritter, Gerhard (1888–1967): German historian; 1924, professor of history, Hamburg; 1925–44 and 1945–56, professor, Freiburg; 1934, participated in the Confessing Synod, Barmen, and 1936, Dahlem; 1942–43, member of the Freiburg circle, which prepared a memorandum for a post-Nazi political system; November 1944–April 1945, imprisoned—6, 7, 8, 16, 17

Ritter, Karl Bernhard (1890–1968): 1925–45, student chaplain, Marburg; representative of the Protestant liturgical movement; 1931, cofounder of the Protestant Brotherhood of Michael, whose head he remained until 1937; 1952, dean, Marburg—11, 12, 14, 17 (for vol. 13)

Ritter(-Müller), Petra: German scholar of Old Testament and Catholic theology—6

Roberts, David: 1939, professor of the philosophy of religion, Union Theological Seminary, New York, where Bonhoeffer met him—15

Roberts, Sir Frank Kenyon: British diplomat; from December 1940, first secretary in the British Foreign Office—16

Robertson, Edwin Hanton (1912–2007): British Baptist pastor, translator, and author of works on Bonhoeffer—2, 6, 7, 8, 12

Robertson, W. Lewis: secretary of the Federal Council of the Evangelical Free Churches of England—13

Robespierre, Maximilien Marie Isidore de (1758–94): French lawyer and revolutionary—7

Robinson, Edward: cotranslator of Heidigger's *Being and Time*—2

Robinson, Henry Wheeler (1872–1945): British Baptist theologian and Old Testament scholar—16

Robinson, James M.: American scholar of New Testament and early Christianity—2, 10

Robinson, John: bishop of the Church of England and author of *Honest to God*—8

Rocha, Bogumil: 1933, pastor, Berlin—12

Rocholl, Arnold: 1933, spoke in the same radio series in which Bonhoeffer gave his address on the führer—12

Rockefeller, John D. (1839–1937): American oil magnate and philanthropist; benefactor of Riverside Church in New York—10

Rockwell, William Walker: 1925–42, librarian at Union Theological Seminary, New York—15

Roeder, Manfred (1900–1971): German lawyer; during the Third Reich, his legal career culminated in his position as military prosecutor for the military high court; 1942, supervisory judge of Air District III/IV Berlin; 1942, charged with investigating the case against Rudolf von Scheliha and against the Rote Kapelle resistance group; April 3, 1943, ordered by the military high court to investigate the *Depositenkasse* case; April–August 1943, directed the interrogations of Hans von Dohnanyi, Dietrich Bonhoeffer, and others; September 1943, prepared the indictment against Dietrich Bonhoeffer; late 1943/early 1944, relieved as lead investigator; January 1944, head judge of Air Fleet 4; May 1944, chief judge; December 1944, judge general; 1949, released from U.S. custody—4, 6, 7, 8, 16, 17

Roediger, Conrad (1887–1973): lawyer; 1914, in the Foreign Ministry; 1934, in that ministry's cultural section; 1936, leave of absence for political reasons; during the war, adviser for international law in the Foreign Ministry; 1946, teaching appointment in Tübingen; 1951, judge in the Federal Constitutional Court—13

Roger II of Sicily (1095–1154): grand count of Sicily; of Norman ancestry; 1130, king of Sicily; waged war against the Byzantine emperor Manuel Comnenus—9

Roggelin, Holger: German pastor; author of work on Franz Hildebrandt; coeditor of *DBW* 10—10, 11, 13

Rohde, Erwin (1845–98): German classicist—17 (for vol. 9)

Rohkrämer, Martin: German historian; author of works on Barth—15

Röhling: pastor (not otherwise identified)—15

Rohloff, Miss: 1924, Sabine Bonhoeffer's violin teacher—9, 17 (for vol. 9)

Rohls, Jan: professor of Protestant theology, Munich; scholar of the Reformation—14

Röhm, Eberhard: German religious educator and editor—10, 15, 16

Röhm, Ernst (1887–1934): 1923, before the Hitler putsch, helped found the storm troopers [Sturmabteilung, or SA] and the NSDAP; 1931, chief of staff of the storm troopers; 1933, Reich Minister without portfolio; July 1, 1934, murdered after the so-called Röhm putsch—13, 14

Rohr: Confessing Church pastor in Neuwedell (in the Grenzmark); leading member of the Berneuchens—14

Rohr, Fritz Robert von (1916–41): son of Ehrengard von Rohr, Ruth von Kleist-Retzow's sister; lawyer; 1941, killed in action as a paratrooper on Crete —16

Rohrbach, H.-C.: author of work on student chaplains—11

Rohrer, Kurt (1904–92): 1933–69, pastor; acquaintance of Dietrich Bonhoeffer—9

Röhricht, Eberhard (1888–1969): 1919, pastor, Froßneuendorf near Frankfurt an der Oder, Brandenburg; 1927–59, Berlin-Dahlem; 1933, cofounder of the Pastors' Emergency League—10, 12, 13, 15

Röhrig, Hans: Pomeranian Confessing Church pastor; from 1931, Stedkow near Belgard—14, 16

Röhrsheim, Ludwig: teacher at the German school in Barcelona—10, 14

Romberg, Hermann (1886–1977): Confessing Church pastor, Wiesbaden-Dotzheim—14

Rondinello, Niccolo (1500–1561): fifteenth-century Italian religious painter —9

Roon, Ger van: Dutch historian, author of works on the European resistance —13, 16

Roosevelt, Franklin Delano (1882–1945): 1932–45, thirty-second president of the United States—6, 8, 15, 16, 17

Roosevelt, Theodore (1858–1919): 1901–09, twenty-sixth president of the United States—10

Rörer, Georg (1492–1557): 1525, deacon at the city church, Wittenberg; 1937, given permission by Elector Johann Friedrich to work on Luther's writings—14

Roscellin von Compiègne (Roscellinus) (1050–1124): French philosopher; representative of early scholastic nominalism—2

Rose, Eugen (1909–2003): winter 1935–36, participated in the second Finkenwalde session; 1937–70, pastor (until 1945 in Gröben/Teltow)—8, 14, 15

Rosenau, Hugo: 1926, pastor, Hohen-Neuendorf—12

Rosenbaum, Peter: member of Bonhoeffer's "Thursday circle" for youth—10

Rosenberg, Alfred (1893–1946): National Socialist ideological propagandist and politician; author of *The Myth of the Twentieth Century*, a widely popular book advocating National Socialism; 1933, head of the NSDAP Foreign Office; November 1941, Reich minister for the occupied eastern territories; 1946, condemned to death at the Nuremberg trials and executed—6, 13, 14, 15

Rosenstock-Huessy, Eugen: sociologist—1, 2

Rosenzweig, Franz (1886–1929): Jewish philosopher and theologian—2
Rösicke, Rosemarie: secondary school student in Barcelona—10
Rößler, Alice Jutta, née Rauth: wife of Helmut Rößler—10
Rößler, Diethelm Walter: son of Alice and Helmut Rößler—10
Rößler, Dietrich: professor (emeritus) of practical theology, Tübingen—14
Rößler, Helmut (1903–82): German Protestant theologian; one of Bonhoeffer's fellow students in Berlin; 1929–32, pastor, Beveringen/Ost-Prignitz; 1933–39, pastor, Heerlen, Holland; 1939–41, director of the preachers' seminary, Düsseldorf; 1942–45, consistory official there; 1944, member of the Provisional Church Administration of the Rhineland Church; 1948–68, member of the governing church council in the Rhineland—1, 2, 5, 6, 8, 9, 10, 11, 12, 13, 14
Rößler, Konstantin (1820–96): German writer; 1860, publicist for the Prussian government; 1892, legation officer in the Foreign Ministry; grandfather of Helmut Rößler—10
Rößler, Walter: consul; father of Helmut Rößler—10
Rost, Leonhard (1896–1979): 1929, private lecturer in Old Testament, Berlin; 1935, professor, Berlin; 1938, Greifswald; 1946, Berlin; 1956, Erlangen; 1965, retired—13
Rotelle, John E.: translator of works of Augustine—8
Rot(h)ermund: probably the inspector of the Berlin student dormitory "Johanneum"—10
Roth, Erich: government counselor and SS major; head of the Group IV B 1 (which spied on the Catholic Church) in the Reich Central Security Office; September 22–23, 1941, adviser at the Reich Central Security Office conference held for personnel involved in church affairs—16
Rothacker, Erich (1888–1965): philosopher and psychologist; 1928–54, professor, Bonn—2, 8
Rothe, Hans: German novelist and dramatist—8
Rothe, Richard (1799–1867): Protestant theologian, ethicist, and dogmatician; 1837–49 and 1854–67, professor of theology, Heidelberg; 1849–54, Bonn; developed a speculative systematic theology and advocated the sublimation of the church in a cultural state—1, 6, 8, 9, 14, 16
Rothfels, Hans (1891–1976): German historian and specialist on the Bismarck era—7, 16
Röthlisberger-Pestalozzi, Esther: daughter of Rudolf and Gertrud Pestalozzi —16
Rothmann, Miss: 1923, mentioned in a letter; not otherwise identified—9
Rothmund, Heinrich (1888–1961): 1919, chief of the Swiss police department dealing with immigrants; 1929, head of the police section of the Swiss Justice and Police Department in Bern; 1954, retired—16

Rothuizen, Gerard T. (1926–88): Dutch theologian; author of several works on Bonhoeffer—4, 6, 8
Rott, Annie, née Reining: wife of Wilhelm Rott—16
Rott, Wilhelm (Willy) (1908–67): from Düsseldorf; 1930, studied under Karl Barth in Bonn; 1935–37, following parish ministry in the Rhineland, academic inspector at the first Zingst/Finkenwalde preachers' seminary; 1937, appointed to the Provisional Church Administration in Berlin; 1943, military service with the intelligence office of the High Military Command; 1945, interned in the Mossberg camp, Upper Bavaria; 1946, pastor, Coblenz; 1959, superintendent there—8, 14, 15, 16, 17
Rouner, Leroy S. (1930–2006): professor of religion and philosophy, Boston University—8
Rousseau, Jean-Jacques (1712–78): French political and moral philosopher and educational theorist—1, 6, 9, 14, 15
Rubba, Miss: 1922, mentioned in a letter; not otherwise identified—9
Rubens, Peter Paul (1577–1640): Dutch baroque painter—8
Rubinow, I. M.: author of article in U.S. biweekly, *The Survey*—10
Rückeberg: congregational council member in Barcelona—10
Rückert, Friedrich (1788–1866): German poet and oriental philologist—13
Rückert, Hanns (1901–74): 1925–28, adjunct lecturer in church history, Berlin; 1928, professor of church history, Leipzig; 1931–66, Tübingen —10, 13
Rückert, Leopold Immanuel (1797–1871): Protestant theologian and privy church official; from 1844, professor, Jena; critical-rationalistic exegete —1
Rüdel, Hugo (1868–1934); from 1909–33 he was conductor and director of the Berlin cathedral choir—17 (for vol. 9)
Rudi, Uncle: *see* Goltz, Rüdiger Graf von der
Rüdiger, Horst (1908–84): German scholar of ancient literature, German studies, and Romance studies—6
Rüdin, Ernst (1874–1952): German-speaking physician; from 1930, professor of psychiatry, Munich; pioneer of National Socialist eugenics—6
Rudl, Maja: assisted German *DBW* 15 editor Dirk Schulz—15
Rudolph, Kurt: German scholar of gnosticism—14
Ruhbach, Gerhard (1933–99): German theologian, church historian, and philologist—14
Ruhenstroth, Renate, née von Hase: daughter of Hans Karl von Hase—9
Ruland, Ludwig (1873–1951): German moral theologian; incorporated pastoral medicine into moral theology—6
Rümmelein, Gregor (formerly Heinrich) (1904–85): Benedictine monk in the Ettal monastery in Upper Bavaria—16

Rumscheidt, Barbara: former lecturer in pastoral theology at Atlantic School of Theology; translator of numerous works, including part of *DBWE* 8—8

Rumscheidt, Martin: professor emeritus of theology, Atlantic School of Theology; translator of numerous works, including part of *DBWE* 8; member of *DBWE* editorial board—2, 8, 10, 16

Runestam, Arvid (1887–1967): Swedish theologian and ecumenist; 1917, lecturer, Uppsala; 1923, professor of systematic theology, Uppsala; 1937–56, bishop of Karlstadt; 1957, retired—13, 16

Runze, Georg (1852–1938): German theologian; professor of philosophy, ethics, and theology, University of Berlin—12

Rüppell, Hanns: theology student in Berlin under Bonhoeffer; winter semester 1932–33, attended Bonhoeffer's lectures on contemporary systematic theology; pastor, Bad Nenndorf—11, 12

Rupprich, Katharina: wife of Detlef Albers—10

Rushbrooke, James Henry (1870–1947): British Baptist pastor with close personal ties to Germany; 1928–39, general secretary of the British section of the World Alliance for Promoting International Friendship through the Churches; 1934–35, president of the National Council of the Evangelical Free Churches in Great Britain—13

Russell, Arthur T. (1806–74): British Anglican bishop and hymnist—12, 14

Russell, Bertrand (1872–1970): British mathematician and philosopher; 1910, appointed professor at Cambridge; 1916, dismissal because of his pacifism; 1944, reappointed; 1950, Nobel Prize in Literature—3, 10

Rust, Bernhard (1883–1945): 1909–30, secondary school teacher, Hannover; National Socialist politician; 1925, regional Nazi party leader [*Gauleiter*] of Hannover-North; 1928–40, of Hannover-South and Braunschweig; 1933, Prussian minister and, after 1934, Reich and Prussian Minister for Science, Training, and Public Education; May 1945, committed suicide—12, 13, 14, 16, 17

Rütenik, Reinhard (1904–85): 1933, theology student, Berlin; 1935–36, participated in the second Finkenwalde session; 1936, pastor, Dahme, Mark Brandenburg; 1946–78, Gebersdorf near Dahme—12, 14

Rüter, Martin: 1933, legation officer with the German embassy in London—10, 13

Ruth: biblical character—8

Ruttke, Falk: lawyer; professor of race and law—6

Rütz, Ruth von: educator; 1940–41, in charge of Berlin school children in Ettal in Upper Bavaria—16

Ruysdael, Salomon van (ca. 1600–1670): Dutch painter—8

Ryder: colleague of Baron Bruno Schröder—13, 17 (for vol. 13)

Sabazios: Phrygian deity; worshiped as the god of agriculture and of life and as a physician, especially in connection with birth—10

Sabellius: early third-century monarchian theologian, possibly of Roman origin; 220, excommunicated—16

Sabinus, Titus Flavius Vespianus (40–81 C.E.): father of the martyred Clemens; prefect of Rome during Nero's persecution of the Christians—12

Sack, Alfons: attorney; 1933, official defense attorney for Ernst Torgler in the Reichstag fire trial—8

Sack, Karl (1896–1945): lawyer; 1934, joined military justice department; 1937, minister counselor in the Reich War Ministry; 1938, military high court councilor; 1938, began work with Hans von Dohnanyi in the Fritsch trial; 1942, chief of the army legal section in the High Military Command; minister director and general staff judge; from 1942, in close contact with Friedrich Justus Perels; September 8, 1944, arrested; April 9, 1945, executed in Flossenbürg—8, 16, 17

Sackmann, Jakobus (Jobst) (1643–1718): 1674, field chaplain, Trier; 1680, pastor, Limmer near Hannover; author of popular, humorous sermons that provoked both merriment among listeners and disapprobation among officials—15

Sahm, Ulrich: German journalist; concentration on church and Middle Eastern affairs—8

Saint-Simon, Claude Henri de Rouvroy, Comte de (1760–1825): French social critic and reformer; representative of utopian socialism—1, 6, 9

Salmen, Walter: German musicologist—17 (for vol. 9)

Salomon, Elfriede, née Weber: wife of Otto Salomon—16

Salomon, Otto (pseudonym: Otto Bruder) (1889–1971): publisher, bookseller, and writer; 1922–38, editor for Chr. Kaiser Verlag, Munich; 1935, prohibited from writing because of Nazi race laws; 1938, emigrated to Switzerland; on several trips to Switzerland for the *Abwehr*, Bonhoeffer stayed with him; 1939–48, worked with the World Council of Churches to help prisoners of war; after 1948, editor for different Swiss publishers; 1950–58, editor of Zwingli publishers—6, 7, 13, 16, 17

Sams, Eric (1926–2004): British musicologist, cryptologist, and Shakespeare scholar—8

Samuel: biblical character—5, 14

Sánchez Sarto, Luis: Bonhoeffer's Spanish tutor in Barcelona; employee at the publisher Labor Editoria in Barcelona—10

Sancho Panza: character in Cervantes's *Don Quixote*—7, 8

Sandegren, Paul H. A. (1887–1970): 1913, doctoral candidate in theology; 1915–23, missionary, southern India; 1926, secretary of the mission

board of the Swedish church (Svenska Kyrkans Missionstyrelse); 1928, pastor, St. Mary's, Stockholm; 1931, general secretary of the Swedish section of the World Alliance for Promoting International Friendship through the Churches; 1933, participated in that organization's conference in Sofia—11, 12

Sanden: church official—10

Sander, Erwin (1911–43): from Unna in Westphalia; 1938, participated in the collective pastorate in Groß-Schlönwitz; 1938, assistant pastor, Kieckow, district of Belgard; 1939, in Mennighüffen, Westphalia; October 30, 1943, killed in action as a lieutenant on the eastern front—15, 16

Sanderhoff, Mr. and Mrs.: neighbors and caretakers of the Bonhoeffers' vacation home in Friedrichsbrunn, Harz—9, 10, 11

Sanderson, J. Burdon: cotranslator of nineteenth-century English edition of Hegel's *Lectures on the Philosophy of Religion*—8

Santa Ana, Julio de: Brazilian theologian and ecumenist—8

Santayana y Borras, George de (1863–1952): U.S. writer and philosopher of Spanish descent; 1872, emigrated to the United States; from 1889, at Harvard University; 1907–12, professor of philosophy, Harvard; independent scholar; a critical realist influenced by Platonism; critic of the North American lifestyle—6, 7, 10, 16

Santmire, H. Paul: U.S. Lutheran pastor, college chaplain, and scholar; author of works on theology and ecology—6, 10

Sapphira: biblical character—9, 14, 15

Sarah: biblical character—15

Sargent, Sir Orme Garton (1884–1962): from 1939, deputy state secretary in the Northern Department of the British Foreign Office—16

Sas, Jacobus Gijsbertus: colonel; 1939–40, Dutch military attaché in Berlin —16, 17

Saß, Gerhard: pastor, Pomerania—15

Sasse, Fritz (1889–1956): 1918, pastor, Lazarus church, Berlin; 1932, in Krahne, district of Lehnin—12

Sasse, Hermann (1895–1976): 1920, pastor, Templin; 1923, Oranienburg; 1928, Berlin; from 1931, editor of the *Church Yearbook*; with Reinhold Krause, organized the working group of theologians and national economists; 1933–46, professor of church history, history of dogma, and symbolism, Erlangen; 1933, worked on the Bethel confession; 1934, member of the Lutheran Council; 1948, left the Bavarian regional church and joined the Old Lutheran (Free) Church; 1949, professor, Lutheran Seminary, North Adelaide, southern Australia—11, 12, 13, 14

Satan (Lucifer): rebellious fallen angel in the Bible; synonym for the Devil—2, 12

Sattert, Mr.: state commissioner for Bonhoeffer's *Abitur* examination—9
Saturninus: second-century Syrian gnostic—12
Saud: *see* Ibn Saud
Sauer, Wolfgang: author of work on the church in Württemberg—16
Sauerbruch, Ernst Ferdinand (1875–1953): surgeon; director of the Charité in Berlin—8
Saul: biblical character—5, 14, 15
Saunders, G. H.: assistant secretary of the National Council of Evangelical Free Churches in England—13
Saussure, Jean de (1899–1977): Swiss Reformed theologian; 1930, at the École de Calvin, Geneva; September 4, 1941, invited by Visser 't Hooft to meet with Dietrich Bonhoeffer; 1945, professor of practical theology, Lausanne; 1948, delegate of the Swiss churches in Amsterdam; 1950, pastor, St. Pierre's, Geneva—16, 17
Sauter, Johannes (1891–1945): German philosopher—1
Saxer, Ernst: Swiss scholar of the Reformation—8
Sceva: biblical character—15
Schaaff, Martin: from Berlin-Treptow; 1935–36, participated in the second Finkenwalde session; pastor, Buchholz near Fürstenwalde; military service; from 1952, pastor, Berlin—15
Schabert, Otto: author of book on Baltic martyrs—9, 10
Schäble, Walter: author of a 1950 work on the church—16
Schacht, Horace Greeley Hjalmar (1877–1970): German economic and financial politician; 1908, chair of the board at the Dresden Bank; 1916, director of the National Bank; 1918, cofounder of the German Democratic Party; 1923, 1924–29, and 1933–39, Reich currency commissioner; 1923–30 and 1933–39, president of the Reich Bank; 1934–37 (resigned in 1937), Reich Minister of Economics; 1935, appointed by Hitler as General Plenipotentiary for the War Economy; 1937–43, Reich minister without portfolio; from 1938, contact with the resistance; after July 20, 1944, arrested and sent to Dachau; together with Dietrich Bonhoeffer in the Gestapo prison on Prinz-Albrecht-Strasse and in the transport to Lower Bavaria; 1945, liberated; 1946, acquitted in Nuremberg; 1947, sentenced to eight years work camp; 1950, released; thereafter financial and political adviser and bank owner—10, 13, 14, 16
Schachtschneider: pastor (1937)—14
Schackla: senior military chaplain, Stettin—15
Schade: pastor in Dobrilugk—10
Schade, Karl August Friedrich: 1930, associated with Bonhoeffer's second theological examination—10

Schade, Rudolf G. (1908–2000): professor of history and philosophy, Elmhurst College; met Bonhoeffer during his time at Union Seminary, New York, summer 1939—10

Schaeder, Anna: wife of Erich Schaeder—17 (for vol. 12)

Schaeder, Erich (spelled "Schäder" in vol. 10) (1861–1936): 1894, professor of systematic and New Testament theology, Königsberg; 1895, Göttingen; 1899, Kiel; 1918, Breslau; representative of theocentric theology: 2, 10, 11, 12, 17 (for vol. 12)

Schaeffers, Sylvester: Catholic priest mentioned in Max-Peter Meyer's letter to Bonhoeffer—15

Schäfer, Gerhard (1923–2003): German church historian and director of the regional church archive, Baden-Württemberg—13

Schäfer, Wilhelm (1868–1952): German writer; representative of a nationalist interpretation of history focused on *Volkstum*—10

Schäfer, Wilhelm (b. 1900): May 23–July 24, 1926, student in Berlin; member of Harnack's seminar—9

Schaff, Philip: German American theologian and religious historian—1, 2, 8

Schäffer, Mr.: Karl-Friedrich Bonhoeffer's piano teacher—9

Schäffle, Albert Eberhard Friedrich—1

Schairer, J. B.: during 1930s, author of nationalist theological works—14

Schalke, Max (1874–1954): from 1912, pastor, Berlin—12

Schanz, Martin (1842–1914): professor of classical philology, Würzburg—9

Scharf, Kurt (1902–90): 1928, pastor, Friesack, Mark; 1933–46, pastor, Sachsenhausen near Oranienburg; 1935, president of the Brandenburg Council of Brethren and of the Confessing Synod of the Confessing Church, Mark Brandenburg; 1938, chair of the conference of Councils of Brethren; repeatedly arrested; 1941, drafted into military service; 1945, head of the Brandenburg section in the Berlin-Brandenburg consistory; 1952, pastor, Berlin; 1957, chair of the advisory council of the Evangelical Church of the Union; 1961, chair of the advisory council of the Evangelical Church of Germany; 1966–76, bishop of the Evangelical Church, Berlin-Brandenburg (from 1973, only for West Berlin)—8, 12, 14, 15, 16

Scharffenorth, Ernst-Albert: studied Protestant theology in Bethel, Bonn, and Heidelberg; until 1969, studied sociology in Heidelberg and Berlin; 1984, ThD under Heinz Eduard Tödt; from 1973, academic senior councilor on the theological faculty, Heidelberg; coeditor of *Heidelberger Untersuchungen zu Widerstand, Judenverfolgung und Kirchenkampf im Dritten Reich*; research focuses on contemporary church history and political ethics—12

Scharffenorth, Gerta: German theologian at the Protestant Institute for Interdisciplinary Research (FEST), Heidelberg—6
Scharl, Emmeran: Catholic youth chaplain, Bavaria; founder of a populist Catholic movement there—8
Scharlemann, Robert P.: U.S. theologian; interpreter of Paul Tillich—2
Scharling, C. J.: 1934, participant from Copenhagen at the Fanø youth conference—13
Scharnhorst, Gerhard Johann David (1755–1813): Prussian military leader and reformer—10
Scharpff, Walter (b. 1894): physician; winter semester 1912–13, member of the Hedgehog fraternity; May 1954, wrote the obituary for Rüdiger Schleicher in *The Hedgehog's Snout*—9
Scharrer, Ernst: German neuroscientist—8
Schattenmann, Johannes: Bavarian New Testament scholar; recipient of fellowship at Union Theological Seminary preceding Bonhoeffer—11
Schauer, Friedrich (1891–1958): pastor in Pütte near Stralsund; until summer 1936, member of the Pomeranian Council of Brethren; head of the St. Michael's brotherhood in Pomerania; 1936, left the Council of Brethren—14
Scheeben, Matthias Joseph (1835–88): German Catholic theologian—11
Scheel, Karl: Confessing Church pastor, St. Mary's, Köslin, Pomerania; 1937, garrison chaplain at the general command there; after 1945, pastor, Weingarten—16
Scheel, Otto (1876–1954): historian of the Reformation; 1919, Tübingen; from 1924, Kiel—1, 8, 11
Scheffel, Viktor von (1826–86): German poet—7
Scheffler, Burckhard: director of the Bonhoeffer Haus, Berlin—11
Scheffler, Johann (Angelus Silesius) (1624–77): Silesian theologian and poet; 1653, converted to Catholicism—11, 12, 16
Scheffler, Karl (1869–1951): prominent German art critic—9
Scheidemann, Philipp (1865–1939): Social Democratic Party politician and journalist; November 11, 1918, proclaimed the Weimar Republic; February–June 1919, first minister president of the Weimar Republic; resigned in protest against the Versailles Treaty; 1920–25, mayor of Kassel—9
Scheidt, Samuel (1587–1654): organist, composer of important organ works—8
Schein, Johann Hermann (1586–1630): composer; from 1616, predecessor of J. S. Bach as choirmaster in the Leipzig St. Thomas Church—8
Scheler, Max (1874–1928): German philosopher; 1900, postdoctorate and lecturer, Munich; 1919–28, professor of philosophy, Cologne; from 1928, Frankfurt am Main; applied Husserl's phenomenological methods to

ethics and to the philosophy of culture and religion—1, 2, 6, 10, 11, 13, 14

Schellenberg, Walter (1900–1952): lawyer; 1939–42, deputy head and, 1942–44, head of Office VI (political secret service) in the Reich Central Security Office; ultimately SS brigade leader and major general of the Waffen SS; sentenced in Nuremberg to six years in prison; 1950, released from prison—16

Scheller, Heinrich: coauthor of volume on Karl Bonhoeffer—8

Schelling, Friedrich Wilhelm Joseph (1775–1854): German idealist philosopher; 1798–1803, professor, Jena; 1803, Würzburg; 1806, after problems with the government, retired to Munich; 1820–26, lecturer, Erlangen; 1827, professor, Munich; 1841, in Berlin to counteract the influence of Hegel's disciples—1, 2, 9, 12

Schellong, Dieter: German church historian—8

Schelsky, Helmut (1912–84): prominent German sociologist—10

Schemelli, Georg Christian (1676–1762): German cantor and hymnal editor —14

Schempp, Paul (1900–1959): 1925, tutor and instructor, Tübingen seminary; 1929, city pastor, Waiblingen; 1933, dismissed for political reasons; 1934, pastor, Iptingen; dismissed for criticizing the church political position of his bishop; 1939, military service; 1946, pastor, Reformed church, Stuttgart; 1958, professor of systematic and practical theology, Bonn—9, 13

Schenk, Dietmar: German musicologist—17 (for vol. 9)

Scherer, Paul (1892–1969): pastor and prominent preacher, Holy Trinity Lutheran Church, New York; 1945–60, professor of homiletics, Union Theological Seminary, New York—15

Scherffig, Wolfgang: engaged in illegal theological training for the Rhineland Confessing Church during the years of the Third Reich; later pastor in Düsseldorf and Essen—13, 14, 16

Sherriff, Robert Cedric (1896–1975): British playwright, author of *Journey's End*—10

Scherzl, Simon (1896–1959): Redemptorist priest, Munich; applied a Dutch method of domestic proselytization in southern Germany, as described in his book *Compelle intrare*—16

Scheven, Karl von: city superintendent, Greifswald; December 1935, head of the Pomeranian church committee; 1947, bishop, Greifswald—14, 16

Schian, Martin (1869–1940): Protestant professor of practical theology and church superintendent—14

Schieder, Julius (1888–1964): 1935–58, district dean of Nuremberg; member of the Reich Council of Brethren—14

Schiller, Friedrich von (1759–1805): German poet, playwright, critic, and historian; influenced by Kantian philosophy, especially by Kant's ethics—6, 7, 8, 9, 10, 11, 13, 14, 15, 16

Schilling, Otto (1874–1956): Catholic moral theologian—1, 6, 8, 16

Schindler, Dietrich (1880–1948): Swiss legal scholar; professor of public law, constitutional law, and international law, Zürich; lived in Zollikon near Zürich—16

Schinkel, Karl Friedrich (1781–1841): architect and painter—11

Schirach, Baldur von (1907–74): National Socialist politician; 1927, head of the National Socialist Student Federation; 1931–40, Reich Youth führer for the Nazi party; from June 1933, Youth führer for the German Reich; published poems in the spirit of the National Socialist movement; 1940–45, regional leader [*Gauleiter*] and Reich governor of Vienna; in 1946, at the Nuremberg war crimes trials, sentenced to twenty years in prison, which he served in Berlin-Spandau, for participation in the deportation of Jews; 1966, released—7, 13

Schirmer, Michael (1606–73): hymnist; friend of Paul Gerhardt—13

Schjørring, Jens Holger: professor of systematic theology, Aarhus, Denmark—12

Schlabrendorff, Fabian von (1907–80): lawyer and economist; 1932–33, assistant to state secretary Herbert von Bismarck in the Reich Ministry of the Interior; state trainee in various local and regional courts; 1939, entered military service as first lieutenant in the reserves; 1941, aide-de-camp on the staff of (his cousin) Major General Henning von Treschkow in the Army Group Center; March 13, 1943, part of an aborted assassination attempt on Hitler; after July 20, 1944, arrested and held in the Gestapo prison on Prinz-Albrecht-Strasse in Berlin; spring 1945, taken to Flossenbürg; liberated from a prisoner transport in Tirol; after the war, attorney and notary in Wiesbaden; 1967–75, judge in the Federal Constitutional Court, Karlsruhe—8, 16, 17

Schlabritzky, Karl (1886–1939): high consistory official and lawyer, Evangelical Consistory of the Mark Brandenburg, Berlin—10, 11

Schlagowsky, Erwin (1911–95): 1935–36, participated in the second Finkenwalde session; 1936–37, pastor—14

Schlarb, Fr. Ph.: congregational council member, German Reformed St. Paul's Church, London—13

Schlatter, Adolf (1852–1938): Protestant theologian born in Switzerland; professor of systematic theology and New Testament exegesis, Berne,

Greifswald, Berlin and finally Tübingen; 1923, Bonhoeffer attended his classes; despite Schlatter's positive attitude toward National Socialism in 1933, Bonhoeffer held him in high regard as a biblical scholar—2, 4, 6, 8, 9, 10, 11, 12, 13, 14, 16

Schlatter, Theodor (1885–1971): son of Adolf Schlatter; taught at the theological school in Bethel from 1923 to 1933—17 (for vol. 12)

Schlegel, Friedrich von (1772–1829): German philosopher, classical philologist, critic, and writer; with his brother, August Wilhelm, founder of the early Romantic school in Germany—7

Schlegel, Heinz (1908–88): 1935–36, participated in the second Finkenwalde session; 1937–71, pastor—14

Schleicher, Christine: *see* Korenke, Christine Elisabeth

Schleicher, Dorothee: *see* Bracher, Dorothee Sabine Julie

Schleicher, Hans-Walter Karl Otto Rüdiger: Bonhoeffer's nephew, Renate Bethge's brother; son of Rüdiger and Ursula Schleicher; March 14, 1949, married Anja Eva, née Ritschl; father of Rüdiger, Johannes, Andreas, and Ursula; physicist; eventually director of the Control Commission of EURATOM—6, 7, 8, 9, 13, 15, 16

Schleicher, Jörg (1904–77): brother of Rüdiger Schleicher; engineer and architect; later actor; studied architecture at the Technical College in Stuttgart; later was an architect in Berlin; built the houses of the Bonhoeffer and Schleicher families on Marienburger Allee; later he was an actor in Tübingen, Augsburg, and Munich—8, 9

Schleicher, Kurt von (1882–1934): general; June 1932, Reich minister of the armed forces; December 1932–January 1933, Reich chancellor; June 30, 1934, murdered during the Röhm putsch—12, 17

Schleicher, Otto: lived in Stuttgart; father of Jörg and Rüdiger Schleicher—9

Schleicher, Renate: *see* Bethge, Renate Ursula Gertrud Paula

Schleicher, Rüdiger (1895–1945): son of the physician Dr. Otto Schleicher; 1919, entered Württemberg civil service; May 15, 1923, married Ursula, née Bonhoeffer; father of Hans-Walter, Renate (married name Bethge), Dorothee (married name Bracher), and Christine (married name Korenke); German lawyer: 1922, appointed to the Reich Ministry of Transport, Berlin; 1933, entered the Reich Air Transportation Ministry, until 1939, head of the legal department there; 1939, honorary professor and head of the Institute of Aviation Law, University of Berlin; participated in the conspiratorial resistance against the National Socialist regime; October 4, 1944, arrested; imprisoned in the Lehrter Strasse prison in Berlin; February 2, 1945, sentenced to death by the People's Court; April 24, 1945, executed by firing squad in Berlin-Moabit—4, 6, 7, 8, 9, 10, 12, 13, 14, 15, 16, 17

Schleicher, Ursula Clara Julia Hanna, née Bonhoeffer (1902–1983): Dietrich Bonhoeffer's sister; May 15, 1923, married Rüdiger Schleicher—7, 8, 9, 10, 15, 16

Schleiermacher, Friedrich Daniel Ernst (1768–1834): German philosopher, theologian, and translator (Plato); from 1809–10, Reformed pastor, Trinity Church, Berlin, and professor of theology at the newly established university there; generally regarded as the founder of modern liberal Protestant theology—1, 2, 5, 9, 10, 11, 12, 13, 14, 15

Schlemihl, Peter: character and story by Adelbert von Chamisso, published in 1814; sells his shadow to a mysterious man in gray for an allegedly inexhaustible fortune but is reviled and persecuted; refuses the man's offer to return the shadow if Schlemihl will yield his soul to the man; misery ends when Schlemihl discovers "seven-league boots" and devotes himself to scientific inquiry (i.e., to useful endeavor)—6

Schlemmer, Hans (1885–1958): Protestant educator and politician—14

Schleunes, Karl A.: German-born historian; author of works on the Nazi era—15

Schlier, Heinrich (1900–1978): German theologian; member of the Confessing Church; 1928–35, private lecturer in New Testament, Jena and Marburg; 1935, withdrawal of the *venia legendi* (authorization to teach at university after postdoctoral lecturing qualification); winter 1935, lecturer and head of the seminary, Wuppertal; 1940, pastor, Lutheran Confessing Church, Elberfeld; 1945, professor of New Testament and church history, Bonn; 1952, requests and is granted emeritus status; 1952–68, honorary professor, Bonn; 1953, conversion to Catholicism—4, 14, 15, 16

Schlingensiepen, Ferdinand: 1948–53, studied theology in Wuppertal, Bonn, Heidelberg, and Edinburgh; 1953, doctorate in theology; 1954–59, pastor of the German community in Bradford, Yorkshire; 1959–69, with the Protestant Church of the Union in Berlin; 1969–88, director of the Diakoniewerk, Dusseldorf-Kaiserswerth; 1972, proposed founding the International Bonhoeffer Society at its first congress in Kaiserswerth—8

Schlingensiepen, Johannes (1898–1980): 1930–50, pastor, Wuppertal-Unterbarmen; 1933, member of the Confessing Church leadership in the Rhineland and director of theological training of the Confessing Church there; 1933–45, member of the Rhineland Council of Brethren; 1945, superintendent, Barmen; 1950, high church official, Evangelical Church, Rhineland; 1945–68, director of theological education there—8, 14, 16

Schlink, Edmund (1903–84): German theologian; 1935–39, lecturer at the theological college in Bethel until its closure in 1939 by the National

Socialist regime; respected theological teacher and pastor of the Confessing Church; 1945, appointed professor of systematic and ecumenical theology, Heidelberg; 1962–65, official observer of the Evangelical Church of Germany at Vatican II—6, 14, 16

Schlund, Mrs. D., and Emma: members of the congregational council, German congregation, Sydenham, London—13

Schlunk, Martin (1874–1958): director, North German Mission Society; professor of mission studies, University of Tübingen—11

Schlunk, Wolfgang (1912–44): son of the mission scholar Martin Schlunk; winter semester 1932–33 and summer semester 1933, studied theology in Berlin and Tübingen; thereafter studied philosophy; 1936, doctorate; 1944, killed in action as a lieutenant in France—12

Schmid, Ernst Fritz (1904–60): German musicologist; 1937, left the civil service and taught privately; 1940–45, military service; 1951–58, president of the German Mozart Society—17 (for vol. 9)

Schmid, Ewald: born in Stuttgart; studied in Tübingen and Berlin; October 20, 1925–September 21, 1926, member of Harnack's seminar—9

Schmid, Fritz (b. 1904): son of Wilhelm Schmid; Bonhoeffer's fellow student in Tübingen; studied natural science—9

Schmid, Heinrich (1811–85): German scholar of the Lutheran confessional tradition—3, 4, 6, 8, 9, 10, 14, 16

Schmid, Lore, née Delbrück (1890–1983): daughter of the historian Hans Delbrück and sister of Emmi Bonhoeffer (née Delbrück, married to Klaus Bonhoeffer), Max, and Justus Delbrück; wife of the surgeon Dr. Heinz Schmid; lived in Herrliberg near Zürich—16, 17

Schmid, Lotte: wife of Ernst Schmid—17 (for vol. 9)

Schmid, Manfred Herman: Mozart scholar; son of Ernst Schmid—17 (for vol. 9)

Schmid, Wilhelm (1859–1951): 1891–1926, professor of classical philology, Tübingen; member of Hedgehog fraternity; father of Fritz Schmid; author of a history of Greek literature—9

Schmidhuber, Wilhelm Adolf (1898–1965): economist, brewery owner, and Portuguese honorary consul in Munich; captain in the Luftwaffe reserves; 1939, assigned to the Military Intelligence Office VI in Munich, directly accountable to the Military Intelligence Office section I/Aviation Berlin; in conspiratorial contact with Josef Müller, Hans von Dohnanyi, and Dietrich Bonhoeffer; 1942, arrested in the currency *Depositenkasse* affair related to the "Operation 7" rescue; February 12, 1944, sentenced by the military high court to four years in prison; 1955, honorary consul, Mexico—8, 16, 17

Schmidt: pastor (1937)—14
Schmidt, Carl (1868–1938): church historian; 1901, academic official, Prussian Academy of Science; 1928, professor, Berlin—10
Schmidt, Friedrich: teacher and National Socialist politician; 1933, deputy regional Nazi party leader [*Gauleiter*] and member of parliament, Stuttgart; as a German Christian also a member of the Württemberg church congress; 1937, head of the central educational office of the NSDAP; 1940, author of *The Reich as Task*; 1942, chief of staff of the Labor Office East of the NSDAP; SS brigade leader—16
Schmidt, Gerhard: mentioned in letter from Theódore de Félice—12
Schmidt, Hans (1877–1953): 1914, professor of Old Testament, Tübingen; 1921, Giessen; 1928, Halle—3, 14
Schmidt, Hans-Wilhelm (1903–91): private lecturer, Bethel; professor of systematic and New Testament theology, Vienna and Erlangen—10
Schmidt, Jürgen: author of works on the Church Struggle—12, 13
Schmidt, Karl Ludwig (1891–1956): 1921, professor of New Testament, Giessen; 1925, Jena; 1929, Bonn; 1933, dismissed for political reasons (member of Social Democratic Party); pastor, Switzerland; 1935–53, professor of New Testament, Basel; 1927–37, editor of the journal *Theologische Blätter*, 1945–53 of the *Theologische Zeitung*; worked in the Swiss group of the Free Germany movement—5, 11, 12, 14, 16
Schmidt, Kurt Dietrich (1896–1964): German theologian; 1929, professor of church history, Kiel; 1934, member of the Lutheran Council; 1935, dismissed because of active participation in the Confessing Church; 1936, theological instructor, Mission Seminary, Hermannsburg; 1948, professor at the seminary, Hamburg; 1953, professor, University of Hamburg—4, 6, 12, 13, 14, 15
Schmidt, Martin Anton: professor emeritus of theology, Basel—11
Schmidt, Traugott: German biblical scholar—1, 2, 4, 11, 14
Schmidt, Walter (1913–2000): from Wittenberg; 1938, participated in the collective pastorate, Köslin; 1939, assistant pastor, Priorau; 1946, pastor, Salzfurthkapelle; 1978, retired—8, 16
Schmidt, Wolfgang (1909–45): from Pomerania; 1936, vicar, Stettin; summer 1937, participated in the fifth Finkenwalde session; 1937–39, predicant, Stettin; 1940, pastor, Boldekow/Anklam; 1945, missing in action—8, 15
Schmidt-Lange, Anne: U.S. translator and scholar of Mennonite history; primary translator of *DBWE* 11—10, 12
Schmidt-Ott, Friedrich (1860–1956): German legal scholar; 1917–18, Prussian minister of culture—10

Schmiedel, Paul Wilhelm (1851–1935): New Testament scholar; from 1890, professor in Jena—1

Schminck-Gustavus, Christoph U.: author of work on Bonhoeffer's summary "trial" and execution—16

Schmitt, Carl (1888–1985): German expert in constitutional law; 1921, professor, Greifswald; 1922, Bonn; 1926, Berlin (senior business school); 1932, Cologne; 1933–45, professor, University of Berlin; influential in promoting Nazi interpretation of constitutional law in early years of the Third Reich—12

Schmitt, Franziskus Salesius: Catholic patristics scholar—2, 12

Schmitt, Kurt Paul (1886–1950): 1921–33, general director, Allianz Insurance company, Berlin; 1931–33, member of the provisional Reich economic council; June 1933–July 1934, Reich minister of economic affairs; leave of absence for health reasons, although remained a Prussian state counselor until 1945—13

Schmitz, Elisabeth (1893–1977): historian, theologian, and educator; Confessing Church member; author of the 1935 memorandum to the Confessing Church leadership demanding that the church speak out about the persecution of German Jews—15

Schmitz, Otto (1883–1957): 1910, private lecturer in New Testament theology, Berlin; after 1912, director of the Protestant preachers' seminary, Basel; 1916, professor of New Testament theology, Münster; 1934, forced retirement; director of the Confessing Church preachers' seminary, Bielefeld, and lecturer at the theological college, Bethel; 1938–51, director of the Johanneum; after 1945, also lecturer (after 1951 full-time) at the seminary in Wuppertal—1, 11, 13, 14

Schmöckel, Hans Werner: Confessing vicar, Berlin-Lichterfelde—14

Schmolck, Benjamin (1672–1737): hymnist—9

Schneckenburger, Matthias (1804–48): theologian—14

Schneemelcher, Wilhelm (1914–2003): church historian, ecumenist, editor of the *New Testament Apocrypha*—10, 11, 14

Schneidemesser, Johannes von (1881–1934): 1919–34, pastor, Lazarus Church, Berlin—12

Schneider, Gerhard (1914–41): 1933, theology student, Berlin—12

Schneider, Helmuth: professor of social and economic history, military affairs, history of classical scholarship, Kassel—10

Schneider, Paul ("the preacher of Buchenwald") (1897–1939): Rhineland pastor and member of the Confessing Church; 1926, pastor, Hochelheim-Dornholzhausen; from 1934, Dickenschied, Hunsrück; 1937, arrested by the Gestapo in his parish and taken to Buchenwald; July 18, 1939, murdered in Buchenwald—15, 17

Schneider, Reinhold (1903–58): Catholic writer and historical author; 1936, prohibited from publishing—6, 8, 16

Schneider, Thomas Martin: director, Institute for Protestant Theology, Coblenz—12

Schneidhuber, Thea: widow of the Munich police president who was murdered on June 30, 1934; "non-Aryan" convert to Catholicism; under the pseudonym Thea Graziella, wrote literary contributions and film reviews for the Catholic church newspaper in Munich; served as courier to the Vatican and other Catholic offices for Johannes Neuhäusler; 1941, arrested in Breda, Holland, as an informant for a Catholic news service; taken with her mother to the Ravensbrück concentration camp and killed there—16

Schnepel, Ernst: author of work about Christians in war—15

Schniewind, Julius (1883–1948): 1921, professor of New Testament, Halle; 1927, Greifswald; 1929, Königsberg; 1935, Kiel; 1936, again in Halle; 1934, member of the Lutheran Council—14, 16, 17 (for vol. 12)

Schnurmann, Anneliese: psychoanalyst; childhood friend of Susanne Bonhoeffer; 1932, financed Dietrich Bonhoeffer's youth center in Charlottenburg; had to emigrate to England because of the National Socialist race laws; worked with Anna Freud in the Hampstead Clinic in London—9, 10, 11, 12, 15, 16

Schober, Franz von (1798–1882): German poet—8

Schoch: secretary in the World Council of Churches in Geneva—16

Schoenberg, Arnold (1874–1951): Austrian-born American composer—11

Schöffel, Simon (1880–1959): 1904, court chaplain to the Prince of Erbach-Schönberg, Hesse; 1906, catechumen, Nuremberg; 1909, pastor, Schweinfurt; 1920, dean there; 1922–54, senior pastor, Hamburg; May 1933–March 1934 (dismissal) and 1946–54, bishop, Hamburg; July 20–September 27, 1933, member of the Provisional Church Administration; September–November 1933 (resignation), clerical adviser to the Reich Church Administration; 1934, member of the Lutheran Council—12, 13, 17 (for vol. 13)

Scholder, Klaus (1930–85): German church historian of the Church Struggle—1, 6, 10, 11, 12, 13, 14, 15, 16

Scholl, Hans (1918–43): medical student; leading member of the White Rose student resistance group in Munich; February 22, 1943, executed with his sister, Sophie—16, 17

Scholl, Sophie (1921–43): student; member of the White Rose; February 22, 1943, executed with her brother, Hans—16, 17

Schollmeyer, Matthias: German scholar of the theology in Bonhoeffer's prison fiction—2, 6, 7, 8

Scholten, Paul: Dutch lawyer—16

Scholz, Heinrich (1884–1956): 1910, private lecturer in systematic theology, Berlin; 1917, professor, Breslau; 1919, philosopher of religion at the university in Kiel; from 1928, in Münster—1, 2, 11

Scholz, Wilhelm von (1874–1969): German novelist, lyricist, and actor—8, 17 (for vol. 9)

Schomerus, Johannes (Hans) (1902–69): 1926, pastor, Hildesheim; 1927, Alfeld an der Leine; 1928, pastor, Wahrenholz, Hannover; 1936, cathedral predicant, Braunschweig; 1938, head of the preachers' seminary, Wittenberg; 1945, pastor, Reinbek; 1948–51, editor of *Christ und Welt*; 1951–67, active in the Evangelical Academy of the Bavarian Church, Herrenalb; from 1965, its director—12, 14

Schönberger, Gustav: 1926, pastor, Ronsdorf near Wuppertal; 1929, German pastor at the Hamburg Lutheran Church, London-Dalston; 1939, military service; 1945–51, pastor, Offenbach-Bürgel and employed in the regional church archives in Darmstadt—13, 15

Schöne, Georg (1875–1960): son of Richard and Helene Schöne, friends of the Bonhoeffer family; Berlin surgeon; 1934, dismissed for political reasons—8, 15

Schöne, Helene, née Härtel (1844–1928): neighbor of the Bonhoeffers in Berlin; widow of Richard Schöne, general director of the Prussian museums in Berlin; a cousin of Karl Alfred von Hase—9, 10

Schöne, Johanna (1878–1920): painter and sculptor; daughter of Richard and Helene Schöne—9

Schöne, Richard (called "the old Schöne") (1840–1922): professor of archaeology; general director of the Royal (Prussian) Museums in Berlin; distant relative of Paula Bonhoeffer; lived across the street from the Bonhoeffers' first Berlin home on Wangenheimstrasse; married to Helene, née Härtel, a cousin of Karl Alfred von Hase; friend of Richard Volkmann-Leander; father of Georg, Johanna, Clara, and Friedrich—8, 9

Schöne, Wolfgang: German art historian—15

Schönemann, Friedrich (1886–1956): professor of American studies, Berlin; after 1945, independent scholar—8

Schönfeld, Johannes Otto Leopold (Hans) (1900–1954): economist and theologian; 1920, studied theology and economics; 1926, doctorate, Kiel; 1929, academic assistant at the International Institute for Sociology, Geneva; 1930, ordination and service as assistant pastor, German Lutheran congregation, Geneva; 1931–46, head of the research department in the World Council of Churches; 1948–49, high church official and ecumenical adviser, Church Foreign Office of the Evangelical Church of Germany, Frankfurt am Main—8, 11, 12, 13, 14, 15, 16, 17

Schönherr, Albrecht (1911–2009): 1931–33, among the circle of students around Bonhoeffer in Berlin; 1934, joined the Confessing Church; 1935, participated in the first Zingst/Finkenwalde session and active in the House of Brethren; 1935, ministry, Greifswald; 1936, ordination by the Confessing Church; 1937, pastor, Brüssow (where August von Mackensen was patron of this church); 1947, superintendent, Brandenburg/Havel; 1951, director at the seminary there; 1963, general superintendent of the church district of Mark Brandenburg [Kurmark], Eberswalde; 1967, bishop; 1973–81, bishop of Berlin-Brandenburg; 1969–81, head of the Conference of Church Leadership of the Federation of Evangelical Churches in the German Democratic Republic; 1981, retired—2, 3, 4, 5, 8, 9, 10, 11, 12, 13, 14, 15, 16, 17

Schönherr, Hilde, née Enterlein (1912–62): studied philosophy and theology in Berlin; 1932–33, among the circle of students around Bonhoeffer in Berlin; summer semester 1933, attended Bonhoeffer's lectures on Christology; 1934, participated in the Fanø youth conference; 1936, married Albrecht Schönherr in a service performed by Dietrich Bonhoeffer; organist and choral director, from 1940, curate, Brüssow—3, 12, 13, 14, 15, 16, 17

Schönhöffer, Johannes (1885–1966): Catholic theologian; monsignor with the Propaganda Fide in Rome—8

Schönmetzer, Adolf (1910–97): German Jesuit scholar and educator—2, 14

Schönrock (Finefrock) (FP): character in the novel, pastor—7

Schopenhauer, Arthur (1788–1860): German philosopher; radical pessimist; 1813, doctorate, Jena; principle work was *Die Welt als Wille und Vorstellung*, which emphasized the primacy of will over intellect; anticipated the psychology of the subconscious—1, 11

Schott, Emil (1871–1932): headmaster in Ulm; from winter semester 1889–90, member of Hedgehog fraternity—9

Schott, Erdmann (1900–1983): 1930, private lecturer in systematic theology, Greifswald; 1953, professor, Halle—14

Schraa, Rudolf: 1936, mentioned in connection with the Council of Brethren in Stettin—14

Schrader, Wolfgang (1910–78): from East Prussia; 1935, participated in the first Zingst/Finkenwalde session; pastor, Kuhz near Prenzlau; 1938, military service, ultimately as a lieutenant; 1945, pastor, Stuttgart-Mühlhausen; 1948–63, Berlin-Spandau; 1963, retired—15, 16

Schreiber: pastor (not otherwise identified)—15

Schreiber, August Wilhelm (1861–1945): 1900, head missions inspector of the North German Mission Society, Bremen; high consistory official, Church Federation Office, Berlin; 1914, director of the German Protestant

Mission Society, Berlin; 1925, official in the Church Federation Office; 1933–37, returned to the North German Mission Society in Bremen, honorary commissarial director—10, 11, 12

Schreiber, Matthias: author of work on Friedrich Perels—8, 16

Schreiner, Helmuth (1893–1962): 1926, head of the Johannes Seminary, Berlin-Spandau; 1931–37 (dismissed), professor of practical theology, Rostock; 1934, member of the Lutheran Council; 1938–55, head of the Westphalian deaconesses' institute, Münster; 1946–57, professor of practical theology, Münster—12, 14

Schreiner, Karl Heinz: 1927, ordination, assistant pastor, Nuremberg/Steinbühl; 1930, German pastor, Liverpool; 1935, Cairo; 1944, Twente, Holland; 1947, pastor, Kelheim, Bavaria—13

Schreitmüller, August: creator of the monument *Die Wacht*, unveiled in Spandau in 1922—9

Schrenk, Viola: German pastor—17 (for vol. 12)

Schrey: from Baden; SS lieutenant [*Obersturmführer*]; October 1944, conducted interrogations of, among others, Constantin von Dietze—16

Schröder, Alfred (1910–91): 1937, participated in the fifth Finkenwalde session; assistant pastor, Berlin; 1938, pastor, Röntgental; 1945, Berlin; 1954–63, regional youth chaplain in Berlin; 1963–75, high consistory official—15

Schröder, Baron Bruno (1867–1940): banker; 1893, joined the bank of his uncle J. Henry Schröder & Co. in London; 1895, named owner of the bank, becoming one of the earliest German private bankers in England; 1904, named Prussian baron for his contributions to Hamburg's welfare; 1914, at the outbreak of World War I, immediately naturalized because of the significance of his bank for the British economy; trustee of various German relief and welfare organizations; 1937, honorary doctorate, University of Hamburg; as the chair of the Association of German Evangelical Congregations in Great Britain and Ireland, he supported Bonhoeffer in Londond—13, 14, 15

Schröder, Hermann (1913–42): from Bremen; young Confessing Church theologian; 1937–38, participated in the collective pastorate, Groß-Schlönwitz; 1942, killed in action on the eastern front—15, 16

Schröder, Konrad: teacher at the German school and director of the choral club in Barcelona—10

Schröder, Winfried: author of article on pantheism—8

Schroeder, Edward H.: U.S. Lutheran pastor and professor emeritus, Valparaiso University, Concordia Seminary, and Christ Seminary-Seminex—14

Schroeder, Johannes: from 1906, pastor, Berlin-Steglitz—12

Schröter (Herr): neighbor of the Dreß family, Berlin-Dahlem—8
Schröter, Christoph Gotthard (1699–1782): organist and inventor, a contemporary of J. S. Bach; considered with Bartolomeo Cristofori and Gottfried Silbermann to be an inventor of the pianoforte—9
Schröter, Dorothea: *see* Hase, Dorothea von
Schröter, Friedrich-Ernst: Confessing Church theologian from Halle/Saale; 1936–37, participated in the fourth Finkenwalde session; according to Bonhoeffer's Finkenwalde newsletter of November 22, 1941, wounded on the eastern front—14, 15, 16
Schrötter: German consul in Barcelona—10
Schübel, Albrecht: author of work on military chaplains—8
Schubert, Ernst August Wilhelm (1876–1943): 1920–28, pastor of the German parish in Rome; pastor, St. Nicolai Church, Berlin; 1928–41, pastor at the Church of the Twelve Apostles, Berlin; after 1936, commissioner and church council member, Church Foreign Office, Berlin—9, 10, 11
Schubert, Franz Peter (1797–1828): Austrian composer and exponent of Romanticism—7, 8, 9, 13, 16
Schubring, Wilhelm (1875–1945): from 1918, pastor, Berlin-Stadt I; general secretary of the Protestant association, Berlin—10, 12
Schul: congregational council member in Barcelona—10
Schulenburg, Friedrich Werner Count von der (1875–1944): German diplomat; 1934–41, ambassador in Moscow; in contact with the political resistance; after July 20, 1944, arrested; November 10, 1944, executed—16
Schultz, Hermann (1836–1903): Protestant theologian—11
Schultz, Siegfried: from 1914, pastor, Berlin-Neukölln—12
Schultz, Walter (1913–87): from Berlin Wilmersdorf; 1938, participated in the collective pastorate in Groß-Schlönwitz; pastor, Stettin—15, 16
Schultz, Walther (1900–1957): 1928, pastor, Badendiek; 1933, German Christian leader; 1934–45, bishop of Mecklenburg; 1939–45, member of the Confidential Council of Clerical Advisers of the German Evangelical Church; 1952–57, pastor, Schnackenburg/Elbe—15, 17
Schulz: 1933, pastor in Berlin—12
Schulz, Dirk: German Protestant theologian and pastor; editor of *DBW* 15—6, 14, 15
Schulz, Frieder: liturgist; "spiritual father" of the Protestant liturgy in Germany—14
Schulz, Georg (1889–1954): 1917, pastor, Sydow, Saxony; 1922, founder and first head of the Sydow Brotherhood; 1925, pastor, Drackenstedt near Magdeburg; 1931, Wuppertal-Unterbarmen; 1933, member of the Pastors' Emergency League; 1936–44/45, pastor, Falkenhagen, Pomerania; 1945–54, instructor of religion, Hilchenbach, Westphalia—11, 12

Schulz, Johann Abraham Peter (1747–1800): German composer—14, 16
Schulz, Robert: 1925–27, National Socialist propagandist and organizer in Mecklenburg and Pomerania; SS-*Oberführer*; from 1930, member of parliament—14
Schulz, Wilfried: active member of the German section of the International Bonhoeffer Society—11
Schulze, Bertha (1896–1987): November 20, 1925–July 24, 1926, student in Berlin; doctoral student and senior member of Harnack's seminar—3, 9, 11, 12, 13
Schulze, Gerhard (1913–41): from Halberstadt; 1938, participated in the collective pastorate in Groß-Schlönwitz; pastor, Letzlingen near Gardelegen/Altmark; summer 1941, killed in action on the eastern front—15, 16
Schulze, Martin: naval captain; October–December 1933, worked closely with Martin Niemöller in the Pastors' Emergency League—13
Schulze, Otto: Berlin pastor, member of the Pastors' Emergency League—12
Schulze zur Wiesche, Paul (1905–87): attorney in Düsseldorf; from 1934, member of the Council of the Evangelical Confessing Synod in the Rhineland; active in various legal matters on behalf of the Confessing Church—16
Schumacher, Erich (1908–45): 1936, in Finkenwalde; 1945, killed in action —14
Schumann, Clara Wieck (1819–96): prominent nineteenth-century pianist and composer; married to the composer Robert Schumann—9
Schumann, Friedrich-Karl (1886–1960): 1914, pastor; 1924, private lecturer in systematic theology; 1929, professor of systematic theology, Giessen; 1932, professor of systematic and practical theology, Halle; 1933, joined the NSDAP; 1933, participated in the Wittenberg national synod; July 20–September 27, 1933, member of the Provisional Church Administration; 1948, head of the Evangelical Research Academy in Hemer; 1951–55, professor, Münster—1, 2, 10, 12, 13, 17 (for vol. 12)
Schumann, Robert Alexander (1810–56): German composer—7, 8
Schümer, Anna (b. 1904): November 25, 1925–April 26, 1926, studied in Berlin; prior to that at the University of Jena; member of Harnack's seminar—9
Schur, Werner (1888–1950): professor of ancient history, Breslau and Heidelberg—8
Schürer, Emil (1844–1910): Protestant theologian and scholar of religious studies; 1890, final edition of one of his primary works, *Geschichte des jüdischen Volkes im Zeitalter Jesu Christi* (A history of the Jewish people in the time of Jesus), in which he drew from primary sources and rigorously applied the historical-critical method to the New Testament as well as to

early church history, emphasizing for the first time the Jewish roots of Christianity and focusing also on the history of Judaism and its various relationships with Christianity; founder of the periodical *Theologische Literaturzeitung*, which he later coedited with his friend Adolf von Harnack —12

Schürmann, Heinz (1913–99): German New Testament scholar; active in the Youth Association for Decisive Christianity—11

Schütz, Alfred (1899–1959): Austrian-American philosopher and sociologist —8

Schutz, Erwin (1907–42): from Pomerania; 1938, participated in the collective pastorate in Groß-Schlönwitz; 1939, pastor, Groß-Schlönwitz; until his marriage in April 1939, put his vicarage residence at the disposal of the collective pastorate; 1942, killed in action at Leningrad—15, 16

Schütz, Heinrich (1585–1672): German composer—5, 8, 16

Schütz, Paul Wilhelm Lukas (1891–1985): German theologian; from 1910, studied theology, philosophy, and art history, Berlin and Jena; 1914, doctorate; 1914–18, military service; 1922, doctorate in theology; 1925–40, pastor, Schwabendorf, Hesse; 1930–37, private lecturer in Protestant ethics and dogmatics, Giessen; 1940–52, head pastor, St. Nicholaus, Hamburg; 1941–45, military service; 1952, statement of dissent to the regional church council of the Lutheran Church of Hamburg and early retirement; 1953, moved to Söcking near Starnberg—6, 8, 12, 15

Schutz, Wiltrud: widow of Erwin Schutz—16

Schwabach, Mrs.: acquaintance of Bonhoeffer in Berlin—10

Schwartz, Paul: professor of history and education, Berlin—9

Schwarz: 1936, pastor, Stralsund—12, 14

Schwarz, Albert: author of study on the Weimar Republic—9

Schwarz, Dr.: physician; distant relative of Bonhoeffer's who was in the NSDAP—14

Schwarz, Prof.: in Budapest; not otherwise identified; apparently in contact with Johannes Neuhäusler—16

Schwebel, Gerhard: pastor, Berlin—10

Schwebel, Johannes (1874–1942): from 1923, pastor, Berlin—12

Schwedler, Hanns-Uwe: author of work on Gossner mission—16

Schweitzer, Albert (1875–1965): Swiss-born Protestant theologian, philosopher, physician (of tropical diseases), missionary, and music scholar; 1902, lecturer, Strasbourg; from 1913, missionary physician in Lambarene (Gabon, French Equatorial Africa); contributed significantly to the study of the question of the historical Jesus; recipient of Nobel Peace Prize—4, 6, 9, 10, 11, 12, 14, 16

Schweitzer, Friedrich: professor of practical theology and religious education, Tübingen—14

Schweizer, Alexander (1808–88): Swiss pastor and professor of practical theology—14

Schwencke, Friedrich: from 1916, pastor, Berlin-Treptow—12

Schwenckfeld von Ossig, Kaspar (1489–1561): Silesian nobleman; joined Luther's reformation but was more inclined to spiritualism; his adherents, the Schwenckfeldians, wanted to live as disciples of Christ consistent with the Sermon on the Mount; they were persecuted in the seventeenth century; 1734, remnants of the community emigrated to Pennsylvania—4, 6, 14, 15

Schwerin von Krosigk, Johann Ludwig (Lutz) Count (1887–1977): German politician; 1929, minister director, Reich Ministry of Finance; 1932–45, Reich Minister of Finance; 1949, sentenced in Nuremberg to ten years imprisonment; 1951, released—13, 16

Schwöner: privy councilor; not otherwise identified—10

Scott, Jamie S.: professor of interdisciplinary studies in literature and religion, York University, Canada—8

Scriban, Julius (referred to as Patriarchate): archimandrite of Bucharest; vice president of the Romanian section of the World Alliance for Promoting International Friendship through the Churches; spring 1943, mentioned by Dietrich Bonhoeffer in the "camouflage letter"—16

Seagell: not otherwise identified (London)—15

Sedlmair, Willibald (formerly Alfred): Benedictine monk in Ettal, Upper Bavaria; monastery senior—16

Seeberg, Alfred (1863–1915): New Testament scholar; professor, Berlin and Leipzig—9

Seeberg, Erich (1888–1945): son of Reinhold Seeberg; German theologian; 1914, military chaplain; 1920, professor of church and dogmatic history, Königsberg; 1924, Breslau; 1926–27, Halle; 1927, successor of Karl Holl, Berlin—2, 6, 9, 10, 11, 12, 13

Seeberg, Reinhold (1859–1935): German theologian and doctoral adviser to Dietrich Bonhoeffer; 1885, professor, Dorpat; 1889, professor of systematic theology, Erlangen; 1898, Berlin—1, 2, 3, 4, 6, 8, 9, 10, 11, 12, 14, 15, 16

Seeberger, Erhard: from 1929, pastor, Berlin-Tempelhof—12

Seebold, Hermann: catechetical scholar—10

Seeckt, Johannes Friedrich (Hans) von (1866–1936): German military officer, nationalist, and monarchist; helped found the Black Reichswehr during the 1920s—17

Seedorf(f), Hermann: from 1927, pastor, Berlin—12

Seeger, Reinhard: author of essays on Marx and Engels—11, 14

Seeger, Ulrich: 1931–33, academic inspector at the preachers' seminary, Frankfurt/Oder; 1936, pastor, München-Gladbach; 1951–58, director of the preachers' seminary, Barmen; 1958, regional church official, Düsseldorf—12

Seehaus, Joachim: Pastor, Fehrbellin parish in Brandenburg until 2004—14

Seeler, Richard (1906–82): assistant pastor of the Confessing Church, Helbra —14

Segerstedt, Torgny (1876–1945): 1913, professor, Stockholm; 1917, editor in chief of the *Göteborg Handels und Sjöfarts Tidning*—16

Sehling, Emil (1860–1928): German professor of church law—14

Seidler: unidentified, in letter to Ernst Cromwell—14

Seither: student at the German school in Barcelona—10

Seligman, Herbert J. (1891–1984): author, journalist; 1919–32, director of publicity for the NAACP—10

Selke, Karl: Confessing pastor, Striche/Grenzmark—14

Sellin, Ernst (1867–1946): 1897, professor of Old Testament, Vienna; 1908, Rostock; 1913, Kiel; from 1921, Berlin; 1935, emeritus—9, 10, 12, 15

Selnecker (also Schnellenecker), Nikolaus (1528–92): 1558–68, moderator (general superintendent), Leipzig; court preacher, Braunschweig; hymnist; also an accomplished organist—14

Selschopps, Frau: widow of Wilhelm Lütgert's brother—10

Sembritzki, Inge, née Karding: from Berlin-Zehlendorf; as a student, worked in Siegmund-Schultze's social working group in east Berlin; 1932, among the circle of students around Bonhoeffer in Berlin; 1934, participated in the Fanø youth conference; passed the first theological examination; later school teacher in Flensburg and pastor in the regional church women's programs, Schleswig-Holstein—12, 13

Senarclens, Jacques de (1914–71): Swiss Reformed theologian; director of the Centre Protestant d'Études, Geneva; 1960, professor of dogmatics, Geneva; editor of the French edition of Karl Barth's *Church Dogmatics* —16, 17

Seneca, Lucius Annaeus ("the younger") (ca. 4 B.C.E.– 65 C.E.): Roman statesman, philosophical author, and poet; 65, forced to commit suicide—6, 9, 10, 17 (for vol. 9)

Senfl, Ludwig (1486–1542): composer of spiritual choral music—13

Senftleben, Otto: lawyer; 1940–42, ministerial adviser; group leader "S" (pastoral counseling) in the Army High Command—8

Sennacherib (701–681): Assyrian high king; 701, subjugated the kingdom of Judah and besieged Jerusalem under King Hezekiah—13

Senz, Dr.: Bonhoeffer family doctor—9

Severus, Septimius (146–211 C.E.): 193–211, Roman Emperor—9

Seydel, Dorothea: wife of Gustav Seydel—16

Seydel, Gustav Paul Heinrich Karl (1910–43): from Berlin; 1936, vicar, Fehrbellin; summer 1936, participated in the third Finkenwalde session; 1937, assistant pastor, Sachsenhausen under the synod head Kurt Scharf; 1942, married Dorothea, née Frick; 1942, assistant pastor, Berlin-Steglitz; October 20, 1943, killed in action at Zaporozh'ye in the Ukraine—8, 14, 15, 16

Seyfang, Dr.: rector of the German school in Barcelona—10

Seymour: novelist—10

Seymour, E. A.: director of the church choir at the German Reformed Church of St. Paul in London—13

Shakespeare, William (1564–1616): British dramatist and poet—6, 12, 13, 16

Shapiro, James: author of book on Oberammergau—15

Sharp: boardinghouse proprietor in London—15

Shaw, George Bernard (1856–1950): Irish playwright and critic—10

Shaw, Marvin C.: author of study of naturalistic theism—12

Sheed, Frank J.: translator of Augustine—8

Sheldon, Charles M. (1857–1946): U.S. social reformer and Congregational minister; early advocate of civil rights for African Americans; best known for his 1897 inspirational book *In His Steps: What Would Jesus Do?*—15

Shem: biblical character—12

Sherover, Miles (1896–1976): Polish-American Jewish businessman and journalist, author of article on loans to Russia read by Bonhoeffer at Union Seminary—10

Sherriff, Robert Cedric (1896–1975): British playwright, author of *Journey's End*—10

Sherman, Franklin: U.S. Lutheran theologian and interfaith leader; 1962, wrote early explication on Bonhoeffer's *Act and Being*—2

Shimei: biblical character—14

Shinn, Roger L. (1917–2013): Reinhold Niebuhr Professor Emeritus of Social Ethics, Union Theological Seminary in New York—10

Shippey, Alma: first African American student enrolled at Warren Wilson College, North Carolina—10

Shreeve, Esther: daughter of Franz Hildebrandt—11

Sickingen, Franz von (1481–1523): knight of the German Reich, predatory baron during the late Middle Ages; outlawed in 1515 but powerful enough to ignore his sentence—10

Sieden, Julius von (1884–1938): 1927, church superintendent, Schwerin; 1933, compulsory transfer to Malchin—14

Siegele-Wenschkewitz, Leonore (1944–99): German church historian—14

Siegfried: prince and protagonist in the first part of the Middle High German heroic epic poem, the *Nibelungenlied*—12

Siegfried, Carl Gustav Albert (1830–1903): German professor of theology—9

Siegmund-Schultze, Friedrich (1885–1969): Protestant theologian, social activist, and labor unionist from Berlin; 1908, licentiate in theology, Marburg; 1909–14, secretary of the committee for fostering the relationship between Great Britain and Germany; 1910–11, pastor, Friedenskirche, Potsdam; 1911, founder and head of the Social Work Association in east Berlin; 1913–33, editor of the *Eiche*; 1914, cofounder of the International Fellowship of Reconciliation and of the World Alliance for Promoting International Friendship through the Churches; 1914–45, secretary of the German board of Faith and Order; 1925–33, professor of social ethics and pedagogy, Berlin, head of the German headquarters for youth ministry, Berlin; 1926, honorary professor in Berlin; 1933, dismissed from office and deported by the Gestapo to Switzerland for his aid to Jews; 1948–57, director of the Dortmund school of social pedagogy; 1948, professor, Münster—6, 7, 9, 10, 11, 12, 13, 14, 16, 17

Sifton, Elizabeth: editor at Farrar, Straus & Giroux publishers; daughter of Reinhold Niebuhr—11

Sigwart, Christoph (1830–1904): professor of philosophy, Tübingen—1, 9

Silas: biblical character—5, 14

Silesius: *see* Scheffler, Johann

Silvanus (also Silas): biblical character—14

Simeon: biblical character—9, 14, 15, 16

Simmel, Georg (1858–1918): philosopher, sociologist—1, 8, 11

Simmons, Paul D.: U.S. Baptist theologian and ethicist—14

Simon: *see* Wellnhofer, Simon

Simon Peter: *see* Peter

Simon the Zealot: biblical character—4

Simon, Ludwig-Wilhelm (1905–95): 1935, pastor, Wies; 1937, Mannheim; 1964–69, instructor of religion, Schopfheim, Baden—12

Simonides (556–468 B.C.E.): early Greek poet—6

Simons: assistant headmaster at the Friedrich Werder Gymnasium, Berlin-Grunewald; member of the examination commission for Bonhoeffer's *Abitur*—9

Simons, Walter (1861–1937): 1920–21, Reich foreign minister; 1922–29, president of the Reich Court; 1928, honorary professor of international law, Leipzig; 1925–36, president of the Evangelical Social Congress;

1930–33, member of the German Evangelical Church Council; long and active member of the World Alliance for Promoting International Friendship through the Churches; 1934, participated in the Fanø conference —11, 13

Simson, Werner von: lawyer; grew up in Berlin closely acquainted with the Bonhoeffer family; 1935, adviser at the Berlin Supreme Court; 1939, moved to England; 1965, lecturer, and after 1968, professor of public law, Freiburg/Breisgau—16

Singer, Friedrich W. (1873–1934): 1892, ordination and emigration to India, worked with the Basel mission society; 1901, director of a brick factory in India; 1907, with the German Evangelical Seamen's Mission in South Shields, Great Britain; 1912, pastor, South Shields; 1915, in Neubeckum, Westphalia; 1921–33, pastor of the German congregation, Sydenham, London, and from 1925, also of German Reformed St. Paul's Church, London; 1933, retired—12, 13

Singh, "Sadhu" Sundar (1889–1929): Indian Christian of Sikh parentage, popular in the West through travels in the 1920s—10, 14

Sirach, Jesus Ben (Son of): author of Wisdom of Sirach—5

Sister (FP): proposed character for drama—7

Skovgard, Hans: member of the Danish section of the World Alliance for Promoting International Friendship through the Churches—11

Slocombe, George (1894–1963): British journalist—10

Smart, James, D. (1906–82): Canadian who taught history of theology at Union Theological Seminary, New York—2, 15

Smemo, Johannes: Norwegian theologian; 1934, rector, Practical Theological Seminary in Oslo; 1946, bishop, Agder; 1951, Oslo—16

Smend, Rudolf (1851–1913): professor of Old Testament, Basel and Göttingen—9

Smid, Marijke: historian at the Protestant Institute for Interdisciplinary Research (FEST), Heidelberg; scholar of Dohnanyi circle and Church Struggle—8, 12, 16

Smidt, Udo (1900–1978): 1925, pastor, Rysum, East Frisia; 1930, Reich patron of the Federation of German Bible Circles; 1934, pastor, Bremerhaven-Lehe; 1934–51, also youth pastor of the Evangelical Reformed Church in northwest Germany; 1951, director of the Reformed preachers' seminary, Wuppertal; 1958–70, superintendent, Detmold—11, 14

Smith, Neville Horton: 1955, British translator of the first edition of Bonhoeffer's *Ethics*—2, 6

Smith, Robert Pearsall (1827–98): Quaker, revivalist preacher; manufacturer in Philadelphia—11

Smith, Ronald Gregor: Scottish theologian; as director of SCM Press in London, he introduced translations of Bonhoeffer to the English-speaking world—1, 2, 3, 5, 7, 8, 9, 12
Snyder, Louis L. (1907–93): American scholar of the Third Reich—15
Sockman, Ralph Washington (1889–1970): pastor of Christ Church on Park Avenue; 1928–62, prominent radio preacher on *National Radio Pulpit*—15
Socrates (ca. 469–399 B.C.E.): Greek philosopher in Athens, teacher of Plato —1, 2, 6, 7, 8, 10, 12, 13
Soden, Hans von (1881–1945): German Protestant church historian and New Testament scholar; from 1918, professor, Breslau; 1924–45, professor, Marburg; 1933, member, Pastors' Emergency League; 1934, member, Reich Council of Brethren—6, 9, 13, 16, 17 (for vol. 12)
Soden, Hermann Baron von (1852–1914): Lutheran theologian, pastor; from 1913, professor of New Testament, Berlin—8
Söderberg: Swedish cleric; 1942, pastor of the Swedish congregation, London—16
Söderblom, Bror-Carl: son of the archbishop Nathan Söderblom—16
Söderblom, Margaretha: wife of Bror-Carl Söderblom; later divorced—16
Söderblom, Nathan (1866–1931): Swedish Protestant theologian; 1894–1901, legation pastor, Paris; 1901, professor for the history of religions, Uppsala; 1912 and 1914, also in Leipzig; 1914–31, archbishop of Uppsala; 1919, his planning prompted the founding of the ecumenical movement for Practical Christianity (Life and Work); leading historian of religion —1, 10, 14
Sodoma—See Bazzi, Giovanni
Söhlmann, Fritz (1905–77): after studying theology, became a journalist and editor; coeditor of the periodicals *Der Vormarsch* (1932–33) and *Junge Kirche* (1933–41 and 1949–50); 1950, head of the regional youth office, Hannover—11, 12, 13, 14, 15
Sohm, Rudolph (1841–1917): church lawyer—1, 4, 14
Sohnius, Georg (1551–89): professor, Marburg and Heidelberg—9
Solf, Hanna (1887–1954): widow of the diplomat Wilhelm Solf; her house was the meeting place of a conservative tea society; January 1944, arrested after denunciation by a Gestapo spy—8, 16
Sölle, Dorothee (1929–2003): studied philosophy, theology, and comparative literature; 1972, postdoctoral lecturing qualification, Cologne; 1975–87, professor at Union Theological Seminary, New York—8
Solomon: preacher, author of Ecclesiastes—4, 5, 13, 14
Solon (born ca. 640 B.C.E.): Greek statesman—10

Soloviev, Vladimir (1853–1900): Russian philosopher of religion; from 1875, teacher, Moscow; from 1880, St. Petersburg; 1881, prohibited from teaching after advocating a reprieve for the murderer of the Czar; after 1881, freelance author and publicist—6

Sombart, Nikolaus: author of work on German culture—9, 10

Sombart, Werner (1863–1941): German political economist; from 1890, professor, Breslau; from 1906, Berlin—1, 7, 10

Sommer, Jakob Karl (Carl) Ernst (1911–81): German ecumenist; 1968–77, bishop of the Methodist Church in Germany—14

Somos, E.: from Budapest; 1934, participated in the Fanø youth conference —13

Sonderegger, Franz Xaver (b. 1898): police official; 1936, criminal secretary, Ludwigshafen; 1939, transferred to the Gestapo in Berlin; 1942, SS second lieutenant; 1943, assigned to military prosecutor Dr. Roeder in the *Depositenkasse* affair (investigating currency irregularities leading to the arrest and interrogation of Hans von Dohnanyi, Dietrich Bonhoeffer, and other prisoners) in the military high court; 1944, criminal commissar; assigned to the "special commission July 20" in the Reich Central Security Office; August 1945, interned; 1948, sentenced to seven years in prison—8, 16, 17

Sontheimer, Kurt: professor emeritus of political science, University of Munich—11

Sonya: *see* Marmeladova, Sonya Semyonovna

Soosten, Joachim von: German theologian; editor of *DBW* 1—1, 2, 9

Sophia: in gnostic speculation, figure variously associated with the feminine aspects of God, the mother of God's son, or the human soul—12

Sophocles (ca. 496–406 B.C.E.): Greek tragedian—6, 9

Sørensen (Soerensen), Henrik (1882–1962): Norwegian painter; friend of Bishop Berggrav—16

Sorum, Jonathan D.: author of work on *Discipleship*—4

Soule, George: U.S. economist; 1930s, on the editorial staff of the *New Republic* magazine—10

Spaemann, Robert: German philosopher and professor (emeritus), University of Munich—16

Spalatin, Georg (actually Burckhardt) (1484–1545): from Spalt near Nuremberg; humanist, Reformation theologian; friend of Luther, tutor of Frederick the Wise—8, 14

Spann, Othmar (1878–1951): Austrian sociologist and philosopher—1

Sparn, Walter: German theologian—17 (for vol. 12)

Sparring-Petersen, Wilhelm August Alfred Gunnar: Danish theologian and ecumenist; 1926–56, pastor, Copenhagen; 1957–69, church provost,

Copenhagen; 1923–48, secretary of the Danish section of the World Alliance for Promoting International Friendship through the Churches; 1937–48, member of that organization's executive committee, and from 1939, of the Danish section of the World Council of Churches; 1940–65, board member of the Nordic Ecumenical Institute Sigtuna; 1957–69, provost—13, 16

Spates, Thomas G. (1890–1988): professor of engineering, Yale University; vice president of General Foods—10

Speck, J.: 1934, Berlin participant in the Fanø youth conference—13

Speckhardt, Hugo Karl (1893–1949): lawyer; March 1941, military high court; specialist in the Reich War Legal Office; 1943, military prosecutor for the military high court—8, 16

Speer, Albert (1906–81): architect; 1934, commissioned by Hitler's staff with city planning; 1937, general architectural inspector for the Reich capital of Berlin; 1942, Reich minister for arms and wartime production; 1946, sentenced to twenty years in prison as a war criminal—16

Speirs, Ebenezer Brown: cotranslator of nineteenth-century English edition of Hegel's *Lectures on the Philosophy of Religion*—8

Spencer, Herbert (1820–1903): British philosopher; viewed evolution as the unifying principle of all the sciences—1, 9, 12

Spener, Philipp Jakob (1635–1705): a leading representative and author of Lutheran pietism; 1666, pastor, Frankfurt am Main; 1670, established private devotional circles (*collegia pietatis*); 1675, published his programmatic writing on pietism, *Pia desideria*; 1686, senior court chaplain, Dresden; 1691, provost, St. Nicholaus, Berlin; laid considerable stress on charitable works; subject of polemical attack from orthodox circles—5, 9, 10, 11, 14

Spengler, Lazarus (1479–1534): Nuremberg town clerk and supporter of the Reformation—12

Spengler, Oswald (1880–1936): German philosopher and historian of culture—3, 6, 7, 8, 9, 10, 14

Spenlein, Georg: Martin Luther's fellow monk; recipient of letters from Luther—14

Sperl, Carolyn: staff member, Hartford Seminary Library, Connecticut—1, 6, 7

Sperling, Marga: summer semester 1933, attended Bonhoeffer's lectures on Christology—12

Sperna Weiland, Jan: Dutch theologian—7

Sperry, Willard L.: professor of practical theology, Harvard—15

Spielbauer, Josef: Catholic priest—16

Spinoza, Baruch (Benedictus de) (1632–77): from a Marrano Jewish family that emigrated from Portugal to Holland; philosopher—1, 2, 8

Spitta, Karl Johann Philipp (1801–59): theologian and hymnist (the two-volume *Psalter und Harfe*, 1833–43)—1, 14

Spitz, Lewis (1922–2000): U.S. Luther scholar and historian on the Reformation—15

Sporleder, Ulrich: 1938, appointed by the East Prussian Council of Brethren as an assistant pastor in Marienburg; 1939, drafted into military service; 1944, killed in action as a captain and company leader on the eastern front—16

Sprague, Rosamond: U.S. professor of philosophy—10

Spranger, Eduard (1882–1963): German cultural philosopher and educator; 1911, professor of philosophy and pedagogy, Leipzig; 1920, Berlin; from 1946, Tübingen—1, 2, 6, 14

Sproul, Barbara: professor of religion, Hunter College—3

St. Leger, James: author of work on Grotius—8

Staats, Reinhart: studied theology in Tübingen, Berlin, and Göttingen; 1964–69, pastor, Wieda/Harz; 1965, doctorate, Göttingen; 1973, post-doctoral lecturing qualification in church history, Heidelberg; 1976–84, professor, Heidelberg, thereafter in Kiel; 1991, honorary doctorate, Lund; primary editor of *DBW* 10—3, 8, 9, 10, 11, 12, 14

Stace, Walter Terence (1886–1967): British-born philosopher; author of works on mysticism—3

Stadelmann, Rudolf (1902–49): beginning in winter semester 1920–21, member of the Hedgehog fraternity; later, professor of history—9, 11

Stadelmann, Walter: from Bavaria; student of Karl Barth; 1931–32, attended Bonhoeffer's lectures in Berlin

Stadler, Franz Thomas (1881–1946): Catholic priest; 1920–35, ministry, Munich-Untergiesing; 1935, appointed Monsignor; 1936, cathedral pastor and chair of the diocesan charity association—16

Staedler (Städler), Johannes (1911–41): from East Prussia; 1939, participated in the collective pastorate in Köslin; 1941, killed in action on the eastern front—16

Staehelin, Ernst (1889–1970): 1924, professor of theology, Basel—14

Stael, Germaine de, née Necker (1766–1817): French writer; fled Paris during the revolution; 1794, returned and maintained a salon for leading intellectuals; 1803, exiled by Napoleon, lived in her chateau in Coppet on Lake Geneva; 1816, returned to France—4

Staemmler, Wolfgang (1889–1970): 1929, superintendent, Halle; 1931, academic director of the provincial Saxon preachers' seminary, Frankfurt/Oder; 1934, pastor, Großkugel near Halle; member of the provincial

Saxon Council of Brethren; 1934, prohibited from speaking publicly; 1935, expelled; 1936, member and, from 1940, president of the Old Prussian Council of Brethren; 1939, arrested and expelled from the district of Merseburg and forbidden from speaking publicly; 1941, arrested and sentenced to one year in prison for violating these terms; 1944, sentenced to three years; 1945, provost of Wittenberg; 1945–50, academic director of the preachers' seminary, Wittenberg—5, 6, 8, 10, 14, 15, 16, 17

Staewen, Gertrud (1894–1987): Berlin welfare worker and social educator; 1922, met Karl Barth; until 1933, worked in Friedrich Siegmund-Schultze's social working group in east Berlin; 1931/32, attended Bonhoeffer's lectures; secretary, Burckhardt House; member of the Dahlem Confessing congregation; active with her friends Helene Jacobs and Melanie Steinmetz in illegally aiding persecuted Jews; 1943, fled to Pomerania to avoid arrest; after the war, member of the *Unterwegs* circle; voluntary lay chaplain, Tegel prison—11, 12, 13, 16

Stahl, Friedrich Julius (originally F. J. Jolson-Uhlfelder) (1802–61): German legal philosopher and politician; from a Jewish family; 1819, became a Lutheran—1, 6, 16

Stahlberg, Alexander (Alla) (1912–94): businessman; son of Walter and Spes (née von Kleist-Retzow) Stahlberg; initially worked in his father's business in Stettin; 1932–33, assistant in the office of Franz von Papen; 1935, entered military service; lieutenant and aide-de-camp during the war, ultimately working as an adjutant of General Field Marshal von Manstein—16

Stahlberg, Ruth Roberta: *see* Heckscher, Ruth Roberta

Stahlberg, Spes, née von Kleist-Retzow (1888–1973): daughter of Ruth von Kleist-Retzow; wife of the Stettin manufacturer Walter Stahlberg; 1920, divorced from him; moved to Berlin with her three children, Ruth Roberta, Alexander, and Hans Conrad—16

Stähler, Gerhard (1911–89): 1938, participated in the collective pastorate, Köslin; 1947, pastor, Osternburg; 1961, Bonn—15

Stählin, Leonhard (1911–42): nephew of Wilhelm Stählin; 1940, licentiate in theology, Halle; 1942, intended to contribute to a commemorative volume for Karl Jaspers's sixtieth birthday being planned by Otto Hammelsbeck; 1942, killed in action on the eastern front—16

Stählin, Rudolf: son of Wilhelm Stählin; studied theology in Erlangen, Berlin, Basel, Münster, and London; 1939–45, military service and pastor; 1947–56, professor of practical theology, Augustana Institute, Neuendettelsau; 1956–76, pastor, Munich—11, 12

Stählin, Wilhelm (1883–1975): father of Rudolf Stählin; 1910–26, pastor; 1922–23, founding member of the Evangelical Brotherhood of Michael

and of the Berneuchen circle; 1926–58, professor of practical theology, Münster; 1945–52, bishop of the Evangelical Lutheran Church, Oldenburg—5, 8, 12, 13, 17 (for vol. 13)

Stainer, John (1840–1901): British chorister and hymnist—13

Stalin, Joseph Vissarionovich (1879–1953): Soviet revolutionary statesman and political leader; after 1924, dictator of the Soviet Union—6, 8, 16, 17

Stange, Carl (1870–1959): conservative Lutheran theologian; Althaus's successor in Göttingen—1, 11

Stange, Erich (1888–1972): 1911, vicar, Lyon; 1913, pastor, Pulsnitz, Saxony; 1917, Leipzig; 1921–37, honorary secretary of the Universal Christian Council for Life and Work; 1921–54, Reich patron of the Protestant Young Men's Association in Germany (dismissed in 1933); 1929, secretary of the conferences of the Lutheran World Convention; 1934, expelled from the NSDAP; 1940–54, pastor, Kassel; 1957, retired and founded Protestant telephone counseling program—1, 11, 12, 13, 14

Stapel, Wilhelm (1882–1954): nationalist and anti-Semitic political journalist; 1919–38, editor of the monthly *Deutsches Volkstum*; author of the 1932 *Der christlicher Staatsmann: ein Theologie des Nationalismus*—10, 11, 12, 13, 14, 16

Stassen, David: translator of Heinz Eduard Tödt, *Authentic Faith: Bonhoeffer's Theological Ethics in Context*—7

Staude, Joachim (Jochen) (1911–41): from Letzlingen near Gardelegen; winter 1938–39, participated in the collective pastorate, Groß-Schlönwitz; summer 1941, killed in action on the eastern front—15, 16

Stauffenberg, Claus Schenk Count von (1907–44): career military; 1944, colonel and chief of the general staff of the commander in chief of the reserve army; July 20, 1944, attempted to assassinate Hitler; shot to death that day in the courtyard of the Bendlerstrasse offices—16, 17

Staupitz, Johann von (1468–1524): helped found Wittenberg University; 1502, professor, Wittenberg; 1503–20, vicar general of the German Augustinians; teacher, patron, and father confessor of Martin Luther before the latter's break with the Roman Catholic Church; 1522, entered the Benedictine order—10, 14, 15

Steck, Karl Gerhard (1908–83): 1932, vicar; 1936, lecturer at the Confessing Church preachers' seminary, Frankfurt am Main; 1943, pastor; 1948, seminary inspector; 1953, professor of Protestant theology, Frankfurt am Main; 1963, professor of systematic theology, Münster—11

Steckel, Karl: church historian—14

Steele, Pierre H: 1931, youth secretary of Life and Work; secretary of the youth commission of the Universal Christian Council for Life and Work—11

Steere, Douglas V. (1901–95): prominent U.S. Quaker—10

Steffen, Gustav: German sociologist—1

Steffen, Mr.: 1927, one of the Bonhoeffers' neighbors in Friedrichsbrunn—9

Stegener Petersen, H.: member of the Danish section of the World Alliance for Promoting International Friendship through the Churches—11

Stegmann, Josua (1588–1632): German theologian and professor of philosophy—14

Steiger, D. von: not otherwise identified (Switzerland)—15

Steil, Ludwig (1900–1945): 1929, pastor, Holsterhausen, Westphalia; member of the Westphalian Council of Brethren and participant in the Confessing Synod of the German Evangelical Church; September 1944, arrested for his protests against Nazism; January 1945, died in Dachau—16

Stein, Edith (Teresa Benedicta of the Cross) (1891–1942): German philosopher and religious author; student of Edmund Husserl; 1922, converted to Catholicism from Judaism; 1923, joined Carmelite order at Cologne; died in Auschwitz; attempted to synthesize Thomism and phenomenology in *Endliches und ewiges Sein* (Finite and eternal being)—1

Stein, Fritz: musicologist; from 1933, director of the Berlin Music Academy—16

Stein, Heinrich Friedrich Karl Baron von und zum (1757–1831): Prussian politician; 1807–08, minister of foreign affairs, accomplished many reforms in government and civil service; abolished serfdom; assisted Scharnhorst and Gneisenau in army reorganization; forced to resign by Napoleon—10

Steiner: 1986, pastor, Lazarus Church, Berlin—12

Steiner, Dr.: autumn 1933, contacted Bonhoeffer through Karl-Friedrich Bonhoeffer; 1933–34, in London—13

Steiner, Robert: German-born pastor, Rondebosch United Church, Cape Town; author of dissertation on Bonhoeffer—10

Steiner, Rudolf (1861–1925): Austrian philosopher and founder of the anthroposophical movement—10, 16

Steinert, Hans (1913–44): from Christianstadt-Bober; 1938–39, participated in the collective pastorate, Groß-Schlönwitz; 1944, killed in action—15

Steiniger, Hermann Otto Ewald: 1927, assistant pastor, Westphalia; 1928, ordination; 1929, German pastor and seamen's pastor, South Shields, New Castle, Sunderland, and Middlesborough; 1935, pastor, Melbourne, Australia—13

Steinmann, Theophil (1869–1950): Moravian theologian; 1919–40, lecturer in systematic theology, Herrnhut—12

Steinmeyer, Franz Ludwig (1811–1900): German preacher and practical theologian—14, 15

Steltzer, Theodor (1885–1967): German politician; 1920–33, regional representative, Rendsburg; 1936, secretary of the Michael brotherhood, Marburg and Hamburg; 1939, military service as a reserve officer; from 1940, in Norway; contact with the Kreisau circle and with the Norwegian opposition; January 1945, arrested; 1945, cofounder of the Christian Democratic Union (CDU) political party; 1946–47, first minister president of Schleswig-Holstein—16

Stephan, archbishop of Bulgaria: noted by Dietrich Bonhoeffer as an ecumenical contact—16

Stephan, Johannes: from 1931, pastor, Berlin-Spandau—12

Stephanie, Elisabeth: staff member at the Evangelisches Zentralarchiv, Berlin—14

Stephany, Werner: German diplomat; 1942, consul first class; head of the courier department in the Foreign Ministry—16

Stephen: biblical character—4, 14, 15

Stephen I: 254–57, bishop of Rome—14

Stern, Fritz: historian of Germany—8, 12

Stern, William (1871–1938): German-born philosopher and psychologist—1

Steudel, Johann Christoph Friedrich (1779–1837): Protestant theologian —11

Steuernagel, Carl (1869–1958): 1895, lecturer; 1907, professor of Old Testament, Halle; 1914–35, professor, Breslau; 1946–48 (retirement), professor, Greifswald; follower of Julius Wellhausen; editor of *Zeitschrift des Deutschen Palästina-Vereins*—9

Stewart, Edith Ann (1894–1973): author of biography of Francis Xavier that Bonhoeffer used for a talk, possibly at Abyssinian Baptist Church—10

Stewart, George Craig: 1930–40, Episcopal bishop of Chicago—15

Stickelberger-Eder, Margrit: Weimar-era author of novel on World War I —10

Stier, Alfred: cantor in Sangerhausen, author of a work on church choral music—14

Stier, Ewald (1864–1946): German Protestant theologian—10

Stifter, Adalbert (1805–68): Austrian writer and painter; born in Bohemia; at first a landscape painter, but in 1840 began publishing his writing, which articulated a simultaneous recognition and rejection of violence, a sensitive perception of nature; his novel to which Bonhoeffer often refers, *Witiko*, contains violent episodes but on the whole expresses a tone of serenity and dignity; the character of Witiko, who establishes himself

as a great landlord and nobleman, is always marked by absolute integrity, and his rule by justice and compassion—6, 7, 8, 14, 16

Stinger, Mrs. (1936): mentioned by Gerhard Vibrans in 1936 letter—14

Stinnes, Hugo (1870–1924): founder of the German Consortium for Mining and Shipping—9

Stock, Konrad: German theologian—9

Stockdale, George M.: pastor, St. James Methodist Church, Madison Avenue and 126th Street, New York City—10

Stockhausen, Jonas von: 1521–32, town mayor of Nordhausen—6

Stockmayer, Otto (1838–1917): German Protestant theologian; 1862–75, pastor in various free church congregations; 1874, after the "holiness movement" conference in Oxford, became a leading member of the holiness movement—11

Stoecker, Adolf (1835–1909): German pastor and conservative politician, known for his anti-Jewish polemics; 1874–89, court and cathedral preacher, Berlin; founder of the Christian Social Workers Party; 1879–98, member of the Prussian parliament; 1881–93, member of the national parliament—6, 11, 12, 14

Stoevesandt, Hinrich: son of Karl Stoevesandt; Barth scholar; after 1971, director of the Karl-Barth-Archiv, Basel—4, 12, 16

Stoevesandt, Karl (1882–1977): German physician and Confessing Church member; chair of the Bremen Council of Brethren; close friend of Karl Barth's; refused to join Nazi physicians' organization and lost his position —11

Stoevesandt, Klara, Dr.: Barth scholar—11

Stöhr, Hermann (1898–1940): member of the International Fellowship of Reconciliation founded in 1914, which encouraged conscientious objectors to engage in practical service on behalf of peace; 1940, executed for refusing to serve in the German army—6, 10, 14, 16

Stoker, Hendrik Gerhardus: pupil of Max Scheler; developed an emotive theory of conscience—2

Stokmann, Gerritdina (Dita): wife of Werner Koch—15

Stoldt: June 19, 1940, mentioned by Dietrich Bonhoeffer during a visitation in Aulenbach near Insterburg (ordination); not otherwise identified—16

Stoll, Christian (1903–46): pastor and later high church official, Munich; from May 1936, member of the advisory council of the Evangelical Lutheran Church of Germany and of the Reich Council of Brethren—14

Stolzenburg, Arnold (1887–1966): from 1921, assistant to Reinhold Seeberg and lecturer in systematic theology, Berlin; from1927, untenured university professor; 1933–45, professor (successor to Arthur Titius) and

tenured dean; from 1933, high consistory official in the Evangelical High Church Council of Berlin—9, 10, 11, 12, 13

Storch, Martin: author of work on Barth—8

Storm, Theodor (1817–88): German poet and author of short stories; in his historical short stories, the dramatic intensification is often motivated by inexplicable extraneous occurrences rather than by a conflict with the characters themselves; he portrayed the delicacy of human relationships with humor and melancholy, often focusing on the human dependence on environment and heredity, and even grappling with the question of euthanasia in one of his later pieces—7, 8, 13

Storr, Gottlob Christian (1746–1805): Protestant theologian—11

Stott, Douglas W.: U.S. Germanist and translator—6, 8, 9, 10, 11, 12, 13, 14, 15, 16

Strang, Lord William (Colville): from 1939, state undersecretary in the British Foreign Office—16

Stranger (FP): character in drama, representative of Death—7

Strasser, Otto (1897–1974): National Socialist politician; 1933, emigrated after breaking with Hitler—12

Stratenwerth, Gerhard (1898–1988): 1926, personal colleague of Friedrich von Bodelschwingh in Bethel; August–November 1933, edited the Bethel confession; 1934, pastor, Dortmund; 1938, imprisoned; 1939–45, military service; 1946, helped establish the social office of the Westphalian Church; 1948–66, vice president of the Church Foreign Office of the Evangelical Church of Germany, Frankfurt am Main—12, 14

Strathmann, Hermann (1882–1966): 1918–48, professor of New Testament, Erlangen; 1919–20, 1946–50, member of the Bavarian parliament; 1920–32, member of the national parliament—2, 5, 14, 16

Straus, Erwin (1891–1975): Jewish physician, a colleague of Karl Bonhoeffer at the Charité hospital; Bonhoeffer tried unsuccessfully to keep him on staff—8

Straus, Leonore, née Schnurmann: born in Karlsruhe; sister (twelve years older) of Anneliese Schnurmann, whom she raised after the early death of her parents; wife of the Berlin physician Dr. Moritz Straus, with whom she emigrated to Brazil in 1939 and to the United States in 1941—16

Straus, Moritz: Berlin physician; husband of Leonore, née Schnurmann; 1939, forced to emigrate because of the National Socialist race laws—16

Strauß, David Friedrich (1808–74): German New Testament scholar; demonstrated the impact of Christian faith on the Gospel tradition; applied Hegelian dialectic to the interpretation of the Gospels—9

Strauß, Richard (1864–1949): German composer and conductor—7, 11, 16

Strecker: pastor (1937)—14

Strecker, Johannes (1885–1966): 1934, pastor, Wusterhausen/Neustettin; 1940, arrested, charged with subversion of the war effort—8

Strege, Martin: Confessing Church pastor, Pomerania—14, 15

Streicher, Julius (1895–1946): National Socialist politician; 1925–40, regional leader or *Gauleiter* of the National Socialist Party in Franconia; 1946, executed—6

Streitberger, J. or V.: 1933, member of the election committee of the German Reformed St. Paul's Church in London—12, 13

Stresemann, Gustav (1878–1929): German statesman; 1918, founded the German National People's Party; 1923, chancellor of Germany; 1923–29, minister of foreign affairs; 1926, shared Nobel Peace Prize with Aristide Briand—9, 10

Strigel, Victorinus (1524–69): Reformation theologian; 1563, professor, Leipzig; 1567, Heidelberg; wrote extensively on philosophical and historical as well as on theological subjects—2

Strindberg, August (1849–1912): Swedish author—11

Strobel, Fr.: member of the congregational council, German Reformed St. Paul's Church in London—13

Strohm, Christoph: German theologian and Bonhoeffer scholar; professor of church history; coeditor, *DBW* 11—4, 6, 8, 11, 12, 14, 15, 16

Strohm, Theodor: studied theology and economics at Erlangen, Göttingen, Frankfurt am Main, and Berlin; 1957, first theological examination; 1961, doctorate in sociology; thereafter director of studies at the Protestant institute in Villigst and academic assistant at the Institute for Christian Social Sciences in Münster; 1967, doctorate; 1968, postdoctoral lecturing qualification and admission as lecturer in theology, University of Münster; 1969–70, professor of theology, Heidelberg; 1970–77, professor and director, Institute of Religious Social Ethics, Berlin seminary; 1977–82, professor and director of the Institute of Social Ethics, University of Zürich; since 1982, professor of practical theology and social ethics, and since 1986, director of the Diakoniewissenschaftliche Institut, both at the University of Heidelberg; since 1980, president of the committee of social order of the EKD; publications on theology and politics, peace, and church social services—16

Strong, Josiah (1847–1916): U.S. Protestant clergyman; one of the founders of the social gospel movement—15

Strong, Tracy (1915–2013): U.S. ecumenist; secretary general of the World Alliance of the YMCA; contacts to Adam von Trott—16

Strub, Werner: provided editorial information for *DBWE* 6—6

Strünck, Theodor (1885–1945): lawyer; 1937, military service; captain in the Military Intelligence Office; part of the resistance circle around General Oster; August 1, 1944, arrested; April 9, 1945, executed in Flossenbürg —16

Strunk, Reiner: German theologian—4

Struwe, Erna: housemother in Finkenwalde, Groß-Schlönwitz, and Sigurdshof—14, 15

Stuiber, Alfred: German patrologist—12

Stumm, Karl Ferdinand (1836–1901): from 1888, Baron von Stumm-Halberg; entrepreneur and politician, founder of important companies in the steel industry—9

Stupperich, Robert (1904–2003): studied theology with Bonhoeffer, Tübingen; 1932, licentiate in theology, Berlin; 1942, lecturer in eastern European history, Berlin; 1946–72, professor of church history, Münster; editor of the critical edition of Melanchthon's works—1, 9, 10, 12

Sturm, Julius (pseudonym for J. Stern) (1816–96): theologian and author; mainly religious poetry, also patriotic poetry—8, 10

Sturm, Marcel (1905–50): 1929–39, pastor, Hüningen, Alsace; 1934, French participant at the Fanø youth conference; 1945, Reformed military bishop with the French occupation forces in Germany—13

Suárez, Francisco de (1548–1617): Spanish Jesuit theologian and philosopher —1, 2, 14

Sudermann, Daniel (1550–ca. 1631): private tutor in various aristocratic families; from 1585, tutor of the students living in the "Brethren House" in Strasbourg; follower of Kaspar Schwenckfeld and of the earlier mystics, whose writings he edited and published—14

Suderow, Pastor: Berlin pastor—11

Suetonius (Gaius Suetonius Tranquillas) (ca. 69–ca. 140 C.E.): Roman biographer and historian—9

Süleyman Ibrahim II (1642–91): Ottoman emperor; son of Ibrahim I; as emperor fought the Austrians over Bulgaria, Serbia, and Transylvania; 1691, died in battle—9

Sulze, Emil (1832–1914): Lutheran pastor, author of works on parish life and structure—14

Sundar Singh: *see* Singh, "Sadhu" Sundar

Süselbeck, Heiner: German pastor and theologian—8

Suso, Henry (1295–1366): German Dominican mystic—12

Süßbach, Willy: "non-Aryan" Confessing Church pastor attacked by SA thugs in Berlin-Brandenburg; later emigrated to Ceylon (Sri Lanka)—4, 14

Süßmilch, Johann Peter (1707–67)—1

Sutz, Dora, née Vogt: wife of the Swiss pastor Erwin Sutz—11, 16

Sutz, Erwin (1906–87): Swiss Reformed pastor and theologian; 1925–30, studied under Emil Brunner (Zürich) and Karl Barth (Zürich); 1928–29, student, Münster, where Barth taught; 1930–31, fellowship at Union Theological Seminary, New York, where he became Bonhoeffer's friend; after 1933, pastor in Wiesendangen, Switzerland; 1940, Rapperswil; 1946, Zürich; postwar, director for eighteen years of the Zürich theological working group—2, 3, 4, 5, 6, 8, 10, 11, 12, 13, 14, 15, 16, 17

Svendsen: *see* Bonnevie-Svendsen, Conrad

Svetaketu: in the Upanishads, son of sage Uddalaka—11

Swithie: at Union Seminary; not otherwise identified—10

Sydow, Reinhold von (1851–1943): German lawyer and politician—9

Sylten, Werner (1893–1942): pastor, Thuringia; dismissed for political reasons as the head of a welfare home supported by the Thuringian church; from 1938, worked in the Berlin "Grüber office," ultimately as its deputy head; February 27, 1941, arrested; May 1941, taken to Dachau; September 26, 1942, moved to Schloß Harthein institution, where he was murdered —16

Symeon: variant reading of Simeon (Luke 2:25); *see* Simeon—1

Tacitus, Publius Cornelius (ca. 55–ca. 117 C.E.): Roman orator, politician, and historian—1, 4, 9

Tafel, Karoline Friederike, née Oswald (1805–89): Bonhoeffer's great-grandmother—13

Tafel, Leonhard (1800–1880): great-great-uncle of Dietrich Bonhoeffer; one of the four Württemberg Tafel brothers; a philologist and preceptor at the Latin school in Schorndorf; emigrated to the United States where he was pastor of the Swedenborgian "New Church"—7

Tagore, Rabindranath (1861–1941): Indian poet, philosopher, and painter; 1913, Nobel Prize in Literature; founded the religious school Shantiniketan near Calcutta—13, 16

Tait, Mr.: spoke at Gland ecumenical conference; not identified—11

Tal, Uriel: professor of contemporary Jewish history at Tel Aviv University, author of numerous works on National Socialism and anti-Semitism—11

Talbot, Edward Keble (1877–1949): British Anglican priest; 1910, member of the Community of the Resurrection, Mirfield, of which he was the superior when Bonhoeffer visited there in 1935—13, 17 (for vol. 13)

Talleyrand, Charles Maurice Duke of Talleyrand-Périgord (1754–1838): French diplomat—8

Tappert, Theodore G. (1904–73): U.S. church historian; edited and translated *The Book of Concord*—5

Tarde, Jean-Gabriel de (1843–1904): French sociologist and criminologist —1

Tardieu, André (1876–1945): premier of France from November 3, 1929–February 17, 1930, March 2–December 4, 1930, and February 20–May 10, 1932—11

Tarter, Brent: historian and archivist, University of Virginia—6

Tasso, Torquato (1544–95): Italian poet; subject of a play by Goethe—10, 14

Tatian (120–180 C.E.): Christian writer and apologist; studied under Justin Martyr; later adopted the heretical doctrines of the Encratites—1, 9

Taul, Jaak (1905–2007): prominent Lutheran Estonian pastor; chair of the Lutheran Council of Great Britain and Dean of Britain's Estonian congregations; elected Estonian ecumenical youth secretary, 1933—12

Tauler, Johannes (1300–1361): German mystic; Dominican—15

Tausch, Friedrich (1892–1958): 1929–47, pastor, Berlin-Tempelhof; November 1933, district leader of the Berlin German Christians; 1936, leading figure in the Alliance for German Christianity (Bund für Deutsches Christentum)—13

Tawney, Richard Henry (1880–1962): British economist—12

Teitel, Ruti G.: Ernst C. Stiefel Professor of Comparative Law at New York Law School and Visiting Professor at the London School of Economics, Global Governance; authority on international human rights, transitional justice, and comparative constitutional law—11

Temple, William (1881–1944): British church leader and ecumenist; 1921, bishop of Manchester; 1929, archbishop of York; 1937, chair of the World Church Conference for Faith and Order in Edinburgh; 1942, archbishop of Canterbury; as archbishop, he was outspoken against the Nazi genocide of the Jews; opposed George Bell's approach to postwar Germany —12, 15, 16

Teneromo: journalist who was well acquainted with Leo Tolstoy—9

Tentler, Thomas N.: church historian of the Reformation—5

Terboven, Josef (1898–1945): bank official and National Socialist politician; 1933, regional Nazi party leader [*Gauleiter*] in Essen; 1935, president of the Rhine province; 1939, Reich defense commissar of Military District VI (Münster); 1940, Reich commissar for Norway; 1945, presumably committed suicide—16, 17

Teresa of Ávila, Saint (1515–1582): Spanish mystic and writer; major figure in the Catholic Reformation—10

Tersteegen, Gerhard (1697–1769): Protestant hymnist, pietist, and poet; of humble origin, became an itinerant preacher in the lower Rhine district; wrote more than a hundred hymns, some of which have remained in regular use—4, 8, 10, 14, 15

Tertullian (Quintus Septimius Florens Tertullianus) (ca. 160–ca. 230 C.E.): African theologian from Carthage; a father of the Latin church; author of works defending Christianity, polemical treatises, and treatises on morals and discipline—1, 4, 6, 7, 8, 9, 11, 12, 14, 16

Teschendorff (family): congregation members in Barcelona—10

Tessenow, Heinrich (1876–1950): 1920, professor of architecture at the Technical College, Berlin-Charlottenburg—11

Tetsch, August (1909–45): summer 1936, participated in the third Finkenwalde session; pastor; June 1940, conscripted into the military; killed in action—8, 14

Thaddaeus (disciple): biblical character—4

Thadden-Trieglaff, Reinold von (1891–76): estate owner in Trieglaff and Gruchow, Pomerania; until 1920, in local politics; 1929, vice president of the Pomeranian Provincial Synod and member of the Old Prussian General Synod; until 1933, Prussian member of parliament (representing the German National People's Party); 1934, leading member of the Confessing Church, head of the Pomeranian Confessing Synod and of the Pomeranian and Reich Councils of Brethren; with Paul Humburg, founder of the German "evangelical weeks" during the Church Struggle, which were held in 1935, 1936, and 1937; 1941, military service as an officer on the staff of General von Falkenhausen in Brussels; 1942–44, commandant of Löwen (Belgian); 1949, founder of the German Protestant Kirchentag and until 1964 its president—14, 15, 16

Thales of Miletus (ca. 624–546 B.C.E.): early Greek philosopher, mathematician, astronomer, and politician—2, 9

Thälmann, Ernst (1886–1944): German communist leader—11

Thamer, Hans-Ulrich: historian; author of works on the Nazi era—15

Thecla: martyr and saint—7

Theile, Johannes (1892–1964): 1927, pastor, Staaken-Dorf near Berlin—12

Theodore the Tanner: second-century Christian theologian, previously Jewish—15

Theophilus (of Antioch): early Christian writer—3

Theseus: in Greek mythology, founder and King of Athens—17 (for vol. 9)

Thiel, Hermann: 1935, participated in the first Zingst/Finkenwalde session—14

Thiel, Wulf: 1934, academic inspector at the preachers' seminary, Naumburg am Queis; 1936, member of the second Provisional Church Administration of the Confessing Church; 1937, together with Oskar Hammelsbeck, head of the catechetical institute, Berlin; 1949–54, instructor in practical theology at the seminary in Berlin; 1956, superintendent—12, 14

Thielicke, Helmut (1908–86): German Protestant theologian, educator, and writer; studied theology and philosophy in Greifswald, Marburg, Erlangen, and Bonn; 1936, lecturer in systematic theology, Erlangen; professor, Heidelberg; 1940, dismissed because of his membership in the Confessing Church; 1941, pastor, Ravensburg; temporary prohibition against public speaking and publication; 1942–45, head of the theological office of the Württemberg church in Stuttgart, where he also came into contact with the resistance group around Carl Goerdeler; 1945, professor of systematic theology, Tübingen; 1951, rector, Tübingen; 1954, professor, Hamburg; 1960, rector—8, 16

Thiemann, Ronald (1946–2012): U.S. professor of theology and of religion and society, Harvard—6

Thierfelder, Jörg: professor of pedagogy, author of numerous works on the German Church Struggle—15, 16

Thieß, Frank (1890–1977): author of psychological and, later, historical novels, also of political and literary essays—8, 14

Thilo, Valentin (1607–62): German hymnist and professor of rhetoric, Königsberg—6, 10, 14

Thimme, Hans (1909–2006): 1935–47, pastor, Spenge; 1947–57, supervisor of the preachers' seminary in Kupferhammer; from 1957, various church leadership positions; 1969–77, president of the Evangelical Church of Westphalia—14

Thimme, Heinrich: student in the Marienburg Confessing congregation, later in Tilsit; June 16, 1940, mentioned by Dietrich Bonhoeffer during a stay in Tilsit; killed in action on the eastern front—16

Thimme, Ludwig: 1905, pastor, Osterwald; leader of the communal movement [*Gemeinschaftsbewegung*] in Hannover—1, 11

Tholuck, Friedrich August Gottreu (1799–1877): 1821, postdoctoral lecturing qualification in theology, Berlin, though with difficulties, especially from Schleiermacher; 1826, student chaplain, Halle—4, 14

Thom, Karl (1900–1935): 1925, pastor, Pustamin, district of Rügenwalde; June 1933, representative of state commissar Jäger in the church province of Pomerania; assistant consistory adviser, Stettin; after the church elections, president of the provincial synod; October, named bishop of Cammin (not installed); cultural administrator of the NSDAP in eastern Pomerania; regional head of the Pomeranian German Christians—13

Thoma, Hans (1839–1924): painter and graphic artist—8

Thomas: biblical character—4, 12, 15, 16

Thomas, George F. (1899–1977): Christian ethicist and philosopher; first professor of religious thought, Princeton Theological Seminary—10

Thomas, Norman Mattoon (1884–1968): U.S. theologian; 1928, socialist presidential candidate—10

Thomas à Kempis (of Kempen) (ca. 1379–1471): Dutch mystic and ascetic writer; 1399, became Augustinian; 1413, ordained; associated with the *devotio moderna*; author of *Imitatio Christi*—3, 4, 5, 8, 11, 15

Thomas Aquinas (ca. 1225–74): Italian philosopher and Dominican theologian; from 1252, taught in Paris and elsewhere; from 1262, head of the new course of general studies in Naples; 1322, canonized; 1567, declared a Doctor of the Catholic Church; his use of Aristotelian categories had a formative influence on Roman Catholic theology—1, 2, 3, 5, 6, 8, 9, 11, 12, 14, 16

Thomasius, Christian (1655–1728): German lawyer, legal scholar, and philosopher—11, 12

Thomasius, Gottfried (1802–75): Lutheran theologian; member of the Erlangen school—15

Thomson, Samuel Harrison (1813–82): Methodist and creationist; professor of mathematics and mechanical philosophy, Hanover College—11

Thomte, Reidar: editor of Kierkegaard—2, 6

Thor: Germanic deity—12

Thorwaldsen, Bertel (1770–1844): Danish sculptor; most famous religious work is the group of *Christ and His Apostles* (1821–42)—1

Thumm, Hermann: teacher and Bonhoeffer's boardinghouse neighbor in Barcelona—10

Thurman, Wallace (1902–34): African American novelist of the Harlem Renaissance—10

Thurmann, Horst (1911–99): summer 1937, participated in the third Finkenwalde session; member of the House of Brethren; 1937, pastor, Cologne; 1940, arrested; 1941, incarcerated in Dachau—8, 14, 16, 17

Thurneysen, Eduard (1888–1977): Swiss Reformed theologian; 1911–13, secretary of the YMCA, Zürich; 1913–20, pastor, Leutwil and Dürrenäsch (Kanton Aargau); 1920–27, in Bruggen near St. Gallen; 1927, at the Basel cathedral; 1929, lecturer; 1941, professor of practical theology, Basel; since 1913, friend of Karl Barth; cofounder of dialectical theology; coeditor of *Zwischen den Zeiten*, then of *Theologische Existenz heute*—1, 2, 9, 11, 12, 13, 14, 16

Thyagaraju, A. F.: Indian national living in London; participated in the Fanø youth conference—13

Thyestes: in Greek mythology, son of Pelops and Hippodamia—17 (for vol. 9)

Tiberius Claudius Nero Caesar Augustus (42 B.C.E.–37 C.E.): 14–37, second Roman emperor—6

Tielsch, Dr.: presumably the family doctor of the Kleist-Retzow family in Kieckow; not otherwise identified—16

Tietz, Christiane: German professor of theology; author of numerous works on Bonhoeffer; president, International Bonhoeffer Society, German section—10, 12

Tiling, Magdalene von (1877–1974): 1917–39, chair of the Association for Protestant Religious Instruction and Education; 1921–30, member of the Prussian parliament; 1923, chair of the Alliance of Protestant Women's Associations of Germany; 1933, dismissed; 1930–33, member of the national parliament, represented the German National People's Party—14

Tilitzki, Christian: author of work on legal philosophy during Weimar era—16

Tillich, Ernst (1910–85): 1932–33, among the circle of students around Bonhoeffer in Berlin; 1933, vicar under Jacobi and Niemöller; 1934, assistant for systematic theology, Berlin; participated in the Fanø youth conference; later illegal journalistic activity; 1936–39, arrest and imprisonment in Sachsenhausen for leaking the Provisional Church Administration memorandum to Hitler to the foreign press; emigration to Czechoslovakia; after 1945, helped establish public welfare relief; 1949–51, lecturer and departmental head for philosophy, German Institute for Politics, Berlin; also commentator for the Radio in the American Sector (RIAS) in Berlin; 1959, entrepreneurial adviser—12, 13, 14

Tillich, Paul (1886–1965): during World War I, military chaplain; 1916, lecturer, Halle; with Günther Dehn and others, founded the circle of religious socialists; 1919, lecturer in systematic theology, Berlin; 1924, professor of systematic theology and philosophy, Marburg, 1925, Dresden and Leipzig, 1929, Frankfurt am Main; 1933, left Nazi Germany because of his dismissal for political reasons (religious socialist); 1933–37, guest lecturer, and 1937–55, professor at Union Theological Seminary, New York; 1955–62, at Harvard; 1962–65, in Chicago; after World War II, widely influential in the United States—1, 2, 6, 8, 9, 10, 11, 12, 13, 14, 15

Tillmann, Fritz (1874–1953): German theologian, advocated basing moral theology on a biblical foundation; from 1913, professor, Bonn—6

Tilp, Walter: 1942, major, *Abwehr* troop 320 with the Armed Forces High Command 10 in Italy, where he was Eberhard Bethge's superior officer; from September 1944, lieutenant colonel—8

Timmermanns, Felix (1886–1947): Flemish writer known primarily for his idyllic regional novels; also wrote short stories, plays, travel tales, autobiographical works, and romanticized biographies—14, 15

Timothy: biblical character—4, 5, 14, 15

Tindal, Matthew (1657–1733): English deist; influential in the Enlightenment —11

Titian (Tiziano Vecelli) (1477–1576): Italian painter; chief master of the Venetian school—9

Titius, Arthur (1864–1936): 1891, private lecturer, Berlin; 1895, professor of systematic theology, Kiel; 1906, Göttingen; 1921–33, Berlin—1, 3, 10, 11, 12, 13, 14

Titus: biblical character—15

Todt, Fritz (1891–1942): engineer; leading Nazi who oversaw the Todt Organization, which used slave labor for major engineering projects—14

Tödt, Heinz Eduard (1918–91): after school graduation, from 1937–39, military service; 1939–45, action at the front; 1945–50, Soviet prisoner of war; 1951–57, studied theology in Bethel, Basel, Göttingen, and Heidelberg, earning doctorate in theology; 1947–61, theological director of Protestant institute in Villigst near Schwerte an der Ruhr; after 1963, professor of systematic theology, ethics, and social ethics, University of Heidelberg; 1983, emeritus, then directed research seminar on contemporary church history; 1978–85, chair of the International Bonhoeffer Society, West German section; from 1985 until his death, chair of the editorial board of the *DBW*—2, 4, 6, 7, 8, 10, 11, 12, 14, 15, 17

Tödt, Ilse (b. 1930): studied anthropology and indigenous religions at the Technical University, Hannover, at the Universities of Göttingen, Hamburg, and Frankfurt, and at Ohio State University; 1957, doctorate, Göttingen; 1957, married Heinz Eduard Tödt; since 1961 at the Protestant Research Institute (FEST) in Heidelberg, concentrating on editing and translating, above all many volumes of the *DBW*; since 1992, member of the *DBW* editorial board; 1995, honorary doctorate in theology, University of Basel—2, 3, 4, 5, 6, 7, 8, 9, 10, 12, 14, 15, 16, 17

Toland, John (1670–1722): British writer, philosopher of religion during the Enlightenment; main work: *Christianity Not Mysterious* (1696); one of the most influential representatives of deism—8

Toller, Ernst (1893–1939): German author and dramatist of Jewish descent; member of the Independent Social Democratic Party of Germany (USPD); 1918, participated in the Bavarian communist revolt in Munich; 1919–24, in prison, where he wrote revolutionary expressionist plays that gained much attention during the 1920s; 1933, deprived of his citizenship by the National Socialist regime because of his Jewish ancestry, went into exile; 1939, committed suicide in a New York hotel—6, 7, 10

Tolstoy, Count Leo Nikolayevich (1828–1910): Russian novelist, aesthetic philosopher, moralist, and Christian mystic—1, 4, 9, 10, 11, 13, 15

Tomkins, Oliver (1908–92): British Anglican ecumenical leader and secretary of Faith and Order—15

Tomlin, James William Sackett (1871–1959): 1899–1911, missionary, Australia; 1928, canon, Salisbury; 1929, warden, St. Augustine's College, Canterbury—13

Tonn, Heinz (1911–56): from Stettin; 1939, participated in the collective pastorate, Sigurdshof; 1941, assistant pastor, Woltin, district of Greifenberg, Pomerania; 1953, pastor, Dortmund; 1954, Handorf-Hornheide near Münster—15

Tönnies, Ferdinand (1855–1936): 1908–33, professor of sociology and philosophy, Kiel—1, 6, 10, 11, 14

Toomer, Jean (1894–1967): leading writer in the Harlem Renaissance and author of *Cane*—10

Torczyner, Harry (Naphthali Herz Tur-Sinai) (1886–1973): Israeli scholar of Semitics, biblical scholar, and translator—9

Torm, Frederik (1870–1953): 1903, professor of New Testament, Copenhagen; until 1939, participated in conferences of the Luther Academy in Sondershausen; deputy chair of the conservative Kirkeligt Landsforbund; chair of the Danish Israel Mission; provided aid to Jewish refugees from National Socialism—14

Torquemada, Juan de (1388–1468): Spanish theologian and Dominican; 1433, papal theologian at the Council of Basel; contributed considerably to ecclesiastical papal policy—11

Torvik, Lois: editor, Fortress Press—2

Toscanini, Arturo (1867–1957): Italian musical conductor; appointments in Milan, New York, Bayreuth, Salzburg; known for his dynamic interpretations of Beethoven, Verdi, and Wagner—10

Toureille, Pierre C. (1900–1976): French Reformed pastor, theologian, and ecumenist; 1931–39, with Bonhoeffer, one of the youth secretaries of the World Alliance for Promoting International Friendship through the Churches (for Romance Europe, Poland, and Czechoslovakia); participated in numerous ecumenical conferences, including the World Alliance conference in Sofia in 1933; 1938–39, international secretary of the World Alliance; 1940, appointed by Marc Boegner to be head of pastoral ministry to Protestant foreign refugees in France and North Africa; member of the resistance in France and in Czechoslovakia; 1945, foreign pastor, Breslau; 1947, doctorate, Breslau, pastor and lecturer, United States; 1955, missionary in the Belgian Congo; 1961, teacher, France; 1966–74, European secretary of the Leprosy Mission in Morges (Switzerland)—11, 12, 13, 16

Tourneur, Maurice: French film director—15

Tow, Maxwell: retired United Methodist minister and author of book on Franz Hildebrandt—10

Toynbee, Arnold Joseph (1886–1975): British historian and historical philosopher; professor, London University; director of studies, Royal Institute of International Affairs (Chatham House); 1939, director of the Foreign Research and Press Service; 1943, responsible for merging the latter with the Political Intelligence Department (PID) in the form of the Foreign Office Research Department (FORD); also a member of the English Peace Aims Groups founded by William Paton in 1940—16

Trakl, Georg (1887–1914): Austrian expressionist poet—10

Traub, Gottfried (1869–1956): conservative nationalist Protestant theologian and politician, follower of Erich Ludendorff—10

Traub, Hellmut (1904–94): student and friend of Karl Barth; Confessing Church pastor, Fürstenwalde and Potsdam; summer 1939, represented Bonhoeffer in the collective pastorate in Sigurdshof while Bonhoeffer was in the United States; Bonhoeffer and Bethge also refer to him as "Potsdam(er)"; after 1945, pastor in Glinde, Hamburg-Volksdorf, and Stuttgart—15

Trebesius, Hulda (1907–80): from Halle; 1934, member of the Brotherhood of Assistant Pastors and Vicars of the Province of Saxony, Confessing Church; 1936, ordination in the provincial Saxon Confessing Church; commissioned with church women's groups; 1940, compulsory national service labor in a factory; 1948, pastor, Uchtspringe; 1972, retired—14, 16

Treitschke, Heinrich von (1834–96): German historian, known for his nationalism, anti-Semitism, and glorification of war—16

Trentepohl, Friedrich (1909–2002): 1935–36, participated in the second Finkenwalde session; 1936–74, pastor—14, 15

Tresckow, Henning von (1901–44): nephew of Ruth von Kleist-Retzow; career military; 1941, major general in the staff of the Army Group Center; 1943, chief of staff of the Second Army; heavily involved in the military resistance movement; July 21, 1944, committed suicide after the failed assassination attempt against Hitler—16

Treviranus, Hans-Heinrich: confirmed by Bonhoeffer in London—13

Tribe, Reginald Herman: British clergyman; 1925–43, director of the Society of the Sacred Mission in Kelham, England—13

Trible, Phyllis: U.S. biblical scholar—3

Triepel, Heinrich (1868–1946): professor of constitutional and international law; teacher of Gerhard Leibholz—10

Trillhaas, Wolfgang: contributor to *Zwischen den Zeiten*; 1933, lecturer in practical theology, Erlangen; 1946, professor of practical theology, later of systematic theology, Göttingen—13, 14

Trilling, Wolfgang (1925–93): German Catholic theologian and New Testament scholar—6

Troeltsch, Ernst (1865–1923): German Protestant theologian, philosopher, and historian; 1892, professor, Bonn; 1894, professor of systematic theology, Heidelberg; 1915, professor of cultural, historical, social, and Christian religious philosophy, Berlin, succeeding Wilhelm Dilthey; 1919–21, state secretary in the Prussian Ministry of Culture—1, 3, 4, 6, 8, 9, 10, 11, 12, 14, 15, 16

Tromm, Bruno: from 1926, pastor, Berlin—12

Trophimus: biblical character—15

Trott zu Solz, Adam von (1909–44): German diplomat; 1931, completed law degree; 1931–33, Rhodes scholar in Oxford; 1933–36, magistrate posts, Kassel and Hamburg; active at an early date in the political resistance abroad; turned down political job at chemical corporation IG Farben; 1937–38, study year in China; 1939, legation officer in the information section of the Foreign Ministry; participant in the Kreisau circle; 1939–44, used position in Foreign Office to travel to the United States, France, Britain, Scandinavia, Switzerland, and Italy on behalf of the anti-Nazi conspiracy; July 25, 1944, arrested; August 15, 1944, executed—7, 8, 16, 17

Truchseß, Christoph Baron von: son of Dietrich and Hedwig von Truchseß —8

Truchseß, Dietrich (Ditze) Baron von (1900–1979): estate owner in Bundorf in Lower Franconia; during the war, stationed in Bamberg as captain in the reserves; August 1944, included in the investigations of the "July 20 special commission," since Count Stauffenberg had designated him to be a contact officer in the Military District Command XIII (Nuremberg); imprisoned in the Tegel military detention center—8, 16, 17

Truchseß, Hedwig Baroness von, née Rotenhan: married to Dietrich Baron von Truchseß—8, 16, 17

Trudinger, Peter: senior lecturer in biblical studies, Flinders University, Australia—14

Tryon, Harold Harrison (1877–1963): 1925, professor of church history, Union Theological Seminary, New York—10, 15

Tschuschner: unidentified member of Harnack's seminar—9

Tübben, Ludwig: 1910–35, professor at the Technical College, Berlin; 1931–June 30, 1933, rector, and July 1935, senate member there—12

Tuchel, Johannes: German historian; research on concentration camps, Nazi era—16
Tucker, A. R.: Anglican bishop of Uganda—16
Tucker, Gene M.: U.S. biblical scholar—3
Tur-Sinai, N. H.: *see* Torczyner, Harry
Turne, Willi: from 1931, pastor, Berlin-Moabit—12
Turner, William (1775–1851): British landscape painter—8
Turretin, Francis (1623–87): Reformed theologian—3
Twardowski, Fritz von (1890–1970): 1922, in the Foreign Ministry; 1928–35, embassy officer in Moscow; 1935–43, Foreign Ministry in Berlin (also head of the Cultural Section); 1943–45, general consul of Istanbul; 1946, in the Hamburg section of the Central Office of Relief Work of the Evangelical Church of Germany; 1950, its head; 1952–56, ambassador in Mexico—14
Tweedie-Stodart: participant at the Fanø conference—13
Tychicus: biblical character—15
Tyconius (d. ca. 400): Donatist theologian—1
Tyldesley, Michael: author of study on twentieth-century communal movements—11, 14
Tyrannus: biblical character—14
Tyrrell, George (1861–1909): Irish Jesuit scholar and modernist theologian; 1906, expelled from the Catholic Church—15

Uckeley, Alfred (1874–1955): Protestant theologian and pastor; 1902, licentiate in theology; 1905, postdoctoral lecturing qualification and private lecturer, Greifswald; 1910, professor of practical theology and church history, Königsberg; 1934, Marburg, where he was transferred as a National Socialist supporter to counter opposition to Nazism among the university's faculty—10
Uddalaka (Aruni): sage in the Upanishads—11
Uhl, Licentiate (Budapest): reviewed Bonhoeffer's book *Creation and Fall*—13
Uhl, Willo: German theologian—2
Uhland, Ludwig (1787–1862): ballad poet; one of the leading members of the Swabian school of the Romantic movement—8
Uhlhorn, Gerhard (1826–1901): Protestant theologian; high consistory official; 1878, abbot of Loccum—8
Ulbricht, Mr.: (not identified, in Cromwell letter)—17 (for vol. 13)
Ulpian(us), Domitius (ca. 170–228): Roman lawyer; 228, murdered—6, 15
Ulrich (FP): character in the drama and the novel—7

Uncle Rudi: *see* Goltz, Rüdiger
Ungnad, Arthur: German scholar of ancient languages—10
Urbain, August: from 1909, pastor, Berlin—12
Uriah: biblical character—14
Utsugi, Tamotsu: Japanese Presbyterian pastor; 1930, student at Union Theological Seminary, New York; 1932, pastor in Nakamura Church (northern Japan); 1935, Reien Church, Tokyo; 1945, superintendent there; 1966, assistant professor at the Teikyo College there—12
Ussher, James: seventeenth-century Irish archbishop—3
Uzzah: biblical character—14

Vahlen, Theodor (1869–1945): from 1933, minister director and office head of the science section in the Reich and Prussian Ministry for Science, Training, and Public Education; from 1935, professor, Berlin—14
Vahlke, Mrs.: (Lagendorf) not otherwise identified—15
Vaihinger, Hans (1852–1933): German philosopher; from 1884, professor, Halle; Kant scholar and ethicist; 1911, main work, *Die Philosophie des Als Ob* (The philosophy of the "as if")—11
Valdes, Petrus (Petrus Waldus) (1140–ca. 1215): founder of the Waldensian movement—10
Valentin, Wolfgang: confirmed by Bonhoeffer in London—13
Valentin(us) (second century): Egyptian gnostic theologian and founder of the sect of Valentinians; arguably the most influential gnostic—12
Van Buren, Paul M. (1924–98): U.S. theologian; influenced by Bonhoeffer; late work focused on Jewish-Christian relations—6
Vandenhoeck: fellow student of Hans Christoph von Hase—10
Van Dusen, Henry Pitney (1897–1975): U.S. theologian and ecumenist; 1928, professor of systematic theology, Union Theological Seminary, New York; 1945, president there; U.S. delegate at ecumenical conferences —10, 15, 16
Van Dyck, Anthony (1599–1641): Flemish painter—15
Vansittart, Sir Robert Gilbert (1881–1957): British politician; 1930–41, state undersecretary in the British Foreign Office—16
Vasconcellos, Traute de, née von Hase: daughter of Hans Karl Paul Stanislaus von Hase—9
Vaughn, Teri: staff, Hartford Seminary; assisted with *DBWE* 1—1
Veckenstedt, Eberhard (1909–45): from Berlin-Lichterfelde; 1937, participated in the fifth Finkenwalde session; pastor, Berlin-Dahlem; 1942, Berlin-Lichterfelde; November 1945, died as a prisoner of war —15
Vedder, Wilhelm: Confessing Church pastor, Pomerania—14, 15

Veerkamp, Dieter: German scholar of ethnology, German philology, and art history—6

Vehse, Julius (1867–1940): from 1911, pastor, Berlin—12

Velásquez, Diego Rodríguez de Silva y (1599–1660): Spanish baroque painter—8, 9

Velde, Theodor Hendrik van de: Dutch physician and writer—16

Venske, Herbert: Pomeranian Confessing Church pastor; from 1934, in Muttrin, district of Belgard—16

Verdi, Giuseppe (1813–1901): Italian opera composer—10

Verges, Maria: member of the Finkenwalde Confessing congregation; lived in Altdamm, Fürstenstrasse 7, where Dietrich Bonhoeffer stored his library and manuscripts after the preachers' seminary was closed down —16

Very, Francis G.: author of work on Corpus Christi processions—10

Vibrans, Elisabeth: *see* Bethge-Vibrans, Elisabeth

Vibrans, Gerhard (1907–42): from Annarode/Harz; October 28, 1934, one of the signers of the Wittenberg preachers' seminary protest letter; as a result, banned (with his cousin Eberhard Bethge) from the Wittenberg preachers' seminary on the order of the Reich bishop; vicar under his father, Karl Vibrans, in Annarode, Harz; summer 1935, participated in the first Zingst/Finkenwalde session; 1936, pastor, Rosian; 1940, military service in France; 1941, married Elisabeth Trebesius; February 3, 1942, killed in action on the eastern front—4, 8, 14, 15, 16, 17

Vibrans, Karl (1870–1959): husband of Sophie, née Bethge; father of Gerhard Vibrans; 1919–32, pastor, Redekin and Wegeleben an der Bode near Halberstadt; 1932, Annarode (Eastern Harz); 1939, Ballenstedt—16

Vibrans, Karl-Friedrich: brother of Gerhard Vibrans; physician in Berlin —15

Vick, Valerie: editorial assistant, Hartford Seminary—7

Victoria Eugénie von Battenberg (1887–1969): 1906–31, queen of Spain—10

Vierkandt, Alfred Ferdinand (1867–1953): German sociologist; 1921–53, professor in Berlin; known for creating philosophical foundations for sociology—1

Vietinghoff, General Heinrich von: from 1943, commander of the German Tenth Army in Italy—8

Viëtor, Karl (1892–1951): literary historian—10

Vilmar, August Friedrich Christian (1800–1868): German theologian, literary historian, regional parliamentary representative; from 1855, professor, Marburg; pursued a specifically Hessian Lutheranism against Prussian control of Hesse—1, 4, 6, 7, 8, 14, 15, 16

Vilmar, Wilhelm (1870–1942): from 1916, director of the Friedrich Werder Gymnasium, Berlin-Grunewald; later Bonhoeffer's German teacher; a frequent guest of the historian Hans Delbrück—9

Viol, Alfred (1912–42): young Confessing Church theologian; 1938–39, participated in the collective pastorate in Köslin; 1942, killed in action as a lieutenant on the eastern front—16

Violet, Bruno (1871–1945): from 1917, pastor, Berlin—12

Visarion, Monsignor: September 1933, Albanian participant in the Sofia conference of the World Alliance for Promoting International Friendship through the Churches—12

Vischer, Eberhard (1865–1946): father of Wilhelm Vischer; New Testament scholar, Basel—9, 14

Vischer, Friedrich Theodor von (1807–87): German author, literary historian, and philosopher; 1837, professor, Tübingen; 1855, Zürich; 1866, Tübingen—6

Vischer, Wilhelm (1895–1988): Swiss Reformed theologian; 1928–34, lecturer in Old Testament at the theological college, Bethel; came into conflict with National Socialism, specifically on the "Jewish question"; 1933, worked on the Bethel confession; 1934, dismissed for political reasons, returned to Switzerland; 1934–37, pastor, Lugano and Basel; 1936, postdoctoral lecturing qualification, Basel; 1936–46, lecturer, Basel; 1947–65, professor of Hebrew and Old Testament, Montpellier—3, 6, 12, 14, 16

Visser 't Hooft, Willem Adolf (1900–1985): Dutch Reformed theologian; 1924, theological doctorate; 1924, secretary of the World Alliance of the YMCA; 1925, participated in World Conference for Life and Work in Stockholm; 1931, secretary in the World Christian Student Federation; 1933, its general secretary, 1936, its president; from 1937, helped establish the World Council of Churches; 1937, participated in the World Conference of Churches in Oxford, which he organized together with Oldham, and in Edinburgh; 1938, general secretary of the nascent World Council of Churches; 1939, chair of the first World Conference of Christian Youth in Amsterdam; 1948–66, general secretary of the World Council of Churches; 1968, its honorary president—6, 8, 11, 12, 14, 15, 16, 17

Vits, Ernst (1868–1939): 1895, pastor; 1925–34, general superintendent of Neumark and Niederlausitz; head of the evangelical consistory of Mark Brandenburg; represented the consistory at Bonhoeffer's theological examinations; November 15, 1931, ordained Bonhoeffer; 1934, retired—9, 10, 11, 12

Vivaldi, Antonio (1680–1743): Italian violinist and composer—8

Vives, Juan Luis (1492–1540): Spanish humanist—8

Voelz, Helmut (1910–78): summer 1935, participated in the first Zingst/Finkenwalde session; 1939, pastor, Kietzig/Stargard; 1937–74, pastor—8, 14

Voes, Hendrik: one of Luther's fellow Augustinians (Antwerp); burned to death at the stake for his Protestant inclinations—14

Vogel, Heinrich Rudolf Gottfried (1902–89): German theologian and pastor, active in the Confessing Church; 1928, pastor and prison chaplain, Oderberg/Mark; 1932, pastor, Dobrikow; 1934–36, participated in the confessional synods; 1933, joined Pastors' Emergency League; 1935, private lecturer and 1941–44, director of the illegal Confessing Church seminary, Berlin; 1941, convicted and imprisoned after the trial of the examination board of the Old Prussian Union Council of Brethren; 1941, prohibition against publishing; 1946–72, professor of systematic theology, Berlin and Humboldt University—6, 8, 12, 13, 14, 15, 16

Vogel, Traugott: German theologian—4, 6

Vogelsang, Erich (1904–44): 1929, private lecturer in church history and church music, Königsberg; National Socialist Luther specialist; 1933, adviser to Reich Bishop Ludwig Müller on the Protestant departments at Prussian universities; 1937, professor, Giessen—12

Vogt, K.: 1932, student of Bonhoeffer in Berlin—12

Vogt, Paul (1900–1984): Swiss pastor; founder and head of the Swiss Relief Agency for the Confessing Church in Germany; 1943, refugee chaplain—6, 16

Voigt, Martha (1897–1970): German theologian, one of the first women to obtain the theological degree; 1926–40, worked at Burckhardthaus, Berlin; represented the Protestant Reich Association of Young Women at the Provisional Bureau for Ecumenical Youth Work—11

Voigt, Paul: 1933, member of the election committee of the German congregation, Sydenham, London; treasurer of the congregational council there; 1935, chair—12, 13, 14

Volk, Ludwig: author of a study on the Bavarian church during the Nazi era—12

Volkmann, Antonie (Toni): Italian-born adopted daughter of Richard von Volkmann(-Leander); first cousin of Karl Alfred von Hase; novelist—8, 9

Volkmann (Volkmann-Leander), Richard von (1830–89): German author and surgeon; surgeon general of the Prussian army; son of Alfred Volkmann and Adele, née Härtel; first cousin of Karl Alfred von Hase—9

Voltaire (François-Marie Arouet) (1694–1778): French writer; celebrated French philosopher; violently opposed to the Catholic Church—4, 14

Volz, Paul (1871–1941): theologian—14

Von Klemperer, Klemens (1916–2012): L. Clark Seelye Professor of History (emeritus), Smith College, Massachusetts—8, 14, 16
Vosberg, Klaus: 1937, in Finkenwalde; 1938–73, pastor—14
Voß: pharmacist; 1936, member of the Council of Brethren, Mecklenburg —14
Voss, Johann Heinrich (1751–1826): German poet and translator of Homer, among others; 1781, translated the *Odyssey* and, in 1793, the *Iliad*—7
Voßberg, Martin (1908–98): Confessing Church pastor, Pomerania—15
Vries, Jan de (1890–1964): scholar of Nordic religion, literary history, and linguistics—10
Vulpius, Melchior (1570–1615): German composer of church music—5
Vurpillot, Émile: French pastor; author of work on church—1
Vyschefslavzeff, Prof.: emigrated from Russia, lived in Paris; 1934, participated in the plenary assembly of the Universal Christian Council for Life and Work—13

Wach, Joachim (1898–1955): German scholar on the history of religions—16
Waetjen (Wätjen), Eduard: Berlin attorney; shared an office with Helmuth von Moltke in the Military Intelligence Office of the High Military Command; 1944, vice-consul in Zürich with a commission from the Military Intelligence Office; in contact there with Allen W. Dulles and the U.S. secret service OSS; after July 20, 1944, remained there despite orders to return to Germany; 1945–46, worked in the Bureau Intermedière in Geneva; 1945, participated in the church conference in Treysa—16
Waetzhold, Wilhelm: German art historian—15
Wagner, Horst: reporting legation officer in the Foreign Ministry, Gruppe Inland II B office (which monitored Jewish activities)—8, 16
Wagner, Richard (1813–83): German composer—6, 8, 11
Wahl, Hans (1900–1946): 1928, joined the NSDAP; from 1930, lawyer for the German Evangelical Church Federation Office; 1933, squad leader in the Nazi Sturmabteilung (SA); 1934, senior church official in the Church Foreign Office of the German Evangelical Church; 1938, senior consistory official—11, 12, 13, 15
Walbaum: name and address (Alexandrinenstrasse 101, tel. 17 30 72) entered in Eberhard Bethge's 1940 calendar; not otherwise identified—16
Walcha, Helmut: organist, church musician—8
Wälde, Paul (1913–42): from Frankfurt am Main; 1936–37, participated in the fourth Finkenwalde session; pastor, Zorndorf near Küstrin; January 20, 1942, killed in action as a lieutenant on the eastern front—16

Waldmann: East Prussian pastor; June 13, 1940, mentioned by Dietrich Bonhoeffer in connection with his visit in Schakendorf, district of Niederung in East Prussia; not otherwise identified—16
Walker, James J. (1881–1946): Democratic mayor of New York City 1925–32 —10
Walker, Kenneth: Baptist minister, London—13
Walker, N. (or W.): Baltic person mentioned in a letter in connection with Karl-Friedrich Bonhoeffer—9
Walker, Williston (1860–1922): U.S. church historian—12
Wallace, Edgar (1875–1932): British author of criminal stories—10
Wallace, George (1919–98): 1963–67 and 1971–87, governor of Alabama; leading segregationist for much of his political career—6
Wallau, René H.: German Protestant pastor and church musician—1
Waller, Balten: mentioned in 1936 ecumenical letter—14
Walpole, Hugh (1884–1941): British narrative author—8
Walter, Franz: German moral theologian; during the 1930s, outspoken opponent of euthanasia—6
Walther, Arnold Friedrich (1880–1938): German theologian and orientalist; author of article about Harnack's *Wesen des Christentums*—11
Walther, Christian: mid-twentieth-century German theologian—9
Walther, Gerda (1897–1977): German philosopher—1
Walther, Johannes: different author of article about Harnack's *Wesen des Christentums*—11
Walther, Wilhelm (1846–1924): Protestant theologian—11
Walther von der Vogelweide (ca. 1170–1230): Middle High German poet; Minnesinger—8
Walzer, Michael: U.S. philosopher and cultural critic—6
Wapler, Rudolf: summer 1937, participated in the fifth Finkenwalde session; 1938, assistant pastor in Schinne and Gehrden; 1940, conscripted into the military; missing in action—8
Ward, Harry Frederick (1873–1966): U.S. Methodist pastor and theologian; 1913, professor of Christian ethics, Boston; 1918–41, Union Theological Seminary, New York; 1920–40, head of the American Civil Liberties Union; advocate of dialogue between Christianity and workers; Bonhoeffer took his ethics course at Union—10, 12
Warmblut (Mrs. Warmblood) (FP): character in the novel—7
Warmuth, Georg: professor of Old Testament, Kiel—9
Warner, Christopher Frederick Ashten: 1942, counselor, head of the Northern Department in the British Foreign Office—16

Washington, Booker Taliafero (1859–1915): African American writer and teacher; rector of the Tuskegee Institute—10

Washington, George (1732–97): first president of the United States—10

Watkins, Vernon (1906–67): British poet and translator—11

Watson, D. B.: from Leeds, England; 1934, participant at the ecumenical youth meeting in Fanø; recorded protocols of the meetings—13

Watson, John Broadus (1878–1958): U.S. psychologist; 1908, professor, Baltimore; 1920, independent scholar; primary founder of behaviorism—10

Webber, Charles Clarence (1892–1982): U.S. Methodist theologian; 1923, pastor, New York; 1927, taught courses on "church and community," Union Theological Seminary, New York—10

Weber, Alfred (1868–1958): German national economist and sociologist—6

Weber, Dr.: legation officer first class in the Foreign Ministry, political section I—16

Weber, Elfriede: *see* Salomon, Elfriede

Weber, Gotthilf (1900–1987): 1928, pastor, Haiterbach, Württemberg; 1931, director, Evangelical Volk Alliance, Stuttgart; 1933, with the regional section of the Protestant Church Services in Stuttgart; 1934–35, on the executive committee of the Confessing Church in Bad Oeynhausen; 1935, member of the Reich Council of Brethren and representative of Westphalian church president Koch; 1936, pastor, Schwenningen; 1934–36, participated in the Confessing Church synods in Barmen, Augsburg, and Bad Oeynhausen; 1947, dean, Göppingen; 1950–67, Stuttgart-Bad Cannstatt—13, 14

Weber, H.: member of the congregational council, German Reformed St. Paul's Church in London—13

Weber, Hans Emil (1882–1950): 1913, professor of systematic theology, Bonn; considered as a possible successor to Reinhold Seeberg in Berlin; 1935, Münster; 1946, Bonn—8, 9, 10

Weber, Jutta: deputy director of the Handschriftenabteilung, Staatsbibliothek, Berlin—11

Weber, Manfred: on the staff of Chr. Kaiser Verlag—11, 17

Weber, Marianne (1870–1954): writer and women's rights advocate; wife of Max Weber—15

Weber, Max (1864–1920): German social economist, economic historian, and sociologist; contributed to the sociology of knowledge and to the sociology of religion; professor, Heidelberg and other German universities —1, 4, 6, 8, 9, 10, 11, 12, 15

Weber, Miss: identity unknown—9

Weber, Otto (1902–66): 1928–33, lecturer at the seminary, Elberfeld; 1933, its director; July 1933, member of the newly formed constitutional com-

mittee; 1933, joined the NSDAP; May 1933 until after the Sports Palace rally in November 1933, member of the German Christians; 1934, Reformed clerical adviser of the Reich Church Administration of the German Evangelical Church; 1934, professor of Reformed theology, Göttingen—12, 13, 14, 17 (for vol. 13)

Weckerling, Rudolf: from Wiesbaden; 1933–34, exchange student, Richmond College, London, where he met Dietrich Bonhoeffer; 1934, vicar of the Confessing Church, Wiesbaden; 1935, Giessen; worked in the upper Hessian district Council of Brethren; 1938, arrested; expelled from Hesse; 1939, pastor, Eschbach near Usingen; 1940, expulsion and arrest; 1941, military service; 1943, married vicar Helga Zimmermann; 1945, pastor, Berlin-Spandau; 1953, student chaplain at the Technical College, Berlin; simultaneously worked in the ecumenical institute in Berlin; 1964, pastor of the German congregation, Beirut; 1976, pastor, Berlin-Neukölln—13, 16

Weddingen, Otto von: famous submarine commander; lived in Boltenhagen —9

Wedell, Gertrud, née Bonhoeffer (1895–1979): Bonhoeffer's cousin; 1919, married the attorney Dr. Hans Wedell; 1939, emigrated to England (with Bonhoeffer's mediation); directed home for "non-Aryan" pastors, Hastings; 1942, active in the Wistow Training Center for Post-war Christian Service; 1946, with Hans Wedell, headed Oakenrough, an ecumenical center; 1950, returned to Düsseldorf—11, 13, 14, 16

Wedell, Hans (1881–1964): son of the Düsseldorf city rabbi Abraham Wedell; converted to Protestantism; 1910, patent attorney, Düsseldorf; 1919, married Gertrud, née Bonhoeffer; attorney at the regional upper court, Düsseldorf; from 1934, legal adviser to the Rhineland Confessing Church; 1935, banned by Nazi racial laws from practicing law; 1935, studied theology at the seminary in Wuppertal, Basel, and 1938, Union Theological Seminary, New York; 1940, pastor in the Congregational Church in the United States; 1946, returned to his family in England; warden of Oakenrough, an ecumenical center; 1950, returned to Düsseldorf; ecumenical academic adviser to the Rhineland church—13, 14, 15

Wedemeyer, Hans von (1888–1942): estate owner in Pätzig and Klein Reetz, Neumark; husband of Ruth, née von Kleist-Retzow; member of the Berneuchen circle; August 22, 1942, killed in action near Stalingrad as a major and a battalion leader of an infantry regiment—7, 8, 15, 16, 17

Wedemeyer, Hans-Werner von: younger brother of Maria von Wedemeyer —8

Wedemeyer, Maria von (1924–77): daughter of Hans and Ruth von Wedemeyer; Ruth von Kleist-Retzow's granddaughter; 1938–42, pupil at the

Wieblingen country boarding school near Heidelberg (run by Elisabeth von Thadden); 1942, secondary school examination and diploma; January–June 1943, worked as a Red Cross nurse in Hannover; January 1943, engagement to Dietrich Bonhoeffer; July–August 1943, medical leave in Seefeld, district of Pyritz, Pomerania; September–December 1943, temporary worker in Kniephof while supporting her mother in Pätzig; from January 1944, worked as a teacher at the Magdalenenstift in Altenburg, Thuringia, and as a private teacher in Bundorf, Lower Franconia; October 1944–January 1945, stayed with Dietrich Bonhoeffer's parents in Berlin; January 31, 1945, led a refugee transport to the West with her siblings and six other people; then journeyed to various concentration camps looking for Dietrich Bonhoeffer; from 1946, studied mathematics in Göttingen; 1948, scholarship to Bryn Mawr College in the United States; 1949, married Paul-Werner Schniewind; emigrated to the United States; children: Christopher (b. 1950), Paul (b. 1954); worked in data processing; 1959, after her first marriage failed, married Barton Lee Weller; divorced in 1965; 1969, head of system analysis at the Honeywell Corporation in Boston; 1975, group leader there for the technical section; 1977, died in Massachusetts General Hospital in Boston—4, 5, 6, 7, 8, 10, 12, 14, 15, 16, 17

Wedemeyer, Maximilian von (1853–1905): father of Hans von Wedemeyer—8

Wedemeyer, Maximilian von (1922–42): son of Hans and Ruth von Wedemeyer; 1938, confirmed by Dietrich Bonhoeffer in Kieckow; October 26, 1942, killed in action on the eastern front—6, 8, 15, 16, 17

Wedemeyer, Ruth von, née von Kleist-Retzow (1897–1985): daughter of Ruth von Kleist-Retzow; 1918, married Hans von Wedemeyer at the Pätzig estate; children: Ruth, Alice (married name von Bismarck), Maximilian, Maria, Hans-Werner, Christine (married name Beshar), Werburg (married name Doerr), Peter Christian; 1945, fled to Westphalia, and later to Hannover—6, 7, 8, 16

Wedemeyer, Ruth-Alice von: *see* Bismarck, Ruth-Alice von

Wegner, Armin Theophil (1886–1978): writer, pacifist; 1933, imprisoned after writing open letter to Hitler protesting the anti-Jewish measures; Bonhoeffer wrote Niebuhr to help him leave Germany; 1936, exiled in Italy—13

Wehler, Hans-Ulrich: German historian—10

Wehrhan, Fritz (1872–1951): 1904, ordination, assistant pastor, Roneck (Royewy), Posen; 1907, seamen's pastor, Genoa; 1911–44, pastor at the German-Evangelical Christ Church with the filial Church of St. Mark and the Lutheran Church of St. Mary in London; January 1945, retired—13

Wehrung, Georg (1880–1959): 1920, professor of systematic theology, Münster; 1927, Halle; 1931–46, Tübingen—12

Weichert, Ludwig (1887–1936): 1926–28, missions inspector for the Berlin Evangelical Mission Society in various German foreign congregations in Africa; 1929, in Berlin; 1932, member of the Reich leadership of the German Christians as a specialist on mission questions; May 1933, contact between the Reich administration and the "Kapler committee"; May 31, 1933, left the German Christians—12

Weidemann, Alfred: from 1938, worked in the Army High Command, general office of the reserve army section; from October 1, 1943, head of the "pastoral counseling" group in the Army High Command; 1943, General Major—8

Weigert, Erich (1872–1943): director of the regional court; closely acquainted with the Bonhoeffer family—9, 10

Weigert, Maria: *see* Brendel, Maria

Weinel, Heinrich (1874–1936): Lutheran New Testament scholar—10, 12

Weiser, Arthur (1893–1978): 1930, professor of Old Testament, Tübingen—13

Weiß, Bernhard (1827–1918): German New Testament critic and theologian; 1863–77, professor of New Testament exegesis, Kiel; 1877–1908, Berlin—1, 4

Weiss, Johannes (1863–1914): German New Testament theologian, son of Bernhard Weiß; 1888, private lecturer, Göttingen; 1890, associate professor, Marburg; 1895, full professor; from 1908, Heidelberg; member of the history of religions school—6, 8, 9

Weiße, Michael (1488–1534): hymnist and cantor, Jungbunzlau; 1531, assembled a collection of hymns for the Moravian Brethren written for one voice only, since the Brethren regarded the blending of parts and instrumental accompaniment to be immoral—5, 14

Weiße, Wolfram: professor of education, University of Hamburg; author of works on religion and political change—12

Weißel, Georg (1590–1635): hymnist—14

Weissler (Weißler), Friedrich (1891–1937): legal civil servant and member of Confessing Church; 1933, dismissed from his position as Magdeburg regional court director because of his "non-Aryan" background; 1934, legal officer with the Provisional Church Administration; 1936, head of the chancellery of the Provisional Church Administration; October 1936, arrested when the memorandum to Hitler was leaked to the foreign press; February 1937, transferred to Sachsenhausen, where he was murdered—15

Weizsäcker, Carl Friedrich Baron von (1912–2007): physicist, scientific theoretician, philosopher—2, 4, 8, 9, 13, 16

Weizsäcker, Carl Heinrich von (1822–99): German New Testament scholar and church historian; 1889, chancellor, Tübingen University—4

Welker, Michael: professor of systematic theology (dogmatics), Heidelberg; doctorate in theology, Tübingen; doctorate in philosophy, Heidelberg; postdoctoral lecturing qualification, Tübingen; 1983–87, professor, Tübingen; 1987–91, Münster; from 1991, Heidelberg; 1985, guest professor, McMaster University; 1988, 1995, and 1997, Princeton; director of the international scholarly forum, University of Heidelberg; publications include *Gottes Geist: Theologie des Heiligen Geistes*, 1992 (Eng. trans. 1994); *Kirche im Pluralismus, Kaiser*, 1995; *Schöpfung und Wirklichkeit: Warfield Lectures, Princeton 1991/92*, 1995 (Eng. trans. 1997)—11, 14, 15

Wellhausen, Julius (1844–1918): Biblical exegete, Orientalist, and historian; 1870, lecturer, Göttingen; 1872, professor of Old Testament, Greifswald; 1882, resigned on conscientious grounds; private lecturer in Semitics, Halle; 1885–92, professor of Semitics, Marburg; 1892–1913, Göttingen; proponent of higher criticism, supported the relative dating of component documents of the Pentateuch; precursor of form criticism—3, 10, 11, 15

Wellnhofer, Simon (formerly Rudolf): Benedictine in Ettal, Upper Bavaria —16

Wendel, Ernst Georg: author of work on Bonhoeffer's homiletics—2, 3, 4, 5, 7, 10, 12, 14

Wendland, Heinz-Dietrich (1900–1992): 1920, private lecturer, Heidelberg; 1929, professor of dogmatics, Heidelberg; 1934–36, student chaplain, Heidelberg; 1937, professor of New Testament theology and Christian social ethics, Kiel; 1939–45, navy chaplain; 1955, professor and director of the Institute for Christian Social Sciences, Münster—12, 13, 14, 16

Wendland, Paul (1864–1915): professor of classical philology, Kiel and Göttingen; scholar of early Christianity and Hellenistic culture—9

Wendland, Traugott (1869–1942): from 1911, pastor, Berlin-Steglitz—12

Wendland, Walter: from 1916, pastor, Berlin—12

Wendtlandt, K.: 1935–36 (until January 1936), in second Finkenwalde session —14

Wengert, Timothy: U.S. Lutheran professor of Reformation history—1, 5, 6, 13, 15

Werbeck, Alfred: from 1931, pastor, Berlin-Moabit—12

Werder, Karl Ludwig: 1926, pastor, Berlin—12

Werdermann, Hermann (1888–1954): 1927, pastor at the St. Lazarus hospital and deaconess home, Berlin; 1923, private lecturer in practical the-

ology, Berlin; 1929, professor of religious education at the Pedagogical Academy, Hamm—10

Wergin, Kurt (1900–1973): Berlin attorney and notary; friend of Klaus Bonhoeffer; 1934, dismissed as company lawyer for the Berlin transportation authority for failing to join the NSDAP; provided aid for persons persecuted for political reasons or reasons of origin; participated in "Operation 7"; September 16, 1943, appointed as Bonhoeffer's defense lawyer—8, 16, 17

Werkmeister: German consul in Barcelona—10

Werner, Arnold: Swedish pastor; secretary of the Swedish Ecumenical Committee; April 17, 1942, Dietrich Bonhoeffer visited him in Stockholm—16

Werner, Friedrich (1897–1955): German lawyer; from 1930, Nazi party city council member at Berlin municipal and district levels; active member of the German Christians from the beginning; 1933–45, Reich Church–appointed director of the Evangelical Church of the Old Prussian Union and of the German Evangelical Church; in this capacity he directed the Church Chancellery, Berlin—6, 12, 13, 15, 16, 17

Weschke, Eugen: pastor—14

Weselovius, Christian: hymnist—14

Wesenberg, Paul (1895–1944): from 1931, pastor, Berlin—12

Wesley, John (1703–91): founder of the Methodist movement—10, 11

Wessel, Horst (1907–30): German student; from 1926, member of the NSDAP; abandoned his studies to join the Sturmabteilung (SA); 1930, died after an armed attack on him; the militant, anti-Semitic song he composed, "Die Fahne hoch" (Raise high the flag), known as the "Horst-Wessel-Lied" (Horst Wessel song), became the Nazi anthem—6, 16

Wessling, Miss von: name and address (Königsberg, Hinterroßgarten 11) noted in Dietrich Bonhoeffer's 1940 calendar for East Prussia; not otherwise identified—16

West, Charles C.: U.S. professor of Christian ethics, Princeton Theological Seminary, and Bonhoeffer scholar—5, 6, 7

West, Michael: former editor in chief of Fortress Press; since 2011, publisher, World Council of Churches—17

Westcott, Brooke Foss (1825–1901): British New Testament scholar and editor of a critical edition of the Greek New Testament; 1890, consecrated bishop of Durham—4, 6

Westman, Knut Bernhard (1881–1967): Swedish missions scholar; 1918, secretary of the World Alliance for Promoting International Friendship through the Churches; 1930, professor for mission history, Uppsala—16

Westring, Claes: 1941–45, Swedish consul general in Oslo—16

Wette, Wolfram: military historian, Freiburg—10

Weymann, Ursula: 1932, student of Bonhoeffer in Berlin—12

Weymarn, Alexander von: 1933–49, head of the press and information office of the World Council of Churches in Geneva—8

Weynand, Udo (1904–25): student of philosophy and law, Tübingen; Bonhoeffer's fraternity brother—9, 17 (for vol. 9)

Whaley, John (1927–2005): renowned translator of Goethe—14

Whitburn, Lawrence: director of the church choir, German congregation, Sydenham, London—13, 15

Whitburn, Mrs., née Lokies: sister of Hans Lokies; an active member of the Confessing Church and director of church mission work, Berlin—15

White, Gaylord: 1930–31, professor of mission studies and field placement during Bonhoeffer's studies at Union Theological Seminary—10, 11

White, Walter F. (1893–1955): African American civil rights advocate; executive secretary, NAACP—10

Whitehead, Alfred North (1861–1947): British/American mathematician and philosopher; 1924, lecturer at Harvard; teacher of Bertrand Russell—10, 15

Wichern, Johann Hinrich (1808–81): Protestant theologian, spiritual father of the executive committee of Inner Mission—11

Wichmann, Georg (1910–74): 1936, participated in the third Finkenwalde session; after 1945, pastor in Berlin—14, 15

Wick: superintendent (1935)—14

Wickersham, George W. (1858–1936): attorney general from Taft administration, appointed by President Hoover to preside over the commission to study the effects of the Eighteenth Amendment, which established Prohibition—10

Wickham, Lionel R.: lecturer (emeritus) of patristics, faculty of divinity, Cambridge University—12

Widmann, Richard (1900–1979): German pastor; 1930, cofounder of the Ecclesiastical-Theological Society, which became tied to the Confessing Church in Württemberg—6, 9

Wieacker, Franz (1908–94): legal historian; 1937, professor, Leipzig; 1948, Freiburg im Breisgau; 1953, Göttingen—8

Wiebering, Joachim: German theologian; publications on ecclesiology, theological ethics, and Bonhoeffer—6

Wiechert, Ernst (1887–1950): author; opponent of National Socialists; 1938, sent to a concentration camp for some months—8, 15

Wieck, Richard: from 1912, pastor, Berlin—12

Wied, Prince Victor zu (1877–1946): 1934–43, envoy in Stockholm—14

Wiedemann, Fritz: captain; from 1935, adjutant in the Reich chancellery; January 1939, transferred to San Francisco as consul general—15

Wiegandt, Manfred H.: German American human rights attorney—12

Wieman, Henry Nelson (1884–1975): professor of religious philosophy, Chicago—12, 15

Wieneke, Friedrich (1892–1957): 1920, archdeacon in Soldin, Neumark; 1930, cathedral pastor there; 1929, joined the NSDAP; 1932, member of the Reich leadership of the German Christians as a specialist for theology and secondary schools; 1933, senior consistory official in the Evangelical High Church Council in Berlin; 1934, temporary oversight of the German Evangelical Church chancellery, then assigned to the evangelical consistory in Magdeburg; 1945, pastor, Hain and Steinbrücken, Stolberg; 1949, Alt-Töplitz—12, 13, 14

Wienken, Heinrich (1883–1961): Catholic theologian; 1921, director of the German Caritas Association; 1937, titular bishop and coadjutor of the diocese Meißen; head of the commissioner's office of the Fulda bishops' conference; 1951, bishop of Meißen—16

Wienstein, Richard (1892–1937): 1929, ministerial counselor in the Reich chancellery—12

Wiese, Karl (1883–1974): from 1925, pastor, Berlin—12

Wiese, Leopold von (1876–1969): German sociologist and professor—1

Wiesner, Werner (1902–74): 1928, academic inspector at the Reformed seminary, Halle; 1933, dismissed; assistant pastor in the Reformed church, Memel; 1940, met there with Dietrich Bonhoeffer; 1941, military service; 1945, private lecturer, and 1948, professor of systematic theology, Göttingen—16

Wilamowitz-Möllendorf, Ulrich von (1848–1931): German classical philologist—17 (for vol. 9)

Wilbert: 1932, senior secretary in the church administration involved with Bonhoeffer's appointment as an assistant pastor—11

Wild, E. and H. von: attended Bonhoeffer's 1929 lectures in Barcelona—10

Wild, Mrs.: 1922; not otherwise identified—9

Wilde, Gerhard: 1921, pastor, Schönwaldau, Silesia; 1931, Stolzenhagen, Pomerania; end of 1933, suspended because of his protests against the German Christians; 1940–45, pastor, Schillersdorf; later lived in Espelkamp, Westphalia—13

Wilde, Joachim (1902–56): 1932, missions inspector with the Berlin Mission Society—12

Wiles, Maurice (1929–2005): British theologian—12

Wilhelm I (1797–1888): 1861, king of Prussia; 1871, also German emperor —14

Wilhelm II (1859–1941): king of Prussia and German emperor—10, 11

Wilkens, Klaus: German theologian and ecumenical leader; publications include several Bonhoeffer studies—6

Will, Dr., née Hystock: friend of Paula Bonhoeffer and Elisabeth von Hase; her husband worked at the German embassy in Mexico—10

William of Occam (ca. 1285–ca. 1349): British scholastic philosopher and Franciscan; initiator of the nominalist doctrine that the real is always individual rather than universal, and that universals have no real existence but are only abstract terms—2, 15

Williams, Roger (1604–83): British Baptist; founder of Rhode Island; 1639, severed all church connections and accepted no creed, maintaining instead a fundamental belief in Christianity—15

Williams, R. R.: British clergyman; during the war, worked in the Ministry of Information, Religious Division; 1942, he supported Bishop George K. A. Bell with information prior to Bell's trip to Sweden—16

Willkie, Wendell (1892–1944): U.S. politician; 1940, unsuccessful Republican presidential candidate against Roosevelt—16

Willnow, Ursula Marianne: daughter of a consulate secretary at the German embassy in London; July 24, 1934, Bonhoeffer baptized her—13

Wilm: SS lieutenant [*Obersturmführer*], worked in department IIB3 (political churches) of the Reich Central Security Office—16

Wilm, Ernst (1901–89): 1929, pastor, Lüdenscheid; 1931, Mennighüffen; 1939, member of the Westphalian Council of Brethren; 1941, arrested for protesting the euthanasia measures; May 1942–January 1945, in Dachau; 1948, president of the Evangelical Church in Westphalia; 1969, retired—16

Wilm, Walter (1893–1957): 1928, provincial youth chaplain, Mark Brandenburg; 1930, chaplain with the executive committee for Inner Mission, Berlin; 1932, pastor, Dolgelin, district of Seelow; 1935–37, member of the executive committee of the Reich Church—12

Wiltshire, Susan Ford: professor of classics, Vanderbilt University; consultant, *DBWE* 2—2

Winant, John Gilbert: U.S. ambassador in London—16, 17

Winckelmann, Johann Joachim (1717–68): German archaeologist and art historian; 1754, became a Catholic; from 1755, lived in Italy—6, 8

Wind, Renate: German professor of biblical theology; author of biography of Bonhoeffer—4, 12, 16

Windelband, Wilhelm (1848–1915): German philosopher, founder, with Heinrich Rickert, of the southwest German school of neo-Kantianism with its attendant philosophy of values—1, 2, 6, 11

Windthorst, Ludwig (1812–91): spokesperson for the Center Party during the period of the Kulturkampf (1871 conflict in the German Empire between the state and the Roman Catholic Church)—11

Winkelmann, Heinz (1907–2002): from Berlin; 1938, participated in the collective pastorate in Köslin—15

Winkler, Robert (1894–1983): 1928, professor of systematic theology, Heidelberg; 1934, Breslau; 1946, curate, Bad Steben; 1947, pastor, Kitzingen; until 1959, professor, Erlangen—2, 12

Winkworth, Catherine (1829–78): British-born hymnist, translator, and educator—4, 5, 10, 12

Winnig, August (1878–1956): German politician and author, trained as a mason; 1913, chair of the German construction workers union; 1919, president of East Prussia; March 1920, removed from office and excluded from the Social Democratic Party for having joined the Kapp putsch; autobiographical writings portray his turn from Marxism to Christianity —6

Winter, Marion: *see* Yorck von Wartenburg, Marion

Winterfeld, Christian Friedrich Hans von (1913–40): son of Friedrich von Winterfeld and Christine, née von Rohr; May 15, 1940, killed in action as a first lieutenant and company commander at Reaucourt—16

Winterhager, Jürgen Wilhelm (1907–89): student of philosophy and theology, Cambridge; 1931, joined the World Alliance for Promoting International Friendship through the Churches; 1931–33, among the circle of students around Bonhoeffer; 1932, doctorate in church history, Cambridge; 1932, academic head of the German section of the World Alliance for Promoting International Friendship through the Churches, Berlin; 1933–34, spent several weeks as Bonhoeffer's guest in London; 1934, participated in the Fanø youth conference; 1935, participated in the Chamby conference; Bonhoeffer's colleague in the Ecumenical Youth Secretariat; 1936, ordained by Otto Dibelius; 1937, pastor, Hohenauen; 1947, director of the department of ecumenical studies at the seminary, Berlin; doctorate, Eden Theological Seminary, St. Louis; 1961, professor of ecumenical studies, seminary in Berlin—4, 10, 11, 12, 13, 14

Wintzer, Friedrich: author of works on practical theology—14

Wintzingerode, Count von: Prussian landowner—14

Wirsing, Giselher (1907–75): journalist; 1933–41, editor in chief of the *Münchener Neueste Nachrichten*; 1933–39, editor of the *Tat*; 1954–70, editor in chief of *Christ und Welt*—12

Wirth, Albrecht (1866–1936): German nationalist author of travelogues—10

Wirth, Günter: professor, Berlin—10

Wirth, Hermann Felix (1885–1981): Dutch historian; studied in Berlin and Basel; during World War I, volunteered for military service in the German army; 1919, returned to the Netherlands; active in the nationalist youth movement; 1933, professor, Berlin; active in the German Christians —10

Wise, Stephen Samuel (1874–1949): U.S. Jewish leader; prominent rabbi in New York—10

Wisløff, H. E.: Norwegian theologian and pastor—16

Wissing, J. C.: council member, secretary, and treasurer of the Dutch section of the World Alliance for Promoting International Friendship through the Churches; 1933, participated in that organization's conference in Sofia —11, 12

Witkop, Philipp (1880–1942): German writer and literary critic—10, 11

Witte, Johannes (1877–1945): 1931, professor of mission studies, Berlin—12, 16, 17 (for vol. 12)

Witte, Leopold: biographer of F. A. G. Tholuck—14

Witte, Otto Karl Emil (1893–1966): bishop of Hamburg; after World War I, closely affiliated with *völkisch* movements; later opponent of National Socialism; 1934–36, professor of systematic theology and New Testament, Hamburg; 1937, dismissed; 1948–54, lecturer in New Testament, Hamburg; 1959, bishop of Hamburg; 1960, professor, Hamburg; 1964, retired —4, 5, 15

Wittig, Joseph (1879–1949): Catholic theologian; professor, Breslau; 1926, excommunicated; 1946, rehabilitated—10

Witzleben, Erwin von (1881–1944): career military; 1935–38, commander in Military District III (Berlin); 1939, commander of the First Army; 1940, general field marshal; 1942, recalled as the commander in chief of Army Group D in France; had contacts with the military opposition; July 21, 1944, arrested; August 8, 1944, executed in Berlin-Plötzensee—16

Wobbermin, Georg (1869–1943): German Protestant theologian; 1907, professor of systematic theology, Breslau; 1915, Heidelberg; 1922, Göttingen; 1935, Lütgert's successor in Berlin; member of the German Christians—10, 11, 12, 14

Woelfel, James: professor of philosophy and religion, University of Kansas —3

Woestehoff, Julie: U.S. Germanist and educator—13

Wohlrab, Rolf: coauthor of German work on the Church Struggle—14

Wojhoski, Barbara: one of the general editors of the *DBWE*—8, 10, 11, 12, 13, 14, 15, 16, 17

Wolf, Asta: wife of Ernst Wolf—16

Wolf, Erik (1902–77): German legal scholar; 1930, professor of church law, legal philosophy, and constitutional philosophy, Freiburg im Breisgau; member of the Confessing Church; 1942–43, member of the Freiburg circle and participant in the Freiburg memorandum; 1944, arrested; after 1945, worked on the reestablishment of the Evangelical Church of Germany—6, 16, 17

Wolf, Ernst (1902–71): German theologian and leading member of the Confessing Church; 1927, lecturer, Heidelberg; 1928, professor, Rostock; 1930, Kiel and Freiburg; 1931, professor of historical theology, Bonn; 1935, transferred to Halle as disciplinary measure; 1945, professor, Göttingen; 1954, editor of the new edition of Dietrich Bonhoeffer's dissertation *Sanctorum Communion*, and 1956, Bonhoeffer's postdoctoral dissertation, *Akt und Sein*, both for Chr. Kaiser Verlag—1, 2, 3, 6, 8, 11, 12, 13, 14, 16, 17

Wolf, Hugo (1860–1903): Austrian composer; master of the art song, of which he composed over three hundred—7, 8

Wolff: 1931, consistory official—3, 11

Wolff, Christian Baron von (1679–1754): German philosopher and mathematician; professor in Halle and Marburg; science adviser to Peter the Great; chief German spokesperson of the Enlightenment—11

Wolff, Karl (1900–1984): 1933, Himmler's adjutant, chief of the personal staff of the *Reichsführer* SS; 1942, SS *Obergruppenführer* and general in the Waffen SS; 1943, military governor in northern Italy; March 1945, independently contacted Allen Dulles in Switzerland and thus brought about the surrender of Army Group C in northern Italy in April 1945—16

Wolford, A.: member of the congregational council, German Reformed St. Paul's Church in London—13

Wolfram von Eschenbach (ca. 1170–1200/20): Middle High German poet; main work: *Parzival*—8

Wolgast, Eike: German church historian and archivist—6

Wollenweber, Martha: author of work on August Vilmar—16

Woltersdorf, Ernst Gottlieb (1725–61): hymnist—15

Wörishöffer, Sophie (1838–90): German novelist—14

Worringer, Wilhelm (1881–1965): German art historian and professor—9

Wotquenne, Alfred (1867–1939): German musicologist—7

Wrede, William (1859–1906): 1893, professor of New Testament, Göttingen; 1895, Breslau; influenced by the history of religions school, approached New Testament theology from the standpoint of the history of traditions; work is foundational for form criticism and the modern search for the historical Jesus—9, 11, 12

Wright, John: British Methodist pastor; 1934, student at Richmond College—13

Wright, Jonathan R. C.: British author of works on political science, including a study of the German Protestant church during the Weimar period—10

Wucher, Albert (1920–2010): German historian—9

Wulczyn, Heidi: author of article on Martin Bucer—14

Wunder, Gerd: coauthor of work on Bonhoeffer family tree—11

Wundt, Max (1879–1963): German idealistic philosopher in the tradition of Kant, Fichte, and Hegel; son of Wilhelm Wundt; from 1929, professor, Tübingen—9

Wundt, Wilhelm (1832–1920): philosopher, physiologist, and psychologist; from 1875, professor, Leipzig; represented a comprehensive, realistic worldview inclined toward voluntaristic idealism—9

Wünsch, Georg (1887–1964): controversial Protestant theologian and journalist; representative of early liberal Protestantism—12

Wünsche, Matthias: German Catholic priest, active in Jewish-Christian dialogue—10

Wünscher: pastor—12

Wurm, Theophil (1869–1953): 1920, dean, Reutlingen; member of the Württemberg parliament, representing the German National People's Party; 1927, prelate, Heilbronn; 1929, Württemberg church president; 1933–49, bishop of the Evangelical Church of Württemberg; 1934, member of the Reich Council of Brethren and of the Lutheran Council; 1945–49, chair of the Council of the Evangelical Church of Germany—13, 14, 16, 17

Wurmbach, Adolf: author of a nativity play—13

Wüstenberg, Ralf K.: professor of Protestant theology, University of Flensburg; 1995, doctorate, Berlin; from 1988, member of the International Bonhoeffer Society—4, 8, 14

Wycliffe, John (ca. 1324–84): British philosopher, theologian, and reformer; 1356, academic instructor; 1382, interrogated at a synod in Oxford; 1415, posthumously condemned as a heretic at a council in Constance—1, 10, 11, 14

Wyller, Trygve: professor of theology, University of Oslo—8

Xavier, Francis (1506–52): 1506–52, Spanish missionary; 1525–34, studied in Paris, where he met Ignatius of Loyola, whom he aided in founding the Jesuit order; pioneered idea that the missionary must adapt to local customs and language—10

Xenophon (ca. 430–ca. 355 B.C.E.): Greek historian, author, soldier, disciple of Socrates—9

Yahweh: biblical divine name—12
Yanitsch: noted by Dietrich Bonhoeffer as a possible ecumenical contact as the Romanian minister of culture; not otherwise identified—16
Yoder, John Howard (1927–97): U.S. Mennonite theologian and ethicist—6
Yorck von Wartenburg, Helene Countess, née Kalckreuth (1852–1925): daughter of Stanislaus Count von Kalckreuth and Anna Eleonore, née Cauer; sister of Bonhoeffer's grandmother Klara von Hase and Pauline, Countess von Kalckreuth; Bonhoeffer's great-aunt; married Hans Count Yorck von Wartenburg, a godfather of Bonhoeffer—7, 9
Yorck von Wartenburg, Marion Countess, née Winter: classmate of Bonhoeffer; wife of Count Peter Yorck von Wartenburg, who participated in the conspiracy against the Nazis and was murdered by the regime—9
Yorck von Wartenburg, Paul Count: estate owner in Klein-Oels, Silesia; member of the Silesian Council of Brethren and of the Silesian Confessing Synod; 1939, member of the Old Prussian Council of Brethren; 1939–41, military service; seriously wounded on the eastern front; 1942, contact with Helmuth von Moltke; with Dietrich Bonhoeffer, member of the theological synodal commission "*primus usus legis*"; July 21, 1944, arrested in Marienbad; until the end of April 1945, interned in Sachsenhausen; 1946–49, worked within the relief organization of the Evangelical Church of Germany; 1950, with the World Council of Churches in Geneva; 1953–66, diplomatic service—16
Yorck von Wartenburg, Peter Count, JD (1904–44): 1936, adviser to the Reich commissioner for price controls; 1939, drafted as a reserve officer; 1942, with the economic staff (east) of the High Military Command; from 1940, in close contact with Helmuth von Moltke, and alongside Moltke a leading member of the Kreisau circle; after July 20, 1944, arrested; September 8, 1944, executed—9, 16
Young, Josiah: U.S. professor of systematic theology, Wesley Theological Seminary, Washington, D.C.; author of work on Bonhoeffer and Harlem —10, 15

Young, Owen D. (1874–1962): U.S. lawyer and businessman; after World War I, set up the reparations plan—10
Yoxthiemer, George: 1930, minister of a U.S. church where Bonhoeffer preached—10

Zabarella, Giacomo (Jacopo) (1532–89): late Aristotelian; author of the influential *Libri quattuor de methodo*—9
Zacchaeus: biblical character—5, 8, 14

Zacharias: cabinetmaker; socialist; often a guest and helpful in the Bonhoeffer family because of his views and familiarity with the mood among workers—8

Zahn, Theodor von (1838–1933): German Lutheran New Testament and patristics scholar; professor at various universities, ultimately in Erlangen —1, 9

Zahn-Harnack, Agnes von (1884–1950): daughter of Adolf von Harnack—9, 10, 11, 12, 14

Zanchi, Jerome (1516–90): Calvinist theologian—2

Zänker, Otto (1876–1960): 1925, general superintendent of the Saxon church province for the parishes of Breslau and Oppeln; 1933, bishop of Breslau; 1934, on the Lutheran Council; 1941, dismissed from office for supporting the Confessing Church and forced to retire; after 1945, in Bielefeld—12, 14

Zankow, Stefan: Bulgarian Orthodox theologian; 1905, doctorate, Sofia; 1918, doctorate in law, Zürich; 1920, general secretary of the Holy Synod of the Bulgarian Orthodox Church; 1923–50, professor of church law and Christian sociology, Sofia; 1926, provost of the Alexander Newski Cathedral, Sofia; member of the executive committee of the World Alliance for Promoting International Friendship through the Churches; 1932, its international secretary; 1933, participated in the organization's conference, Sofia; 1934, Bulgarian delegate and adviser at the World Alliance Conference in Fanø; 1950, professor at the theological academy, Sofia —12, 13, 16

Zarathustra (Zoroaster) (ca. 628–ca. 551 B.C.E.): Persian founder of Zoroastrianism, a dualistic religion centered on the conflict between good and evil—2, 11

Zarnack, Hulda (1883–1977): from 1933, head of Burckhardt House in Berlin—11, 12

Zebedee brothers: biblical characters—9

Zechariah: biblical character—14

Zedekiah: biblical character—9

Zedlitz-Trützschler, Robert Count von (1837–1914): grandfather of Maria von Wedemeyer; president of Silesia, Posen, and Hesse; Prussian minister of culture—8

Zehrer, Eva-Maria: German historian—6

Zeiger, Ivo Alois (1898–1966): German Jesuit; from 1928, in Rome; professor of church law and history at the papal Gregoriana University; 1939–48, rector of the German-Hungarian Collegium Germanicum in Rome. As an adviser to Pius XII and later to Bishop Aloysius Muench, Zeiger was

an advocate of compromise, if not sympathy, with the Nazi regime—16, 17

Zeller, Winfried (1911–82): church historian; attended some of Bonhoeffer's lecture courses in Berlin—11

Zenke, Robert (1911–41): from Kolberg; 1935, participated in the first Zingst/Finkenwalde session; Confessing Church pastor, Altwigshagen near Anklam; 1936, at St. Mary's, Köslin; 1941, killed in action on the eastern front—14, 15, 16

Zerner, Ruth: 1957–58, Fulbright fellowship, Free University of Berlin; 1962, PhD in modern German history, University of California, Berkeley; 1962–68, professor of history, Hunter College, City University of New York; after 1968, associate professor of history, Lehman College, City University of New York—4, 7, 8, 10

Zernoff, Nicolas: Russian theologian; emigrated to Paris; 1934, participated in the Fanø youth conference—11, 13

Zerubbabel: biblical character—14

Zeruiah: biblical character—14

Zeus: father of the gods, highest of the Greek gods—8, 10, 12, 17 (for vol. 9)

Zezschwitz, Carl Adolf Gerhard von (1825–86): professor of practical theology ("Erlangen theology")—14

Zezschwitz, Gertrud von: member of a well-known aristocratic family with a history of military leadership—9

Ziegner, Oskar: religious educator; follower of Gogarten—14

Ziehen, Theodor (1862–1950): German philosopher, psychologist, and psychiatrist; professor in Utrecht, Berlin, and, after 1917, Halle—10

Zielinski, Kurt: 1933, one of Bonhoeffer's confirmands—12

Ziemer: 1933, pastor, Berlin—12

Ziller, Tuiskon (1817–82): German educator; main proponent of Johann Herbart's educational philosophy; from 1863, professor, Leipzig—14

Zillessen, Alfred: with Karl Arper, author of book on church liturgy—14, 15

Zimmer: 1931–32, participant in Bonhoeffer's seminar "The Idea of Philosophy and Protestant Theology"—11

Zimmerman: worker at Berlin-Charlottenburg youth club, 1932—12

Zimmermann, Christian-Matthias: son of Wolf-Dieter Zimmermann; Maria-Claudia's twin—8

Zimmermann, Helga: 1932, student of Bonhoeffer in Berlin; theological degree; 1937, illegal ordination in the Confessing Church; 1943, married Rudolf Weckerling—12

Zimmermann, Jens: professor of English; Canada Research Chair in Religion, Interpretation and Culture, Trinity Western University—8

Zimmermann, Maria-Claudia: daughter of Wolf-Dieter Zimmermann; Christian-Matthias's twin—8

Zimmermann, Max Georg: art historian—9

Zimmermann, Richard (1877–1945): 1927, pastor and superintendent, Berlin—12

Zimmermann, Wolf-Dieter (1911–2007): German pastor; 1932–33, student of Bonhoeffer, Berlin; summer 1936, participated in the third Finkenwalde session; 1936, special commission for the Old Prussian Council of Brethren; 1938, pastor under General Superintendent Otto Dibelius; from 1939, "illegal" pastor; 1946, in Berlin-Tegel, and cofounder of the "Unterwegs" circle and editor of the periodical *Unterwegs*; 1954, broadcast commissioner, Protestant Church in Berlin-Brandenburg and head of the Berlin Protestant radio service—1, 3, 5, 6, 7, 8, 9, 10, 11, 12, 13, 14, 15, 16

Zimmermann-Wolf, Christoph: member German Society for Pastoral Counseling—8

Zimri: biblical character—15

Zinn, Elisabeth: *see* Bornkamm, Elisabeth

Zinzendorf, Nikolaus Ludwig Count von (1700–1760): religious leader influential among the Moravian Brethren; bishop of the Moravian Brethren in Herrnhut, a colony of Hussite refugees on his estates in Saxony; emphasized religious feeling—2, 5, 9, 14, 15, 16

Zipfel, Friedrich: German historian; works on Church Struggle and resistance—16

Zippel, Bruno (1884–1945): 1937, pastor, Borken, district of Prussian Eylau, East Prussia; 1940, represented pastor Potschka, Kuckerneese; June 9, 1940, Dietrich Bonhoeffer mentions him during his visit there—16

Zippel, Hans-Henning (1909–43): 1934, member of the Brotherhood of Assistant Pastors and Vicars of the Province of Saxony, Confessing Church; 1936, ordination, Halle; worked with the Provincial Council of Brethren, Magdeburg, responsible for work with students; husband of Ingeborg, née Koch; 1943, killed in action on the eastern front—8, 14, 15, 16

Zippel, Ingeborg (née Koch) (1914–76): theologian; chaired the Brotherhood of Assistant Pastors and Vicars of the Province of Saxony—8

Zippel, Johannes: from 1932, pastor, Berlin-Steglitz—12

Zischka, Anton (pseudonym: Rupert Donkan): Austrian journalist; his widely read books on economics and world politics reflected National Socialist ideas—6, 15

Zoellner, Wilhelm (1860–1937): 1886, pastor, Friedrichsdorf near Bielefeld; 1897, head of the institute for deaconesses, Kaiserswerth; 1905–31,

general superintendent of Westphalia; 1931, retired; 1934, member of the Lutheran Council; 1935–37, chair of the executive committee of the Reich Church (dissolved in 1937)—4, 11, 12, 13, 14, 17

Zola, Émile (1840–1902): French author—6, 7

Zophar: biblical character—9

Zorilla y Moral, José (1817–93): Spanish poet and dramatist—10

Zuck, Lowell H.: minister, archivist, and former professor of church history, Eden Theological Seminary, St. Louis, Missouri; 2000, Fulbright senior lecturer, Romania—16

Zuckmayer, Carl (1896–1977): German playwright; friend of Karl Barth; 1930, plays banned in Germany—16

Zumpe, Hans: son-in-law of Eberhard Arnold—13

Zündel, Friedrich (1827–91): Protestant pastor and New Testament scholar—9, 10

Zurhellen, Otto: coauthor of book on introducing the Bible to children—14

Zurhellen-Pfleiderer, Else: coauthor of book on introducing the Bible to children—14

Zutt, Jürg (1893–1980): psychiatrist, neurologist; a student of Karl Bonhoeffer in Berlin; MD in psychiatry and neurology; 1933, assistant to Karl Bonhoeffer and lecturer at the Charité hospital in Berlin; 1937, professor; during World War II, director of the West End Clinic (Berlin-Charlottenburg) of the future university neurological clinic of the Free University in Berlin; 1946, professor, Würzburg, and later in Frankfurt am Main—7, 8

Zweig, Emil: German economist, leading personality in Berlin banking circles; professional prohibition as a result of National Socialist race laws; accountant for the Reformed Bethlehem church, Berlin—16, 17

Zweig, Stefan (1882–1942): Austrian biographer, poet, and novelist; between the wars, he lived chiefly in Salzburg; 1934, emigrated to England; 1940, went to Brazil, where, in 1942, he committed suicide out of depression over the destruction of his spiritual home in Europe; best known for his psychoanalytical biographies—7, 10, 12

Zwick, Johannes (1496–1542): German hymnist—8

Zwingli, Ulrich (Huldrych) (1484–1531): Swiss religious reformer, pastor, and theologian in Zürich; influenced by the humanism of his day; exercised considerable influence on the development of the theology of the Reformation—1, 9, 12, 13, 14

Master Index of Subjects

This index includes key historical and theological terms, subjects, and place names from *DBWE* volumes 1–16, as well as from the new documents published in this volume. It is intended to be not a comprehensive or detailed index but rather a guide to refer readers to the respective volumes where these terms appear.

The extensive index of the German edition in *DBW* 17 served as the foundation for this index; the corresponding English *DBWE* volume indexes were then consulted to refine the indexed entries. The criteria for inclusion in this index for the English-language edition were the historical or theological significance of a given term and/or the frequency of citation. The complexities of translation posed a significant challenge, particularly with regard to theological terms, since some key German terms have been translated differently among the *DBWE* volumes or even within a given volume. Conversely, some English terms (e.g., "compassion") may be translations of more than one German term (in this case, *Barmherzigkeit, Erbarmen,* and *Mitleid*). For clarification in such cases, the German terms have been included here in parentheses, but readers will find it helpful, in conjunction with this index, to consult the list of master documents.

The numbers following the indexed terms below refer only to volume numbers. Readers consulting the respective volume indexes will find the corresponding page numbers, cross-references, and subheadings in those volumes. Volume numbers in this index are listed in **bold** wherever an indexed term is central to that volume. An asterisk (*) next to a volume number indicates that the term in question was a significantly indexed entry in the German index volume (*DBW* 17) but was either not indexed at all in the respective *DBWE* volume or was indexed under a different entry. The terms listed at the end of a citation offer alternative terms under which these may have been listed or may appear as subheadings. As an example, the entry below for "devotions" indicates that this was a significant or fre-

quently used concept in *DBW* volumes 5, 14, and 15 (in bold) but was not indexed under that term in the *DBWE* volume indexes for volumes 5, 8, 11, and 16 (*); users of those volumes may, however, find these references under "Daily Texts," sermons, or worship. Some but not all of these cross-references have also been included in this index; readers are in most cases referred to the individual *DBWE* volume indexes.

devotions, religious (*Andacht*), **5***, 8*, 11*, 12, **14**, **15**, 16*.
See also Daily Texts; sermons; worship

Where an entry is associated with a particular individual (e.g., *Abwehr* and Wilhelm Canaris) or a biblical passage (e.g., prodigal son and Luke 15:11–32), readers will also be referred to the master biographical index of names and the master index of scriptural references in this volume. Similarly, some entries include references to particularly relevant texts from Bonhoeffer's writings, lectures, and sermons (see, for example, the entry below for "pacifism"). References to new documents published in this volume list volume 17, followed by the volume number in which the document would have been published had it been available at the time the *DBWE* volume appeared and the document number, for example, 17 (9:2/2a). In many cases, Greek references are listed in the Greek index of a respective volume (sometimes instead of being listed in the full index; readers are advised to check individual volumes in those cases).

a priori, **2**, 4, 5, 8, 9, 10, **11**, 12. In *DBWE see also* religious a priori
abortion, 6
above, **6**, **7**. In *DBWE see also* authority; *Oben und Unten*
from above, 6, 8, 12, 14
and below (ὑπέρ-ὑπό), 4, **6**, **7**, 8, 16
state of being above, 6
absolute, 2, 9, 17 (9, 2/2a)
absolution, 2, 5, 9, 15, 16
absolutism, 6
abstinence (*Enthaltsamkeit*), 4, 5*, 15. *See also* "Biblical Study Seminars on Basic New Testament Concepts: Notes on the Concept of Abstinence" (*DBWE* 15, 2/2.7)
Abwehr, 4, 6, 7, 15, **16**. In *DBWE see also* conspiracy; July 20; Military Intelligence Office; resistance. *See also* Canaris, Wilhelm, in the master biographical index of names

Abyssinian Baptist Church, 2, 6, **10**, 11, 12, 15*. In *DBWE see also* African American churches; Harlem; Negro spirituals; racism; New York

Academic Assistance Council (UK), 13

acedia (*accidie*), 6, 7, 8, 9, 15, 16. In *DBWE see also* depression; *tristitia*

act (*actus*)
- direct, **2**, 4, 6, **10**, **12**, 14, 15
- pure, **2**, **10**
- reflexive, **2**, 4, 6, **10**, **12**

act (*Akt*), **1**, 10, 11, 12
- religious, **1**, 4, 8

Act and Being, 1, **2**, 3, 4, 5, 6, 8, 9*, **10**, 11, 12, 14, 15, 16*

action (*Handeln*), 6, 7, 8*, 9*, 10. In *DBWE see also* responsible action; responsibility
- and consequences, 6
- ethical, 10, 16
- historical, 6
- human, 2
- responsible, 6, 7

action (*Tun*), 4, **6**, 7, 8*, **12**, 14*

activism, 4, 10, 12

actualization, 1, 6. In *DBWE see also* realization

Adam, and Christ, **1**, 2, 6*. In *DBWE see also* "being in Adam"; "human being in Adam"; "humanity in Adam"; "in Adam"
- humanity in (*Adamsmenschheit*), 1, 2, 6, 10, 11, 14
- theological concepts related to, **1**, 2, **3**, 6*, 9*, 10, 11, 16*

adiaphora, 1, 8, 12, 14, 15*, 16

Advent, 7, **8**, 10, 11, 12, 13, 14, 15, **16**
- sermons for, 10, 11, 13, 15

aesthetics, 2, 8

Africa, 7, 8*, 9, 10, 11*, 12, 15, 16
- Africans, 7, 9

African Americans, **10**, 11*, 12, **15**. In *DBWE see also* Abyssinian Baptist Church; Harlem; Negros; Negro spirituals; racial ideology
- African American churches, 6, **10**, 11, 14, **15**.

"After Ten Years" (*DBWE* 8), 6, 7, **8**, 14, 15

agape (ἀγάπη), 1, 5, 6*, 9, 12*, 15; listed under ἀγάπη, 6, 12, 14

air raids (Second World War), 7*, **8**, **16**. In *DBWE see also* Berlin; bombing raids; World War II

Albania, 12

Allah, 9

Allied forces (WWII), **8**, 15, **16**. In *DBWE see also* World War II

altar, 7*, 11*, 12. In *DBWE see also* God; throne and altar

Altona confession (1933), 12

altruism, 6*, 8*, 16

ambition (*Ehrgeiz*), 2, **7***, 9, 10, 14*, 15, 16*

America, 1, 6, 8, 10, 12, 14, **15**, 16*. In *DBWE see also* "Protestantism without Reformation" (*DBWE* 15); Union Theological Seminary; United States
- Bonhoeffer's 1939 diary, 15
- Bonhoeffer's 1939 visit, 15
- churches in, 11

American Civil Liberties Union, 12
American Committee for Christian German Refugees, 15
Amsterdam, 6*, 8*, 10, 11*, 15, 16
Anabaptists, 1, 9, 10, 12, 13, 14, 15
anarchy, 7, 8, 13, 16*
Anfechtung, 2, 5, 7, 10, 12. In *DBWE see also* temptation; tribulation
angels, 3, 5, 7*, 12, 14, 16*
anger, 4, 7
Anglican churches, 15, 16, 17 (13, 1/208a). In *DBWE see also* Anglo-Saxon theology; Canterbury; Chichester; Church of England. *See also* Bell, George, in the master biographical index of names
animals, 1, **3**, 6, 7*, 8
Ansbach Memorandum (1934), 6, 14*, 16. *See also* Elert, Werner, in the master biographical index of names
anthropology, **2**, 5, **10**, 12, 15. In *DBWE see also* "The Anthropological Question in Contemporary Philosophy and Theology" (*DBWE* 10, 2/7); "Dogmatic Exercises on 'Theological Anthropology'" (*DBWE* 12, 2/2); human being; theology
  biblical, 3
  philosophical, 2, 10
  theological 1, 2, 3, **10**, 12
"Anthropological Question in Contemporary Philosophy and Theology, The" (*DBWE* 10, 2/7), 3, 5*, 8, **10**, 14, 17 (9, 1/99b) (title of earlier English translation: "Man in Contemporary Philosophy and Theology")
anthroposophy, 10, 16
Antichrist, 1, 4, 6, 9, 10, 11, 12, 13*, **14**, 15*, 16*. In *DBWE see also* Hitler, Adolf (both in volume indexes of subjects and in the master biographical index of names)
anti-Judaism (theological), 5*, 10, 12, 16. In *DBWE see also* Ansbach Memorandum; German Christians; Institute for the Study and Eradication of Jewish Influence on German Church Life; Godesberg Declaration; Pharisees
anti-Semitism, 1, 3, 6, 9, 10, 12, 14, 15, 16. In *DBWE see also* Aryan laws; Jews, persecution of; National Socialism
anxiety (*Angst*), 2, 3, **6**, 7*, **8**, 10, 11*, 12, 13*, 15*. In *DBWE see also Anfechtung*; fear
apocalypse, 4, 9, 13*, 14, 16. In *DBWE see also* judgment; Last Judgment. *See also* the master index of scriptural references: Revelation
apologetics, 8, 10, **11**, 12, 14, 15*, 16*
apostles, 1, 4, 6, 11*, 12, **14**, 16. In *DBWE see also* disciples. *See also* the master index of scriptural references

Apostles' Creed, 1, 4, 6, 8, 9, 10, 11, **14, 15**. In *DBWE see also* confessional writings; creeds; Small Catechism
apostolic succession, 9, 14, 15*
Arabs, 9*, 10. In *DBWE see also* Africa
arbitrariness (*Willkür*), **6**, 7*, 16*. In *DBWE see also* government, under law of God
arcane discipline, 2, 4, 5, 7*, **8**, 11*, 14. In *DBWE see also* *Arkandisziplin*; "discipline of the secret"
Armed Forces High Command (Oberkommando der Wehrmacht), 8, 15, **16**. *See also* military; military intelligence
Armistice Day, 10
arrest (Bonhoeffer's), 4*, 6*, 8, 14*, 15*, **16**. In *DBWE see also* conspiracy; imprisonment; National Socialism; prison
of other conspirators, 16
arrogance, 4, 6, 7 , 10, 12, 15. In *DBWE see also* pride
art, 1*, 6, 7, **8**, 9, 10, 12, 15, 16
Aryan, as racial ideology, 3, 6, 12, 13, 16. In *DBWE see also* anti-Semitism; National Socialism
Aryan legislation (state racial laws), **12**, 14, **15**. In *DBWE see also* National Socialism; Nuremberg laws
Aryan paragraph/clause (church racial law), 4, 5, 7, **12**, **13**, 14, 15, 16, 17 (12, 1/106a) In *DBWE see also* Church Struggle; Confessing Church; Erlangen *Gutachten*; Marburg *Gutachten*; "non-Aryan" pastors; Pastors' Emergency League
identification card, 8
Ascension Day, 1, 4*, **8**, 12, **13**, 14, 15, 16. *See also* "Reflection on the Ascension" (*DBWE* 16, 2/2)
asceticism, 1*, 2, **4**, 6, 10, 11*, 12, 13, 14, 15. In *DBWE see also* "The Hiddenness of Practicing Piety" (*DBWE* 4)
Ash Wednesday, 10
assassination (of Hitler), 7, **8**, 15, **16**. In *DBWE see also* conspiracy; July 20; resistance; tyrannicide. *See also* Canaris, Wilhelm, and Stauffenberg, Claus von, in the master biographical index of names
assistant pastorate (*Vikariat*), **10**, 11*, 13*, 14. In *DBWE see also* Barcelona; pastoral ministry
Association of the German Evangelical Congregations in Great Britain and Ireland, **13**. In *DBWE see also* church; Bradford; London; Great Britain; pastors; St. Paul's; Sydenham
atheism, 2, 6, 11, 12
Atlantic Charter (1941), 16
atonement, 2, 6, 10, 12, 14
Augsburg, 1935 synod, 14
peace of (1555), 16
Augsburg Confession (1530), 1, 2, 4, 6, 11*, **12**, **14**, **15**, **16**. In *DBWE see also* confessional

writings. *See also* "Lecture Course on Lutheran Confessional Writings" (*DBWE* 14, 2/2)
Apology, 4, 12, **14**
Art. 4, 2
Art. 12, 1, 2, 4
Art. 16, 4
Art. 25, 4
Austria, 6, 8*, 10*, 11, 12, 13, 14, 15, 16. In *DBWE see also* *Anschluß*
authority (*Autorität*), **1**, 3*, 4, 5, 6, 7, 8, 9, 11*, **12**, 13, **14**, 16. In *DBWE see also* above and below; obedience; state; world. *See also* "Authority and Freedom in the Empirical Church" (*DBWE* 1)
from above and below, 12;
divine, 16
of the office, 6, **12**
papal, 16
parental, 14
political, 12, 13, 14, 16
responsibilities limiting, 6
authority (*Obrigkeit*), **4**, **6**, 7, 9, 10*, **12**, **14**, 15, **16**. *See also* church, authority of; church/state issues; government; vicarious representative action (*Stellvertretung*)
antichristian, 16
to Christ, 6, 16
and the church, 6, 16
duties of, 16
foundation of, 16
as mandate, 6, 8, 16
obedience to, 6, 14, **16**
office of, 12, 16
of the sword, **12**, 14, 16
tyrannical, 14, 15
worldly, 12, 14, 15, 16
authority (*Vollmacht*), 3*, 4, 7, 11*, 13, 14, 16
autonomy (*Autonomie*), 2*, 6, **8**, 9, 11, 12, 14, 16
ethical, 14
Kantian, 6
worldly, 5, 6
autonomy (*Eigengesetzlichkeit*), **6**, 11, 14, 16. In *DBWE see also* freedom; "world come of age"
Avignon, 10
Avila, 10

Baal, 3
Babylon, 8, 9, 12, 14, 15, 16*
Bad Oeynhausen, 8, 13*, **14**. In *DBWE see also* Confessing Church; legalization; Oeynhausen. *See also* "From Barmen to Oeynhausen" (*DBWE* 14, 2/14)
synod of (1936), 14
Balkans, 8*, 9, **12**, 14, 16
Baltic region, 7*, 8*, 9, 10, 12, 13, 14, 15, 16
bans, by Nazi state against Bonhoeffer and the churches, 16. In *DBWE see also* Confessing Church, state measures against; Nazi state; Third Reich
baptism, 1, 2, 4, 6, 7, **8**, **9**, 10, 12, 13, 14, 15, **16**. *See also* "Baptismal Homily on Joshua 24:15" (*DBWE* 13, 3/11); "Baptism Sermon on

Ephesians 5:14" (*DBWE* 11, 3/14); "Baptism Sermon on 1 John 4:16" (*DBWE* 11, 3/9); "New Testament Examination on Baptism" (*DBWE* 9, 2/17a); "Pastoral Duties: Baptismal Homilies" (*DBWE* 14, 2/23.1); "A Theological Position Paper on the Question of Baptism" (*DBWE* 16, 2/14); "Thoughts on the Day of Baptism of Dietrich Wilhelm Rüdiger Bethge, May 1944" (*DBWE* 8, 2/145)
grace of (*Taufgnade*), 4, 14, 16
homilies, 3, **8**, **11**
infant baptism, 2, 4, 8, 9, 10, 13, 14, 16
of Jews, 12
Baptist churches, 1, 10, 13, 14, 15, 16. In *DBWE see also* Abyssinian Baptist Church
Baptist World Alliance, 13
Barcelona, 1, 2, 3, 4, 6, 7, 8, **10**, 11, 12, 13*, 15, 16. In *DBWE see also* church, Foreign Office; German people, abroad;
Bonhoeffer's time as assistant pastor, 2, **10**
Barmen, 9*, 12, 13, 15
Barmen confession/declaration of faith (1934), 1, 3, 4, 6, 12, **13**, **14**, **15**, 16. In *DBWE see also* Confessing Church; Dahlem synod; legalization; *status confessionis*. *See also* "From Barmen to Oeynhausen" (*DBWE* 14, 2/14); "On the Question of Church Communion" (*DBWE* 14, 2/19)
Barthians, 9*, 10, 11*, 13*, 14. In *DBWE see also* Barmen confession; Bonn; theology, study of; universities
Basel, 6, 8*, 10, 11*, 12, 14, 15*, 16
Basel conference (1933), 12
Bavaria, 4, 8, 9, 12, 14, 15, 16
regional church in, 12, 13, 14
Bayreuth, 10, 13
BBC. *See* British Broadcasting Corporation
Beatitudes, 4, 6, 12, 15. In *DBWE see also* Sermon on the Mount
beauty (*Schönheit*), 3, 7*, **8**, 13, 15*
Beer Hall Putsch (1923), 7*, 9, 14
being (*Sein*), 1, **2**, 3*, **6**, 11*, **12**, 14, 16. In *DBWE see also* becoming; *Dasein*
in Christ, 10
for others, 1, 8, 14
being a stranger (*Fremdlingschaft*), 4*, 10, **12**, **15***. In *DBWE see also* church-community; faith
Belgium, 10, 13* 14, 16
"below" (*Unten*), 6, 8*, 7, 12*, 14. In *DBWE see also* "above and below"
Benedictines, 5*, 10, 16. In *DBWE see also Ethics*; Ettal; monasticism
Bergli (Pestalozzi summer home), 11*, 12, 14, 15*
Berlin, 2, 3, 4, 6, 7, 8, 9, 10, 11, **12**, **13**, 14, 15, **16**, 17. In *DBWE see also* Berlin-Brandenburg; Dahlem; Humboldt

University; Friedrich Wilhelm University; Technical College; Technical University
1936 Olympics, 7, 13
Bonhoeffer family home, 7, 8, 14, 15, 16
Grunewald, 7, 8, 10, 11, 12, 16, 17 (9, 1/80a, 94b; 2/2a)
Technical University, 10, 11, 12, 13*
University of, 2, 5, 9, 10, 11, **12**
Berneuchen book, 11
Berneuchen movement, 5*, 6, 8, 11, 12, 14, 16
Bethel (institution for epileptics near Bielefeld), 6, 7*, 9, **12**, 13, 14, 16, 17 (12, 1/106a). *See also* Bethel confession; in the master biographical index of names Bodelschwingh, Fritz von, and Braune, Paul
theological college there, 12, 14
Bethel confession, 4, 6, **12**, 13, 14, 16, 17 (12, 1/106a). In *DBWE see also* "The Bethel Confession" (*DBWE* 12)
betrayal (*Verraten*), 7, 8, 13*, 14. In *DBWE see also* traitor; treason
beyond (*Jenseits*), 2, 3*, 4*, 8*. In *DBWE see also* God; heaven; Sermon on the Mount
Bible, 1, 2, 3, 5, 6, 7, 8, 9, 10, 11, 12, 13, 14, 15, 16. In *DBWE see also* circular letters; exegesis; Finkenwalde; preaching; proclamation (*Schriftauslegung*); word of God
Bible studies by Bonhoeffer, 13, **14**, **15**, **16**
and church, 3, 12, 15
and confession, 13
exegesis of, 16
fallibility of, 9
reading, 9, 12, 14, 15
and revelation, 9
Biesenthal, 5*, 11, 12
biology, 3, 8, 11, 12*
birth, 7*, 8*, 14*, 15
birthdays, 4*, 8, 9*, **13**, 14*, 15, 16
bishop, 5, 12, 15, 16. In *DBWE see also* Church Struggle; German Evangelical Church; regional churches; Reich bishop
office of, 5, 12
Black Forest, 7*, 8, 9*, 17 (9, 1/80a)
blackmail (*Erpressung*), 6*, 8
Blankenburg alliance, 11
blasphemy, 4, 7, **9**, 12, 15, 16
blessedness (*Seligkeit*), 1*, 4, 5*, 10*, 13, 16*. In *DBWE see also* Beatitudes; righteousness; Sermon on the Mount
blessing (*Segen*), 3, 5*, 6*, 7*, 8, 9, 11*, 12, 13, 14*, 15, 16
Bloestau (Confessing church seminary until 1937), 8*, 14, 15, **16**
blood, 6, 7*, 11*, 12, 13*, 14, 15. In *DBWE see also* blood and soil; German Christians; National Socialism
"blood and soil," 3, 6, 8, 12

Germanic understanding of, 6, 15
shedding of, 14
B-minor mass. *See* Mass in B Minor
body, bodily life (*Leib*, σῶμα), 1, 3, 4, 5*, 6, 7*, 8*, 9, 10, **12**, 13*, 15, 16. In *DBWE see also* Christology; human
Bolshevism, 6, 12, 14, 16. In *DBWE see also* Communism
Bonhoeffer student circle (Berlin), **12***, 13, 16*. In *DBWE see* Berlin, student community groups; Berlin University, Bonhoeffer's students; students
Bonn, 1*, 2, 4, 6, 10, 11, 12, 13, 14, 15, 16
Book of Concord, 5, 9, 14, 16. In *DBWE see also* Epitome; Formula of Concord; Large Catechism; Smalcald Articles; Small Catechism
boundary (*Grenze*), 1, **2**, 3, 5*, 6, 7*, **8**, 10, 11*, **12**, 14*, 16*. In *DBWE see also* limits
absolute, 10
national and racial, 14
the other person as, 3, 17
of theology, 2
bourgeoisie/bourgeois values (*Bürgertum*), 4, 6, 7*, 8, 9*, 11, 13. In *DBWE see also Bürgertum*; church, bourgeois; citizens/citizenship; Enlightenment; middle class; social class; upper class
Bradford (congregation), 12, 13
Brandenburg, 12, 15*, 16. In *DBWE see also* Berlin-Brandenburg; churches; consistory; Council of Brethren
consistory governance of, 10, 11*, 12
mission conference (1932), 11*, 17 (12, 1/106a)
bread, 3, **5**, 14
daily bread, 4, 5, 14
for the hungry, 6*
of life, 5
Bremen, 9*, 10, 15
Breslau (Wroclaw), 6*, 7, 8, 9*, 11*, 12, 14, **16**
Breslau Confessing synod (1936), 14
Breslau Confessing synod (1943), 6, 8
Britain. *See* Great Britain
British Bible Society, 13
British Broadcasting Corporation (BBC), 8, 15, **16**. In *DBWE see also* BBC; Great Britain; radio
broadcasts to Germany, 16
British people. *See* Great Britain
brotherhood (*Bruderlichkeit*), 6*, 7, 14, 15, **16**. In *DBWE see also* community; Council of Brethren; fellowship; Finkenwalde
Brotherhood (*Bruderschaft*) of Young Theologians, 8, 11, 12, 14, 15, 16. In *DBWE see also* Bruderrat; Finkenwalde; "illegal" seminarians; Pomerania
Christian, 5

brothers, 3, 4, 5, 6*, 8, 9, 11, 12, 13*, 14, 13, 16. In *DBWE see also* brotherhood; brothers and sisters; circular letters; Council of Brethren; fellowship; Finkenwalde; House of Brethren; kindred; neighbor; the "other"; pastors; seminarians
- animals as, 3
- contempt for, 4
- fallen in war, 16
- godless, 12, 13
- Jewish, 6, 12, 14, 16
- love for, 14, 15*
- "non-Aryan", 13
- relationship between, 16

"Brown Synod" (1933), 12, 13, 17 (12, 1/106a). In *DBWE see also* Pastors' Emergency League; Wittenberg
Bruay en Artois, 13, 16
Bruderhof community, 6, 10, **13**, 14. *See also* Arnold, Hardy and Eberhard, in the master biographical index of names
Brunswick (Braunschweig), 8, 15*
Bucharest, 8
Buchenwald, 6, 7, 8, 15, **16**
Budapest, 6*, 12, 13*, 16
Buddhism, 1, 9*, 10
Bulgaria, 6*, 12, 14, 16
bullfights, 10
Burckhardt House, 8, 16. In *DBWE see also* Dahlem
bureaucracy, church. In *DBWE see* church; Church Foreign Office; Church Struggle; consistory; German Evangelical Church, leadership; Old Prussian Union church
business, 8, 14*
"By Powers of Good" (poem), **8**, 16. In *DBWE see also* poetry

Caesarea Phillipi, 4, 12
Calvinism, 2, 6, 9, 10, 11, 12, 13*, 14. In *DBWE see also* Reformed Church
camaraderie, 7*, 8*, 12. In *DBWE see also* brotherhood; fellowship
Cambridge, 13, 15, 16
- conference (1931), 10, **11**, 12, 14, 16

camouflage letter (1943, backdated to 1940), **16**
Canaan, 3, 10, 12, 14*, 15
Canada, 14, 16
Canterbury. *See* Lang, Cosmo, and Temple, William, in the master biographical index of names. In *DBWE see also* archbishop of Canterbury
cantus firmus, 8
capax infiniti, 2, 10
Capernaum, 8, 14*
capitalism, 1*, 6, 10, 11, 12
Carmen (opera), 10
Carthage Synod (third century), 16
Casablanca, 9*
- Casablanca conference (1943), 16

casuistry, **6**, 8, 9, 12, 16
Catalog of Vices, 4*, 6*, **14**, 15. *See also* "Concrete Ethics in Paul" (*DBWE* 14, 2/22)

catechesis, 1, 7, 10, 14; on Matthew, 9. *See also* "Lecture on Catechesis" (*DBWE* 14, 2/11)
catechetics, 12, 14, 15
  catechetical lectures (1935–37), 8*, **14**, 15
catechism, 4, 6, 9, 10, 11, 12, 14, 15*. In *DBWE see also* catechetical instruction *or* catechetical lessons; Council of Trent
  Luther's Large Catechism, 4, 14, 16
  Luther's Small Catechism, 4, 12, 14; Roman, 4, 6, 14
categories, 11; sociological, 2, 12
Catholic Church. *See* Catholicism; Roman Catholic Church
Catholicism, 1*, 2, 4, 6, 8, 9, 10, **11**, 12, 13*, 14, 15, **16**. In *DBWE see also* Roman Catholic Church
  defense against Catholicization, 5
Catholics, 4, 8, 10, 12, 13*, 14, 15
Caux, 14. In *DBWE see also* Moral Rearmament
celibacy, 8*, 10, 15*
censors, censorship, 5, 16, 17 (12, 1/106a)
Center Party, 12. *See also* Röhm Putsch; Roman Catholic Church
Central Welfare Office for German Jews (Zentralwohlfahrstelle der deutsche Juden), 12 (also listed there as Jewish Welfare Association)
certainty (*Gewißheit*), 1*, 3*, 4*, 5*, 6*, 12, 13*, 14, 15, 16
Chalcedon, Council of, 2, 6, 8, **12**, 15
Chamby sur Montreux, 8, 14. In *DBWE see also* ecumenical organizations; Life and Work
  1935 conference, 14
  1936 conference, 14, 15, 16*
chaos, 3*, 6, 7, 8*, **12**, 15*, 16*
chaplaincy. *See* military chaplaincy; student chaplaincy
character, 6*, 7, 12, 14, 17. In *DBWE see also* "After Ten Years"; shame;
charism, 4
charisma, 14
charity (*Wohltätigkeit*), 1, 7*, 10*, 13*. In *DBWE see also* beneficence; social work
Charity Fund Committee (London), 13
Charlottenburg, 2. In *DBWE see also* Berlin-Charlottenburg
chastity (*Keuschheit*), 4, 6, 8*, 14*, 17 (9, 2/2a). In *DBWE see also* virtue
cheap grace, **4**, 6, 7*, 10, 12, 14, 15, 16. In *DBWE see also* costly grace; grace, cheap
cheerfulness (*Heiterkeit, Hilaritas*), 8
Chicago, 8*, **10**, 15
  Chicago theological school of thought, 12, 15
Chichester, 6, 8*, 12, **13**, 14, 15, **16**. In *DBWE see also* Bell, George, in the master biographical index of names

child, children, 1*, **2**, 3, 4, 6, 7, **8**, 9, **10**, **12**, **13**, 14, **16**
  faith of, 12, 16
  of God, 4, 5*, 6, 9, 12, 14, 16
children's worship, 1*, **9**, **10**, 13. *See also* "Homily for the Children's Service" (*DBWE* 10, 3/16)
  catechism, 7, 9, 10
chiliasm, 9, 10, 11*, 12, 15
China, 6, 10, 11, 12, 14, 15, 16
Chr. Kaiser publishers, 8, 13*, 15*, **16**. In *DBWE see also* Kaiser publishers
Christ, 1, 2, 3, 4, 5, 6, 7, 8, 9, 10, 11, 12, 13, 14, 15, 16. In *DBWE see also* Barmen declaration; Christology; Jesus Christ; preaching; proclamation; resurrection; revelation; *solus Christus*; vicarious representative action (*Stellvertretung*). *See also* "Christ, Reality, and Good" (*DBWE* 6)
  ascension of, 15
  being in Christ, 1, **2**, **4**, 5, 6, **9**, 14
  birth of, 6, 8, 12, 14, **15**, **16**
  body of, **1**, **4**, 5, 6, 9, 10, 12, 13, **14**, **15**, 16
  as brother, 4, 5, 11, 12
  commandments of, 6, 8, 10, 16
  cross of, 1, 2, 3, **4**, 5, 6, 8, **10**, **11**, **12**, 13, **14**, **15**, 16
  crucifixion of, 1,6, 8, 12, 15, 16
  death of, 3, **4**, 5, **9**, 11, **14**, 15
  demands on us, 6, 12, 15, 16
  discipleship, **4**, 5, 6, 12, **14**
  existing as church-community, **1**, 2, 3, 4, 5, 6, 9, 10, **11**, 12, 13, 14, 15
  as God become human (*menschgewordene*), 4, 6, 12, 16
  as human being, 2, 8, 16, 6, 11, 12
  humiliation (*Erniedrigung*) of, 5, 9, 10, **12**, 16
  kingdom of, 1, 6, 9, 12, 13, 14, 15
  life of, 6, 14
  as Lord, 7, 12, **14**, 15, **16**
  as Lord of the religionless, 8
  lordship/dominion of, 9, 11, 14, 15, 16
  love of, 1, 4, 6, 8, 9, 10, 13, **15**, **16**
  as the new humanity, 2, 6, 11
  omnipresent, 5, 16
  for the other, 8
  in the other, 5, 11
  participating in, 4, 8, 14
  present, **4**, 6, 10, 11, **12**, **14**, 16
  proclamation of, 2, 6, 12, 16
  as radical, 6
  reality of, 1, 6
  resurrection of, 1, 2, 3, 4, 5, 6, 7, 8, 9, 10, 11, 12, 13, 14, 15, 16
  the risen Christ, 12, 14, 16
  second coming, 2, **4**, 6, 9, 11, 12, 13, **14**, 15, 16
  as son of God, 12, 14, 116
  suffering of, 5, 8, 12, 16
  transfiguration of, 4, 9, 14, 15
  as vicarious representative (*Stellvertreter*), 5, 11
  who is Christ for us today, 7, 8
  word of, 1, **4**, **5**, 6, 7, 13, 14, **15**, 16
"Christ and Peace" (1932 lecture, *DBWE* 12), 6, 10, 11*, **12**

Christendom (*Christenheit*), 6, 8*, 11*, 12, 13, 15, **16**
ecumenical, 13
in Europe, 13
in the United States, 6
in the West, 6
Christian, the (*das Christliche*), 6, 7, 8, 12, 13, 14
Christian Century, 10, 15
Christian community (anthroposophical), 10, 14, 16
Christianity (*Christentum*), 1, 2, 4, 5, 6, 7, 8, 9, 10, 11, 13, 14, 15, **16,** 17 (13, 1/208a). *see also* German Christians; "nonreligious Christianity"; practical Christianity; "religionless Christianity"; "world come of age"; "worldly Christianity"
aristocratic, 8
Christian life, 15
dogmatic, 6
early, 1, 6, 11, 14, 16
German, 14
persecution of, 13
practical, 6, 9
radical, 6
in Rome, 6
this-worldliness of, 5, 7, 8, 16, 15
unconscious (*unbewusstes*), 2, 6, 7, 8
in the United States, 15
Christians, 5, 6, 7, 8, 11, 12, 13, 14, 15, **16**. In *DBWE see also* Aryan paragraph; Christ; gentiles; German Christians; Jewish Christians
and Germans, 13
"non-Aryan", 14
Russian, 14, 15
and the state, 13
in the United States, 10, 15
worldly, 8
worldly responsibility of, 16
"Christians and Heathens," (*DBWE* 8), 7, 8. In *DBWE see also* "Christians and Pagans"
Christian-Social movement, 12, 14
"Christ in the Psalms" (1935, *DBWE* 14), 14
Christmas, 8, 9, 10, 11*, 12, 13, 14, **15**, **16**. *See also* "Supplements to the Monthly Letters from the Confessing Church Council of Brethren in Pomerania to Its Pastors: Meditation on Christmas" (*DBWE* 15, 3/10.1)
carols, 10, 13, 16
Christmas Eve, 8*, 13, 14
pageant, 10, 13.
Christmas Oratorio (Bach), 9
Christocentrism, 4, 5, 6, 13
Christology, 1, 2, 3, 4, 6, 7, 8, 9, 10, 11, **12**, 14, 15, 16. *See also* "Lecture on Christ in the Psalms" (*DBWE* 14, 2/5)
critical, 12
of the early church, 12, 15
reformed, 16
Christology lectures (1933), 1, 2, 3, 4, 5*, **6**, 7, 10, **12**, 14, 15. In *DBWE see also* "Christ the Center"
Christ the Center (early translation of Bonhoeffer's 1933 Christology lectures), 2, 7
church, **1**, 2, 3, 4, 5, 6, 7, **8**, 9, 10, 11, 12, 13, 14, 15, **16**. *See also* Catholic Church;

church-state; Church Struggle; Confessing Church; ecumenical movement; Federal Council of Churches; free churches; liturgy; proclamation; Reformation; Reich Church; *Volkskirche*. *See also* "Address in Gland" (*DBWE* 11, 2/17); "Lecture: 'The Visible Church in the New Testament'" (*DBWE* 14, 2/8); "The Nature of the Church" (*DBWE* 11, 2/9); "What Is Church?" (*DBWE* 12, 2/7)
Anglican, 6, 11, 12, 13, 14, 15
attendance, 4*, 6, 7, 12, 13
boundaries, 4, 15
as Christ, 2, 6, 12
of Christ, 3, 8, 16
as collective person, 1, 9
communion, 15
concept of, 1, 2, 9, 10, 11, 13, 16*
constitution of, 1, 12, 14, 16, 17 (12, 1/106a)
crisis of, **10**, 16*
Dutch, 16
duty of, 16
elders, 14, 15, 16
empirical, **1**, 2, 9, 11
Episcopal, 10, 15
freedom of, 7
German, 12, 13, 14, 15
institutional, 2
invisible, 1, 9, 14, 15
liturgical agendas of, 14, 15
Lutheran, 12, 13, 14, 15, 16
as mandate, 6, 8, 16
nature of, 10, **11**, 12, 13, 14
in New Testament, 1, 14
in Norway, 16
orthodox, 6, 8
for others, 1, 8
political action of, 12
Protestant (*evangelisch*), 4, 6, 8, 9, 11, 12, 13, 14, 15, 16
Reformed, 12, 14, 15, 16
renewal of, 14, 16
Russian Orthodox, 1, 12, 16
scope of, 14
Scottish, 12;
space of, 4, 6, 8, **14**
and state, 1, 4, 6, 11, **12**, 14, 15 **16***
and synagogue, 15
triumphant, 1, 9, 12
in the United States, 6, 10, 15, 16;
unity of, 1, 9, 11, 13, 14, 15
universal, 13
visible, 1, 6, 9, 11, 12, 13, 14, 16
word of, 1, 12, 14, 16
and the world, 1, 6, 8, 11, 14, 15, 16
church, early, 3, 4, **12**, 14, 15, 16. In *DBWE see also* ancient church; church fathers; early church
church, social ministries (*Diakonie*), 6, 8, 14. In *DBWE see also* diaconate; pastoral care
"Church and the Jewish Question, The" (*DBWE* 12), 13, 15, 16
church chancellery, 12, 13, 15, 16
church committees (1935-37), **14**, 15, 16. In *DBWE see also* Church Struggle; Old Prussian Union Church
church communion (*Kirchengemeinschaft*), 6, 10, 12*, 13*, 14, 15*. *See also*

ecumenical movement; "On the Question of Church Communion," (*DBWE* 14, 2/19), 6, 8, **14**
church-community (*Gemeinde*), 1, **2**, **4**, 6, 7*, 8, 9, 10*, 11, 12, 13*, 14, **15**, 16*
building of, 4, 14. In *DBWE see also* community; congregation; *Gemeinde*
church discipline, 1*, **4**, 6, 14, 15*
church elections, 12, 13*, 16. In *DBWE see also* elections, church
Church Federation (Kirchenbund). *See* German Evangelical Church Federation
Church Foreign Office, 8, **13**, 14, 16*. In *DBWE see also* German Evangelical Church
church government, 12, 13*, 14, 15, 16
church history, 1, 6, 9, 10, 13*, 15*, 16. In *DBWE see also* history, church
Church of the Old Prussian Union, 1*, 5*, 12, **13, 14, 15, 16***, 17 (12, 1/106a). In *DBWE see also* Confessing Church; Constitution of the Church of the Old Prussian Union; Old Prussian Union Church; Prussia
church schism, 12, 13*, 14, 15, 16*. In *DBWE see also* Church Struggle; schism
Church-Social Federation (after 1918), 11
Church Struggle (*Kirchenkampf*), 4, 5, 6, 7, 8, 9, 10, 11, 12, **13**, 14, **15**, **16**, 17 (12, 1/106a); 17 (13, 1/208a). In *DBWE see also* Aryan paragraph; Barmen synod; Confessing Church; Dahlem synod; Finkenwalde; German Christians; intact churches; Reich Church. *See also* "Bonhoeffer's Sketch for His Statement 'From Barmen to Oeynhausen'" (*DBWE* 14, 2/14); "Draft Proposal for a Reorganization of the Church after the 'End of the Church Struggle'" (*DBWE* 16, 2/16); "Essay and Discussion on Church Communion" (*DBWE* 14, 2/19); "Expert Opinion on 'False Teaching' in the Confessing Church" (*DBWE* 14, 2/20); "Lecture on the Path of the Young Illegal Theologians of the Confessing Church" (*DBWE* 15, 2/5)
church tax, 1, 15
Ciernohorské Kúpele, 3, 4, **11**, 12, 16. *See also* "On the Theological Foundation of the Work of the World Alliance" (*DBWE* 11, 2/14)
Cimade (French resistance/rescue organization), 16. *See also* Le Chambon
circular letters (from Finkenwalde), 4*, **15**, 16. *See*

also Finkenwalde, circular letters
circumcision, 8, 16
citizens/citizenship (*Bürger, Bürgertum),* 1*, 4*, 6, 7, 8*, 10, 11, 12, 14, **16**. In *DBWE see also* bourgeoisie; class; Christians; civic community; civil courage; community; Enlightenment; middle class
  Christians as, 8
city/cities (πόλις), 6, 7, 8, 13*, 14
civil courage, 7, 8, 10
civil rights, 10, 12, 14, 15, 16. In *DBWE see also* civil liberties; church-state relationship
Civil War (U.S.), 6*, 12, 15, 16. *See also* slavery; United States
class (social), 1, 3, 6, 7*, 8*, 9, 10, 12, 16. In *DBWE see also* bourgeoisie; citizens; social class; society
clergy. *See* ministry; pastors
clericalism, 6, 8, 16
collections (in church), 13, 14, 15*, 16*. In *DBWE see also* church collections; Confessing Church, collections; Himmler Decree (1937)
collective pastorates (1937–40), 4, 5*, 8, 14, **15**, **16**. In *DBWE see also* Groß-Schlönwitz; Köslin; Sigurdshof
collective person, **1**, 2, **6**, 9, 16. In *DBWE see also Gesamtperson, Kollektivperson*
collectivism, 1, 5*, 6, 12
Columbus, Ohio, 15
comfort (*Trost*), 3, 6, **8***, 10, 11*, 13*, 14*, 16
"coming of age" (*mündig werden*), 2, 6*, 7, 8*, 12*, 14, 16*. In *DBWE see also Mündigkeit;* "world come of age"
  religious, 14
command (*Befehl*). In *DBWE see also* authority (*Obrigkeit*); commandments; God, commands of; Ten Commandments
  apostolic, 14
  of Christ, 4
  concrete, 4*, 6, 11, 12, 14
  fulfilled in history, 6, 15
  of God, 3, 4*, **6**, 7, 8*, 9, 10, **11***, **12**, 13, **14**, **15***, 16*
  of peace, 3, 11, 12, 13
  understanding, 4*, 14
commandment(s), 3, 4, 6, 7, 9, 10, 15, 16. In *DBWE see also* command; Decalogue; Ten Commandments
common good (*Gemeinwesen*), 7, 8*, 16
communal movement (*Gemeinschaftsbewegung*), 1, 11*, 14, 15. In *DBWE see also* communitarianism
communion. *See* Lord's Supper
Communism, 6, 11, 12, 13*, 14, 15, 16. In *DBWE see also* proletariat; workers
community (*Gemeinschaft*), **1**, 2, 3, 4, **5**, 7, 9, 10, 12, 13, 15, 16, 17 (9, 1/99b). *See also* church-community; communion; fellowship

compassion (*Barmherzigkeit*), 3, 4, 6, 7, 8, 10, 13*, **15***, **16***. *See also* grace; mercy

compassion (*Erbarmen*), 4, 9

compassion (*Mitleid*), 1, 7, 8, 11*, 14*, 16*. In *DBWE see also* pity

concentration camps, 6*, 7, 8, 12, 13*, 14, 15, **16**. In *DBWE see also* Auschwitz; Buchenwald; Dachau; Flossenbürg; Sachsenhausen

Concordat, Bavarian (1924), 9; Reich (1933), 12

Concordia Seminary, 10

Concord of Worms (1122), 8

concreteness, 1*, 2, 6, 11, **12**. *See also* "The Concrete Commandment and the Divine Mandates" (*DBWE* 6, 388–94); "Concrete Ethics in Paul" (*DBWE* 14, 2/22). In *DBWE see also* action; concretion

of ethics, 14

conduct (*Wandel*, περιπατεῖν), 4 (in Greek index, translated in this volume as "journeying"), 14

Confessing Church, 1, 2, 4, 5, **6**, 7, 8, 9, 10, 11, 12, **13**, **14**, **15**, **16**. In *DBWE see also* Aryan paragraph; Augsburg; Bad Oeynhausen synod; Barmen synod; Church of the Old Prussian Union; Church Struggle; Dahlem synod; ecumenical movement; Finkenwalde; German Christians; German Evangelical Church; Halle synod; legalization controversy; Leipzig synod; Pastors' Emergency League; Young Reformation Movement. *See also* "The Confessing Church and the Ecumenical Movement" (*DBWE* 14, 2/6); "Expert Opinion on 'False Teaching' in the Confessing Church" (*DBWE* 14, 2/20); "Lecture on the Path of the Young Illegal Theologians of the Confessing Church" (*DBWE* 15, 2/5)

congregations and regions, 16

Council of Brethren, 8, 13, 14, 16

emergency law in, 4, 8, 14, 15, 16

and German Christians, 12, 13, 14, 15

and Nazi state, 12, **13**, 14, 15, 17 (12, 1/106a; 13, 1/208a)

preachers' seminaries, 4, 5, 14, 15

synods, 13, 14, 15, 17 (12, 1/106a)

theological education in, 4, 13, **14**, **15**

"Confessing Church and the Ecumenical Movement, The" (*DBWE* 14, 2/6), 13, 14. *See also* "Lecture in Ciernohorské Kúpele: On the Theological Foundation of the Work of the World Alliance" (*DBWE* 11, 2/14)

confession (*Konfession*), 9, 12, 13, 14, 16

confessionalism, 14, 16

confession, personal (*Beichte*), 1, 2, 4, **5**, **6**, 7, 8, 9, 10, 11, 12, **14**, **15**, 16. *See also* "Lectures on Personal Confession" (*DBWE* 14, 2/24); "Outline for a Homily for Personal Confession on Proverbs 28:13" (*DBWE* 14, 3/4)
  Catholic practice of, 9
confessional writings (*Bekenntnisschriften*), 5, **12**, 13*, 14, 15, **16**. In *DBWE see also* Augsburg Confession; Book of Concord; catechism; Formula of Concord; Heidelberg Catechism; Smalcald Articles. *See also* "Lecture Course on Lutheran Confessional Writings" (*DBWE* 14, 2/2)
  Lutheran, 4, 14, 16
  of the Reformation, 5, 14
  Reformed church, 14
confession of faith (*Bekenntnis*), 1, 2, 4, **5**, 6, 8, 10, 11, **12**, **13**, **14**, **15**, 16, 17 (9, 2/2a). In *DBWE see also* Apostles' Creed; Augsburg Confession; Barmen synod; Bethel confession; Confessing Church; confession, personal; confessional texts; confession of guilt; Dahlem synod; Lutheran; Nicene Creed; Reformation. *See also* "The Bethel Confession" (*DBWE* 12, 2/15)
  and the church, 13, 15, 16
  and discipleship, 13
  Lutheran confessions, 4, 12, 14, 15
confession of guilt (*Schuldbekenntnis*), 15. In *DBWE see also* guilt; "Unfinished Draft of a Pulpit Pronouncement following the Coup, end of 1942" (*DBWE* 16, 2/15)
confession of sin (*Sündenbekenntnis*), 3, 4, 5, 8, 14, 15
Confessions
  Gallica, 14
  Scottish, 14
  second Swiss (Helvetica), 1, 14
Confidential Council of Clerical Advisors (Geistliche Vertrauensrat, after August 1939), 15, 16 (translated there as Confidential Spiritual Council)
confirmation instruction, 1, 7, 8*, 9, 10, 11, 12, 13, **14**, 15, **16**. In *DBWE see also* catechetical instruction. *See also* "Catechetical Outlines" (*DBWE* 14, 2/4); "Confirmation 1938" (*DBWE* 15, 3/3); "Lecture on Confirmation Instruction" (*DBWE* 14, 2/27)
confirmation students, 7, 10, 11, 12, 13, 14, 15
congregational council, Barcelona, 10
congregational discipline (*Gemeindezucht*), 4, 15, 16*. In *DBWE see also* church, discipline; congregational order; discipline. *See also*

"Lecture and Discussion on the Power of the Keys and Church Discipline" (*DBWE* 14, 2/29); "Lecture: 'Congregational Development and Church Discipline in the New Testament'" (*DBWE* 14, 2/28)
Congregationalists, 10, 13*, 15
congregations, 12, 13, **16**. In *DBWE see also* church; church-community; parish
conscience (*Gewissen*), 1, **2**, 3, 4*, **6**, 7, **8**, 9, **10**, 11, 12, 13, 14, 15, 16. *See also* "Catechetical Outlines: Conscience" (*DBWE* 14, 2/4.3)
 and decision, 14.
conscientious objection, objectors, 4, 5*, 12, 13, 14, 15. In *DBWE see also* International Fellowship of Reconciliation; military; pacifism. *See also* Stöhr, Hermann, in the master biographical index of names
consciousness (*Bewußtsein*), 1, **2**, 6, 7, 10, 11*, 12. *See also* self-consciousness
 Christian, 9
 and God, 2;
 religious, 11
 species-consciousness, 1
 and transcendence, 2
conservatism, 1, 6, 11*, 12, 14*, 15
consistory (Old Prussian Union), 10, 12*, 14, 15, **16**. In *DBWE see also* church, governance; Old Prussian Union church
conspiracy (resistance), **6**, 7, **8**, 9, 12, 15, **16**. *See also Abwehr*; coup; *Despositenkasse* affair; ecumenical movement; July 20; resistance
constitution. *See also* church, constitution of; Weimar Republic
 Prussian (1850), 9
 U.S., 6, 15
contemplation, 2. In *DBWE see also* monasticism; prayer
continuity, 3, 8*, 12
 of revelation, 2
contraception, 6, 10, 16*. In *DBWE see also* birth control
contrition, 1*, 3, 4, **9**, 12
conversion (*Umkehrung*), 4*, 5, 8, 10, 11, 12, 13*, **14***, 15, 16
 of Jews, 9, 12
convictions, 6*, 7
Copenhagen, 8*, 11*, 12, 13, 14, 16
cor curvum in se (heart turned in upon itself), **2**, 3, 5, 10, **12**
Corpus Christi, 6, 9, **10**
costly grace, 4, 6, 7, 8, 10*, 12, 14, 15*. In *DBWE see also* cheap grace; grace, costly
Council of Brethren, 4, 5, 8*, 14, **15**, **16**. In *DBWE see also* Confessing Church; Finkenwalde; Pastors' Emergency League; underground pastorates
coup, 5*, 8*, 12, **16**. In *DBWE see also* conspiracy; July 20; resistance. *See also* "Friedrich Justus Perels: Draft of a Church Constitution following the Coup"

(*DBWE* 16, 2/17);
"Unfinished Draft of a Pulpit Pronouncement following the Coup" (*DBWE* 16, 2/15)
courage, 2, 7, 8, 9, 10*, 12, 13*, 15, 16*
covenant (*Bund*), 2, 4*, 9, 10, 12, 14, 15, 16. In *DBWE see also* mosaic covenant; Old Covenant
covenantal love, 3
eternal, 14, 15; with God, 2, 7, 14, 15
with God's people, 4*, 10, 12, 14
Noahide, 14
people of the, 12 (*Bundesvolk*)
sign of God's love, 16
cowardice, 7, 8*, 12, 13, 15
creation, 1, 2, **3**, 4, 5, 6, 8, 9, 10, **11**, 12, 13, 14, 15, 16. In *DBWE see also* creator; creature; orders of creation; orders of preservation. *See also* "Theses: The Discernible Nature of the Order of Creation" (*DBWE* 11, 2/8)
new (καινὴ κτίσις), 11, 12, 14
and preservation, 3, 4
and redemption, 6
and the resurrection, 3
Creation and Fall, 2, **3**, 4, **6**, 7*, 8, 10, 12, 13, 14, 15, 16, 17 (9, 1/99b)
creation history, 3, 16
Creator (God), 1, 2, **3**, 6, 8*, 9, 10, 11, 12, 13*, 14*, 15*, 16. In *DBWE see also* God
and the created, 1, 3, 4, 9, 12, 14
praise for, 3, 5
creature (*Geschöpf*), 1, **2**, 6, 9, 12, 14, 16*
as own being, 3
creature (*Kreatur*), 3*, 6, 12, 14, 15*, 16*. In *DBWE see also* creation
new (καινὴ κτίσις), 1, 6, 9, 12, 16
crimes, 6, 7*, 16. In *DBWE see also* Jews, persecution of; National Socialism; Nazi regime; Third Reich
Nazi crimes against humanity, 6, 7*
Croall Lectures, 15
cross of Christ, 1, 2, 3, 5, 6, 7, 8, 9, 10, 11*, **12**, 13, 14, 15, 16*. In *DBWE see also* Christ; crucifixion; Jesus Christ; resurrection
crucifixion/crucified one, 1, 4, 10, 12, 16
cultural Protestantism, 6, 14, 15*. In *DBWE see also* Protestantism
culture (*Bildung*), **6**, 7, 8, 10, 11*, 12, 14, 16. In *DBWE see also* character formation; cultivation; education; mandates
as mandate, 6
culture (*Kultur*), 1, 2, **6**, 8, 9, 10, 11*, **10**, 12, 13*, 14*, **16**, 17 (9, 1/99b). In *DBWE see also* barbarization; *Bildung*
barbarization of, 7, 12
Christian, 6, 14
as mandate, 6
curiosity (*Neugier*), 7, 8*
curse (of God), 3, 4*, 6, 7*, **12**, 14, 15*

cynicism, 6, 7*, 8, 10, 15, 16
Czechoslovakia, 5*, 6, 10, 11, 12, 13*, 14, 15, 16. In *DBWE see also* Sudetenland

Dachau, 8, 14, 15
Dahlem, 8, 12, 13, 14, 15, 16. In *DBWE see also* Berlin-Dahlem; St. Anne's Church; *also* Niemöller, Martin, in the master biographical index of names
- 1934 Confessing synod (October), 4, 5, 6, 8, **13**, **14**, 15, 16
- 1934 Prussian synod, 13
- 1935 synod, 14

daily bread. *See* bread
Daily Texts (*Losungen*), **5**, 6*, **8**, 10*, 11*, 13*, 14*, 15, **16**. In *DBWE see also* Moravian church. *See also* "Devotional Aids for the Moravian *Daily Texts*" (*DBWE* 16, 3/4)
- Bonhoeffer's meditations on, 9, 16

Damascus, 9, 15*
dance, 8*, 9, 10
Danzig, 10, 14, 15, 16
Darwinism, 8, 10
Dasein, **2**, 3*, 10, 16, 17 (9, 2/2a). In *DBWE see also* being; "exists, that which" (3); presence (16)
- autonomy of, **2**
- for the other, 5*, 6*, 7, 8*, 13

Dassel, ecumenical conference (1933), 12. In *DBWE see also* "Discussion Paper for the Ecumenical Conference in Dassel" (*DBWE* 12, 2/10)
day, 3, 5, 14, 16
death, 1, **2**, **3**, 4, 5, 6, **7**, **8**, **9**, **10**, 11, **12**, 13, **14**, 15, **16**, 17. In *DBWE see also* dying; funeral; killing. *See also* "Biblical Study Seminars on Basic New Testament Concepts: Notes on Death" (*DBWE* 15, 2/2.8); "Lecture Fragment on Death and Justification" (*DBWE* 14, 2/15.2 and 3); "Literary Attempt on the Theme of 'Death'" (1932), 11, 2/22
- as enemy, 7, 8, 15
- longing for, 7, 9, 17
- spiritual, 5, 9

"Death of Moses, The" (poem), 7, **8**, 16
decadence, 6, 7
Decalogue (Ten Commandments), 4, **6**, 7, 8, **9**, 10, 12, 14, 15, **16**. In *DBWE see also* commandments; Ten Commandments. *See also* "Exposition on the First Table of the Ten Words of God" (*DBWE* 16, 3/5)
- eighth commandment, 14, 16
- fifth commandment, 4, 6, 12, 14
- first commandment, 4, 8, 9, 12, 14, 15, 16
- fourth commandment, 4, 6, 8, 9, 14, 16
- ninth commandment, 14
- second commandment, 14, 16
- seventh commandment, 14
- sixth commandment, 4, 14
- tablets of, 6, 12, 16
- tenth commandment, 4, 14
- third commandment, 7, 14, 16

decay, 4*, 6, 7. In *DBWE see also* decomposition
deception (*Täuschung*), 16
decision/decisiveness, 1, **2**, 4*, 6, 7, 8*, 9*, 10, 12, 13, **14**, **15***, **16**. In *DBWE see also* conscience; ethics; responsibility
  church decisions, 4, 8*, **14**, 15
  ethical, 6
  of faith, 13, 15
Declaration of Independence, 6
Declaration of the Rights of Man, 6
deconstruction, 2
Dehn affair, 11, 12. *See also* Dehn, Günther, in the master biographical index of names
deism, 8, **11**
democracy, 1, 3, **6**, 7, 10, **12**, 14, 15, **16**
  concept of, 10
  in the United States, 6, 15
demons, 9, 12, 13, 14, 17. In *DBWE see also* devil; Satan
  the demonic, 6, 10, 14, 16
demythologization, 6, 8, 16
Denmark, 6, 10, 11*, 12, 13, 14, 15, **16**. In *DBWE see also* Copenhagen; Danish bishops; Fanø
denominations, 4, 10*, 12*, **15**. In *DBWE see also* "Protestantism without Reformation" (*DBWE* 15, 2/6)
denunciation, 6
deportation of the Jews. *See* Jews, deportations of
Depositenkasse affair, **16**. In *DBWE see also* conspiracy; Operation 7; resistance. *See also* Schmidhuber, Wilhelm, in the master biographical index of names
despair, 6, 7, **8**, 9, **12**
desperation (*Verzweiflung*), 3, 6, 7*, 8, 11*, 12*, 15*, 16*. In *DBWE see also* despair
determinism, 6, 10, 17 (9, 2/2a). *See also* "Course Paper: The Character and Ethical Consequences of Religious Determinism" (*DBWE* 10, 2/14)
Deus absconditus, 1*, 9, 10, 14. In *DBWE see also* God
  etsi Deus non daretur, 3, 8*
Deus ex machina, 8. In *DBWE see also* God
devil, 2, 3, 4, 5, 6, 7, 8*, 9, 11*, 12, 13*, 14, 15, 16 In *DBWE see also* Satan
  calling by name, 14;
  in the guise of an angel, 12
  reign of, 6, 14
devotions, religious (*Andacht*), **5***, 8*, 11*, 12, **14**, **15**, 16*. In *DBWE see also* Daily Texts; Finkenwalde; meditation; prayer; sermons; worship
diaconate, 9, 12*, 14, 16. In *DBWE see also* church, social ministry; pastoral care
dialectic(s), 1*, 2, 3, 6, 8*, 9, 10, 11, **12**, 13*, 14
dialectical theology, **2**, 6, 9, 10
diary (Bonhoeffer's), 9, 10, 15
  1924 visit to Rome, 9, 17 (9, 1/80a)
  1939 in New York, 15
  descriptions in the novel, 7
diaspora, 5, 9

dichotomy (*Zwiespalt*), 4, 6*, 15
dictatorship, 6, 12, 16. In *DBWE* *see also* authoritarianism; National Socialism; Third Reich. *See also* "The Younger Generation's Altered View of the Concept of Führer" (*DBWE* 12, 2/8)
dignity (*Würde*), 4, 6, 7, 8*, 9*, 14*
disarmament, 6*, **11**, 12, 13*. In *DBWE see also* conscientious objection; League of Nations; pacifism; war
discernment (*Scheidung*), 4*, 6, 8, 14, 15*, 16
disciples, 1, 2, 4, 6, 7*, 8*, 12, 14*, 15, **16**
discipleship, **4**, 7, 8, 9, 10, 11, 12, 13, **14**, 15, 16
  call to, 4, 14
  and scriptural principle (*Schriftprinzip*), 4
Discipleship (book), 1, 2, 3, 4, 5, **6**, 7, 8, 10, 12, 13, 14, 15, 16. In *DBWE see also Cost of Discipleship*
disciplina arcani, 1, 4, 5, 7. In this index and in *DBWE see also* arcane discipline and "discipline of the secret"
discipline (*Zucht*), 2, 4, 5, 6, 7, 8, 9, 12, 13*, 14*, **16**. In *DBWE see also* church discipline; congregational discipline; doctrinal discipline; power of the keys. *See also* "Lecture and Discussion on the Power of the Keys and Church Discipline" (*DBWE* 14, 2/19)
  lack of, 6, 14, 15
"discipline of the secret," 1, 4, 5, 7. *See also* arcane discipline
discrimination, 10*, 15. In *DBWE see also* Aryan legislation; prejudice
disobedience, 3, 4, 8, 14*, 16
dissertation (licenciate degree), 9, **10**. In *DBWE see also* licentiate. *See also* Seeberg, Reinhold, in the master biographical index of names
divorce, 6, 16. In *DBWE see also* marriage
docetism, 4, 12, 14, 15
doctor. *See* physician
doctrinal discipline (*Lehrzucht*), 4, 12, 14*, 15*
doctrine (*Lehre*), 1, 2, 4, 6, 7, 9, 11, 12, 13*, 14*, 15, 16. In *DBWE see also* Two Kingdoms
  false, 4, 12, 14
  pure, 1, 2, 12, 13, 14
dogma, 2, 8*, 10, 11, 12, 14, 15*
  dogmatism, 13
dogmatics, **1***, 2, 3, 6, 8*, **9**, **10**, 11*, 12, 14, 15, 16. In *DBWE see also* church dogmatics; doctrine; ethics; teaching
  Catholic, 2, 6, 9, 11
  of the early church, 9, 10, 12, 14
  Lutheran, 2, 9, 16
donatism, 14
doubt (*Zweifel*), 12, 15, 16, 17 (9, 2/2a)
doxologies, 15
dream(s), 5*, 7, 8, 16
Dresden, 8, 14, 16
drive (*Trieb*), 1, 6, 11*, 16*
dualism, 2, 6, **9**
Dusseldorf, 9*, 11*, 13, 14, 16

duty, 6, 12. In *DBWE see also* obligation; responsibility
dying, 3, 6, 7, 8, 10*, 11*, 12, 13*, 15*, 16*. In *DBWE see also* death; funerals

early Christianity. *See* Christianity, early
earth, 2, 3, 4*, 5, 7*, 8, 10, **12**, 13, 14, 15, 16*
  as mother, 3, 12, 17 (9, 2/2a)
Easter, 1, 3, 4, 7, **8**, 9, **10**, 11*, 12, 13*, 14, **16**, 17 (9, 1/99b)
  Easter message, 10. *See also* "Reflection on Easter: Resurrection" (*DBWE* 16, 2/1)
East Prussia, 7, 8, 10, 13*, 14*, 15*, **16**. In *DBWE see also* Finkenwalde; Old Prussian Union Church; Pomerania
ecclesia, 1, 4, 9, 12, 14. In *DBWE see also* church; church-community; ecclesiology
  Catholic concept of, 9
ecclesiology, 1, 3, 4, 6, 8, 10, 12, 14, 15
economy, 6, 10, 11, 12, 13*, 15*, **16**
  Christian, 16
ecumenical movement, 1*, 2, 3, 4, 5*, 6, 8, 9, 10, 11, 12, **13**, 14, **15**, **16**. In *DBWE see also* ecumenism; Edinburgh; Faith and Order; Federal Council of Churches; Geneva; Life and Work; Oxford; World Alliance; World Council of Churches. *See also* "Discussion Paper for the Ecumenical Conference in Dassel" (*DBWE* 12, 2/10); "Essay on the Confessing Church and the Ecumenical Movement" (*DBWE* 14, 2/6); "Lecture in Ciernohorské Kúpele: On the Theological Foundation of the Work of the World Alliance" (*DBWE* 11, 2/14); "Reports on Ecumenical Work" (*DBWE* 11, 2/1–2); "Texts from Ecumenical Work" (*DBWE* 11, 11–19). *See also* Bell, George; Freudenberg, Hans; Keller, Adolf; Visser 't Hooft, Willem, in the master biographical index of names
  Bonhoeffer's work in, 6, 11, 12, **13**, 16
  concept of, 6, 10
Ecumenical Working Group. *See* German Ecumenical Working Group
Eden, garden of, 3
Eden Theological Seminary (St. Louis), 15, 16
Edinburgh, 11*, 13, 15, 16, 17 (13, 1/208a)
  Faith and Order conference (1937), 14, 15
  World Mission Conference (1910), 14
education, 6, 7*, 8, **9**, 10, 16
ego, 2, 3, 6, 7, 10, 12, 15, 17
egoism/egocentricity, 2, 3, 6, 7, 8, 9, 12
Egypt, 8, 6, 10, 12, 14, 15, 16
Eiche, Die **11**, 12. In *DBWE see also* Siegmund-Schultze,

Friedrich, in the master biographical index of names
Eisenach, 11, 12, 14, 15
Eisenacher Bund, 11
"either/or", 6,* 8*, 10, 13
Elberfeld, 14, 15, 16
church college, 14
preachers' seminary, 14
elderly, the, 7*, 14
and youth, 7, 14
election (*Erwählung*), 1, 2, 3, 4*, **6**, 7, **9**, 12, **14**, 15*, 16*
elections, 6, 12, 16*. *See also* church elections; Nazi Germany; Reich bishop; Weimar Republic
Elmau, 4, 9
Elmhurst (U.S.), 15, 16
emigrants, 10*, 13, 14. In *DBWE see also* refugees
emigration (from Nazi Germany), 4*, 8*, 15, **16**. In *DBWE see also* Jews; refugees
emotion, 1, 10
empirical church. *See* church, empirical
Enabling Act (*Ermächtigungsgesetz* of March 23, 1933), 12
encounter, 2. In *DBWE see also* brotherhood; fellowship
end (*Ende*), 4. In *DBWE see also* eschatology; eschaton; last day; last things
of all things, 5*, 6*, 12
eschatology, 6, 9, 16
end (*Eschaton*), 3, 9
enemy, enemies (*Feind, Feinde*), **4**, 5, 6, 7, 8*, 10, **12**, **14**, **15**, 16. In *DBWE see also* enmity
love for, 4, 5, 6, 8*, 9, 10, 12, 14, 15, 16
engagement (to Maria von Wedemeyer), 8, **16**
England. *See* Great Britain
English language, **10**, 13
enlightenment, sexual, 10, 14
Enlightenment, the, 1, 5, 6, 7, 8, 9*, 10, 11*, **12**, 13, 14
enmity (*Feindschaft*), 4, 6, 7, 12, 16*
Enthusiasm (*Schwärmerei/ Schwärmertum*), 1, 2, 4, 5*, 6, 10, 11, 12, 13, 14, 15, 16*
Enthusiasts (*Schwärmer*), 4, 6, 7, 12, 14, 15, 16
Ephesus, 8*, 14, 15
Epiphany, 15. *See also* "Supplements to the Monthly Letters from the Confessing Church Council of Brethren in Pomerania to Its Pastors: Meditation on Epiphany" (*DBWE* 15, 10.2)
Epiphany Synod (1939), 4*, **15**
Episcopal Church (U.S.A.), 15, 16. In *DBWE see also* Anglicans
epistemology (*Erkenntnistheorie*), 1, **2**, 4, 6*, 9, 10, 11
Epitome. *See* Formula of Concord
Epsom Conference (1932), 11
equality (*Gleichheit*), 1, 6, 7, 8*, 9*
Erlangen, 2, 6, 11, 12, 13*, 14, 17 (12, 1/106a)
school, 11, 12
eros, 5, 10
and agape, 1
and pathos, 4, 5
erotic love, 1
error, 12, 14*, 15*, 16
eschatology, 1, 2, 3, 4, 6, 8, **9**, 10, 11, 12, 13*, 14, 15, 16. *See also* "Paper on Early Lutheran

Eschatology" (*DBWE* 9, 2/12); "Seminar Paper on Church and Eschatology" (*DBWE* 9, 2/9)
eschatological hope, 15
Essen (city), 15
essence (*essentia*), 2
essence (*Wesen*), 11*, 16. In *DBWE* *see* nature
estate(s) (*Stand/Stände*), 6, 8*, 12, 14*
spiritual 6, 15*
eternal life, 6, 8, 9, 10. *See also* life
eternity, 1, 2, **4**, 6, 7, 8*, 9, **10**, 11*, 12, 13, **14**, 15, 16
Ethics, 1, 2, 3, 4, 5, **6**, 7, **8**, 9, **10**, **11**, 12, 13*, 14, 15*, 16. In *DBWE see also* "Basic Questions of a Christian Ethic" (*DBWE* 10, 2/3); "Concrete Ethics in Paul" (*DBWE* 14, 2/22); "Is There a Christian Ethic?" (*DBWE* 11, 2/10); "The Religious Experience of Grace and the Ethical Life" (*DBWE* 10, 2/15); "Study on 'Personal' and 'Objective' Ethics" (*DBWE* 16, 2/13)
Catholic, 6, 8, 16
Christian, 3, 6, 8, 10, 11, 12, 14, 15*, 16
concrete, 4, 6, 12, 14
Jewish, 9
Lutheran, 12
political, 4, 6, 10, 12, 16
problems of, 6, 7, 11
Protestant, 4, 6, 16
theological, 3, 11
Ethics (Bonhoeffer's 1940–43 manuscripts), 1, 2, 3, 4, 5, **6**, 7, **8**, 9, 10, 11, 14, 15, **16**
Ethics notes (Bonhoeffer's *Zettelnotizen* for his planned book), **6**, 7
ethno-nationalism, 12. In *DBWE see also* Aryan ideology; fascism; German Christians; National Socialism; *völkisch* movement
Ettal, 4, 5*, **6**, 8, **16**. In *DBWE see also* monasteries
Europe, 6, 7*, 8, 9, **10**, 11*, 12, 14, 15, **16**
euthanasia (Nazi T-4 murders of the disabled and mentally ill), 4, **6**, 7*, 8*, 9*, 15, **16**
Evangelical Church of Germany, 5. *See also* German Evangelical Church
Evangelical Theology/Evangelische Theologie (publication), 13, 14, 16*
evangelization (*Volksmission*), 4*, 12, 14, 15, **16**. In *DBWE see also* church, missions; church renewal movement; missionary work
evil (*das Böse*), 1, 2, 3, 4, **6**, 7, **8**, **10**, 11*, 13, **12**, **14**, 15, **16**, 17 (9, 2/2a). In *DBWE see also* "After Ten Years" (8); good and evil
banality of, 7
overcoming, 4, 9
radical nature of, 1, 14
evil/bad will (*Bosheit*), 6, 7, 8, 16
Evil One (*der Böse*), 3, 4, 6, 8, 9, 12, 14, 15. *See also* devil;

fall of humanity; good and evil; Satan
evolution, 3, 9, 11, 12. In *DBWE see also* Darwinism
excommunication, 1, 11*, 14, 16
exegesis, 1, 3, 5, 14, 15*, 16. In *DBWE see also* Bible; hermeneutics; proclamation; Scripture; sermons. *See also* "Bible Study Class on Fundamental New Testament Concepts" (*DBWE* 14, 2/9); "Bible Study on the Letters of Timothy (Student Notes)" (*DBWE* 14, 3/16); "Biblical Study Seminars on Basic New Testament Concepts" (*DBWE* 15, 2/2); "Exposition on Romans 9–11" (*DBWE* 14, 3/6); "Lecture on Contemporizing New Testament Texts" (*DBWE* 14, 2/7); "Meditation on Psalm 119" (*DBWE* 15, 3/9); "Practical Exercises in Homiletics" (*DBWE* 14, 2/3)
exemption. *See* military exemption
existence, **2**, 3, 4, 5*, 8*, 10, **12**, **14**, 16*. In *DBWE see also* being; *Dasein*
  bourgeois, 6*, 7, 8*, 12, 14
  Christian, 4, 6, 14
  and discipleship, 4
  worldly, 16
existentialism, 6*, 8, 12
exorcism, 14, 15
exousia, 4*, 15, 16
experience (*Erfahrung*), 5*, 7*, 8*, 9, 11*, 12, 13, 16*
  religious, 2, 9, 10, 11
experience (*Erlebnis*), 1, 2, 8*, 10, 11*, 14

fairy tales, 3, 6*, **10**, 13, 14*, 15. In *DBWE see also* fantasy
Faith and Order movement, 11, 12, 13, 14, **15**. In *DBWE see also* ecumenical movement; Lausanne conference (1927)
faith/belief (*Glaube*), 1, **2**, 3, **4**, 5, 6, **7**, 8, 9, 10, 11, **12**, **13**, 14, 15, **16**. In *DBWE see also* confession; *fides*
  act of, 2, 14
  experience of, 11
  and hope, 1, 6, 8
  and obedience, 2, 4, 6, 9, 12, 13, 14
  and seeing (*Schauen*), 1, 3
fall (*Abfall*), the, 1, 2, **3**, 4, 6, 7, 8, 10, 12, 14, 15*, 16. In *DBWE see also* apostasy; fallenness; fall of humanity
  of Adam, 15
  Lucifer's, 3
fall (*Sündenfall*), the, 1, 3, 4, 6, 7, 8, 10, 12, 13, 15*, 16
false doctrine or teaching (*Irrlehre*), 4, 12, 13*, 14, 15, 16. In *DBWE see also* Barmen confession; Church Struggle; Confessing Church; German Christians; heresy; Reich bishop. *See also* "Expert Opinion on 'False Teaching' in the Confessing Church" (*DBWE* 14, 2/20); "From Barmen to Oeynhausen" (*DBWE* 14, 2/14); "The Visible Church in the New Testament:

Section on False Teaching" (*DBWE* 14, 2/8.5)
false gods (*Götzen*), 3, 6, 7*, 8*, 9*, 11*, 12*, 14, 15*, **16**. In *DBWE see also* German Christians; heresy; idolatry
worship of, 8, 14, 15, 16
family, 9, 10, 12, 15, 16. In *DBWE see also* Bonhoeffer family; mandates; marriage; *also* listings for individual Bonhoeffer family members in the master biographical index of names
Bonhoeffer's, 1, 4*, 5*, 6, 7, 8, 9, 11*, 12, 13, 14, 15, 16
Jewish, 7, 16
as mandate, 6, 16
fanaticism, **6**, 7*, 8, 14, 16, 16
Fanø, 3, 4, 6, 10, 12, **13**. *See also* "Theses Paper for the Fanø Conference: The Church and the Peoples of the World" (*DBWE* 13, 2/2); "Address to the Fanø Conference" (*DBWE* 13, 2/3)
1934 ecumenical conference, 11, **13**, **14**
1934 Youth Conference, **13**
fantasy, 3, 8, 16*. In *DBWE see also* fairy tales
and reality, 9
fasting, 4, 8*
and prayer, 14
fate (*Schicksal*), 1*, 6, **8**, 10*, 11*, 12, 13*, 14*, 15, 16, 17. In *DBWE see also* destiny
of Germany, 8, 14*, 15
father, 6, 7, 8*, 9, 11*, 12, 14*, 16*. In *DBWE see also* Bonhoeffer, Karl, in the master biographical index of names
father-son problem, 12
relationship to children, 16
fatherland, 1*, 4*, 7*, 11*, 13*, 14, 15, 16. In *DBWE see also* Germany; patriotism; *Vaterland*
love for, 6, 10, 13
traitors against, 6
Faust, 3, 17 (9, 2/2a)
fear (*Furcht*), **8**, 12, 13, 14
Federal Council of Churches (U.S.), 10, 11, 12, 13, 15, 16
feelings, 8, **9**, 11, 14*. In *DBWE see also* emotion
fellowship (κοινωνία), 1, 2*, 3*, 4, **6***, 7*, **8***, 9*, 10, 11*, 12, 13*, **14**, 15, **16**. In *DBWE see also* brotherhood; community; Finkenwalde; *Life Together*; *Volksgemeinschaft*
among brothers, 13, 15
with Christ, 4, 6, 15, 16
in the church-community, 4, 14
concept of, 1
of the cross, 4, 15
ecumenical, 6, 8, 16
of God, 1, 4
of love, 1, 9
religious, 1, 9, 11
of the saints, 4, 9, 12, 13, 14, 15
and society, 1, 9
Fellowship of Reconciliation. *See* International Fellowship of Reconciliation
fiancée. In *DBWE see also* engagement. *See also*

Wedemeyer, Maria von, in the master biographical index of names
in Bonhoeffer's prison fiction, 7*
letters to Maria von Wedemeyer, 8*, 16
Fifth Implementation Decree (December 2, 1935), 4*, 14, 15
Finkenwalde, 1, 3, **4**, **5**, 6, 8, 10, 11, 12, 13, **14**, **15**, **16**. In *DBWE see also* preachers' seminaries; theological education
1936 trip to Sweden, 13, 14
circular letters, 14, 15
Confessing Church there, 4, 14
House of Brethren, 4, 5, 8, 14, 15
retreats, 4, 5, 14
theological seminary, 3, 4, 5, 6, 7*, 8, 9*, 10, **14**, 15, 16
Finland, 9*, 13*, 16
Fleischwerdung (becoming flesh), 8*, 12*, 15*. In *DBWE see also* becoming human; bodily existence; Christ; Christology; incarnation; Logos
Flensburg, 9*, 14, 16
flesh (σάρξ), 2, 4, 8, 10*, 11*, **12**, 14, 15, 16*
and blood, 14, 15
and spirit (πνεῦμα), 4, 14, 15
Flossenbürg, 2, 5, 7*, 8, 16
forbearance (*Tragen*), 5
foreign ministry (Germany), 13, 16. *See also* Germany, Foreign Office
Foreign Office (church), 8, **13***, 14, 16. In *DBWE see also* Church Foreign Office; German Evangelical Church, Foreign Office. *See also* Heckel, Theodor, in the master biographical index of names
forgetfulness, 6, 8, 16
forgiveness (*Vergebung*), 1, 2, 3, 4, **5**, **6**, 7, 8, **9**, **10**, **11**, **12**, 13, 14, 15, 16
between nations, 6
daily, 14
revelation in forgiveness, 12
form (*Gestalt*, μορφή), 3, 4, 12*, 14*. In *DBWE see also Gestalt*
of Christ, 4, 6
transformation of, 4, 6
Formula of Concord, 4*, 6, 8, 9, 10, **12**, 13, **14**, **15**, 16. In *DBWE see also* Book of Concord
fornication (*Hurerei*), 4, 6, 14*, 15*
"Fortune and Calamity" (poem), 7*, 8
France, 6, 7*, 8, 9, 10, 11*, 12, 13, 14, 15, **16**
Frankfurt am Main, 5, 9*, 10, 11*, 13, 14
Frankfurt an der Oder, 4, 8*, 10, 15
Confessing parish there, 14
police prison, 4, 14
free churches, 12*, **13**, 14, 15, 16
free will, 1, 2, 6, 14, 17 (9, 2/2a). In *DBWE see also* will
freedom, 1, **2**, **3**, 4, 5, **6**, **7**, **8**, 9, 10, **11**, **12**, 13, **15**, **16**. *See also* church, freedom of; democracy; free will; responsibility
of Christians, 6, 7, 14
of the church, 12, 13, 15, 16
created for human beings, 3

from the law, 6, 9, 12, 14
for the other, 3
religious freedom, 15, 16
Freiburg circle, 6, **16**
Freiburg im Breisgau, 8*, 9*, 10, 16
Freiburg memorandum (1942/43), 16. In *DBWE see also* Freiburg circle. *See also* Dietz, Constantin von, in the master biographical index of names. *See also* "Preparations for the Freiburg Memorandum" (*DBWE* 16, 1/205)
French Revolution, 6, 7, 11*, 12, 15. In *DBWE see also* the Enlightenment
Friedrich-Wilhelm University. *See* Humboldt University; University of Berlin
"Friend, The" (poem), **8**
friend(s), friendship, 1, 5*, 6, **7**, **8**, 9, **10**, 12, 13, 15*, **16**
fruit (καρπός), 4, 14*, 16*. In *DBWE see also* "New Life in Paul: Bonhoeffer's Notes on Conduct, Growth, and Fruit" (*DBWE* 14, 2/15.6)
führer, 4*, 7, 8, 10, 11, **12**, 14, 16. In *DBWE see also* National Socialism; Third Reich. *See also* "The Führer and the Individual in the Younger Generation" (*DBWE* 12, 2/9); "The Younger Generation's Altered View of the Concept of Führer" (*DBWE* 12, 2/8)
as ideological principle, 5, 7, **12**, 13, 15, 17 (12, 1/106a)
"Führer and the Individual in the Younger Generation, The" (*DBWE* 12), 8, 15
fundamentalism, 10, 15
funerals, 10, 13, 14, 15*, 16. In *DBWE see also* funeral sermons (*DBWE* 13, 3/21; *DBWE* 16, 3/2) and "Pastoral Duties: Funeral Homilies" (*DBWE* 14, 2/23.3)
Bonhoeffer's own wishes, 8
Füreinander, 1, 5, 7. In *DBWE see* being; "being-for-each-other"
future, **2**, 6, 7, **8**, 12*, 16

Galilee, 4, 9*, 11, 15
Geist, 1. In *DBWE see also* intellect; spirit
generational differences, 7*, 8*, 10*, **12**, 14. In *DBWE see* parents; teachers; youth movement
Genesis, Luther's lectures on, 2, 3
Geneva, 6, 7*, 8, 10, 11, 12. In *DBWE see also* ecumenical movement; World Council of Churches
1932 disarmament conference, 12
gentiles (*Heiden*), 1, 4, 6, 8*, 10, 12, 14, 15, 16. In *DBWE see also* pagans/paganism
German Academic Exchange Service (DAAD, or Akademischer Austauschdienst), 10, 11*, 16
German Christians, 3, 4*, 6, 8, 10, 11, **12**, **13**, **14**, **15**, 16, 17 (12, 1/106a). In *DBWE*

see also "Ayran" theology; Church Struggle; Confessing Church; consistories; Germanism; German Protestantism (4); Godesberg Declaration (1939); National Socialism; Old Prussian Union church; Teutonic Christianity (4). *See also* "Essay and Discussion on Church Communion" (*DBWE* 14, 2/19)
church opposition to, 13
principles of, 13
Sport Palace rally (1933), 13
in Thuringia, 13, 14, 16
German Christian Student Association, 9, 11, **12**, 13*, 14
ecumenical working group, 4*, 12
German Democratic Republic, 8
German Ecumenical Working Group, 11, 12
German Evangelical Church, 10, 11, 12, 13, 14, 15, 16, 17 (12, 1/106a). In *DBWE see also* church; Church Struggle; Confessing Church; consistories; ecumenical movement; Evangelical Church; German Christians; laws; Lutheran churches; Ministry of Church Affairs; Reich bishop; spiritual ministry
ecumenical ties, 14
leadership of, 12, 13, 15, 16
German Evangelical Church, Foreign Office, 8, 13*, 14*, 16. In *DBWE see also* Church Foreign Office. *See also* Heckel, Theodor, in the master biographical index of names
German Evangelical Church, overseas congregations. *See* Association of the German Evangelical Congregations in Great Britain and Ireland
German Evangelical Church Committee, 10, 12
German Evangelical Church Federation (*Kirchenbund*, from 1922), 10, **12**, 13, 14, 16*
constitution, 11
law concerning Germans abroad, 13
German Evangelical Church Mission Committee, 12
German Faith Movement (*Glaubensbewegung*), 13, 14
Germanization, 4, 14*. In *DBWE* 4 *see also* "Germanism vs. Christianity"
German language, 8*, 10, 13*. In *DBWE see also* Luther German
German National People's Party (Deutschnationale Volkspartei), 10, 12
German people, 6*, 8*, 10, 11*, **12**, 14, 15*, **16**. *See also* German Evangelical Church, Foreign Office; Germany
abroad, **10**, 11, 12, **13**, 16
conformity of, 10
treatment of in Italy, 9
German Protestant missions, 13, 16. In *DBWE see also* evangelization; German

Evangelical Church, missions; Gossner Mission; Inner Mission; missions; *Volksmission*

German Reich (1933–45). *See* Third Reich

German Student Association, 12

Germany, 1, 3, 6, 7, 8, 9, 10, 11, 12, 13, 14, 15, **16**
- culture and heritage, 12, 13
- future of, 7, 10, 16
- nationalism, 4, 6, 7, 8
- political unrest in, 9

Gesamtperson, 1, 2*, 14. In *DBWE see also* collective person; *Kollektivperson*

Gestapo, 4*, 5, 6, 7, **8**, 12, 13, 14, **15**, **16**, 17 (13, 1/208a)

Gethsemane, 4, 8, 14, 15

gifts (*Gaben*), 7, 15*, 16*. In *DBWE see also* Christ; God
- of Christ, 15
- and duties, 6, 9
- of God, 6, 7, 15, 16

Gland conference (1932), **11**, **12**. In *DBWE see also* World Alliance. *See also* "Address in Gland" (*DBWE* 11, 2/17)

Gleichschaltung, 6*, 12, 13, 14, 15, 16, 17 (9, 1/80a). In *DBWE see also* German Christians; Germanization; National Socialism; nazification; Third Reich
- of the churches, 4

glory (*Herrlichkeit*), 10*, 12, 16. In *DBWE see also* "Draft of a Lecture on the Theme of 'Glory'" (*DBWE* 16, 2/4)

glory (*Ruhm*, καύχημα), 4*, 14*, 16

gnosis (γνῶσις), 3, 9, 12, 14

goal (*Ziel*), 7*, 8, 16

God, 1, 2, 3, 4, 5, 7, 8, 9, 10, 11, 13, 16. In *DBWE see also* becoming human; Christology; godlessness; *Menschwerdung*; revelation; word of God; worship service. *See also* "Essay: Concerning the Christian Idea of God" (*DBWE* 10:2/16)
- the Almighty, 8, 9, 10, 14
- become human, 6, 15
- compassion, 6, 7, 12
- concept of, 1, 3, 4, 11
- confidence in, 4, 8, 12, 13
- death of, 2, 10, 14
- denial of (*Leugnung*), 16
- distance of, 3, 4, 7, 14
- dominion of (*Herrschaft*), 1, 11, 12, 14, 15, 16
- faithfulness (*Treue*), 6, 8, 11, 12, 14, 15
- as father, 3, 4, 9, 13, 14, 16
- freedom of, 2, 3, 12, 14, 15, 16
- goodness of, 6, 7, 8, 11, 16
- grace of, 1, 9, 4, 14, 16
- guidance of, 8, 16
- in heaven, 4, 7
- honor of, 8, 9, 10, 11, 14
- and the human being, 10, 13, 17 (9, 2/2a)
- justice of, 4, 6, 8, 9, 10, 14, 15
- law of, 1, 6, 8, 12, 14, 16
- as Lord, 2, 14, 15, 16
- love of, 1, 3, 4, 6, 7, 9, 10, 12, 13, 15, 16
- mockery of, 12
- in other human beings, 1, 8
- peace of, 3, 8, 10, 11, 12, 13, 14, 15, 16

people of, 1, 3, 4, 5, 10, 12, 14, 15, 16
presence, 6, 10, 11, 14, 16
reality of, 6
rule of, 1
trinitarian, 5, 15, 16
will of, 1, 3, 4, 6, 17, 13, 9, 10, 11, 13, 14, 15, 16
works of, 3, 4, 14, 15, 16
and the world reality, 1, 6
wrath of, 1, 4, 6, 8, 9, 10, 12, 13, 14, 15, 16
Godesberg Declaration (1939), 15
godlessness, 1*, 3*, 4*, **6**, 7, 9, 10, **12**, 14*, 15*, 16. In *DBWE see also* false gods; German Christians; God; idolatry; paganism
godparents, 8, 10, 14, 15*, 16. In *DBWE see also* baptism
gods, 6, 7*, 8*, 9, 10, 14, 17. In *DBWE see also* false gods
Golgotha, 3, 4, 8*, 10, 11, 12, 13*, 14. In *DBWE see also* crucifixion
good, the, 2, 4*, 6, 7, 8*, 10, **12,** 13, 14, 15*, **16**
being, 6
doing, 4, 6, 7
and evil, 6, 10
of God/Christ's, 3, 4, 6
goodness, 8
human beings, 3, 4, 6
good and evil, 1, **3**, 4, **6**, 7*, **10**, **12,** **13**, 14, 15*, 17 (9, 2/2a). In *DBWE see also* evil
ignorance of, 3, 4, 6, 12
knowledge of, 1, 3, 4, 6, 15
Good Friday, 3*, 8, 9, **10**, 12, 13, 14
good news (*Botschaft*), 11*, 12
Christian, 10, 11*. In *DBWE see also* Easter message; gospel
good works, 4, 6, 9, 14, 15*, 16. In *DBWE see also* good deeds; works
gospel, 1, 2, 3, **4***, 6, 7*, 8, 9, 10, **11**, 12, **13**, 14, 15, 16. *See also* law and gospel; proclamation. *See also* the master index of scriptural references
proclamation of, 6, 11, 13, 16
Gossner Mission, 8, 14, 15, **16**
Göttingen, 4, 5, 8, 10, 12, 13, 14, 15, 16
government (*Obrigkeit*), **6**, **16**. In *DBWE see also* authority; mandates; state
government (*Regierung*), 7, 8, 10
grace (*Gnade*), 1, **2**, 3, **4**, 5, **6**, 7, 8, 9, **10**, 11, 12, 13, **15**, **16**. In *DBWE see also* cheap grace; costly grace. *See also* "Course Paper: The Religious Experience of Grace and the Ethical Life" (*DBWE* 10, 2/15)
and discipleship, 4
God's, 7, 11, 12, 13, 15, 16
proclamation of, 6, 11, 14
Grand Inquisitor (from *The Brothers Karamazov*), 6*, 14*. *See also* Dostoyevsky, Fyodor, in the master biographical index of names
gratitude (*Dankbarkeit*), 1*, 5*, 6, 7, **8**, 10, 14, **15**, **16**. In *DBWE see also* offering; thankfulness; thanksgiving.

See also "Biblical Study Seminars on Basic New Testament Concepts: Notes on the Concept of Gratitude" (*DBWE* 15, 2/2.9); "Reflection: On Gratitude among Christians" (*DBWE* 16, 2/5)
Great Awakening (*Erweckungsbewegung*), 14
Great Britain, 6*, 7*, 8*, 9*, **10**, 11*, 12, 13*, 14, **15**, **16**, 17 (13, 1/209a). In *DBWE see also* Anglo-Saxon; Britain; Church of England; England; London parishes. *See also* Bell, George, in the master biographical index of names
  British people, 7*, 8*, 10*, 11, 15
Great Britain, Foreign Office, 16
Greece, 11*, 12, 16
  Greeks, 2, 10, 16
greed (*Habgier*), 4, 6, 14*, 16
Gregorian chant, 4, 5*
Greifswald, 10, 12, 13*, **14**, 15*. In *DBWE see also* theological faculties
grief (*Trauer*), 10*, 14*, **16**
Grisebach circle (Jena), 2
Groß-Schlönwitz, 4, 8*, 14, **15**, 16
  collective pastorates (1937–39), 8, 15
Grüber office, 16
guidance (*Weisung*), 12, 13, 14*, 15*, 16
guilt (*Schuld*), 1, 2, 3, 4, 5, 6, 7, **8**, 10, 11*, 12, 13, 15, 16, 17 (9, 2/2a)
  acknowledgment of, 1, 6
  consciousness of, 9, 11, 16
Gütersloh, 8*, 15
"Gypsies." *See* Roma

Haarlem (Holland), 12, 15*
Habilitation (postdoctoral dissertation), 2, 3, 9, **10**, 11, 16, 17 (9, 1/94b). In *DBWE see also Act and Being*; degree, postdoctoral. *See also* "Inaugural Lecture: The Anthropological Question in Contemporary Philosophy and Theology" (*DBWE* 10, 2/7)
habitus, 2, 4*, 8*, 9*, 11*, 12, 15
Hague, the, 9*, 11, 13
Halle an der Saale, 2, 6, 8*, 10, 11*, 12, 13*, 14, 16
  Confessing synod (1937), 14, 16
Hamburg, 8*, 9*, 10, 12, 13, 14*, 16
Hannover/Hanover, 8*, 9*, 10, 13, 14, 15, 16
happiness (*Glück*), 1, 4, **6**, **7**, 8, 10, 12, 13*, 14*, 15*, 16*
"happy exchange," 14
Harlem, 6, 10, 11, 12. In *DBWE see also* Abyssinian Baptist Church; New York
Harvard University, 6*, 10, 15, 16
Harz Mountains, 7, 8, 9*, 10, 14, 15, 16
hatred (*Haß*), 3*, **4**, 6, 7*, 9, 12, 13*, **14***, 15*, 16. In *DBWE see also* enemies
Hauteroda, 14
Havana, 10
healing (*Heilung*), 4*, 9, 12, 14, 15, **16**
health, 6, 7*, **8**, 14

heart, 1*, 7*, 8, 12, 13*, 14*, 16. In *DBWE see also cor curvum in se*
pure, 12, 13
heathen (*Heiden*), 12, 13. In *DBWE see also* gentiles; pagans
heaven, 2, 3, 5*, 9, 12, 13*, 16
and earth, 3, 13
new, 12
Hebrew, 9
Hebrew scriptures, 12
Hedgehogs (fraternity), 9, 10, 17 (9, 1/80a)
"Hegel's philosophy of religion" (1933), 3, 6*, 12
Heidelberg, 9*, 10, 12, 13, 14, 16
Heidelberg Catechism, **14**, 15
Heidelberg disputation, 8
Helbra, 14
hell, 2, 5*, 7, 8*, 9, 12, 13, 15, 16
Hellenism, 4, 9, 14. In *DBWE see also* Greece; Greeks
helle Ton, Der (songbook), 14, 15
heresy, 4, 10, 11*, **12**, **13**, 14, 16. In *DBWE see also* error; false teaching; German Christians
docetic, 12, 15
donatist, 14
Ebionite, 12
modalistic, 12
Monophysitic, 12
Nestorian, 12
heritage (*Erbe*), 6, 7, 8, 9
historical, 6
Jewish, 5
"Heritage and Decay" (*DBWE* 6, 103–34), 16
hermeneutics, 4, 5*, 6, **8**, 14*
heroes, 12, 14, 15
the heroic, 9, 17 (9, 1/99b)
heroism, 6, 12, 13*
Herrschaft. See God, dominion of; lordship
Hesse-Nassau, 14*
heteronomy, 2, 6, 11
hiddenness (*Krypsis*), 2
hiddenness (*Verborgenheit*), 1, 4, 6*, 8, 10*, 13*, 14*, 15*. In *DBWE see also* God, hiddenness of
Hilaritas, 8, 10. *See also* cheerfulness
Hilfswerk, 16. *See also* Gruber office
Hindsgavl (Hindsgaul) conference, 14, 15
historicity, 1, **2**, 6, 9, 12, 14*
historiography, 1, 16
history, **1**, 2, 3, 4*, **6**, **7**, 8, **9**, 10, 11, 12, 13*, 14*, 15, **16**. In *DBWE see also* "History and Good" (*DBWE* 6:219–99)
philosophy of, 9, 11, 16
of religions, 11
of salvation, 5
history of religions school, 1*, 3, 9*, 10, 11
"History of Twentieth-Century Systematic Theology" (*DBWE* 11, 2/3), 2, 3, 8
Hitler, Adolf. *See also* assassination; Beer Hall Putsch; July 20; National Socialism; tyrant, tyrannicide; Weimar Republic. *See also* "The Führer and the Individual in the Younger Generation" (*DBWE* 12:2/9); "The Younger Generation's Altered View of the Concept of Führer" (*DBWE* 12, 2/8). *See also* Hitler, Adolf, in the

master biographical index of names
Bonhoeffer family attitudes toward, 7
church leaders meet in 1934, 13
and *Führer* principle, 12
July 20 attempt on his life, 7, **8**, 15, 16
Hitler Youth, 6, 7, 12, 13, 14, 16
Holland, 6, 8, 11*, 12*, 13*, 14, 15, 16. In *DBWE see also* Netherlands
Holocaust, 6, 8
Holy Scripture, 3, 4*, 5, 6, 7*, 8, 9, 11*, 12*, 13*, 14, 15, 16 In *DBWE see also* Bible; exegesis; meditations; proclamation; Scripture; sermons
Holy Spirit (πνεῦμα ἅγιον), 1, 2, 3, **4**, 5*, 6, 8, **9**, 10, 11, 12, **13**, 14, **15**, 16. In *DBWE see also* Trinity. *See also* "Bible Study Class on Fundamental New Testament Concepts: Bonhoeffer's Notes on Holy Spirit" (*DBWE* 14, 2/9); "Lecture: 'The Visible Church in the New Testament: Section on Holy Spirit and Church-Community'" (*DBWE* 14, 2/8.4); "Seminar Paper on the Holy Spirit according to Luther" (*DBWE* 9, 2/10)
offices of, 4, 14, 15
Homburg Synod (1526), 14
homeland (*Heimat*), 2, 6*, 7*, 8*, 10*, 13*, 14, 15*, **16***. In *DBWE see also* Fatherland; Germany; native land
homesickness, 7, **8**, 15, 16
home visits (in ministry), 10*, 11*, 14. In *DBWE see also* pastoral care. *See also* "Lecture on Pastoral Care" (*DBWE* 14, 2/12)
homiletical lectures (1935-37), 4, 5, 8*, 10, **14**, 15. In *DBWE see also* "Lecture on Homiletics" (*DBWE* 14, 2/10)
homiletics, 4, 14, 15. In *DBWE see also* preaching; proclamation; sermons; theological exercises
homiletical exercises, **14**:2/13, 2/17, 2/25
homoousia, 12. In *DBWE see also* Christology
honor, 4, 6, 7, 8, 9, 12, 13*, 16*
hope, 1, 3, 5*, 6, 7, **8**, 9, 10, 12, 13, 14*, 15, 16
hopelessness, 12, 13
House of Brethren (*Bruderhaus*), 5*, 8, 15, 16. In *DBWE see also* Brothers' House; Council of Brethren; Reich Council of Brethren
Howard University, 10
hubris, 6, 8*, 10
Huguenots, 14
human being, 1, 2, 3, 5, 6, 7, 8, 9, 10, 11*, **12**, 13*, 15, 16, 17 (9, 1/96c; 1/99b; 2/2a). In *DBWE see also* Adam; becoming human; humanity; humankind; human race
being human (*Menschsein*), 3, 6, 8
contempt for, 4, 7, 8
as creator, 3, 4, 6

as fallen, 3
the new human (καινὸς ἄνθρωπος), 2, 4, 6, 9, 12, 14, 15
the old human, 2, 9, 12, 14, 15
sin of, 1
as whole person, 6, 8, 14, 15
humanism, 6, 7, 8, 9, 10, 11, 12, 14, 15
humanity, 1*, 2, 4, **6**, 7, 8, 9, **11**, **12**, 13, 14, 15*, 16*. In *DBWE see also* "new humanity"
the new, 2, 4, 6, 7, 9, 10, 11, 12, 14
human nature, 3, 4, 5*, 8*, 12, 13, 14, 15*, 16*. In *DBWE see also* human being; human condition; humanity
human rights, **6**, 12, 15, 16
Humboldt University. *See* University of Berlin
humiliation (*Erniedrigung*), 7, **12**
of Christ, 2, 4, 12
humility (*Demut*), 4, 5*, 6, 7, 8, **9**, 10, 11*, 13, 15, 16
and arrogance, 4
of the theologian, 2
humility (*Niedrigkeit*, ταπείνωσις), 12, 14. *See also* humiliation
humor, 8
Hungary, 6, 12, 13, 14, 16
hunger, 1, 5*, 7, 8, 9, 10, 11*, 12
hymnals, 13, 14, 16. In *DBWE see also Der helle Ton*; *Evangelisches Gesangbuch*
hymns, 8, 12, **13**, **14**, **15**. In *DBWE see also* Negro spirituals. *See also* "Presentation on the History of the Protestant Hymn" (*DBWE* 14, 2/21)
hypocrisy, 4, **6**, 8, 13*, 14*, 15, **16**
"I," **2**, 3, 6, 7*, 8*, 9, 10, 11*, 12, 14*, 15. In *DBWE see also* Adam; ego; Id; I-You relationship
idea, 3*, 4*, **6**, 7, 9, 11*, **12**, 14*, 15*
idealism, 2, 6, 7, 9, **10**, 11*, 12, 14*, 15, **16**
German philosophy of, **1**, 2, 3, 4, 6, 8, 9, 10, 11*, 12, 14*, 15
ideals, 1, 4*, 7, 11*, 12, 14*, 15, 16*
ideology, 4*, 6, 12, 13*, 14, 16*. *See also* German Christians; National Socialism
idolatry (*Vergötterung*), 2, 3, 4, 6, 7, 8, 9, 10, **12**, 15*, 16. In *DBWE see also* false gods; idol
"illegal" pastors (Confessing Church), 14, **15**, **16**. In *DBWE see also* Bad Oeynhausen; Confessing Church; Dahlem synod; legalization. *See also* "Lecture on the Path of the Young Illegal Theologians of the Confessing Church" (*DBWE* 15, 2/5)
illusion, 1, 7*, **8**, 10, 11*, 12, 16*
image (*Ebendbild*), 3, 9. In *DBWE see also* God, image of; *imago Dei*
of Christ, 4
of God, 1, 2, **3**, 4, 6, 9, 12, 14
Imitatio Christi/Imitation of Christ, 4, 5, 6, 8, 9
immanence, 2, 11, 12
immediacy (*Unmittelbarkeit*), 4, 5, 14*
imperative, ethical, 6, 10*, 14*, 16*
imperialism, 12, 16
impressionism, 11

imprisonment, 8, 14*, **15**, **16**. In *DBWE see also* arrest; Lehrter Strasse; Moabit; prison; Tegel
inaugural lecture (1930), 3, **10**, 15. In *DBWE see also* "The Anthropological Question in Contemporary Philosophy and Theology" (*DBWE* 10, 2/7)
incarnation (*Inkarnation*), 1, 2, 4, 6, 8, 10, **11**, 12, 13, 14, 15, 16. *See also Menschwerdung*/ becoming human; *Fleischwerdung*/becoming flesh
India, 6, 8, 9, **10**, 11, 12, **13**, 14, 15, 16. In *DBWE see also* Round Table conference
  Bonhoeffer's interest in visiting, 10, 11, 12, 13, 14
individual (*Individuum*), 1, 6, 7, 9, 11*, **12**, 15*, 16
individual, the (*das Einzelne*), **1**, 3*, 4, 6, **7**, 10, 12, 13*, 14, 15*. In *DBWE see also* human being; individualism; person; personhood
  and the church-community, 1, 2
  and humanity, 2
  isolated, 6
individualism, **1**, 5*, 6, 8, 9, 10, 11, 12, 13*, 14*, 15
Industrial Revolution, 6
industry, 6, 9, 13
infinity/the infinite, 3, 8*, 10, 11*, 12
injustice, 7, 11*, 12, 13*, 14, 15, 16, 17 (9, 2/2a). In *DBWE see also* justice
inner life, 2, 4*, 5*, 6*,7, 8*, 12, 14*. In *DBWE see also* inwardness
Inner Mission, 11, 13*, 14, 16, 17 (12, 1/106a). In *DBWE see also* church, social ministry; diaconical work; mission; service
  Apologetic Central Office (1919–35), 11, 12*
innocence (*Unschuld*), 3, 6, 14*, 15*
innocent, the, 6, 14, 15*
Inquisition, 10
inspiration, 6, **9**, 14*
Institute for the Study and Eradication of Jewish Influence on German Church Life, 15, 16
intact churches, 13. *See also* church, Lutheran; Church Struggle; Hannover/Hanover; Lutheran churches; Munich; Württemberg
intellectual life, 6*, 7, 8, 12*, 14*
intercession or intercessory prayer, 1, 4*, **5**, 8*, 10, 11, 12, 13*, **14**, 15, 16. In *DBWE see also* prayer
  Confessing Church list, 15
Interchurch Aid (ecumenical). *See* World Council of Churches
internationalism, 10, 12, 13*, 14
International Association for Liberal Christianity and Religious Freedom, 14
International Fellowship of Reconciliation, 10, 11*, 14*. *See also* Stöhr, Hermann, in the master biographical index of names

International Jewish Christian Alliance (London, after 1925). *See* Jewish Christians
interpretation, 1, 8*. In *DBWE see also* exegesis; nonreligious interpretation; Scripture, interpretation of
  philosophical, 10
interrogations (of Bonhoeffer and other conspirators), 8*, **16**
intimacy, 16
Ireland, 8*, 14
irrationality, 6, 9*, 11*
Islam, 9, 10*
isolation (*Isolierung*), 1. *See also* loneliness; solitude
Israel (biblical), 1, 4, 8, 9*, 10, 11, 12, 14*, 15, 16
  people of, 4, 6, 12, 14, 15, 16
  as people and church, 12
  prophecy, 3
Italy, 6, **8**, **9**, 10, 12, 13, 14, 15, **16**, 17. In *DBWE see also* resistance; Vatican
  Bonhoeffer's 1924 diary of his visit, 9, 17
  Bonhoeffer's travels for the conspiracy, **16**
  fascism in, 10
  Italian language, 9, 10, 13
Ius divinum/humanum, 15. *See also* natural law
I-You relation (*Ich-Du*), **1**, 2, 5, 6, 10, 12, 15*

Japan, 6, 9, 11*, 12, 13, 14, 15, 16
Jena, 2, 12, 16
Jenseits, 3, 4*, 8
Jerusalem, 4, 7*, 9, 10, 12, 13*, **14**, 15, 16
  1928 World Mission Conference, 14
  heavenly, 4, 8, 9
Jesuits, 14*, 16
Jesus, 1, 2, **6**, 7, **9**, **10**, **13**, **16**. In *DBWE see also* Christ; Christology; Jesus Christ
Jewish Christians, 4*, 9, **12**, 13, 14, 15, 16, 17 (13, 1/209a). In *DBWE see also* Aryan laws; baptism; Pastors' Emergency League
"Jewish question," 10, **12**, 13, 14, 16. In *DBWE see also* Aryan paragraph; Church Struggle; Confessing Church; synods. *See also* "The Church and the Jewish Question" (*DBWE* 12, 2/13); "The Jewish Question as Status Confessionis" (*DBWE* 12, 2/14)
Jewish Welfare Association. *See* Central Welfare Office for German Jews
Jews, 1, 3, 4*, 5, **6**, 7, 8, 9, 10, 11, 12, 13, 14, 15, **16**. In *DBWE see also* anti-Semitism; Aryan laws; Jewish Christians; Jewish Welfare Association; Judaism; Kristallnacht; National Socialism; November pogrom; Operation 7
  baptized or converted, 4*, 12, 14, 16
  Christian attitude toward, 12, 17 (12, 1/106a)

conversion of, 9
crying out for, 4*, 5;
culture (*Judentum*), 3, 4*, 8, 9, 11, 12, 14, 15
deicide charge, 12
deportations of, 6, 7, 15, **16**
German Jews, 9
and Greeks, 7, 9
persecution and deportations of, 10, 15, 16
Polish, 9
propaganda against, 14
religious, 16
temple Judaism, 14
"Jonah" (poem), 8, 16
Jordan River, 15
joy (*Freude*), 1, 4, 5*, 6*, 7, **8**, **9**, 10, 12, 13, 14, **15**, **16**. *See also* "Biblical Study Seminars on Basic New Testament Concepts: Notes on the Concept of Abstinence" (*DBWE* 15, 2/2.5); "'Joy' in Early Christianity: A Commemorative Paper for Adolf von Harnack" (*DBWE* 9, 2/11)
in God, 12, 15
Judaism, 3, **9**, 11, 12, 15, 16, 17 (12, 1/106a)
judge (*Richter*), 6, 7, 11, 12, 14*, 15
judgment (*Gericht*), 2, 4*, 5, 7*, 8, **9**, 10, 11, 12, 13, 16
of Christ, 4, 6, 11, 13
final, 16
God's, 1, 3, 4, 5, **6**, 7, 8, 9, 10, **11**, 12, 14, 15, 16
wrathful, 4, 15, 16
judgment day, 4, 5, 6, 8*, 9, 12, 13, 15*, 16. In *DBWE see also* last days; Last Judgment
July 20 attempt on Hitler's life, 7*, **8**, 15*, **16**. *See also* assassination; conspiracy; resistance; tyrannicide
Junge Kirche, 11*, 12, 13, 14, 15, 16
justice (*Gerechtigkeit*, δικαιοσύνη), 3, 4, **6**, 7, **8**, 9, 10, 11, 12, 13, 14, 15, 16, 17 (9, 2/2a). In *DBWE see also* righteousness
justice (*iustitia*), 9, 11
alien, 9, 11, 14*
civil, 4, 10, 12, 14*, 16
justification, 1, 2, 4, 5, **6**, 8, **9**, **10**, 11, 12, 13, 14, 15, 16. *See also* "Lecture: 'New Life in Paul'" (*DBWE* 14, 2/15)
doctrine of, 2, 4, 9, 10, 11, 14, 16
faith alone, 4, 5, 8, 10, 13, 14, 15, 16
and Luther, 5, 10
and salvation, 1, 4, 14
of the sinner, 4, 6, 12, 14, 15

kaiser, 6*, 9, 12, 14
Kantianism, 11
Kassel, 5, 7, 8*, 11, 14*, 15
Kelham, 5, 13, 14, 15*, 17 (13, 1/209b). In *DBWE see also* monasticism
kenosis, 12
kerygma, 3, 4, 15*
Kieckow estate, 7, 8, 14, 15, 16. In *DBWE see also* Kleist-Retzow, Ruth von, in the master biographical index of names
Kiel, 4*, 14
killing (*Tötung*), 6. In *DBWE see also* euthanasia; murder
kingdom of God, 1, 3, 4, 5, 6, 7*, 8*, **9**, 10, 11, **12**, 13, 14, 15, 16. In *DBWE see also* God,

kingdom of; kingdom of heaven. *See also* "Thy Kingdom Come! The Prayer of the Church-Community for God's Kingdom on Earth" (*DBWE* 12, 2/11)
concept of, 6, 9
on earth, 3, 8, 11, 12, 15
Kings, 8*, 12, 14, 15*, 16. In *DBWE* *see also* the master index of scriptural references
Klein-Krössin, 6, 8, 15, **16**
knowledge (*Erkennen/Erkenntnis*), **2**, 3, 4*, 6, 7*, 8, 9, 11*, **12**, 13, 14. In *DBWE see also* epistemology
knowledge (*Wissen*), **2**, 3, 6, 7*, 10, 11*, 13, 14*. In *DBWE see also* good and evil; scholarship (*Wissenschaft*)
and God, 3, 6
Königsberg, 6*, 8, 12, 14*, 16
Köslin, 8, 14*, 15, 16. In *DBWE see also* collective pastorates; Confessing Church
collective pastorate, 15
Kristallnacht (1938 pogrom), 5*, 7, 9*, 15, 16. In *DBWE see also* Crystal Night; Jews, persecution of; November 1938 pogrom; pogroms

La Borcaderie (1936 conference), 14
Lambeth Conference (1930), 10
language (*Sprache, Sprachen*), 1, 3, 7, 8*, **9**, 10, 12, 13, 14*, 15*, 16*. In *DBWE see also* nonreligious language
Last Judgment, 4, 5, 6, 9, 10, 11, 12, 13, 14, 15*
Last Supper, 1
Lausanne, 12, 14
Faith and Order conference (1927), 10, 11*, 12, 14
law, 1, 2, 3, 4, 5, **6**, 7, 8*, **9**, 10, 11*, **12**, 14, 15, **16**, 17 (9, 2/2a). In *DBWE see also* *nomos* (νόμος). *See also* "Disputation on Preaching the Law" (*DBWE* 14, 2/26)
fulfillment of, 4, 12, 14, 15, 16
and Gospel, 2, 4, 5, 6, 9, 11, 12, 13, 14, 15, 16
of the old covenant, 4, 8, 12
Law for the Prevention of Hereditary Diseases (July 14, 1933), 3, 6*, 12*, 13. In *DBWE see also* euthanasia; sterilization
Law for the Protection of the German Evangelical Church (September 24, 1933), 4*, 14. In *DBWE see also* Church Struggle
Law to Restore Order in the German Evangelical Church (*Maulkorberlass*, or "muzzling decree" [1934], 13, 14 (date listed incorrectly there as 1935)
laypeople. In *DBWE see* church, laity in
League of German Girls (BDM), 14
League of Nations, 6, 10, 11, 12, 13
Lebensgemeinschaft, 1, 4, **5**, 13. In *DBWE see also* life-community
Lebensraum, 4, 10, 14, 15. In *DBWE see also* living space

Le Chambon, 12, 16
legalism, 4, 5*, 14, 15*, 16. In *DBWE see also* law
legalization, 4*, 8, 14, **15**, 16. In *DBWE see also* Church Struggle; Confessing Church; Finkenwalde; illegals
Lehrter Strasse prisons, 8*, 15*, 16. In *DBWE see also* Berlin; imprisonment; prisons
Leipzig, 6, 8, 11*, 13*, 14, 15, 16
Leszno (Lissa), 7, 8
Letters and Papers from Prison (*DBWE* 8), 1, 2, 3, 4*, **5**, 6, 7, 9*, 10, 12, 16, 17 (9, 1/99b)
letters, Bonhoeffer's prison, 8, 12, 15*
Levites, 14
liberal, 1, 8*, 10, 12, 15*, 16
liberalism, 6, 9, 10, 11*, 12, 14, 15, 16
liberal theology, 2, 5, 10, 12, 13, 14, 16
liberation, 3, 7, 16
libido, 14
lies/lying, 3, 4*, 6, 7, 8, 10, 12*, 13*, 14*, 16*. In *DBWE see also* "What Does It Mean to Tell the Truth?" (*DBWE* 16, 2/19)
life, 1*, 2, 3, **6**, 7, 8, 9, 10, **12**, 12, 13*, 15, 16, 17 (9, 2/2a). In *DBWE see also* being; *Dasein*; human being
  Christ as, 3, 4, 14
  Christian, 6, 8, 10, 13, 14, 15, 16
  in community, 8, 10, 14, 15
  earthly, 8, 13, 15, 16
  eternal, 6, 7, 9, 10, 12, 13, 14, 15, 16
  fullness of, 6, 8
  inner, 12, 14
  for others, 7, 8
life, bodily, 6. In *DBWE see also* natural law
Life and Work movement, 1, 6, **11, 13**. In *DBWE see also* ecumenical movement; International Christian Council for Life and Work; Oxford; Stockholm; Universal Christian Council on Life and Work
life-community (*Lebensgemeinschaft*), 1
life-principle (*Lebensprinzip*), 1
life together, 7, 8
Life Together, 1, 4, **5**, 8, 10, 12, 14, 15, 16
"life unworthy of life" (euthanasia), 4*, 6, 9*, 15*. In *DBWE see also* euthanasia
limit(s) (*Grenze*), 1, **2**, **3**, 6, 7, 10, **12**, 17 (9, 1/99b). In *DBWE see also* boundary
Lippe, 16
Lisbon, 14*, 16
literature, 8, 10, 15*. *See also* "Reading Notes for the Seminar 'Ethical Viewpoints in Modern Literature'" (*DBWE* 10, 2/11)
liturgy, 1, 8, 10*, 12, 13*, 14, 15, 16
  Catholic, 5*, 9
Lobetal. *See* Bethel institutions
Lodz, 16
logic, 6, 9, 11, 13*
Logos (λόγος), 2, 6*, 9, 12, 14, 15, 16
  doctrine of, 9

London, 2, 4, 6, 7, 8, 9*, 10, 11*, 12, **13**, 14, **15**, 16
  Bonhoeffer's ministry (1933–35), 5, 6, 7, 12, 13, 14
  German congregations, 13
  other pastors, 13
loneliness (*Einsamkeit*), 1, 2, 5, 6, 8, 9, 10, 12, 13, 15, 16*
longing (*Sehnsucht*), 7, 8*
Lord (Herr), 6, 7*, 14, 15*, 16. *See also* Christ; God
Lord's Prayer, 1, 3, 4, 5, 6, 10, 11, 14, 15, 16. *See also* "Catechesis in the Second Theological Examination on the Fifth Petition of the Lord's Prayer" (*DBWE* 10, 3/21)
Lord's Supper (*Abendmahl*), **1**, 3, 4, 5, 6, 8, 9, 11, 12, 13*, **14**, **15**, 16. In *DBWE see also* communion; Holy Communion; sacrament. *See also* "Lectures on Personal Confession: Personal Confession and Lord's Supper" (*DBWE* 14, 2/24.1); "Supplements to the Monthly Letters from the Confessing Church Council of Brethren in Pomerania to Its Pastors: Theological Reflection on the Lord's Supper" (*DBWE* 15, 3/10.3)
  doctrine of, 14, 15, 16
Louvain, 13
love (agape, ἀγάπη), **1**, 3, 4, **5**, **6**, **7**, 8, 9, 10, 11*, 12, 13, 14, 15, **16**, 17 (9, 2/2a)
  commandment, **1**, 9, 10, 11, 12
  for God, 4, 6, 8, 15
  for human beings, 3, 4, 7, 8;
Love Letters from Cell 92, 1, **8**, **16**
loyalty (*Treue*), 6*, 7, 8, 10, 11*, 12, **13**, 14*, 15, 16. In *DBWE see also* allegiance; loyalty oath
  swearing an oath, 6, 8, 16
loyalty oath (*Treueid*), 4*, 8. In *DBWE see also* oath
  to Hitler, 5, **15**, 16
  in Japan, 16
Lübeck, 9
Lucifer, 3, 12*, 15*. In *DBWE see also* devil; evil; Satan
Lund, 8*, 14, 16
lust, 4, 8*, 10*, 14*, 15, 16. In *DBWE see also* longing; temptation
Lutheran Church. In *DBWE see also* Elmhurst; Missouri Synod
  Lutheran Council (Germany), 13, 14
  Lutheran World Federation, 14, 16
  in the United States, 10
Lutheranism, 4, 6, 11*, 12, 13, 14, 15, **16**
  Lutherans, 4, 6, 8, 12, 14, 15
  Lutheran theology, 2, 4, 8, 9, 11*, 12, 13*, 14, 15, 16
  Luther renaissance, 10, 14
  orthodox, 1
Luther Bible, 7, 8*, 12, 14, 15*. In *DBWE see also* Bible; Nestle Bible
Luxembourg, 12, 16
  study conference, **13**
lynching, 10, 15
Lyon, 8, 10
  Council of Lyon (1274), 14*

Macedonia, 14*, 17 (9, 2/2a)
Machiavellianism, 6, 8*
machines, 6, 7*, 10, 11*, 12. In *DBWE see* industrialism; Industrial Revolution; technology
Madrid, **10**, 16
Magdeburg, 7*, 8, 9*, 14, 15, 16
magic, 9, 14, 15*, 16*
Magna Carta, 6
Magnificat, 14*, 16
Majorca, 10
Malmö, 14*, 16
Malta, 9
Malvern (1941 conference), 16
mandates, 3, **6**, 8, 12, **16**
Marburg, 8, 9*, 10, 12, 14, 15*, 16*, 17 (12, 1/106a)
Maria Laach, 10, 11
marriage, **1**, **3**, 4, **6**, 7, **8**, 10, 11*, 12, 13, 14, 15, **16**. In *DBWE see also* family; mandates. *See also* "Wedding Sermon from the Prison Cell" (*DBWE* 8, 1/18); "Wedding Sermon on 1 Thessalonians 5:16–18" (*DBWE* 14, 3/12); "Wedding Sermon on John 13:34" (*DBWE* 14, 3/15)
  doctrine of, 6
  as mandate, 6, 8, 16
martyrdom, 4, 6, 8, 9, 10, 12, 13, 14*, 15, **16**
martyrs, 7, 8, 9, 10, 12, 13*, 14*, 15*
Marxism, 6, 7, 10, 12. In *DBWE see also* Bolshevism; Communism; workers
Maryland, 6, 15
Mass (Catholic), 1, 6, 9*, 10, 14, 16*. In *DBWE see also* Roman Catholicism
Mass in B Minor (Bach), 1*, 7, 8*, 16
mass movements, 1, 6, 7, 8*, 10, 11*, 12*. In *DBWE see also* masses
materialism, 2, 7, 10, 13, 14*
mathematics, 3, 6, 14*
Mecklenburg, 7*, 8, 9*, 12, 14*
Mediator (Christ), 1, 2, 4, 5*, 6*, 9, 11*, 12, 14*, 15*. In *DBWE see also* Christ, as mediator
meditations (on Scripture), 4, **5**, 6, 8, 12, 14, **15**, 16. In *DBWE see also* Daily Texts; exegesis; meditations. *See also* "Guide to Scriptural Meditation" (*DBWE* 14, 3/14)
melancholy, 7, 9*, 12*. In *DBWE see also acedia*; sadness
Memel, 16
memorandum to Hitler (1936), 14, 15*. In *DBWE see also* Hitler memorandum. *See also* Koch, Werner, and Weissler, Friedrich, in the master biographical index of names
Memorial Day (Volkstrauertag), 10, 11, 14
men, 8*, 10, 14, 15
  and women, 1, 3, 6*, 7, 10
Menschwerdung (becoming human), 3*, 4*, 5*, 6*, 8, 12, 15*, 16*. In *DBWE see* Christ; Christology; God; Jesus; incarnation
mercy (*Barmherzigkeit*), 4, 6, 7, 8, 15, 16. In *DBWE see also* compassion; grace
mercy (*Erbarmen*), 1, 9
mercy (*Gnade*), **12**, 15

Messiah, 4, 5*, 6, 10, 12, 14. In *DBWE see also* Christ; Christology
metanoia (μετάνοια), 8
  in Greek indexes in 6, 8, 9, 14
metaphysics, 1, 2, 5, 8, 9, 10, 11, 12*, 15*
method, 2, 3*, 6, 8, 10, 11*, 12*, 14*, 15*, 16*. In *DBWE see also* dialectics
  historical-critical, 3, 5, 9
Methodism, 4, 8, 11*, 12, 14
Methodist Church, 6*, 10, 12, 13, 14, 15, 16
  Methodist College, Richmond (UK), 5
Mexico, 8, 10, 11*, 16
Middle Ages, 1, 2, **6**, 8, 10, 15
middle class, 1, 7, 8. In *DBWE see also* bourgeoisie; class
military (*Wehrmacht*), 7, 8, 9, 15, 16. In *DBWE see also* Armed Forces High Command; Germany, military; military intelligence; United States; war
  call-up (*Musterung*), 15, 16
  chaplaincy, 8, 12, 15, 16
  conscription, 15
  exemption (Bonhoeffer's), 6, 8, 16
  oath to, 15
  recruiting station, 15, 16
  requirement, 4*, 15, 16
  wartime civilian service (Germany), 8, 16
Military Intelligence Office (*Abwehr*), 4, 6, 7, 8, 15, **16**
  Bonhoeffer's work for, **6**, **8**, 15, **16**
military prison, 7*, 8. In *DBWE see also* imprisonment; prison
military service (*Wehrdienst, Militärdienst, Waffendienst*), 4*, 6, 7, 8, 9, 12, 13, 14*, 15, **16**. *See also* conscientious objection; desertion; military (*Wehrmacht*)
  avoidance of, 8, 16
  conscription, 15, 16
mind-body relation, 2
Ministry of Church Affairs(Reichskirchenministerium), 4*, 8, 14, 15, **16**. In *DBWE see also* church committees; Church Struggle; German Evangelical Church; intact churches; Reich bishop; Reich Ministry of Church Affairs. *See also* Kerrl, Hans, in the master biographical index of names
Ministry of Culture (Prussia), 12, 13, 17 (12, 1/106a)
Ministry of Information (British), 16
Ministry of Justice, 13
Ministry of the Interior, 13, 16
ministry/pastoral service (*Dienst/Dienen*), 1, 3, 4, **5***, 6*, 7*, 8, 10, **12**, 13*, **14**, **15**, 16. In *DBWE see also* church; clergy; offices; pastorate; service
minorities, 10, 12
Minsk, 8
miracle (*Wunder*), 6, 8, 9, 12, 13, 14, 16
Mirfield (UK), 5, **13**, 14, 17 (13, 1/208a, 209a). In *DBWE see also* monasteries

misery (*Elend*), 6, 7, 8*, 12, 16*. In *DBWE see also* suffering
misfortune (*Unglück*), 7, 8*, 9*, 16*
Missa solemnis (Beethoven), 8
mission(s) or mission work, 1, 4, 8*, 9, 10, 11*, 12, 13*, 14, 15, 16. In *DBWE see also* church, missions; church renewal movement; evangelization; *Volksmission*. *See also* "Sketch for a Lecture by Eberhard Bethge: The Significance of Mission to Non-Christians for the Church Renewal Movement" (*DBWE* 16, 2/7); "Thesis Fragment: What Do We Learn from the Mission to Non-Christians?" (*DBWE* 16, 2/8)
missionary, 10, 12, 14, 15*, 16
Missouri Synod church, 10
Miteinander, 1. In *DBWE see also* being; "being-with-each-other"
Moabit prison, 8, 10, 15
models (*Vorbilder*), 1, 4*, 7*, 8*, 14, 15*, 16*
modernity, 10
modesty/humility (*Bescheidenheit*), 7, 8, 16
  false, 7
monad, 1
monarchy, 11*, 12, 16. In *DBWE see also* Hohenzollern; kaiser
monasticism, 1*, 4, 5, 6, 8*, 9, 10, 12, 13*, 14, 16. In *DBWE see also* community, monastic; Ettal; Kelham; Mirfield; monasteries
monism, 1, 2
Monte Cassino, 8*, 9
Montserrat, 10
morality/moralism/moral values, 1, 2, 6, 7, 8, 9, 10, 11*, 12, 13, 14, 16, 17 (9, 2/2a)
Moral Rearmament, 4, 6, 10, 14. In *DBWE see also* Oxford Group Movement. *See also* Buchman, Frank, in the master biographical index of names
moral theology, 6, 16*. In *DBWE see also* morality; theology
Moravian Church (*Herrnhut*), community (*Brüdergemeinde*), 4, 7, 8, 9, 10, 16. In *DBWE see also* Daily Texts
Morocco, 9, 10
motherhood, 6*, 7, 10, 12*, 14*, 16*. In *DBWE see also* family; marriage
movements, 12. In *DBWE see also* mass movements; names of individual movements
Mündigkeit, 8, 16. In *DBWE see also* "world come of age"
Munich, 6, 7*, 8, 9*, 12, 13, 14*, 15, **16**. In *DBWE see also* *Abwehr*
  Munich agreement (1938), 6, 15
Münster, 6, 11*, 12, 14*
murder, 3, 4, 6, 10, 14*
music, 5*, 6*, 7, **8**, 10, 11*, 12, 13, 14*, 15*, **16**, 17 (9, 1/80a, 95a, 94b, 96c, 99b). In *DBWE see also* hymns. *See also* Schmid, Ernst, in the master biographical index of names
  playing music, 7, 8, 9, 10, 17
Muslims, 8, 9, 10
mysterium (μυστήριον), 1, 4, 14

mystery (*Geheimnis*), 1*, 3, 4, 5*, **6**, 7*, 8, 10, 11*, **12**, 13, 14*, 15*
mystery cults (Greek and oriental), 9
mysticism (*Mystik*), 1, 2, 4, 6, 8, 9, 10, 11*, 12, 14*, 15*, 16*
myth, 3, 4, 10, 12, 14*, 15
  German myths of redemption, 3, 8, 15*
mythologization, 6. In *DBWE see also* demythologization. *See also* Bultmann, Rudolf, in the master biographical index of names
mythology, 3, 4, 6, 8*, 9, 12, 17 (9, 2/2a). In *DBWE see also* Greek mythology

Namibia, 7
nation(s), 1, 6, 7, 9, 11*, **12**, 13, 16*
  German, 6, 12
National Council of the Evangelical Free Churches (London), 13
National Socialism, 1, 2, 3, 4, 5, **6**, 7, **8**, 9, 10, 11, **12**, **13**, 14, **15**, **16**, 17 (12, 1/106a). In *DBWE see also* anti-Semitism; Aryan laws; German Christians; Jews; Nazi state; Nazism; Nuremberg laws; resistance; storm troopers
  adherents of, 6, 7, 8, 10, 11, 12, 13, 14, 15
  antichurch measures, 5, 6, 15, 16
  ideology, 3, 4, 6, 11, 15
  regime, 3, 4, 5, 7, 8, 10, 12, 14, 15, 16
  rise to power, 4, 7
  state, 1, 7, 8, 12, 13, 14, 16
National Socialist Workers Party (*NSDAP*), 6, 8, 9, 10, 11, 12, 13, 14, 15, 16, 17 (12, 106a). In *DBWE see also* Nazi party
  overseas organization, 13
National Synod (September 27, 1933), 12, 13, 16
nationalism, 6, 10, 11, **12**, 13, 14, 16. In *DBWE see also* Germany; National Socialism
natural, the, 1, 3, 4, **6**, 8*, 12, 15*, 16. In *DBWE see also* natural law
natural law (*Naturrecht*), 1, **6**, 8*, 9, 11, 12, 14, 15, **16**
natural sciences, 1, 3, 6, 7*, 8*, 10*, 11, 12, 13
natural theology, 3, 9, 15
nature, 1, 2, 4, 7, 8, 9, 10, 11, **12**, 13, 14, 15*, 16, 17 (9, 2/2a). In *DBWE see also* creation; human nature
  created, 3
  divine, 15
  experience of, 9, 10
  and grace, 6
"Nature of the Church, The" (1932), **11:2/9**; 1, 2, 3, **5**, 6*, 11, 14*. In *DBWE see also* church, nature of; referenced in *DBWE* 10 as "The Essence of the Church"
Nazi Germany, opposition to, 8*, 12, 13, **16**. In *DBWE see also* Confessing Church; conspiracy; German church; National Socialism resistance
necessity (*necessitas*), 3*, 6, 8, 11

Negro church. *See* African American church
Negro spirituals, 5*, 7*, **10**, 15*. In *DBWE see also* spirituals
neighbor (*Nächste*), 1, 2, 4*, 6*, 7, 8*, 10, **12**, 13, 16
love for, 1, 5, 6, 8, 9, 10, 11, 12, 13, 16
neo-Hegelianism, 2
neo-Kantianism, 2, 6, 10, 11
Neoplatonism, 9, 11
neues Leid, Ein, 5*, 8*, 14. *See also* hymnals
neutrality, 6*, 14, 15*
"neutrals" (in the Church Struggle), 14, 15. In *DBWE see also* intact churches; Lutherans. *See also* Marahrens, August; Meiser, Hans; Wurm, Theophil, in the master biographical index of names
New Decalogue, 6, 9*, 10, 12
New England, 15
new humanity, 1, 2
New Order, The (1941; Paton book), 16
New Orleans, 10
New Oxford movement, 6*, 11
New Testament, 1, 2, 3, 4, 6, 7, 8, 9, 10, 11, 12, 13*, 14, 15, 16, 17 (12, 1/106a). In *DBWE see also* exegesis; Holy Scripture; Nestle Bible. *See also* the master index of scriptural references
New Testament lectures (1935–37), 4, 7*, 8*, **14**. In *DBWE see also* New Testament
Newcastle (England), 11*, 13
newspapers, 7, 8, 11*, 16*
New York, 2, 4, 6, 7, 8, **10**, 11*, 12, 13, 14, **15**, 16. In *DBWE see also* Union Theological Seminary
Nicaea, council of (325 CE), 10, 12, 14, 15*
Nicene Creed, 4, 10, 12, 15
"Night Voices" (poem), 7*, **8**
nihilism, 6, 8*, 15, 16*. In *DBWE see also* nothingness
nominalism, 1, 2, 9, 15
nomism, 6*, 10, 14, 15*
nomos, 12, 15 (in Greek index); of Christ, 2
"non-Aryans", 5, 12, 13, 14, 15, **16**. In *DBWE see also* Aryan laws; Jewish Christians; racial laws
nonreligious interpretation, of biblical concepts, 2, 3, 6, 7, **8**. In *DBWE see also* interpretation, nonreligious
nonreligious language, 8
nonviolence, 10, 12, 13. In *DBWE see also* conscientious objection; pacifism; resistance. *See also* Gandhi, Mohandas, in the master biographical index of names
norm, **6**, 10, 14*
Normandy, 8, 16
North Africa, 7, 9
North America, 6, 10, 12, 14. In *DBWE see also* Canada; United States
North Sea, 7, 9
Norway, 7, 11*, 13*, 16. In *DBWE see also* Fanø. *See also* Henriod, Henry-Louis, in the master biographical index of names

nothingness (*Nichts*), 3, 6, 7*, 15*, 16, 17 (9, 2/2a)
nous (νοῦς), 12
Novi Sad (1933 ecumenical conference), 12, 13
numinosity, 9*, 11
Nuremberg, 6, 12, 13, 15, 16
Nuremberg Laws (1935), 14, 15, 16. In *DBWE see also* Aryan legislation; Jews, persecution of; National Socialism; Steglitz synod

oath, 4, 6, 13, 14, 15, 16. In *DBWE see also* loyalty oath
obedience (*Gehorsam*), 1, 2, 3, **4**, **6**, 7, 8, **9**, 10, 12, 13*, **14**, 15, **16**
Oberammergau, 13, 16
Oberlin (U.S.), 15
object, 1, 2
objective/objectivity, 2, 3*, 6, 8, 9, 12*, 13*, 16
  objective spirit, **1**
obligations (*Pflichten*), 6*, 8, 10, 14*. In *DBWE see also* duty
occultism, 7, 8, 15*
Oeynhausen. See Bad Oeynhausen
offices (usually: of ministry (*Amt/Ämter*), 1, 5*, 6, 7, 9, **12**, 13*, 14, 15*, 16*. In *DBWE see also* ministry; pastoral office
  apostolic, 14
  authority of, 11*, **12**
  ethics of, 10
  person who holds office, 4, 6, 14, 15, 16
  of preaching, 2, 9
oikumene. See ecumenical movement
Old Protestant (*altprotestantisch*), 9*, 14. In *DBWE see also* dogmatics; orthodoxy; scholasticism
Old Prussian Union Church, 4*, 5, 10, 11*, 12*, 13*, 14, **15**, **16**. In *DBWE see also* Brandenburg; church; collective pastorates; consistories; east Prussia; Pomerania; preachers' seminaries; Prussia; regional churches; Rhineland; Saxony; Westphalia
  "Brown Synod" (September 1933), 12, 13, 14, 16, 17 (12, 1/106a)
  Confessing Church in, 12, 13, 14, 15, 16
  German Christians in, 13, 16
  governance of, 10, 11, 12, 13, 14
Old Testament, 1, 3, 4*, 5, 7, 8, 9, 10, 11, 12, 13*, 14, **15**, 16. In *DBWE see also* covenant; faith; Holy Scripture; law; prophets. *See also* the master index of scriptural references
  and New Testament, 5, 9
Olympics (1936), 4, 7, 13*, 14, 15. In *DBWE see also* Berlin Olympics
omnipresence, doctrine of, 12. In *DBWE see also* God
"On the Theological Foundation of the Work of the World Alliance" (*DBWE* 11, 2/14; 1932), 3, 6*, 9*, 11. In *DBWE see also* Ciernohorské Kúpele; World Alliance

ontology, **2**, 10, **12**
Operation 7 (1943 rescue), 8, **16**
opportunism, 13
optimism, 6, 8, 12*, 13*
Oranienburg, 14. In *DBWE see also* Sachsenhausen. *See also* Scharf, Kurt, in the master biographical index of names
orders (*Ordnungen*), 4*, 6, 7, 8*, 10, 11, **12**, 13*, 14, 15*, 16*. In *DBWE see also* mandates
  of Christian life, 14, 16
  in the church, 4*, 6, 8*, 14, 15, 16
  in the congregation, 14, 15
  earthly, 14, 16
  of God, 3, 6, 10, 11, 15, 16
  of life, **6**, 7, 12, 16
  natural, 4*, 16
  powers of, 6, 16
  of state, 15, 16
  worldly, 4*, 6, 9, 12, 13, 14, 16
orders of creation (*Schöpfungsordnungen*), 1, 3, 4*, 5, *6*, 10, 11, 12, 13, 14, 15, 16. In *DBWE see also* Church Struggle; German Christians; orders of preservation
orders of preservation (*Erhaltungsordnungen*), 3, 4, 5, 6, 8, 10, 11, 12, 14, 15, 16. In *DBWE see also* Church Struggle; German Christians; orders of creation
ordination, 2, 5, **10**, 11*, 12, 13*, 14, 15, 16
Orient, 9, 10, 13*. In *DBWE see also* the East
origin (*Ursprung*), **6**, 10, 13*, 16*
original sin, 1, 2*, 3*, 5*, 6, 9*, 10, 11*, 12, 14, 15*, 16. In *DBWE see also* sin
Orthodox churches 1, 11*, 14, 15*
orthodoxy, 1, 10, 12, 13, 14, 15. In *DBWE see also* "age of orthodoxy"
  Lutheran, 5, 7, 8, 14
  old Protestant, 2, 3, 9, 11
Oslo, 8*, 16
other, the, **1**, 2, **3**, 4*, **5**, 6, 7, 8, 10, 12, 14. In *DBWE see also* Christology; love
Oud Wassenaar meeting (1919), 11
Oxford, 6, 8, 11, 12, 14, 15, 16. *See also* "Assessment by Hans Schönfeld for the Ecumenical Advisory Committee of the Provisional Church Administration" (*DBWE* 14, 1/6)
  Life and Work Conference (1937), 13, 14, 16
Oxford Group movement, 4, 6, 8, 10, 14. *See also* Buchman, Frank, in the master biographical index of names

pacifism, 4, 6, 10, 11, 12, **13**, 14, 15, 16. In *DBWE see also* Christ; conscientious objection; Fanø; peace; Sermon on the Mount
pagans, paganism (*Heidentum*), 4, 9, 10, 13, 14, 15. In *DBWE see also* Tannenberg movement; Teutonic Christianity. *See also*

Ludendorff, Erich and Matilde, in the master biographical index of names
in National Socialism, 4, 14, 16
pain, **3**, 6, 7, **8**, 16
painting (*Malerei*), 8*, 9, 10
Palestine, 8, 10
Palm Sunday, 8, 9, 12, 13. *See also* the master index of scriptural references
Pan, 9*, 10
pan-Germanism, 16. *See also* Germany; nationalism
pantheism, 1, 8, 11*, 14*
papacy, 6, 8, 12, 14. *See also* pope
parable, 9, 14, 16
Paraclete, 9, 14*, 15
paradise, 3, 10, 12, 13, 14*, 15, 16
paradox, 1*, 2, 3, 4, 6, 8*, 9, 10, 11*, 12, 14*, 15*
parents, 6, 7, 8*, 9*, 13, 14, 15*, 16. *See also* Bonhoeffer, Karl, and Bonhoeffer, Paula, in the master biographical index of names
Paris, 8*, 10, 11, 14, 15, 16
1934 and 1935 youth conferences, 13
parishioners, 7, 10, 14, 14*, 15*, 16*. In *DBWE see also* church-community; congregation; pastoral care
participation in (*Teilhabe*), 8*. In *DBWE see also* Christ; Christianity; *Stellvertretung*; worldliness
in Christ, 4*, 14*
in Germany's fate, 8
in God's suffering, 8
in worldly life, 2*, 8
passion, 12, 14, 15, 16*. In *DBWE see also* Christ, passion of
of Christ*, 3, 4*, 8, 12, 13
passion (*Leidenschaft*), 6, 7*, 8*, 9
passivity, 4*, 6, 16*
"Past, The" (poem), 7, **8**
pastoral care, 1, 4, 5*, 6, 8*, 11, 12, 14, 15, 16*. In *DBWE see also* care, pastoral; ministry; pastoral office. *See also* "Lecture on Pastoral Counseling" (*DBWE* 15, 2/1a)
Lectures on Pastoral Care (*DBWE* 14, 2/12 and 2/23), 4, 5*, 8*, 14, 15, 16*
pastoral counselor, 8*, 11, 12, 13, 14, 15. In *DBWE see also* chaplaincy; student chaplain
pastoral office or ministry (*Pfarramt*), 10, 11, 12*, 13, 14, 15*, 16*. In *DBWE see also* Catholic Church; Confessing Church; "illegals"; legalization; ministry; ordination; pastoral care; pastors; theological education; vocation. *See also* "Lecture: 'The Visible Church in the New Testament: The Space of the Pastoral Offices and Gifts and of Christian Life'" (*DBWE* 14, 2/8.6)
pastoral theology, 14, 16*. In *DBWE see also* theology
pastorate, **12**, 14, **16***. *See also* clergy; ministry, office of; office (*Amt*); pastoral care; pastoral office

pastors, 1, 4, 5*, 6, 7*, 8*, 9, 10, 11, **12**, **13**, 14, 15*, 16. In *DBWE see also* chaplains; church; church-community; clergy; Confessing Church; German Evangelical Church; intact churches; ministry; Pastors' Emergency League
- disciplinary measures against, 13, 14
- "non-Aryan", 4, 12, 13, 14
- overseas, 10, 13
- vocation of, 8, 14
- wives of, 8, 14, 15, 16

Pastors' Emergency League, 4, 12, **13**, 14, 16. In *DBWE see also* Aryan paragraph; Council of Brethren; synods. *See also* Niemöller, Martin, in the master biographical index of names
- chancel proclamation (1934), 13
- Wittenberg declaration (1933), 13

path (*Weg*), 15, 16
- preparing the way, 6*, 14, 16*

pathos, 4

patience (*Geduld*), 6, 7, 8*, 9, 13*, 15, 16. *See also* "Biblical Study Seminars on Basic New Testament Concepts: Notes on the Concept of Abstinence" (*DBWE* 15, 2/2.3)

Patmos, 8, 14

patriarchalism, 1

patriotism, 1*. In *DBWE see also* country, love of; Germany

Pätzig, **8**, 16

peace (*Friede*), 1, 3, **4**, 5, 6, 7, **8**, 9, **10**, 11, **12**, **13**, 14, 15, **16**, 17 (9, 2/2a). In *DBWE see also* Christ; Christology; Fanø; pacifism; war. *See also* "Biblical Study Seminars on Basic New Testament Concepts: Notes on the Concept of Peace" (*DBWE* 15, 2/2.6); Lecture on "Christ and Peace" (*DBWE* 12, 2/6); Fanø addresses "The Church and the Peoples of the World" (*DBWE* 13, 2/2 and 2/3)
- Christian message of, 13
- conspiracy peace aims and feelers, 16
- on earth, 13, 15
- eschatological, 15
- peace movements, 10, 13, 15
- in the world, 7, 12, 13, 15

pecca fortiter, 2, 3, 4, 10, 12, 14, 15

pedagogy, 6, 7*, 11*, 14*, 16*. In *DBWE see also* catechetical instruction; confirmation; education

Pelagianism, semi-, 2, 9, 10

penance (*Buße*), 2, 10, 15

penitence (*Buße*), 2, 14, 15

Pentecost, 1, 4, 8, 9, 10, 11*, 13*, **14**, 15, 16. *See also* "Pulpit Announcement on Pentecost Sunday 1936" (*DBWE* 14,1/75)

penultimate (*Vorletztes*), 4, 6, 8, 10, 12*, 16. In *DBWE see also* ultimate

peoples (*Volk*), 1, 3, 4*, 6, 7, 8*, 10, 11*, 12, 13*, 14, 15*, 16*. In

DBWE see also Lebensraum; nations
German, 6, 11, 12, 14, 15, 16
of God, 5
Jewish, 12, 15
of the Old Testament, 14
Western, 6, 16
person, 1, **2**, 5, 6, 9, 10, 11*, 12, 14*, 16*. In *DBWE see also* collective person; personhood
Christian concept of, 1, 9
concept of, 1, 2
personal, the, 6, 7*, 10, 13. In *DBWE see also* objective. *See also* "A Study on 'Personal' and 'Objective' Ethics" (*DBWE* 16, 2/13)
Bonhoeffer's personal life, 8
personality, 2, 7, 9, 10, 11*, 12, 13*. In *DBWE see also* character formation; education
personality cult, 5, 11
pessimism, 9, 12, 13*. In *DBWE see also* optimism
Pharisees/pharisaical (φαρισαῖος), 4, 6, 8*, 9, 10, 12, 14, 15*, 16, 17 (9, 1/99b)
phenomenology, 1, 2, 6, 10, 12
Philadelphia, 7, 10, 11*, 15*. *See also* Tafel family in the master biographical index of names
philosophy, 1, **2**, 3, 6, 7, 8, 9, **10**, 11, **12**, 13*, 15, 16. In *DBWE see also* "On Euripides's Philosophy,"17 (9, 2/2a)
Christian, 1, 2, 9, 10, 16
dialectic, 10
Greek, 17 (9, 2/2a)
idealist, 1, 4
of religion, 3, 10, 11
transcendental, 2, 11
phraseology, 2, 8, 9, 10, 15*. *See also* "Turning Away from the Phraseological to the Real: A Personal Recollection," by Hans Christoph von Hase (*DBWE* 10:591–605)
physician, 6, 7*, 8*, 14, **16**. In *DBWE see also* medicine. *See also* "The Best Physician" (*DBWE* 16, 2/9)
pietism, 1, 5, 6, 8, 9, 10, 11, 12, 13, 14, 15, 16
pietists, 4, 8, 10, 11, 14
piety (*Frömmigkeit*), 2, 3, 4, 5, 7, 8, 9, 10, 11*, 12, 13*, 14, 15, 16
plebiscite, 9. In *DBWE see also* Saar plebiscite
pneuma (πνεῦμα), 14 (12, 14, 15 in Greek index)
and *sarx* (σάρξ), 5 (14, 15 in Greek index)
pneumatology, 4*, 5, 14, 15. In *DBWE see also* eschatology
poetry, **8**, **9**, 16. In *DBWE see also* individual poem titles
Poland, 6, 8, 10, 11*, 12, 13*, 14, **15**, 16
invasion of (1939), 7*, 15
police, 8*, 16. In *DBWE see also* Gestapo
polis (πόλις), 4*, 12, 14, **16**
political, the, 1, 4*, 6, 7, 8*, 10, 11*, 13*, 14*, 16. In *DBWE see also* ethics; theology
political theology, 12, 15. In *DBWE see also* ethics; theology
political ethic, 6, 8, 10
politics, 6, 7, 8, 10, 11*, 12, 13*, 14*, 15*, 16. In *DBWE see also*

churches; Church Struggle; Nazi state
and Sermon on the Mount, 6
Pomerania, 6, 8*, 10, 13*, 14, **15**, 16. In *DBWE see also* Confessing Church; Council of Brethren; Finkenwalde; Old Prussian Union Church
church province in, 13, 14, 15, 16
poor, the, 5, 6, 7, 8, **14**, 16. In *DBWE see also* poverty; the Sermon on the Mount
pope, 1, 4, 9, 11*, 12, 14, 15, 16. In *DBWE see also* papacy; Vatican
1924 papal audience, 9
"positive Christianity," 6*, 12*, 14. In *DBWE see also* Barmen declaration; German Christians; ideology; idolatry
positivism, 2, 6, 8, 9*, 11*, 14*, 15, 16
"positivism of revelation" (*Offenbarungspositivismus*), critique of Barth, 1*, 2, 5*, **8**, 9*. In *DBWE see also* revelation
possibility, 1, **2**, 3, 4, 6, 8, 10
postdoctoral dissertation. *See Habilitation*
Potsdam, 7*, 8, 10, 12, 15*, 16
poverty, 1, **4**, 6*, 7, 8*, 9, 10, **13**, 14, 16. In *DBWE see also* poor
and presence of God, 13
voluntary, 4
power (*Macht*, ἐξουσία), 2, 3, 4*, 5*, 7, 8, 10, 11, **12**, 13, 14, 15*, 16, 17 (9, 2/2a)
demonic, 13, 14
misuse of, 7
political, 14
powerlessness, 8
power of the keys, 4, 11*, 14, 15, 16*. *See also* "The Power of the Keys and Church Discipline in the New Testament" (*DBWE* 14, 2/29)
powers (*Gewalten*), 4*, 6, 7, 11, 13, 14, 16
pragmatism, 6, **10**, 11, 12, 15
Prague, 8, 10, 11*, 14, 15, 16
1939 occupation of, 15
conference (1928), 6
Prague agreement (1942), 16
praxis, 10, 14
prayer (*Gebet*), 1, 2, 4, **5**, 6, 7, **8**, **9**, **10**, 11*, 12, 13, 14, **15**, 16. In *DBWE see also* intercessory prayer; Lord's Prayer. *See also* "Prayers for Prisoners: Evening, Morning, Prayer in Particular Need" (*DBWE* 8, 2/76–78)
as discipline, 14, 17 (13, 1/208a)
times, 14
Prayerbook of the Bible (*DBWE* 5), 14, 15, 16
prayer liturgy (Sudeten crisis), 15
praying/prayer (*Beten*), 2, 7, 8, 11*, 12. In *DBWE see also* fasting; prayer (*Gebet*)
and the doing of justice, 5, 7, 8
waiting for God's time, 8, 15
preacher, 2, 6, 7, 11*, 12, 14, 15*, 16*
preachers' seminary, 10, 13, **14**, **15**, 16. In *DBWE see also* Bethel; Elberfeld; Finkenwalde; underground pastorates

preaching (*Predigen*), **1**, **2**, 4, 5, 7*, 8, 9, 10, 11, 12, 13, 14, **15**, **16**. In *DBWE see also* preacher; preachers' seminaries; proclamation; sermons. *See also* "Examination Paper: The Meaning and Choice of a Biblical Text for the Sermon in the Worship of the Congregation" (*DBWE* 10, 2/5)
predestination, 1, **2**, 3*, 4, 6, 8, **9**, 10, 11, 12*, 14, 16
presbyter (πρεσβύτερος), 10*, 14, 15*
Presbyterian Church, 15
press, 6, 12, 13, 14*, 16
  foreign, 13
  National Socialist*, 10, 14*, 15*
pride (*Hochmut*), 4, 5, 6, 9, 10, 14*, 15*, 16. In *DBWE see also* arrogance
pride (*Stolz*), 3, 7, 8, 11, 12, 14*
priest, 1, 10, 11, 12, 14, 15*
priesthood, 14*, 15
  of all believers, 1, 6, 11, 15
  general, 5, 11, 14
  Levite, 14*
primal state, 1, 3
Princeton, 15
principles, 3*, 4*, **6**, 7*, 8, 9, 10, 11*, 12, 14*, 15*
  Christian, 11, 13, 15
  ethical, 3, 10, 14*
Prinz Albrecht Strasse 8 prison (Gestapo prison), 7, 8
prison, 4, 7, **8**, 10, 12, 13, 15, **16**. In *DBWE see also* antichurch measures; Gestapo; imprisonment; *Letters and Papers from Prison*; Lehrter Strasse; Moabit; National Socialism; Prinz Albrecht Strasse; Tegel. *See also* "Report on Experiences during Alarms" (*DBWE* 8, 2/80); "Report on Prison Life after One Year in Tegel" (*DBWE* 8, 2/131)
  Bonhoeffer's imprisonment, 4, 7, 8, 14*, 16
  Bonhoeffer's report on prison conditions (1944), 7, 8
  Bonhoeffer's writings in prison, 4, 15
  permission for visitors, 7, 8
prisoner of war camps, 8
prisoners, 6, 7, 8, 15*, 16
privilege, 4*, 6, 8, 9, **12**, 14*
probation (theological *Bewährung*), 15, 16*. *See also* "Biblical Study Seminars on Basic New Testament Concepts: Notes on the Concept of Probation" (*DBWE* 15, 2/2.4)
proclamation (*Verkündigung*), 2, 4, 6, 9, 10, 11, **12**, 13*, 14, 15, 16. In *DBWE see also* homiletics; preaching; sermon. *See also* "Lecture Sections concerning the Space of Proclamation and the Space of the Pastoral Offices" (*DBWE* 14, 2/28)
  as divine mandate, 6
prodigal son, 6, 10, 12
profane, the, 6, 14*
progress, 1, 9, **10**, 11, 12, 15*
Prohibition (U.S.), 6, 10, 12, 15
proletariat, 1, 6*, 7, 8, 9, 10*, 11*, 12, 13*. In *DBWE see*

also capitalism; socialism; unemployment; workers
promise (*Verheißung*), 1, 2, 3, 4*, 5*, 8*, 9, 10*, 12, 13, 14*, 16*. In *DBWE see also* prophecy
of discipleship, 4
of eternity, 13
and fulfillment, 9, 12, 14
propaganda, 4*, 6, 7*, 12, 14*, 15, 16. In *DBWE see also* National Socialism
prophets, 1, 3, 7*, 10, 11*, **12**, 13, 14, 15, 16. In *DBWE see also* "Israelite prophets." *See also* the master index of scriptural references. *See also* "The Tragedy of the Prophetic and Its Lasting Meaning" (*DBWE* 10, 2/1)
prophecy, 8, 9, 14
Protestantism, 3, 4, 8, 9, 11, **12**, 13, 14, 15, 16. In *DBWE see also* church
orthodoxy, 1
"Protestantism without Reformation" (*DBWE* 15, 2/6; 1939), 6, 10, **15**, 16
providence (*Vorsehung*), 6*, 9, 12, 13, 14, 16
Provisional Bureau for Ecumenical Youth Work (*Mittelstelle*), **11**, 12
Provisional Church Administration (November 22, 1934–February 19, 1936), 13*, 14, 15, **16**
Prussia, 6, 9, 10, 11*, 12, 13, 14, 16*. In *DBWE see also* Old Prussian Union Church
Psalms, **5**, 9*, 10, 12, 14, 15, 16. *See also* the master index of scriptural references. *See also* "Homiletical Exercises on Psalm 50" (*DBWE* 14, 2/13.1); "Lecture on Christ in the Psalms" (*DBWE* 14, 2/5); "Meditation on Psalm 119" (*DBWE* 15, 3/9); Sermons on Psalm 42, 90, 58 (*DBWE* 14 3/1, 3/11, 3/19); Sermon on Psalm 62:2 (*DBWE* 10, 3/7); Sermon on Psalm 63:3 (*DBWE* 11, 3/1); Sermon on Psalm 98:1 (*DBWE* 13, 3/8); Sermon on Psalm 127:1 (*DBWE* 9, 3/5)
exegesis of, 5, 9
of revenge (*Rachepsalmen*), 5, 14, 159
psychoanalysis, 3*, 5*, 14, 15*. In *DBWE see also* psychology; psychotherapy
psychology, 1, 2, 4*, 5, 6, 8, **9**, 10, 11*, **12**, 13*, 14, 15, 16*, 17
public sphere (*Öffentlichkeit*), 1, 4*, 6, 8, 12, 14*, 15*, 16*. In *DBWE see also* polis
punishment (*Strafe*), 1, 6, 7*, 8*, 16*
purity, 4, 6, 7, 8*, **10**, 13*, 16*
Pyrenees, **10**

Quakers, 4, 5, 9, 10, 12, 13, 14*, 15, 16. *See also* Jehle, Herbert, in the master biographical index of names
quietism, 3, 10

rabbinic literature, 1
rabbis, 4*, 10

race, 4, 6, 9, 10, 11*, **12**, 13, 14, 15*, 16. In *DBWE see also* anti-Semitism; Ayran laws; Nazi ideology; racial laws; racism
racial laws, 9, 11*, 15*, 16*. In *DBWE see also* Aryan laws; National Socialism; Nuremberg; racial laws
racism (U.S.), **10**, 15
radicalism, 4*, 6
  and compromise, 6, 7, 8
radio, 8, 12, 13, 15*. In *DBWE see also* BBC
rationalism, 6, 9, 10, 11*, 12, 13, 14. In *DBWE see also* reason
rationing (wartime), 8
Ravensbrück, 16
realism, 1, 2, 6, 10, 15, 17
reality (*Tatsache*), 8, 9
reality (*Wirkliche, Wirklichkeit*), **1**, **2**, 3, 4, **6**, 7, 8, 9, 10, 11*, **12**, 13*, 14*, 15*, 16. In *DBWE see also* penultimate; ultimate
  concept of, 2
realization (*Erkenntnis*), 1, 2, 3, 6, 8*
rearmament, 8*. In *DBWE see also* Germany, military; Moral Rearmament
reason (*Vernunft*), 1, **2**, 3, 4*, **6**, 8, 9, 10, 11*, 12, 13*, 14, 15*, 16, 17 (9, 2/2a). In *DBWE see also* knowledge; understanding
  practical, 2, 11
  and revelation, 9, 11
reason (*Verstand*), 6, 7, 11*, 13*, 14, 16
rebirth (*Wiedergeburt*), 2, 6, 8, 9, 11*, 14*, 15*, 16
reconciler, God as, 2, 14, 16. In *DBWE see also* God
reconciliation (*Versöhnung*), 1, 2, 3, 4, **5**, **6**, 7, 8, 9, 10, 11*, 13, 14, 15, 16
Red Cross, 8
Redeemer, 2, 6, 14, 16*. In *DBWE see also* Christ
redemption, 1, 4, 5*, 6, 8, 9, 10, **11**, **12**, 13, 14, 15, 16
reflection, 2, 10, 12
Reformation, 1, 2, 4, 5, 6, 7*, 8, 9, 10, 11*, **12**, 13, 14, **15**, **16**. In *DBWE see also* confessions; Lutheran. *See also* "Protestantism without Reformation" (*DBWE* 15, 2/6)
Reformation Day, 8, 12, 13
Reformed Church, 2, 4*, 6, 8, 11*, 12, 13, 14, 15, 16
Reformers, 4, 8*, 10, 12, 14, 15*
refugees, 8, **13**, 15, 16, 17 (13, 1/209a, 210a). In *DBWE see also* American Committee for Christian German Refugees; emigration; relief agency
Regensburg, 8, 16
regional churches (*Landeskirchen*), 9*, 12, 13*, 14, 16. In *DBWE see also* German Evangelical Church; Landeskirchen
Reich bishop, 12, 13, 14, 16, 17 (12, 1/106a). In *DBWE see also* Church Struggle; consistory; German Christians; Reich Church. *See also* Bodelschwingh, Friedrich von; Müller,

Ludwig, in the master biographical index of names
Reich Central Security Office, 8, **16**
Reich Chamber of Literature (Schriftstumskammer), 8*, 15, 16
Reich Chancellery, 12, 13, 14, 15, 16. In *DBWE see also* Third Reich
Reich Church, 12, **13**, 14, 15, 17 (13, 1/208a). In *DBWE see also* Aryan paragraph; Church Foreign Office; Church Struggle; Confessing Church; consistory; German Christians
- government of, 12, 13, 14

Reich Church Committees (1935–37), 14, 15, 16
Reich Church Constitution (July 1933), 12, 13, 16
Reichstag elections
- July 1932, 11, 12
- March 1933, 12
- November 1932, 12
- September 1930, 10, 11

Reich War Court, 6*, 8, 16
rejection (*Verwerfung*), 4, 12, 14*
relativism, 8*, 12, 17 (9:2/2a)
religion, 1, 2, 3*, 4, 5, 6, 7, 8, 9, **10**, **11**, **12**, 13*, 14, 15, 16*, 17
- concept of, 5, 6
- critique of, 10
- history, 1, 9, 11
- natural, 1, 2, 8
- positive, 11
- and revelation, 1, 2, 5, 10
- secular, 12
- syncretism, 19
- *völkisch*, 12

religionless Christianity, 5*, 6, 7, **8**, 15, 16. In *DBWE see also* Christianity, nonreligious; "world come of age"
religiosity, 2, 8, 10, 11*, 12, 14*, 15*
religious community, 1
religious education or instruction, **10**, 11, 12, 14*, 16. *See also* catechetical instruction; confirmation
religious historical method, 10, 11. *See also* history of religions school
religious socialism, 4, 8, 10*, 12*, 14, 16. In *DBWE see also* socialism
remembrance, 2, 8*, 14
Remembrance Sunday (*Totensonntag*), 8, 9, **10**, 12*, 13
Renaissance, 6, 8, 10, 11*, 12
renunciation (*Verleugnung*), 4, 9, 12, 15*, 16
reparations, 9, 10, 11*
repentance (*Buße*), 1, 2, 4, 6, 7, 8, 9, 11*, **12**, 13, 14, 15, 16. In *DBWE see also* penance; penitence
- call to, 14
- Catholic sacrament of, 2, 9
- discipline, 14, 16
- Repentance Day, 8, 9, 10, 13
- sermon about, 10, 14, 16
- worship service of, 13

repression, 6
resignation, 6, 8, 11, 14*, 15*, 16
resistance (*Widerstand*), 1, 2, 3, 5, 6, 7, **8**, 11*, 12, 13, 14*, 15, **16**. In *DBWE see also Abwehr*;

conspiracy; July 20; *Letters and Papers from Prison*; Reich Central Security Office
armed, 14
Christian right to, 16
nonviolent, 10, 13
right to, 6
and submission, 8
during Third Reich, 1, 5, 6, 7, 8, 9, 13, 14, 15, 16
responsibility, 1, 2, 4, 5, **6**, 7, **8**, 9, 10, 11*, **12**, 13*, 14*, 15, 16*, 17 (9, 2/2a). In *DBWE see also* action; responsible action
as free response to God, 6
political, 16
resurrection, 1, **2**, 3, 4, 5, 6, 7, 8, **9**, 10, 11, 12, 13, **14**, 15, 16. *See also* "Reflection on Easter: Resurrection" (*DBWE* 16, 2/1)
of the body, 15, 16
Catholic concept of, 9
of the dead, 3, 4, 6, 8, **14**, 15, 16
retreats, 12, 14*, 15*. In *DBWE see also* Finkenwalde
revelation, 1, **2**, 3, 5, 6, 7*, 8, **9**, 10, **11**, **12**, 13, 15, 16
book of, 4
in Christ, 5, 6, 13, 14
concept of, **2**, 9
and Holy Scripture, 9, 13
revenge, 7, 15, 16*, 17 (9, 2/2a)
revolution, 4, 6, 7, 10, 11*, 12, 13*, 14*, 16. In *DBWE see also* Germany; National Socialism
American, 6, 12, 15
German, 4, 7, 12, 13, 14, 16
Russian, 9, 11
after World War I, 6, 10
Rhineland, 8, 9, 13*, 14, 15, 16
as church province, 13, 14, 15
Richmond College (UK), Methodist college, 5, 8*
righteousness, 1, 2, **4**, **5**, 8, 9, 10, 11, **12**, **16**. *See also* "Catechetical Outlines: Righteousness" (*DBWE* 14, 2/4.4)
righteous ones (*Gerechten*), 7, 8, 9, 12, 14
Rights (*Rechte*), 4*, 6, 7*, 8*, 11*, **12**, 14*, 15*, 16*. In *DBWE see also* civil rights; constitution; human rights
for bodily life, 6
free expression, 7
natural, 6, 16
state, 16
"Right to Self-Assertion" (*DBWE* 11, 2/6; 1932), 3*
rite vocatus. See vocation
ritual (*Kultus*), 1, 8, 11*, 13*, 14, 15*
Röhm purge (1934), 8*, 14*. *See also* Röhm, Ernst, in the master biographical index of names
Roma (ethnic Sinti), 6, 7*, 10*
Roman Catholic Church, 1, 2, 3, 4, 5, 6, 8, 9, 10, 11, 12, 13*, 14, **15**, **16**. In *DBWE see also* Catholicism; pope; St. Peter's; Vatican. *See also* "Paper on 'The Catholic Church' for the 'Thursday Circle'" (*DBWE* 9, 3/14)
Roman Empire, 4, 6, 15, 16
Romania, 11, 12*, 16

Romanticism, 1, 6, 8, 9, 11*, 12, 15*, 16, 17 (9, 1/96c)
Rome (city), 1*, 4, 6, 8, 9, 10, 11*, 12, 13, 14, 15*, **16**, 17. In *DBWE see also* St. Peter's
  Bonhoeffer's 1924 visit, 9, 17 (9, 1/80a)
Rostock, 12, 14*, 15*
Round Table, The (periodical), 13
Round Table Conference (1930–32, London, about India), 10, 13. In *DBWE see also* India. *See also* Gandhi, Mohandas, in the master biographical index of names
Ruhr region, 9, 16*
Russia, 4*, 6, 7*, 8, 9, 10, 11*, 12, 13*, 14, 15*, **16**

SA (Sturmabteilung), 12, 13, 14, 15, 16, 17 (12, 1/106a). In *DBWE see also* storm troopers; Sturmabteilung
Saar region, 9, 13, 15; 1935 plebiscite, 13, 17 (13, 1/208a)
Sabbath, 5, 6, 7, 14*, 16
Sabellianism, 16
Sachsenhausen, 8, 14*, **15**, 16. In *DBWE see also* concentration camps
sacrament(s), 1, 2, 3, 4, 5, 6, 8, 9, 10, **11**, **12**, 13, 14, 15, 16
sacred, the, 4*, 7, 8*, 14, 16. In *DBWE see also* sanctity
sacrifice, 1, 5*, 6, 7, 8, 10, 11, 12, 13, 14, 15, 16
  for the brothers, 11
  in Catholicism, 9
  and death, 9, 13
  willingness, 12
sadness (*Traurigkeit*), 6*, 8*, 14*, 15, 16. In *DBWE see also* *acedia*; melancholy; *tristitia*
saints (*Heilige*), 1, 4, 6, 8, 14, 13*, 15
  images of, 7, 9
Sakrow, **8**, 16
salvation (*Heil*, σωτηρία), 1, 2, 4, 5, 6, 8, 9, 10, 11, **12**, 13*, **14**, **15**, **16**. *See also* "Doctrinal Examination on the Certainty of Salvation" (*DBWE* 9, 2/17)
Salvation Army, 7
salvation history, 1, 5*, 9, 14
Salzburg, 9, 14*, 16
Samaritan, 9, 16*
sanctification (*Heiligung*, ἁγιασμός), 1, 3, **4**, 5, 8, 9*, 10, 11, 12, 13*, 14, 15, 16
sanctity (*Heiligkeit*), 1, 3*, 6, 9, 10, 14, 15*
Sanctorum Communio, **1**, 2, 3, **4**, 5, **6**, 8, 9, **10**, **11**, 12, 13*, **14**, 15, 16, 17 (9, 1/94b, 99b)
Satan, 2, 3, **4**, 7*, 8, **9**, 12, 14, **15**, 16
Saxony, province of, 13*, 8, 14, 15*, 16
Scandinavia, 8*, 14, 16. In *DBWE see also* Denmark; Sigtuna; Sweden
  Bonhoeffer's travels for the conspiracy, 7*, 16
schism, **12**, 13, 14, 16
Schlawe (Pomerania), 6*, 8, 14, **15**, **16**
Schleswig-Holstein, 9
scholarship (*Wissenschaft*), 2*, 6, 7*, 8, 10, 11*, 12, 14*, 16. In *DBWE see also* academia; scholarly work; science

scholasticism, 1, 2, 9, 10, 11, 16
Catholic, 9
Schwäbisch Hall, 9*, 11*, 15, 16
science, 3, 6
Scotland, 7*, 10, 13*, 14, 15*, 16, 17 (13, 1/208a)
Scottish confession (1560), 14*. In *DBWE see also* tyrannicide
Scottsboro case, 6, 10, 12
Scripture, 1, 4, 6, **9**, 11, 15. In *DBWE see also* exegesis; Holy Scripture; proclamation; Word
allegorical, 9, 14
exegesis of, 8, 14, 15
historical-critical, 14
reading of, 5
sealing (*Versiegelung*), 4, 14
second coming of Christ, 1, 6, 16
sects, 1, 7*, 10, 11*, 12, 14*, 15*
secularism, 5, 6, 10, **12**, 14, 15*
process of, 6, 10, 11
secularization, 4*, 6, 11, 15, 16
security (*Sicherheit*), 4*, 6, 7, 10, 11*, 12, 13, 14*, 15
self, **2**, 3, 9, 10, 12, 13
self-assertion, 4, 6. In *DBWE see also* self-determination. *See also* "The Right to Self-Assertion" (*DBWE* 11, 2/5)
self-consciousness, 1, 2, 6, 12
self-denial, 4, 6, 12, 15, 16
selfishness, 4
self-justification, 1, 4, 5, 6, 10, 13, 15*
selflessness, 6, 8*, 16
self-love, 1, 6, 8, 13, 16
Selly Oak (UK), 5, 8*, 13
senses, 2, 8, 10, 12, 16. In *DBWE see also* sensations
separation (*Trennung*), 8*, 16. In *DBWE see also* church/state
from sins, 4
seriousness (*Ernst*), 2, 6, 13*, 16
exegesis of, 4
sermon(s), 1, 2, 4, 6, 7, 8, 9, 10, 11*, **12**, 13, 14, 15, 16. In *DBWE see also* homiletics; preaching; proclamation; word of God
baptismal sermons, 8, 11, 13
Bonhoeffer's 1943 sermon, 6, 7*, 8
meditations for, 8, 14, 15, 16
office of, 6, 11, 12, 14, 15, 16
and sacrament, 1, 2
wedding sermons, 8, 16
Sermon on the Mount, 2, 3*, **4**, 5, **6**, 8, 9, 10, **11**, 12, **13**, **14**, 15, 16. In *DBWE see also* Beatitudes. *See also* the master index of scriptural references
serpent, **3**, 4*, 11*, 12, 13*
in paradise, 3, 6, 14
service (*Dienst*), **5**, 6, 9, 12, 16
sexuality, 1, 3, 4, 6, 8, 10, 11*, 12, 14, 15
shame, 1, 3, 4*, 7, 6, 8, 14*, 15*, 16
shepherd (pastoral/*Hirt*). *See* pastoral care
Sicily, 8, 9
sickness, 6*, 7, 8*, 12, 13*, 14, 15, 16. In *DBWE see also* illness; physician
patients, 6, 8, 10, 14
sicut deus, 3, 4*, 6, 7, 12, 14, 15*
Sigtuna, 6, 14, 16
Sigurdshof, 8, 14*, **15**, 16
collective pastorate there, 8, 15

silence (*Ruhe*), 3, 7, 8, 14*
silence (*Schweigen*), 3*, 4*, 6, **7**, 8, 10, 12, 14*, 16*
Silesia, 9, 16. In *DBWE see also* Upper Silesia
 church in, 13
simple, simpleness (*Einfalt*), 6, 7, 8*, 10, 13*, 15*, 16*. In *DBWE see also Einfalt*
 quality of, 4, 6, 14, 15
simplicity (*Einfachheit*), 6, 7, 8, 14
sin(s), **1**, **2**, 3, 4, 5, **6**, 7, 8, **9**, 10, 11*, **12**, 13, **14**, **15**, **16**, **17**. In *DBWE see also* confession of sins; forgiveness; original sin; penitence; repentance; sinners. *See also* "Biblical Study Seminars on Basic New Testament Concepts: Notes on the Concept of Abstinence" (*DBWE* 15, 2/2.1)
 acknowledgment of, 5, 9, 11, 16
 being without sin, 6, 14, 15
 deadly, 14, 15;
 against Holy Spirit, 9, 14, 15
 sinfulness, 2, 3, 4, 5, 6, 9, 12, 14*, 15*
 sinlessness, 6, 11*, 12, 14*
 of weakness, 6, 8, 15
 willful, 8, 15, 17
 worldly, 4, 16
Sinai, 9, 12, 14*
singing, **5**, 8*, 14, 15. In *DBWE see also* hymns; music
sinner(s), 1, 2, 3*, 4, **5**, 6, 7*, 8, 9, 12, 13*, 14*, 15, 16. In *DBWE see also* confession of sins; forgiveness
 God's love for, 15
 justification of, 8, 12, 14*
Sinti (Roma), 6
slavery, 4, 6, **7**, 12, 15, 16
Smalcald Articles, 4*, 12*, 14, 15, 16. In *DBWE see also* Book of Concord
Small Catechism, 6, 9, 10, 12, **14**, 15, 16
Social Democrats, 9*, 11*, 12
social gospel, 6, 10, 11, 12, 13, 15. *See also* "The Social Gospel" (*DBWE* 12, 2/4; Bonhoeffer's 1932 memorandum), 6, 11, **12**, 14
socialism, 1, 6, 9, 10, 11, 12, 13*, 16
socialists, 9, 10, 12. *See also* religious socialists
sociality, **1**, 2, 3, 7*, 9, 11*, 13, 14*. In *DBWE see also* basic-relation and social basic-relation; collective person; community; "other"; person
social philosophy, **1**
Social Working Group (Soziale Arbeitsgemeinschaft Berlin-Ost), 9*, 10*, 12*. *See also* Siegmund-Schultze, Friedrich, in the master biographical index of names
society (*Gesellschaft*), **1**, 5, 6, 8, 9, 10, 11, 12, 13, 16. In *DBWE see also* community
 order of, 6, 10, 11, 12, 15
Society of the Sacred Mission (Kelham), 5, 14, 15, 17 (13, 1/208a, 209a). In *DBWE see also* Kelham
sociology, **1**, 2, 9, 10, 11*, 12*. In *DBWE see also* church; *Sanctorum Communio*
 Christian, 1, 2, 17 (9, 1/94b)
 Protestant, 10

Sofia (Bulgaria), 8. In *DBWE* *see also* World Alliance
1933 conference, **12**, 13*, 16
soldiers, 4*, 6, 7*, 8*, 9, 10, 14*, 15*, **16**. In *DBWE see also* military; war
solidarity, 1, 6, 12, 13*, 14*, 15, 16
solitude (*Alleinsein*), **2**, 3*, 5, 7*, 8, 10, 11*, 12*, 16. In *DBWE see also* alone; aloneness (*Alleinigkeit*); humankind, solitude and loneliness; loneliness
solitude (*Einsamkeit*), 1, 2
and community, 6
solus Christus, 13, 14. In *DBWE see also* Barmen declaration; Christ alone; Christology
Song of Songs, Christian exegesis of, 3, 8*. *See also* the master index of scriptural references
songs (*Lieder*), 5, 7*, 8*. In *DBWE see also* hymns; singing
soteriology, 10, 12
soul (ψυχή), 1, 3, 4, 5, 7*, 8, 9, 10, 11, 12, 13*, 14*, 15, 16, 17
South Africa, 3, 6, 7, 8, 12, 13, 14
South America, 10, 11*, 13, 14
Soviet Union, 6, 10, 12*, 13, 15, 16
Spain, 8, 9, **10**, 12, 14, 16
spirit (*Geist*, πνεῦμα), 1, 2, 3, 4, 6, 7, 8, 9, **10**, **11**, 12, 13, 14, 15, 16*
objective, **1**, 9, 14
spirituality, 16
spiritualism, 6, 12, 15. In *DBWE see also* Enthusiasm
spiritualization, 5
in Catholicism, 9
Spiritual Ministry (Geistliches Ministerium; July–November 1933), 13
spirituals (hymns), **10**, 15. In *DBWE see also* Negro spirituals
sport, 1, 7, 9, 10, 12, 15*. In *DBWE see also* Olympics
Sport Palace Rally (1933), 13
SS (Schutzstaffel), 16. In *DBWE see also* Gestapo; Nazi party; Waffen-SS
Stahlhelm, 10
Stalingrad, 6, 7, **16**
Stalinism, 4, 16
standards (*Maßtab*), 6, 7, 8*, 14*
St. Anne's Church (Annenkirche), Dahlem, 8*. *See also* Dahlem
state (*Staat*), 1, 4, **6**, 7, 8, 9, **11**, **12**, 13, 14, 15*, **16**. In *DBWE see also* church and state; mandates; National Socialism; orders of creation; orders of preservation; statesman; treason. *See also* "A Theological Position Paper on State and Church" (*DBWE* 16, 2/10), 6, 16
Christian, 12, 16
and church, 1, 4, 6, 9, 10, 11, **12**, 13, 14, 15, 16
citizenship, 6, 14
concept of, 16
doctrine of, 16
and God, 9, 12, 16
as mandate, 8
office of, 11, 12
power of, 12, 16
preservation of, 13

separation from, 6, 9, 10, 11, 15, 16
totalitarian, 6, 12, 14, 16
state of being created (*Geschöpflichkeit*), 2, 3, 6. In *DBWE see also* creation; human being
statesman, 6, 12, 14*
"Stations on the Way to Freedom" (poem), 3, 7, **8**, 16. In *DBWE see also* poems
status confessionis, **12**, 14, 15. In *DBWE see also* Barmen declaration; Confessing Church. *See also* "The Jewish-Christian Question as Status Confessionis" (*DBWE* 12, 2/14)
Steglitz (Berlin), 8*, 12, 14*, 15. In *DBWE see also* Confessing Church, synods of; synods
1935 Synod, 4*, 14*
1938 synod, 15
1939 synod, 15
Stellvertretung. *See* vicarious representative action
sterilization, **6**, 12, 16
compulsory, 6, 13*
Stettin (today: Szczecin), 4*, 8, 10, 12, 14, **15**, **16**
Steyler Mission, 16
St. Gallen, 7*
St. George's congregation, 13, 14*. *See also* London, German congregations
St. Louis (Missouri), 10, 15
St. Mary's congregation, 13
St. Matthew Passion, 7, 8, 9*, 10, 16
Stockholm, 7, 11*, 13*, **14**, 15, **16**. In *DBWE see also* ecumenical movement; Finkenwalde; Life and Work
Life and Work conference (1925), 1, 6, 9*, 10, 11, 12, 14
stoicism, 1, 2
storm troopers. *See* SA
St. Paul's congregation (London), 8*, 12, 13, 14, 15. In *DBWE see also* churches; London
St. Peter's (Rome), 8, 9*, 12, 13
Stralsund, 14*, 15
strength (*Kraft*, δύναμις), 6, 7, 8*, 9, 11*, 14, 15*, 16
strikes (labor), 9, 12. *See also* labor movement
struggle (*Kampf*, ἀγών), 1, 3*, 4, 6, 11*, 12, 13*, 14, 15*, 16. In *DBWE see also* strife
student chaplaincy, 10, 11*, 12, 13*, 16. In *DBWE see also* chaplaincy; Technical College
students, 6, 10, 11*, **12**, 13, 16, 17 (12, 1/106a). In *DBWE see also* Bonhoeffer student circle; Hedgehogs; student chaplaincy; Tübingen; University of Berlin
African-American, 10
organizations of, 9, 11, 12
stupidity (*Dummheit*), 6, 7, 8
stupidity (*Torheit*, μωρία), **14**, 16
Stuttgart, 8, 9, 10, 13*, 14, 16
Stuttgart Declaration of Guilt (1945), 6
Stuttgart Jubilee Bible, 15, 16
subject, 1, **2**, 6, 10, 11*
subject/object dialectic, 1, 2, 9
subjectivity, 2, 6, 9, 11
success (*Erfolg*), **6**, 7, **8**, 12*, 13*, 15*

Sudan, 9
Sudeten crisis (1938), 5*, 15. In *DBWE see also* prayer liturgy
suffering (*Leiden*), 1, 2, **4**, 5, **6**, 7, **8**, 9, 10, **12**, **13**, 14, 15, **16**. *See also* "Seminar Paper on Suffering in Job" (*DBWE* 9, 2/14); "Examination Paper: What Is Paul's View on Earthly Suffering?" (*DBWE* 10, 2/6)
suicide, 3*, 4, **6**, **7**, 8, 9, 10, 12, 14, 15, 16
sun, 7*, 8*, 10
superbia, 5, 14*, 15*
superman (*Übermensch*), 6, 10, 11. *See also* Nietzsche, Friedrich, in the master biographical index of names
superstition, 8, 9, 13*. In *DBWE see also* occult
surrender (*Hingabe*), **1**, **6**, 7*
suum cuique, 6, 15
Sweden, 6, 8, 11*, 12, 13, 14, 15, **16**
Swedish consulate, Berlin, 14, 16. *See also* Forell, Birger, in the master biographical index of names
Switzerland, 7*, 8, 9, 10, 11*, 12, 13*, 14, 15, **16**. In *DBWE see also* ecumenical movement; Geneva
  and Bonhoeffer's travels to for the conspiracy, 6, 16
sword, 6, 12, 14*
Sydenham congregation, 4*, 5, 8, 12, **13***, 14, 15. In *DBWE see also* London, congregations
Sydow brotherhood, 5, 7*, 12
Sylt, 7, 9
sympathy, 1
synagogue, 9, 10, 11*, 12, 14, 15, 16*. In *DBWE see also* Judaism
syncretism, 9, 10
synods, 1, 12, 14, **15**, 16*. In *DBWE see also* Barmen; "Brown Synod" (1933); Confessing Church; Dahlem; Old Prussian Union Church
  Confessing: Sixth (1938/Berlin-Nikolassee), 15; Sixth (1938/Berlin-Steglitz), 15; Seventh (1938/Epiphany/Berlin-Nikolassee) 15; Eighth (1939/Exaudi/Berlin-Steglitz), 15
  in the United States, 10
Synoptic Gospels, **4**, 9, 12, 14*
systematic theology, 2, 3, 6, 10, 11. In *DBWE see also* theology. *See also* "The History of Twentieth-Century Systematic Theology" (*DBWE* 11, 2/3)
  and ethics, 6

Talmud, 4, 9
Tannenberg association, 12, 14*. In *DBWE see also* neopaganism. *See also* Ludendorff, Erich and Matilde, in the master biographical index of names
tax collector (Luke 19), 6, 7*, 9, 10, 12*, 14*, 15*. *See also* the master index of scriptural references
taxes, 9, 13, 14*, 16

Technical College (Berlin-Charlottenburg), 2, **10, 11, 12**, 13, 15
technology, 3, 6, 8, 11*, 12, 14*. In *DBWE see also* Industrial Revolution; machine
  serving its own ends, 6, 9
Tegel prison, 6, 8, 9, 13, 14, 15, **16**. In *DBWE see also* imprisonment; prison
  notes, 7
  visits to Bonhoeffer, 8
  Wehrmachtuntersuchungsgefängnis Seidelstrasse 3, 6, 7, 8, 10, 14, 15, 16
temple, 4, 6, 12, 16*
  of God, 9, 14, 16
  of the Holy Spirit, 16
temple (Jerusalem), rebuilding of, 5, 14
temporality, 2, 9
temptation (*Anfechtung*) 1*, **2**, 7, 8, 9*, 10, 12, 14. In *DBWE see also Anfechtung*; spiritual assaults; testing; tribulation
temptation (*Verführung*), 16
temptation (*Versuchung*), 3, 4, 5, 8, 9, 13*, 14*, **15**, 16, 17 (9, 2/2a). *See also* "Bible Study on Temptation" (*DBWE* 15, 2/4), 3; Biblical Study Seminars on Basic New Testament Concepts: Notes on the Concept of "Temptation" (*DBWE* 15, 2/2)
  of Christ, 6, 15
  to suicide, 6, 8
Ten Commandments, 4, 8, 9, **16**. In *DBWE see also* commandments; Decalogue
tennis, 5*, 9, 10, 15
Teutoburg Forest, 7
thanksgiving, 5, 10. In *DBWE see also* gratitude; thankfulness
Times (London), 13, 14*
theater, 7, 8*, 9
theocracy, 6, 10
theodicy, 6, 9, 10, 14*, 15, 17 (*DBWE* 9, 2/2a)
theologians, 2, 8, 9, 10, 11*, **12**, 13*, 14, 15, 16*. In *DBWE see also* Bonhoeffer student circle; collective pastorates; Confessing Church; ecumenical movement; "illegal" pastors; theological education; theology students; Union Theological Seminary
  training of, 12, 13, 14, 15
theological anthropology, 3. In *DBWE see also* anthropology, theological
theological education, 12, 13*, 14, 15, 16*. In *DBWE see also* collective pastorates; Confessing Church, examination committees; Finkenwalde; preachers' seminaries; theological examinations
theological education, university faculties, 5, 13, 16. In *DBWE see also* Berlin University; Erlangen; Giessen; Halle; Kiel; Marburg; Münster; Rostock; Tübingen
theological examinations, 13*, 15, 16*
  Bonhoeffer's first, 9, 10
  Bonhoeffer's second, 10

theological exercises, 3, 4*, 12, 14*
homiletical, 4, 14, 15
meditative, 12
Theological Society
Karl Barth's, 11
Adolf von Harnack's, 10
Theologische Blätter, 14*, 16
Theologische Existenz heute, 5, 12, 13, 14, 16
theology, 1, **2**, 3, 6, 7, 8, 9, 10, **11**, **12**, 13, 14, 15, **16**. In *DBWE see also* academic theology; anthropology, theological; Chicago school; Christology; ecclesiology; ecumenical movement; German Christians; systematic theology; Union Theological Seminary *See also* "Lecture on the Theology of Karl Barth and the Situation in Germany" (*DBWE* 13, 2/4); "Theology and the Congregation" (*DBWE* 16, 2/6);
as academic discipline, 2, 3, 9, 10, 11, 12, 13, 14, 16
Anglo-Saxon, 6, 11, 15
authority of, 16
of Barth, 13
of Bultmann, 16
Catholic, 9, 15, 16
of crisis, 10, 11
of the cross, 1, 4, 5, 10, 14, 16
dialectical, 1, 2, 5, 6, 9, 10, 11, 12, 13, 14
discipline of, 14, 16
dogmatic, 11
and ethics, 6
humanist, 10
and incarnation, 16
liberal, 1, 2, 5, 6, 8, 10, 11, 12, 113, 14, 16
liberation theology, 8
Lutheran, 4, 12, 16
natural, 3, 6, 8, 9, 13, 14, 15, 16
practical, 10, 14, 16
reformed, 1, 12
in the United States, 10, 14
völkisch, 14
theology, Bonhoeffer's studies. In *DBWE see also* academic theology; *Habilitation*; *Sanctorum Communio*; Union Theological Seminary; University of Berlin
Berlin, 9, 10, 12, 15, 16, 17 (9, 1/80a; 12, 1/106a)
New York, 10
Rome, 9, 16
Tübingen, 9, 10, 15, 16.
"Theology of Crisis and Its Attitude toward Philosophy and Science, The" (*DBWE* 10, 2/17), 2, 10
theology students, 1, 11*, 12, 16. In *DBWE see also* "What Should a Student of Theology Do Today?" (*DBWE* 12, 2/17)
Third Reich, 4, 6, 7, 8, 10, 12, 13*, 14, 15*, 16*. In *DBWE see also* bans; churches; Confessing Church, state measures against; decrees; führer; laws; Ministry of Foreign Affairs (Auswärtiges Amt); Ministry of the Interior; National Socialism; Nazi state; Reich Chancellery
policies toward churches, 3, 12, 13*, 16

Thirteenth Implementation Decree (March 2, 1937), 4, 15*
Thirty Years War (1618–48), 6, 7, 8, 9, 12, 14
thought/thinking (*Denken*), **2**, 3, 8*, 9, 10, 11*, **12**, 15*, 16*
  and action, 8
  Anglo-Saxon, 15
  autonomy of, 2
  Catholic, 11, 12
  devout, 13
  dialectical, 2
  existential, 2
  of fallen humanity, 3
  Greek, 12
  individualistic, 2, 10
  Jewish, 10, 12
  modern, 13
  obedient, 2
  objective, 8
  Old Testament, 8
  philosophical, 2, 6, 10
  political, 15
  profane, 2
  Protestant, 12, 15
  rationalist, 6
  responsible, 8
  theological, 10, 11
  volkisch, 15
  Western, 6
  and will, 6
throne and altar, 6, 11*, 16. In *DBWE see also* church and state; two kingdoms
Thüringia, 7, 8, 16
"Thy Kingdom Come" (*DBWE* 12, 2/11), 3*, 6, **12,** 15
time, times (*Zeit, Zeiten*), 1, 2, 3, 6, **8**, 10, 14*, 15*, 16*. *See also* "Lecture on Contemporizing New Testament Texts" (*DBWE* 14, 2/7)
  contemporary, 7, 8
  and eternity, 6, 9
  final days, 6, 15, 16
  fullness of, 7, 8
  revelation, 1
  zeitgeist, 10
Titanic, 4, 6
titanism, 4, 9
Toledo (Spain), 8*, 10, 15*
tolerance, **6**, 8, 15, 16*
Torgau, 8, 16
torture, 6, 7, 8*
totalitarianism, demands of, 6, 7, 13, 16
tower of Babel, 9*, 10, 12, 14*. In *DBWE see also* Babylon. *See also* the master index of scriptural references
tradition, 1, 7, 8*, 9, 10, 15*, 16*. In *DBWE see also* culture; Germany; parents
  bourgeois, 7, 8*
  principle of, 14*
tragedy, 6, 8, 10, 12, 15*. *See also* "The Tragedy of the Prophetic and Its Lasting Meaning" (*DBWE* 10, 2/1)
tragic, the, 6
traitor, 7, 14. *See also* betrayal; treason
transcendence, 1, **2**, 5*, 8, 10, 11, 12. In *DBWE see also* God; metaphysics; philosophy;
  experience of, 8
transcendentalism, 1, **2**, 11*
transubstantiation, 15

treaty/treaties, 1, 6, 12*, 13*, 15*. In *DBWE see also* Versailles, Treaty of
tree of life, **3**, 6, 12, 14. In *DBWE see also* good and evil; paradise
Trent, 8, 9*
  Council of, 14
trials, 16
  Bonhoeffer's, **8**, 16
  Niemöller's, 15
tribulation (*Anfechtung*) 5*, 7*, 8*, 14, 16*. In *DBWE see also Anfechtung*; spiritual assaults; temptation
  and faith, 2
  in Luther, 9
Trinity, 3, 4, 7, 8, **9**, 10, 11, 12, 13, **14**, 15, 16. In *DBWE see also* Holy Spirit. *See also* "Lecture: 'The Visible Church in the New Testament: Indwelling of the Trinity'" (*DBWE* 14, 2/8.3)
  doctrine of, 9, 11, 13, 16
  immanent and economic, 9, 14
Trinity Sunday, 13
Tripoli, 9, 10
tristitia (sadness), 6*, 7, 8, 9. In *DBWE see also acedia*; melancholy
triumphalism, 6, 12
trust (*Vertrauen*), 6, 7, **8**, 13*, 16*
truth (*Wahrheit*), 1, **2**, 3, 4, 5*, 6, **7**, **8**, 9, 10, 11*, **12**, 13, **14***, **15***, 16. *See also* "Fragment of an Essay: What Does It Mean to Tell the Truth?" (16, 2/17), 7, 8
  concept of, 8, 10, 16
  general, 4, 12, 14
  of God, 3, 6, 7, 11, 15, 16
  and love, 6, 14
  recognizing, 6, 14
  standing in truth, 2
  telling the truth, 6, 7, 8, 9, 16
truthfulness (*Wahrhaftigkeit*), 4, 6, 7, 8*, 13, 14, 15, 16
Tübingen, 2, 6, 7, 8*, 9, 10, 12, 13, 14, 15, 16, 17 (9, 1/80a, 85a, 94b)
Tunis, 8, 16
Turkey, 11, 16
Turks, 9, 14
Tuscany, 8
two kingdoms, 6, 15, 16
two natures, doctrine of, 4, 10, 12
tyrannicide, 6, 14
tyranny, 6, 7, 8, **12**, 14, 15*, 16. In *DBWE see also* authoritarianism; dictatorship; tyrannicide
  of National Socialism, 16
tyrant, 6, 12, 13*, 14*, 15. In *DBWE see also* tyrannicide; tyranny

UK classification, 8, 16. *See also Abwehr*; military conscription
Ukraine, 8
Ulm declaration (1934), 13
ultimate/last things (*das Letzte*), 2, 5*, **6**, 8*, 10, **12**, 14*, 15, 16. In *DBWE see also* "last things"; penultimate
ultimate reality, 6, 12. In *DBWE see also* penultimate; reality
Unam Sanctam (1302 papal bull), 6
una sancta, 12, 16
unbelief, 4, 5, **6**, 7, 11*, 14*, 16
Uncle Rudy (code name for war), 8, 15*, 16

unconscious Christianity, 7, 8
understanding (*Verstehen*), 1*, **2**, 6, 9, 11*, 16*. In *DBWE see also* epistemology; knowledge
unemployment, **10**, 11*, 12, 15
Union Theological Seminary, 1, 2, 4, 6, 7, **10**, 11, **12**, 13, 14, **15**, 16
  Bonhoeffer's 1930/31 studies, **10**
Unitarians, 12, 14, 15
United States, 6, 7, 8, **10**, 11, 12, 13, 14, **15**, **16**. *See also* America; American Civil Liberties Union; Declaration of Independence; New York; racism; Union Theological Seminary
  Bonhoeffer's 1939 visit, 15
  Bonhoeffer's comments about, 8*, 10, 11, 15, 16
  churches in, **10**, **15**, **16**
  Civil War, 12, 15
unity (*Einheit*), 1, **6**, 7, 8*, 9, 10, 11, **12**, 13*, 14, 16
universalism, 1
universities, 1, 7, 10, 11*, 12, 13, 14, 15, 16. *See also* University of Berlin; individual listings for cities
  Basel, 11, 14
  Berlin, 3, 4, 6, 8, **11**, 12, 13, 14, 15, 16
  Bonn, 1, 6, 11, 12, 14
  Columbia (N.Y.), 10, 15
  Erlangen, 11, 12
  Frankfurt am Main, 11
  Freiburg, 3
  Giessen, 12, 15
  Göttingen, 10, 11
  Greifswald, 14
  Halle, 11
  Hamburg, 12
  Heidelberg, 9, 10, 15
  Kiel, 14
  Leeds, 12
  Marburg, 12
  Münster, 6, 11, 14
  Rome, 9
  Rostock, 12
  Tübingen, 14, 15
  Yale, 15
University of Berlin. In *DBWE s ee also* students; theological faculties; universities
  Bonhoeffer's assistantship, 2, 10, 11, 16
  Bonhoeffer's inaugural lecture (1930), 2, 10
  Bonhoeffer's lectureship, 2, 3, 4, 5, 6, 7, 10, 11, 12, 13, 14, 15
  Charité (clinic), 8, 9, 14, 15
  student associations, 4, 12, 14
  students, 3, 4, 7, 11, 12, 13, 14, 16
  theological faculty, 1, 9, 10, 12, 14, 17 (12, 106a)
Unter dem Wort (weekly publication), 13
Upper Silesia, 8*, 9
Uppsala, 13*, 14, 16. In *DBWE see also* Sweden
usus legis, 14*, 16. *See also* "A Theological Position Paper on the Primus Usus Legis" (*DBWE* 16, 2/18)
  philosophical, 9
  primus, 6*, 14*, 16
  tertius, 12, 14, 16
utilitarianism, 1, 6, 14
utopia, 6*, 12, 14*

value, values (*Wert, Werte*), 1, **2**, 6, **7**, 8*, 9, 10, 11*, 12*, 14*. In *DBWE see also* morality; standards
vanity (*Eitelkeit*), 6, 7, 9, 12*, 14, 15, 17
Vatican, 6, 8, 9, 12, 14*, 15, 16
  Vatican Council, First (1869–70), 2; Second (1962–64), 14*
vengeance (*Vergeltung*), 4*, 5, 6, 15, 16. In *DBWE see also* revenge
verdict (*Urteil*), 6, 7, 11*. In *DBWE see also* interrogation; prison; trial
Verkündigung und Forschung (magazine), 12*, 15*, **16**
Versailles treaty (1919), 4, 6, 9, 10, 11, 12, 16. In *DBWE see also* Treaty of Versailles
vicariate. *See* assistant pastorate
vicarious representative action (*Stellvertretung*), 1, 2, 4*, 5, **6**, 8*, 9, **11**, 12*, 14, 15, 16. In *DBWE see also* Christ; Christology; *Stellvertretung*
  Christ as *Stellvertreter*, 9
  God as *Stellvertreter*, 16
vices, 4
Vienna, 8, 11*, 12, 13*, 16*
"view from below", 6, 7*, **8**. In *DBWE see also* "After Ten Years" (*DBWE* 8, prologue)
violation (*Vergewaltigung*), 5, 6*. In *DBWE see also Vergewaltigung*
violence, 4, **6**, 7, 8, 10, 12, 13, 15, **16**
virgin birth, 8*, 9, 10*, 12*
Virginia (U.S.), 6, 15
virtue (*Tugend*), 4, 6, **8**, 10, 12, 14*, 16, 17 (9, 2/2a)
vitality, 3, 6, 8, 12
vocation (*Beruf /Berufung*), 1, **6**, 7*, 8, 9, 10, **11,** 12, 13*, 15, 16*. In *DBWE see also* discipleship, call to; ministry; rite vocatus
  and responsibility, 6
  worldly, 4, 6, 8, 14
vocation (*Vocation*), 14. *See also* "Literary Attempt on the Theme of 'Vocation'" (*DBWE* 11, 2/21)
völkisch ideology (ethnonationalism), 2, 4*, 6, 10, **11**, **12**, 13, 14, 15. In *DBWE see also* anti-Semitism; Aryan ideology; German Christians; Germanic myths; National Socialism
Volksgemeinschaft, 4*, 6, 10, 11, 12, 14, 16
Volkskirche, 1, 4, 10, 11, 12, 13, 14, 15, 16. In *DBWE see also* church-of-the-people
  Israel as, 4
Volksmission, 16. In *DBWE see also* church renewal movement; evangelization
Volksnomos, 12, 13*
voluntarism, 2, 3*, 6, 8*. In *DBWE see also* will
voluntary association, **1**, 2
Vorwärts (newspaper), 9
vow (*Gelübde*), 4, 5, 8, 9, 14*. In *DBWE see also* loyalty oath; oath

Waffen-SS, 16
Wandsbecker Bote (publication), 13
war, 1, 3, 4, 6, **7**, **8**, 9, 10, 11, 12, 13, 14, 15, **16.** In *DBWE see also* conscientious objection;

peace; World War I; World War II. *See also* "Lecture on War" (*DBWE* 10, 2/9); "Reading Notes for the Seminar 'Ethical Viewpoints in Modern Literature: War Literature'" (*DBWE* 10, 2/11.1)
Warsaw, 8
Warthegau, 6, 15*, 16
Washington, D.C., **10**
way A and B (Church Struggle decisions), 15
weakness (*Schwäche*), 6, 7, 8*, 12, 13, 14*, 16*
wealth, 1
weapons, 7*, 13, 15*
  God's word as, 15
  philosophical and moral, 7
wedding (*Hochzeit*), 3*, 7, 8, 10, 13, 14, 15*, 16*. In *DBWE see also* marriage
Weimar (city), 8*, 13, 14*, 15
  Disputation of, 2
Weimar Republic, 3, 6, 9, 10, **11**, 12, 16. In *DBWE see also* Beer Hall Putsch; Hitler
West, the, **6**, 8, 11*, 12
Westerburg, 1932 conference, **11**, 12
Westminster Confession, 14
Westphalia, 10, 11*, 13*, 15, 16. In *DBWE see also* Bad Oeynhausen
  church province, 14, 15
  Confessing Church synods: March 1934, 13; April 1934, 14; 1648 Treaty, 6, 7
"Who Am I?" (poem), 7, 8
Wiesbaden, 10, 14*, 16
will, **1**, **2**, 3, 4*, 6, 7, 8, 9, 10, 11*, 13*, 14*, 17
  evil, 1, 4
  free, 1, 2, 4* 14, 15, 16
  good, 1, 3, 6
  human, 3, 13, 16
  unfree, 4, 10
wisdom (*Weisheit*), 6, 9, 12, 13, 14, 15, 16
witness, 5*, 6, 13, 12, 14*, 16*
Wittenberg, 1, 8, 9*, 11*, 12, 14*. In *DBWE see also* Pastors' Emergency League
woman, women, 1, 3, 4, **7**, 8, 10, 12, 14, 15, 16*
word (of God), **1**, 2, 3, 4, **5**, 6, 7*, 8, **9**, 10, 11, **12**, **13**, 14, **15**, 16. In *DBWE see also* Logos; preaching; proclamation; Scripture; theology
  in Christ, 5, 15
  hearing of, 3, 13
  of Holy Scripture, 4, 6, 9, 10, 14
  and human words, 3, 4, 5, 9, 12, 14, 15
  in our hearts, 3, 14
  power of, 4, 16
  proclamation of, 11, 13, 16
  and sacrament, 1, 2, 5, 9, 12, 14, 15, 16
work (*Werk*), 3, 4*, 5, 6, 7, 8, 9, 10, 11*, 12, 14, 15, 16
  academic, 10, 11, 16
  of the church, 10, 11, 16
  and community, 5
  as mandate, 6, 8, 16
  theological, 10, 16
worker(s), 1, 4*, 6, 7, 8, 9, 10, 11*, 12, 13. In *DBWE see also* labor movement; proletariat; unemployment

Working Group of Theological and National Economists (Arbeitsgemeinschaft von Theologen und Nationalokonomen), 11
works, 1*, 2, 4*, 6, 8, 9, 11*, 12, 13*, 14*, 15, 16. In *DBWE see also* good works; justification. *See also* "Lecture: 'New Life in Paul'" (*DBWE* 14, 2/15)
  justification by or "works-righteousness" (*Werkgerechtigkeit*), 2, 5, 12, 15, 16
  and the Law, 4, 14, 16
world, 2, 3, 4, 5, **6**, 7, 8, 9, 10, 11*, 12, 13, 14, 15, 16
  Anglo-Saxon, 6, 16
  come of age, 5, 8, 14
  fallen, 3, 12, 16
  godless, 6, 8, 16
  material, 5, 6, 8
  new, 3, 4, 6, 8, 12, 14
  order, 9
  worldliness, 3, 4, 5, 6, 7, **8**, 10, 11, 12, 14. In *DBWE see also* worldliness
World Alliance for Promoting International Friendship through the Churches, 4, 6, 8, 10, **11**, **12**, 13, 14, 16. In *DBWE see also* ecumenical movement. *See also* "On the Theological Foundation of the Work of the World Alliance" (*DBWE* 11, 2/14)
  Austrian branch, 11
  British branch, 13
  Committee on Minorities, 12
  Dutch branch, 13
  Executive Committee, 13
  French branch, 12
  German branch, 11, 13
  Management Committee, 11, 13
  Norwegian branch, 11
  Swedish branch, 11
  Youth Commission, 11, 13, 14
  Youth Secretariat, 6, 10, 11, 13, 14
World Alliance for Promoting International Friendship through the Churches conferences. In *DBWE see also* names of individual conferences. *See also* "Lecture in Ciernohorské Kúpele: On the Theological Foundation of the Work of the World Alliance" (*DBWE* 11, 2/14); "Report on a Conference of the World Alliance in Cambridge" (*DBWE* 11, 2/1); "Report on the Youth Conference of the World Alliance in Epsom" (*DBWE* 11, 2/11); " Reports on Youth Conferences of the World Alliance" (*DBWE* 11, 2/18 and 2/19)
  Baltic (1933), 11
  Basel (1933), 12
  Bruay (1934), 13
  Cambridge (1931), 11, 12
  Chamby (1935, 1936), 14
  Ciernohorské Kúpele (1932), 11, 12
  English-French, 11
  Epsom (1932), 11
  Fanø (1934), 13
  German-French, 11, 12

German-Polish, 12;
Gland (1932), 11, 12
La Borcaderie (1936), 14
Luneray (1933), 12
Paris (1934, 1935), 14
Sofia (1933), 12, 13
Westerburg (1932), 12
World Church Conference. *See* Faith and Order; Life and Work
world come of age, 2, 3, 5*, **8**, 16. In *DBWE see also* autonomy; "come of age"; *Mündigkeit*; world, autonomy of
World Conference of Christian Youth (1939), 14
World Council of Churches (in process of formation), 4, 6, 8, 11*, 12*, 13, 14, 15, 16. In *DBWE see also* ecumenical movement; Geneva; World Alliance. *See also* Visser 't Hooft, Willem, in the master biographical index of names.
1948 founding of, 10, 16
Research Department, 13, 14
world history, 1*, 8, **10**, 11*, 14*, 16*
as battle between God and Satan, 9
World Mission Conference (1928), 14
World Student Christian Federation, 12, 13, 14, 16
worldview, 6, 8, 9, **11**, 12, 13, 14*
World War I, 1, 2, 3*, 4*, 6, 7, 8, 9, 10, 11*, 12, 14, 15, 16. In *DBWE see also* Treaty of Versailles; war
and Germany, 9, 10
postwar generation, 12
war guilt, 10, 11*
World War II, 1, 2, 5, 7*, **8**, 10, 14*, 15, **16**
worry (*Sorge*), 4, 8, 13, 14*, 16*
worship service (*Gottesdienst*), **1**, 3, 4, 5, 6*, 7, 8, 9, 10, 11*, 12, 13, 14, 15, 16. In *DBWE see also* catechetical instruction; children's worship; intercessory prayer; prayer; sermons
wrath (*Zorn*), 1, 3, 7, 8*, 11*, 14*, 15. In *DBWE see also* God
Wuppertal, 4, 14, 15, 16. In *DBWE see also* Barmen; Elberfeld; pietism
Württemberg, 9*, 11*, 12, 16
Council of Brethren, 13
Ecclesiastical-Theological Society, 9
regional church, 12, 13, 14, 16
Württemberg Ecclesiastical-Theological Society (Confessing Church organization), 15. In *DBWE see also* Württemberg. *See also* Diem, Hermann, in the master biographical index of names

X-Report (1940), 16. In *DBWE see also* Zossen files

Yahweh, 3, 9*, 10
yellow star, 16. *See also* Jews, persecution of; "non-Aryan" Christians
yes, of God, 6, 8*
to life, 6

"You," 1, **2**, 10. *See also* "I-You" (*Ich-Du*)

Young Men's Christian Association (YMCA), 8*, 10, 11, 12, 13*, 14, 15, 16

Young Plan (1930), 10, 11

Young Reformation Movement, **12**, 13

Young Women's Christian Association (YWCA), 14, 15

youth, 1, 6*, 7, 8, 9*, 10, 11, **12**, 13, 14, 15, 16. In *DBWE see also* confirmation; Hitler Youth; younger generation; youth movement

  Finkenstein Bund, 17 (9, 1/80a)

  youth work, **10**, 11, 13

Youth Commission (ecumenical). *See* World Alliance

youth movement (*Jugendbewegung*), 1, 7, 9, 10, 11, 12, 17 (9, 1/80a)

Yugoslavia, 10, 11, 12, 16

Zeitschrift für Kirchengeschichte, 14

Zettelnotizen. See Ethics notes

Zingst, 4, 5, 14, 15, 16

Zion, 14

Zion church (Berlin), 11

Zossen files, 8, 13, 16

Zürich/Zurich, 8*, 9*, 11, 12, 13, 14, 15, 16, 17 (9, 1/80a)

Zwinglianism, 14

Zwischen den Zeiten (publication), 1, 10, 12, 13

Corrigenda

The following are corrections to the published *DBWE* volumes. Most were sent to Fortress Press in 2012 so that the corrections could be made for future digital editions. Corrigenda discovered since 2012 have also been added here.

***DBWE* 2**

31, line 11 from top, insert page numbers in text in parentheses as follows: "interpretation of revelation in terms of act (pp. 81–103) or in terms of being (pp. 103–9)"

31, line 7 of text from bottom, insert page numbers as follows: "are drawn together into one (pp. 109–35)"

32, line 8 from top: insert page numbers as follows: "in our final chapter (pp. 136–61)"

50, line 2 from bottom: replace "existential" with "existentiell"

70, *DBWE* ed. note 78, should read: "I think therefore I am"

92, line 16 from top: replace "'existentially' ['existentiell']" with "in an existentiell sense"

94, last line: replace "existentially" with "in an existentiell sense"

95, line 2 from top: replace "existential" with "existentiell"

95, line 8 from bottom: replace "existential" with "existentiell"

99, line 18 from top: replace "existential" with "existentiell"

113, first line: replace "existentially" with "in an existentiell sense"

114, line 6 from bottom should read: "it remains past, of no interest in an existentiell sense"

114, last line: replace "existential" with "existentiell"

117, line 10 from top: replace "existential" with "existentiell"

124, line 10 from top: replace "existential" with "existentiell"
124, last line of text should read: "logically this knowing has three forms: as unbelieving,[67] as existentiell,"
124, ed. note 67 should read: "The German editor corrected this to read 'believing' [*DBW* 2:122, n. 58], but this would render the three forms of knowledge (unbelieving, existentiell, and ecclesial) as two forms, since Bonhoeffer at the top of p. 126 identifies 'believing' and 'existentiell'"
126, line 5 from top: replace "existential" with "existentiell"
129, line 12 from bottom: replace "existential" with "existentiell"
131, line 9 from top: replace "existential" with "existentiell"
131, line 10 from top: replace "existential" with "existentiell"
131, last line: replace "existential" with "existentiell"
132, line 3 from top: replace "existential" with "existentiell"
133, line 7 from top: replace "existential" with "existentiell"
136, line 5 from top: replace "existential" with "existentiell"
145, line 7 from bottom: replace "existentially" with "in an existentiell sense"
211: Add the following name: Augustine
214: correct entry: "Möller, Michael F." (not "Müller")

***DBWE* 4**

29, lines 2 and 3, and p. 352: "Otto Salomon" (not "Solomon")
61, line 8 and ff. from bottom, revise to read: "He does not want what Jesus wants; he does not even want what he himself wants"
67, par. 2, lines 11–12: "Only the believers obey—that is said to the obedient person inside the believer. Only the obedient person believes: this is what is said to the believer in his obedience"
141, ed. note 147, last line of the page, revise to read: "which reports that the galley proofs for"
244, last line of text, delete "in"; should read: "has to say about a secular vocation"
313, line 10 from top: replace "a commemorative conference to mark Bonhoeffer's seventieth birthday" with "a conference on the seventieth anniversary of Bonhoeffer's birth"
329 and 350, correct entry: "Jean Bethke Elshtain" (not "Bethge")
357, references to the German Christians (Deutsche Christen) from pp. 31, 295–96, have erroneously been placed under "German Protestantism."

***DBWE* 5**

32, line 15 from below, revise to read: "The Christ in one's own heart is weaker than the Christ in the word of a brother. The Christ in one's heart is uncertain; the Word is certain"

39, line 8 from top, revise as follows: delete "self-centered"; should read: "The essence of emotional community is darkness"

42, par. 2, line 1, revise as follows: delete "merely"; should read: "There is, likewise, an 'emotional' love of neighbor"

44, par. 2, line 8, revise sentence as follows: "It will respect the boundary of the other, which is placed between us by Christ, and it will find full community with the other in the Christ who alone binds us together"

55, par. 2, line 5, revise to read: "All the things of which the Psalter speaks, which individuals can never fully comprehend and call their own, live only in the body of Christ as a whole"

101, par. 2, sentence 3, revise to read: "Christians could rid themselves of this burden if they didn't release the other person but did violence to him, stamping him with their own image"

206, correct entry: Halkenhäuser, Johannes

207, correct entry: Nehemiah

***DBWE* 6**

282, ed. note 135, line 2, Greek term should read: παραίνεσις

284, ed. note 143, last line: delete "es"; should read: "the word *geschiet*, 'happens'"

287, par. 2, line 2, bracketed German should read: "[verwirklicht]"

314, ed. note 55, Greek term should read: πρὸς

349, ed. note 45, line 2, remove hyphen in bracketed German: [bürgerlich saturierten]

389, ed. note 2: last line of note, correct citation to read: "[*DBW* 16 (2/13): 560–61]"

***DBWE* 7**

10, ed. note 36, should read: "See below p. 167, ed. note 110"

73, ed. note 1, line 3, should read: "60 above" (not 160)

104, ed. note 32, should read: "*In Zitz*" (title in bibliography is correct)

125, ed. note 11: should read "the twentieth century" instead of "this century"

169, ed. note 118: correct Paton book title is *The Church and the New Order*
256: The Sombart title should be *Deutscher Sozialismus*
270, entry for Mozart, Wolfgang Amadeus, dates should be: (1756–91).
270, entry for Niemöller, Martin, line 1 should read: "naval officer in World War I"
272, entry for Salomon, Otto, should read: "(pseudonym: Otto Bruder)"
273, entry for Stifter, Adalbert, should read: "Austrian writer and painter"
273, entry for Storm, Theodor, should read: "German poet and short story author"

***DBWE* 8**

19, par. 3, line 8 from bottom, should read: "by the publication in 1963"
136, ed. note 11, line 4, should read: "Winfried" (not "Winfrid")
155, line 6 from top, and ed. note 6, should read: "Münnich" (Middle High German spelling of Mönch) (not "Münich")
155, ed. note 6, next to last line, should read: "stinging desert sand"
419, line 4 from bottom (Poem: "The Past"), revise to read: "as privet berries make the hawk moth drunk at night"
446, ed. note 2 should read: *Love Letters from Cell 92*
495, line 5 from top: replace "The other-worldly" with "That which is beyond [das Jenseitige]"
501, line 4 from bottom, should read: ". . . nor again the Greek god-human form [Gott-Menschgestalt] of the 'human being in itself,' but 'the human being for others,' therefore the Crucified One."
503, line 1, first word, should read: "perceived" (not "preceived")
544, ed. note. 20, should read: "Winfried" (not "Winfrid")
730, entry for "gratitude": delete third entry (p. 11)

***DBWE* 9**

152, last line of letter, should read: "Heussi" (not "Heußi")
157, ed. note 2 (first instance), should read: Georg Warmuth (not "Wasmuth")
170, letter 101, last three sentences should be deleted (they are repeated at top of p. 171); delete: "But he is a touchingly concerned cousin. When he saw that it was pointless, he gave up trying to convert me. In return, he wanted to"
180, letter 110, ed. note 2, the date-of-entry stamp should be corrected to read: "Superintendent's Office, Köll . . . Diestel"
405, 408, and 670, should read: "Strauß" (not "Strauss")

429, line 16 from bottom, should read: "according to chapters 13, 16, 19, 31" (no semicolon)
634, correct entry: Barabbas
646, entry for Frederick II should read: Frederick II ("the Great") (1712–86): 1740–86, king of Prussia
656, entry for Paul Kraus, should read: Göppingen (not "Göttingen")
652, should read: Heussi (not Heußi)
656, should read: Köhler, Wolfgang (instead of "Prof.")
664, line 12 from bottom at the line break, should read: Consul
647: biogram for Georg Konrad, delete final line: "defense counsel for Hans von Dohnanyi in his court-martial case"

***DBWE* 10**

32, ed. note 147, should read: "*DBW* 17"
44, ed. note 189, should read: "1/109a, 1/115a, 1/115b, 1/117a"
295, line 8, should read: "Easter Monday"
421, ed. note 8, should read: "[Correct: *The Souls of Black Folk.* Bonhoeffer also misspells the author's name, which is Du Bois.—CG]."
491, line 8 from bottom, should read: "not the distant, but the nearby God, that is Easter"
491, line 3 from bottom, should read: "Yet the yearning grows for the time when"
492, line 4 from top, should read: "for which hundreds of thousands of hands greedily reach out"
493, line 9 from top, should read: "by which thinking [geistig] beings connect"
493, lines 15–16 from top, should read: "it says this in different ways to every person . . . one thing to a child and another to a man"
545, lines 3–4 from top, should read: "rejoice around the Christmas tree"
597, line 7 from top, should read: "Piety was a private matter"

***DBWE* 11**

vi and 67, with regard to document 18a, should read: "Appointment" (not "Assignment").

***DBWE* 12**

112, line 7 from bottom, should read: "Central Welfare Office for German Jews" (not "Jewish Welfare Association").
313, ed. note 34, lines 2–3, should read: "from Paul, which is 'in the likeness of sinful flesh.'"

348, first line of first full paragraph, should read: "agreed on an inelegant formulation" (replace "unpretentious" with "inelegant").

356, ed. note 171, should read: "'fleshly form,' or 'likeness of flesh.' [These paragraphs develop . . .]"

459, line 9 from bottom, should read: "all the things our lives depend on"

463, line 14 from top, should read: "unreal or general terms"

478, line 17 from top, should read: "the center of the people's life"

496, n. 54, line 7, should read: "their emancipation"

530, reference to Paul Lehmann papers should read: "Paul Lehmann Collection, Special Collections, Princeton Theological Seminary Library, Princeton, New Jersey"

571, entry for Burlingham, should read: "member of the Management Committee"

575, entry for Albert Einstein: capitalize "Prize"

653, entry for "Liberation of the Jews" should be revised to read "Emancipation of the Jews" and reordered accordingly (i.e., under E).

DBWE 13

xv (table of contents), 22. Fragment of a Wedding Sermon, correct page number: 410

296, line 9, should read: "Philipp" (not "Philip").

359, last par., 6 lines from bottom, should read: "In this service you will serve each other"

359, last par., 4 lines from bottom, should read: "If aught but death"

368, par. 2, last sentence, should read: "means something entirely different for Jesus from what it means"

383, par. 1, last sentence, should read: "What is totally different is its object"

460, correct entry: "Herbert Anzinger"

DBWE 14

309, ed. note 6, should read: "Benckert's" (not "Benkert's").

1018, entry for April 20–24, title of Bonhoeffer's lecture should read: "On the Question of Church Communion" (not "Fellowship").

1204, column 1, fourth entry from bottom for Confessing Church, correct to read: "taking up collections" (not "collecting taxes").

1215, revise entry as follows: "Law to Restore Order in the German Evangelical Church (1934), implementation of"

***DBWE* 15**

25, entry for January 9–15, should read: "Ecclus. 50:24–26."

355, line 13 from top, replace "Mark 18:26" with "Matt. 18:26."

362, line 15 from top, should read: "Philippians 4:5" (not "4:4").

381, line 2, should read: "Hos. 14:2 'the fruit of our lips'"

423, ed. note 40, should read: "Eph. 4:15–16"

451, end of ed. note 26, should read: "from each other.—VB]"

467, line 16 from top, should read: "lest you become murderers"

468, line 13 from bottom, should read: "but the other person is in danger"

468, line 8 from bottom, should read: "Be worthy of respect, not only toward the respectable" . . . "peaceable, not only with the peaceful"

468, last line, should read: "yearns to dwell among friends"

469, lines 3–4 from top, should read: "Their devout members"

469, line 13 from top, should read: "a more peaceful word and deed than preaching about"

469, line 2 from bottom, should read: "for all of human nature screams for revenge"

470, line 4 from top, should read: "and bids me:"

477, line 19 from bottom, should read: "very much at its beginning"

479, par. 2, line 16, should read: "the hearts of his children"

480, line 6 from top, should read: "Now I know that you won't leave me"

480, par. 2, line 4, should read: "demands the engagement of one's entire life"

535 (ed. note 28), 617, and 654, should read: "Dürig, Walter" (not "Düring")

629, delete "Eccles. 50:2426" (the reference is to Ecclus./Jes. Sirach on the next page and is cited there correctly).

630, first book of Old Testament Apocrypha, should read: "Tobit" (not "Tobias")

637, col. 2, line 1, should read: "4:5" (not "4:4").

***DBWE* 16**

1, last line, should read: "town of Memel"

12, par. 2, line 2, delete the following sentence: "It ended with the defeat of the German Sixth Army at Stalingrad in the winter of 1941–42 and with Hitler's dismissal of Brauchitsch as commander in chief of the army on December 19, 1941"; replace with: "This second stage ended after the German offensive bogged down outside of Moscow in December 1941 and Hitler dismissed Brauchitsch as commander in chief of the army on December 19, 1941."

36, ed. note 1, line 6 from bottom, revise bracketed insert to read: "[Measured by (Stifter's book) *Indian Summer.*—MB]"

65, line 10 from top, add bracketed text: SS-Major [Sturmbannführer]

93, line 3 of letter 35, should read: "I will send you my telephone bill!"

107, ed. note 3, last line, should read: "Kyrie, 27"

184, letter 104, line 10, should read: "which reads, 'Civil servants, scholars, clergy'"

185, ed. note 1, delete first sentence in bracketed insert; replace with: "[MBK (Verlag für Missions- und Bibel-Kunde, or "Publisher for Mission- and Biblical-knowledge") was the name of a publishing house in 1941. According to the contemporary . . .]"

260, ed. note 4: replace note ("Bultmann's *New Testament and Mythology* triggered a decades-long discussion about the demythologization of New Testament concepts; cf. Eberhard Jüngel's introduction to the 1988 German edition.") with the following: "*Offenbarung und Heilsgeschehen* included the essay 'Neues Testament und Mythologie' (New Testament and mythology), which triggered a decades-long discussion about the demythologization of New Testament concepts; cf. Eberhard Jüngel's introduction to the 1988 German edition."

329, ed. note 4, should read: "Röhricht" (not "Röhrig")

687, entry for April 4, should read: "Bonhoeffer spends Easter in Kieckow. Norwegian Lutheran church issues 'Kirkens Grunn' in protest against the Quisling government; many Norwegian bishops and pastors arrested."

727, entry for vol. 12, place of publication: Gütersloh

743, entry for *Die Religion in Geschichte und Gegenwart,* should read: "7 vols."

778, entry for Georgii, should read: "Wolf" (not "Wolfgang")

790, entry for "James the Zebedee" should read: "James, son of Zebedee"

797, entry for "Kübarth, Frau" should read: "Kübarth, Mrs."

824, entry for Strong should read: "Strong, Tracy" (not "Tracey")

825, entry for von Thadden, should read: "Reinold" (not "Reinhold")